EDUCATIONAL PSYCHOLOGY 95/96

Tenth Edition

Editor

Kathleen M. Cauley
Virginia Commonwealth University

Kathleen M. Cauley received her Ph.D. in educational studies/human development from the University of Delaware in 1985. Her research interests center on applying cognitive developmental research to school learning. Currently, she is studying children's mathematical understanding in classrooms that are implementing the National Council of Teachers of Mathematics Standards for Mathematics.

Editor

Fredric Linder
Virginia Commonwealth University

Fredric Linder received an A.B. in American civilization from the University of Miami, Florida, a M.A. in psychology from the New School for Social Research, and a Ph.D. in educational psychology from the State University of New York at Buffalo. His research and publications focus on the values, locus of control, and cognitive learning styles of students.

Editor

James H. McMillan
Virginia Commonwealth University

James H. McMillan received his bachelor's degree from Albion College in 1970, his M.A. from Michigan State University in 1972, and his Ph.D. from Northwestern University in 1976. He has reviewed and written extensively on many topics in educational psychology. His current interests are classroom assessment and school report cards.

Cover illustration by Mike Eagle

Annual Editions
A Library of Information from the Public Press

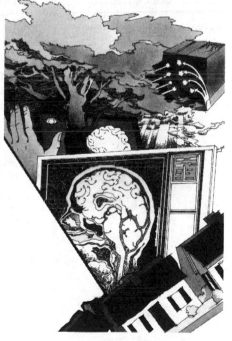

The Dushkin Publishing Group/
Brown & Benchmark Publishers
Sluice Dock, Guilford, Connecticut 06437

The Annual Editions Series

Annual Editions is a series of over 65 volumes designed to provide the reader with convenient, low-cost access to a wide range of current, carefully selected articles from some of the most important magazines, newspapers, and journals published today. Annual Editions are updated on an annual basis through a continuous monitoring of over 300 periodical sources. All Annual Editions have a number of features designed to make them particularly useful, including topic guides, annotated tables of contents, unit overviews, and indexes. For the teacher using Annual Editions in the classroom, an Instructor's Resource Guide with test questions is available for each volume.

Printed on Recycled Paper

VOLUMES AVAILABLE

Africa
Aging
American Foreign Policy
American Government
American History, Pre-Civil War
American History, Post-Civil War
Anthropology
Archaeology
Biology
Biopsychology
Business Ethics
Canadian Politics
Child Growth and Development
China
Comparative Politics
Computers in Education
Computers in Business
Computers in Society
Criminal Justice
Developing World
Drugs, Society, and Behavior
Dying, Death, and Bereavement
Early Childhood Education
Economics
Educating Exceptional Children
Education
Educational Psychology
Environment
Geography
Global Issues
Health
Human Development
Human Resources
Human Sexuality
India and South Asia

International Business
Japan and the Pacific Rim
Latin America
Life Management
Macroeconomics
Management
Marketing
Marriage and Family
Mass Media
Microeconomics
Middle East and the Islamic World
Money and Banking
Multicultural Education
Nutrition
Personal Growth and Behavior
Physical Anthropology
Psychology
Public Administration
Race and Ethnic Relations
Russia, the Eurasian Republics, and
    Central/Eastern Europe
Social Problems
Sociology
State and Local Government
Urban Society
Violence and Terrorism
Western Civilization,
    Pre-Reformation
Western Civilization,
    Post-Reformation
Western Europe
World History, Pre-Modern
World History, Modern
World Politics

Cataloging in Publication Data
Main entry under title: Annual Editions: Educational Psychology 1995/96.
        1. Educational psychology—Periodicals. 2. Teaching—Periodicals.
I. Cauley, Kathleen M., *comp.*; Linder, Fredric, *comp.*; McMillan, James H., *comp.*
II. Title: Educational psychology.
ISBN 1–56134–398–6   370.15′05   82–640517

Tenth Edition

Printed in the United States of America

Editors/ Advisory Board

To the Reader

In publishing ANNUAL EDITIONS we recognize the enormous role played by the magazines, newspapers, and journals of the *public press* in providing current, first-rate educational information in a broad spectrum of interest areas. Within the articles, the best scientists, practitioners, researchers, and commentators draw issues into new perspective as accepted theories and viewpoints are called into account by new events, recent discoveries change old facts, and fresh debate breaks out over important controversies.

Many of the articles resulting from this enormous editorial effort are appropriate for students, researchers, and professionals seeking accurate, current material to help bridge the gap between principles and theories and the real world. These articles, however, become more useful for study when those of lasting value are carefully *collected, organized, indexed,* and *reproduced* in a *low-cost format,* which provides easy and permanent access when the material is needed. That is the role played by *Annual Editions.* Under the direction of each volume's *Editor,* who is an expert in the subject area, and with the guidance of an *Advisory Board,* we seek each year to provide in each *ANNUAL EDITION* a current, well-balanced, carefully selected collection of the best of the public press for your study and enjoyment. We think you'll find this volume useful, and we hope you'll take a moment to let us know what you think.

Educational psychology is an interdisciplinary subject that includes human development, learning, instructional strategies, intelligence, motivation, assessment, and classroom management. It also gives special attention to the application of this knowledge to teaching.

Annual Editions: Educational Psychology 95/96 is presented in six units. An overview precedes each unit and explains how the articles in the unit are related to the broader issues within educational psychology. The first unit presents issues central to the teaching role. The authors discuss the challenges of responding to calls for educational reform and the role of research in meeting those challenges.

The second unit is concerned with child and adolescent development and covers the cognitive, social, and emotional components of development. The articles in this unit examine the developmental implications of early childhood programs for teachers, the social forces affecting children and adolescents, and the personal and social skills needed to cope with school learning and developmental tasks.

The third unit, concerning exceptional and culturally diverse students, focuses on the learning disabled, the gifted, and minority students. All of these students are different in some way and require an individualized approach to education. The articles in this unit review the characteristics of these children and suggest programs and strategies to meet their needs.

The fourth unit includes articles about theories of learning and instructional strategies. The different views of learning, such as information processing, behaviorism, and constructivist learning, represent the accumulation of years of research on the way humans change in thinking or behavior due to experience. The principles generated from each approach have important implications for teaching. These implications are addressed in a section on instructional strategies, covering such topics as instructional methods, authentic instruction, computer-aided teaching, learning styles, and discovery methods.

The topic of motivation is perhaps one of the most important aspects of school learning. Effective teachers need to motivate their students both to learn and to behave responsibly. How to manage children and what forms of discipline to use are issues that concern parents as well as teachers and administrators. The articles in the fifth unit present a variety of perspectives on motivating students and discuss approaches to managing student behavior.

The articles in unit six review assessment approaches that can be used to diagnose learning and improve instruction. The focus is on grading practices and appropriate uses of standardized tests. Performance based assessment is introduced as a promising new approach to classroom measurement.

This tenth edition of *Annual Editions: Educational Psychology* has been revised so as to present articles that are current and useful. Your responses to the selection and organization of materials are appreciated. Please fill out and return the prepaid article rating form on the last page of the book.

Kathleen M. Cauley

Fredric Linder

James H. McMillan
Editors

Unit 1

Perspectives on Teaching

Three selections discuss the importance of research and the value of scientific inquiry to the teaching process.

Unit 2

Development

Six articles examine how social interaction in the classroom influences child and adolescent development.

The concepts in bold italics are developed in the article. For further expansion please refer to the Topic Guide and the Index.

Unit 3

Exceptional and Culturally Diverse Students

Seven articles look at the problems and positive effects of educational programs for learning disabled, gifted, and culturally diversed children.

The concepts in bold italics are developed in the article. For further expansion please refer to the Topic Guide and the Index.

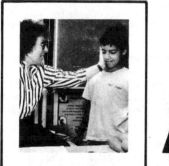

Unit 4

Learning and Instruction

Twelve selections explore the important types of student/teacher interaction.

The concepts in bold italics are developed in the article. For further expansion please refer to the Topic Guide and the Index.

Unit 5

Motivation and Classroom Management

Seven selections discuss student control and motivation in the classroom.

The concepts in bold italics are developed in the article. For further expansion please refer to the Topic Guide and the Index.

Unit 6

Assessment

Six articles discuss the implications of educational measurement for the classroom decision-making process and for the teaching profession.

The concepts in bold italics are developed in the article. For further expansion please refer to the Topic Guide and the Index.

Topic Guide

This topic guide suggests how the selections in this book relate to topics of traditional concern to educational psychology students and professionals. It is useful for locating articles that relate to each other for reading and research. The guide is arranged alphabetically according to topic. Articles may, of course, treat topics that do not appear in the topic guide. In turn, entries in the topic guide do not necessarily constitute a comprehensive listing of all the contents of each selection.

TOPIC AREA	TREATED IN:	TOPIC AREA	TREATED IN:
Family Structure	5. Helping Children Develop Self-Control 9. At-Risk Students and Resiliency	**Objectives**	37. Developing a Personal Grading System 38. Creating Tests Worth Taking
Gifted Children and Youth	12. Ability Grouping 13. Meeting the Needs of Your High-Ability Students	**Performance Assessment**	38. Creating Tests Worth Taking 39. Performance Assessment
Grading	37. Developing a Personal Grading Plan	**Portfolio Assessment**	40. Planning for Classroom Portfolio Assessment
Grouping Students	12. Ability Grouping 23. Synthesis of Research on Cooperative Learning	**Positive Reinforcement/ Praise**	19. Rewards of Learning 20. Rewards versus Learning 21. Sticking Up for Rewards
Humanistic Education	22. Return of Character Education 23. Synthesis of Research on Cooperative Learning	**Problem Solving**	17. Remembering the Forgotten Art of Memory 18. Mind's Journey from Novice to Expert 28. Link between Technology and Authentic Learning
Individual Differences	26. Culture/Learning Style Connection		
Information Processing	17. Remembering the Forgotten Art of Memory 18. Mind's Journey from Novice to Expert	**Questioning**	25. Optimizing the Instructional Method
Learning Styles/ Strategies	26. Culture/Learning Style Connection	**Reflective Practice**	3. Where Can Teacher Research Lead?
Mainstreaming	11. Enabling the Learning Disabled	**Resiliency**	9. At-Risk Students and Resiliency
Memory	17. Remembering the Forgotten Art of Memory	**Self-Efficacy/ Self-Reliance**	9. At-Risk Students and Resiliency
Minority Students	14. What We Can Learn from Multicultural Education Research 31. Educating and Motivating African American Males	**Social Development**	4. Myths Associated with Developmentally Appropriate Programs 5. Helping Children Develop Self-Control 7. Encouraging Positive Social Development in Young Children 22. Return of Character Education
Moral Development	5. Helping Children Develop Self-Control		
Motivation	29. Choices for Children 30. Motivating Underachievers 31. Educating and Motivating African American Males	**Standardized Tests**	41. Putting the Standardized Test Debate in Perspective
		Teacher Beliefs	14. What We Can Learn from Multicultural Education Research
Multicultural Education	14. What We Can Learn from Multicultural Education Research 15. Authentic Multicultural Activities 16. Student Diversity 26. Culture/Learning Style Connection	**Technology**	27. Paradigm Shifts in Designed Instruction 28. Link between Technology and Authentic Learning
		Values	22. Return of Character Education
Norms	37. Developing a Personal Grading System		

Perspectives on Teaching

The teaching-learning process in schools is enormously complex. Many factors influence pupil learning—such as family background, developmental level, prior knowledge, motivation, and of course, effective teachers. Educational psychology investigates these factors to better understand and explain student learning. We begin our exploration of the teaching-learning process by considering the teaching role, particularly as it is being defined in the educational reform movement.

In the first article, Dorothy Kerzner Lipsky suggests that current reform efforts are inadequate because they fail to focus on the student. She believes that student learning will increase only by "giving students respect, building upon their knowledge, providing them control over the learning process and appropriate materials, helping them see the connection between subjects, and encouraging cooperation among students." Constance Kamii, Faye Clark, and Ann Dominick echo these sentiments as they discuss a constructivist perspective on the goals in *America 2000*.

Another perspective in the reform of education is that teachers need to engage in more systematic inquiry—or research. As the professional development schools envisioned by the Holmes group and others are established, teacher research will become more widespread. As the next selection illustrates, teacher researchers are important to implementing educational change. Rita Wright Johnson gives testimony to the value of classroom research for improving teaching.

Educational psychology is a resource for teachers that emphasizes disciplined inquiry, a systematic and objective analysis of information, and a scientific attitude toward decision making. The field provides information for decisions that are based on quantitative and qualitative studies of learning and teaching, rather than intuition, tradition, authority, or subjective feelings. It is our hope that this aspect of educational psychology is communicated throughout these readings, and that as a student you will adopt the analytic, probing attitude that is a part of the discipline.

While educational psychologists have helped to establish a knowledge base about teaching and learning, the unpredictable, spontaneous, evolving nature of teaching suggests that the best they will ever do is provide concepts and skills that teachers can adapt for use in their classrooms. The issues raised in these articles about the impact of the reform movement on teachers help us understand the teaching role and its demands. As you read articles in other chapters, consider the demands they place on the teaching role as well.

Looking Ahead: Challenge Questions

Describe several of the roles teachers are expected to perform.

In your opinion, is educational reform addressing the right issues? Explain your position.

As educational reform progresses, what new demands do you think it will place on teachers?

How does research, either teacher research or formal educational research, improve teaching?

We Need a Third Wave of Education Reform

Dorothy Kerzner Lipsky

Dorothy Kerzner Lipsky is Superintendent of Schools, Riverhead (NY) Central School District.

In the last ten years we've seen two waves of school reform. The first, following in the wake of *A Nation at Risk* (released in 1983), focused on external factors—higher standards (strengthened graduation requirements, competency statements, no pass/no play, and attendance rules), new—and often mandated—curricula, strengthened teacher-certification requirements, and expenditure increases of more than a thousand dollars per pupil between the '82/'83 and the '87/'88 school years. We are in the midst of a second wave of reform that focuses on the roles of adults—teacher empowerment, school-based management, and parental choice. It shifts the locus of attention from state capitals to local schools, and from mandated activities to collaborative, cooperative, and protracted efforts. What we need today is a third wave of reform, a comprehensive effort that places the student at the center of reform.

As generations of teachers have realized, they cannot learn for their students; it is the student who must do the learning. Giving students respect, building upon their knowledge, providing them control over the learning process and appropriate materials, helping them to see the connection between subjects, encouraging cooperation among students—these are the necessary predicates to increases in student learning, the bases for significant improvement of our schools.

From *Social Policy,* Winter 1992, pp. 43-45. © 1992 by Social Policy Corporation. Reprinted by permission.

The fundamentals of this third wave have already been tested. What we need now is a coordinated effort to:

Respect students: Students do their best when they feel respected. Yet, most often schools operate from a deficit model, one that concerns itself with student weaknesses and what the student does *not* know. Instead, we should be building programs on the strengths and capacity of students. Adoption of the effective schools literature's correlate of high expectations for all students is a starting point. The necessary correlate is that schools must be responsible for assuring that success.

Engage students in learning: The traditional concept of schooling, not significantly changed in spite of several reform movements, puts the student in a passive role as the recipient of teaching: the student is a vessel into which the school pours knowledge. A third wave of reform should place the student at the center, as an active, engaged worker. The learning process must become less one of memorizing answers, and more one of discovery and higher-level thinking. It should be the doing of science, the seeing of mathematics as a tool, the understanding of reading as a way for each learner to construct knowledge and to gain pleasure. Engaging students in the work of learning is the basis for new instructional strategies and curriculum efforts. Cooperative learning and peer tutoring promote collaboration among students. Involving all students in the preparation of material, sharing information with other students, acting as tutors, monitoring their own performance—these and other activities have been found to offer both affective and cognitive benefits. And for students themselves "at risk," a population of particular concern, studies show that tutoring programs have even higher degrees of success.

Learning for a lifetime: Students cannot learn all they will need to know for the rest of their lives in the short years of schooling. A new wave of reform must go beyond the equation of learning with schooling. One way of doing this is through community service, which provides both a forum for out-of-classroom learning and is an expression of the respect that comes from expecting things of students. We should also develop the concept of a community-referenced curriculum more broadly; usually limited to students labelled severely impaired, learning in community settings makes sense for all students.

Doing it right from the start: Presently, when a student has failed to learn something identified by the school and teacher as important, the teacher's and school's response is to look for some deficit in the child or parent—often in a sociological or psychological framework. The present division between "regular" and "special" education is an example of this formula. In a third wave of reform, we would recognize student failure as a failure of the school to meet the student's needs, and to engage her or him in the work of learning. As industry has long recognized, it is considerably more expensive to fix something done wrong than to make sure you do it right the first time.

Making parents and community partners: Showing respect for the students also means letting students see their parents as people held in esteem by the school. Developing student education in partnership with parents, reporting regularly to parents, developing opportunities for family-learning activities, using the expertise of parents, and creating opportunities for students to learn in the community are a few ideas that have already been tested and could be expanded.

In seeking to involve parents, however, schools often view them as para-teachers, junior partners to the school. This is misguided. The partnership is not one of junior and senior, nor even one of alike. Parents and school professionals bring the strengths of their differences to the joint task of education. Showing respect means including parents of *all* children in such programs, not just those from a particular social, economic, or racial group.

New roles for school adults: At the school organizational level, respect for students is expressed by staff knowing them as individuals and valuing their involvement. Large, anonymous schools need to be changed to assure that each child is known as an individual. School days should be organized so there are regular opportunities for small groups of youngsters to meet with adults. The district office should function more as a service agency staffed by facilitators and coordinators than as an enforcement agency staffed by police officers. Similarly, state education departments must shift their role from bean counter and prescriber to standard setter and monitor—as is beginning to develop in Kentucky.

Placing students at the center of school reform is not a solution to every problem. It will not by itself overcome racism, sexism, handicappism, or class divisions. It will not substitute for needed funds nor personnel of competence and dedication. Nor does it offer specific prescriptions for the needed changes in American education. Rather, it is a point of view, a concept, a set of relationships. Working out ways to implement this concept—recognizing the central and unique role of the student as the producer of learning—can be the necessary change that powers a third wave of school reform, one that establishes schools that serve and succeed for all students.

The Six National Goals

A Road to Disappointment

The people who set goals for education seldom take into account scientific knowledge about how children acquire knowledge and moral values — and the six national goals formulated in 1990 are no exception, these authors charge.

....

CONSTANCE KAMII,
FAYE B. CLARK, AND
ANN DOMINICK

CONSTANCE KAMII is a professor in the Department of Curriculum and Instruction at the University of Alabama, Birmingham; FAYE B. CLARK is an assistant professor in the School of Education, Samford University, Birmingham; and ANN DOMINICK is a fourth-grade teacher at Shades Cahaba Elementary School, Homewood, Ala.

MANY FACTORS can be cited to explain the meager results of the reform efforts of the past decade. The quick-fix approach to accountability that led only to attempts to raise test scores and increase graduation requirements and a variety of other reasons have been mentioned in recent years. Many people are calling for bolder, fundamental, systemic changes, especially changes that bring true innovation into the classroom. A factor seldom mentioned is the need for coherent goals that are based on the best scientific theory available today about how human beings acquire knowledge and moral values. Such goals are of the utmost importance in education reform because, if our ob-

Illustration by Mario Noche

From *Phi Delta Kappan*, May 1994, pp. 672-677. © 1994 by Phi Delta Kappa. Reprinted by permission of *Phi Delta Kappan* and the authors.

jectives are poorly conceived, the rest of our efforts will be misdirected.

Goals in education are usually defined by groups of people who have the power to decide what outcomes are desirable. The people who set these goals seldom take into account scientific knowledge about how children acquire knowledge and moral values. They usually formulate goals based on tradition and on their own values and priorities. The six national goals that were formulated by President Bush and the National Governors' Association are no exception.[1]

In contrast to our political leaders, Jean Piaget started out by conceptualizing only one broad aim for education — the development of autonomy.[2] Our purpose here is to argue that, unless we have a set of goals coherently formulated with autonomy as the overall aim, the results of the second decade of reform will once again be disappointing. Piaget's conception of autonomy as the aim of education was a result of his application of his theory, constructivism, which is a scientific theory supported by 60 years of research all over the world.[3]

Since autonomy in the Piagetian sense means something different from what we often understand by the term, we will first explain what Piaget meant by autonomy. Then we will discuss autonomy as the aim of education — and the drastic changes in classroom practices that this goal entails. We will also point out the inadequacies of the six national goals.

PIAGET AND AUTONOMY

In common parlance, autonomy means the *right* of an individual or group to be self-governing. When we speak of Palestinian autonomy, we are referring to this kind of political right. In Piaget's theory, however, autonomy refers not to the right but to the *ability* of an individual to be self-governing — in the moral as well as in the intellectual realm. Autonomy is the ability to think for oneself and to decide between right and wrong in the moral realm and between truth and untruth in the intellectual realm by taking all relevant factors into account, independently of rewards or punishments. The opposite of autonomy in the Piagetian sense is heteronomy. Heteronomous people are governed by someone else because they are unable to think for themselves.

Moral autonomy. An extreme example of moral autonomy is the struggle of Martin Luther King, Jr., to obtain civil rights for African Americans and others. King was autonomous enough to take relevant factors into account and to conclude that the laws discriminating against African Americans were unjust and immoral. Convinced of the need to make justice a reality, he fought to end the discriminatory laws in spite of the police, jails, dogs, fire hoses, and threats of assassination. Morally autonomous people are not governed by rewards and punishments.

An extreme example of moral heteronomy is the affair of the Watergate cover-up. The perpetrators went along with what they knew to be morally wrong to reap the rewards that President Nixon could bestow on those who helped in the cover-up.

In *The Moral Judgment of the Child*, Piaget cited more commonplace examples of autonomy and heteronomy.[4] He interviewed children between the ages of 6 and 14 and asked them, for example, why it is bad to tell lies. Young heteronomous children replied, "Because you get punished when you tell lies." Piaget asked, "Would it be okay to tell lies if you were not punished for them?" The young children answered yes. Their judgment of matters of right and wrong was obviously governed by others.

Piaget also made up many pairs of stories and asked children which one of the two children in the stories was the worse. The following is an example of such a pair.

> A little boy . . . goes for a walk in the street and meets a big dog who frightens him very much. So then he goes home and tells his mother he has seen a dog that was as big as a cow.
>
> A child comes home from school and tells his mother that the teacher had given him good marks, but it was not true; the teacher had given him no marks at all, either good or bad. Then his mother was very pleased and rewarded him.[5]

Young children systematically manifested the morality of heteronomy by saying that it was worse to say, "I saw a dog as big as a cow." Why was it worse? Because dogs are never as big as cows, and adults do not believe such stories. Older, more autonomous children, however, tended to say that it was worse to say, "The teacher gave me good marks" *because* this lie is more believable. For more autonomous children, a believable lie is worse than one that is so outlandish that people will not be deceived.

All babies are born helpless and neither autonomous nor heteronomous. But young children are initially dependent on adults and, therefore, become heteronomous. Ideally, they become increasingly autonomous as they grow older. As they become more autonomous, they become less heteronomous. In other words, to the extent that children become able to govern themselves, they are governed less by other people.

In reality, however, human development does not happen in this ideal way. Most people do not attain their potential, and many stop developing at a low level. This observation can easily be confirmed in our daily lives. Newspapers are filled with stories about corruption in government and dishonesty in business practices, as well as with items dealing with drug trafficking, theft, assault, and murder.

The important question for parents and teachers is, What causes certain children to become more autonomous than others? Piaget's answer to this question was that adults reinforce children's heteronomy when they use rewards and punishments, thereby hindering the development of autonomy. By refraining from using rewards and punishments and by instead exchanging points of view with children, we can foster the development of autonomy, he said.

For example, if a child tells a lie, an adult could punish the child by saying, "No dessert tonight." Alternatively, the adult could look the child straight in the eye, with both affection and skepticism, and say, "I *really* can't believe what you are saying because . . . (state the reason). And when you tell me something next time, I am not sure I'll be able to believe you. . . . I want you to go to your room (or seat) and think about what you might do to be believed next time." Children want to be trusted, and, when they are confronted with this kind of statement, they are likely, over time, to come to the conclusion that it is best for people to deal honestly with each other.

In general, punishment leads to three possible outcomes. The first outcome is a weighing of risks. Children who are punished will learn to calculate their chances of getting caught the next time and to weigh the price they might have to pay against their chances of getting caught. The second possible outcome is, interestingly, the opposite of the first

2. Six National Goals

one: blind obedience. Sensitive children will do anything to avoid being punished. Thus by completely conforming to the rules, they give the impression that punishment works. The third outcome of punishment derives from the second: revolt. Many "model" children surprise everyone by beginning to cut classes, to take drugs, and to engage in other acts that characterize delinquency. Their reason for switching to these behaviors is that they are tired of living for their parents and teachers and think that the time has come for them to start living for themselves.

Piaget was realistic enough to say that it is sometimes necessary to impose restrictions on children. However, he made an important distinction between *punishment* and *sanctions by reciprocity*. Depriving the child of dessert for telling a lie is an example of a punishment, because the relationship between the lie and dessert is completely arbitrary. Telling children that we cannot believe what they said and sending them away to think about how they can be believed next time is an example of a sanction by reciprocity. Sanctions by reciprocity are directly related to the act that we want to discourage and to the adult's point of view. They have the effect of motivating the child to construct rules of conduct from within, through the coordination of viewpoints. Other examples of sanctions by reciprocity — such as excluding the child from the group, depriving the child of the thing he or she has misused, and having the child make restitution — can be found in *The Moral Judgment of the Child* and in *Young Children Reinvent Arithmetic*.[6]

Piaget's theory about how children acquire moral values is fundamentally different from traditional theories and from common sense. In the traditional view, the child is believed to acquire moral rules and values by *internalizing* them from the environment. According to Piaget, children acquire moral convictions not by absorbing them directly from the environment but by *constructing* them from the inside, through the exchange of points of view with people who are close and important to them. For example, no child is taught that it is okay to tell lies if one is not punished for them. Yet young children construct this belief as they try to make sense out of what adults say and do. Fortunately, they continue to construct other relationships, and many children ultimately conclude that

lies are bad even if one is not punished for them.

The exchange of viewpoints between adults and children fosters the development of autonomy by enabling the children to consider relevant factors, such as other perspectives. When children can take relevant factors into account, especially other people's rights and feelings, they construct from within the rule of treating others as they wish to be treated by them. A person who has constructed this conviction from within cannot lie in situations like the Watergate affair — no matter what reward may be offered.

Many behaviorists and others believe that punishment is bad because it is negative and that rewards are positive and good. However, rewards do not make children any more autonomous than punishment. Children who help their parents only to get money and those who fill out worksheets only to get stickers are governed by someone else, just as much as those who behave well only to avoid being punished.

Money, candy, and stickers are rewards because they are attractive objects used to manipulate or control children. By contrast, honest praise and expressions of appreciation are part of human relationships involving the exchange of points of view. Just as it is necessary to express disbelief when a child is not telling the truth, it is desirable to communicate our pleasure and appreciation when children behave in especially praiseworthy ways. Praise is thus different from rewards, such as money and stickers, but it too can be used in insincere, manipulative ways. Praise can thus degenerate into a reward, just as an expression of disbelief can turn into an angry, punitive act.

Autonomy is often confused with adopting a laissez-faire attitude. However, when one takes such relevant factors into account as the rights and feelings of other people, one is not free to break promises, tell lies, or act inconsiderately or irresponsibly.

Intellectual autonomy. In the intellectual realm, too, autonomy means the ability to govern oneself by being able to take relevant factors into account in deciding what is true or untrue. Copernicus provides an extreme example of intellectual autonomy. (The same applies to inventors of any other revolutionary theory.) Copernicus invented the heliocentric theory when nearly everybody else believed that the sun revolved around the earth. He was ridiculed off the stage but was

autonomous enough to remain convinced of his own idea. An intellectually heteronomous person, by contrast, believes unquestioningly what he or she is told, including illogical conclusions, slogans, and propaganda.

A more common example of intellectual autonomy is the case of a child who used to believe in Santa Claus. When she was about 6, she surprised her mother by asking, "How come Santa Claus uses the same wrapping paper as we do?" Her mother's explanation satisfied her for a few minutes, but she soon came up with the next question: "How come Santa Claus has the same handwriting as Daddy?" This child had her own way of thinking, which was different from what she had been taught.

According to Piaget, the child acquires knowledge in a way similar to the way a child acquires moral values: by *constructing* knowledge from within, rather than by internalizing knowledge directly from the environment. Children may accept what they are told for a time, but they are not passive vessels that merely hold what is poured into their heads. Children construct knowledge by creating and coordinating relationships. When the child described above put Santa Claus into a relationship with everything else she knew, she began to feel that something was wrong somewhere. When children are not convinced by what they are told, they rack their brains to make sense of these "facts."

Unfortunately, children are not encouraged to think autonomously in school. Teachers use rewards and punishments in the intellectual realm to get children to give "correct" responses. An example of this practice is the use of worksheets. For example, in first-grade arithmetic, if a child writes "4 + 4 = 7 ," most teachers mark this answer wrong. The result of this kind of teaching is that children become convinced that only the teacher (or someone else) knows which answers are correct. Furthermore, when we walk around a first-grade classroom while children are working on worksheets and stop to ask individual children how they arrived at particular answers, they typically react by grabbing their erasers — even when their answers are perfectly correct! Already many children have learned to distrust their own thinking. Children who are thus discouraged from thinking critically and autonomously will construct less knowledge than those who are confident and do their own thinking.

If a child says that 4 + 4 = 7, a better reaction is to refrain from correcting him or her and inquire instead, "How did you get 7?" Children often correct themselves as they try to explain their reasoning to someone else. The child who tries to explain his or her reasoning has to decenter in order to make sense to the other person. Trying to coordinate his or her point of view with that of another person makes the child think critically, and this often leads to a higher level of thinking.

Another way of dealing with a child's correct or incorrect answer to 4 + 4 is to ask the class, "Does everybody agree?" The exchange of points of view among peers stimulates critical thinking, which leads to a higher level of reasoning. In

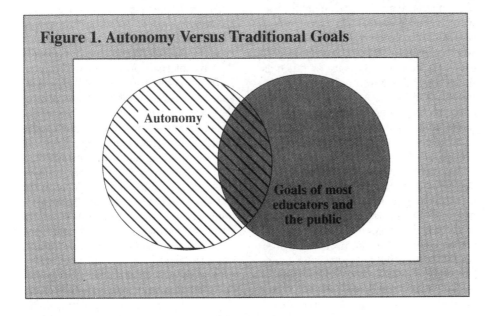

Figure 1. Autonomy Versus Traditional Goals

the following section, we argue that we must replace the conformity and obedience that are now valued in schools with an education that emphasizes the honest, critical exchange of viewpoints.

AUTONOMY AS THE AIM OF EDUCATION

Figure 1 is our interpretation of the relationship of autonomy, the goal Piaget set for education, to the goals of most educators and the public. In the circle on the right, labeled "goals of most educators and the general public," we would put those goals that resulted in our memorizing words and their definitions just to pass one test after another. All of us who succeeded in school achieved this success by memorizing an enormous number of words without necessarily understanding them or caring about them. The

shaded part also includes the moral heteronomy that schools generally reinforce by using rewards and punishments.

A more accurate label for the circle on the right would have been "heteronomy." However, we did not use that label because today's educators do not consciously set out to foster children's heteronomy. Indeed, most educators (to say nothing of the general public) have not even heard of autonomy and heteronomy. Nevertheless, they unwittingly manipulate children with rewards and punishments, thereby reinforcing children's heteronomy.

In the intersection with the circle labeled "autonomy," we put those things we learned in school but did not forget after the test. The ability to read and write,

to do basic arithmetic, to read maps and charts, and to situate events in history are examples of what we learned in school that we did not forget after cramming for tests. The little bit of moral autonomy we have managed to build came mostly from our homes, but schools have also made a contribution to this development. *When fostering moral and intellectual autonomy becomes our aim, educators will work hard to increase the area of overlap between the two circles.*

The six national education goals for the year 2000 were conceived within the circle on the right in Figure 1. There is nothing new in these six goals. Everybody agrees on the values they endorse. However, because they are not guided by an overall goal based on scientific theory, the six goals are fragmentary, some-

times contradictory, and conspicuous in their lacunae.

Goal 2 — increasing the graduation rate to 90% — would be easily fulfilled if autonomy were the aim of education and if schools were better adapted to today's students. All adolescents want to become competent and socially respectable, but they drop out of school when classes seem irrelevant and coercive. If high school curricula were relevant and interesting to students, we would find it unnecessary to preach the value of a high school diploma.

The aims of Goal 3 — demonstrating competency in challenging subject matter and being prepared for responsible citizenship — are already included within the idea of autonomy as the aim of education, but they are conceptualized differently. A teacher whose aim is to foster autonomy does not teach English, mathematics, science, history, and so on merely to prepare students for "responsible citizenship, further learning, and productive employment in our modern economy." Intellectual pursuits should enable individuals to make sense of the world and to become competent human beings. Of course, competent individuals are likely to be good citizens and good workers, and educators need to pay closer attention to what sense individuals are making of the world during each hour in every subject.

Goal 4 — to be first in the world in math and science — would be eliminated because mathematics and science are already included in Goal 3, and being first in the world is not a valid goal for education. Our goal should be to turn out young people who can make sense of mathematics and science and who like these subjects. Another reason for eliminating Goal 4 is that it contradicts Goal 2. If 90% of the students stayed in high school, it would certainly not be possible to be "first in the world in mathematics and science achievement" by the year 2000.

Goal 5 — dealing with adult literacy and lifelong learning — would be eliminated, too, because literacy and "knowledge and skills" are already included in Goal 3. Goal 5 makes us wonder whether the governors viewed it as a special goal for the part of the student population that traditionally consists of low achievers.

Goal 6 — that schools be safe, orderly, and free of drugs and violence — would also be eliminated if autonomy were the aim of education because individuals who can take relevant factors into account do not take drugs or resort to violence. The statement that every school in America "will offer a disciplined environment" also reveals a traditional way of thinking. Schools cannot *offer* a disciplined environment. A disciplined environment has to be *created from within* by students and teachers — together.

The lacunae in the six national goals are conspicuous. Nowhere in the formulation of these goals is any attention paid to young people's sense of self, to their relationships with other human beings, to their making sense of the world, or to their mastering of their environment by becoming creative problem solvers.

The social and moral qualities necessary for successful employment, such as dependability, initiative, and a sense of responsibility, are totally absent from the six national goals. These qualities are part of autonomy, which is prevented from developing in most schools and in many homes today. Since heteronomous parents raise heteronomous children, public schools must assume a major role in breaking the cycle of heteronomy.

In a multicultural society, autonomy as the aim of education has the special advantage of not specifying the particular values that we want youngsters to have. We cannot predict, for example, whether an autonomous child will have the values and priorities associated with an environmentalist or those that characterize an industrialist. While we cannot predict what specific virtues and aspirations the child will have, we can be sure of two things about all autonomous people: 1) they will have thought deeply about the factors relevant to any decision, and 2) through exchanging viewpoints, they will have constructed certain basic values, such as taking the rights and feelings of others into account, negotiating solutions in situations of conflict, and basing decisions on what is morally right rather than on anticipated rewards or punishments.

AUTONOMY IN CLASSROOM LIFE

Classrooms today are all too often heteronomous environments in which teachers control children and push them through uninspiring textbooks. Below we specify and illustrate three practices that can be observed throughout the day when the teacher's aim is to develop autonomy in children.

1. *Encouraging children to make decisions and to enforce their own rules.* The traditional role of the teacher is to control children by telling them what to do and by giving them ready-made rules. But children who are always controlled by others can only learn to be controlled. If we want children to be able to make their own decisions and to feel responsible for those decisions, it is best to allow them to make decisions from an early age. For example, a third-grade teacher asked her class to decide how many minutes each student should be allotted to give an oral book report. The children initially decided on 10-minute reports. Then they considered relevant factors, such as the fact that this would take a total of three hours and 40 minutes for the 22 students in the class. Deciding that this was much too long, they next considered five minutes and finally settled on three-minute reports. Having to make such a decision also made for an excellent math lesson, motivated by a genuine need to know.

Children often make exactly the same rules and decisions that the teacher would have made. However, the fact that children have made a rule or decision makes an enormous difference in their commitment to it. Children tend to understand and respect the rules they make. In the course of making a rule, they also come to know that *their* opinions are respected, and they are then more likely to respect the opinions of others, including adults.

To cite another example, teachers often announce that they will give a lower grade or a zero to a paper that is turned in late. By contrast, a teacher whose aim is the development of children's autonomy presents the problem to the class and asks for suggestions about the best way to deal with the problem. The group may make the same rule as the teacher, but this rule will have been constructed by the group out of a personally felt need of its members. Someone may even ask the person whose paper was late, "Do you want me to call you in the evening to make sure you're doing your homework?" The very fact of participating in such a discussion helps children take relevant factors into account as they learn how to make good decisions. Whole-class discussions are much more powerful in motivating students from within than the rewards and punishments teachers usually use.

2. *Fostering intrinsic motivation.* Traditional teaching tries to transmit knowledge through well-organized, "objective," and uninspiring textbooks, with assistance from tests, grades, and other forms of rewards and punishments. The result is that most of us remember such terms as cosine and neutron and such names as the Second Continental Congress. However, we may have only the vaguest notion of what these words mean.

Constructivism, a scientific theory, coupled with the development of autonomy as the aim of education, recognizes that human beings have an intrinsic desire to make sense of the world and that they learn best when they are personally curious, deeply involved, or in a social situation that requires them to take and defend a position. As Piaget pointed out, children work hard when they have intriguing questions to answer and problems to solve. If teaching truly appealed to the human desire to make sense of things, the memorization and the rewards and punishments used today would become outdated. Nor would we forget most of what we "learned" in school.

To take an example from the teaching of American history, a teacher whose goal is children's development of autonomy might ask students to prepare for a debate. With respect to the Second Continental Congress, for instance, a good debate might be between a position in sympathy with the loyalists (loyal to the British Crown) and a position opposing them. Students would have to be extremely well-informed, logical, and critical to participate in such a debate. They might, for example, read biographies of such figures as John Adams, Joseph Galloway, and Thomas Jefferson and come to know the uncertainties and agonies each individual faced as well as the façades and strategies each employed under various circumstances. Having to coordinate subjective perspectives in a debate makes history much more alive and unforgettable than does the "objective," dull textbook. If children are allowed to change sides in the middle of a debate, this especially motivates them to understand both sides of an issue.

3. *Encouraging children to exchange viewpoints.* An essential part of Piaget's theory is the importance of social interaction for the construction of knowledge and moral values. In fact, Piaget pointed out that science has been constructed over the centuries through the exchange

of points of view among scientists. Science is a social enterprise.[7]

Let us return to the example given above of 4 + 4. If in response to the answer "8" the teacher refrains from saying, "That's right," but asks instead, "Does everybody agree?" the class has to come to its own conclusion through the exchange of ideas. If a child says that 4 + 4 = 7, the teacher should also ask if everybody agrees and encourage the subsequent debate. Children *will* arrive at the truth in mathematics if they debate long enough, because nothing is arbitrary in mathematics. In traditional classrooms, the teacher's role is to reinforce correct answers and to correct wrong ones. But children stop thinking and debating when the teacher assumes the responsibility of judging which answer is correct.

If the reader asks any fourth-grader why he or she works from left to right in long division but not in addition, subtraction, and multiplication, the answer is likely to be: "That's the way the teacher told us to do it." In most elementary schools today, mathematics is taught with intellectual heteronomy as the unintended goal of education. If long division were taught through honest, critical debate about each step, there would be no need for all the repetition and worksheets that are now endlessly imposed on children.[8]

A similar situation exists in the social/moral realm. In the case of a conflict between two children in class, traditional teachers tell the parties to "stop it" and to pay attention to the lesson. The result is often that the conflict continues when the teacher's back is turned. A teacher whose aim is autonomy is likely to tell the students to step away from the group to negotiate a solution. If negotiation (the exchange of viewpoints) is encouraged from an early age, children become surprisingly good about settling their disputes.

If two kindergartners are fighting over a toy, for example, traditional teachers preach the virtue of sharing and specify how the toy will be shared. A teacher who fosters the development of autonomy, however, may say to the children, "I don't know what to do, but what I do know how to do is to keep the toy for you until *you* decide on a fair way to solve this problem." As noted earlier, children often decide that neither of them should get the toy. This outcome may be the same as the adult's taking the toy away because they "don't know how to play nicely with it." From the standpoint of the development of the children's autonomy, however, there is a world of difference between their making the decision and an adult's imposition of the same decision.

Most educators and most of the public today think that the hour for English is only for English, that the hour for math is only for math, and so on. They also view the drug problem, AIDS, teenage pregnancies, and violence as separate issues, to be dealt with apart from academic subjects. However, drug abuse, unsafe sex, and violence are all symptoms of heteronomy. As noted earlier, children who can take relevant factors into account do not take drugs or resort to violence to settle conflicts. In the classroom, students develop or are prevented from developing intellectually as well as socially and morally. And the intellectual and social/moral domains are inseparable. A classroom cannot foster the development of autonomy in the intellectual realm while suppressing it in the social and moral realms.

Traditional education begins with a list of desired outcomes and seeks to produce results through the use of pep talks and the promise or threat of rewards or punishments. Piaget's theory, constructivism, coupled with the idea of autonomy as the aim of education, reflects the belief that the education of human beings requires a much deeper, longer-range perspective that is different from the mindset necessary to produce quality cars.

Education that aims to produce autonomy is better suited for life in a democracy than traditional education, which fosters conformity. A long-lasting, successful democracy requires informed, autonomous citizens who consider relevant factors in voting for laws and representatives who make those laws. Autonomy goes far beyond equipping youngsters with "the knowledge and skills necessary to compete in a global economy." If all the public schools in the United States educated children for autonomy during every hour of the 13 years the children are in school, the nation's prisons would be less crowded, the federal deficit and the drug problem would be more amenable to control, and we would be working more positively to solve many of our human and social problems.

1. *America 2000: An Education Strategy* (Washington, D.C: U.S. Government Printing Office, 1991), pp. 62-66.
2. Jean Piaget, *To Understand Is to Invent* (1948; reprint, New York: Viking, 1973).
3. For example, the experiments described in Jean Piaget and Alina Szeminska, *The Child's Conception of Number* (1941; reprint, London: Routledge and Kegan Paul, 1952) have been replicated in Africa, Asia, Australia, North America, and South America.
4. Jean Piaget, *The Moral Judgment of the Child* (1932; reprint, New York: Free Press, 1965).
5. Ibid., p. 148.
6. Ibid.; and Constance Kamii, *Young Children Reinvent Arithmetic* (New York: Teachers College Press, 1985).
7. Jean Piaget and Rolando Garcia, *Psychogenesis and the History of Science* (1983; reprint, New York: Columbia University Press, 1989).
8. For further detail on a constructivist approach to primary arithmetic within the context of autonomy as the overall goal, readers should refer to the following books and videotapes by Constance Kamii, published by Teachers College Press, New York, N.Y.: *Young Children Reinvent Arithmetic* (1985); *Young Children Continue to Reinvent Arithmetic, 2nd Grade* (1989); *Young Children Continue to Reinvent Arithmetic, 3rd Grade* (in press); *Double-Column Addition: A Teacher Uses Piaget's Theory* (videotape, 1989); *Multiplication of Two-Digit Numbers: Two Teachers Using Piaget's Theory* (videotape, 1990); and *Multidigit Division: Two Teachers Using Piaget's Theory* (videotape, 1990).

Where Can Teacher Research Lead? One Teacher's Daydream

Improved instruction, more reflective learners, professional growth, and collegial sharing—all can result from involving teachers in classroom research.

Rita Wright Johnson

Rita Wright Johnson is a Teacher at Franklin Middle School, Fairfax County Public Schools. She can be reached at 12504 Reign Court, Herndon, VA 22071.

It's 4 o'clock in the morning. One of those occasions when I wake up two hours before the alarm is set to go off and can't get back to sleep. My mind drifts back to the previous day, when my teacher-researcher group spent our last "day out."

As members of a collaborative teacher-researcher group, funded and supported by Fairfax County Public Schools, we are each given five administrative leave days during the year to work on research projects. The Office of Research and Policy Analysis provides two support personnel to guide us through the research process. While making final plans for completing our yearly reports, we feel a camaraderie that teachers rarely experience—a moment without competition, refreshing and nonthreatening.

A Morning Muse

On this day we take part in a "read-around." Even though I've experienced sharing in other collaborative research groups, it is new every time.

Each teacher brings a freshness that is never duplicated. As each of us discuss personal research, others join in with similar experiences.

Two teacher researchers who teach elective courses voice similar problems in motivating a student to take elective courses as seriously as required courses. Several of the others, who share the same student, say that he reacts more positively when he is in close physical reach of the teacher. One experience leads into another until all teachers have contributed some of their findings.

Our principal—who has joined us to hear our findings—leaves reluctantly to return to school for the lunch period. She has sensed the importance of what we are learning about ourselves as professionals, about our teaching, and, most important, about our students.

In my own classroom research, I am exploring strategies for working with learning disabled students who are mainstreamed into one of my science classes. As I determine the success or failure of each strategy I try, I adjust my lessons to enable students to be more successful learners.

For example, during my data collection, I find that learning disabled students work well with other students in cooperative groups. In addition to learning from other members of the group, they contribute capably to the group task. After collecting and analyzing data about their interactions, I eventually conclude that cooperative learning is a successful strategy to use with all my students.

What goes through my mind in the wee hours of this morning is that the concept of "reflective practice" may have far-reaching applications. What if college professors actually carried on teacher-research to determine successful strategies in their teaching? They could introduce it to their students, who then could use reflective practice to improve their learning throughout college and later for greater productivity in whatever career they choose. Further, what might the potential applications be for reflective practice for employees in business, industry, and government?

With all of these exciting ideas running through my mind, I have to share them, so I nudge my sleeping husband. His company is doing something like collaborative reflective practice. Executives have been meeting in groups and subgroups to explore ways to cut waste and improve productivity. We have discussed the similarity many times over dinner.

"Paul, who thought of that method you are using at the office?"

"Our new president," he mumbled. "He has a book by a Japanese author." (He turns over and covers his head with the blanket.)

I press on. I can't let Paul fall back asleep and leave me alone in my thoughts. "I've been thinking that what you do is a lot like teacher-research and could be applied to many different occupations—including the government.... Well, what do you think?"

"No," he mumbles, "it isn't the same. The Japanese use this method in businesses, and it goes all the way down to the bottom of the corporate ladder. If you used their method, then your students would be doing it, too."

"That's an interesting thought. But I think they are doing it—researching their own learning, I mean. Yes, they are! At the beginning of a group project, I ask them to list the ingredients needed for collaboratively producing a successful project. Then, I tell them to use as many of the ingredients as possible during their work. The elements they identify include listening to everyone's ideas, staying on task, and respecting others' feelings.

"Next they evaluate their final group projects by writing about the activity in learning logs. They write about any specific problems that delayed their progress and describe how the group solved them. Then, when beginning the next group project, they draw on this information. Finally, my students write about what they learned from the project.

"That's reflective learning," I add,

"And it is similar to reflective teaching, which is what teacher-researchers do."

Obviously I'm not going to get any more out of Paul at this time of night. He has fallen back into sleep.

Back to Reality

The next morning, there isn't time to continue our discussion. I'm ready to leave for school, where 28 7th graders are waiting to find out if they can choose their favorite endangered species to research for a report.

Later that day, my thoughts focus on the impact of my research on my teaching. I know that changes are taking place because of the research. Five years ago, when I joined a collaborative teacher-researcher group at Hughes Intermediate School to explore teaching and learning, I came across a research question that changed my teaching forever: *Can writing-to-learn strategies improve the achievement of students in my science classes?*

Although I had tried a few writing activities the previous year at the request of our principal, I hadn't seen value in the activities. After joining the teacher-research group, however, I read some articles about using writing-to-learn in science and wanted to explore it further. My research topic became: *What happens when 7th graders use writing-to-learn in science?*

That year I experimented with the process. My 7th grade science students completed their assignments in "learning logs." In my own research log, I wrote about what was happening as they wrote. I chose four students, who I felt represented a cross section of my class, and read their learning logs regularly. Each month I met with the research group and shared what was happening. During these exchanges, other teachers helped me analyze the data. By the end of the year, I had a lot of evidence showing how writing had involved these students in science learning.

The activity that stood out the most was the writing that occurred after my students had viewed films. I had

always printed up sheets of questions for students to answer after watching films. Then one day a former student stopped by. Noticing that I had scheduled a science film for the day's activity, she remarked that when she was in my class, she had hated the films because of having to answer the questions afterwards. Surprised that she had disliked the activity so much, I decided to take a closer look at this strategy.

As I observed students viewing films, I discovered that they were so busy taking notes that they were missing much of the valuable information. When I asked my students to listen carefully—but not take notes because there would be no questions—they were able later to write pages of information, even using new vocabulary, that showed what they learned. By letting them share aloud their writings, I found that they wrote more and became enthusiastic about their writing. Not only did they learn more, but they also enjoyed watching the films when they didn't have to answer the questions.

After this illuminating lesson, I threw away all of the question sheets. Not only do I not have to spend time developing questions for each film or video I show, but my students are learning more from the writing activities. The success of this activity encouraged me to search for further ways to use writing-to-learn with my students.

Sharing Teacher Research

As I reflected on my experience as a teacher-researcher that first year, I knew that there were even deeper questions being answered than the one my research focused on: What happens when a teacher looks at her own classroom to discover what learning is taking place? What happens when students look at their own learning? What happens when a teacher shares research results with other teachers?

I shared my findings in our teacher research group. Writing-to-learn soon became a common thread in the research reports we wrote at the end of the year. Other teacher-researchers had found the strategy to be effective in their classrooms as well.

The following year we formed a Writing-to-Learn Research Group to interest other teachers in the process. Six other teachers joined the group, which I led, to continue research about using writing-to-learn in science, math, English, and creative writing.

Over the months, the sharing continued. Our final report, in the form of a poster, displayed a large tree with branches indicating where we had tried writing-to-learn with our students in various ways that year. We had many copies of the "Branch Out and Use Writing-to-Learn" poster printed and gave them to our faculty. Many still hang in the teachers' workrooms and in some classrooms. We also presented the posters at workshops in the county and in surrounding school districts. Some posters even made it to the National Science Teachers' Convention. Recently, at the request of my principal, I shared the posters with the faculty at my present school. Six teachers requested more information about writing-to-learn in their subject areas. At least two of them said, "I used some of your ideas the very next day."

The next way I shared my research with other teachers was through writing. My article "Using Writing-to-Learn with Films" was published in *Science Scope* (October 1991), a National Science Teacher Association publication. When I ran into other science teachers I knew from other parts of Fairfax County, they remarked that they had seen my article and successfully tried writing-to-learn with films in their classes. And so, in addition to my students and myself learning from the research experience, my colleagues were also learning. Staff development was growing out of my research.

Not only have teachers learned from my research, but I also have learned from other teacher-researchers' findings. For example, a first-time teacher-researcher in our group, a speech clinician, gave a learning styles inventory to her students. After her students and their parents eagerly received the results, she modified some of her teaching strategies to more closely match her students' learning styles. She also began working with some students individually to improve their speech.

The experiences she shared with the group caused me to reflect on my own teaching strategies and the learning styles of my students. Teacher research *again* had led to new knowledge, changed instructional practice, involved students in reflecting on their own learning, and encouraged colleagues to learn from one another.

Daydreaming Again

The changes I see taking place in my own teaching and that of other teacher-researchers confirm my belief in the value of reflective practice. As I begin to drift into another pleasant reverie, I imagine what would happen if senators, representatives, and all our government leaders actually reflected about how they operate in committees and in the larger group. It seems to me that others could profit from taking a closer systematic look at what they do to appraise its effectiveness.

I begin to formulate in my mind the letter I will write to the President of the United States. Reflective practice could solve the "educational crisis," I speculate—and who knows what might happen to the national debt! I envision myself in an elegant waiting room. Deep in thought, I hear the receptionist repeat her invitation: "Mrs. Johnson, the President will see you now!"

Development

- Childhood (Articles 4–7)
- Adolescence (Articles 8 and 9)

The study of human development provides us with knowledge of how children and adolescents mature and learn within the family, community, and school environment. Educational psychology focuses on the description and explanation of the developmental processes that make it possible for children to become intelligent and socially competent adults. Psychologists and educators are presently studying the idea that heredity and environment influence cognitive, personal, social, and emotional development.

Jean Piaget's theory regarding the cognitive development of children and adolescents is perhaps the best known and most comprehensive. According to this theory, the perceptions and thoughts that young children have about the world are often prelogical and premoral. When compared to adolescents and adults, children think about moral and social issues in a unique way. Children need to acquire cognitive, moral, and social skills in order to interact effectively with parents, teachers, and peers. If human intelligence encompasses all of the above skills, then Piaget may have been correct in saying that human development is the child's intelligent adaptation to the environment.

Today the cognitive, moral, social, and emotional development of children takes place in a rapidly changing society. A child must develop a sense of self-worth and autonomy as well as a strong sense of family, in order to cope with the changes and become a competent and socially responsible adult. The article by Marjorie Kostelnik presents ways teachers can provide children with appropriate experiences that enhance their development while the articles by Judith Schickedanz, Janet Kuebli, and Donna Sasse Wittmer and Alice Sterling Honig discuss the social and emotional needs of children.

Adolescence brings with it the ability to think abstractly and hypothetically and to see the world from many perspectives. Adolescents strive to form goals and to achieve a sense of identity, but they often become frustrated and feel alienated from the adult world. The kinds of adults they want to become and the ideals they want to believe in sometimes lead to conflicts with parents and teachers. Adolescents are also sensitive about espoused adult values versus adult behavior. The articles in this unit discuss the social and personal problems that confront adolescents, as well as suggest ways the family and school can help meet the needs of adolescents.

Looking Ahead: Challenge Questions

What are some of the social pressures and risks children face in growing up? How can parents and teachers help children to develop a sense of competence and self-esteem?

How can teachers provide children and adolescents with experiences that promote their cognitive, moral, social, and emotional development?

Describe the societal and personal problems adolescents face. What is meant by resiliency?

How can the middle school provide a balance between the physical, cognitive, and affective aspects of learning and development for adolescents?

Unit 2

MYTHS Associated with Developmentally Appropriate Programs

Marjorie J. Kostelnik

Marjorie J. Kostelnik, president of the Michigan Association for the Education of Young Children, is a professor of Family and Child Ecology at Michigan State University and program supervisor of the Child Development Laboratories on campus. She is editor of Teaching Young Children Using Themes, *published in 1991 by Good Year Books.*

It seems everywhere early childhood practitioners turn these days, people are talking about developmentally appropriate practice and programs. The term 'developmentally appropriate' has become prominent in journal articles, books, the media, professional newsletters, conference presentations, publishers' materials and manufacturers' advertising. Teachers and administrators, theoreticians and researchers, parents and politicians have all become involved in the 'developmentally appropriate' programs discussion. The problem is, not everyone means the same thing when they use the term. In fact, the phrase developmentally appropriate is becoming a catch word people use to describe almost anything and everything associated with early childhood education. The same terminology may be used to justify such incompatible notions as 'readiness' programs for children and programs that advocate giving children the 'gift of time'—structuring children's learning experiences within narrowly defined parameters and not structuring them at all—grouping children by ability and grouping children by almost any criteria other than ability. These inconsistencies have led to much confusion about what developmentally appropriate programs entail (Walsh, 1991).

In the absence of true understanding, myths have sprung up to explain what it all means. These myths represent collective opinions that are based on false assumptions or are the product of fallacious reasoning. Some have evolved from people's attempts to simplify a complex phenomenon, resulting in oversimplification to the point of inaccuracy. Others have resulted from people's intuitive interpretations of child behavior or superficial understanding of child development and learning-related theories and research (Spodek, 1986). Still more myths have been created as a way for people to make finite and absolute, a concept that is in fact open-ended and amenable to many variations. Unfortunately, these myths are widespread; causing misunderstandings and anxiety among practitioners and the public. What follows are a few of the most common ones I have encountered both in this country and abroad.

MYTH: *There is one right way to implement a developmentally appropriate program.*

REALITY: When talking about developmentally appropriate practice with any group of practitioners it is not unusual to hear statements like, "You always use learning centers." "You never use whole group instruction." "You always let children determine the content of the lesson." "You never correct children." "You always let children figure out their own spellings for words." "You never use lined paper." Likewise, teachers and administrators may ask, "Is it ever okay to show children how to hold a pencil?" "Is it wrong to spell words for children when they ask?" "Exactly when should we introduce cursive writing?" These kinds of pronouncements and queries represent efforts to establish single, correct approaches to instruction. They are based on the belief that one method of teaching suits all children and all situations. Unfortunately, the reality is that teaching is complex; there is no one solution that fits every circumstance. On the contrary, individual teaching episodes can and should be qualified by "It depends" (Newman and Church, 1990). It depends on such variables as what the child's current level of comprehension might be, what experiences the child might have had, and the kinds of previous knowledge and skills the child brings to the situation. Contextual elements including time, human resources, the physical environment, material resources, and the values and expectations of the school and community must also be factored in. The goals, strategies and standards school personnel finally choose are all affected by these constraints. Hence, every educational decision requires judgement—judgements by teachers and administrators—made on the spot or over time, but always with certain children in mind. This means practitioners must continually weigh out what they do in relation to their knowledge about how children develop and learn. To translate that knowledge into actual teaching strategies, they must be willing to explore a variety of practices in the classroom and to allow themselves to make mistakes. Moreover, teachers will have to continually examine their assumptions and learn from the children as they evaluate the effectiveness of their teaching. What meets the needs of several children in a group may not be appropriate for others. What was optimal for last year's class, may not be so this year. One's search, then, is not simply for 'right' answers but for the best answers to meet the needs of children representing a wide

These myths represent collective opinions that are based on false assumptions or are the product of fallacious reasoning.

range of abilities, learning styles, interests and backgrounds. Finally, teachers, too, differ from one another and require flexibility to develop an approach to teaching that is compatible with their beliefs and comfortable for them as well as for their students. These variations in both children's and teacher's needs necessitate differences in the programs designed to meet them. Hence there is no one model that is best for all.

MYTH: *Developmentally appropriate practice requires teachers to abandon all their prior knowledge and experience. Nothing they have learned or done in the past is acceptable in the new philosophy.*

REALITY: It is not only a daunting prospect, but an affrontive one, for seasoned practitioners to contemplate returning to novice status in their pursuit of developmentally appropriate practice. Those who approach the idea in this frame of mind are understandably discouraged and/or resistant. However, the facts of the matter are, few experienced teachers require a total 'make-over' to become more developmentally appropriate in their practices. The knowledge of children and teaching they have gained over the years will serve as the foundation from which they

can examine their pedagogical beliefs and instructional practices. In addition, since the concept of developmental appropriateness has evolved from past educational trends, most teachers are already implementing numerous philosophically compatible strategies and activities in their classrooms. Some practitioners simply need 'permission' to continue. Others need help recognizing their own strengths. In either case, teachers are most successful making the transition to more developmentally appropriate practice when they build on what they know.

MYTH: *Developmentally appropriate classrooms are unstructured classrooms.*

REALITY: Some people make this claim because they equate structure with rigidity and so shun the term. Others envision a classroom in which chaos reigns. Both interpretations are based on misinformation. Structure refers to the extent to which teachers develop an instructional plan, then organize the physical setting and social environment to support the achievement of educational goals (Spodek, Saracho and Davis, 1991).

By this definition, developmentally appropriate classrooms are highly structured. Both teachers and children contribute to their organization. Teachers generate educational goals for students based on school-wide expectations tempered by their understanding of individual children's needs, abilities and interests. All of the activities and routines of the day are purposefully planned to promote these goals. Keeping their instruc-

Every educational decision requires judgement—judgements by teachers and administrators—made on the spot or over time, but always with certain children in mind.

tional plan in mind, teachers determine the arrangement of the furniture, what specific materials to offer children, the nature and flow of activity, the approximate time to allocate to various instructional segments, and the grouping of children throughout the session. As teachers interact with children they observe them, listen to them, instruct them, guide them, support them and encourage them. Consequently, while teachers carefully consider long-range objectives, their moment-to-moment decision-making remains fluid in order to capitalize on input from the children (Newman and Church, 1990). Children ask questions, suggest alternatives, express interests and develop plans that may lead the instruction in new directions. In this way, overall instructional goals are merged with more immediate ones, thereby creating a flexible, stimulating classroom structure.

Developmentally appropriate classrooms are active ones in which both teachers and students learn from one another. Such learning requires a constant interchange of thoughts and ideas. As a result, there are times during the day when many people are talking at once or when several children are moving about the room at one time. To the untrained eye these conditions may appear chaotic, but a closer look should reveal children on-task, constructively involved in their own learning. If children are wandering aimlessly, screaming indiscriminately or racing from place to place, the environment is not conducive to learning, and so is developmentally inappropriate.

MYTH: *In developmentally appropriate classrooms, teachers don't teach.*

REALITY: This myth stems from the stereotypic idea that teachers are people who stand up in front of a group of students, telling them what they need to know. And, that

the teacher's most important duties consist of assigning work to children and checking for right and wrong answers. According to this scenario, teachers are always directive and center-stage. People who envision teachers this way may not recognize all the teaching that is going on in a developmentally appropriate classroom. For example, teachers create physical environments and daily schedules that enable children to engage in purposeful activity. Curricular goals are frequently addressed through pervasive classroom routines such as dressing to go outside, preparing for snack and cleaning-up. Although some whole group instruction takes place, teachers spend much of their classroom time moving throughout the room working with children individually and in small informal groups. During these times, they influence children's learning indirectly through the provision of certain activities in which the focus is on children's self-discovery and exploration. They also teach children directly, using a variety of instructional strategies. Teachers initiate learning activities as well as respond to children's initiatives. They pose questions, offer procedural suggestions, suggest explorations and provide information. As opportunities arise, instructors present children with challenges that help them move beyond their current understandings and strategies (Newman and Church, 1990). Additionally, teachers constantly reflect on what is happening in the classroom. They make judgements about children's progress and introduce variations or changes in focus as children's needs warrant. All of these activities are essential teaching behaviors.

Teachers are most successful making the transition to more developmentally appropriate practice when they build on what they know.

MYTH: To be developmentally appropriate, elementary teachers and administrators will have to 'water down' the traditional curriculum. Children will learn less than they have in the past.

REALITY: This myth is based on two assumptions: (1) that all learning is hierarchical in nature, and (2) that the curriculum offered in many elementary schools today is sufficient in scope. Neither is correct.

Learning can be characterized as occurring in two directions, vertically and horizontally. Vertical learning is hierarchical; it can be likened to climbing a ladder. A person starts at the base and gradually moves upward, pausing now and then or even vacillating between rungs, but with little veering off to the sides. This kind of learning piles fact or skill on top of the other. As the learner proceeds higher and higher, the result is an increase in the number and complexity of the facts and skills he or she has attained.

Horizontal learning, on the other hand, is conceptually based. An analogy that comes to mind is that of casting a net in all directions, then drawing it back in. Within this framework, experiences occur more or less simultaneously, and the role of the learner becomes that of making connections among these experiences. Horizontal learning implies a deepening understanding of the world through the development of increasingly elaborate concepts.

Both vertical and horizontal learning are essential to human understanding. The former expands one's quantity of knowledge and skills, the latter contributes to their quality. Neither should be emphasized to the detriment of the other. Yet, the lock-step nature of the curriculum in many primary schools promotes vertical learning to the exclusion of concept development. Curriculum guides delineate a vertical scope and sequence for every subject. Children are continually pushed upward, even when they show signs of inadequate comprehension. If children need more time to consolidate their understandings (an example of horizontal learning), they are identified as 'falling behind' or 'at-risk' for potential failure. Conversely, when children complete the scope and sequence for a given subject in a particular grade, they are encouraged to continue their vertical climb into the next grade level rather than spending time on strengthening the linkages among the bits and pieces of knowledge they have acquired. The fundamental flaw in all this is that children in the early years are establishing the conceptual base from which all future learning will proceed. Their need for a solid, broad foundation, and hence much horizontal learning, is great. The breadth of the conceptual base children form influences how well they eventually perform in school. The narrower the base, the fewer connections children are able to make among the bits and pieces of knowledge that they encounter over time. The broader the base, the more comprehensive their learning. More of a balance in the curriculum, with both kinds of learning being addressed and valued, is a fundamental tenet of developmentally appropriate programs. This would result, not in children learning less, but in children learning better.

Similarly, the past decades have witnessed a narrowing of the elementary curriculum. Many schools have gone from a holistic approach to learning that includes social, physical, cognitive, and aesthetic aims, to one that focuses almost solely on isolated academic skills such as tracing letters and memorizing number facts (Peck, McCaig and Sapp, 1988). The beliefs underlying developmentally appropriate programs are that the curriculum needs to be expanded to include experiences related to all aspects of child development. Again, this is not a cry to limit children's learning but to broaden it. The result will not be a 'watered down' program, but a richer, more comprehensive one.

MYTH: *Developmentally appropriate programs can be defined according to dichotomous positions. One position is always right, the other position is always wrong.*

REALITY: The dichotomies, Process-focused versus Product-focused, Child-initiated versus Adult-initiated, Socially-oriented versus Cognitively oriented, are some of the ones people typically refer to when talking about developmentally appropriate programs. Such discussions tend to treat these variables as polar opposites. As a result, the items on the left, above, are usually defined as 'good', 'desirable' and 'appropriate'; those on the right, as 'bad', 'undesirable', and 'inappropriate'. Furthermore, because the categories are mutually exclusive, they imply that developmentally appropriate programs are 100 percent process-focused with no thought given to products; that children initiate all learning episodes and adults initiate none; that social development is more important than cognition. None of these assertions are true. Developmentally appropriate programming is not an all or nothing proposition. For example, process learning is very important to children and should be highly valued by teachers. The satisfaction a child gains from painting is more important than the degree to which his or her picture represents the adult's notion of reality. However, anyone who has watched young children proudly show-off their work knows that products are sometimes important too. Likewise, many, many activities in the developmentally appropriate classroom come about through child exploration and initiation. Yet, others are introduced by the teacher as a way to spark children's interest in something new. Furthermore, although social development cannot be ignored, neither can cognitive pursuits. To elevate one above the other denies the integrative nature of child development. Consequently, it is more accurate to envision variables such as these along continuums. Rather than calling to mind issues of all or none, yes or no, good or bad, a continuum suggests that educational planning is really a matter of degrees and balance. Developmentally appropriate programs are both varied and comprehensive. They enable children to engage in the kinds of experiences they need at a given time. Such experiences will fall in different places along the continuum, depending on the child, and will differ from time to time.

MYTH: *Academics have no place in developmentally appropriate programs.*

REALITY: Academics represent the traditional content of the schools. In most people's minds this encompasses reading, writing and arithmetic. Proponents of this myth believe young children are not 'ready' for academics. They proudly announce that students in their programs are not expected to read or use numbers or write. Opponents point to the myth as a sign that children who participate in developmentally appropriate programs are not 'learning' the essentials. They worry that such children will lack critical skills necessary for achievement. Both claims are based on an overly nar-

23

> While teachers carefully consider long-range objectives, their moment-to-moment decision-making remains fluid in order to capitalize on input from the children. Children ask questions, suggest alternatives, express interests and develop plans that may lead the instruction in new directions.

row interpretation of academic learning. They equate academics with technical subskills (e.g., reciting the ABC's or writing out numerical equations) or with rote instruction (e.g., emphasis on worksheets and drill). Each of these definitions is too narrow in scope. They confuse concepts with methods and ignore how reading, writing and number-related behaviors and understandings emerge in young children's lives. Children do not wait for elementary school to demonstrate an interest in words and numbers. They manifest literacy-related interests as infants when they mouth a book or 'pat the bunny', and again as toddlers when they beg, "read it again." Likewise, young children count—one cookie . . . two shoes . . . three candles on the birthday cake. They compare—"Which has more? . . . Who still needs some?" Children calculate—"Will it fit?" "Now I have two, I need one more." These kinds of activities form the beginnings of literacy and mathematical thinking—the true essence of academics.

Children continue on in this manner as they mature, seeking new knowledge and skills as their capacities to know and do increase. Thus, there is no specific time before or after which such learning is either appropriate or inappropriate. These evaluative labels are better applied to the parameters within which academics are defined and the strategies teachers use to address academic learning. Programs that focus on isolated skill development and that rely on long periods of whole group in-

struction or abstract paper-and-pencil activities do not meet the needs of young children. Those that emphasize concepts and processes, that utilize small group instruction, active manipulation of relevant, concrete materials and interactive learning provide a solid foundation for academics within a context of meaningful activity. Using children's interests and ways of learning as guides, early childhood teachers do four things to promote academic learning. First, they understand the broad nature of literacy and mathematics and are familiar with the concepts, processes and content that they comprise. They recognize that reading is more than reciting the alphabet or making letter-sound associations out of context; that writing is not the same as penmanship; that mathematics goes beyond rote memorization of number facts. Second, they recognize manifestations of academic interest and exploratory behavior in the children they teach (e.g., "Teacher, what does this say?" "How many do we need?" "Look what I made." etc.). Third, teachers provide concrete materials and relevant experiences to enhance children's academic learning (e.g., They read to children often and invite children to respond and interpret the story. They sing songs, read poems, and play rhyming games in which sound associations are addressed. They give children materials to sort, sequence, count, combine or divide and make estimations about. They offer children many ways to express themselves both orally and

in writing). Fourth, teachers introduce new information, materials, and problems that stimulate children to make observations and comparisons, to question, to experiment, to derive meaning, to make predictions and from which to draw their own conclusions. In this way academics become an integral part of classroom life.

MYTH: *Developmentally appropriate programs are suitable for only certain kinds of children.*

REALITY: Some people believe that the notion of developmental appropriateness only fits young children, or middle-class children, or Euro-American children, or children who have no special needs. This is a fallacy. While specific details of what is appropriate for children will vary from population to population and from child to child, the principles guiding developmentally appropriate programs are universally applicable. To put it another way, one might ask, "For what children is it appropriate to ignore how they develop and learn? For what child is it inappropriate to treat him or her as an individual?" If the answer is none, then there is no group for whom the basic tenets of developmental appropriateness do not apply.

MYTH: *Developmental appropriateness is just a fad, soon to be replaced by another, perhaps opposite, trend.*

REALITY: One cannot blame prac-

Academics are an integral part of classroom life.

titioners for being skeptical about the potential longevity of any new idea in education. Teachers and administrators perceive that theirs is a profession in which instructional practices come and go with predictable regularity. Cyclic trends are also common, with ideas gaining notoriety for a time, then fading from the scene, only to reappear years later in a newly packaged form. It is not surprising, therefore, that many practitioners figure developmental appropriateness is simply a 'retread' of previous ideas or that others think, "This too shall pass." In either case, their motivation to embrace this philosophy is seriously reduced because practitioners assume its influence will not last long.

As with any myth, there is some truth to these assertions. Yet there are also flaws in this reasoning. First, developmental appropriateness does share similarities with previous trends in early childhood education, but it also differs markedly from those trends. Building on what went on before, developmental appropriateness does not duplicate the past. Consequently, the concept represents an evolution in professional thinking that will continue to emerge over the coming decades. In other words, early childhood educators are not simply revisiting old ideas. They are integrating the truths of previously developed hypotheses with other, newer understandings. The result has been the creation of an enhanced concept that is uniquely suited to modern times.

Additionally, one reason why trends come and go is that old technologies are constantly being replaced by newer ones. This is a natural occurrence because people are constantly discovering better ways to do things. If developmental appropriateness is treated merely as a technology encompassing specific materials (e.g., unifix cubes or Big Books) and particular activities (e.g., choral reading or Math Their Way tubbing), it could suffer the same fate, for there is no reason to believe that we will not continue to find ways to improve instructional practices in the future. On the other hand, if developmental appropriateness is conceived of as a philosophy, it will not be technology bound. Certain basic assumptions and beliefs will prevail, regardless of how we choose to operationalize them. In other words, the essence of developmental appropriateness is not simply what we do, but how we think—how we think about children and programs; what we value children doing and learning; how we define effectiveness and success. If developmental appropriateness transcends technology and moves to this higher conceptual plane, then its influence is likely to endure.

References

Newman, J.M., & Church, S.M. (1990). Myths of whole language. *The Reading Teacher, 44*(1), 20–26.

Peck, J.T., McCaig, G., & Sapp, M.E. (1988). *Kindergarten policies: What is best for children?* Washington, DC: NAEYC.

Spodek, B. (1986). *Today's kindergarten.* New York: Teachers College Press.

Spodek, B., Saracho, O.N., & Davis, M.D. (1991). *Foundations of early childhood education.* Englewood Cliffs, NJ: Prentice Hall.

Walsh, D.J. (1991). Extending the discourse on developmental appropriateness. *Early Education and Development, 2*(2), 109–119.

This article is an adaptation of a chapter by Marjorie Kostelnik in *Developmentally Appropriate Practice for Early Education: A Practical Guide* by M.J. Kostelnik, A.P. Whiren, and A.K. Soderman, being published by Charles Merrill, Westerville, Ohio.

An earlier version of this article appeared in *The Beacon,* Newsletter of the Michigan Association for the Education of Young Children. [Volume XI, Number 1]

Helping Children Develop Self-Control

Judith A. Schickedanz

Judith A. Schickedanz is a Professor in the School of Education, Boston University.

The apparent causes of children's violent behavior are well known. Children are often witnesses of violence committed by one adult against another, and are themselves frequent victims of abuse or neglect. Gunfire has become commonplace in cities. Gangs and drugs are other destructive forces. During the times when not directly affected by real violence, many children watch violent television programs. Finally, child socialization, both within the family and at school, seems weaker today than in years past, and many adults seem incapable of making sacrifices for the sake of their own or someone else's children.

It is no wonder that today's children create difficult challenges for their teachers, or that teachers feel physically and emotionally exhausted at day's end. For many years, I have worked with urban preschool and kindergarten teachers, sometimes spending two or three days a week in their classrooms. I know firsthand about teachers' exhaustion. And I understand what they mean when they say, "Children today are violent and lack self-control." But I also think that some of the difficulties in classrooms emerge because teachers themselves are unaware of children's potential for developing social competence, including self-regulation.

A cognitive-developmental view of social development has dominated early childhood teachers' thinking about children's social and moral development for several decades. Therefore, teachers sometimes have been less effective in promoting self-regulation in children than they might have been. Teachers cannot, and must not, be blamed for the larger societal forces that play havoc with children's lives. They cannot be expected to work miracles. But neither can we ignore the potential good that teachers can achieve; in fact, teachers should be considered an important element in the effort to improve children's self-control.

Child Socialization: Theory, Research and Practice

Beginning in the 1960s, ideas about child socialization were influenced dramatically by Piaget's cognitive-developmental theories. According to this theory, moral development is necessarily a late occurrence because it depends on, and emerges from, well-developed capacities for logical reasoning and social role-taking (Piaget, 1977). Also, skill in social role-taking—the adoption of different perspectives—depends on interaction with people of equal status (Piaget, 1977).

Piaget used several tasks to gauge moral development by probing children's reasoning. To study children's understanding of rules, he observed them as they played marbles, asked them to teach him

to play and questioned them about the origin of the rules (Piaget, 1977). He examined children's understandings of intentions by telling stories and then asking the children to make and explain judgments about them (Piaget, 1977). Kohlberg, a follower of Piaget, also asked children to make judgments and explain their reasoning about moral dilemmas (Kohlberg, 1969).

Logical reasoning, however, is not the young child's strength. Requiring children to reveal their social understanding through verbal explanations puts them at a big disadvantage in demonstrating their budding competence. Not surprisingly, young children, especially preschoolers, perform poorly on most of these tasks (Piaget, 1977).

Another requirement for moral development, beyond building children's capacity to engage in logical reasoning, is developing skills in social perspective-taking. Cognitive-developmentalists believe development of this skill requires social interaction in situations of "mutual respect" (i.e., among peers or with adults who don't "pull rank"). Piaget stated that "the sense of justice, though naturally capable of being reinforced by the precepts and the practical example of the adult, is largely independent of these influences, and requires nothing more for its development than the mutual respect and solidarity ... among children themselves" (Piaget 1977, p. 190). Young children's poor grasp of the rules of marbles was, he believed, a result

From *Childhood Education*, Annual Theme Issue, 1994, pp. 274-278. Reprinted by permission of Judith A. Schickedanz and the Association for Childhood Education International, 11501 Georgia Avenue, Suite 315, Wheaton, MD. © 1994 by the Association.

of their "unilateral respect" for the older children and adults who taught them the rules. Because the younger children had not participated in rule formation, they viewed the rules as external and, therefore, did not understand or abide by them.

Kohlberg (1969) expressed similar views: "Family participation is not unique or critically necessary for moral development . . . other primary groups stimulate more development" (p. 399). Given children's "unilateral respect" for their parents, Kohlberg found parent-child interaction was not ideal for mutual role-taking. Kohlberg recommended "intense peer group interaction, supervised by a group leader." He observed high levels of moral reasoning among adolescents living in an Israeli kibbutz where they had "low interaction with parents" (1976, p. 400). The kibbutz leaders included the adolescents in decisions about many daily activities.

Considerable research has been conducted on peer interaction since the early 1970s, perhaps because of its primary importance in cognitive-developmental theory. Many researchers have wondered how social behavior differs among children who have been judged by peers to be popular, neglected or outcast. Results from many studies show that rejected children tend to be aggressive and self-centered. They also are more likely to infer hostility from their peers' behavior even when this may not be the case (Hudley & Graham, 1993).

Social skills researchers, like cognitive developmentalists, have focused on reasoning—children's understanding of others' views and intentions. While some of these researchers recognize anger, they attribute its cause to perceptions of the social situation. To reduce anger and the resulting aggression, children are trained to interpret situations differently (Hudley & Graham, 1993) and to improve their participation, cooperation and communication skills (Oden & Asher, 1977).

The Impact of Cognitive-Developmental Theory

Early childhood educators are continually told that children's interaction with peers is very important, while interaction with adults is less important. After hearing that "obedience is not enough" (Kamii, 1984), educators may wonder if it is desirable at all. They have been cautioned that "unless handled positively, discipline of any kind may be perceived by the child as punishment . . . children of 3 to 8 years of age are still just beginning to learn the advanced skills of seeing things from another person's perspective" (Gartrell, 1987, p. 55).

Furthermore, professionals have been encouraged not to get too involved in children's conflicts. Oken-Wright (1992) encourages teachers to use a "teacher behavior continuum" (TBC) developed by Wolfgang and Glickman (1980). Oken-Wright urges teachers to intervene initially in children's conflicts in a way that gives children complete control. If this fails, the teacher intervenes in ever-increasing amounts, finally taking complete control only if necessary. As an example, a child excluded from a school sandbox reported her mistreatment to the teacher, who asked, "What do you suppose you could do if you want to play there?" The child said that she could ask the other child. The teacher and child returned to the sandbox, whereupon the first child "invited" the second child to play. According to the author, this invitation was extended while a "non-judgmental" adult looked on (Oken-Wright, 1992, p. 18).

In this case, however, it is inaccurate to say that the adult was "non-judgmental." When the teacher asked the child what she could do to play in the sandbox, the teacher implied her belief that the child had the right to play in the sandbox and that the other child had been wrong to exclude her. The adult made the moral decision, while the child was responsible only for finding a solution to the specific conflict.

Many authors explicitly tell teachers not to make moral decisions. For example, Hitz and Driscoll (1988) note their agreement with Kamii's (1984) view that praise is a reward and "like other forms of reward [it] discourages children from judging for themselves what is right or wrong" (p. 9). They imply that moral decisions should be left to the children. Ironically, to give praise, sometimes teachers first must make a decision about what behavior is right or desirable. Instead of telling a child that he is nice because he shared with a classmate, Hitz and Driscoll advise teachers to say, "José, I noticed that you shared today with Alice," leaving José to decide if he was "nice" (p. 12).

Because teachers cannot determine easily the child's intent in many situations, it is wise to describe the child's desirable behavior and leave it at that. In addition, young children can become overly concerned about what the teacher thinks of them, rather than their behavior. Whatever the approach used to praise children, teachers first must make a moral judgment. A teacher wouldn't comment on sharing if she did not consider sharing to be more desirable than not sharing. Because such comments usually are accompanied by smiles and a pleasant tone of voice, most young children probably know that the teacher holds sharing in high regard.

Because researchers recommend that teachers allow children to make their own moral judgments, the teachers often conclude that they should remove themselves completely from children's conflicts. Even in situations where a teacher knows a child has been wronged, the teacher might not intervene in order to provide the child with crucial experience in making moral judgments and solving conflicts. Often the child continues to complain to the teacher about the transgression and may start whining, crying or throwing a tantrum. The teacher does not realize, perhaps, that his own reluctance to take a stand in the situation confuses and undermines the child, making it difficult for the child to act.

It is true that children's skills in handling conflicts can be limited if adults think of all the solutions, or completely intercede to solve a dispute. But research (and human experience) does not show any benefits to children when adults remove themselves completely from children's conflicts or refuse to take a stand on what is right or wrong.

Evidence That Moral Development Begins Early
Cognitive-developmental theorists, as we have seen, assume that social understandings, especially the development of awareness about other people's feelings and thoughts, emerge late in development. Dunn (1988) questioned this assumption:

Do we conclude that for a child the crucial development—the understanding that other people have feelings and minds like his or her own, yet also different—is extremely slow? Children develop their powers of communication, understanding and thought, their emotional security and their sense of themselves, within a complex social framework: do they nevertheless fail to grasp the nature of the moods, interests and relationships of others who share that world, or the ground rules of that world, until they are 5 or 7 years old? (p. 3)

Children only 2 years old will attempt to comfort a parent in distress (Dunn, 1988; Zahn-Waxler & Radke-Yarrow, 1982). At first, they use simple strategies, such as offering their own comfort objects to the parent or patting the parent. As they develop, they find another person to help and they locate objects or materials they have seen used when people are hurt (i.e., first aid items).

Very young children's other behaviors also indicate social competence, including judgments about violations of a standard and awareness that others make social judgments and hold opinions. In Dunn's study (1988), children not yet 3 years old called their mother's attention to a sibling's wrongdoing. A study by Zahn-Waxler, Radke-Yarrow, Wagner and Chapman (1992) demonstrated that 2-year-olds responded differently in situations where they caused someone's distress as opposed to situations where they witnessed but did not cause distress. In other studies, babies as young as 8 or 9 months used a "social reference"—perhaps by reading their mothers' social signals—to ascertain their reaction to a stranger or a novel toy (Klinnert, 1981; Walden & Baxter, 1989).

> ## When rejecting parents express negative emotion, their children do not absorb moral lessons or internalize standards.

Other researchers have also documented the abilities that very young children bring to social situations. Kagan (1981) noted some advances in relevant cognitive abilities during the last half of children's second year. At this stage, the child becomes able to "infer the cause of an event" and begins to "expect events to have antecedents." As a result, the child "automatically generates cognitive hypotheses as to causes" (p. 124). The 2-year-old is also "self-aware," and can judge his or her "competence to attain a goal defined by a standard" (p. 129). In addition, the child is able "to generate ideas of goals and to hold them in awareness . . . He becomes aware of the fact that he can initiate, cease, and monitor his actions" (p. 135).

Zahn-Waxler, et al. (1992), summarized the abilities of the very young child. They concluded that the very young child has "a) the cognitive capacity to interpret the physical and psychological states of others, b) the emotional capacity to affectively experience the other's state and c) the behavioral repertoire that permits the possibility of trying to alleviate discomfort in others" (p. 127).

Although the skills of young children do not match those of older children, their competence is substantial enough to provide a substratum upon which moral development can take hold. Researchers working outside of the cognitive-developmental tradition think reason is not the basic starting point of moral development. In their view, emotion is the key.

Emotion and Moral Development
Those emphasizing the role of emotion in moral development consider conscience to be of central importance. Conscience, the internalization of standards, is what causes the child to "restrain antisocial or destructive impulses, even in the absence of surveillance" (Kochanska, 1993, p. 325). Kochanska summarizes the origins of moral development from this point of view:

The foundations of the moral self derive from repeated early interactions with consistently available—not threatening, as suggested by early psychoanalysis—caregivers. During the continual, early affective exchanges, a young child develops a sense of connectedness and the ability to read others' emotions and to react with distress, empathy and prosocial activity to others' distress. . . . Simultaneously . . . an older infant and toddler begins to internalize first prohibitions. Parents communicate their prohibitions by expressing anger, disapproval or warning during the process of affective communications. Because the child has established a bond . . . with the parent . . . such emotional signals function as inhibitors of forbidden acts—first, when the parent is physically present and can be referenced, and later . . . when the parent is absent. Thus, the roots of internalization are in the process of the early affective communication between parents and the child—transgressions become highly affectively charged events due to the parents' subtle affective signals. Caregivers endow the act of wrong-doing with affective significance because they express negative emotion. . . . (p. 326)

Research provides some support for this view. In virtually all of the attachment studies, parents who score high on measures of warmth and nurturance have children who are securely attached (Ainsworth, Blehar, Waters & Wall, 1978). Furthermore, these children later show the most skill in peer interactions and comply easily with parental and teacher requests (Matas, et al., 1978; Sroufe, 1982; Stayton, Hogan & Ainsworth, 1971). These behaviors are early indices of later self-regulation, which is a good predictor of mature conscience (Kochanska, 1991).

In other studies, Hoffman (1988) and Baumrind (1968) found that the affective climate of parenting influences children's subsequent social and moral behavior. Baumrind identified two kinds of parents who exerted control over their children. The authoritative parent "exerts firm control at points of parent-child divergence. . . . She uses reason as well as power to achieve her objectives. She does not base her decisions on group consensus or the individual child's desires; but also, does not regard herself as infallible" (Baumrind, 1968, p. 261). An authoritarian parent, in contrast, "favors punitive, forceful measures to curb self-will at points where the child's actions or beliefs conflict with what she thinks is right conduct" (Baumrind, 1968, p. 261). Authoritarian parents "value obedience as a virtue" (p. 261), forgetting that compliance shown only in the face of authority is not the final goal. When parents focus only on obedience, their discipline is harsh and they often convey a message of rejection.

When rejecting parents express negative emotion, their children do not absorb moral lessons or internalize standards. Authoritative parents, on the other hand, are effective because they express negative emotions in a larger context of overall acceptance of their children (Baumrind, 1972). Kochanska (1993) stresses that caregivers must be "consistently available and non-threatening," but that "caregivers endow the act of wrong-doing with affective significance because they express negative emotion." In other words, parents must create an affective climate in which children are certain of the parent's love and unwavering acceptance.

Research on temperament provides further evidence of the central role of emotion in social and moral development. Kagan, Reznick and Gibbons (1989) have documented biological differences among children in their tendencies to be inhibited or uninhibited. Other researchers (Dienstbier, 1984) have wondered if these emotional tendencies lead to different responses to parents' socialization. For example, they asked if inhibited children fare better under low power-assertion parenting conditions because they respond to subtler cues, and because too much power will divert their attention away from internal feelings of distress toward external controls. Conversely, will uninhibited children be less sensitive to low power-assertion because it fails to induce enough emotional distress to cause the child to attend to a parent's reasoning about prohibitions? Recent research suggests that the answer is yes. In one study (Kochanska, 1991), uninhibited children whose parents exerted little authority had a more poorly developed conscience at ages 8 to 10 than did inhibited children with the same socialization history.

One study examined preschool children to learn how well their understanding of moral rules ver-

sus appropriate moral emotions predicts actual moral behavior. Differences in moral rule understanding predicted poorly, while differences in the attribution of appropriate moral emotions predicted well (Asendorpf & Nunner-Winkler, 1992). Children's knowledge of how one would *feel* seems to play a more important role in children's moral behavior than the knowledge of how one should *behave* in certain situations.

Summary and Implications for Practice

Research and theory from outside the cognitive-developmental tradition can broaden the early childhood teacher's view of young children's capacity for social and moral learning. The research is compelling in demonstrating: a) the central role adults play in children's social and moral learning; b) the early emergence of the basic language and cognitive underpinnings necessary for social and moral learning, and of aspects of social and moral learning itself and c) the importance of emotion in early social and moral development.

1. Think carefully about your place in children's conflicts. Do not hesitate to let children know when you think certain behavior is right or wrong, but incorporate their ideas to right a wrong.

2. Emphasize the effects on others of children's appropriate and inappropriate behavior. Adults must, at times, express negative emotions when prohibitions and standards are violated. It is never excusable or effective, however, to belittle children, be punitive or hold a grudge.

3. Use enough authority-assertion to get a child's attention in a situation where a prohibition or a standard has been violated. Deal with individual children in private as much as possible, adapting levels of authority-assertion to individual needs.

4. Provide interesting activities. Prevent unnecessary conflicts by

providing adequate materials. The ability to share materials and wait for a turn does not develop well in children accustomed to deprivation.

5. Avoid the trap of thinking that you cannot begin implementing your curriculum until children's social and emotional behavior is under control. Kounin's (1970) research with kindergartners indicated that a challenging and interesting program is an excellent way to solve children's behavior problems.

6. Use tactics that make compliance easier for young children. Keep rules to a few basic, necessary and understandable ones. Organize the classroom to make cleaning up easy. Give children some choice, while enforcing expectations. Enable children to predict events and expectations by being consistent and following a daily routine.

7. Give reasons for your prohibitions, but do not wait for their agreement as a condition for following through. Baumrind's (1968) effective, authoritative parent "does not base her decisions on group consensus or the individual child's desires," although this parent does "share with the child the reasoning behind her policy" (p. 168).

8. Interact with children as they play. Adult interaction increases children's learning. In addition, it is essential to the development of teacher-child affective bonds (Moss, 1992).

9. Ask yourself how you teach children to keep promises. This is an effective means of thinking about the nature of good conscience.

References

Ainsworth, M. D. S., Blehar, M. D., Waters, E., & Wall, S. (1978). *Patterns of attachment.* Hillsdale, NJ: Lawrence Erlbaum.

Asendorpf, J. B., & Nunner-Winkler, G. (1992). Children's moral motive strength and temperamental inhibition reduce their immoral behavior in real moral conflicts. *Child Development, 63,* 1223-1235.

Baumrind, D. (1968). Authoritarian vs. authoritative parental control. *Adolescence, 3,* 255-272.

Baumrind, D. (1972). Socialization and instrumental competence. In W. W. Hartup (Ed.), *The young child: Reviews of research (Vol. 2)* (pp. 202-204). Washington, DC.: National Association for the Education of Young Children.

Dienstbier, R. A. (1984). The role of emotion in moral socialization. In C. Izard, J. Kagan & R. B. Zajonc (Eds.), *Emotions, cognitions and behaviors.* New York: Cambridge University Press.

Dunn, J. (1988). *The beginnings of social understanding.* Cambridge: Harvard University Press.

Gartrell, D. (1987). Punishment or guidance? *Young Children, 42,* 55-61.

Hitz, R., & Driscoll, A. (1988). Praise or encouragement? *Young Children, 43,* 6-13.

Hoffman, M. L. (1988). Moral development. In M. H. Bornstein & M. E. Lamb (Eds.), *Developmental psychology: An advanced textbook* (2nd ed.). Hillsdale, NJ: Lawrence Erlbaum.

Hudley, C., & Graham, S. (1993). An attributional intervention to reduce peer-directed aggression among African American boys. *Child Development, 64,* 124-138.

Kagan, J. (1981). *The second year: The emergence of self-awareness.* Cambridge, MA: Harvard University Press.

Kagan, J., Reznick, J. S., & Gibbons, J. (1989). Inhibited and uninhibited types of children. *Child Development, 60,* 838-845.

Kamii, C. (1984) Viewpoint: Obedience is not enough. *Young Children, 39,* 11-14.

Klinnert, M. (1981). *The regulation of infant behavior by maternal facial expression.* Unpublished doctoral dissertation, University of Denver, Denver, CO.

Kochanska, G. (1991). Socialization and temperament in the development of guilt and conscience. *Child Development, 62,* 1379-1392.

Kochanska, G. (1993). Toward a synthesis of parental socialization and child temperament in early development of conscience. *Child Development, 64,* 325-347.

Kohlberg, L. (1969). Stage and sequence: The cognitive-developmental approach to socialization. In D. A. Goslin (Ed.), *Handbook of socialization: Theory and research* (pp. 347-480). Chicago: Rand McNally.

Kohlberg, L. (1976). Moral stages and moralization. In T. Lickona (Ed.), *Moral development and behavior: Theory, research, and social issues* (pp. 31-53). New York: Holt, Rinehart & Winston.

Kounin, J. (1970). *Discipline and group management in classrooms.* New York: Holt, Rinehart & Winston.

Matas, L., Arend, R. A., & Sroufe, L. A. (1978). Continuity of adaptation in the second year of life: The relationship between quality of attachment and later competence. *Child Development, 49,* 547-556.

Moss, E. (1992). The socio/affective context of joint cognitive activity. In L. T. Winegar & J. Valsiner (Eds.), *Children's development within social context (Vol. 2)* (pp. 117-154). Hillsdale, NJ: Lawrence Erlbaum.

Oden, S., & Asher, S. (1977). Coaching children in social skills for friendship making. *Child Development, 48,* 495-506.

Oken-Wright, P. (1992). From tug of war to "let's make a deal": The teacher's role. *Young Children, 48,* 15-20.

Piaget, J. (1977). *The moral judgment of the child.* (M. Gabain, trans.). Harmondsworth, England: Penguin. (Original work published in 1932.)

Sroufe, L. A. (1982). Attachment and the roots of competence. In H. E. Fitzgerald & T. H. Carr (Eds.), *Human development: Annual Editions,* Guilford, CT: Dushkin.

Stayton, D., Hogan, R., & Ainsworth, M. D. (1971). Infant obedience and maternal behavior: The origins of socialization reconsidered. *Child Development, 42,* 1057-1069.

Walden, T. A., & Baxter, A. (1989). The effect of context and age on social referencing. *Child Development, 60(6),* 1511-1518.

Wolfgang, C., & Glickman, C. (1980). *Solving discipline problems: Strategies for classroom teachers.* Boston: Allyn & Bacon.

Zahn-Waxler, C., & Radke-Yarrow, M. (1982). The development of altruism: Alternative research strategies. In N. Eisenberg (Ed.), *The development of prosocial behavior* (pp. 109-137). New York: Academic Press.

Zahn-Waxler, C., Radke-Yarrow, M., Wagner, E., & Chapman, M. (1992). Development of concern for others. *Developmental Psychology, 28,* 126-136.

Young Children's Understanding of Everyday Emotions

Janet Kuebli

Janet Kuebli, M.S., is a doctoral student in the Department of Psychology at Emory University in Atlanta, Georgia, where she is studying parent–child narratives about children's emotional experiences.

*This is one of a regular series of Research in Review columns. This column was edited by **Laura E. Berk**, Ph.D., professor of psychology at Illinois State University.*

W hat young children understand about emotion states and behaviors is of importance to early childhood educators who deal with children's feelings every day. Children, like adults, experience many emotions in the course of each day. Strong emotions arising from their own experiences may be very confusing for children. Children also have to make sense of other people's emotional reactions or feelings; therefore, we often try to help children talk about their own and others' feelings. We think of this especially when children encounter traumatic life events, such as when a child's parents divorce or someone in the family is very sick or dies.

Children may also need help in understanding everyday emotions. Teachers and parents may, for example, suggest ways that children can cope with feelings of distress, fear, or shyness on the first day of school or explain how it is possible to feel sad and happy at the same time about moving to a new school. Sometimes we urge children to talk about their anger or sadness as a way of handling minor daily conflicts and disappointments. By helping children to understand emotions, we hope to help them channel their feelings in self-enhancing ways and also prepare them to deal with similar experiences in the future.

As children mature, we also expect them to master their emotions to some extent. Learning to express some feelings and how to mask others are common everyday lessons in children's lives. Hochschild (1983) calls this learning how to do "emotion work." Getting along with others often means handling feelings in a socially acceptable fashion. Children who get mad because they have to wait their turn or who laugh at a crying child who has taken a fall and skinned a knee sometimes are encouraged to think about how others feel. A child who overexuberantly boasts about being a winner may be urged to remember how it also feels to be the loser. In some cases the ability to regulate and manage emotions tells us that a child is ready for new challenges.

Over the last decade, researchers have shown keen interest in the nature of children's understanding of emotion, especially as it relates to social–cognitive development. Much of this work has concerned school-age children. Results from these studies suggest, not sur-

At the heart of the studies with younger children are two related issues. The first concerns identifying links between early developments in emotion understanding and language.

prisingly, that emotion understanding becomes more complex and sophisticated during elementary school. At these ages, for example, children begin to appreciate the fact that they can experience more than one emotion at a time (Carroll & Steward, 1984; Donaldson & Westerman, 1986; Harter & Buddin, 1987; Wintre, Polivy, & Murray, 1990). They also begin to take into greater account the situations that cause emotional reactions (Barden, Zelko, Duncan, & Masters, 1980; Strayer, 1986; Brody & Harrison, 1987; Camras & Allison, 1989). At this time children's skill in hiding their feelings also shows considerable improvement (Saarni, 1984, 1985; Davis, 1992), as does their understanding of emotions that involve self-evaluations, such as pride, guilt, and shame (Graham, Doubleday, & Guarino, 1984; Graham, 1988; Harter & Whitesell, 1989).

© Subjects & Predicates

Emotion-understanding studies with younger children are by comparison less common. New research, however, has begun to yield information both about what younger children know about emotions and how this understanding may develop. At the heart of the studies with younger children are two related issues. The first concerns identifying links between early developments in emotion understanding and language. The second issue centers on how children's emotion understanding is socialized in the course of children's interactions with others. One major conclusion derived from these studies is that conversations about feelings are an important context for learning about emotions and how to manage them.

This article considers the general nature of emotional experience first. The focus turns next to several studies

---

The second issue centers on how children's emotion understanding is socialized in the course of children's interactions with others.

---

on children's early emotion vocabulary and concepts, followed by research on how emotions are discussed by young children with others. The studies described here,

while not exhaustive of the work in this area, provide a selective overview of what is known about emotion understanding in young children. Finally, I suggest ways that teachers can use these findings to facilitate children's understanding of their own and others' feelings.

Emotional experience

According to Lewis (Lewis & Michalson, 1983; Lewis, 1992), it's useful to think of emotional behavior as consisting of a variety of components. One of these components, *emotional experience,* refers to how individuals interpret and evaluate their emotions. Other components include (a) emotion states and (b) their expressions, which may be conveyed either verbally or through nonverbal changes in facial expressions, physical posture, or movement. The componential model of

---

One major conclusion derived from these studies is that conversations about feelings are an important context for learning about emotions and how to manage them.

---

emotion proposes that our emotional experiences, states, and expressions do not always correspond to each other. On some occasions we may be unaware of our emotions or simply unable to name the particular feelings we are having. At other times we might intentionally express one emotion while experiencing a different feeling, or we might recognize our feelings but lack insight into the reasons for having them.

Among these various emotion components, emotional experience is considered the most cognitive (Lewis & Saarni, 1985) because it relies upon basic mental processes of attention, perception, and memory. We cannot begin, thus, to understand our feelings until we pay attention to them. Emotional experience further entails arriving at cognitive judgments and insights about our own emotion states and expressions. Emotional experience, in effect, depends upon being able to introspect or reflect upon ourselves (Lewis, 1992). Cognitive processes that underlie emotional experience essentially bring our emotions into consciousness and provide the basis for our having emotional experiences.

The developmental timetable for the emergence of various emotion states and expressions has already been well documented (e.g. Campos, Barrett, Lamb, Goldsmith, & Stenberg, 1983). Newborns, for example, display joy, interest, disgust, and distress; around eight months most babies show surprise, anger, fear, and sadness (Stenberg, Campos, & Emde, 1983; Izard & Malatesta, 1987). Embarrassment, empathy, pride, shame, and guilt only begin to appear at the end of infancy, usually after the age of 18 months. Much less is

Some Characteristics of Young Children's Emotion Language and Understanding

Approximate age of child	Description
Birth to 18 months	display emotions and respond to emotions in others at preverbal stage use emotion cues of others to guide own responses to new or ambiguous situations do not produce or comprehend emotion terms with a few exceptions
18 to 20 months	use first emotion words in vocabulary (e.g. cry, happy) begin to discuss emotions spontaneously in conversations with others
2 to 3 years	increase emotion vocabulary most rapidly correctly label simple emotions in self and others, and talk about past, present, and future emotions talk about the causes and consequences of some emotions and identify emotions associated with certain situations use emotion language in pretend play
4 to 5 years	show increased capacity to verbally reflect on emotions and to consider more complex relations between emotions and situations understand that the same event may call forth different feelings in different people and that feelings sometimes persist long after the events that caused them demonstrate growing awareness about controlling and managing emotions in accord with social standards
6 to 11 years	exhibit conceptual advances in their understanding of complex emotions (e.g. pride and shame) and of mixed or multiple emotions show marked improvements in the ability to suppress or conceal negative emotional reactions and in the use of self-initiated strategies for redirecting feelings take into fuller account the events leading to emotional reactions

known about the developmental course of emotional experience and understanding. The components model of emotion, however, suggests that it is not necessary for emotional states, expressions, and experience to develop in lock-step fashion all together. This model may explain why children have emotions and express them before they are able to reflect upon and understand their feelings (Michalson & Lewis, 1983; Lewis, 1992).

Researchers hypothesize that a fundamental prerequisite underlying emotional experience is having a *self-concept;* that is, children need a sense of an "I" who owns and knows her or his own emotion states and expressions in order to experience them. Even prior to forming a self-concept, however, children acquire several important cognitive skills related to self-understanding, which may also underlie their capacity for emotional experience. Collectively these skills are known as self-referential behaviors. They are first evident at ages between 15 and 24 months and include acquiring (a) an awareness of oneself as separate from others, (b) knowledge that objects independent of oneself have a permanent exist-

ence, (c) a sense of oneself as a causal agent, and (d) the ability to visually recognize oneself (Bertenthal & Fisher, 1978; Lewis & Brooks-Gunn, 1979; Sroufe, 1979; Kagan, 1981; Harter, 1983; Lewis, Sullivan, Stanger, & Weiss, 1989). Harter (1983) refers to these developments as contributing to the formation of an "existential self." Existential awareness of self forms the foundation for the child's initial self-concept. Together, these cognitive abilities enable children to make themselves objects of thought. Thereafter, emotional experience probably develops gradually, most likely in concert with changes in children's self-concepts. Emotions are, thus, integral to children's sense of who they are, helping them to form their own personal views of the world around them.

Learning words and concepts for emotions

Emotion theorists suspect that learning to talk is another critical factor in the development of emotional experience; acquiring word labels for emotions is re-

We cannot begin to understand our feelings until we pay attention to them.

garded as particularly important for developments in children's understandings of emotions. Certainly, parents refer to emotions in conversations with their children, almost from birth. Emotion communication enables others to draw attention to children's expressions of emotion. No doubt, this communication accelerates the development of emotional experience and understanding (Izard & Malatesta, 1987). Children's emotional self-understanding may start with being able to name emotion states and behaviors. From maternal reports, diary studies, and direct observations, we know that children begin to use emotion terms around the ages of 20 to 24 months (see Bretherton, Fritz, Zahn-Waxler, & Ridgeway, 1986 for a review of research on how children learn to talk about emotions). By 36 months children use emotion words to talk about both themselves and others, and in reference to events in the present, past, and future (Bretherton & Beeghly, 1982).

To learn about children's first emotion words, Bretherton and Beeghly (1982) gave mothers of 28-month-olds a list of terms for emotions as well as for mental states (e.g. knowing, remembering, dreaming), physiological states (e.g. hunger, fatigue), and perceptual states (e.g. seeing, hearing, tasting). Mothers indicated which words on the list their children used. At this age about 75% of the children had acquired the emotion words *mad* and *scared*, and well over half used *happy* and *sad*. Nearly all of the children used the emotion-behavior term *cry;* however, *surprise,* apparently a late acquisition, was reported for only 13% of the children. Additionally, children used emotion words to refer to both self and others, rather than only to self or only to others. This suggests that children's early emotional understanding of themselves and others may be closely related rather than developing separately. Finally, emotion terms were more common than mental-state words but less frequent than words for perceptual or physiological states. Notably, however, children talked about causes for emotions more often than causes for other kinds of states of being. This finding underscores the importance of emotional understanding as central to how children make sense of what happens to them.

In several experimental studies, researchers have looked at preschoolers' ability to label facial expressions. Michalson and Lewis (1985), for example, asked two- to five-year-olds "What kind of face" another child was making in a series of snapshots. They found that children knew the labels for *happiness* and *sadness* at earlier ages than they knew the terms for *anger, surprise, disgust,* or *fear.* In fact, children did not produce many verbal labels at all until after age three, and even by five years of age children had difficulty naming the surprise, disgust, and fear expressions. When asked to point to the face that matched the emotion label given by the experimenter, however, children as young as two demonstrated they knew something about the situations in which certain facial expressions were likely. Seventy percent of two-year-olds matched the happy face with a birthday-party drawing. These results tell us that children's early knowledge of some emotional situations may considerably outpace their ability to talk about those emotions. Less than half of the two- and

three-year-olds, however, matched the sad and disgust faces with the correct pictures; whereas, the majority of the four- and five-year-olds made the correct match. This more gradual development trend in understanding negative emotions has also been observed in several other studies (e.g. Borke, 1971; Glasberg & Aboud, 1982; Reichenbach & Masters, 1983).

Clearly, preschoolers become more adept at talking about their own and others' emotions. The largest and most rapid increase in the number of terms children have for emotions occurs between the ages of two and three (Ridgeway, Waters, & Kuczaj, 1985), but children continue to acquire new emotion words after this time. During the preschool period, caregivers also increasingly urge children to "use words" rather than act out their feelings. Research shows that young children are learning more than just an emotion vocabulary. Specifically, children learn more about the nature of emotional processes, including new insights about the causes and consequences of feelings.

Denham and Zoller (1993) were particularly interested in what preschoolers think causes various emotions. The two researchers showed children puppets with happy, sad, fearful, or angry faces and then asked them to think of what would make the puppets "feel that way." Results showed that the children more often associated

---

Emotional experience further entails arriving at cognitive judgments and insights about our own emotion states and expressions.

---

happiness with nonsocial causes (e.g. playing or going somewhere without reference to being with others) than with social ones. By contrast, the reasons children gave for sadness and anger were mostly social in nature. Children said that being hurt or left by others caused sadness, for example; their reasons for anger included being punished, fighting, or not liking someone else. Interestingly, neither social nor nonsocial reasons were given for feeling fearful; instead, children said fear was caused by make-believe creatures, such as monsters or ghosts. One notable gender difference in the responses was that girls gave more reasons for sadness than did boys. This outcome is intriguing in light of research with adults and adolescents in which females report thinking about sadness in relation to themselves and experiencing depression more often than do males (Brody, 1984; Conway, Giannopoulos, & Stiefenhofer, 1990).

Some preschoolers also have begun to recognize that a single event sometimes causes different feelings in different people. In one study (Gove & Keating, 1979) three- and five-year-olds heard a short story in which only one of two characters won a game. All of the older children, but only two thirds of the younger ones, judged that the victor would feel happy, while the loser would be sad in this social situation. This result is somewhat at odds

Emotional experience, in effect, depends upon being able to introspect or reflect upon ourselves.

with what Denham and Zoller found, but the differences may be products of the methods used in the two studies. In addition, although preschoolers demonstrate an increasing ability to reason about the causes and consequences of single emotions, few children prior to the age of five grasp the concept of mixed or conflicting feelings. That is, while preschoolers may say that one feeling can follow another one sequentially, they tend to deny that two different emotions can be experienced simultaneously (Harter & Buddin, 1987). Even after short training about mixed emotions, four- and five-year-olds have shown little improvement in their understanding of mixed emotions (Peng, Johnson, Pollock, Glasspool, & Harris, 1992). Younger children's greater difficulty with multiple feelings may be tied to their limitations in the cognitive skills necessary for integrating opposing emotions.

Socialization of emotion understanding

Studies on children's emotion concepts have sought to document at what ages children demonstrate higher levels of understanding about emotions. Other research has focused on identifying experiences in children's lives that influence the particular forms emotion understandings can take. A key assumption is that children's insights into their own emotions are socially shaped in important ways (e.g. Lutz, 1985; Gordon, 1989). Whereas research on the content of emotion concepts has concentrated on older children, studies examining how emotions are socialized have usually been conducted with younger children.

The goal of emotion socialization is usually to redirect or change the way children spontaneously express their emotions to conform more closely with social rules or conventions. Sometimes this means substituting one feeling for a different one, as when we smile after receiving a disappointing gift (Saarni, 1984) or look on the bright side of things that worry or sadden us. Saarni (1985; Saarni & Crowley, 1990) outlines three general classes of processes by which emotions may be socialized. First, *direct* socialization refers to occasions when others chide or praise children's immediately prior emotional behaviors. In this case an adult's behavior reinforces the child's expression of emotions. Reinforcement, either reward or punishment, gives children explicit information about the way certain emotions are valued by others. Didactic teaching is another direct form of socialization often used with children to convey social conventions for expressing emotions. A child may be told, for example, that "girls don't brag" about their successes or that "boys don't cry" about their failures.

Emotions are also socialized *indirectly*. A classic example is when a child imitates someone else's emotional reactions, such as one child's fearful reluctance to try

something new being copied by another child who only moments before was a willing and eager participant. We can view this situation, in part, as a case in which one person's emotional reactions are "catching." There are times when uncontrolled laughter seizes a group of children in this way or sadness sweeps through a classroom. Adults also provide ready models, of course, for children's emotional reactions. Research shows that children faced with a situation in which they do not know how to react will scan a caregiver's face in search of cues for the appropriate emotional response. This behavior, known as social referencing, has been studied extensively with infants. One study, for example, showed that eight-month-olds' reactions to a stranger were influenced by their mothers' immediately prior emotional reactions toward that person (Feinman & Lewis, 1983). Although fewer studies have considered this phenomena among preschoolers, the notion in all cases is that children learn about emotion states, expressions, and events by watching others and imitating their emotional behaviors.

A third channel for emotion socialization involves *expectancy communication*. For Saarni and Crowley (1990) emotion expectancies are beliefs about how emotions should be felt and expressed that are conveyed to children, verbally or nonverbally, in advance of particular events in which children's own emotional reactions are called forth. Saarni and Crowley liken the process to hypnosis, in which adults, first, plant "suggestions" in children's minds about how to respond in certain situations. If children subsequently encounter the same or similar situations, they may use this information to guide their own emotional responses. In this way children remember and act upon at later points in time the information previously acquired about emotions. So, when we tell young children, for example, about how we felt afraid (or excited) at their age, going on a ferris wheel ride or sleeping away from home the first time, these verbal suggestions may be internalized as expectancies upon which children subsequently rely. By such means, Saarni and Crowley (1990) contend, strategies for managing emotions initiated "outside" the child are imported into children's own private, emotional lives.

A general, theoretical framework for studies on emotion socialization is found in the works of Cooley (1902), Mead (1956), and Vygotsky (1978), who each discussed links between emotion, self, and cognition. These writers proposed that (a) we become conscious of ourselves through how others know us and (b) consciousness is forged, in large part, through social activity and discourse. Mead, for example argued that self-consciousness only arises when we take on the attitudes of others toward ourselves. He wrote

> the child can think about his conduct as good or bad only as he reacts to his own acts in the remembered words of his parents. (1913, p. 146)

The imagined judgments of others "drawn from the communicative life" (1902, p. 179) were also essential to Cooley's *looking-glass self:*

> in imagination we perceive in another's mind some thought of our appearance, manners, aims, deeds,

© Blendi Reynolds

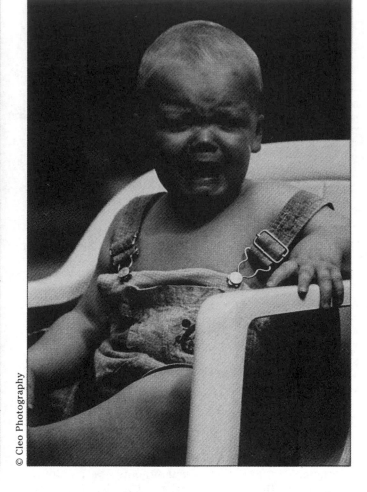

© Cleo Photography

character ... and are variously affected by it. (1902, p. 184)

Although Vygotsky did not explicitly write about emotion development, he believed that children became self-conscious by using

the same forms of behavior in relation to themselves that others initially used in relation to them. (1981, p. 157)

In particular, Vygotsky stressed the role that everyday social speech plays in children's development.

Contemporary researchers speculate that asking about emotions provides children with "reflective distance" from feeling states themselves (Stern, 1985; Bretherton et al., 1986; Dunn, Brown, & Beardsall, 1991). Discussing emotions is thought to distance children from the rush and immediacy of affective responses. Distancing gives children space in which to interpret and evaluate their feelings and to reflect upon causes and consequences.

Emotion discourse may further allow adults and children to work out socially acceptable meanings of feeling states. Especially significant may be the way adults attribute meaning to children's own emotional behavior and development (Lutz, 1983). The way we talk about emotions with children, thus, has the potential to uniquely organize and transform their emotional lives.

Researchers also assume that preschoolers begin to formulate emotion concepts specific to their own culture or subculture (Lutz, 1983; Lutz & White, 1986; Miller & Sperry, 1987). From this perspective emotion concepts are viewed as embedded in broader cultural knowledge about situations and social relationships. How children come to understand emotions will presumably depend on the particular cultural vocabulary and meaning systems available to children for talking about emotions (Levy, 1984; Lutz & White, 1986; Gordon, 1989) and on existing social norms about ways emotions should be felt and expressed.

Cognitive processes that underlie emotional experience essentially bring our emotions into consciousness and provide the basis for our having emotional experiences.

Both psychologists and anthropologists have studied how emotions are variously viewed and talked about in different cultures. There is evidence that emotions downplayed or left undefined in some cultures are central to how other cultures make sense of experiences. Cross-cultural comparisons indicate that Americans and Chinese, for example, identify different types of causes for pride (Stipek, Weiner, & Li, 1989), and Japanese culture emphasizes shame more than other groups do (Lewis, 1992). Americans also report experiencing emotions longer and more intensely than do Japanese sub-

---

Children use emotion words to refer to both self and others, rather than only to self or only to others. This suggests that children's early emotional understanding of themselves and others may be closely related, rather than developing separately.

---

jects (Matsumoto, Kudoh, Scherer, & Wallbott, 1988). In contrast to the Western culture's sense of sadness as an emotion, Tahitians classify sadness as a physical illness or body state (Levy, 1984). How adults approach childrearing, moreover, is thought to be related to their knowledge and beliefs about emotions (Lutz & White, 1986; Miller & Sperry, 1987; Markus & Kitayama, 1991). Yet, until recently, few researchers have directly observed adult–child conversations about emotions. The few studies so far have, not surprisingly, focused mostly on how mothers talk with young children.

Miller and Sperry (1987), for example, interviewed three working-class mothers of two-and-one-half-year-old daughters and observed how they socialized anger and aggression. Notably, the mothers led lives in which violence and aggression were all too commonplace; they typically discussed these events in their daughters' presence but usually while talking to other family members or friends. It is striking that at least one child's own stories about anger and aggression were closely patterned after her mother's recollections. In this way what children overhear others relating about emotional events may be one context for learning about emotions. Miller and Sperry observed a second important context—episodes of anger between mothers and daughters. Mothers sometimes intentionally provoked their daughters' anger by teasing or trading insults with them as a way of teaching the girls how to stand up for themselves. Miller and Sperry also found that, rather than talking explicitly about the emotional state of anger itself, families referred to those emotion behaviors that only indirectly expressed anger (e.g. *fight, hit, punch*).

Children's interactions with their mothers and a sibling have been examined by Dunn and her associates. Their analyses of these three-way interactions included tracking how the amount and kind of emotion talk that

---

Some preschoolers have begun to recognize that a single event sometimes causes different feelings in different people.

---

occurs in the home changes as young children grow older. One study's home observations conducted when younger siblings were 18 and 24 months old revealed that family members' references to emotion states and to their causes and consequences increased over time (Dunn, Bretherton, & Munn, 1987). Mothers' comments during these interactions usually served to guide or explain children's feelings rather than simply to bring attention to children's emotions. This suggests that mothers, consciously or not, actively worked at shaping their children's emotional experiences, much like the mothers in the Miller and Sperry study. Moreover, the more frequently mothers and older siblings referred to feeling states at the 18-month visit, the more often the younger child talked about emotions at the 24-month visit. In other research Dunn and Kendrick (1982) found that two- and three-year-olds whose mothers commented more often about a new baby's feelings were more likely to have friendly interactions with that sibling one year later.

Dunn has also examined sibling conflicts as contexts for emotion socialization. Between the ages of 14 and 36 months, younger siblings' ability to tease and upset their older siblings appears to increase significantly (Dunn & Munn, 1985; Dunn, Brown, & Beardsall, 1991). This finding demonstrates how young children are learning to anticipate and influence others' feelings. Dunn et al. (1991) further found that mothers and children who

---

The way we talk about emotions with children has the potential to uniquely organize and transform their emotional lives.

---

engaged in more frequent emotion talk were more apt to also discuss the causes and consequences of siblings' disputes. Finally, three-year-olds from families with more emotion talk showed a better understanding of others' emotions three years later at age six. These results provide additional support for the contention that emotion talk provides an important context for learning about feelings.

Together, these studies indicate that exposure to different types and amounts of emotion talk may be related to individual differences in children's emotion understanding (Gordon, 1989). Especially intriguing in this regard are reports of differences in how mothers talk about emotions with daughters and sons. In the

Applications for Early Childhood Educators

For educators and parents, it is certainly not earthshaking to find that children learn about emotions from us; but, emotions are sometimes so "close to the skin" and fleeting that it is easy for feelings to slip out of one's conscious awareness. Becoming conscious of the roles we play in children's emotion socialization empowers us to provide children with better opportunities in their daily lives for understanding themselves and others. Teachers have some unique occasions for structuring children's activities in ways that can encourage children to talk about their own and others' emotions. Consider the following recommendations for meeting this objective.

1. Evaluate whether the emotional climate of the classroom itself is conducive to expressing emotions. In other words, caregivers need to legitimate children's feelings in order for children to feel it is acceptable to talk about and reflect upon their emotions. Leavitt and Power (1989) contend that we give meaning to children's emotions when we recognize and respond to their feelings. Essentially this means entering into authentic emotional relationships with children and regarding them as "emotional associates" (Leavitt & Power, 1989, p. 37) who are capable of interpreting and understanding their own and others' emotions.

2. Consider the physical environments in which children may learn about feelings. Play centers no doubt vary in the opportunities they afford for emotional engagement and reflection. Family-living or dramatic-play sections, for example, may encourage children to act out social interactions into which emotions figure. Well-stocked play centers can also provide sources of suggestions to children's imaginations for reworking earlier emotional altercations or experiences. Either from the sidelines or as players ourselves, adults can observe the way individual children play out emotion scripts dramatically. Introduce themes and ask questions that prompt children to vicariously explore the causes and consequences of emotions. Similarly, puppets and dolls are excellent vehicles for emotion play.

3. The arts center provides another valuable context for emotion conversation. Encourage children to make pictures that tell about personal events in their lives. This idea, borrowed from therapists who work with disturbed children, adapts well for children whose "troubles" are within the typical range of life experiences. Children might be encouraged to "draw about the time when . . ." they were upset with another child, afraid of something new, and so forth. Engaging children in conversations about their pictures, either as they are being created or afterwards, can give children chances to reflect upon their emotions. Children can also dictate the stories and feelings that go with their pictures. Older children may want to construct longer picture stories, several pages in length. Sometimes, children will enjoy "reading" back their picture stories to someone else, either during group times or on their own to other children and teachers.

4. Stories written for children are yet another readily available resource for talking about emotions. Books can be selected that show other children being emotional and dealing with their feelings (some titles well suited to this activity are suggested at the end of this article). Children and teachers can discuss the causes and consequences of story characters' emotions and then link them with children's own experiences. Certainly, other media (e.g. TV, movies, plays, children's magazines) provide similar options.

5. Tape recorders and video equipment can be used advantageously as well. Children might audiotape or videotape each other telling stories in which they recreate emotions. Subsequent viewing of these mini productions can serve as a springboard for later discussion about choices children have in responding to their own or others' emotions. Audiovisual projects can also be sources of collaborative production and pride. We show children that we value their emotions if we put the emotion work they do in projects of this sort on display for others to see and share. Invite parents or other classes for a film showing, or put on loan children's story tapes for other children's listening.

6. Dealing with children's quarrels and disputes offers a final classroom context in which children can develop their understanding of emotions. Fighting children learn more about anger and aggression if we do more than simply separate them. Ask each child to "tell what happened" from his or her perspective without interruption by the other participant(s). Teachers can convey back what the child says, asking for any corrections or clarifications before calling on the other child to tell her or his part in the altercation. All children should be urged to examine their personal contributions to the conflict. Teachers can also ask children to talk about how the events made them feel and how they think the other child feels, along with what they each could do differently next time. In this way teachers can help children to manage their feelings rather than simply to suppress or deny them; by doing so, Leavitt and Power (1989) claim that we enhance children's ability to develop authentic emotional understandings and relationships.

study by Dunn et al. (1987), for example, references to emotions were more frequent in mother–daughter, than mother–son, conversations at both 18 and 24 months; and by 24 months girls also talked about feeling states more often than boys did. Gender differences have also

---

How children come to understand emotions will presumably depend on the particular cultural vocabulary and meaning systems available to children for talking about emotions.

---

been reported by Fivush (1989; 1991). Reasoning that conversations about past emotions might provide even more reflective distance, Fivush asked mothers to talk with children about specific events in their child's past. In one study with 30- to 35-month-olds, Fivush (1989) found that mothers attributed more talk about sadness to daughters and more talk about anger to sons. Mother–daughter conversations also focused more on feelings, whereas mother–son pairs were more apt to discuss causes and consequences for emotions.

When fathers talk about the past with young children, they, too, seem to talk differently about emotions with daughters than with sons. Kuebli and Fivush (1992) found that both mothers and fathers of 40-month-olds talked about a greater number and variety of emotions with daughters than they did with sons; again, sadness was more often a topic in conversations with girls. At the age of 40 months, differences were not yet apparent in how boys and girls talked about emotions. Mother–child interviews conducted just before the children started kindergarten, however, revealed that the number of girls' references to emotions nearly quadrupled over this time, whereas boys' references had remained about the same (Kuebli & Fivush, 1993). These results suggest that girls' and boys' emotional lives may be socialized in somewhat different ways. In related research, moreover, adult women were found to be more likely than men to say they are emotional, to value the

expression of emotions, and to report experiencing a variety of emotions (Allen & Hamsher, 1974; Allen & Haccoun, 1976; Balswick & Avertt, 1977; Fitzpatrick & Indvik, 1982).

Conclusion

Research on young children's emotion understanding and socialization is still very new. Based on what we know so far, however, we can expect that children will show individual differences in the kinds of emotion understandings they possess. Differences will be apparent among children of different ages and even in the rate at which age-mates gain new insights into emotions; moreover, children's family backgrounds and histories are likely to translate into different ways of conceptualizing and using emotions. Cross-cultural evidence on emotion understanding should make teachers particularly sensitive to multicultural variation in the ways emotions figure in children's lives. Despite the differences, however, research also suggests that the basic processes by which children learn about emotions are similar, although much more needs to be learned about the nature of these mechanisms. What is, perhaps, fundamentally important is realizing that a great deal of what young children understand about feelings is apparently learned in the informal curriculum provided by their social interactions with others. Emotions frequently are at the heart of these interactions, and children may greatly benefit when we direct their attention to talking about these experiences.

Between the ages of 14 and 36 months, younger siblings' ability to tease and upset their older siblings appears to increase significantly. This finding demonstrates how young children are learning to anticipate and influence others' feelings.

Four processes by which emotions are socialized are
(1) chiding or praising children's immediately prior emotional behaviors;
(2) giving direct instruction regarding social conventions for expressing emotion ("girls don't brag about their successes");
(3) modeling emotion states, expressions, and events—children watch and imitate; and
(4) communicating expectancies, verbally or nonverbally, directly to the child or within his hearing ("when I was your age I was afraid the first time I slept away from home").

Books About Emotions for Young Children

Many books for young children afford opportunities for adults and children to talk about emotions. The following titles are good examples of books in which emotional themes are central to the story.

Carle, E. (1977). *The grouchy ladybug.* New York: Harper & Row.

Carlson, N. (1988). *I like me!* New York: Viking Kestrel.

Clarke, G. (1991). *. . . along came Eric.* New York: Lothrop, Lee, & Shepard.

Cole, J. (1990). *Don't call me names!* New York: Random House.

Engel, D. (1989). *Josephina hates her name.* New York: Morrow Junior.

Godwin, P. (1993). *I feel orange today.* New York: Firefly.

Gretz, S. (1981). *Teddy bears' moving day.* New York: Four Winds.

Havill, J. (1989). *Jamaica tag-along.* Boston: Houghton Mifflin.

Hazen, B.S. (1981). *Even if I did something awful.* New York: Atheneum.

Lakin, P. (1985). *Don't touch my room.* Boston: Little, Brown.

Macdonald, M. (1990). *Little hippo starts school.* New York: Dial.

Mayer, M. (1983). *I was so mad.* Racine, WI: Western Publishing.

Noll, S. (1991). *That bothered Kate.* New York: Puffin.

Sharmat, M.J. (1983). *Frizzy the fearful.* New York: Holiday House.

Stevenson, J. (1983). *What's under my bed?* New York: Greenwillow.

Viorst, J. (1972). *Alexander and the terrible, horrible, no good, very bad day.* New York: Atheneum.

Waber, B. (1972). *Ira sleeps over.* Boston: Houghton Mifflin.

Wells, R. (1988). *Shy Charles.* New York: Dial.

Wilhelm, H. (1990). *A cool kid—like me!* New York: Crown.

References

Allen, J.G., & Haccoun, D.M. (1976). Sex differences in emotionality: A multidimensional approach. *Human Relations, 29*(8), 711–722.

Allen, J.G., & Hamsher, J.H. (1974). The development and validation of a test of emotional styles. *Journal of Consulting and Clinical Psychology, 42*(5), 663–668.

Balswick, H., & Avertt, C.P. (1977). Differences in expressiveness: Gender, interpersonal orientation, and perceived parental expressiveness as contributing factors. *Journal of Marriage and the Family, 39*(1), 121–127.

Barden, R.C., Zelko, F., Duncan, S.W., & Masters, J.C. (1980). Children's consensual knowledge about the experiential determinants of emotion. *Journal of Personality and Social Psychology, 39*(5), 968–976.

Bertenthal, B.I., & Fisher, K.W. (1978). Development of self-recognition in the infant. *Developmental Psychology, 14*(1), 44–50.

Borke, H. (1971). Interpersonal perception of young children: Egocentrism or empathy. *Developmental Psychology, 5*(2), 263–269.

Bretherton, I., & Beeghly, M. (1982). Talking about internal states: The acquisition of an explicit theory of mind. *Developmental Psychology, 18*(6), 906–921.

Bretherton, I., Fritz, J., Zahn-Waxler, C., & Ridgeway, D. (1986). Learning to talk about emotions: A functionalist perspective. *Child Development, 57*(3), 529–548.

Brody, L.R. (1984). Sex and age variations in the quality and intensity of children's emotional attributions to hypothetical situations. *Sex Roles, 11*(1/2), 51–59.

Brody, L.R., & Harrison, R.H. (1987). Development changes in children's abilities to match and label emotionally laden situations. *Motivation and Emotion, 11*(4), 347–365.

Campos, J.J., Barrett, K.C., Lamb, M.E., Goldsmith, H.H., & Stenberg, C. (1983). Socioemotional development. In M. Haith & J.J. Campos (Eds.), *Handbook of child psychology: Vol. 2. Infancy and developmental psychobiology* (pp. 783–915). New York: Wiley.

Camras, L.A., & Allison, K. (1989). Children's and adults' beliefs about emotion elicitation. *Motivation and Emotion, 13*(1), 53–70.

Carroll, J.J., & Steward, M.S. (1984). The role of cognitive development in children's understanding of their own feelings. *Child Development, 55*(4), 1486–1492.

Conway, M., Giannopoulos, C., & Stiefenhofer, K. (1990). Response styles to sadness are related to sex and sex-role orientation. *Sex Roles, 22*(9/10), 579–587.

Cooley, C.H. (1902). *Human nature and the social order.* New York: Scribner's.

Davis, T.L. (1992, April). *Sex differences in the masking of children's negative emotions: Ability or motivation?* Paper presented at the Human Development Conference, Atlanta, GA.

Denham, S.A., & Zoller, D. (1993). *"When mommy's angry. I feel sad": Preschoolers' causal understanding of emotion and its socialization.* Manuscript submitted for publication.

Donaldson, S.K., & Westerman, M.A. (1986). Development of children's understanding of ambivalence and causal theories of emotions. *Developmental Psychology, 22*(5), 655–662.

Dunn, J., Bretherton, I., & Munn, P. (1987). Conversations about feeling states between mothers and their young children. *Developmental Psychology, 23*(1), 132–139.

Dunn, J., Brown, J., & Beardsall, L. (1991). Family talk about feeling states and children's later understanding of others' emotions. *Developmental Psychology, 27*(3), 448–455.

Dunn, J., & Kendrick, C. (1982). *Siblings: Love, envy and understanding.* Cambridge, MA: Harvard University Press.

Dunn, J., & Munn, P. (1985). Becoming a family member: Family conflict and the development of social understanding in the second year. *Child Development, 56*(2), 480–492.

Feinman, S., & Lewis, M. (1983). Social referencing at ten-months: A second-order effect on infants' responses to strangers. *Child Development, 54*(4), 878–887.

Fitzpatrick, M.A., & Indvik, J. (1982). The instrumental and expressive domains of marital communication. *Human Communications Research, 8*(3), 195–213.

Fivush, R. (1989). Exploring sex differences in the emotional content of mother–child conversations about the past. *Sex Roles, 20*(11/12), 675–691.

Fivush, R. (1991). Gender and emotion in mother–child conversations about the past. *Journal of Narrative and Life History, 1*(4), 325–341.

Glasberg, R., & Aboud, F. (1982). Keeping one's distance from sadness: Children's self-reports of emotional experience. *Development Psychology, 18*(4), 287–293.

Gordon, S.L. (1989). The socialization of children's emotions: Emotional competence, culture, and exposure. In C. Saarni & P.L. Harris (Eds.), *Children's understanding of emotion* (pp. 319–349). New York: Cambridge University Press.

Gove, F.L., & Keating, D.P. (1979). Empathic role-taking precursors. *Developmental Psychology, 15*(6), 594–600.

Graham, S. (1988). Children's developing understanding of the motivational role of affect: An attributional analysis. *Cognitive Development, 3*(2), 71–88.

Graham, S., Doubleday, C., & Guarino, P.A. (1984). The development of relations between perceived controllability and the emotions of pity, anger, and guilt. *Child Development, 55*(2), 561–565.

Harter, S. (1983). Developmental perspectives on the self-system. In E.M. Hetherington (Ed.), *Socialization, personality and social* development, Vol IV, Handbook of Child Psychology (pp. 275–385). New York: Wiley.

Harter, S., & Buddin, B.J. (1987). Children's understanding of the simultaneity of two emotions: A five-stage development acquisition sequence. Developmental Psychology, 23(3), 388–399.

Harter, S., & Whitesell, N.R. (1989). Developmental changes in children's understanding of single, multiple, and blended emotion concepts. In C. Saarni & P.L. Harris (Eds.), Children's understanding of emotion (pp. 81–116.). Cambridge, England: Cambridge University Press.

Hochschild, A.R. (1983). The managed heart: Commercialization of human feelings. Berkeley: University of California Press.

Izard, C.E., & Malatesta, C.A. (1987). Perspectives on emotional development I: Differential emotions theory of early emotional development. In J.D. Osofsky (Ed.), Handbook of infant development (2nd ed.), (pp. 494–554.) New York: Wiley.

Kagan, J. (1981). The second year: The emergence of self-awareness. Cambridge, MA: Harvard University Press.

Kuebli, J., & Fivush, R. (1992). Gender differences in parent–child conversations about past emotions. Sex Roles, 27(11/12), 683–698.

Kuebli, J., & Fivush, R. (1993, March). Children's developing understanding of emotion and mind. Paper presented at the biennial meetings of the Society for Research in Child Development, New Orleans, LA.

Leavitt, R.L., & Power, M.B. (1989). Emotional socialization in the postmodern era: Children in day care. Social Psychology Quarterly, 52(1), 35–43.

Levy, R.I. (1984). Emotion, knowing, and culture. In R.A. Shweder & R.A. LeVine (Eds.), Culture theory: Essays on mind, self, and emotion (pp. 214–237). Cambridge, England: Cambridge University Press.

Lewis, M. (1992). Shame: The exposed self. New York: The Free Press.

Lewis, M., & Brooks-Gunn, J. (1979). Social cognition and acquisition of self. New York: Plenum.

Lewis, M., & Michalson, L. (1983). Children's emotions and moods. New York: Plenum.

Lewis, M., & Saarni, C. (1985). Culture and emotions. In M. Lewis & C. Saarni (Eds.), The socialization of emotions (pp. 1–17). New York: Plenum.

Lewis, M., Sullivan, M.W., Stanger, C., & Weiss, M. (1989). Self-development and self-conscious emotions. Child Development, 60(1), 146–156.

Lutz, C. (1983). Parental goals, ethnopsychology, and the development of emotional meaning. Ethos, 11(4), 246–262.

Lutz, C. (1985). Cultural patterns and individual differences in the child's emotional meaning system. In M. Lewis & C. Saarni (Eds.), The socialization of emotions (pp. 37–53). New York: Plenum.

Lutz, C., & White, G.M. (1986). The anthropology of emotions. Annual Review of Anthropology, 15, 405–436.

Markus, H.R., & Kitayama, S. (1991). Culture and the self: Implications for cognition, emotion, and motivation. Psychological Review, 98(2), 224–253.

Matsumoto, D., Kudoh, T., Scherer, K., & Wallbott, H. (1988). Antecedents of and reactions to emotions in the United States and Japan. Journal of Cross-Cultural Psychology, 19(3), 267–286.

Mead, G.H. (1913). The social self. In A.J. Reck (Ed.), Selected writings: George Herbert Mead (pp. 142–149). Chicago: Chicago University Press.

Mead, G.H. (1956). On social psychology: Selected papers. Chicago: The University of Chicago Press.

Michalson, L., & Lewis, M. (1985). What do children know about emotions and when do they know it? In M. Lewis & C. Saarni (Eds.), The socialization of emotions (pp. 117–139). New York: Plenum.

Miller, P., & Sperry, L.L. (1987). The socialization of anger and aggression. Merrill-Palmer Quarterly, 33(1), 1–31.

Peng, M., Johnson, C., Pollock, J., Glasspool, R., & Harris, P. (1992). Training young children to acknowledge mixed emotions. Cognition and Emotion, 6(5), 387–401.

Reichenbach, L., & Masters, J.C. (1983). Children's use of expressive and contextual cues in judgments of emotion. Child Development, 54(4), 992–1004.

Ridgeway, D., Waters, E., & Kuczaj, S.A. (1985). Acquisition of emotion-descriptive language: Receptive and productive vocabulary norms for ages 18 months to 6 years. Developmental Psychology, 21(5), 901–908.

Saarni, C. (1984). An observational study of children's attempts to monitor their expressive behavior. Child Development, 55(4), 1504–1513.

Saarni, C. (1985). Indirect processes in affect socialization. In M. Lewis & C. Saarni (Eds.), The socialization of emotions (pp. 187–209). New York: Plenum.

Saarni, C., & Crowley, M. (1990). The development of emotion regulation: Effects on emotional state and expression. In E.A. Blechman (Ed.), Emotions and the family: For better or for worse (pp. 53–73). Hillsdale, NJ: Erlbaum.

Sroufe, L.A. (1979). Socioemotional development. In J.D. Osofsky (Ed.), Handbook of infant development (pp. 462–516). New York: Wiley.

Stenberg, C., Campos, J., & Emde, R. (1983). The facial expression of anger in seven-month-old infants. Child Development, 54(1), 178–184.

Stern, D. (1985). The interpersonal world of the infant. New York: Basic.

Stipek, D., Weiner, B., & Li, K. (1989). Testing some attribution-emotion relations in the People's Republic of China. Journal of Personality and Social Psychology, 56(1), 109–116.

Strayer, J. (1986). Children's attributions regarding the situational determinants of emotion in self and others. Developmental Psychology, 22(5), 649–654.

Vygotsky, L.S. (1978). Mind in society: The development of higher psychological processes. Cambridge, MA: Harvard University Press.

Vygotsky, L.S. (1981). The genesis of higher mental functions. In J.V. Wertsch (Ed.), The concept of activity in Soviet psychology. Armonk, NY: M.E. Sharpe.

Wintre, M.G., Polivy, J., & Murray, M.A. (1990). Self-predictions of emotional-response patterns: Age, sex, and situational determinants. Child Development, 61(4), 1124–1133.

For further reading

Berk, L.E. (1985). Research in review. Why children talk to themselves. Young Children, 40(5), 46–52.

Frieman, B.B. (1993). Separation and divorce: Children want their teachers to know—meeting the emotional needs of preschool and primary school children. Young Children, 48(6), 58–63.

Kemple, K.M. (1991). Research in review. Preschool children's peer acceptance and social interaction. Young Children, 46(5), 47–54.

Pellegrini, A.D., & Glickman, C.D. (1990). Measuring kindergartners' social competence. Young Children, 45(4), 40–44.

Rogers, D.L., & Ross, D.D. (1986). Encouraging positive social interaction among young children. Young Children, 41(3), 12–17.

Rousso, J. (1988). Talking with young children about their dreams: How to listen and what to listen for. Young Children, 43(5), 70–74.

Solter, A. (1992). Understanding tears and tantrums. Young Children, 47(4), 64–68.

Warren, R.M. (1977). Caring: Supporting children's growth. Washington, DC: NAEYC.

Zavitkovsky, D., Baker, K.R., Berlfein, J.R., & Almy, M. (1986). Listen to the children. Washington, DC: NAEYC.

Encouraging Positive Social Development in Young Children

Donna Sasse Wittmer and Alice Sterling Honig

Donna Sasse Wittmer, Ph.D., is assistant professor in early childhood education at the University of Colorado in Denver. She has had extensive experience directing, training in, and conducting research in early childhood care and education programs.

Alice Sterling Honig, Ph.D., professor of child development at Syracuse University in Syracuse, New York, was program director for the Family Development Research Program and has authored numerous books, including Parent Involvement in Early Childhood Education *and* Playtime Learning Games for Young Children. *She directs the annual Syracuse Quality Infant/ Toddler Caregiving Workshop.*

Editor's note: *This two-part review presents techniques for teachers and parents, schools and communities, to promote young children's social development. Supportive research findings are often cited to back up the techniques suggested. In Part 1, suggestions refer to interpersonal interactions of caregivers with individual children or small groups of children. Techniques in Part 2 (to be published in a subsequent issue of* Young Children) *target entire classrooms as well as broader systems, such as centers, schools, families, and communities.*

An earlier version of this article was presented at NAEYC's Annual Conference in Denver, Colorado, in November 1991. Portions of this article have been adapted from Prosocial Development in Children: Caring, Sharing, & Cooperating: A Bibliographic Resource Guide *by Alice Sterling Honig and Donna Sasse Wittmer (1992).*

A toddler, reaching for a toy, got his finger pinched in the hinge on the door of a toy shelf in his child care classroom. He cried loudly; his pacifier fell from his mouth. Another toddler, obviously distressed by the sounds of pain coming from his playmate, picked up the pacifier and held it in the crying toddler's mouth in an apparent attempt to help and comfort the injured toddler.

This example, shared by a child care provider, is one of many exciting prosocial events that have been observed in young toddlers, preschoolers, and primary-age children as they interact together in group settings. Caregivers of young children notice events such as the one above as they live and work with very young children. If adults implement curriculum that promotes interpersonal consideration and cooperation in children, we see even more of these behaviors.

Social development was seen as the core of the curriculum in nursery schools and kindergartens until a cognitive emphasis was brought into the field in the late 1960s; social development has recently been getting renewed attention by early childhood education leaders. Skilled teachers of young children implement prosocial goals for young children as they attempt to facili-

tate children's positive social interactions. Prosocial goals that teachers emphasize include

- showing sympathy and kindness,
- helping,
- giving,
- accepting food or toys,
- sharing,
- showing positive verbal and physical contact,
- comforting another person in distress,
- donating to others who are less fortunate,
- showing concern
- responding to bereaved peers,
- taking the perspective of another person,
- showing affection, and
- cooperating with others in play or to complete a task.

The adults in children's lives play an important role in helping children develop these prosocial attitudes and behaviors.

Not surprisingly, if caregivers and teachers take time to encourage, facilitate, and teach prosocial behaviors, children's prosocial interactions increase and aggression decreases (Honig 1982). In an interesting study, children who attended, from 3 months to kindergarten, an experimental child care program that focused on intellectual growth were rated by their kindergarten teachers as more aggressive than a control group of children who attended community child care programs during their preschool years for less amount of time (Haskins 1985). But when a prosocial curriculum entitled "My Friends and Me" was implemented, the next groups of child care graduates did not differ in aggression rates from control-group children. Emphasizing and encouraging prosocial behaviors made a difference in how children learned to interact and play with each other. A number of other intriguing research studies concerning teacher educators and curriculum intended to enhance positive social development in young children are described in our book *Prosocial Development in Children: Caring, Sharing, & Cooperating*.

Social development was seen as the core of the curriculum in nursery schools and kindergartens until a cognitive emphasis was brought into the field in the late 1960s; social development has recently been getting renewed attention by early childhood education leaders.

Focus on prosocial behaviors: Value, model, and acknowledge

Need it be said? What the adults who are important in children's lives value, model, and encourage in children influences them. What values do we value and encourage?

Value and emphasize consideration for others' needs. Children become aware at an early age of what aspects of life their special adults admire and value. Research on toddlers (Yarrow & Waxler 1976) and boys with learning disabilities (Elardo & Freund 1981) shows that when parents encourage their children to have concern for others, the children behave more prosocially.

As every experienced teacher knows, emphasizing the importance of children helping others whenever possible results in children undertaking more helping activities (Grusec, Saas-Kortsaak, & Simultis 1978). Children whose parents esteem altruism highly are more frequently considered

by peers as highly prosocial (Rutherford & Mussen 1968).

Model prosocial behaviors. "Practice what you preach," "Do as I say, not as I do," and "Monkey see, monkey do" are tried-and-true sayings that remind us that children model many behaviors that we do—and do not!—want them to imitate. Adults who model prosocial behaviors influence children's willingness to behave prosocially (Bandura 1986). A teacher who patiently tied his toddlers' shoelaces day after day observed that toddlers who saw a peer tripping over laces would bend down and try to twist their

friend's sneaker laces in an attempt to help. Bryan (1977) stresses that children imitate helping activities whether the models are living people or fictional characters. Over the years, modeling has proven more powerful than preaching. Traditionally we have called it *setting a good example*. How caregivers and parents act—kind, considerate, and compassionate, or cruel, thoughtless, and uncaring—influences young children to imitate them.

Children who frequently observe and are influenced by family members and teachers who behave prosocially will imitate those special adults. "Mama," ob-

---

If adults implement curriculum that promotes interpersonal consideration and cooperation in children, we see even more of these behaviors.

---

served 3-year-old Dana, "that was a very good job you did buckling my seat belt." How often Mama had used just such encouraging words with her preschooler!

Label and identify prosocial and antisocial behaviors. We all love it when our positive deeds are acknowledged. Notice the positive interactions, however small, that occur between children and encourage them through your comments. When adults label behaviors, such as "considerate toward peers" and "cooperative with classmates," children's dialogues and role-taking abilities increase (Vorrath 1985). Rather than just saying "That's good" or "That's nice" to a child, be specific in identifying prosocial behaviors and actions for children. Saying

"You are being helpful" or "You gave him a tissue, he really needed it to wipe his nose" will be most helpful to children.

Attribute positive social behaviors to each child. Attributing positive intentions, such as "You shared because you like to help others" or "You're the kind of person who likes to help others whenever you can," results in children donating more generously to people in need (Grusec, Kuczynski, Rushton, & Simultis 1978; Grusec & Redler 1980).

After 8-year-olds had shared their winnings from a game with "poor" children, the children who were given positive attributions (e.g., "You're the kind of person who likes to help others whenever you can"), as op-

posed to social reinforcers (just being told that it was good to share with others), were more likely to share at a later time (Grusec & Redler 1980).

Skilled teachers personalize attributions so that each child feels special. Say such things as "You are a very helpful person," "You are the kind of person who likes to stick up for a child who is being bothered," and "You really try to be a buddy to a new child in our class who is shy at first in finding a friend."

Children from punitive homes may need help understanding how to make attributions that are true rather than assuming that others have evil intentions. For example, you might ask, "Did your classmate step on your homework paper in the school-yard to be mean or to keep it from blowing away?" Focus children's thinking on attributes and intentions of others' actions as a way to prevent children from unthinkingly lashing out at others in angry response.

Notice and positively encourage prosocial behaviors, but do not overuse external rewards. In research by Rushton and Teachman (1978), social reinforcement for sharing increased sharing among young children even when the experimenter was no longer present. Goffin (1987) recommends that teachers notice when children share mutual goals, ideas, and materials, as well as when they negotiate and bargain in decision making and accomplishing goals. When caregivers and parents use external reinforcement too much, however, children's prosocial behaviors may decrease. Fabes, Fultz, Eisenberg, May-Plumlee, and Christopher (1989) reported that mothers who like using rewards may undermine their children's internalized *desire* to behave prosocially by increasing the salience of external rather than internal rewards.

Teachers have reported that offering stickers for prosocial be-

As every experienced teacher knows, emphasizing the importance of children helping others whenever possible results in children undertaking more helping activities. Children whose parents esteem altruism highly are more frequently considered by peers as highly prosocial.

haviors to one child in a classroom often backfires when other children become upset that they didn't also get stickers. A kindergarten child went home from school one day and told his grandmother, "I've got it figured out now. First you have to be bad, and then good, and then you get a sticker." Commenting on positive behaviors and attributing positive characteristics to children rather than using external rewards help young children internalize prosocial responses.

Encourage understanding of children's own and others' feelings and perspectives

Skilled teachers understand how to do these things:

Acknowledge and encourage understanding and expression of children's feelings. The ability to empathize with a peer who is experiencing sadness, anger, or distress may depend on a child having had a prior similar experience with those feelings (Barnett 1984). Children from ages 3 to 8 are becoming aware of *happy feelings* (3½ years), *fear* (3½ to 4 years), and *anger and sadness* (3 to 8 years) (Borke 1971).

Caregivers need to help children put feelings into words and to understand their feelings. Teachers can acknowledge and reflect children's feelings by making comments such as "It seems as if you are feeling so sad" or "You look like you are feeling angry. You want my attention *now*. As soon as I change

Luanne's diaper, I can read to you." This calm observation by a child care provider wiped the thunder off a toddler's face. He looked amazed that his teacher had understood his feelings. He relaxed when she reassured him with a promise to come back in a few minutes and read with him.

Facilitate perspective- and role-taking skills and understanding others' feelings. Helping young children notice and respond to the feelings of others can be quite effective in teaching them to be considerate of others. A preschool teacher kneeled to be at eye level with a child who had just socked another child during a struggle for a bike. The teacher pointed out the feelings of the other child: "He's very sad and hurt. What can you do to make him feel better?" The aggressor paused, observed the other child's face, and offered the bike to the crying child.

A child's ability to identify accurately the emotional state of another, as well as the empathic ability to experience the feelings of another, contribute to prosocial behavior. Children who are altruistic and more willing to help others display more empathy and perspective-taking skills (a cognitive measure) (Chalmers & Townsend 1990).

Feshbach (1975) reported that two training techniques that promoted understanding in children of other children's feelings were *role playing* and *maximizing the perceived similarity* between the observer and the stimulus person. The latter is what antibias education is about.

Encourage children to act out stories dramatically. Children who act out different stories become aware of how the characters feel. Switching roles gives children a different perspective on the feelings and motives of each character. Acting out roles, as in "The Three Billy Goats Gruff" or "Goldilocks and the Three Bears" gives children a chance to understand each story character's point of view (Krogh & Lamme 1983). A first- or second-grade class may want to write a letter of apology from Goldilocks to the Bear family!

Trovato (1987) created the puppets "Hattie Helper," "Carl Defender," "Robert Rescuer," "Debra Defender," "Kevin Comforter," and "Sharon Sharer" for adults to use to help young children learn prosocial behaviors with other children. Crary (1984) also promotes the use of puppets for teachers and children to use in role playing different social situations that may arise in the classroom.

Perspective taking is not enough to ensure children's development of prosocial behaviors. Children who are low in empathy but high in perspective taking may demonstrate Machiavellianism (a tendency to take advantage in a negative way of knowledge concerning another person's feelings and thoughts) (Barnett & Thompson 1985). Although Howes and Farber's (1987) research with toddlers ages 16 to 33 months of in child care showed that 93% of toddlers responded prosocially to peers who showed distress, George and Main (1979) reported that abused toddlers looked on impassively or reacted with anger when a playmate was hurt or distressed. Vulnerable children urgently need help understanding and acknowledging their range of often very strong feelings and empathizing with other people's feelings.

Helping young children notice and respond to the feelings of others can be quite effective in teaching them to be considerate of others.

Use victim-centered discipline and reparation: Emphasize consequences. Other-oriented techniques focus a child on the effects of hurtful and antisocial behaviors, such as hitting or pinching. Results of a study of how children learned altruism at home revealed that parents of the most prosocial toddlers had emphasized the negative consequences of their toddlers' aggressive acts on other children (Pines 1979). Point out the consequences of the child's behavior. Emphasize to the aggressor the results of hurtful actions upon another person. Choose statements such as "Look—that hurt him!" "He is crying" and "I cannot let you hurt another child, and I do not want anyone to make you hurt; we need to help each other feel happy and safe in this class."

Help children become assertive concerning prosocial matters. If a child has high-perspective-taking skills and is assertive, then the child is likely to be prosocial. In contrast, if a child has high-perspective-taking skills and is timid, then the child is less likely to be prosocial (Barrett & Yarrow 1977). In the book *Listen to the Children* (Zavitkovsky, Baker, Berlfein, & Almy 1986, 42), the authors shared a true story about two young girls, Dolores and Monica, who were washing their hands before lunch. Eric was waiting for his turn to wash his hands. Out of the blue, he shouted crossly into Monica's face, "You're not pretty." The author and observer reported that out of the stillness came Dolores's firm voice, "Yes, she is. She looks just right for her." Dolores was demonstrating both perspective-taking skills— knowing that Monica's feelings were hurt—and prosocial defending skills. As teachers notice and acknowledge prosocial behaviors, children's self-confidence concerning prosocial interactions will increase.

Acknowledge and encourage understanding and expression of children's feelings. Facilitate perspective- and role-taking skills and understanding others' feelings.

Encourage problem solving and planfulness for prosocial behaviors

You have heard this before, but it takes time, effort, and planfulness to *do* it.

Encourage means–ends and alternative-solution thinking in conflict situations. Help children think through, step-by-step, their reasoning about how to respond when they are having a social problem with a peer. What are the steps by which they figure out how to get from the conflict situation they are in to peaceful, friendly cooperation or a courteous live-and-let-live situation? Shure (1992) provides daily lessons for teachers to help children discover when their feelings and

wishes are the *same* or *different* from other children's, or whether *some* or *all* of the children want to play the game that *one* prefers. Teachers who use these daily lesson plans with emphasis on encouraging children to think of alternative solutions to their social conflicts and to imagine the consequences of each behavior or strategy they think of can help aggressive and shy children become more positively social within three months. Increased positive social functioning is associated with children's ability to think of more strategies rather than with the quality of the social solutions they devise (Shure & Spivak 1978).

Use Socratic questions to elicit prosocial planfulness and recognition of responsibility. When a child is misbehaving in such a way as to disturb his own or class progress, quietly ask, "How does that help you?" This technique, recommended by Fugitt (1983), can be expanded to encourage group awareness by asking the child, "How is that helping the group?" or "How is that helping your neighbor?" This strategy is designed to help children recognize and take responsibility for their own behaviors.

Show pictured scenes of altruism, and ask children to create verbal scenarios. Show children pictured scenes of children being helpful, cooperative, generous, charitable, patient, courteous, sharing, and kind. Working with a small group of children, call on each child to make up a scenario or story about the child or children in the picture. Ask, "What do you think is happening here?" Be sure to help children become aware of how the child being helped feels and how the child who has been helpful or generous will feel about herself or himself.

Provide specific behavioral training in social skills. Cartledge and Milburn (1980) recommend defining skills to be taught in behavioral terms assessing children's level of competence. Then teach the skills that are lacking, evaluate the results of teaching, and provide opportunities for children to practice and generalize the transfer of these new social skills to other situations.

McGinnis and Goldstein use structured "skillstreaming" strategies to teach prosocial skills to preschool (1990) and elementary

© The Growth Program

Encourage means–ends and alternative-solution thinking in conflict situations. Help children think through, step-by-step, their reasoning about how to respond when they are having a social problem with a peer. What are the steps by which they figure out how to get from the conflict situation they are in to peaceful, friendly cooperation or a courteous live-and-let-live situation?

school (1984) children. Skills such as listening, using nice talk, using brave talk, saying thank you, asking for help, greeting others, reading others, waiting one's turn, sharing, offering help, asking someone to play, and playing a game are a few of the "beginning social skills" and "friendship making skills." Other skills help children deal with feelings and provide them with alternatives to aggression. Preschool

children who received training and were encouraged to (1) use politeness words, (2) listen to who is talking, (3) participate with a peer in an activity, (4) share, (5) take turns, and (6) help another person have fun were more sociable in the training classroom and at follow-up (Factor & Schilmoeller 1983).

Teaching concern for others is a familiar idea to teachers of children from infancy through 8 years!

Place a child who is experiencing social problems with a friendly, socially skilled playmate, preferably a younger one, to increase the social isolate's positive peer interactions.

Use positive discipline for promoting prosocial behaviors and less aggression

We have to educate children about socially desirable behaviors, as about many other things.

Use positive discipline strategies, such as induction and authoritative methods. When teachers use positive discipline techniques—such as reasoning, use of positive reinforcement, and empathic listening—and *authoritative* strategies (Baumrind 1977)—loving, positive commitment to the child plus use of firm, clear rules and explanations—children are more likely to behave prosocially. The more nonauthoritarian and nonpunitive the parent, the higher the child's level of reasoning (Eisenberg, Lennon, & Roth 1983). Discipline that is *emotionally intense but nonpunitive* is effective with toddlers (Yarrow & Waxler 1976).

Positive discipline: A protection against media violence. As one might guess, a relationship has been found between parents' positive discipline techniques and the effects of prosocial and antisocial television programs on children. Using Hoffman's terms to describe parenting styles, Abelman (1986) reported that parents who are most *inductive* (who use reasoning) and who rarely use love withdrawal or power assertion have children who are *most* affected by prosocial and *least* affected by antisocial television. The reverse is also true. Positive discipline, then, is a powerful buffer against the negative effects of antisocial media materials.

Respond to and provide alternatives to aggressive behaviors. This has been a basic principle of nursery and kindergarten education since their beginning. Writing much more recently, Caldwell (1977) advises caregivers not to ignore aggression or permit aggression to be expressed and assume that this venting will "discharge the tension." For example, bullying that is ignored does not disappear. Caldwell writes, "In order to control aggression, we must strengthen altruism" (1977, 9). Teach children what they can do to help others feel good.

Redirect antisocial actions to more acceptable actions. A child who is throwing a ball at someone may be redirected to throw a beanbag back and forth with another child.

Teach angry, acting-out children to *use words* to express feelings. When children are feeling aggrieved, tell them, "Use your words" instead of hurtful actions. Help children learn "I" statements to express their feelings or wishes and to express how they perceive a situation of distress or conflict (Gordon 1970). Give children words and phrases to use, such as "I feel upset when our game is interrupted," "I cannot finish my building if you take away these blocks," or "I was using that Magic Marker first. I still need it to finish my picture."

Ask children to restate classroom rules about not hitting or hurting others (Honig 1985). Preschool children, however, may interpret the rules from an egocentric viewpoint and not always understand the reasons for rules. Deanna, a preschooler, went home from school and told her mother, "Matthew pinched me." After talking about the classroom rule, "Don't pinch or hit back," Deanna's mother tried to get Deanna to problem-solve other solutions to the problem, such as telling Matthew that it hurt when he pinched. The next day, when her mom picked her up from school, Deanna reported angrily, "Matthew pinched me back." When asked why she pinched him, Deanna restated the classroom rule, "That doesn't matter; he's not supposed to pinch me back."

Offer children choices. This is another "basic" of professional work with young children. Toddlers and preschoolers struggling to assert newly emergent autonomy cooperate more easily with caregiver requests if they feel empowered to make choices. Adults can decide on the choices to be offered. For the toddler having trouble settling at naptime, the offer "Would you like to sleep with your head at this end of your cot or the other end?" may empower him enough to decide cheerfully just how he wants to lie down for naptime. Gilligan observed that "The essence of the moral decision is the exercise of choice and the willingness to accept responsibility for that choice" (1982, 58). Often adults forget that if they carefully craft choices, children may more readily cooperate in the home and in the classroom. During snacktime adults can offer a choice of "darker or lighter toast," "apple or orange juice" to the finicky eater who generally resists food simply set down without her being allowed some choice. When children want to practice throwing a small basketball into a preschooler-size net, discuss the need for a turn-taking rule and offer a choice: "Do you want to take two or three throws for your turn?" Later, comment on how the children followed the rule. Ask them how they think the rule helped their game go more peaceably.

Provide opportunities for social interactions through play—pair "social isolates" with sociable children

Place a child who is experiencing social problems with a friendly, socially skilled playmate, preferably a younger one, to increase the social isolate's positive peer interactions (Furman, Rahe, & Hartup 1978). Pair an assertive, gregarious, but gentle child (who is the recipient of many prosocial overtures and is likely to offer help and friendliness) with a very shy child.

Create good adult–child relationships

Children learn to enjoy being with other people when they experience adults who are positive, caring, loving, and responsive. When adults respond to a child in affectionate, kind, empathetic ways, the child learns how to be a communicative partner who knows how to take turns, listen, negotiate, and help others; common sense tells us that this is logical. Park and Waters (1989)

found that two children who had experienced affirmative first relationships with their mothers engaged in more harmonious, less controlling, more responsive, and happier play together than did children who had not experienced positive first relationships.

Provide body relaxation activities

Create a relaxed classroom climate to further harmonious interactions. Relaxation exercises can restore harmony when children are fussy or tense. Back rubs help. Sand play and water play promote relaxation in some children who have a difficult time acting peaceably.

© The Growth Program

Offer children choices. This is another "basic" of professional work with young children. Toddlers and preschoolers struggling to assert newly emergent autonomy cooperate more easily with caregiver requests if they feel empowered to make choices. Adults can decide on the choices to be offered.

Children may lie down on mats and wiggle each limb separately, in turn, to relax and ease body tension. Many classical music pieces, such as the Brahms *Lullaby* or Debussy's *Reverie*, can be useful in helping children imagine peaceful scenes. Focused imagery activities can reduce tensions. Have children close their eyes and imagine being in a quiet forest glade, listening to a stream flow nearby and feeling the warm sunshine on their faces.

Group movement to music adds another dimension of relaxation. Dancing partners need to tune in to each other's motions and rhythmic swaying as they hold hands or take turns imitating each other's gestures.

Use technology to promote prosocial behaviors

Unlike most of the familiar principles for promoting social development reviewed in this article, *this* idea will be new to many teachers. Videotape children who are behaving prosocially to facilitate sharing. A video camera in the classroom can help promote altruism. Third-grade children viewed videotapes of themselves and models in situations involving sharing. This technique was effective in increasing sharing immediately following training and one week later (Devoe & Sherman 1978). Maybe some teachers who like trying new things will try this idea with *younger* children.

Conclusion

As teachers focus on and facilitate prosocial behaviors, the whole ambience of a classroom may change. As teachers model kindness and respect, express appreciation for prosocial actions, promote cooperation, teach children how their behaviors affect others, point out each child's prosocial behaviors with admiration to the other children, and encourage children to help each other, prosocial deeds and attitudes will increase. Adults' interactions with young children make a powerful difference in the atmosphere and climate of the classroom.

References

Abelman, R. 1986. Children's awareness of television's prosocial fare: Parental discipline as an antecedent. *Journal of Family Issues* 7: 51–66.

Bandura, A. 1986. *The social foundation of thought and action: A social cognitive theory.* Englewood Cliffs, NJ: Prentice Hall.

Barnett, M. 1984. Similarity of experience and empathy in preschoolers. *The Journal of Genetic Psychology* 145: 241–50.

Barnett, M., & S. Thompson. 1985. The role of perspective-taking and empathy in children's Machiavellianism, prosocial behavior, and motive for helping. *The Journal of Genetic Psychology* 146: 295–305.

Barrett, D.E., & M.R. Yarrow. 1977. Prosocial behavior, social inferential ability, and assertiveness in young children. *Child Development* 48: 475–81.

Baumrind, D. 1977. Some thoughts about childrearing. In S. Cohen & T.J. Comiskey (Eds.), *Child development: Contemporary perspectives.* Itasca, IL: F.E. Peacock.

Borke, H. 1971. Interpersonal perception of young children: Egocentrism or empathy? *Developmental Psychology* 5: 263–9.

Bryan, J.H. 1977. Prosocial behavior. In H.L. Hom, Jr., & P.A. Robinson, eds. *Psychological processes in early education.* New York: Academic.

Caldwell, B. 1977. Aggression and hostility in young children. *Young Children* 32 (2): 4–14.

Cartledge, G., & J.F. Milburn, eds. 1980. *Teaching social skills to children.* New York: Pergamon.

Chalmers, J., & M. Townsend. 1990. The effects of training in social perspective taking on socially maladjusted girls. *Child Development* 61: 178–90.

Crary, E. 1984. *Kids can cooperate: A practical guide to teaching problem solving.* Seattle, WA: Parenting Press.

Devoe, M., & T. Sherman. 1978. A microtechnology for teaching prosocial behavior to children. *Child Study Journal* 8 (2): 83–92.

Eisenberg, N., R. Lennon, & K. Roth. 1983. Prosocial development: A longitudinal study. *Developmental Psychology* 19: 846–55.

Elardo, R., & J.J. Freund. 1981. Maternal childrearing styles and the social skills of learning disabled boys: A preliminary investigation. *Contemporary Educational Psychology* 6: 86–94.

Fabes, R.A., J. Fultz, N. Eisenberg, T. May-Plumlee, & F.S. Christopher. 1989. Effect of rewards on children's prosocial motivation: A socialization study. *Developmental Psychology* 25: 509–15.

Factor, D., & G.L. Schilmoeller. 1983. Social skill training of preschool children. *Child Study Journal* 13 (1): 41–56.

Feshbach, N. 1975. Empathy in children: Some theoretical and empirical considerations. *The Counseling Psychologist* 5: 25–30.

Fugitt, E. 1983. *"He hit me back first!" Creative visualization activities for parenting and teaching.* Rolling Hills Estates, CA: Jalmar.

Furman, W., D.F. Rahe, & W.W. Hartup. 1978. Rehabilitation of low-interactive preschool children through mixed-age and same-age socialization. In H. McGurk, ed., *Issues in childhood social development.* Cambridge: Methuen.

George, C., & M. Main. 1979. Social interactions of young abused children: Approach, avoidance, and aggression. *Child Development* 50: 306–18.

Gilligan, C. 1982. *In a different voice.* Cambridge, MA: Harvard University Press.

Goffin, S.G. 1987. Cooperative behaviors: They need our support. *Young Children* 42 (2): 75–81.

Gordon, T. 1970. *Parent effectiveness training.* New York: Wyden.

Grusec, J.E., & E. Redler. 1980. Attribution, reinforcement, and altruism. *Developmental Psychology* 16: 525–34.

Grusec, J., P. Saas-Kortsaak, & Z. Simultis. 1978. The role of example and moral exhortation in the training of altruism. *Child Development* 49: 920–3.

Grusec, J., J. Kuczynski, P. Rushton, & Z. Simultis. 1978. Modeling, direct instruction, and attributions: Effects on altruism. *Developmental Psychology* 14: 51–7.

Haskins, R. 1985. Public school aggression among children with varying day care experience. *Child Development* 56: 689–703.

Honig, A.S. 1982. Research in review. Prosocial development in children. *Young Children* 37 (5): 51–62.

Honig, A.S. 1985. Research in review. Compliance, control, and discipline. Part 1. *Young Children* 40 (2): 50–8.

Honig, A.S., & D.S. Wittmer. 1992. *Prosocial development in children: Caring, sharing, & cooperating: A bibliographic resource guide.* New York: Garland.

Howes, C., & J. Farber. 1987. Toddlers' responses to the distress of their peers. *Journal of Applied Developmental Psychology* 8: 441–52.

Krogh, S., & L. Lamme. 1983 (January–February). Learning to share: How literature can help. *Childhood Education* 59 (3): 188–92.

McGinnis, E., & A. Goldstein. 1984. *Skillstreaming the elementary school child: A guide to prosocial skills.* Champaign, IL: Research Press.

McGinnis, E., & A. Goldstein. 1990. *Skillstreaming in early childhood. Teaching prosocial skills to the preschool and kindergarten child.* Champaign, IL: Research Press.

Park, K., & E. Waters. 1989. Security of attachment and preschool friendships. *Child Development* 60: 1076–81.

Pines, M. 1979. Good Samaritans at age two? *Psychology Today* 13: 66–77.

Rushton, J.P., & G. Teachman. 1978. The effects of positive reinforcement, attributions, and punishment on model induced altruism in children. *Personality and Social Psychology Bulletin* 4: 322–5.

Rutherford, E., & P. Mussen. 1968. Generosity in nursery school boys. *Child Development* 39: 755–65.

Shure, M.B. 1992. *I can problem solve: An interpersonal cognitive problem-solving program.* Champaign, IL: Research Press.

Shure, M., & G. Spivack. 1978. *Problem-solving techniques in childrearing.* San Francisco: Jossey-Bass.

Trovato, C. 1987. Teaching today's kids to get along. *Early Childhood Teacher* 34: 43.

Vorrath, H. 1985. *Positive peer culture.* New York: Aldine.

Yarrow, M.R., & C.Z. Waxler. 1976. Dimensions and correlates of prosocial behavior in young children. *Child Development* 47: 118–25.

Zavitkovsky, D., K.R. Baker, J.R. Berlfein, & M. Almy. 1986. *Listen to the children.* Washington, DC: NAEYC.

Developmentally Appropriate Middle Level Schools

M. Lee Manning

M. Lee Manning is Assistant Professor, Department of Educational Curriculum and Instruction, Darden College of Education, Old Dominion University, Norfolk, Virginia

E ducation theorists have suggested that learners' developmental levels should provide the basis for school curricular, instructional and organizational practices, as well as the overall teaching/ learning environment. While insightful theories have been offered regarding physical, psychosocial and cognitive development, the process of translating theories into practice has been somewhat slow, especially beyond the elementary school years.

Recognition of early adolescence as a legitimate developmental period is a hopeful sign. The 1990s have ushered in a new emphasis on improving schools for young adolescents. The growing middle level school movement represents a commitment to base school practices on the developmental needs of 10- to 14-year-olds. To support this effort, ACEI's *Developmentally Appropriate Middle Level Schools* examines young adolescents' physical, psychosocial and cognitive characteristics and suggests develop-mentally appropriate educational experiences. An abstract of this forthcoming book follows.

Time for Appropriate and Decisive Action

For decades, the role of schools for 10- to 14-year-olds remained unclear. The problem may have resulted from the mindset that elementary school should address the education needs of the childhood years and secondary school focus upon the adolescent years. Except for serving as a transition between the two, the middle level school lacked a clear rationale.

Several factors have contributed to the increased emphasis on developmentally responsive middle level schools. First, early adolescence has now been accepted as a legitimate developmental period (Thornburg, 1983). Second, the middle level school has progressed beyond its infancy and has developed to a stage where genuine improvements are possible. Third, the contemporary emphasis on reforming middle level schools to be more responsive to the needs of young adolescents can be seen in many forms: *Turning Points* (Carnegie Council on Adolescent Development, 1989), *Making the Middle Grades Work* (Children's Defense Fund, 1988), *Caught in the Middle* (California State Department of Education, 1987) and *What Matters in the Middle Grades* (Maryland State Department of Education, 1989). Fourth, the formation of ACEI's Division for Later Childhood/Early Adolescence demonstrates a commitment to young adolescents and their education.

Young Adolescents' Developmental Characteristics

Young adolescents' developmental characteristics have been clearly defined. Physical characteristics include a marked increase in body growth, readily apparent skeletal and structural changes (bones growing more rapidly than muscles), widely varying developmental rates, onset of puberty, faster development in girls than boys and increases in physical endurance. Psychosocial characteristics include increased social interactions and concern with friendships, shifting allegiance from parents and teachers to peers, constant examination of development and the overall "self," quests for freedom and independence and fluctuating self-concept. Cognitive characteristics include increased abilities to think hypothetically, abstractly, reflectively and critically and to make reasoned moral and ethical choices. Some young adolescents develop from Piaget's concrete operations stage to the formal operations stage.

From *Childhood Education*, Vol. 68, No. 5, Annual Theme Issue, 1992, pp. 305-307. Reprinted by permission of M. Lee Manning and the Association for Childhood Education International, 11501 Georgia Avenue, Suite 315, Wheaton, MD. © 1992 by the Association.

2. DEVELOPMENT: Adolescence

Educators basing teaching/learning experiences on these and other developmental characteristics should not assume all young adolescents develop at a similar rate. As Thornburg (1982) suggested, diversity is the hallmark characteristic of young adolescents. Considerable differences exist between early and late maturers and shy students and the socially outgoing. In addition, learners may be functioning at various stages of development, from the concrete to the formal operations stage.

Providing Developmentally Appropriate Practices

Once educators commit to developmentally appropriate instruction, actual experiences, methods and materials can be planned. The forthcoming book discusses the "why, how and what" of practices that reflect physical, psychosocial and cognitive development of middle level children.

Physical characteristics of 10- to 14-year-olds suggest the need to provide learning opportunities to master physical skills; develop positive attitudes toward health, fitness and nutrition; and understand drug and tobacco use and abuse. Likewise, activities that stress size, strength, stamina and competition among early and late maturers should be avoided.

Educational experiences that involve social interaction and friendships and develop appropriate sex-role identification address the psychosocial needs of middle level students. Strategies include cooperative learning, teacher and student teams, adviser-advisee programs, cross-cultural grouping and the school-within-a-school organizational model.

Cognitive needs may be met by integrating subject matter across disciplines and providing communities of learning. Strategies include cooperative and experiential learning, proper academic counseling, exploratory programs for studying areas of interest and working in small groups. As middle level school educators plan group instruction, whether large or small, grouping students by ability should be avoided at all costs. Equating ability or achievement levels with development can result in dire consequences for academic achievement, self-concept, multicultural concerns and teacher behaviors (Manning & Lucking, 1990).

Concerns and Issues

The book also addresses several relevant issues and concerns, such as the many differences that distinguish young adolescents from their peers, the need to teach young adolescents about their constantly changing bodies and minds and last, the pressing need to re-engage parents and families in the education of their 10- to 14-year-olds.

Developmentally Appropriate Middle Level Schools staunchly maintains that young adolescents' individual development should be the basis for curricular, organizational and managerial decisions. Reaching these decisions, however, should include consideration of learners' individual, gender, class and cultural differences. Cultural and social class differences may be seen in friendship patterns, identity development, social expectations, learning styles and self-esteem. Similarly, gender differences can be identified in health concerns, social networks, sex-role attitudes and relationship between self-image and school achievement.

Teaching young adolescents about themselves and their development can be one of the greatest contributions a middle level school can make. Subjects to consider are: developmental changes, growing arms and legs, increased hair, deepening voices, rapidly changing friendships, shifts from being parent-centered to peer-centered, feelings of anonymity, effects of peer pressure, perceptions of morals and values, differing levels of thought and varying levels of test-taking abilities. Sometimes, young adolescents feel uncomfortable talking with their parents and often receive inaccurate information from friends. Through curricular content, adviser-advisee sessions, exploratory programs and counseling sessions, educators can explain the normalcy of development and distinguish between false and genuine concerns.

A recent survey of 8th-graders and their parents revealed two-thirds of the students never or rarely discussed classes or school programs with parents and half of the parents had never talked to school officials about academic programs ("Parents Key," 1991). The developmental changes being experienced by 10- to 14-year-olds, the current outcry to improve middle level education and the long overdue recognition that middle level school students need developmentally appropriate educational experiences all point to the acute need to re-engage parents in educational efforts. Parents and teachers working together can enhance the education of learners. Teachers can provide parents with opportunities to play crucial roles in children's health and safety. In addition, teachers can help parents to create a home environment that contributes to school achievement and overall development. Students benefit in their school work, attitudes and aspirations for continued schooling when parents remain knowledgeable partners with the schools in their children's education (Children's Defense Fund, 1988).

Closing Remarks

Developmentally Appropriate Middle Level Schools, to be published by ACEI in 1993, examines young adolescent development and developmentally appropriate educational practices in middle level schools. While providing a preview of the book, this abstract cannot comprehensively explain the entire contents. In addition to ideas discussed, readers will find information such as: putting assessment in its proper perspective, the dangers of ability grouping, the concept of multiple intelligences and re-engaging parents in schools' efforts. Likewise, the book will include a detailed, annotated bibliography and checklist to evaluate educators' responses to young adolescent development.

A major goal of middle level educators during the 1990s and 21st century will be to improve the lives of young adolescents. ACEI's contribution to the improvement of middle level schools can be seen in its decision to publish *Developmentally Appropriate Middle Level Schools* and also in its commitment to be a powerful advocate for all children, infancy through early adolescence.

References

California State Department of Education. (1987). *Caught in the middle.* Sacramento, CA: Author.

Carnegie Council on Adolescent Development. (1989). *Turning points.* Washington, DC: Author.

Children's Defense Fund. (1988). *Making the middle grades work.* Washington, DC: Author.

Manning, M. L., & Lucking, R. (1990). Ability grouping: Realities and alternatives. *Childhood Education, 66,* 254-258.

Maryland State Department of Education. (1989). *What matters in the middle grades.* Baltimore, MD: Author.

Parents key to classroom experience. (1991). *Middle Ground, 18*(4), 1-2.

Thornburg, H. (1982). The total early adolescent in contemporary society. *The High School Journal, 65,* 272-278.

Thornburg, H. (1983). Is early adolescence really a stage of development? *Theory into Practice, 22,* 79-84.

Note to readers: The book *Developmentally Appropriate Middle Level Schools* was published in 1993. If you wish information, please write to: Marilyn Gardner, Director of Marketing, Association for Childhood Education International, 11501 Georgia Avenue, Suite 315, Wheaton, Maryland 20902.

At-Risk Students and Resiliency: Factors Contributing to Academic Success

JAMES H. McMILLAN and DAISY F. REED

James H. McMillan is a professor and Daisy F. Reed is an associate professor—both at the School of Education, Virginia Commonwealth University, Richmond, Virginia. Funds to support this research were received from the Metropolitan Educational Research Consortium. The views expressed are those of the authors and do not represent opinions or beliefs of the members of the consortium.

The increasingly high number of at-risk middle and high school students—those in danger of dropping out of school because of academic failure or other problems—is a major concern in education today. At-risk students show persistent patterns of under-achievement and of social maladjustment in school, leading to their failure to finish high school. Indeed, the national dropout rate averages about 25 percent (Sklarz 1989), and for minorities, that rate is higher, with an average of 30 percent leaving school before they graduate (Liontos 1991). In Texas, the dropout rate for Hispanic Americans is 45 percent. Additionally, students in urban schools have much higher dropout rates than those in other areas: in Boston, Chicago, Los Angeles, Detroit, and other major cities, dropout rates range from 40 percent to 60 percent of the total school population (Hahn 1987).

An interesting approach to helping at-risk students succeed is to examine the notion of "resilience." Despite incredible hardships and the presence of at-risk factors, some students have developed characteristics and coping skills that enable them to succeed. They appear to develop stable, healthy personas and are able to recover from or adapt to life's stresses and problems. These students can be termed *resilient* (Winfield 1991).

In one recent large-scale study, approximately 19 percent of students who could be classified as at-risk became individuals who had success in school, with positive goals and plans for the future (Peng, Lee, Wang, and Walberg 1992). What enables these resilient students to succeed

academically? What can educators and other concerned citizens do to foster these qualities in the 81 percent of at-risk students who do not succeed in school? We believe that much can be learned from studying students who may be classified as at-risk but are resilient, that is, doing well in school despite the odds against them. In this article, we integrate existing literature with our own research that examines resiliency, and then suggest a model to explain resiliency that can be used to better understand why these students have been successful and what can be done to help other at-risk students.

The factors that seem to be related to resiliency can be organized into four categories: individual attributes, positive use of time, family, and school (Peng et al. 1992; McMillan and Reed 1993).

Elements of Resiliency

Individual Attributes

Resilient at-risk students possess temperamental characteristics that elicit positive responses from individuals around them. These personality traits begin in early childhood and are manifested in adolescence as students seek out new experiences and become self-reliant. This begins a cycle of positive reciprocity that enables these students to reach out to other people and expect help. Their positive attitudes are usually rewarded with helpful reactions from those around them. Thus, they come to see the world as a positive place in spite of the difficult issues with which they have to deal. Their positive attitudes include respecting others, coming to class prepared, volunteering for in- and out-of-class assignments, and knowing how to play the school game.

High intrinsic motivation and internal locus of control seem to enable resilient at-risk students to succeed. In their study of 17,000 tenth graders from low-income families, Peng et al. (1992) found that locus of control was a significant predictor of academic success—students with higher academic achievement tended to have a more in-

From *The Clearing House*, January/February 1994, pp. 137-140. Reprinted with permission of the Helen Dwight Reid Educational Foundation. Published by Heldref Publications, 1319 Eighteenth St., NW, Washington, DC 20036-1802. © 1994.

ternal locus of control. They also found that successful students had higher educational aspirations than non-resilient students. In a qualitative study of the perceptions of academically successful at-risk students, many students spoke of satisfaction gained from experiencing success in self-fulfilling activities (McMillan and Reed 1993). These students were motivated by a desire to succeed, to be self-starting, and to be personally responsible for their achievements. They attributed poor performance to internal factors such as a lack of effort, not caring, not trying, not studying as much as they needed to, goofing off, and playing around; most respondents thought that poor performing students could do better if they put in more work and got serious about school. A strong sense of self-efficacy is important; students see themselves as being successful because they have chosen to be so and give much credit to themselves.

Resilient students have clear, realistic goals and are optimistic about the future. They have hope, despite all the negative circumstances in their lives, and confidence that they can achieve their long-range goals. For some students a particularly difficult experience, either direct or vicarious, reinforces the importance of getting an education. These might be called "reality checks" because they seem to motivate students toward positive goals (McMillan and Reed 1993). The reality check may have been dropping out of school, becoming pregnant, being in drug rehabilitation, or some other event or circumstance that showed them that without an education their opportunities would be limited. As a result, these resilient students tend to be very mature in their explanations and goals.

Resilient students do not believe that the school, neighborhood, or family is critical in either their successes or failures. They acknowledge that a poor home environment can make things difficult, but they do not blame their performance on these factors.

Positive Use of Time

In the qualitative study conducted by McMillan and Reed (1993), resilient students were asked about their hobbies, activities, and participation in clubs, church, or other organizations and about how they spend their time. It was clear that they used their time positively and were meaningfully involved in school and other activities. With some exceptions, this involvement was not in a special program or group for at-risk students or students with specific problems. This positive involvement did not leave these students with much spare time. Active involvement in extracurricular events at school and in other areas seems to provide a refuge for resilient students. Hobbies, creative interests, and sports help promote the growth of self-esteem. Being recognized and supported for special talents is also important. In addition, simply being involved in an activity considered special appears to increase self-esteem and a belief in one's ability to succeed (Geary 1988; Werner 1984; Coburn and

Nelson 1989; McMillan and Reed 1993). Such involvement may provide an important social-psychological support system by connecting the students to others in meaningful ways. Success in these activities may be important in enhancing self-esteem by providing recognition and a sense of accomplishment.

Involvement in "required helpfulness" seems to be a factor in resilient students' experiences. Required helpfulness may mean volunteer work in the community, tutoring or buddying at school, or taking care of siblings or otherwise helping at home. These activities seem to lend purpose to the difficult life of an at-risk student and serve to increase their caring about others. They realize there are people that even they can help (Werner 1984; Philliber 1986).

Family Factors

Most resilient at-risk students have had the opportunity to establish a close bond with at least one caregiver who gives them needed attention and support. A sense of trust is developed that is very important in interactions with teachers and peers. This support may be from people other than parents, such as siblings, aunts, uncles, or grandparents who become positive role models. Resilient children seem to be adept at finding these substitute caregivers, much as they are adept at eliciting positive responses from many people around them (Werner 1984).

Family support seems to be an attribute of successful at-risk students. Parents of resilient students have higher expectations for their children's education. Such expectations exert pressure on the children to remain engaged in school and work toward high achievement. These students are more likely to interact with parents, to have more learning materials in the home, and to be involved in out-of-school educational activities than are non-resilient at-risk students (Peng et al. 1992).

Interestingly, family composition seems to have no significant relationship to at-risk students' success or failure (Peng et al. 1992). Students living with both parents do not necessarily have a higher level of resiliency than students in single-parent families or other configurations. Instead, good parent-child relationships and supportive attachments appear to act as protective factors from the environment. Parents who are committed to their children provide informal counseling, support, and help in achieving success. This parental commitment lends a feeling of coherence to the family unit. Werner (1984) maintains that these strong family ties help at-risk students to believe that life makes sense and that they have some control over their own lives. This sense of meaning becomes a powerful motivation for many resilient at-risk students.

Finally, the educational background of parents is related to student resiliency. Peng et al. (1992) found that less than 11 percent of students whose parents had less than a high school education were classified as resilient students as compared with 23 percent of students whose parents had a high school education or beyond.

2. DEVELOPMENT: Adolescence

School Factors

Resilient students seem to find support outside of the home environment, usually in school. They like school, in general, or at least put up with it. Most attempt to involve themselves in classroom discussions and activities. School is more than academics for these students. Most are involved in at least one extracurricular event that becomes an informal source of support. The extracurricular event not only increases involvement, belonging, and self-esteem, it also provides a network of people who have a common bond and work in cooperation with each other (Werner 1984; Coburn and Nelson 1989). Extracurricular events at school, especially sports, seem to mitigate the powerful and widespread peer pressure not to do well. Many resilient students seem to feel they must be involved with a nonacademic activity in order to "fit in" with the majority of students. This involvement maintains the resilient at-risk student's positive engagement in school (Geary 1988).

Teachers play an important role in the success of resilient students. In three qualitative studies, resilient at-risk students mentioned school staff who had taken a personal interest in them as being important to their success (Geary 1988; Coburn and Nelson 1989; McMillan and Reed 1993). Both interpersonal relations and professional competence are important to at-risk students. They cite the following interpersonal qualities of a teacher as important: being caring, having respect for them as persons and as learners, being able to get along with them, listening without being intrusive, taking them seriously, being available and understanding, helping and providing encouragement, and laughing with them. Professional behavior and competence are also important. Resilient at-risk students look for these qualities: the ability to represent and further the goals of the system and the school, a willingness to listen to the motivations behind inappropriate behavior before they discipline, fairness in grading and instruction, praise and encouragement that they can succeed, high expectations, and a willingness to get to know the students personally as well as academically (Werner 1984). Students feel that they can talk to "good" teachers and counselors about almost anything and that the teacher or counselor will listen without judging the student. These counselors and teachers "push" the students and at the same time are very supportive.

Profile of the Resilient Student

Resilient at-risk students have a set of personality characteristics, dispositions, and beliefs that promote their academic success regardless of their backgrounds or current circumstances. They have an internal locus of control and healthy internal attributions, taking personal responsibility for their successes and failures and showing a strong sense of self-efficacy. They feel that they have been successful because they have *chosen* to be successful and have put forth needed effort. Even though they wel-

come and appreciate the efforts of the significant adults in their lives, they do not see these people as being responsible for their success or failure. They credit themselves. They have positive expectations about their abilities and the future, an optimistic perspective with realistic long-range goals. This strong sense of hope is accompanied by a belief that doing well in school is necessary to doing well in life. These students are very mature in their outlook and attitudes and tend to make positive choices about how to use their time.

To develop these characteristics, resilient students have a psychological support system that provides a safety net and encouragement. This system is evident in the way the students are meaningfully connected to others, in or out of school. They are actively involved in positive activities that provide a sense of support, success, and recognition. Activities such as hobbies give these students a reason to feel proud and provide a solace when other aspects of their lives are troubling. Involvement in both academic and extracurricular activities maintains resilient students' positive engagement in school.

Resilient students have adults—usually a parent (more often mother than father) and someone from the school—with whom they have trusting relationships. These adults have high expectations and provide support and encouragement with firmness. Students respect these adults because they obviously care about their welfare.

Thus, there are important environmental factors that contribute to the strong, resilient personalities and beliefs that are critical to these students. These factors are illustrated with the conceptual model in figure 1. The model shows how significant relationships with adults and positive use of time provide encouragement, high expectations, a psychological suport system, and recognition and accomplishment. These environmental factors influence these students so that they develop self-efficacy, goals, personal responsibility, and so forth. It is these traits that make students resilient. The challenge to schools is to provide the relationships and involvement that can foster this development.

Implications for School Personnel

The model suggests several implications for school personnel. First, instructional strategies and techniques, as well as other dimensions of the school environment, must be developed to promote a sense of internal locus of control, self-efficacy, optimism, and a sense of personal responsibility. Teachers should establish reference points where achievement will be identified, and they must continually relate success to effort and ability. Goal setting is also important, particularly setting long-range goals that demonstrate the need to focus beyond one's immediate interests and activities.

Second, teachers, administrators, and counselors need to be trained and encouraged to provide classroom activities and classroom environments that stress high academic achievement while also building students' self-es-

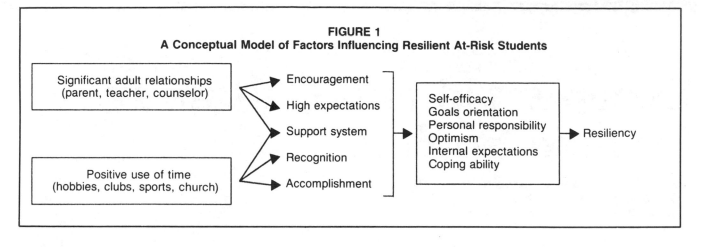

FIGURE 1
A Conceptual Model of Factors Influencing Resilient At-Risk Students

teem and self-confidence. The classroom environment should facilitate time-on-task, student interaction, student success, and positive reinforcement for desired classroom behaviors. Teachers need to be aware of the difference between high expectations and high standards. High expectations involve beliefs about what students are capable of doing and achieving, while high standards do not necessarily suggest that students can reach them. Positive experiences in school help provide students a sense of belonging, bonding, and encouragement.

In addition, extracurricular activities need to be expanded and promoted in schools where there are large populations of at-risk students. As previously mentioned, these activities increase involvement in school. However, many at-risk students will not voluntarily participate in activities because of their general feelings of disconnectedness. Teachers and administrators should develop needed programs and systematically issue personal invitations for at-risk students to join. These programs should include the usual school clubs such as drama, choir, "Future Teachers," "Future Farmers," and others, as well as support groups for various concerns such as adolescent mothers, victims of abuse, children of alcoholic parents, and children of incarcerated parents.

Third, teachers need to be provided with training and encouragement to develop relationships that benefit at-risk children. These students need teachers who are respectful, caring, honest, patient, open-minded, and firm. They also need teachers who understand learning styles, expect positive results, and recognize cultural norms and differences. Perhaps teacher education programs for preservice and inservice teachers need to offer special seminars or classes on working with at-risk populations.

Resilient students give us hope and encouragement, for it is clear that despite unfavorable odds, they have succeeded. We need to learn from them and put into practice what we have learned.

REFERENCES

Coburn, J., and S. Nelson. 1989. *Teachers do make a difference: What Indian graduates say about their school experience* (Report No. RC–017–103). Washington, D.C.: Office of Educational Research and Improvement. (ERIC Document Reproduction Service No. ED 306 071)

Geary, P. A. 1988. *"Defying the odds?": Academic success among at-risk minority teenagers in an urban high school* (Report No. UD-026–258). Paper presented at the annual meeting of the American Educational Research Association, New Orleans, La. (ERIC Document Reproduction Service No. ED 296 055)

Hahn, A. 1987. Reaching out to America's dropouts: What to do? *Phi Delta Kappan* 69(4): 256–63.

Liontos, L. B. 1991. *Trends and issues: Involving families of at-risk youth in the educational process.* ERIC Clearinghouse on Educational Management. Eugene, Oregon: College of Education, University of Oregon. ED 328946

McMillan, J. H., and D. F. Reed. 1993. A qualitative study of resilient at-risk students. Paper presented at the 1993 annual meeting of the American Educational Research Association, Atlanta.

Peng, S. S., R. M. Lee, M. C. Wang, and H. J. Walberg. 1992. Resilient students in urban settings. Paper presented at the 1992 annual meeting of the American Educational Research Association, San Francisco.

Philliber, S. 1986. *Teen outreach: Data from the second year of a national replication.* Paper presented at the 1986 annual national conference of the Children's Defense Fund, Washington, D. C.

Sklarz, D. P. 1989. Keep at-risk students in school by keeping them up to grade level. *The American School Board Journal* 176(9): 33–34.

Werner, E. E. 1984. Resilient children. *Young Children* 40(1): 68–72.

Winfield, L. A. 1991. Resilience, schooling, and development in African-American youth: A conceptual framework. *Education and Urban Society* 24(1): 5–14.

Exceptional and Culturally Diverse Students

- **Educationally Disabled (Articles 10 and 11)**
- **Gifted and Talented (Articles 12 and 13)**
- **Culturally Diverse (Articles 14–16)**

The Equal Educational Opportunity Act for All Handicapped Children (Public Law 94-142) gives disabled children the right to an education in the least restrictive environment, due process, and an individualized educational program that is specifically designed to meet their needs. Professionals and parents of exceptional children are responsible for developing and implementing an appropriate educational program for each child. The application of these ideas to classrooms across the nation at first caused great concern among educators and parents. Classroom teachers whose training did not prepare them for working with the exceptional child expressed negative attitudes about mainstreaming. Special resource teachers also expressed concern that mainstreaming would mitigate the effectiveness of special programs for the disabled and would force cuts in services. Parents feared that their children would not receive the special services they required because of governmental red tape and delays in having their children properly diagnosed and placed.

It is almost two decades since the implementation of Public Law 94-142. Many of the above concerns have been studied by psychologists and educators, and their findings have often influenced policy. For example, research has indicated that mainstreaming is more effective when regular classroom teachers and special resource teachers work cooperatively with disabled children.

The articles concerning the educationally disabled confront many of these issues. Steven Landau and Cecile McAninch describe attention deficit hyperactivity disorder and how parents, teachers, and peers can help. Sally Smith offers several teaching strategies to help meet the needs of learning disabled students in the regular classroom.

Another dimension of exceptional children is the gifted and talented. These children are rapid learners who can absorb, organize, and apply concepts more effectively than the average child. They often have IQs of 140 or more and are convergent thinkers (i.e., they give the correct answer to teacher or test questions). Convergent thinkers are usually models of good behavior and academic performance, and they respond to instruction easily; teachers generally value such children and often

nominate them for gifted programs. There are other children, however, who do not score well on standardized tests of intelligence because their thinking is more divergent (i.e., they can imagine more than one answer to teacher or test questions). These gifted, divergent thinkers may not respond to traditional instruction, may become bored, may respond to questions in unique and disturbing ways, and may appear uncooperative and disruptive. Many teachers do not understand these unconventional thinkers and fail to identify them as gifted. In fact, such children are sometimes labeled as emotionally disturbed or mentally retarded because of the negative impressions they make on their teachers. Because of the differences between these types, a great deal of controversy surrounds programs for the gifted. Such programs should enhance the self-esteem of all gifted and talented children, motivate and challenge them, and help them realize their creative potential. The two articles in this unit on gifted and talented children consider the characteristics of giftedness, and explain how to identify gifted students and provide them with an appropriate education.

The third section of this unit concerns culturally diverse children. Just as labeling may adversely affect the disabled child, it can also affect the child who comes from a minority ethnic background where the language and values are quite different from those of the mainstream culture. The term "disadvantaged" is often used to describe these children, but it is negative, stereotypical, and may result in a self-fulfilling prophecy whereby teachers perceive such children as incapable of learning. Teachers should provide culturally diverse children with experiences that they have missed in the restricted environment of their home and neighborhood. The articles in this section address these cultural differences and suggest strategies for teaching culturally diverse children.

Looking Ahead: Challenge Questions

What are some of the strategies that regular classroom teachers can use to help students deal with their learning disabilities?

Describe the characteristics of children with attention deficit hyperactivity disorder. What are some important

sources of information that can be useful in order to help these students?

Who are the gifted and talented? How can knowledge of their characteristics and learning needs provide them with an appropriate education?

What are some of the cultural differences that exist in our society? How can teacher expectations affect the culturally diverse child? Explain how multicultural education would help teachers deal more effectively with these differences.

Editor's Note: *Most children who are diagnosed by competent mental health professionals as having attention-deficit hyperactivity disorder* do; *but as early childhood educators, we must always ensure that our classrooms are developmentally appropriate and that children are not being inappropriately labeled because our* classroom *is inappropriate.*

Young Children With Attention Deficits

Steven Landau and Cecile McAninch

Steven Landau, Ph.D., is a professor of psychology at Illinois State University. Previously a school psychologist, his research interests include ADHD and problems associated with peer rejection.

Cecile McAninch, M.A., is completing her doctorate in clinical psychology at the University of Kentucky. Her areas of interest include children's self-concept and social cognition.

Three-year-old Jamie was expelled from preschool after frequent fights with other children. If Jamie and the other boys were playing with trucks, Jamie was the first one to start crashes, which escalated into wild behavior. In the sandbox it was always Jamie who threw sand in someone's face or grabbed the shovel from another child. After a month of preschool, Jamie's teacher became worried that Jamie might seriously hurt another child, and she asked Jamie's mother to keep him home.

Jamie's parents were dismayed by this request. They knew that he was a difficult child. They found Jamie hard to manage because he seemed to have an excessive activity level and a short attention span and was prone to numerous temper outbursts. Indeed, he had been "difficult" since infancy; however, they wanted to believe that this was simply a phase he was going through—a difficult period of development—and that he would outgrow these problems sometime soon. They even considered the possibility that Jamie's preschool teacher didn't understand him—that she could intervene more before he became too excited and wound up. These problems were thus simply developmental (i.e., he is just "all boy"), or they were best understood as a function of an intolerant preschool teacher. Maybe a better preschool would be the answer.

Jamie, who was first described by Campbell (1988), is representative of many young children referred for atten-

tion-deficit hyperactivity disorder (ADHD). What is ADHD, and how does it differ from hyperactivity? ADHD is the current psychiatric term used to describe a set of symptoms reflecting excessive inattention, overactivity, and impulsive responding. It is important to note that the presence of these symptoms must be established in the context of what is developmentally appropriate for the child's age and gender group. ADHD is found in 3 to 5% of the childhood population (American Psychiatric Association, 1987) and is clearly a disorder that is far more prevalent in males; sex differences among children referred for treatment average about six males to one female. Because ADHD is the formal diagnostic label from the psychiatric classification scheme (i.e., the *Diagnostic and Statistical Manual of Mental Disorders* [DSM–III–R]; American Psychiatric Association, 1987), this is the term used by family physicians, pediatricians, psychiatrists, and other mental health clinicians. Indeed, all professionals who deal with children, *except* professionals in the public school system, employ the psychiatric classification scheme and, thus, the term ADHD.

The fact that children considered "in need of special services" by their school according to Public Law 94–142 are not required to have a formal DSM–III–R psychiatric diagnosis for placement creates confused communication among parents, school personnel, and community professionals. Confusion is further increased by the fact that the nomenclature pertaining to this disorder has changed several times over the years. The disorder has previously been known as "brain damage syndrome"; "minimal brain dysfunction"; "hyperkinetic reaction to childhood"; "attention deficit disorder (with and without hyperactivity)"; and, most recently, "attention-deficit hyperactivity disorder." Although frustrating for some, this trend of changing terminology clearly represents improved understanding of the disorder (Schaughency & Rothlind, 1991).

Primary symptoms

The preceding overview of evolving terminology makes it apparent that there has been a shift in emphasis regarding what is considered most central to the disor-

The column in this issue was edited by Laura E. Berk, Ph.D., professor of psychology at Illinois State University.

From *Young Children*, Vol. 48, No. 4, May 1993, pp. 49-58. © 1993 by the National Association for the Education of Young Children, 1506 16th Street, NW, Washington, DC. Reprinted by permission.

der. Many researchers agree that a deficit in *sustained attention,* the inability to remain vigilant, represents the area of greatest difficulty for the child with ADHD (Douglas, 1983); thus, children with ADHD show significantly less persistence than their classmates. Even though many teachers use the term *distractible* to characterize their observations of school performance, distractibility implies that the child with ADHD seems unable to select relevant from irrelevant stimuli that compete for their attention (i.e., a *selective attention* deficit). The bulk of current research, however, suggests that their greatest difficulties stem from an inability to *sustain a response* long enough to accomplish assigned tasks, that is, they lack perseverance in their efforts. As a consequence, parents and teachers attribute to them characterizations such as "doesn't seem to listen," "fails to finish assigned tasks," "can't concentrate," "can't work independently of supervision," "requires more redirection," and "confused or seems to be in a fog"—all apparently the result of this inability to sustain attention (Barkley, 1990).

It is important to stress, however, that even though inattention may be the source of some difficulty in a less structured, free-play setting, highly structured academic settings create the greatest problem for these children (Milich, Loney, & Landau, 1982). The specific expectations within a setting and the degree of structure in that setting thus play important roles in determining the presence of the disorder. This may explain, in part, why parents and teachers do not tend to agree when rating the symptoms of these children (Achenbach, McConaughy, & Howell, 1987). Expectations in the home environment are simply different from those at school. This point was recently reinforced in a study by Landau, Lorch, and Milich (1992). These investigators were intrigued by the surprising but frequent parent report that their child with ADHD is able to attend to television (e.g., "What do you mean he can't pay attention in school? He sits glued to the TV for hours!"). In fact, a recent advice column in *Parents* magazine suggested that parents could rule out thoughts of ADHD if their child was able to pay attention to television. Results of the study by Landau and his colleagues indicated that boys diagnosed with ADHD who were extremely inattentive in the classroom were able to attend to educational television programming to a high degree, and their attention was indistinguishable from that of normal agemates under some circumstances. It seems evident that television may hold greater intrinsic appeal than schoolwork for the child with ADHD, plus TV does not represent the historical source of frustration and failure associated with classroom performance. Apparently the nature of the task seems crucial when determining if the child has significant difficulty paying attention.

Related to problems with inattention, children with ADHD are *impulsive;* they experience difficulty *inhibiting* their response in certain situations (Barkley, 1990). As with inattention, impulsivity is a multidimensional construct; it can be defined in several ways (Olson, 1989). Children with ADHD, for example, are impulsive when confronted with academic tasks. They are extremely quick to respond without considering all alternatives; thus they are known as fast but careless and inaccurate problem solvers. This type of response style can have a profound influence on the child's ability to perform in an academic setting. Besides affecting cognitive performance, impulsivity can also manifest itself as an inability to suppress inappropriate behavior. As such, children with ADHD are also known to be high-risk takers, as evidenced by their running out in traffic. In addition, they seem unable to delay gratification (Campbell, Szumowski, Ewing, Gluck, & Breaux, 1982). In school they experience difficulty waiting their turn in line, blurt out answers in class, constantly touch other children, and tend to be undesirable playmates because of their difficulty with turn taking, sharing, and cooperation, and their low tolerance for frustration while playing games (Landau & Moore, 1991).

The third primary symptom involves motor excess, or *overactivity.* Historically overactivity was considered the hallmark characteristic of the disorder and served as the source for the enduring "hyperactivity" label applied to these children. This is probably because overactivity remains the most salient symptom and possibly the symptom most annoying to others. In fact, parents of children with ADHD retrospectively report overactivity to be an early marker of the disorder (Campbell, 1988), even though it is also a common complaint from parents of normal children (Lapouse & Monk, 1958; Richman, Stevenson, & Graham, 1982). As with the other symptoms, overactivity can take many forms but is especially apparent as excessive body movements (both major and minor motor) and vocalizations; for example, these children are described as "always on the go" or "squirmy and fidgety," or as a child who "can't sit still," "hums and makes other odd noises," "talks incessantly," and "climbs excessively" (Barkley, 1990).

When children with ADHD engage in table activities or academic seatwork, they constantly get up and down from the desk (or do all seatwork while standing). Many show minor motor fidgeting, such as pencil tapping or leg shaking, and they seem unable to keep their hands off objects unrelated to the task at hand. During individual psychological testing, children with ADHD can be extremely challenging subjects because they attempt to manipulate the examiner's test materials throughout the evaluation. Finally, they are often overactive and incessantly talkative in the context of social play—behaviors that seem to have a negative effect on peer relations (Landau & Moore, 1991). Again, it is important to remember that setting demands—in particular, the degree of structure in the environment—affect the extent to which these children are problems to their teachers. The child with ADHD may be considered quite troublesome, for example, in a highly structured academic setting, with desks placed in rows and all work to be accomplished in one's seat. In contrast, in the open-classroom setting where cooperative learning is encouraged and children are expected to move about and collaborate with others, the child with ADHD may be less distinctive and disturbing to others (Jacob, O'Leary, & Rosenblad, 1978).

Secondary symptoms or associated characteristics

Children with ADHD experience numerous difficulties that go beyond inattention, impulsive responding, and overactivity. Although these problems are not related to the diagnosis of ADHD, the fact that children with ADHD present these added difficulties accounts for the extreme heterogeneity among ADHD cases.

First, children with ADHD are at elevated risk for problems related to conduct disorder. Although the rates of overlap vary with each study, most investigators agree that at least one half of all children with ADHD also meet diagnostic criteria for conduct disorder. In these children one finds extreme stubbornness, noncompliance, hostility, rule violations, stealing, lying, and aggressive acts (Hinshaw, 1987). Studies of children with ADHD indicate that those who show conduct disorder not only are more difficult to manage as children but also will have more serious adolescent and adult adjustment problems (Weiss & Hechtman, 1986).

Second, many children with ADHD are rejected by their peers (Landau & Moore, 1991). In fact, many boys with ADHD who are not aggressive seem to be more "disliked" than their classmates who are highly aggressive but do not have ADHD (Milich & Landau, 1989), and this negative reputation may be established after only brief contact with unfamiliar children (Pelham & Bender, 1982). This effect on others is not surprising, as children with ADHD tend to be bossy, intrusive, disruptive, and easily frustrated while in the play group. They have few, if any, friends. Peer rejection is a serious outcome of ADHD because children who are rejected early in life tend to be at high risk for many adult adjustment difficulties, including job terminations, bad-conduct discharge from the military, negative contact with police, and psychiatric hospitalization (Parker & Asher, 1987).

Third, children with ADHD are at high risk for achievement difficulties, and many meet special-education placement criteria as learning disabled (McGee & Share, 1988). Because children with ADHD in the academic setting are typically off task, noisy, disruptive, out-of-seat, and do not finish schoolwork or homework, parents and teachers complain of underachievement. These children's work tends to be highly inefficient and disorganized, and their performance often shows great fluctuations.

Finally, these children seem to experience problems dealing with the numerous transitions in school (such as going from recess back to class). They have difficulty adapting their behaviors as situational expectations change (Landau & Milich, 1988). Consequently, there may be a grave discrepancy between actual achievement in school and the child's estimated potential for learning. As children with ADHD accumulate a history of negative feedback from parents, teachers, and peers, it is little wonder that they are also at risk for low self-esteem and depression as they mature.

Effects on the classroom

Children with ADHD can be an extremely negative force in the classroom setting. They tend to evoke numerous negative interactions with their teachers and take teacher time away from other children. They are disruptive to learning activities; try to dominate social situations; and, to make matters worse, do not perform well academically. Indeed, the presence of a child with ADHD in the preschool setting serves as a catalyst for significantly more negative teacher feedback to all children in the classroom (Campbell, Endman, & Bernfeld, 1977).

Causal hypotheses

Many causal explanations for ADHD have been proposed over the years. First, research indicates that the role of genetic transmission must be taken seriously. Parents and siblings of children diagnosed with ADHD are more likely to have the disorder, and studies of twins indicate that identical twins are much more likely to share the disorder than are fraternal twins. Second, researchers are currently working on identifying a neurobiological cause, such as a deficit in the neurotransmitters that control attention, although none has yet been isolated (Hynd, Hern, Voeller, & Marshall, 1991). Third, there is intriguing correlational evidence that maternal smoking and/or alcohol use during pregnancy may be linked to increased risk for ADHD. Fourth, in spite of widespread belief among lay persons and the popularity of the "Feingold Diet" (1975), sugar consumption does *not* seem to be related to the symptoms of ADHD (Wolraich, Milich, Stumbo, & Schultz, 1985). Finally, there is no evidence to suggest that parenting or childrearing is in any way related to the primary symptoms of the disorder; however, some of the secondary problems associated with ADHD (such as conduct disorder and self-esteem problems) may be the consequence of factors in the child's social environment.

Assessment of ADHD

Because symptoms of impulsivity, poor attention, and excessive activity may differ among children with ADHD and across various situations, a multidimensional approach to assessment is necessary. Parent, teacher, and possibly even peer reports, plus observation in the naturalistic setting, are considered in the evaluation of ADHD. This assessment is designed to go beyond offering an actual diagnosis. A comprehensive school-based evaluation should provide data to develop a thorough intervention plan for the child.

Parents

Parents are, of course, an important source of information about children's behavior because they observe the children daily and in a variety of settings. In addition, parents are in a position to notice fluctuations in behavior in response to different situations and varying responses to treatment. Parent reports are not sufficient in the evaluation of ADHD, however, for two reasons. First, parents do not have exposure to the full range of child behavior. They may be unaware of developmental norms and what constitutes age-appropriate behavior. Second, as stated earlier, the symptoms of ADHD may not be as troublesome in the home, a setting that typically is less structured than school. Although parent reports are necessary, information from other sources must be considered as well.

Teachers

Teachers serve as an essential source in the assessment of ADHD, and there are several rating scales by which teachers may easily communicate their knowledge and concerns regarding the child. These scales provide a normative comparison; teachers are asked to rate the degree to which the child's behavior differs from the behavior of other children in the class. Like parents, teachers have almost daily contact with these children. Unlike parents, teachers are also exposed to many other children of the same age and are able to use their *normative perspective* to determine if the referred child is behaving in age-inappropriate ways. In addition, teachers observe these children in unstructured play settings as well as highly structured academic settings, where symptoms of ADHD are more likely to emerge. Teacher input is thus integral in the assessment of ADHD (see Barkley, 1990, for a review of these rating scales).

Naturalistic observation data

An important source of information regarding the child with ADHD—one that has direct implications for treatment planning—involves systematic observation of the child in classroom and play settings. By using previously defined code categories that quantify the amount of time the child with ADHD spends engaged in on-task behavior and in various inappropriate off-task behaviors, it is possible to get *direct* information about how the child is functioning. In addition, it is helpful to collect these data on the same-sex classmates of the child. In this way it is possible to determine that Billy, who presents symptoms suggestive of ADHD, attends to math or storytime 22% of the time, while the other boys in his class attend an average of 84% during that same observation session. Because parent and teacher reports are based on previous contact with the child (i.e., numerous *retrospective* observations) and may be biased by the disruptive nature of the child's behavior, direct observation of the child with ADHD is the only way to provide data on *current* behavior, and these data will facilitate interpretation of the reports from parents and teachers.

Peers

One final area to be considered in the assessment process involves the child's peer interactions. Classroom sociometric assessment, which can provide information about peer popularity and rejection, in combination with measures of social loneliness and social anxiety offers valuable information about the child's social functioning and may highlight areas for intervention (see Landau & Milich, 1990, for a discussion of appropriate measures).

Preschool issues

Special issues arise in the assessment of preschool-age children. Most measures used to diagnose ADHD, for example, are not normed for preschoolers and may be developmentally inappropriate for this age group (Barkley, 1990). Furthermore, high activity level and noncompliance in very young children may either signify

> **Many children with ADHD are rejected by their peers. Children with ADHD tend to be bossy, intrusive, disruptive, and easily frustrated while in the play group. They have few, if any, friends. Peer rejection is a serious outcome of ADHD because children who are rejected early in life tend to be at high risk for many adult adjustment difficulties, including job terminations, bad-conduct discharge from the military, negative contact with police, and psychiatric hospitalization.**

problems or simply represent normal development. In assessing preschoolers, therefore, special emphasis must be placed on the severity and frequency of a disruptive behavior rather than on its presence or absence (Campbell, 1990). Parents who are unaware of developmental norms tend to overreport problems with their children due to unrealistic expectations, thereby engendering additional conflict. On the other hand, some parents may be overly lenient and thus fail to notice potential problems.

Finally, teacher reports of behavior are obviously unavailable for those young children who do not attend preschool. Problems exist, however, even when teacher reports are obtainable (Barkley, 1990). As mentioned earlier, the public school classroom is an important arena in which to assess ADHD due to its structure; preschool settings are generally less structured and can therefore accommodate children with attentional deficits more easily. Preschool-based assessments thus may yield much less informative information than assessments conducted in grade school. Activities of daily living (e.g., eating, dressing) are more likely to be the source of conflict at this age. Even in this area, however, it is important to not confuse the child's normal attempts at autonomy with ADHD-related management difficulties.

Treatment of ADHD

Once assessment has indicated a possibility of ADHD, what can teachers and caregivers do? It is important to remember that children with ADHD benefit from the same environments that all children do; thus, designing classrooms appropriately for the child's development is an important step toward managing the behavior of a child with ADHD. For young children this means a loosely structured environment in which active involvement is an integral part of the learning process. In addition, tailoring work to fit the child's individual needs and encouraging collaboration and cooperation are practices recommended for children with ADHD, as they are for all children.

The two primary methods of intervention are stimulant medication and behavioral management; however, the most effective treatment involves a combination of the two (Pelham, in press).

Medication therapy

The most common treatment for ADHD is medications that stimulate the central nervous system (Barkley, 1990). Research suggests that children with ADHD may not be as sensitive to feedback from the social and physical environment as other children; stimulant medication appears to render these children more sensitive by lowering response thresholds in the nervous system (Barkley, 1989). Ritalin, or methylphenidate (the generic drug name), is the most common stimulant used. Approximately 70 to 75% of children responded positively to this medication, while about one fourth are unaffected (Pelham, 1987); thus, these medications will help many but not all children with ADHD.

Effects of medication. For those children who do respond positively, the effects are immediate and typically quite strong. Attention, impulse control, and short-term memory may all be improved (Barkley, 1990). Children talk less, are less disturbing, follow rules better, and exhibit less aggression (Pelham, 1987). These changes often lead to improved relations with parents, teachers, and peers. As these children become more cooperative, the need for close adult supervision should diminish; however, in spite of substantial reduction in disruptive behavior, the majority of children with ADHD will still show problem behaviors. Medication is thus often helpful, but not sufficient, in managing the disorder.

In addition to reducing disruptive behavior, stimulant medication has been found to help children attend better when involved in organized athletic play with other children (Pelham et al., 1990). Because these activities, such as soccer or T-ball, involve peer interactions, medication may indirectly improve the peer relations and self-esteem of children with ADHD. Even while on medication, however, it is difficult for most children with ADHD to gain peer acceptance (Pelham & Milich, 1984).

Children with ADHD who are on medication are also better able to concentrate on schoolwork. They complete more assignments and are more careful and accurate; thus, they show improved academic *performance* (Barkley, 1990). Medication is much less effective in improving children's scores on academic *achievement* tests, however. In other words, medication does not necessarily help children with ADHD master more difficult tasks and may not directly relate to enhanced learning; thus, academic achievement *per se* appears to be only minimally improved by medication, if at all.

Recently there has been growing interest in the effects of medication on the attitudes and motivation of children with ADHD. Some experts have suggested, for example, that medication may cause children to believe that they are responsible for their own misbehavior—that they must rely on some external agent (the drug) for control of their difficulties. Consequently, when children behave inappropriately or do not succeed at schoolwork, they might conclude that the medication must not be working that day—in other words, these problems are not their fault. In contrast, other researchers suggest that because medication leads to improved performance, children with ADHD may be able to personalize this newly discovered success and thus feel greater responsibility for their own behavior than

if they had not been medicated—they have greater control than before. Although more study is necessary, current results support the second hypothesis: Medicated children with ADHD seem to credit themselves for good performances (i.e., they *internalize* and personalize their successes) while *externalizing* or blaming poor performance on factors beyond their control (Milich, 1993). The fact that these children attribute successes to their personal responsibility, and not to the medication, may contribute to their self-esteem. In summary, medication seems to improve behavior in a variety of ways and may also help children to feel better about themselves.

Despite the important effects of medication, several cautions should be kept in mind. First, as mentioned earlier, not all children with ADHD benefit from stimulant medication. Second, four- to five-year-old children do not experience improvement to the same extent as do older children (Barkley, 1989). In a review of medication studies with preschoolers, Campbell (1985) noted that few benefits were obtained and that side effects, such as increased solitary play and clinging, appeared serious enough to potentially disrupt social development. Third, all of the medication-induced benefits represent short-term effects only; that is, improvements are noticeable only while the child is taking the medication. In the evenings, weekends, and summers, when children are typically not medicated, their symptoms generally return to pretreatment levels; thus medication brings no lasting benefits.

Side effects. Many parents express concern about potential negative side effects of stimulant medication; for example, there is evidence that mild insomnia and lessened appetite, especially at lunchtime, can occur (Barkley, 1990). This latter effect has been thought to lead to suppressed weight and height gains. Research indicates, however, that effects on growth can be corrected by altering dosage and tend to occur only during the first year of medication therapy (Barkley, 1990). Height and weight tend to catch up to age norms in subsequent years even if medication is continued (Mattes & Gittleman, 1983). There is little research on this side effect in pre-school children, however, even though medication is sometimes given to children as young as age three (Campbell, 1990). As a consequence, medication is not recommended for children in this age group. Because medication effects tend to wear off within a four-hour period, most children with ADHD receive a noontime dose to cover their afternoon activities at school. One simple way to avoid the lunchtime appetite loss is to have the child eat lunch prior to taking the afternoon medication dose.

Mild headaches and stomachaches may also occur, but they tend to disappear within a few weeks (Barkley, 1990). These problems, along with mood changes, such as irritability, and individual reactions (e.g., lip licking, rashes) may be alleviated by a simple dosage adjustment. Research indicates that there are no known long-term side effects; for example, these children do not appear to be at increased risk for drug abuse later in life. Any side effects, therefore, tend to be mild, short term, and easily relieved.

One unfortunate consequence of drug treatment is that many parents and teachers tend to rely on medication exclusively and not invest in other, more lasting interventions. Within the past few years, the lay press has expressed alarm about overmedication of children. If parents seek medication for their child to manage home-based behavior problems, this concern may be valid; however, if medication is used to help the child attend to important classroom instruction and adjust well to school, this concern seems to be exaggerated. It is important to remember that medicated children with ADHD, although improved, are not made symptom free. For these reasons, medication is not adequate by itself as a treatment for children with ADHD. The "best practice," based on research, is to combine medication and behavioral treatments in the management of ADHD. This is done not only because medication is insufficient in the treatment of most cases but also because it permits the use of a lower dose of medication. There is strong evidence that a low dose of Ritalin, in combination with behavioral intervention, results in at least the same improvement—and sometimes greater improvement—in the child as does a high dose of Ritalin alone (Pelham, in press). In addition, when the low dose is used, most undesirable side effects can be avoided. In fact, it has been suggested that behavioral interventions be attempted in school *before* thought is given to the use of medication (National Association of School Psychologists, 1992).

Behavioral treatment

Because many children with ADHD demonstrate an inability to follow rules and govern their own behavior (Barkley, 1989), behavioral treatment is necessary for these self-regulatory difficulties. Aspects of successful behavioral intervention include rewarding appropriate behavior, giving effective directions and requests, and using consistent methods of discipline. If teachers can receive assistance from consultants (such as school psychologists) to implement these procedures, most children with ADHD can have their educational and social needs met in the regular education setting. In addition, collaboration with parents is essential because home-based support for school behavior and performance will enhance the success of programs at school.

Appropriate behavior. Many parents and teachers do not think that children should be rewarded simply for "doing what they ought to do," and most children do not need a heavy overlay of rewards to promote acceptable behavior; however, if a child with ADHD seldom engages in an important behavior (such as playing cooperatively), then rewards may be necessary to promote the behavior. As the child learns the behavior, rewards should be gradually removed. Research shows that the use of rewards is particularly helpful when dealing with children who have ADHD (Pelham, 1992). Their inappropriate behavior tends to be extremely compelling; adults cannot ignore it. As a consequence, much of the feedback these children receive from parents, teachers, and peers is expressed as a complaint or reprimand. It is little wonder that many children with ADHD develop self-concept difficulties and depression. Rewarding positive behaviors thus not only encourages the child to continue behaving well but also provides the child with desperately needed success, thereby building self-esteem.

Verbal praise is crucial for a child with ADHD and is especially powerful when the positive behavior is also clarified (e.g., "I like the way you are playing so nicely with the other boys"). Praise may not, however, provide adequate incentive initially due to the child's lower sensitivity to feedback from the social environment; thus, children with ADHD often require more frequent and powerful rewards for a time (Barkley, 1990). At first, parents and teachers may need to give material rewards, along with praise, to teach appropriate behavior; subsequently they may use praise alone to maintain the behavior—for example, smiley faces or gold stars may be given to the child every half hour for engaging in appropriate classroom behavior. A star chart on which different classroom activities (e.g., storytime) are separated as intervals can make implementation of such a reward system easier. To avoid a problem with classroom equity (other children wondering why they do not earn these rewards), the smiley faces could be granted discreetly, perhaps on a special card to be taken home at the end of each day. Even though some teachers may find these procedures intrusive and distracting, the fact remains that the use of behavioral intervention disrupts classroom routine less than does an untreated child with ADHD.

Directions. Unfortunately, the disruptive behavior of children with ADHD causes parents and teachers to often find themselves issuing numerous directives and commands to these youngsters throughout the day. To increase the likelihood that the child will cooperate with adult requests, directions should be specific and brief (Pelham, 1992). Those that are vague or issued in question format (e.g., "Let's get back to work, shall we?") or that involve several directives strung together are not likely to be obeyed. Instead, adults should obtain the child's attention, issue the direction (e.g., "Joey, finish picking up those blocks now"), and wait a few seconds. The child should then be praised for cooperating. Research shows that these techniques are effective. They prevent adult interactions from escalating into impatience and reduce the tendency of children with ADHD to ignore or resist adult direction.

In instances in which a child with ADHD does not respond to adult guidance, school psychologists can work with teachers to implement a variety of other behavioral interventions. Ignoring mildly negative behaviors may prove effective, but often increased adult monitoring and immediate consequences to reduce disruptive acts (e.g., asking the child to sit out an activity) are necessary. If the child engages in aggressive outbursts or is extremely uncooperative, a time-out procedure may also have to be implemented (Barkley, 1990). Consistency is essential for all of these methods to work well.

Daily report card. Parents can serve as an effective back-up to school-based interventions. An important behavior-management strategy involves sending home a brief daily report card reflecting the child's performance for each day (Barkley, 1990). Parents may thus praise the child for success in school, thereby supporting teachers'

Acknowledging teachers' need for effective consultation and collaboration in this area, the National Association of School Psychologists (NASP) recently issued the following position statement describing a "best-practice" approach for dealing with children with attention deficits.

NASP believes that effective intervention should be tailored to the unique learning strengths and needs of every student. For children with attention deficits, such interventions will include the following:

1) Classroom modifications to enhance attending, work production, and social adjustment;

2) Behavioral management systems to reduce problems in arenas most likely to be affected by attention deficits (e.g., large group instruction, transitions, etc.);

3) Direct instruction in study strategies and social skills, within the classroom setting whenever possible to increase generalization;

4) Consultation with families to assist in behavior management in the home setting and to facilitate home-school cooperation and collaboration;

5) Monitoring by a case manager to ensure effective implementation of interventions, to provide adequate support for those interventions, and to assess progress in meeting behavioral and academic goals;

6) Education of school staff in characteristics and management of attention deficits to enhance appropriate instructional modifications and behavior management;

7) Access to special education services when attention deficits significantly impact school performance;

8) Working collaboratively with community agencies providing medical and related services to students and their families.

NASP believes appropriate treatment may or may not include medical intervention. When medication *is* considered, NASP *strongly* recommends:

1) That instructional and behavioral interventions be implemented before medication trials are begun;

2) That behavioral data be collected before and during medication trials to assess baseline conditions and the efficacy of medication; and

3) That communication between school, home, and medical personnel emphasize mutual problem solving and cooperation. (National Association of School Psychologists, 1992)

efforts. In addition, parents should consider using small toys and special activities (e.g., going to a movie) as back-up rewards for positive school performance because these children need rewards of high salience. Parents should target small successes first (e.g., remaining seated throughout storytime) then gradually increase expectations as the child demonstrates mastery.

Preschool issues. Unfortunately, dealing with ADHD symptoms among preschool-age children can be quite a challenge because some of these problems simply represent individual differences in developmental rates. Excessive activity, impulsive responding, and an inability to pay attention—all symptoms of ADHD among school-age children—may not be particularly unusual behaviors for many preschool-age children. Even so, some preschool children receive a diagnosis of ADHD. In these cases—such as Jamie, who was described earlier in this article—parents may feel overwhelmed with the child's discipline problems at home and with aggressive conduct with playmates. The primary symptoms of ADHD *per se* thus do not represent the major source of difficulty, and a diagnosis of ADHD would be premature. Parent training, however, may be an appropriate intervention, in which Jamie's parents are given systematic guidance on how to manage his behavior at home. If Jamie continues to experience difficulties once he reaches school age, when classroom demands require a greater restraint on activity and more persistent attention, a diagnosis of ADHD may be given serious consideration.

Conclusion

ADHD is a problem that has many facets and affects the child in many areas of functioning, including academic performance, interpersonal relations, and emotional well-being. Because of ADHD's complexity, successful treatment requires a multidisciplinary approach reflecting the collaboration of many professionals. Teachers must have assistance in dealing with children with ADHD.

References

Achenbach, T.M., McConaughy, S.H., & Howell, C.T. (1987). Child/adolescent behavioral and emotional problems: Implications of cross-informant correlations for situational specificity. *Psychological Bulletin, 101,* 213–232.

American Psychiatric Association. (1987). *Diagnostic and statistical manual of mental disorders* (3rd ed., revised). Washington, DC: Author.

Barkley, R.A. (1989). Attention deficit-hyperactivity disorder. In E.J. Mash & R.A. Barkley (Eds.), *Treatment of childhood disorders* (pp. 39–72). New York: Guilford.

Barkley, R.A. (1990). *Attention-deficit hyperactivity disorder: A handbook for diagnosis and treatment.* New York: Guilford.

Campbell, S.B. (1985). Hyperactivity in preschoolers: Correlates and prognostic implications. *Clinical Psychology Review, 5,* 405–428.

Campbell, S. (1988, October). *Longitudinal studies of active and aggressive preschoolers: Individual differences in early behavior and in outcome.* Paper presented at the Second Rochester Symposium on Developmental Psychopathology, Rochester, NY.

Campbell, S.B. (1990). *Behavioral problems in preschool children: Clinical and developmental issues.* New York: Guilford.

Campbell, S.B., Endman, M.W., & Bernfeld, G. (1977). Three year follow-up of hyperactive preschoolers into elementary school. *Journal of Child Psychology and Psychiatry, 18,* 239–249.

Campbell, S.B., Szumowski, E.K., Ewing, L.J., Gluck, D.S., & Breaux, A.M. (1982). A multidimensional assessment of parent-identified behavior problem toddlers. *Journal of Abnormal Child Psychology, 10*(4), 569–592.

Douglas, V.I. (1983). Attentional and cognitive problems. In M. Rutter (Ed.), *Developmental Neuropsychiatry* (pp. 280–329). New York: Guilford.

Feingold, B. (1975). *Why your child is hyperactive.* New York: Random House.

Hinshaw, S.P. (1987). On the distinction between attentional deficits/hyperactivity and conduct problems/aggression in child psychopathology. *Psychological Bulletin, 101,* 443–463.

Hynd, G.W., Hern, K.L., Voeller, K.K., & Marshall, R.M. (1991). Neurobiological basis of attention-deficit hyperactivity disorder (ADHD). *School Psychology Review, 20*(2), 174–186.

Jacob, R.B., O'Leary, K.D., & Rosenblad, C. (1978). Formal and informal classroom settings: Effects on hyperactivity. *Journal of Abnormal Child Psychology, 6*(1), 47–59.

Landau, S., & Milich, R. (1988). Social communication patterns of attention-deficit-disordered boys. *Journal of Abnormal Child Psychology, 16,* 69–81.

Landau, S., & Milich, R. (1990). Assessment of children's social status and peer relations. In A.M. LaGreca (Ed.), *Through the eyes of the child* (pp. 259–291). Boston: Allyn & Bacon.

Landau, S., & Moore, L. (1991). Social skill deficits in children with attention-deficit hyperactivity disorder. *School Psychology Review, 20*(2), 235–251.

Landau, S., Lorch, E.P., & Milich, R. (1992). Visual attention to and comprehension of television in attention-deficit hyperactivity disordered and normal boys. *Child Development, 63,* 928–937.

Lapouse, R., & Monk, M. (1958). An epidemiological study of behavior characteristics in children. *American Journal of Public Health, 48,* 1134–1144.

Mattes, J.A., & Gittleman, R. (1983). Growth of hyperactive children on maintenance regimen of methylphenidate. *Archives of General Psychiatry, 40,* 317–321.

McGee, R., & Share, D.L. (1988). Attention deficit disorder-hyperactivity and academic failure: Which comes first and what should be treated? *Journal of the American Academy of Child and Adolescent Psychiatry, 27,* 318–325.

Milich, R. (1993). *Children's response to failure: If at first you don't succeed, do you try, try again?* Manuscript submitted for publication.

Milich, R., & Landau, S. (1989). The role of social status variables in differentiating subgroups of hyperactive children. In L.M. Bloomingdale & J. Swanson (Eds.), *Attention deficit disorder: Current concepts and emerging trends in attentional and behavioral disorders of childhood: Vol. 5* (pp. 1–16). Elmsford, NY: Pergamon.

Milich, R., Loney, J., & Landau, S. (1982). The independent dimensions of hyperactivity and aggression: A validation with playroom observation data. *Journal of Abnormal Psychology, 91,* 183–198.

National Association of School Psychologists. (1992, May). Position statement on students with attention deficits. *Communique, 20,* 5.

Olson, S.L. (1989). Assessment of impulsivity in preschoolers: Cross-measure convergence, longitudinal stability, and relevance to social competence. *Journal of Clinical Child Psychology, 8*(2), 176–183.

Parker, J.G., & Asher, S.R. (1987). Peer relations and later personal adjustment: Are low-accepted children "at risk"? *Psychological Bulletin, 102,* 357–389.

Pelham, W.E., Jr. (1987). What do we know about the use and effects of CNS stimulants in the treatment of ADD? In J. Loney (Ed.), *The young hyperactive child: Answers to questions about diagnosis, prognosis and treatment* (pp. 99–110). New York: Haworth.

Pelham, W.E. (1992). *Children's summer day treatment program: 1992 program manual.* Unpublished manuscript, University of Pittsburgh School of Medicine, Western Psychiatric Institute and Clinic, Pittsburgh, PA.

Pelham, W.E. (in press). Pharmacotherapy for children with attention deficit hyperactivity disorder. *School Psychology Review.*

Pelham, W.E., & Bender, M.E. (1982). Peer relationships in hyperactive children: Description and treatment. In D.C. Gadow & I. Bialer (Eds.), *Advances in learning and behavioral disabilities: A research annual: Vol. 1* (pp. 365–436). Greenwich, CT: JAI.

Pelham, W.E., & Milich, R. (1984). Peer relations in children with hyperactivity/attention deficit disorder. *Journal of Learning Disabilities, 17,* 560–567.

Pelham, W.E., Jr., McBurnett, K., Harper, G.W., Milich, R., Murphy, D.A., Clinton, J., & Thiele, C. (1990). Methylphenidate and baseball playing in children with ADHD: Who's on first? *Journal of Consulting and Clinical Psychology, 58,* 130–133.

Richman, N., Stevenson, J., & Graham, J.J. (1982). *Preschool to school: A behavioral study.* London: Academic.

Schaughency, E.A., & Rothlind, J. (1991). Assessment and classification of attention deficit hyperactivity disorders. *School Psychology Review, 20*(2), 187–202.

Weiss, B., & Hechtman, L.T. (1986). *Hyperactive children grown up.* New York: Guilford.

Wolraich, M., Milich, R., Stumbo, P., & Schultz, F. (1985). The effects of sucrose ingestion on the behavior of hyperactive boys. *Pediatrics, 106,* 675–682.

Enabling The Learning Disabled

Answers to your questions about reaching, teaching, and meeting the special needs of learning-disabled students in the regular classroom

Sally Smith

Sally Smith is the founder and director of The Lab School in Washington, D.C. She is also professor and head of the American University's masters degree program in special education: learning disabilities, and is the author of six books.

Chances are you'll have at least one learning disabled (LD) student in your classroom this year. And if you teach in a district that's already moved toward inclusion (see sidebar "Inclusion"), that number could be higher.

Teaching children with learning disabilities brings with it special joys, and special challenges. To help you manage, INSTRUCTOR went to Sally Smith, founder and director of the Lab School in Washington, D.C., and professor and head of special education at the American University—and asked her to address some of your biggest concerns. Her advice follows.

What does the term *learning disabled* really mean?
Learning disabilities encompass a broad range of neurological problems that are quite distinct from either retardation or emotional disturbances. The LD child is likely to have difficulty with reading, writing, spelling, and math. More sub-

tle—and harder to pinpoint—are difficulties the child will have in attending; concentrating; remembering; organizing; sequencing; coordinating; and distinguishing right from left, letters, and numbers. The ability to make these distinctions is essential in learning the rudiments of reading, writing, and mathematics. If not addressed, a child's academic, emotional, and social development is adversely affected.

What instructional strategies work best with LD students?
LD students need opportunities to apply what they're learning. Ask them to reenact events, draw pictures, collect magazine photos to illustrate topics, construct models, and so on. Follow up with discussions that encourage students to verbalize what they've learned.

Also, whenever possible, show photos that will help students comprehend a topic. All children will enjoy the pictures, but for the LD child—who tends to have disabilities with language and tends to learn visually—pictures can mean the difference between not understanding and understanding a subject.

My LD students have trouble grasping abstract concepts. What can I do?
Turn an abstract idea into something concrete by having kids illustrate the

How can I tell if a student is LD?

Learning disabilities affect 10 to 15 percent of all Americans. According to the Learning Disabilities Association of America, if a child demonstrates a number of these signs, it may mean that he or she should be referred to a psychologist who understands learning disabilities for testing.
Watch the child who:
• is disorganized,
• is easily distracted,
• has a poor attention span,
• overreacts to noise,
• doesn't enjoy being read to,
• has poor hand-eye coordination,
• can't make sense of what he or she hears,
• uses words inappropriately,
• is hyperactive,
• has limited vocabulary,
• is unable to follow simple directions,
• sometimes has poor emotional control,
• has difficulty remembering or understanding sequences, and
• chooses younger playmates or prefers solitary play.

[For a more in-depth look at detection, see the INSTRUCTOR Guide to Early Diagnosis and Referral, September 1993.]

From *Instructor,* July/August 1993, pp. 88-91. © 1993 by Scholastic, Inc. Reprinted by permission.

concept using their bodies, objects, and pictures. For example, to introduce the concept of our government's balance of power, you might begin with balancing exercises—have students use weights to even out a pair of scales. Then you could divide students into threes—to represent the judicial, executive, and legislative branches—and have them clasp hands and gently tug on one another's arms to illustrate the system's give-and-take. Afterward, kids could draw a triangular chart to show the balance of power and discuss a current example of the balance in action.

Especially during the early part of the year, when I'm trying to get to know all the students in my class, I sometimes have trouble remembering each of my LD students' main problem areas. What do you suggest?
Create a handy profile for each student. On separate index cards list each child's strengths, weaknesses, and interests, as well as the classroom-management methods that he or she responds to and the techniques that don't work. Add other information you've discovered about the student, and you'll have a quick reference tool at your fingertips.

How can I help the LD student feel successful?
Break down tasks into as many steps as necessary to ensure that the student can complete each step successfully. By starting with what a youngster can do and then building from there, you'll give the child a boost of confidence. (Hint: Be sure the student understands each step thoroughly before moving on to the next.)

When a student feels overwhelmed or depressed, how can I help?
I give the student tangible proof of his or her progress and commit to working together on trouble spots. On a sheet of paper folded down the middle, I make a column on the left-hand side called "Your Strengths" and write down such observations as: You work hard, you are a good artist, and so on. I read the list aloud to the child. Then I make a column on the right-hand side called "Needs Work" and write down skills the student needs to work on, such as spelling, subtraction, and reading. I read the list aloud. Next I tear the sheet down the middle, hand the list of strengths to the student, and say something like, "You keep the list of

your strengths. I'll keep the list of what you need to work on because it's my job to take care of those things for a while until you can become responsible for them."

Following my oral instructions is difficult for the LD students in my class. What can I do?
First, to reinforce sound, make sure the children are looking at you when you're giving instructions. It helps to stand near them, too. Be sure you speak slowly and loudly enough to be heard and keep your directions clear, precise, and succinct. Also, break down your instructions into simple steps, give only one or two at a time, and ask students to repeat each one aloud. Consider pairing an LD child with a considerate classmate who can check whether the student understands the instructions and can help explain them when he or she doesn't.

Because concrete reinforcement works well for the LD child, consider giving students gold stars or stickers when they follow instructions properly.

INCLUSION—
A Movement That's Gaining Momentum

If you haven't heard of inclusion, you will soon. It's a movement that's gaining ground in schools across the country. It means bringing the special-education teacher into the regular classroom—instead of pulling students out. The regular teacher and special-ed teacher coteach: planning lessons and delivering instruction together and sharing the responsibility for assessing students' mastery.

How does it work? In some schools, students with disabilities are grouped into a single class at each grade level for subjects like reading

and language arts, and the special-education teacher coteaches in that classroom every day. Sometimes special-education teachers split time among several classrooms, perhaps coteaching in social studies in a third-grade class on Mondays and Wednesdays and in a fifth-grade class on Tuesdays and Thursdays, with Fridays set aside as flexible time to be used according to need. Some schools find that coteaching works well when scheduled by units. For example, if a teacher who has mainstreamed students in her class is

teaching a concept that many children find difficult, she might ask the special-education teacher to coteach that concept.

Through coteaching, special-education students avoid the stigma associated with the daily journey in and out of the regular classroom. Their learning is less fragmented, not only because they don't miss any time in the regular classroom, but also because the special-education teacher is better able to relate remediation to regular instruction.

How can I approach the student who is afraid to admit he or she doesn't know something or is afraid to make mistakes?

When you don't know the answer to something yourself, set an example by saying, "I don't know, but we can find out together."

Send the signal to all students that it's okay to make mistakes and that everyone—even teachers—makes them. When kids do something wrong, tell them about mistakes you've made and talk about how you learned from them.

One of my LD students often has trouble finding her way around the school. For example, I have to show her how to find the resource room nearly every day. What can I do?

Pair the student with a classmate who does not have directional difficulty. Or point out landmarks between your classroom and the resource room—such as the green door, the drinking fountain, and the stairs—that the child can use to help her find her way on her own. If the student is a visual learner, have her draw a map of how to get there.

Sometimes I feel angry or frustrated with my LD students. How can I overcome these feelings?

Your feelings are important diagnostic tools because they may reflect students' feelings. When a student is angry, his or her feelings may be contagious. If you realize you're frustrated because the child is, you'll be better able to diffuse a situation and work patiently with a student. So it's important for you to be solidly in touch with your feelings, recognize and acknowledge them, and use them as a barometer to clue you in to what's happening with a student.

I've noticed that humor works well with my LD students. Why?

Nothing dispels tension faster than laughter, because if students can see the funny side of difficult or uncomfortable situations, usually they can find a way out of them. Because LD children tend to feel that others are laughing at them, it's important for these students to see laughter as a relief and means of togetherness—not as a form of punishment.

Teachers who laugh at themselves in an easy, accepting way are important models for children who tend to see themselves with despair or as a source of worry to others. And humor and the absurd can be an effective tool for anything from disciplining to testing.

Is it true that LD students need additional structure?

Yes. Structure means predictability, and predictability helps make LD children feel more comfortable. Although it takes extra work on your part, give your LD students a list of the topics for the day. The list will help them focus and better prepare them to learn.

If You Want To Know More

No Easy Answers: The Learning Disabled Child at Home and School by Sally Smith (Bantam paperback, 1981). To order call (800) 223-6834 or (212) 354-6500.

Succeeding Against the Odds: How the Learning Disabled Can Realize Their Promise by Sally Smith (Tarcher/Perigee paperback, 1992)

The following organizations offer a variety of publications and services. For more information, write or call:

The Learning Disabilities Association of America 4156 Library Rd. Pittsburgh, PA 15234 (412) 341-1515

The Orton Dyslexia Society Chester Building, Suite 382 8600 Lasalle Rd. Baltimore, MD 21286 (410) 296-0232

National Center for Learning Disabilities 99 Park Ave. New York, NY 10016 (212) 687-7211

Ability Grouping: Geared for the Gifted

The anti-tracking movement has given ability grouping a bad name. The two are not the same.

Ellen D. Fiedler, Richard E. Lange, and Susan Winebrenner
From *Roeper Review*

Ellen D. Fiedler is Associate Professor, Gifted/ Talented Masters Degree Program, Northeastern Illinois University, Chicago. Richard E. Lange is Director of Gifted Education, Staff Development, and Assessment, Prospect Heights Public Schools, and Adjunct Faculty Member, College of Education, National-Louis University, Evanston, both in Illinois. Susan Winebrenner is an independent consultant in staff development.

IN the 1990s, the anti-tracking movement has suddenly become anti*ability grouping*, side effects ranging from the Regular Education Initiative for students with learning handicaps to attempts to eliminate programs for highly able or gifted students. The concern is about negative effects of locking certain students into unchallenging classes and locking them out of educational situations that stretch their minds. But, all of the relevant research and its ramifications have not been considered.

There are six common myths about appropriate educational programs for all students, including the gifted:

Myth 1:
Tracking and ability grouping are the same.
Reality:

Tracking separates students into class-size groups using their perceived ability or prior achievement. It results in students being assigned full-time to instructional groups based on a variety of criteria, including presumed ability derived from achievement test scores and teacher observations of classroom performance.

This often means a high-ability group for Teacher A, a middle-ability group for Teacher B, and a low-ability group for Teacher C. Once students are in a track, there is little movement between tracks during a school year or from one school year to another. Consistent placement in the low track leads students to disenfranchisement in a class system where there are clear differences between the "haves" and "have-nots."

Ability grouping is re-grouping students to provide curriculum aimed at a common instructional level. Elementary teachers create more homogeneous reading or math groups while teaching heterogeneous groups for most other subjects. Secondary students may be assigned to high-ability groups in areas of their strengths and to average- or low-ability groups in other subjects. Ability grouping does not imply permanently locking students out of settings that are appropriately challenging; it means placing them with others with similar learning needs for whatever length of time works best.

Myth 2:
Ability grouping is elitist.
Reality:

Most gifted educators work to develop an understanding of giftedness in the context of individual differences rather than superiority—consistent with newly emerging approaches that consider cognitive and affective development as equally important.

Keeping one or two highly gifted students in a classroom of mixed abilities may create snobbery. Scattering gifted students through all classrooms may lead them to feel far superior to classmates and promote arrogance. Unless gifted students can be challenged by intellectual peers, the possibilities that they will develop an elitist attitude might increase.

However, when gifted students are grouped together for instruction, studying with intellectual peers may actually lower self-esteem somewhat. There is nothing so humbling as discovering other students in the group equally capable or more knowledgeable. If one goal of education is to help all students develop a realistic appraisal of their own ability, students need to measure themselves with appropriate yardsticks. Comparisons are more likely to be accurate when made with others of similar abilities.

Interestingly, educators have no qualms about identifying outstanding athletes and providing specialized programs for them. If this is not considered elitist, why should intellectual giftedness be given short shrift?

Myth 3:
Ability grouping inevitably discriminates against racial and ethnic minorities.
Reality:

From *The Education Digest*, January 1994, pp. 52-55. Condensed from *Roeper Review*, 16 (September 1993), pp. 4-7.

71

Gifted educators have made great progress in refining identification methods. Widespread efforts are being made to overcome inequities of over-reliance on standardized test scores and assumptions that too often have been made about students who, although gifted, may not fit the stereotype of high achievers with positive attitudes toward school.

The direction is toward approaches that include studying student behaviors for indicators of gifted potential, with attention on training teachers to do this. Also, behavioral descriptors are used to identify other underserved populations. Preschool and kindergarten children, creative thinkers, nonproductive gifted students, and gifted students with learning disabilities and other handicaps are being screened more accurately.

Eliminating ability grouping because of inequitable identification is throwing out the baby with the bath water. Furthermore, singling out racial and ethnic minorities as the only disenfranchised group is misleading. The intent of gifted programs has not been to exclude certain populations. But identification procedures needed revision, and improved methodologies are already being implemented.

Myth 4:
Gifted students will make it on their own; grouping them by ability does not improve their learning or achievement.
Reality:

Studies confirm what gifted educators have known for years: Gifted students benefit cognitively and affectively from working with other gifted students.

Some studies indicate no increase in achievement test scores for high-ability students grouped together, but they omit gifted students. Robert Slavin's research that recommended heterogeneous grouping for all ability groups systematically omitted data from students in the top 5 percent. Such omissions can lead to dangerous overgeneralizations by interpreters.

Also consider ceiling effects: Grade-level achievement tests fail to reveal growth for students who already perform in the top percentile ranks because they have reached the ceiling of the test—the highest scores attainable

for that age group. Only with instruments designed for older students can actual achievement gains be determined for students in the extreme upper range.

Another critical issue involves the goals of the gifted program and whether its purposes are actually focused on increasing academic achievement. What gifted students learn should be measured by far more comprehensive criteria than increased achievement test scores. Equally important are the development of socialization and leadership skills, experience with complex concepts and challenging learning, and opportunities to pursue topics in great depth. If such a program is more concerned with helping gifted students work together to grapple with global concerns that are complex and substantive, increases in achievement test scores in specific subject areas are not appropriate for measuring success.

Myth 5:
Heterogeneously grouped cooperative learning is most effective for serving all students, including the gifted.
Reality:

The students who may learn the least in a given class are the gifted. So much of what they are asked to learn they may have already mastered. Teachers may then be tempted to use them as classroom helpers or to teach others, robbing the gifted of consistent opportunities to learn through real struggle. This can have a negative impact on them in many ways, including lowered self-esteem. Without regular encounters with challenging material, the gifted fail to learn how to learn and have problems developing study skills for future academic pursuits.

Cooperative learning is designed to be used with either homogeneous or heterogeneous groups. It seems reasonable to allow teachers the flexibility to determine which lessons lend themselves to heterogeneous cooperative learning groups and which to homogeneous cooperative learning groups and make professional decisions to place students accordingly.

Myth 6:
Having gifted students in all classrooms provides positive role

models and will automatically improve the classroom climate.
Reality:

The notion that gifted students in low-ability classrooms will automatically benefit students performing at lower levels rests on questionable assumptions: that the performance discrepancies will be perceived as alterable by the less capable students; that gifted students are consistently highly-motivated high achievers who will inspire others to similar accomplishments; and that gifted students placed in low-ability or heterogeneous classrooms will continue to perform at their peak even when they lack regular opportunities to interact with intellectual peers who can stimulate their thinking. Research indicates that students model their behavior on that of others who are of similar ability and are coping well in school.

Furthermore, heterogeneous grouping may have negative side-effects on both the gifted and others. Gifted students who are a minority of one or who have only one or two classmates whose ability level approaches their own feel either odd or arrogant. If all the other students watch from the sidelines while the smart one provides all the answers, their perceptions of themselves as competent, capable learners suffer.

Equality in education does not require that all students have exactly the same experiences. Rather, education in a democracy promises that everyone will have an equal opportunity to actualize their potential, to learn as much as they can.

Education in a free society should not be a choice between equity and excellence. Providing for formerly disenfranchised groups need not take away appropriate programs from any other group. As the research clearly indicates, gifted students benefit from working together. Therefore, ability grouping for the gifted must continue. While the educational community moves toward heterogeneity for students who benefit more from working in mixed ability groups, it should not deny gifted students the right to educational arrangements that maximize their learning. The goal of an appropriate education must be to create optimal learning experiences for all.

Meeting the Needs of Your High-Ability Students

*Strategies
every teacher
can use*

SUSAN WINEBRENNER

Do you feel you could be doing more to help your gifted and talented students achieve their potential? The four strategies described here will help you engage your most advanced students and develop the abilities of every child.

1. FIND HIDDEN ABILITIES
Student Scenario: Elizabeth

Sixth grader Elizabeth had difficulty reading and writing because of a learning disability, and didn't appear to be gifted. But when I introduced a unit on map skills, Elizabeth approached me after class and said, "You know, Mrs. Winebrenner, I know a lot about maps."

"You do? How did that happen?" I asked.

"I don't know. I just love maps."

"What do you like to do with this love of maps?"

"Well, when my family goes on a vacation, I plan our trip on the map."

"No kidding! Where did you go last year?"

"Yellowstone National Park."

"And how did you get there?"

Elizabeth proceeded to do something I'm not sure I could do—she told me how she had navigated her family to Yellowstone: highway by highway, county by county, state by state. I was amazed.

"Pretty impressive," I said. "I bet the prospect of doing a unit on map skills is not very appealing to you."

"I've thought about that."

"I'll tell you what. I'll give you the end-of-unit test

From *Instructor,* September 1994, pp. 60-65. Adapted from *Teaching Gifted Kids in the Regular Classroom: Strategies and Techniques Every Teacher Can Use to Meet the Academic Need of the Gifted and Talented* by Susan Winebrenner. © 1992 by Free Spirit Publishing. To order the book, call 800-735-7323.

tomorrow, and if you pass it with an A, you'll be able to spend your social studies time on a different activity of your choice." Elizabeth was thrilled.

Next, I offered the same deal to everyone in the class. This is something I've learned to do routinely, so that every student has the opportunity to shine.

Sixteen of my twenty-seven students volunteered to take the pretest. The pretesters knew beforehand that if they did not earn an A, their tests would not count. Two passed with A's—Elizabeth was one of them.

While the class honed their map skills, Elizabeth worked independently, creating a papier-mâché relief map of an imaginary country. Because her learning disability prevented her from writing well, I encouraged her to simply flag the population centers, the natural resources, the manufacturing centers, and so on. When she'd finished her project, she gave an interesting talk about her country that fascinated the class.

Did other students ask to do a project like Elizabeth's? Yes! And I let everyone do one as a culminating activity for the map unit, while Elizabeth acted as a consultant. Imagine the boost to Elizabeth's self-esteem when her classmates turned to her for advice.

CUSTOM-MADE LEARNING

What does Elizabeth's story tell us? It's up to teachers to determine what competencies certain students have, and give them full credit for what they already know. Then we need to decide how to modify the curriculum so that these students will learn something new. Dr. Joseph S. Renzulli of The National Research Center on the Gifted and Talented in Storrs, Connecticut, calls this process "curriculum compacting." Dr. Renzulli, author of *Schools for Talent Development: A Practical Plan for Total School Improvement,* and Linda H. Smith developed the form that follows. Use it to record all the modifications you make for your students.

2. APPOINT RESIDENT EXPERTS
Student Scenario: Joey

Joey, a student in my fifth-grade class, was exceptional in every subject area, but his actual classroom performance left a lot to be desired. He spent most of his time daydreaming, and he seldom completed his homework, yet he always aced the tests. Joey behaved rudely during class discussions, often remarking under his breath to amuse other students.

When Joey's class was about to begin a Civil War unit, I gave him and other students whom I felt could tackle the text on their own a chance to do an independent project on the Civil War during social studies.

I dubbed them "resident experts" and told them they would be responsible for presenting a report on their topic to the class. I gave them each a list of project ideas, but they were free to choose a topic of their own. I also assured all my students that they could do an independent project at the end of the unit.

I asked each resident expert to sign an independent study contract that included the major Civil War concepts I expected them to know, activities related to these ideas, and a timetable of all class quizzes and discussions to assess their progress. (Resident experts take the quizzes and/or participate in discussions along with the other students. Those who do not earn a B or higher, or who display problematic behavior, must rejoin the class until the next quiz. If they achieve a B or higher on the next quiz, they may return to their project. If they don't, they can finish their project when the rest of the class gets school time to work on independent projects.)

You can modify these contracts to include detailed expectations about the quality of the projects you would like students to produce. A contract I designed especially for Joey is shown below.

Unlike the independent study method I used with Elizabeth, the resident-expert strategy is not based on the results of a pretest given to all students willing to give it a try. Instead, teachers use their own judgment, selecting students they feel are capable of developing an in-depth talk, performance, or display of their investigation.

THE COMPACTOR		
Joseph Renzulli & Linda H. Smith		
Student's Name: _____		
Areas of Strength	Methods used to document student's mastery of a skill, competency, chapter, concept, or unit	Activities student will be engaged in as an alternative to the regular class activities

This article is adapted from the book Teaching Gifted Kids in the Regular Classroom: Strategies and Techniques Every Teacher Can Use to Meet the Academic Needs of the Gifted and Talented *by Susan Winebrenner, (Free Spirit Publishing, 1992).*

EVALUATION CONTRACT
Civil War Project

For a grade of "B," use information gathered from other sources. Choose from the ideas below, or design your own with my approval:

1. Research the different types of trains and locomotives that would have been used during the Civil War era. Draw them to scale.
2. Discover the details about the lives of two famous generals, one Union and one Confederate. Comment on at least two similarities you find.
3. Learn several Civil War songs from both sides. Teach one song from each side to the class. Lead the class in a discussion of similarities and differences in the songs.

For a grade of "A," create a unique product that requires high levels of thinking. Choose from the ideas below, or design your own with my approval:

1. Draw the trains of the Civil War era on routes between the major manufacturing centers and four famous battlefields: two in the North and two in the South. Be prepared to discuss how the proximity of the battlefields to the manufacturing centers may have affected the outcome of the war.
2. Create an interview with a famous Civil War general. Include some information that was probably unknown to the general public at the time of the Civil War. Prepare a live interview where you and a friend impersonate the general and the interviewer. Come in appropriate costume.
3. Discover the role that music has played to create and maintain patriotic feelings during wartime. Illustrate your presentation with musical excerpts.

Use this space to describe your project:

#1

I am contracting for a grade of: __A__

Student's signature: __Jocy__

3. PROVIDE A VENUE TO SHOWCASE TALENTS
Student Scenario: Alvin

Alvin was passionate about reading and writing poetry, and he had the talent to match it. But he was reluctant to share his poetry with me or his peers, and kept his work at home. In school, Alvin preferred to work alone, wary of group activities. I needed to showcase Alvin's poetic talent in a way that would make him feel more comfortable with his peers.

One Monday, I announced that Friday would be the first of many Great Friday Afternoon Events and explained how the events would work (see chart, **on next page**). I asked Alvin if he would like to be captain of the poetry team. "I guess so," he replied, nervously.

Within a couple of days, Alvin seemed at ease with the other team members, and the poem the team recited had lots of Alvin-like language and images. The Great Friday Afternoon Events became an effective way to have Alvin and other high-ability students work productively in heterogeneous groups, and gave all students a chance to showcase their talents.

WHO'S GIFTED?
CHARACTERISTICS TO LOOK FOR

Whom teachers consider gifted is changing as we use new tools to measure children's talents and consider a broader range of "gifts," from visual intelligence to affective abilities. (For more about evolving definitions of **giftedness, see next page.) Nevertheless, the partial list of** indicators below, which is organized into three different categories, will help you recognize the high-ability students in your classroom. Gifted students may exhibit many but not all of these qualities.

General
- Has an advanced vocabulary
- Possesses an outstanding memory
- Is curious about many things; asks lots of questions
- Has many interests and hobbies
- Is intense; gets totally absorbed in activities and thoughts
- Operates on higher levels of thinking than his or her age peers
- Perceives subtle cause-and-effect relationships
- Catches on quickly, then resists doing work, or works in a sloppy, careless manner
- Is sensitive to beauty and other people's feelings and emotions
- Possesses an advanced sense of justice
- Sees connections between apparently unconnected ideas and activities
- May prefer to work alone; resists cooperative learning
- May be street-smart while not doing well on school tasks

Creative Thinking
- Displays original ideas
- Is fluent in idea generation and development
- Is able to elaborate on ideas
- Values nonconformity in appearance, thought, etc.

Perfectionism
- Believes he is valued for what he can do rather than who he is
- May cry easily in frustration that her work at school can never be perfect
- Procrastinates to the point that work never even gets started
- Asks for lots of help and reassurance from the teacher

New Ways to Think About Giftedness

Carolyn Callahan, a researcher and teacher at the University of Virginia's Curry School of Education and president-elect of the National Association for Gifted Children, talks with Instructor's *Senior Associate Editor Wendy Murray about giftedness and what teachers can do to encourage the special abilities of every child.*

How has our society's conception of giftedness changed over the years?
In the past, the traditional gifted child was one who possessed exceptional reading and writing skills—a giftedness that everyone could see. This usually meant children who scored well on standardized tests, which was problematic because the tests don't accommodate children's different learning styles. New definitions of intelligence have stretched our definition of giftedness and talent. Now we know we must consider many ways of assessing how children perform, interact with their learning, and problem-solve, beyond just reading and writing, to find out who's gifted.

How can teachers unveil their students' talents?
We need to give children the opportunity to show their strengths in a variety of ways. Can students fix a toy pump? Tell a story dramatically? Create a song? Construct a model of a mathematical principle? We have to combine tests with portfolios, observations, and other performance-based assessments.

What is the most important thing a teacher can do to meet the needs of gifted students?
Differentiate the curriculum! For example, say you're planning a unit on community. Think to yourself, I

have some chidren who need to learn what a community is; I have others who already know. What activities will challenge each group? While one group might explore the community of their family or the local community, the other can compare world communities.

What other strategies should teachers use?
Teach in an interdisciplinary manner, weaving math, literature, science, social studies, and so on, into whatever it is your students are exploring. Ask yourself, How can I structure this unit so that children think about and solve real-world problems?

Here's my favorite example of bringing the real world into school: One kindergarten teacher I know was teaching her class about germs—viruses and bacteria—in all sorts of interesting ways. Still, there was one child who went ten steps further. He wanted to figure out how to stop the spread of flu at school. He designed an experiment where he put up paper cups at the drinking fountain for a certain number of days and noted student absences from school during that period. Then he took the cups away, tracked the absences, and put the data on a graph that showed drinking cups cut down on the number of students absent due to colds and flus. Then he went to the PTA and got it to pay for cups! Never underestimate the learner!

THE GREAT FRIDAY AFTERNOON EVENT

Students, in four teams, present a program to class.
Teams stay intact for four weeks.
Each week, each team has a different task.
Tasks rotate until each team has done each task.

	POETRY Students read or recite a poem of their choice or creation.	DECLAMATION (Readers' Theater) Students present a dramatic reading.	PLAY Students present Readers' Theater or dramatic play.	NEWSCAST Students broadcast a 5–10 minute radio or video show.
WEEK 1	A	B	C	D
WEEK 2	B	C	D	A
WEEK 3	C	D	A	B
WEEK 4	D	A	B	C

Teachers Who Are Good with the Gifted

A team of researchers at the National Research Center on the Gifted and Talented and I recently examined ten U.S. schools that had a reputation for meeting the needs of capable students in regular classrooms. Among other things, we wanted to find out what these successful teachers were doing right. Here's what we found.

In addition to using methods such as curriculum compacting, independent study projects, and heterogeneous-group activities requiring critical thinking, teachers who were most successful with high-ability students possessed these attributes:

● **Trust.** At a northeastern school, we observed a teacher as she showed a group of capable math students how to use protractors to measure degrees in angles. Afterward, she said, "Go through the first four pages of the next chapter. Along the way, *you* decide which problems you need to do to help you understand measurement of triangles."

● **Spontaneity.** In an urban school, a student approached her teacher, a Shakespearean play in hand.

"I know Shakespeare is not very popular at this time, but I really feel he will be appreciated again soon," she said, before asking whether she could share the play with another student. The teacher didn't miss a beat; she told her it was a great idea. This same teacher once put aside what she had planned, to take advantage of a snowstorm. When we walked into her room, students were busy determining the volume of snow that had to be plowed from the school's driveway.

● **Rapport.** One of the most memorable things we observed was watching teachers who clearly enjoy swapping ideas with colleagues. At one school, four teachers of the same grade level meet for dinner at a Mexican restaurant once a week. They refer to these evenings as Ol' Mexico night, and during these dinners they plan their unique "Enrichment Wednesdays," during which they teach special classes designed to address their students' interests. ■

—Karen L. Westberg, Ph.D., The National Center on the Gifted and Talented, Storrs, Connecticut.

4. REDIRECT LEADERSHIP QUALITIES

Student Scenario: Lucy

Twelve-year-old Lucy had unusual leadership abilities. She could think on her feet, persuade others to see her point of view, and inspire classmates to work as a team—when she applied herself. But too often she took the shortcut, dominating discussions and bossing other students around. She needed more structured opportunities to hone her gift for persuasion.

With Lucy in mind, I built an array of group activities into the curriculum, setting aside every Wednesday afternoon to engage in these events. Groups of kids held mock trials (we even invited in a lawyer, who ended up being a great mentor for the children),

worked together to simulate running a business, and planned a city of the future, to mention just a few.

By posing open-ended questions to groups of students (such as: If you were sent to live on a planet, what five people would you need to have along to survive?) every student gets to stretch intellectually, and students like Lucy positively blossom. Lucy relished the intellectual challenge, and her peers enjoyed the chance to make her back up her opinions with facts.

The self-assessment involved in these activities are also valuable for children of every ability who lack confidence. Students assess their own ideas and those of the group, and come to see that these evaluations are as valid as yours.

What We Can Learn from Multicultural Education Research

Educators will be more successful if they understand five variables that matter in working with a diverse student population.

Gloria Ladson-Billings

Gloria Ladson-Billings is an Assistant Professor at the University of Wisconsin-Madison, Department of Curriculum and Instruction, 225 N. Mills St., Madison, WI 53706.

Many findings from multicultural education research can be applied in the everyday world of teachers and administrators. This observation holds regardless of whether the educators work with many students of color or with only a few.

The research shows that five areas matter a great deal in the education of a multicultural population: teachers' beliefs about students, curriculum content and materials, instructional approaches, educational settings, and teacher education. One other area—whether the race and ethnicity of teachers affects student learning—remains unclear.

Beliefs About Students Matter

To begin to see how teacher beliefs affect student achievement, imagine two new teachers. Don Wilson and Margie Stewart are starting their first year of teaching.

Don Wilson. After his first weeks of teaching in an urban school, Wilson is exhausted and uncertain about whether he chose the right profession. His class of 28 fourth graders are African Americans and Latinos. Wilson knows that they have not had many advantages, so he doesn't push them too hard. He wants his students to have fun learning. He worries, though, because many of them don't seem to be

having fun or learning. Many are one or more achievement levels below national averages, and some attend school sporadically, fail to complete homework assignments, and seem unmotivated in the classroom. Although Wilson has sent several notes home expressing concern, parents have not responded. Wilson doubts that he makes any difference in the lives of his students.

> # How teachers think about education and students makes a pronounced difference in student performance and achievement.

Margie Stewart. The first weeks of teaching in a suburban school have been exhausting for Stewart, too, but she is enjoying herself. Of Stewart's 28 third graders, 23 are white, upper-middle-class children. Three of the remaining five are African American, and two are Mexican American (one speaks limited English). In general, the students test at or above grade level on

standardized tests, but the students of color lag behind the others. Stewart is also concerned about José. Because José's English is limited, Stewart must explain everything to him four or five times, and she can seldom work with him one-on-one. She fears that he is a special needs student. Perhaps she will ask the school psychologist to test José.

The research literature suggests that how teachers like Wilson and Stewart think about education and students makes a pronounced difference in student performance and achievement (Apple 1990, Cooper 1979). Winfield (1986) found that teachers expect more from white students than from African-American students, and they expect more from middle-class students than from working- and lower-class students. Teachers often perceive African-American students from working- or lower-class backgrounds as incapable of high-quality academic work. Both Wilson and Stewart are entertaining such thoughts. They are not attributing their problems with students of color to ineffective teaching approaches.

Sometimes, unrecognized or outright racism causes teachers to hold negative beliefs about students of color. A dramatic example from a first-year teacher's journal entry:

> I hate [African-American students'] ethnic attitude and their lingo. I hate to categorize it but ... I am more comfortable with black students who act white (Birrell 1993).

Such negative attitudes toward students of color lower expectations for achievement, which lowers achievement (King and Ladson-Billings 1990, Lipman 1993).

Content and Materials Matter

Teachers who are sincerely committed to multicultural education cannot be satisfied with superficial celebrations of heroes and holidays. This approach to content trivializes multicultural education and conveys the idea that diversity issues come into play only during celebratory moments with foods, fun, and festivals.

In the multicultural festival model, teachers, students, and parents typically spend lots of time and energy preparing for an all-school activity. Students may do background research about a culture, prepare maps, and help create indigenous costumes. Parents may help to prepare various ethnic foods. On the day of the festival, members of the school community go from class to class, visiting the various cultures, sampling the foods, and enjoying dances, songs, and arts and crafts. At the end of the day, everyone agrees that the annual event has been a great success. Then teachers and students go back to their real work.

In the transformative model, on the other hand, multicultural education is not a separate, isolated, once-a-year activity. Instead, the regular curriculum includes a range of cultural perspectives, as in the following two classroom scenarios.

In a primary classroom, the teacher reads several versions of the Cinderella story. One is the familiar European tale by the Brothers Grimm, but other versions are Chinese, Egyptian, and Zimbabwean. The teacher helps students compare the different versions. Similarities include story structure, plot development, moral and ethical dilemmas, and the use of magic. Differences include standards of beauty, settings, use of language, and specific characters. The students absorb the importance of understanding cultural differences and similarities.

In an intermediate history class, students study the African slave trade, but not solely from the perspective of the European traders. They also read a range of primary documents, like the slave narrative called *The Interesting Life of Olaudah Equiano* (it compares slavery in Africa with slavery in the Americas). In addition, the teacher introduces information about the European feudal system. The students compare the lives of enslaved people in Africa, the Americas, and medieval Europe. Finally, they generate analytical questions, such as, What is the relationship between slavery and racism? How could a nation striving for equality and justice permit slavery? Why did some people in Africa participate in the slave trade? And how does the textbook's treatment of slavery compare to primary source material?

The teacher in this class plans to do similar in-depth study when the class studies the displacement of Native Americans, the Spanish mission system, European immigration of the 1890s, and Japanese internment. Although the transformative approach requires redesigning the curriculum, searching for additional materials, and limiting the number of topics taught, the teacher thinks the outcome is worth the effort. Students learn more content and develop a real ability to ask and answer critical questions.

The materials used in classrooms have important effects, too. As Banks' comprehensive literature review (1993a) points out, children are aware of their race and ethnicity at an early age. "If realistic images of ethnic and racial groups are included in teaching materials in a consistent, natural, and integrated fashion," Banks (1993b) concludes, all children "can be helped to develop more positive racial attitudes." Similar results are reported on gender issues (Scott and Schau 1985).

If classrooms use materials that do not portray diverse groups realistically, students are likely to develop, maintain, and strengthen the stereotypes and distortions in the traditional curriculum. Text analysis (a common form of multicultural research) indicates that textbook images and representations exclude, distort, and marginalize women, people of color, and people from lower socioeconomic echelons. A growing proportion of textbooks do include diversity, but their images and representations tend to be superficial and incorrect (Swartz 1992).

Instructional Approaches Matter

Changes to make curriculum content more equitable must be accompanied by changes that make pedagogy even-handed. To ensure "equitable pedagogy," Banks says, teachers must modify instruction to "facilitate academic achievement among students from diverse groups."

> For some teachers, providing more equitable pedagogy may be as simple as using more cooperative learning strategies.

To some teachers, simultaneously dealing with the flood of new materials and modifying instructional approaches seems like an overwhelming task. These teachers think that it is all they can do to teach the new material in old ways. In other classrooms, however, teachers have asked themselves, what one move can I make to ensure that all students have opportunities for success?

For some teachers, providing more equitable pedagogy may be as simple as using more cooperative learning strategies in class. After all, cooperative learning was first developed as a way to create more equitable classroom environments (Cohen and Benton 1988, Slavin 1987).

For other teachers, equitable pedagogy will demand that they use the language and understandings that children bring to school to bridge the gap between what students know and what they need to learn (Au and Jordan 1981, Erickson and Mohatt 1982, Jordan 1985, Vogt et al. 1987). In addition, the total school context must come to accept whatever students have learned and experienced as legitimate knowledge (Irvine 1990, Ladson-Billings 1992, in press). Teachers can further these ends if they spend time in their students' community and apply in the classroom what they learned in students' homes.

Teachers may also profit by learning their students' language. A teacher who knows how to ask and answer basic questions in a second language can often make the classroom a welcoming and psychologically safe environment for speakers of that language. If a teacher becomes sufficiently fluent to teach academic content in English and a student's home language, the teacher tacitly promotes bilingualism and biliteracy (Hornberger 1988).

Educational Settings Matter

Forty years ago, the Supreme Court handed down a landmark decision, *Brown v. Board of Education,* which declared separate schools inherently unequal. Yet now, after years of hard-fought battles to desegregate the nation's schools, most students of color still attend segregated schools (Orfield 1989). Even when students go to desegregated schools, they are resegregated within the school via tracking and ability grouping (Oakes 1985).

For students of color, perhaps more devastating is the lack of access to high-quality education (Kozol 1991). Clearly, as a society, our care and concern for student learning is differentiated along racial, class, and ethnic lines.

To grasp the impact of these inequities, imagine that our new

teachers, Wilson and Stewart, were to participate in a school exchange program. Wilson's students would visit Stewart's class. Then Stewart's class would visit Wilson's. What will each setting informally teach the children?

When Wilson's students arrive at Stewart's school, they are struck by its physical beauty and space. Well-kept grounds have ample playground equipment. Inside the school, the halls gleam, and a lively buzz emanates from the various classrooms. Each brightly lighted classroom has at least one computer. The school library has several computers, CD-ROM, laser disks, and an extensive library of videotapes. The school has many special rooms: a gymnasium, a multi-purpose room, vocal and instrumental music rooms, an art room, and a room for enrichment activities. In each of the rooms is a teacher who regularly works with Stewart's students, freeing her for 45 minutes each day. She uses the time to plan, read, hold parent conferences, and do research.

When Stewart's class visits Wilson's school, they enter an old structure built in the 1920s. Its concrete yard is littered with broken glass, graffiti cover the walls, and the only piece of playground equipment is a netless basketball hoop. Inside the building, the dark halls are eerily silent, since room doors are closed and locked from the inside. There is a room where books are stored, but they are not catalogued because there is no librarian. The entire school shares one VCR and monitor. One of the two 16 mm film projectors is broken. A few filmstrips hide in various closets. The one room that does have computers, listening centers, and film loop machines is the Chapter One lab.

Here, students with literacy and mathematics deficits receive small-group instruction and skill practice for 30 to 45 minutes each day. In a corner of the multipurpose room, 12 gifted students in grades 3 to 5 meet one morning a week with a visiting gifted and talented education teacher. Classroom teachers are responsible for all other instruction, so they rarely have time to plan or confer.

What Stewart's students learn from their encounter is that Wilson's students are underprivileged, and perhaps, undeserving. The students will probably come to see inequities as normal and to equate African Americans and Latinos with poverty.

Meanwhile, Wilson's students learn that material advantages go with being white. Since Stewart's and Wilson's students are all about the same age with similar interests and abilities, the major difference that Wilson's students can see is skin color.

The few students of color in Stewart's class learn that they are very lucky. Under other circumstances, they could be at Wilson's school. Even though they may do poorly in a predominantly white school, they regard being there as a privilege.

Teacher Education Matters

If Wilson's and Stewart's students derive naive conceptions from their exchange visits, the teachers themselves also have trouble making sense of the differences. Neither teacher learned much about cultural variation during preservice preparation (Zeichner 1992, Ladson-Billings, in press).

Wilson took an ESL course, but Stewart did not, and she has José. Both Wilson and Stewart took a required human relations course, but although it presented some historical information about Native Americans, African Americans, Asian Americans, and Latinos, it was silent on European-American cultures and the role of culture in learning and achievement. Both Wilson and Stewart believed, further, that the course was designed to make them feel guilty. As a result, they silently resisted the material, and its impact on their eventual practice was sharply reduced.

As inservice teachers, Wilson and Stewart have had some opportunities to learn about multicultural education, but these have taken the form of fleeting, one-time workshops. The experiences had little or no follow-up, and no one attempted to ensure that teachers applied the new information (Sleeter 1992).

Fortunately, one of Wilson's colleagues is a graduate student who has taken several courses dealing with race, class, and gender issues. He has learned from the experiences of two teachers like Vivian Paley (1979) and Jane Elliot (Peters 1987). Wilson's colleague is impressive because he seems to manage his classes easily, and his students achieve well on tasks that go beyond worksheets and drills. Wilson plans to enroll in a multicultural education course next semester. He hopes to learn something that will help him succeed with students of color.

While Wilson is motivated to change, Stewart is not. Because she is successful with most of her students, she thinks her lack of success with students of color stems from their deficiencies. Stewart's colleagues and the parents of her white students reinforce this belief.

Does the Race and Ethnicity of Teachers Matter?

Whether teachers' race and ethnicity affect student achievement remains an open question. We know that most teachers in the United States are white and that the next largest group, African Americans, comprise less than 5 percent of all public school teachers. We also know that the majority of students in the 25 largest public school systems are students of color.

No empirical evidence, however, indicates that students of color learn better when taught by teachers of color. The most recent review of the literature on African-American teachers (King 1993) finds no connection between teacher race/ethnicity and student achievement. The positive aspect of this finding is that it makes all teachers accountable for teaching all students.

If current demographic trends hold, our student population will become more diverse, while the teaching population remains predominantly white. The implication is that if teachers are to be effective, they will need to be prepared to teach children who are not white. If we are lucky, more teachers will follow Wilson's lead. They will

know that the multicultural education research literature can help them understand themselves, their culture, and the cultures of others, and be more successful with all students.

References
Apple, M. (1990). *Ideology and Curriculum.* 2nd ed. New York: Routledge.
Au, K., and C. Jordan. (1981). "Teaching Reading to Hawaiian Children: Finding a Culturally Appropriate Solution." In *Culture and the Bilingual Classroom: Studies in Classroom Ethnography,* edited by H. Trueba, G. Guthrie, and K. Au. Rowley, Mass.: Newbury House.
Banks, J. A. (1993a). "Multicultural Education for Young Children: Racial and Ethnic Attitudes and Their Modification." In *Handbook of Research on the Education of Young Children,* edited by B. Spodek. New York: Macmillan.
Banks, J. A. (1993b). "Multicultural Education: Development, Dimensions, and Challenges." *Phi Delta Kappan* 75: 22-28.
Birrell, J. (February 1993). "A Case Study of the Influence of Ethnic Encapsulation on a Beginning Secondary School Teacher." Paper presented at the annual meeting of the Association of Teacher Educators, Los Angeles.
Cohen, E., and J. Benton. (Fall 1988). "Making Groupwork Work." *American Educator:* 10-17, 45-46.
Cooper, H. (1979). "Pygmalion Grows Up: A Model for Teacher Expectation Communication and Performance Influence." *Review of Educational Research* 49: 389-410.
Erickson, F., and G. Mohatt. (1982). "Cultural Organization and Participation Structures in Two Classrooms of Indian Students." In *Doing the Ethnography of Schooling,* edited by G. Spindler. New York: Holt, Rinehart and Winston.
Hornberger, N. (1988). "Iman Chay'?: Quechua Children in Peru's Schools." In *School and Society: Teaching Content Through Culture,* edited by H. Trueba and C. Delgado-Gaitan. New York: Praeger.
Irvine, J. (1990). *Black Students and School Failure.* Westport, Conn.: Greenwood Press.
Jordan, C. (1985). "Translating Culture: From Ethnographic Information to Educational Program." *Anthropology and Education Quarterly* 16: 105-123.
King, J., and G. Ladson-Billings. (1990). "The Teacher Education Challenge in Elite University Settings: Developing Critical Perspectives for Teaching in Democratic and Multicultural Societies." *European Journal of Intercultural Education* 1: 15-20.
King, S. H. (1993). "The Limited Presence of African-American Teachers." *Review of Educational Research* 63: 115-149.
Kozol, J. (1991). *Savage Inequalities.* New York: Crown Publishers.
Ladson-Billings, G. (1992). "Reading Between the Lines And Pages: A Culturally Relevant Approach to Literacy Teaching." *Theory into Practice* 31: 312-320.
Ladson-Billings, G. (In press). "Multicultural Teacher Education: Research, Practice, and Policy." In *Handbook of Research in Multicultural Education,* edited by J. A. Banks and C. M. Banks. New York: Macmillan.
Lipman, P. (1993). "Teacher Ideology Toward African-American Students in Restructured Schools." Doctoral diss., University of Wisconsin-Madison.
Oakes, J. (1985). *Keeping Track: How Schools Structure Inequality.* New Haven, Conn.: Yale University Press.
Orfield, G. (1989). *Status of School Desegregation 1968-1986.* (Report of Urban Boards of Education and the National School Desegregation Research Project). Washington, D.C.: National School Boards Association.
Paley, V. (1979). *White Teacher.* Cambridge, Mass.: Harvard University Press.
Peters, W. (1987). *A Class Divided: Then and Now.* New Haven, Conn.: Yale University Press.
Scott, K. P., and C. G. Schau. (1985). "Sex Equity and Sex Bias Instructional Materials." In *Handbook for Achieving Sex Equity Through Education,* edited by S. S. Klein. Baltimore: Johns Hopkins University Press.
Slavin, R. (November 1987). "Cooperative Learning and the Cooperative School." *Educational Leadership* 45, 3: 7-13.
Sleeter, C., and C. Grant. (1988). "An Analysis of Multicultural Education in the United States." *Harvard Educational Review* 57: 421-444.
Swartz, E. (1992). "Multicultural Education: from a Compensatory to a Scholarly Foundation." In *Research and Multicultural Education: From the Margins to the Mainstream,* edited by C. Grant. London: Falmer Press.
Vogt, L., C. Jordan, and R. Tharp. (1987). "Explaining School Failure, Producing School Success: Two Cases." *Anthropology and Education Quarterly* 18: 276-286.
Winfield, L. (1986). "Teacher Beliefs Toward At-Risk Students in Inner-Urban Schools." *The Urban Review* 18: 253-267.
Zeichner, K. (1992). *Educating Teachers for Cultural Diversity.* East Lansing, Mich.: National Center for Research on Teacher Learning.

Avoiding Pseudomulticulturalism

Authentic Multicultural Activities

Gloria S. Boutte and Christine B. McCormick

Gloria S. Boutte is Assistant Professor, Early Childhood Education and Christine B. McCormick is Associate Professor, Educational Research and Psychology, University of South Carolina, Columbia.

Multiculturalism is a term that has appeared frequently in education literature during recent years. Many teachers use the term "multiculturalism," however, only to refer to isolated classroom units. Often these formal lessons center on activities such as cooking ethnic foods, examining Native American artifacts at Thanksgiving or discussing African American achievements during Black History month. Certainly, these lessons have merit; however, since they are often isolated and discontinuous, they are actually "pseudomulticultural" activities. Authentic multicultural activities are ongoing and integrated daily in both informal and formal activities.

Although an abundance of theoretical and research information on multicultural education exists, many teachers find themselves at a loss when seeking practical strategies for implementing an authentic multicultural curriculum. The complexity of this task is due, in part, to the multitude of differences among children. Moreover, understanding and appreciating others' lifestyles is often difficult because limited personal experiences inevitably influence interactions. Perspectives may also be constrained by implicit cultural assumptions (Wilson, 1989). The purpose of this article is to assist teachers in evaluating their views about cultural diversity and provide strategies that may be used in the classroom setting.

Multicultural ideas are "caught" rather than "taught"; that is, multicultural attitudes are developed through everyday experiences rather than formal lessons. Multicultural ideas and activities, therefore, should be thoroughly integrated throughout all activities every day—not only in fragmented units (Hendrick, 1990).

This article discusses six issues that will help teachers evaluate their multicultural views and practices: 1) building multicultural programs, 2) showing appreciation of differences, 3) avoiding stereotypes, 4) acknowledging differences in children, 5) discovering the diversity within the classroom and 6) avoiding pseudomulticulturalism.

Teachers need to consider each issue carefully and examine their own classrooms for pseudomulticultural practices. The commentary includes strategies to help teachers take an authentic multicultural approach. Suggested strategies are based on research, personal experiences and logic.

Building Multicultural Programs

Two basic complementary concepts should guide multicultural classrooms (Lay-Dopyera & Dopyera, 1987): 1) All people are similar in that they have the same basic needs such as water, food, shelter, respect and love and 2) different groups fulfill some of these needs in different ways (different types of houses, diets, etc.). Similarities as well as differences, therefore, should be emphasized in the classroom.

Lay-Dopyera and Dopyera (1987) recommend the following components for multicultural classrooms:

■ *Modeling by teachers.* If teachers show that they value persons of differing characteristics and backgrounds, children will sense and emulate this attitude. Teachers should model acceptance of people who look, dress or speak differently.

From *Childhood Education*, Spring 1992, pp. 140-144. Reprinted by permission of the authors and the Association for Childhood Education International, 11501 Georgia Avenue, Suite 315, Wheaton, MD. © 1992 by the Association.

■ *Curricular inclusion of multicultural heritage.* The curriculum should include religious beliefs, music, art and literature representing many cultures. The teacher should be sensitive to the fact that not all children celebrate Christmas. Some children may celebrate Kwanzaa, Hanukkah or other holidays.

■ *Multicultural literature.* Teachers should use literature that features children of differing racial characteristics, ethnic backgrounds and home circumstances. Literature that promotes stereotypes should not be used. During storytelling or similar activities, teachers should use names representative of different cultures. Avoid the "token" approach where only one person who is not a majority group member is pictured on illustrations.

■ *Multilinguistic experiences.* Children should learn different words that represent the same thing. By integrating both colloquial and non-English expressions into the curriculum, teachers can help children realize the value and fun of knowing different ways to talk. Ask children to name all the ways they know to greet someone (*Hi, Yo, Howdy, Hey, What's up?*). Then list the greetings and discuss possible reactions to unfamiliar expressions. Discussion of differences in the terminology used to refer to parents is also a good beginning activity (e.g., *Mama, Mother, M'dear, Ma*).

■ *Resource persons from different cultures.* Teachers should involve people of many different characteristics and backgrounds in classroom activities. Representatives of various cultural groups within the classroom and the community, such as local merchants, can be invited to the classroom to share African jewelry, Oriental rugs or other cultural goods. Parents may be encouraged to share a family recipe or other family traditions.

Showing Appreciation of Differences

An authentic multicultural approach is based on appreciation of differences in others. Modeling by teachers is therefore critical. Teachers do much more than help children develop basic skills; they unconsciously teach children many things—including their attitudes about people who are different from them. One salient difference found in many classrooms, for example, is a wide variety in speech patterns and dialects. Teachers should pay close attention to how they respond (both verbally and nonverbally) to children who speak differently. Young children may be unaware that they speak or behave in a way incongruent with the larger society. Minority children may inadvertently be discouraged from classroom participation because of teachers' negative reactions to their attempts. For example, if a child says, "Dere go the sto-man," the teacher should avoid interrupting the child to provide the standard English version (i.e., "You mean, there goes a man who works in a store?"). Instead, the teacher should first show appreciation for the child's contribution, then model the standard English version of the sentence or work with the child individually later (depending on the child's age and the situation).

Hispanic, Native American and African American children have been exposed to negative imagery and a sense of invisibility in school materials (Spencer & Markstrom-Adams, 1990). Teachers must make a conscious effort to ensure that all children see positive role models depicted in books, videos and other instructional materials. Children's self-esteem can be adversely affected by negative messages given on a daily basis. When teachers do not show appreciation for children's language and other cultural differences, children may conclude that their culture is inferior. These feelings of inferiority

are not easily overcome and are definitely not alleviated by isolated pseudomulticultural units.

Helping children develop behaviors and attitudes appropriate for survival in the general society while fostering unique cultural behaviors and attitudes is a complex, difficult task. Often, the two cultures may well be contradictory. In some cultures, for example, children are considered rude if they do not say "Sir" or "Ma'am" when speaking to adults. In others, it is inappropriate to maintain eye contact with adults. Multicultural teachers seek to develop an awareness of cultural practices so that the child's behavior is not misinterpreted. Rather than assuming that a child who does not maintain eye contact is sneaky or has poor self-esteem, the teacher may discuss why using eye contact at school is necessary.

In an authentic multicultural classroom, teachers demonstrate an appreciation for different viewpoints. In a social studies class, for example, students might be asked to describe the westward movement from the viewpoints of both American pioneers and Native Americans. Or when discussing the Civil War, viewpoints of Blacks and Whites from both the North and South should be considered. Instructional models (Banks, 1987; Banks & Banks, 1989) are available to assist teachers in showing appreciation for different perspectives. Banks's model emphasizes that, without lowering standards, teachers can examine information from both majority and minority perspectives.

Avoiding Stereotypes

Although most teachers intuitively realize that tremendous variation exists within each ethnic group, pervasive societal stereotypes may negatively influence teacher-child interactions. Multicultural teachers realize that there is no single entity as the "African American," "White," "Asian," "Latino" or "Native American" child. Families' economic status, values, language and degree of acculturation vary significantly within culture and socioeconomic class (Spencer & Markstrom-Adams, 1990).

To illustrate briefly the vast differences found within various ethnic groups, a summary of ethnic compositions in the United States (cited in Harrison, Wilson, Pine, Chan & Buriel, 1990) is presented in Table 1. Although Harrison et al. did not provide a breakdown of Whites, this group is equally as variable. When the differences noted in Table 1 are considered along with others discussed earlier, it becomes clear that stereotypes have no place in the classroom or society. Each child is unique.

Many group stereotypes are derived from covert or overt messages conveyed by the media (education literature included). Current research, for example, reveals the dominance of a troubling stereotype that predicts educational failure for African Americans and educational excellence for Asian Americans (Slaughter-Defoe, Nakagawa, Takanishi & Johnson, 1990). Such information is a disservice to both groups. The behavior of minority group children should be examined and appreciated in terms of what is typical for their culture rather than in comparison to the majority culture (Spencer & Markstrom-Adams, 1990). Despite the implications of models of minority education that assume some children are inferior to others (Harrison et al., 1990; Spencer & Markstrom-Adams, 1990), a child can be different from the rest of the class without being inferior. Differences should be appreciated, not denigrated.

To change stereotypical views of a particular group, the first step is for teachers to evaluate their views and feelings about their own culture and those who are different from them (Lay-Dopyera & Dopyera, 1987). All of us have biases, but it takes a concentrated effort to avoid stereotypical expectations.

To assess stereotypes in the classroom, teachers should record the frequency and type of interactions with each child. Since teachers can't always be completely aware of their behaviors, it might be useful occasionally to videotape classroom interactions. When viewing these videotapes, teachers should pay attention to whether interactions are primarily negative or positive and whether some children receive less attention than others. Are some children allowed more time to respond to questions than others? What is the composition of groups within the classroom (i.e., ability reading or math groups)? Are the "low" ability groups made up primarily of children from a particular ethnic group? If so, procedures used in assigning children to groups need to be reviewed to determine possible ethnic biases.

The realization that America is multicultural and effective communication among different cultures is essential should serve to motivate teachers to become more multicultural. Pseudomulticultural teachers are not preparing children to deal with differences. An initial step for avoiding stereotypes is to recognize and address stereotypes encountered from other teachers, students, administrators and parents. A statement such as "Chinese people eat fried rice and Mexican people eat beans" is pseudomulticultural. Qualifying the statement, however, by saying, "*Some* Chinese people eat fried rice and *some* Mexican people eat beans, but remember that most people eat many different foods" acknowledges variation within cultures.

Acknowledging Differences in Children

Children *are* different. Not only do children differ in physical characteristics, they have different cognitive, social, emotional and physical needs as well. It is precisely these

---

Table 1
Ethnic Compositions in the United States

Ethnic Group	Inclusive Groups
African Americans (not limited to Blacks)	African-Caribbean Native Africans
Native Americans/ Alaskan Natives (over 500 tribes)	Largest tribes include Cherokee, Navajo, Sioux, Chippewa/Aleuts and Eskimos
Asian Pacific Americans	Chinese, Japanese, Korean, Vietnamese, Cambodian, Thai, Filipino, Laotian, Lao-Hmong, Burmese, Samoan and Guamanian
Latino	Mexicans, Puerto Ricans, Cubans, Central and South Americans

Note: From "Family Ecologies of Ethnic Minority Children" by A. O. Harrison, M. N. Wilson, C. J. Pine, S. Q. Chan and R. Buriel, 1990, *Child Development, 61,* 347-362. Copyright 1990 by The Society for Research in Child Development, Inc. Adapted by permission.

Discovering diversity takes creativity, extra effort and diligence on the teacher's part.

differences that teachers must acknowledge and plan for accordingly. The basic premise of multiculturalism is that teachers must acknowledge and build on cultural differences. Some teachers feel uncomfortable mentioning a child's race. Unable or unwilling to see and/or acknowledge differences in children, a teacher may attempt to treat all children the same.

Additional problems arise when children's cultural differences are viewed as deficits rather than assets. Most teachers know that children have diverse needs, but probably do not adapt their teaching strategies because doing so requires a new frame of reference and additional planning. Despite the evidence that minority children do not perform or behave in the same way as their Anglo peers in the classroom (Hale-Benson, 1986), many teachers insist on trying to make the child fit the curriculum. This approach is generally ineffective. By contrast, multicultural teachers try adapting the curriculum to better fit the child's needs. Integrating aspects of the child's culture into the curriculum makes the curriculum more relevant. Children are encouraged to bring pictures of their families, share favorite stories or songs from home or participate in other similar activities. Such activities illustrate the tremendous variations in family compositions, language and traditions.

Discovering Diversity Within the Classroom

Since each child is unique, multicultural teachers must discover specifics about the child and his/her family that facilitate the learning and development of the child. Discovering diversity takes creativity, extra effort and diligence on the teacher's part. This is a teacher's "homework" and should be considered as routine preparation for teaching each year. Authentic multicultural teachers want to understand the children they teach;

therefore, they take the initiative to learn about children's backgrounds.

To be familiar with each child and understand the ecological context from which the child views the world, it is essential that teachers visit the children's homes at least once—preferably at the beginning of the year. Administrators should schedule home visits as part of a teacher's work day. During the visit, teachers should question parents about a variety of topics such as children's favorite activities, special holidays that their family celebrates or "pet" names. Additionally, it is helpful to ask parents to describe a "typical" school day and a "typical" Saturday. After the visit, teachers should visualize themselves living in each child's household for a week. This imagery exercise will provide teachers with a deeper understanding of the children.

Another way to better understand cultures is to observe various cultural differences at malls, grocery stores and other public places. Teachers should closely examine speaking patterns, nonverbal communication, hair styles, clothes fashions, eating preferences and other behaviors. Since variation exists within each ethnic group, a wide range of individuals within the ethnic group should be observed. Teachers need to develop a true appreciation of the richness in differences.

Reading about cultural differences can also add insight. Ethnographic studies on various ethnic groups (Brice, 1988; Erickson & Mohatt, 1988; Wilcox, 1988) provide a more detailed understanding of various cultures. The reader needs to be sensitive to possible unfair stereotypes in the literature. In general, multicultural teachers try to involve as many differ-

ent people from the community as possible. They discover their classroom's diversity by seeking frequent parental input (not just for parent meetings), going on field trips to ethnic restaurants and inviting community members to the class to share information. To avoid stereotyping, it is helpful to invite a number of people from the same culture who serve in different roles.

Avoiding Pseudomulticulturalism
Many teachers mistake the term "multicultural" to mean addressing only the needs of minority children (often limited to African American children). This approach is pseudomulticultural in not considering the needs of all children and in assuming that Anglo children's needs are generally taken care of in the classroom. Variation among Whites exists and should also be illustrated in the classroom. Multicultural teachers invite White parents (as well as other cultures) to the classroom to share their specific cultural heritage.

Multicultural teachers familiarize themselves with the extensive body of research that reveals that children from typically depressed ethnic groups (i.e., African Americans, Latinos and Native Americans) are disproportionately placed in special classes for mentally retarded and the learning disabled and drop out of high school at rates much higher than those of Whites (Murphy, 1986). They are aware that these children tend to score lower than White children on measures of cognitive ability and academic success. Multicultural teachers are not guided by such information; rather, they interpret the information to mean that the differences children bring to school must somehow be accommodated in the classroom. Hence, multicultural teachers seek to meet the needs of all children and expect them to reach their fullest potential.

Multicultural teachers are comfortable teaching children to be bicultural; however, they realize that modeling the behavior from the general culture may need to be accompanied by explanation of the underlying dynamics. Many minority children apparently do not readily assimilate certain behavior characteristics of the "White culture" considered necessary for success in schools and society. In a multicultural classroom, the expectations of the "White culture" need to be articulated in an overt as well as covert manner. Teachers often discuss how some behaviors are acceptable at home but not in other settings. The teacher may point out that when students nod or shake their heads or say "Uh huh" instead of answering questions clearly with a "Yes" or "No," listeners may assume that the children are not interested in the topic being discussed. The teacher may designate times for "relaxed" talk versus "business" talk.

Essentially, multicultural teachers avoid being pseudomulticultural because they have a sincere desire to treat all children with respect in as many ways as possible and as frequently as possible. Teachers who aim to do this will provide the best possible classroom experience for children.

Conclusion

The school brings together children of diverse cultures and backgrounds, and teachers have the tremendous task of teaching them. For many years the "melting pot" conception was widely accepted; people from all parts of the world were expected to give up their cultures and become "American." This has not happened. The realization that America is a multicultural society has prompted an appreciation of differences in social customs, food and even language. Rather than a "melting pot," we actually have a "tossed salad" in which every ingredient maintains its own identity, but adds a new flavor to the whole (Broman, 1982). Authentic multicultural teachers realize that each child possesses different strengths, and that all people have weaknesses. One child may be verbally precocious and another, physically adept. The combination of all strengths results in the best possible environment where each person can help someone else.

Although each person has unique cultural idiosyncrasies, working with people from distinctly different backgrounds makes one more aware of aspects of human activity that are unnoticeable until they are missing or different (Rogoff & Morelli, 1989). In an authentic multicultural classroom, such differences are appreciated. This, however, takes conscientious effort on the teacher's part. If teachers realize that their own cultural idiosyncrasies may seem strange to others, then they may begin to understand that no culture is better—just different.

References

Banks, J. A. (1987). *Teaching strategies for ethnic studies* (4th ed.). Boston: Allyn & Bacon.

Banks, J. A., & Banks, C.A. (Eds.). (1989). *Multicultural education: Issues and perspectives*. Boston: Allyn & Bacon.

Brice, S. (1988). Questioning at home and at school: A comparative study. In G. Spindler (Ed.), *Doing the ethnography of schooling* (pp. 102-131).

Prospect Heights, IL: Waveland.

Broman, B. (1982). *The early years in childhood education*. Boston: Houghton Mifflin.

Erickson, F., & Mohatt, G. (1988). Cultural organization of participation structures in two classrooms of Indian students. In G. Spindler (Ed.), *Doing the ethnography of schooling* (pp. 132-174). Prospect Heights, IL: Waveland.

Hale-Benson, J. (1986). *Black children—their roots, culture, and learning* (rev. ed.). Baltimore: Johns Hopkins Press.

Harrison, A. O., Wilson, M. N., Pine, C. J., Chan, S. Q., & Buriel, R. (1990). Family ecologies of ethnic minority children. *Child Development, 61,* 347-362.

Hendrick, J. (1990). *Total learning* (3rd ed.). Columbus: Merrill.

Lay-Dopyera, & Dopyera, J. (1987). *Becoming a teacher of young children* (3rd ed.). New York: Random House.

Murphy, D. (1986). Educational disadvantagement: Associated factors, current interventions, and implications. *Journal of Negro Education, 55,* 495-507.

Spencer, M. B., & Markstrom-Adams, C. (1990). Identity processes among racial and ethnic minority children in America. *Child Development, 61,* 290-310.

Slaughter-Defoe, D. T., Nakagawa, K., Takanishi, R., & Johnson, D. J. (1990). Toward cultural/ecological perspectives on schooling and achievement in African- and Asian-American children. *Child Development, 61,* 363-383.

Rogoff, B., & Morelli, G. (1989). Perspectives on children's development from cultural psychology. *American Psychologist, 44,* 343-348.

Wilcox, K. (1988). Differential socialization in the classroom: Implications for equal opportunity. In G. Spindler (Ed.), *Doing the ethnography of schooling* (pp. 268-309). Prospect Heights, IL: Waveland.

Wilson, M. N. (1989). Child development in the context of the black extended family. *American Psychologist, 4,* 380-385.

Student Diversity: Implications for Classroom Teachers

Daniel D. Drake

Daniel D. Drake is an associate professor in the Department of Educational Leadership at Cleveland State University and a former principal and community superintendent.

America's call for excellence and equity cannot be answered except in a diverse and culturally rich environment. The changing demographics for students in public schools, especially within metropolitan areas, demand a revised approach to the education process. Harold Hodgkinson's (1986) examination of population trends projected between 1980 and 2000 notes that "these population dynamics can already be seen in many schools. Fully 27 percent of all school students in the United States represent minorities, and each of the nation's 24 largest city school systems has a minority majority."

All classrooms today are becoming more reflective of America's multiracial and multiethnic society. According to Hodgkinson,

The schools of tomorrow may have to be more sensitive to minority differences. Many blacks resent being lumped into a single racial grouping without regard for social and economic status. Similarly, Puerto Ricans do not necessarily enjoy being labeled with Cubans and Mexicans as Hispanics. It is clear that Asian immigrants from Japan, Korea, and Vietnam are very different. All of these groups and subgroups want to retain as much of their culture as possible, which is one reason California provides instructions for connecting a gas stove in English, Spanish, Chinese, Korean, and Vietnamese.

Teachers today work with students from every continent. Such a mixture of students is sure to generate challenges related to diversity. These challenges should be addressed in a way that promotes cooperation and understanding between people of all cultures.

In an article entitled "Multicultural Education: For Freedom's Sake," James Banks (1991/1992) states that "education within a pluralistic society should affirm and help students understand their home and community cultures. However, it should also help free them from their cultural boundaries." Although parents, administrators, and other school support staff serve an important role in helping students to have a meaningful school experience, it is the teachers who are the key to successful learning and character formation. All across America, teachers create the climate for learning within the classroom. Therefore, their awareness and knowledge of the cultural differences of students in the nation's classrooms are critical factors in the educative process. In this article, I will provide suggestions for what teachers can do on Monday morning to enhance the benefits of student diversity.

Creating the most favorable climate for learning is a challenge to teachers because of the numerous variables that are involved, such as interpersonal relationships, the attitudes of students, and the development of the teachers' own abilities to interact with people from different cultures. However, teachers should settle for nothing less than a classroom environment that nurtures and values cultural differences. Valuing language differences, ethnic hairstyles, styles of dress, and attitudes toward authority are all links to addressing cultural diversity in a supportive and understanding manner. An example of attitudes toward authority would be female teachers giving directives to male students who are from a cultural orientation where women are not regarded as authority figures. The challenge is how these teachers can show sensitivity to the students' cultural orientation while using a strategy to elicit the cooperation of the students. Teachers can achieve the goal of developing an excellent learning climate by working creatively in three areas: infusing the curriculum, making instruction

From *The Clearing House*, May/June 1993, pp. 264-266. Reprinted with permission of the Helen Dwight Reid Educational Foundation. Published by Heldref Publications, 1319 Eighteenth Street, NW, Washington, DC 20036-1802. © 1993.

relevant, and implementing meaningful programs. Activities and use of supplemental materials in these areas can be initiated by teachers without policies from outside the classroom.

Infusing the Curriculum

Teachers need to ensure that their curricula are flexible, bias-free, and relevant. For instance, course materials should encompass references to males, females, and people from different ethnic and cultural groups, and teachers should address the concerns and issues of these student populations. In a recent article, Asa Hilliard III (1991/1992) indicates that "the primary goal of a pluralistic curriculum process is to present a truthful and meaningful rendition of the whole human experience." In this frame of reference, teachers should ask themselves this question: Are the study materials reflective of individuals from different cultural groups engaging in similar occupations and social roles? Unless teachers examine the materials with this concern in mind, they could miss the fact that the materials may present an overall impression that promotes a stereotypical bias. Materials on Mexico, for example, may feature what appears to be a harmless illustration of a man in a sombrero and serape dozing against the stucco wall of an adobe hut. But would this be a fair image of Mexicans? What kind of a statement does such a picture make about the people of a land that is steeped in ancient history and rich culture?

J. B. Boyer (1990) and others make a valid point when they say that if the teachers' supplemental curriculum materials ignore the existence of a student's ethnic profile, the learner gets the message that people in that ethnic group have made no contribution to the development of America. Therefore, when teachers select supplemental materials, they should include some ethnic-specific magazines, music, and audiovisuals. Examples would be *Ebony* magazine, rap mu-

sic, and films with Spanish-speaking characters. Teachers can easily work these kinds of materials into any curriculum to establish the fact that they want to develop and maintain a diverse ethnic environment within the classroom.

One way that teachers can receive assistance with their effort to address diversity in the classroom is to consult with advisory committee members and parents. Ask them to discuss aspects of the curriculum that they feel are positive with respect to diversity as well as those that are negative. Teachers should carefully analyze and use the committee's recommendations. Further preparations for working with culturally and ethnically different students include reading literature on their cultural heritage and political and economic development and being familiar with the present day successes and problems of minority groups. Teachers should openly discuss these issues with their students in order to establish a better rapport with them. Such discussions should help in making the students more receptive for learning about different cultures.

Making Instruction Relevant

Teachers need to be aware of their personal attitudes toward culturally diverse students. It is necessary to have this awareness because one's attitudes will be reflected in the instructional process. In her book, Frances Kendall (1983) indicates that teachers pass their own values and attitudes on to students both intentionally and unintentionally during the teaching and learning process. One way teachers can check on their own attitudes and values is to ask themselves a series of questions: Do I respect diversity in American society? Do I accept differences in individuals? Have I ever rejected a student's answer because I did not understand her or his frame of reference? Did I assume that the answer given by a student who used slang was wrong?

Teachers need to develop a mindset that allows them to be accepting of student differences. For instance, teachers should make sure to use examples of minority persons or groups that highlight their successes or respected positions in the community. Such practices have been identified as "culturally relevant teaching." In a recent article, Gloria Ladson-Billings (1990) describes it in this way: "It is the kind of teaching that uses the students' culture to help them achieve success. The teachers work within three important dimensions: their conception of themselves and others, their knowledge, and their classrooms' social structure."

In the development of an ideal classroom, teachers need to solicit the views of students and other advisers who are sensitive to cultural differences. A helpful exercise is to have students identify information that is culturally specific. For example, a social studies class might discuss the issue of a bilingual education program to address the needs of some Hispanics. Then, within the instructional process, put that information in the context of that community of people and have the students respond to it in ways that are meaningful to that culture. The bilingual education issue would be examined by the students in class; they would identify the barriers that could cause problems for Hispanics who are unable to speak or understand English. Because all minority persons do not have the same kinds of concerns or problems, it is unrealistic for teachers to assume that it is possible to address the needs of every student with a single approach. Teachers do not have to be experts on different cultures, but they must be sensitive to the fact that cultural differences must be respected.

Teachers should also provide opportunities for critical-thinking and problem-solving activities where no answers are labeled as incorrect. This allows students to build self-confidence. To the extent possible, teachers should use open-ended statements in their evaluations or case studies that make reference to different groups of students. Teachers' questioning techniques should personally involve the students. This practice will permit the students to respond differently, reflecting their cultural diversity for their fellow students to see and understand. Whenever possible, teachers should use resource persons from the community who are representative of the ethnic make-up of the student population. Teachers should also make sure that bulletin board displays reflect the demographic mix of the community.

A positive relationship between teachers' expectations and students' academic progress will have a positive effect on learning. Research substantiates the fact that if teachers believe that a student cannot learn or improve, then that student will not make progress. This is especially significant in the case of minority students. Therefore, teachers need to guard against giving up on a student because it appears that the student is not capable of understanding. Unconsciously the teacher may be reflecting a bias that believes that "these kinds" of kids will never learn. Teachers who have this fatalistic attitude about the amount of progress minority students can make may not go that extra step to foster school success.

Implementing Meaningful Programs

Students need to see teachers as role models who accept and value diversity. Some things that can affect their perceptions are the tone of a teacher's voice when he or she responds to certain students and the eye contact that the teacher does or does not make with students. The teacher's own belief about the value of cultural differences is reflected in such verbal and nonverbal communications. Kendall (1983) indicates that teachers are indeed role models

for students, and, therefore, they should show respect and concern for all people.

Teachers need to be honest and sincere with their students. Students will sense it. This does not mean trying to become a buddy by using their vernacular and attempting to imitate their behaviors. There should always be a social distance between teachers and students. Teachers must remember that it is far better to respect students' differences than to try to become part of the group.

A concerted effort must be made to avoid segregating students by cultural groups or allowing the students to separate themselves in this manner. Such student groupings can defeat everything else that teachers do to promote a diverse classroom. Seating should be arranged so as to encourage students to interact with one another and accept one another's differences. Role playing, in situations where students can reflect their personal perceptions of a problem and use their cultural outlook to apply a solution, is a viable way to promote the understanding of differences. Such an activity will go a long way toward developing an atmosphere conducive to educating all students.

When evaluating students, teachers need to select student assessment methods that are appropriate for the diverse student population. For instance, teachers should make sure that the language of assessment instruments is free of ethnic or cultural biases, omissions, and stereotypes. Teachers should consider and employ, when possible, multiple approaches to assessing students.

Conclusion

There is no one approach that will allow teachers to meet the needs of all students. Understanding cultural differences is part of a life-long learning process. Teachers must continue to seek opportunities that will help

them to be effective. Further, they should work to become more knowledgeable about their own attitudes toward cultural differences. As professionals, teachers cannot use the excuse of being ignorant about the problems and cultures of African Americans, Asian Americans, Spanish Americans, native Americans, and other minorities. The ethnic texture of our student population is growing more diverse, and teachers must be ready to deal with the challenges that it brings. This means that teachers will need to lean on their support systems (family, administrators, community members) as they engage in proactive ventures that are directed toward developing an ideal classroom for the students and themselves.

The best learning climate will be productive for all students, not just for minority students. In these excellent classrooms, teachers can generate experiences that promote diversity, respect, and acceptance of others while at the same time providing students with the opportunities to learn about the benefits of diversity. American school systems can no longer afford to produce citizens who are unable to value a culturally diverse world and to interact effectively in it.

REFERENCES

Banks, J. A. 1991/1992. Multicultural education: For freedom's sake. *Educational Leadership* (Dec./Jan.): 32–34.

Boyer, J. B. 1990. *Curriculum materials for ethnic diversity*. Lawrence, Kan.: University of Kansas Press.

Hilliard III, Asa G. 1991/1992. Why we must pluralize the curriculum. *Educational Leadership* (Dec./Jan.): 12–14.

Hodgkinson, H. L. 1986. What's ahead for education. *Principal* (Jan.): 6–11.

Ladson-Billings, G. 1990. Culturally relevant teaching: Effective instruction for black students. *College Board Review* (155): 2025.

Kendall, F. E. 1983. *Diversity in the classroom: A multicultural approach to the education of young children*. New York: Teachers College Press, Columbia University.

Learning and Instruction

- Information Processing/Cognitive Learning (Articles 17 and 18)
- Behavioristic Learning (Articles 19–21)
- Humanistic/Social Psychological Learning (Articles 22 and 23)
- Instructional Strategies (Articles 24–28)

Learning can be broadly defined as a relatively permanent change in behavior or thinking due to experience. Learning is not a result of change due to maturation. Changes in behavior and thinking result from complex interactions between individual characteristics of students and environmental factors. One of the continuing challenges in education is understanding these interactions so that learning can be enhanced. This section focuses on approaches within educational psychology that represent unique ways of viewing the learning process and related instructional strategies. Each approach to learning emphasizes a different set of personal and environmental factors that influence certain behaviors. While no one approach can fully explain learning, each is a valuable contribution to our knowledge about the process.

The discussion of each learning approach includes suggestions for specific techniques and methods of teaching to guide teachers in understanding student behavior and in making decisions about how to teach. The articles in this section reflect a recent emphasis on applied research conducted in schools and constructivist theories. The relatively large number of articles on information processing/cognitive learning and instruction, as opposed to behaviorism, also reflects a change in emphasis. Behaviorism, however, remains very important in our understanding of learning and instruction.

Researchers have recently made significant advances in understanding the way our minds work. Information processing refers to the way that the mind receives sensory information, stores it as memory, and recalls it for later use. This procedure is basic to all learning, no matter what teaching approach is taken, and we know that the method used in processing information determines to some extent how much and what we remember. The articles in the first subsection present some of the fundamental principles of information processing.

In cognitive learning, new knowledge is obtained as existing knowledge is reorganized, altered, and expanded. This process is often stimulated when we are presented with information that disagrees or is incompatible with knowledge we already possess. Cognitive learning of this sort is practiced continually by children as they learn about their world; they make discoveries by perceiving things that pique their curiosity or raise questions in their minds.

For years, behaviorism was the best-known approach to learning. Most practicing and prospective teachers are familiar with concepts such as classical conditioning, reinforcement, and punishment, and there is no question that behaviorism has made significant contributions to understanding learning. But behaviorism has also been subject to much misinterpretation, in part because it seems so simple. In fact, the effective use of behavioristic principles is complex and demanding, as debate presented in the articles in this subsection points out.

Humanistic/social psychological learning emphasizes the affective, social, moral, and personal development of students. Humanistic learning involves an acceptance of the uniqueness of each individual, and it stresses character, feelings, values, and self-worth. To the humanist, learning is not simply a change in behavior or thinking; learning is also the discovery of the personal meaning of information. Social psychology is the study of the nature of interpersonal relationships in social situations. In education, this approach looks at teacher-pupil relationships and group processes to derive principles of interaction that affect learning.

Instructional strategies are the teacher behaviors and methods of conveying information that affect learning. Teaching methods or techniques can vary greatly, depending on objectives, group size, types of students, and personality of the teacher. For example, discussion classes are generally more effective for enhancing thinking skills than are individualized sessions or lectures. For this subsection, we have selected some major instructional strategies to illustrate a variety of approaches. The first article in the last subsection shows how appropriate teaching techniques can be applied to develop higher-level thinking skills. This is followed by an article that describes four major instructional approaches. The next article examines the relationship between culture and learning styles, while the growing importance of technology in the classroom is reviewed in the final two articles.

Looking Ahead: Challenge Questions

Compare and contrast the different approaches to learning. What approach do you think is best? What factors are important to your answer (e.g., objectives, types of students, setting, personality of the teacher)?

What are some teaching strategies that you could use to promote greater student retention of material? What is the best way to attract and keep students' attention? Is it necessary for a teacher to be an "entertainer"?

How can a teacher promote positive self-esteem, values, character, and attitudes? How is this related to cognitive learning? How much emphasis should be put on cultivating character or positive student interactions? Do you believe cooperative learning is feasible in the grade level and subject in which you will teach? Why or why not?

What are some examples of discovery-based instructional methods? What are the advantages and disadvantages of using a Socratic style of teaching?

What are learning styles, and how can teachers use learning styles to enhance teaching effectiveness?

How can technology be used productively in the classroom? What learning theories should be used as a basis for instruction that utilizes technology?

REMEMBERING THE FORGOTTEN ART OF MEMORY

THOMAS E. SCRUGGS AND MARGO A. MASTROPIERI

Thomas E. Scruggs and Margo A. Mastropieri are professors of special education at Purdue University. Their book on memory techniques is entitled Teaching Students Ways To Remember: Strategies for Learning Mnemonically, *published in 1991 by Brookline Books, Cambridge, Massachusetts.*

IN THE fifth century B.C., the Greek poet Simonides narrowly escaped death, and in so doing provided the birth of memory strategies. Reciting a poem at a banquet, Simonides was called out of the house for a message. While he was out, the building collapsed, and the diners within were crushed beyond recognition. Asked to help identify the bodies, Simonides noted that he was able to do so by remembering an image of the diners' positions at the table. This inspiration gave birth to the *Method of Loci,* the most ancient of mnemonic techniques.

Ancient Greeks and Romans placed great value on the development of memory skills, partly because the relative lack of printed materials required individuals to commit many things to memory. Throughout the Middle Ages, complex memory strategies took on religious aspects, and sometimes became associated with individuals who dabbled in magic and the occult, such as Giordano Bruno and his secret of "Shadows."

With the development of the printing press, memory skills received less and less emphasis; nonetheless, knowledge of many of these techniques survived, such as those described in 1890 by William James in his *Principles of Psychology.* For a time in American schools, memorization and recitation of inspirational passages and quotations were considered important in developing well-trained minds. Unfortunately, the act of memorizing *per se* is not usually helpful in intellectual development; further, many of the things American schoolchildren were compelled to memorize were decontextualized and therefore of little meaning in themselves. As a result, "memorizing" began to become regarded as a pointless waste of time, as it no doubt was in many cases. Further, "progressive" educators such as John Dewey began rightly to promote the facilitation of "higher-order" thinking skills over the mindless repeti-tion of facts and passages. With the recent renewal of interest in constructivist perspectives and the rise of technological advances in information storage and retrieval, the decline of interest in memory skills has apparently become nearly complete.

With this decline in interest in memory skills, students' memory for important school content also has declined. A recent national report documented the sad fact that American students have become deficient at recall of even the most basic information about history and literature. For example, only one out of three American seventeen-year-olds could place the Civil War within the correct half-century or correctly identify the Reformation or the Magna Carta.

In this article, we wish to provide a different perspective on memory. We define memory skills as techniques for increasing the initial learning and long-term retention of important information. We argue that good memory skills are as important now as they were in Simonides' day; that memory strategy instruction has a very impor-

> ***American Students have become deficient at recall of even the most basic information about history and literature.***

tant place in schools, yet unrealized; and that good instruction in memory strategies enhances, rather than detracts from, the facilitation of "higher-order" skills such as comprehension and critical thinking. Indeed, while there are many important things to learn and do in school, and learning and retaining factual information is only one component of the entire school experience, it is our contention that a strong declarative knowledge base is an absolutely critical first step to "higher-level" skills.

Reprinted with permission from *American Educator,* Winter 1992, pp. 31-37. *American Educator,* the quarterly journal of the American Federation of Teachers.

We also provide brief descriptions of nine strategies for promoting strong memory skills.

WE BECAME aware of the critical importance of good memory skills during the course of our work with students with learning disabilities. Many learning-disabled students have some difficulty with semantic memory, or memory for verbally presented information. Clearly, such students face enormous challenges in courses that require vast amounts of verbal information to be "memorized," such as traditionally taught social studies and science courses. In addition, learning-disabled students usually perform poorly on tests of verbal reasoning or higher-order thinking skills. One explanation why these students with average intelligence may do so poorly on verbal reasoning tasks is that they can remember little verbal information to help them on the task. And, it has been well established that content knowledge is one of the best predictors of performance on reasoning tasks. When we trained students in powerful mnemonic strategies to facilitate memory of the core content, we noticed dramatic improvements in their ability not only to remember content information but also to participate actively in classroom discussions that required thinking actively about the subject.

The relation between knowledge and thinking can be further explained by an example. In a recent national educational performance test, one item presented outlines of four birds and asked students to identify the one that probably lives close to water. Students who make effective use of their reasoning abilities could consider the characteristics of such environments, observe the four bird outlines, and correctly conclude that the long-legged bird, physically equipped for wading, was the most likely choice. However, students who remembered important information about birds and their environments could easily recognize one of the birds as a heron and immediately answer the question. Thus, what is a higher-order thinking task to a student lacking background knowledge is a simple recall task to a student possessing the relevant information. As can be seen, the "reasoning" deck is stacked against the student who has not learned, or cannot remember, critical information.

Memory is not only helpful for facilitating thought about academic subjects. One of us remembers the great difficulties he had learning to sail, until he began to master the highly specialized vocabulary associated with sailing. When terms such as *sheet, jib, starboard,* and *boomvang* became automatic, he began to make rapid progress in sailing. Likewise, we found that students began to make greater progress in vocational skills when they began to learn and remember the specialized vocabulary associated with such areas as rough construction and electricity. Why does verbal knowledge seem to facilitate procedural knowledge, such as sailing and construction? Since we are accustomed to thinking in language, we find it difficult to reflect and elaborate on new information until the relevant language associated with this information has been acquired and remembered. So, it can be seen that a well-established verbal knowledge base is a prerequisite for critical or reflective thinking.

Although memory and attention are not the same thing, it is true that things are not likely to be remembered if they are not attended to in the first place.

Nor can computer data bases take the place of a broad background of knowledge committed to memory. We often here the refrain, "In a few years, all of this will be unnecessary. Students will wear on their arms a computer no larger than a wristwatch but powerful enough to contain all the information known to mankind." The problem with this line of thinking is that one needs a sufficient knowledge base to know *what* to call forth from the computer, to give form to the endless ocean of information. Research has shown that students who have the most firmly established knowledge base are the ones who can most easily assimilate and apply new information.

Unfortunately, it is not only students with learning disabilities who may find themselves weak in prior knowledge. Students from less-privileged economic backgrounds may come to school not having had the same background experiences as other students. Students for whom English is a second language may have more difficulty expressing their knowledge in English. Finally, if recent national reports are considered, many "ordinary" students exhibit a surprising lack of memory for basic information in school subjects. It seems, therefore, that the argument should not be *whether* to teach memory skills, but *how* memory skills can be best taught. Some recommendations are given in the section that follows.

OUR RESEARCH and experience have shown us that there are at least nine ways that teachers can greatly improve the ability of their students to remember. We will summarize these recommendations in order of complexity. The ninth method, promoting mnemonic strategy use, is the most complicated and will require the most explanation.

1. Promote Attention

Although memory and attention are not the same thing, it is true that things are not likely to be remembered if they are not attended to in the first place. This makes attention an important prerequisite to memory.

There are several methods for improving attention. The simplest include direct appeals ("Please pay attention to what I'm about to say") and follow-up ("What did I say was the assignment for tomorrow?"), and physical proximity to students who are likely not to pay attention. Other strategies for promoting attention include intensifying instruction, with enthusiastic teaching, use of high-intensity visual aids, and providing relevant activi-

Teachers who are expert in certain content areas may forget how difficult it is to acquire new speech sounds to represent new concepts or facts.

ties for students, rather than simple listening and note-taking. Teaching is more easily intensified by focusing on a smaller number of critical concepts than by covering a wide range of less important information.

Provide positive feedback for students when they exhibit good attending skills. For more persistent attending problems, teach self-recording of attending, e.g., by having an egg timer go off at random intervals and hav-

ACROSTICS AT HARVARD

SOURED, PERHAPS, by memories of the multiplication tables, college students hate the annual ritual of memorizing the geological time scale in introductory courses on the history of life. We professors insist, claiming this venerable sequence as our alphabet. The entries are cumbersome—Cambrian, Ordovician, Silurian—and refer to such arcana as Roman names for Wales and threefold divisions of strata in Germany. We use little tricks and enticements to encourage compliance. For years, I held a mnemonics contest for the best entry to replace the traditional and insipid "Campbell's ordinary soup does make Peter pale . . ." or the underground salacious versions that I would blush to record, even here. During political upheavals of the early seventies, my winner for epochs of the Tertiary (see table) read: "Proletarian efforts off many pig police. Right on!" The all-time champion reviewed a porno movie called *Cheap Meat*—with perfect rhyme and scansion and only one necessary neologism, easily interpreted, at the end of the third line. This entry proceeds in unconventional order, from latest to earliest, and lists all the eras first, then all the periods:

> *Cheap Meat* performs passably,
> Quenching the celibate's jejune thirst,
> Portraiture, presented massably,
> Drowning sorrow, oneness cursed.

The winner also provided an epilogue, for the epochs of the Cenozoic era:

> Rare pornography, purchased meekly
> O Erogeny, Paleobscene.*

When such blandishments fail, I always say, try an honest intellectual argument: If these names were arbitrary divisions in a smooth continuum of events unfolding through time, I would have some sympathy for the opposition—for then we might take the history of modern multicellular life, about 600 million years, and divide this time into even and arbitrary units easily remembered as 1-12 or A-L, at 50 million years per unit.

But the earth scorns our simplifications and becomes much more interesting in its derision. The

---

*There are two in jokes in this line: *orogeny* is standard geological jargon for mountain building; *Paleobscene* is awfully close to the epoch's actual name—Paleocene.

GEOLOGIC ERAS			
Era	Period	Epoch	Approximate number of years ago (millions of years)
Cenozoic	Quaternary	Holocene (Recent) Pleistocene	
	Tertiary	Pliocene Miocene Oligocene Eocene Paleocene	
Mesozoic	Cretaceous Jurassic Triassic		65
Paleozoic	Permian Carboniferous (Pennsylvanian and Mississippian) Devonian Silurian Ordovician Cambrian		225
Precambrian			570

The geological time scale.

history of life is not a continuum of development, but a record punctuated by brief, sometimes geologically instantaneous, episodes of mass extinction and subsequent diversification. The geological time scale maps this history, for fossils provide our chief criterion in fixing the temporal order of rocks. The divisions of the time scale are set at these major punctuations because extinctions and rapid diversifications leave such clear signatures in the fossil record. Hence, the time scale is not a devil's ploy for torturing students, but a chronicle of key moments in life's history. By memorizing those infernal names, you learn the major episodes of earthly time. I make no apologies for the central importance of such knowledge.

Excerpted with permission from Wonderful Life: The Burgess Shale and the Nature of History, *by Stephen Jay Gould (W. W. Norton & Company, 1989).*

ing students indicate whether or not they were paying attention at that moment.

William James argued, "My experience is what I agree to attend to." Promoting attending will not guarantee improvement in memory, but it is a great place to start.

2. Promote External Memory

One very simple way for students to remember things better is to learn to write them down and refer back when necessary. This is one method of "external memory," which refers to the use of any device outside the student's own mind used to enhance memory. External memory devices include writing things in notebooks, appointment books, or on cards; placing things to be remembered (e.g., books, notes, self-reminders) in prominent places where they will be noticed; and using physical prompts (e.g., a string on the finger, a watch placed on the opposite wrist), which remind students to think of or do some particular thing. One drawback to external memory is that it is not a substitute for truly remembered information, especially in test situations, in which use of such systems is usually considered cheating.

3. Increase Meaningfulness

Students remember familiar and meaningful information much more readily than non-meaningful information; and students often surprise us by what is not meaningful to them. The most usual way of increasing meaningfulness is to develop experiences with the things being learned and to relate new information in some way to things that are already known. For instance, in describing the components of levers, use see-saws, oars, rakes, and wheelbarrows as examples. Tie examples of abstractions, such as "torque," to everyday things the student already understands.

4. Use of Pictures or Imagery

Most information is more easily remembered when it is pictured. Pictures make concepts more concrete, and, therefore, more easily remembered. Pictures allow students to more easily employ their mental imagery, which also facilitates remembering. Pictures can be shown to all students simultaneously on the overhead or opaque projector. If information is only presented verbally, it is less likely to be stored in students' memories as images, and, therefore, may be more difficult for them to retrieve. If it is not possible to show pictures, describe the information clearly and concretely, and encourage students to make pictures in their minds. If they can draw their images clearly, they are more likely to remember them.

5. Minimize Interfering Information

Highlight the most important information and reduce the number of unnecessary digressions. Provide only the most highly relevant examples. Unfortunately, some textbooks present what appears to be an endless string of facts, concepts, and vocabulary for students to memorize; it has been reported that some science textbooks

Research has consistently indicated that mnemonic techniques help students perform better on comprehension tasks.

contain more vocabulary words than are found in foreign language texts! If you do rely on textbooks to cover important class information, prioritize the terminology, facts, and concepts to include those that you consider most important and provide special emphasis on this information.

6. Encourage Active Participation

Concepts are better remembered if students actively manipulate or otherwise act out instances or manifestations of these concepts. For instance, in science, students are more likely to remember about series and parallel circuits if they have actively created these circuits. In social studies, students are more likely to remember information if they assume roles in debating historical issues, such as the U.S. recognition of the Republic of Texas, or current events, such as United Nations policy in the Sudan. Students can also assume roles in historical problem solving, such as problems in pioneer bridge building.

7. Promote Active Learning

Encourage students to reason actively through new information. Promote deductive reasoning when appropriate. Ask students to draw conclusions for themselves rather than simply telling them the information. For example, rather than explaining to students why earthworms are found on the ground after a rainfall, or why the full moon rises shortly after sunset, ask questions intended to lead students to draw the correct conclusions for themselves.

8. Increase Practice and Review

Many teachers require information to be remembered for a weekly or unit test (e.g., spelling, science) but rarely monitor recall of that information after it has been tested. To promote long-term recall of previously learned information, isolate the most critical content and provide brief but regular reviews over a longer time period. Students can review this information individually, question each other with flash cards, ask questions from books, or review with the teacher as a whole class activity. Although finding even small amounts of additional time for such activities may seem unlikely, look for occasions for brief reviews before or after transitions (lunch, recess, assemblies) or while students are standing in line or doing other activities that take minimal mental energy.

9. Use Mnemonic Techniques

Mnemonics are systematic techniques designed to enhance memory, particularly memory for new vocabu-

OKAY, WHO REMEMBERS THE FIVE MAJOR DIVISIONS OF VERTEBRATES?

SCIENCE IS an area in which many students experience frustration and disappointment. There are many causes for this. Although science itself is a fascinating subject, many students may fail to become interested because they fail to learn and remember key concepts and vocabulary. Without this foundation, more advanced learning and meaningful applications are impossible. In other cases, the content may be too complex or abstract for some students to readily grasp. Many advocates of science education have stressed the importance of experiment and discovery in science learning. Nevertheless, many key concepts and vocabulary must first be learned to make later experiment and discovery meaningful.

Mnemonic techniques can be very effective in science teaching, since they help make complex content simpler, abstractions more concrete, and seemingly meaningless information more meaningful.

For example, life science, as typically taught, has much to do with the classification, organization, and description of living things. Therefore, much instruction in life science has to do with learning characteristics and taxonomies. This type of learning easily lends itself to mnemonic instruction.

Vertebrates. The study of vertebrates is a relatively easy unit in life science because students usually are familiar with many of the relevant concepts. In fact, most students are familiar with what a "backbone" is, although they may not know the meaning of the word "vertebrate." In this case, a keyword strategy is helpful in teaching this verbal label for an already-familiar concept.

"Dirt" can be used as a keyword for "vertebrate" because it sounds like the first syllable of vertebrate and can be pictured (e.g., a dirt pile). A picture then can show a backbone (or a vertebrate animal with an obvious backbone) sticking out of a pile of dirt, to help students remember this definition of vertebrate.

There are five major divisions of vertebrates: amphibians, fish, reptiles, birds, and mammals. Two of the five, fish and birds, are almost certainly familiar to students. Therefore, fish and birds can be shown in *mimetic* or representational pictures, and important concrete attributes, such as scales, fins, and feathers, can be portrayed within these mimetic pictures.

Reptiles are also familiar to many students. However, many other students may not know what reptiles are, or they may not know all the different types of reptiles, such as snakes, lizards, turtles, and crocodilians. If reptiles are as familiar to students as birds and fish, they can be presented in a mimetic picture. If they are less familiar, a keyword elaboration will be helpful. In this case, the word "tiles" could be a good keyword for reptiles, because it sounds like the second syllable for reptiles, and can be pictured. A picture depicting reptiles in some relationship to tiles, e.g., a picture of snakes, lizards, turtles, and crocodilians sitting on tiles, or with tiles for scales, or both, could be effective.

Possible keywords could be "bib" for amphibian (*amplifier* may also be good) and "camel" for mammal. "Bib" is an acceptable keyword because, although a short keyword for a long word, bib sounds very much like the accent-ed second syllable of amphibian. Camel is a particularly good keyword because a camel *is* a mammal.

Organization. Much of life science instruction involves teaching which of several types of plants or animals go together. With respect to the *vertebrates* examples, above, students may be required to "have the five types committed to memory." Once the names of these animals have become familiar, a first-letter strategy is appropriate. The first letters of the five vertebrates cannot be combined to make a "real" word, but together they do form the acronym (suggested by Roy Halleran) "FARM-B." Now, FARM-B does not convey any particular meaning to us, other than, say, an unusual name for a farm; nevertheless, with a little practice this can become a very effective mnemonic for retrieving *fish, amphibian, reptile, mammal, bird.* To integrate this idea with the concept "vertebrate," place a picture of each animal on a pile of *dirt* (keyword for vertebrate). Also, to reinforce the keywords in the acoustically transformed animal names, show the amphibian with a *bib*, the reptile on *tiles*, and a camel for the *mammal.*

Excerpted from Teaching Students Ways To Remember: Strategies for Learning Mnemonically.

Types of Vertebrates = Fish, Amphibians (bib), Reptiles (tiles), Mammals (camel), Birds (FARM-B)

lary or terminology, facts, and concepts. They are most effective, and most appropriate, when used to facilitate memory of things that cannot be deduced or otherwise constructed by students. Examples include remembering the seemingly arbitrary speech sounds in new vocabulary or terminology, human conventions, or basic facts such as the number and names of continents or planets.

Teachers who are expert in certain content areas may forget how difficult it is to acquire new speech sounds to represent new concepts or facts. Mnemonics often work by impacting on retrieval of the *acoustic properties,* or sounds, of unfamiliar words. A retrieval route is constructed between the sound of the word and the underlying meaning or conceptualization. Mnemonic techniques have been studied empirically over the past two decades and have been shown to be remarkably facilitative in promoting memory objectives.

In our recent book, *Teaching Students Ways to Remember: Strategies for Learning Mnemonically* (Cambridge, MA: Brookline Books), we describe a variety of effective mnemonic techniques and provide examples of how they can be applied in classroom settings. We will provide here some examples of *keyword, pegword,* and *letter* mnemonic strategies.

Keyword strategies. Keyword strategies are employed by creating an acoustically similar proxy (the keyword) for a new vocabulary word, proper name, fact or concept, and linking the keyword to the relevant associated information through an interactive picture or image. For instance, to help students remember that ranid (rā′nid) refers to the family of typical frogs, create a keyword for ranid that sounds like ranid and is easily pictured, e.g., *rain*. Then, show the rain and the frog interacting in a picture, e.g., a *frog* in the *rain.* Then remind students, when they hear the word ranid, think of the keyword, rain, think of the picture with rain in it, think what else was in the picture, and retrieve the response, *frog.* Have students practice until they can retrieve the information backwards, i.e., frog = ranid. For another example, to help students remember that *olfactory* refers to *sense of smell,* create a keyword for olfactory, e.g., "oil factory," and show or prompt imagery of a *smelly oil factory.* Verbal elaboration is also helpful. In this case, a person could be pictured walking past a smelly oil factory, holding his nose, and commenting, "That *oil factory* is bothering my *olfactory* sense!" When students hear the word olfactory, they can think of the keyword, oil factory, think of the picture of the smelly oil factory, and remember that olfactory referred to sense of smell. Keywords can also be used to promote foreign vocabulary learning and to help remember the names of important people and places in history. In a recent investigation, we found that pictured keywords for place names (e.g., Ticonderoga = Tiger) on maps promoted better recall of historical locations than the place names alone.

Pegwords. Pegwords are rhyming proxies (one is *bun,* two is *shoe,* three is *tree,* etc.) for numbers and are used in remembering numbered or ordered information.

For example, to help students remember that a *rake* is an example of a third-class lever, show a picture of a rake leaning against a *tree* (pegword for three). To help them remember that a wheelbarrow is an example of a second-class lever, show a picture of a wheelbarrow on a *shoe* (pegword for two).

Letter strategies. Letter strategies, particularly acronyms, are the strategies most commonly used by adults to remember things in clusters or series. Most everyone knows the HOMES strategy for remembering the names of the Great Lakes or that the name ROY G. BIV can help retrieve the colors of the spectrum. Acronyms can also be combined with keywords and pegwords. For example, you can help students remember the names of countries in the World War I Central Powers Alliance by using the acronym TAG (T = Turkey, A = Austria-Hungary, G = Germany). This acronym can be linked to the Central Powers by depicting children playing TAG in Central Park (keyword for Central Powers). To remember freedoms guaranteed by the First Amendment to the Constitution, have students think of a contemporary singer who RAPS (R = religion, A = assembly and petition, P = press, S = speech). To effectively tie these freedoms to the First Amendment, portray a singer who RAPS about *buns* (pegword for one).

In addition to acronyms are acrostics, which expand rather than condense representations. One example is *My Very Educated Mother Just Served Us Nine Pizzas,"* to represent the planets in order from the Sun: Mercury, Venus, Earth, Mars, Jupiter, Saturn, Uranus, Neptune, Pluto. Another is "King Phillip's Class Ordered a Family of Gentle Spaniels," to remember the classifications Kingdom, Phylum, Class, Order, Family, Genus, and Species, in order. Letter strategies are helpful whenever information can be clustered and when the information itself is relatively familiar.

IN SPITE of their success in facilitating memory, mnemonic techniques have often been criticized for promoting simple recall at the expense of conceptual understanding. However, research has consistently indicated that mnemonic techniques do not inhibit comprehension and actually help students perform better on comprehension tasks, probably because students employing these techniques can use more information in answering questions. Of course, it is possible to remember information that is not comprehended, and it is advisable to ensure that all information to be remembered is meaningful to students and that coursework is not overloaded with excessive amounts of facts and vocabulary to be memorized. On the other hand, it is not possible to comprehend or use information that is not remembered. To address this potential problem, memory strategies are appropriate.

Good memory skills have benefited humanity for thousands of years, and no doubt will continue to do so for thousands more. Although memory objectives can certainly be overemphasized in school settings, it is time to place appropriate emphasis on the importance of memory in school learning, as well as the skills that allow us to remember effectively.

The Mind's Journey from Novice to Expert

If We Know the Route, We Can Help Students Negotiate Their Way

John T. Bruer

John T. Bruer is president of the James S. McDonnell Foundation, St. Louis, Missouri. This article is adapted, with permission, from his book Schools for Thought: A Science of Learning in the Classroom *(The MIT Press: A Bradford Book). Copyright 1993 Massachusetts Institute of Technology.*

CHARLES IS in the seventh grade. He has an IQ of 70 and reads at the third-grade level. He has had several years of remedial reading instruction in a public school, but seems to make little progress. Charles has sufficient decoding skills to read aloud, but has almost no comprehension of what he reads. He is representative of many students who will fail—students whom our educational system can't reach.

Teachers report that they often see students who are unable to comprehend written language. What is odd is that these children can tell stories and often have no trouble understanding spoken language. This suggests they do have language comprehension skills and at least some background knowledge about the world, but cannot bring these skills and knowledge to bear on written language. Sometimes they can even read aloud, but still have difficulty understanding what they have read. Obviously, standard reading instruction has failed these students in a fundamental way.

On the first day of a new remedial reading program,

the teacher asked Charles to read a short passage about reptiles. To see if he understood the passage, the teacher asked him to formulate a question based on the passage, a question that might appear on a test. Although he tried, he couldn't think of a question and gave up. He had not understood and retained enough of what he had just read to frame a question about it.

After 15 days in the new remedial program, the teacher and Charles repeated this exercise. After Charles had read a passage about Antarctic research, he immediately offered the question "Why do scientists come to the South Pole to study?" By this time he also had raised his comprehension scores on the reading passages from 40 to 75 percent, an average performance level for a seventh-grader. On comprehension tests given in his regular classroom, he improved from the 25th to the 78th percentile in social science and from the 5th to the 69th percentile in science. At the end of the 20-day program he had gained 20 months on standardized reading comprehension tests, and he maintained this improvement long after his remedial instruction ended.

Charles was the beneficiary of *reciprocal teaching,* a method that applies results of cognitive research to reading instruction. To understand what lies behind this method, we have to go back more than three decades to the beginning of what has come to be called the cognitive science revolution.

In 1956, a group of psychologists, linguists, and computer scientists met at the Massachusetts Institute of Technology for a symposium on information science (Gardner 1985). This three-day meeting was the beginning of the cognitive revolution in psychology, a revolution that eventually replaced behaviorist psychology with a science of the mind. In essence, the revolutionaries claimed that human minds and computers are sufficiently similar that a single theory—the theory of computation—could guide research in both psychology and computer science. "The basic point of view inhabiting our work," wrote two of the participants, "has been that the programmed computer and human problem solver are both species belonging to the genus IPS" (Newell and Simon 1972, p. 870). Both are species of the genus *information-processing system;* both are devices that process symbols.

That scientific revolution became a movement, and eventually a discipline, called cognitive science. Cognitive scientists study how our minds work—how we think, remember, and learn. Their studies have profound implications for restructuring schools and improving learning environments. Cognitive science—the science of mind—can give us an applied science of learning and instruction. Teaching methods based on this research—methods that result in some sixth-graders' having a better understanding of Newtonian physics than most high school students, or that, as recounted above, help remedial students raise their reading comprehension scores four grade levels after 20 days of instruction—are the educational equivalents of polio vaccine and penicillin. Yet few outside the educational research community are aware of these breakthroughs or understand the research that makes them possible.

Certainly cognitive science, or even educational research in general, isn't the sole answer to all our educational problems. Yet it has to be part of any attempt to improve educational practice and to restructure our schools. The science of mind can guide educational practice in much the same way that biology guides medical practice. There is more to medicine than biology, but basic medical science drives progress and helps doctors make decisions that promote their patients' physical well-being. Similarly, there is more to education than cognition, but cognitive science can drive progress and help teachers make decisions that promote their students' educational well-being.

In the years following the MIT symposium, cognitive scientists worked to exploit the similarities between thinking and information processing. Allen Newell and Herbert Simon developed the first working artificial intelligence computer program, called the Logic Theorist. It could prove logical theorems using methods a human expert might use. Besides logic, Newell and Simon studied problem solving in other areas, ranging from tic-tac-toe to arithmetic puzzles to chess. Problem solving in each of these areas depends on learning facts, skills, and strategies that are unique to the area. As cognitive scientists say, expertise in each area requires mastery of a distinct knowledge *domain.* Cognitive research began to have relevance for education as scientists gradually started to study knowledge domains that are included in school instruction—math, science, reading, and writing.

In their 1972 book *Human Problem Solving,* Newell and Simon summarized the results of this early research program and established a theoretical outlook and research methods that would guide much of the work that now has educational significance. Newell and Simon argued that if we want to understand learning in a domain, we have to start with a detailed analysis of how people solve problems in that domain. The first step is to try to discover the mental processes, or programs, that individuals use to solve a problem. To do this, cognitive scientists give a person a problem and observe everything the subject does and says while attempting a solution. Newell and Simon prompted their subjects to "think aloud"—to say everything that passed through their minds as they worked on the problems. Cognitive psychologists call these "think-aloud" data *protocols.* Analysis of the protocols allows cognitive scientists to form hypotheses about what program an individual uses to solve a problem. Cognitive scientists can test their hypotheses by writing computer programs based on their hypotheses to simulate the subject's problem-solving performance. If the scientists' analysis is correct, the computer simulation should perform the same way the human did on the problem. If the simulation fails, the scientists revise their hypotheses accordingly and try again. After studying and simulating performances from a variety of subjects, Newell and Simon could trace individual differences in problem-solving performance to specific differences in the mental programs the subjects used.

To be sure they could find clear-cut differences among individual programs, Newell and Simon initially compared the problem-solving performances of experts and novices—which were almost certain to be different—in a variety of domains. In such studies (now a mainstay of the discipline), cognitive scientists consider any individual who is highly skilled or knowledgeable in a given domain to be an "expert" in that domain. The domains can be ordinary and commonplace; they don't have to be arcane and esoteric. In the cognitive scientists' sense of the word, there are experts at tic-tac-toe, third-grade arithmetic, and high school physics. Comparing experts with novices makes it possible to specify how experts and novices differ in understanding, storing, recalling, and manipulating knowledge during problem solving.

Of course Newell and Simon knew that experts in a

domain would be better at solving problems in that domain than novices, but it was not always obvious how experts and novices actually differed in their problem-solving behavior. In one early expert-novice study, Simon and Chase (1973) looked at chess players. One thing we do when playing chess is to choose our next move by trying to anticipate what our opponent's countermove might be, how we might respond to that move, how the opponent might counter, and so on. That is, we try to plan several moves ahead. One might think that experts and novices differ in how far ahead they plan: a novice might look ahead two or three moves, an expert ten or twelve. Surprisingly, Simon and Chase found that experts and novices both look ahead only two or three moves. The difference is that experts consider and choose from among vastly superior moves. When expert chess players look at a board, they see configurations and familiar patterns of pieces; they see "chunks" of relevant information. Novices, in contrast, see individual pieces. The experts' more effective, more information-rich chunks allow them to see superior possible moves and choose the best of these. Chunking, rather than planning farther ahead, accounts for the experts' superiority. Experts process more and better information about the next few moves than novices.

Newell and Simon's emphasis on problem-solving performance and expert-novice differences was a first step toward a new understanding of learning. In short, learning is the process by which novices become experts. As one learns chess, math, or physics, one's problem-solving performance in the domain improves as the programs one uses to solve problems improve. If we know what programs a person first uses to solve problems in a domain, and if we can compare them with the programs the person eventually constructs, we have a measure and a description of what the person learned. We can study learning by tracing changes in the mental processes students use as they progress from novice to higher levels of proficiency. If we have detailed knowledge of these processes, such as the computer simulations give us, we can know not only that learning has occurred but also *how* it has occurred.

Other investigators joined in the program that Newell and Simon had outlined, and the research developed and expanded along two dimensions.

First, the kinds of problems and tasks the scientists studied became more complex. To play games and solve puzzles, even in logic and chess, one has to know a few rules, but one doesn't need much factual knowledge about the world. As cognitive scientists honed their methods on puzzle problems and accumulated insights into how people solve them, they became more ambitious and began applying their methods to more knowledge-rich domains. They started to study problem solving in physics, mathematics, and medical diagnosis. They began to study language skills, such as reading and writing, and how students use these skills to acquire more knowledge. Extending their research into these domains made it applicable to understanding expert and novice performance in school subjects.

Second, the research evolved from merely comparing novices against experts to studying the process by which novices *become* experts. Psychologists began to develop intermediate models of problem-solving performance in a variety of domains. The intermediate models describe how domain expertise *develops* over time and with experience. If learning is the process by which novices become experts, a sequence of intermediate models in a domain traces the learning process in that domain. The intermediate models describe the stages through which students progress in school.

By the mid 1970s, cognitive scientists were studying school tasks over a range of competencies—from novice to expert, from pre-school through college. In many subject areas, our knowledge of students' cognitive processes is now sufficiently detailed that we can begin to describe their performance at every level of competence, from novice to expert. We can describe the normal trajectory of learning in these subject areas. If we understand the mental processes that underlie expert performance in school subjects, we can ask and answer other questions that are important for education. How do students acquire these processes? Do certain instructional methods help students acquire these processes more quickly or more easily? Can we help students learn better? Answers to these questions can guide educational practice and school reform. For example, research in science learning shows that novices—and all beginning students are novices—hold naive theories about how the physical world works. These theories so influence how the students interpret school instruction that the instruction is often ineffective. Curricula based on cognitive research that build from and correct these naive theories can overcome this problem.

Later in this article, we will see how researchers and teachers are applying the new learning theory to create classroom environments in which students are successfully moving along the path from novice to expert. But first let's look at how cognitive scientists work and how their results can contribute to better instructional methods.

II.

Balance-Scale Problems: A Classic Study of Novice-to-Expert Performance

Research on how children learn to solve balance-scale problems illustrates the main ideas, methods, and instructional applications of cognitive science.

Try to solve the balance-scale problem shown in Figure 1. Assume the scale's arm is locked so that it can't rotate around the fulcrum. If I were to unlock the arm, what would happen? Would the scale tip left, tip right, or balance?

This is a tricky problem. Rule IV in Figure 1 gives a set of rules one might use to solve it. Each rule has an IF clause that states the conditions under which the rule is applicable and a THEN clause that states what to do under those conditions. To use these rules, find the rule whose conditions fit the pattern of weights and distances in the problem. You find that P4 is the only rule whose IF clause fits the problem. Its THEN clause tells you to compute torques for each side; that is, for each side, multiply the number of weights by their distance from the fulcrum. Doing that gives $t_1 = 5 \times 3 = 15$ for the left side and $t_2 = 4 \times 4 = 16$ for the right. These new data satisfy the condition for P7; executing its THEN clause gives the correct answer, "Right side down." Some readers might remember the THEN clause in P4 from high school physics as a version of the law of torques: Multiply weight by distance on each arm to find the torque, or rotational force; the side with the larger torque goes down. This simple law solves all balance-scale problems.

The set of rules is an English-language version of a computer program for solving balance-scale problems. It takes as input data about the weight on each side of the scale and the distance of the weight from the fulcrum. The output is the answer for a balance-scale problem: tip left, tip right, or balance. The program is a series of IF-THEN rules. Computer scientists call the IF clauses *conditions,* the THEN clauses *actions,* and the entire IF-THEN statement a *production rule.* They call computer programs written using only production rules *production systems.* Computing devices that execute production systems efficiently have a specific internal structure (or *architecture,* as computer scientists say).

Cognitive scientists claim that the human mind can be described as a computing device that builds and executes production-system programs. In fact, rule IV is a production system an expert would use to solve balance-scale problems. Robert Siegler, a cognitive psychologist, showed that production systems can simulate human performance on such problems (Siegler 1976; Klahr and Siegler 1978; Siegler and Klahr 1982). He also showed that a series of increasingly complex production systems can model the way in which children gradually develop expertise on balance-scale problems from ages 5 through 17. Children learn, says Siegler, by adding better rules to their production systems. Proper instruction, he goes on to show, can help children acquire these better rules.

The beauty of the balance-scale task for developmental psychology is that it is complex enough to be interesting but simple enough for exhaustive task analysis. Two variables are relevant: the amount of weight on each arm and the distance of the weight from the fulcrum. There are three discrete outcomes: tip left, tip right, and balance. There is a simple law, the law of torques, that solves all balance-scale problems, though few of us discover this law on our own. If weight and distance are the only two relevant variables and if the scale either tips or balances, there are only six possible kinds of balance-scale problems:

■ balance problems—equal weight on each side and the weights at equal distances from the fulcrum;

■ weight problems—unequal weight on each side and the weights at equal distance from the fulcrum;

■ distance problems—equal weight on each side and the weights at unequal distances from the fulcrum;

■ conflict-weight—one side has more weight, the other side has its weight at a greater distance from the fulcrum, and the side with greater weight goes down;

■ conflict-distance—one side has more weight, the other side has its weight at a greater distance from the fulcrum, and the side with greater distance goes down;

■ conflict-balance—one side has more weight, the other side has its weight at a greater distance from the fulcrum, and the scale balances.

Siegler called the last three types "conflict" problems, because when one side has more weight but the other side has its weight farther from the fulcrum one can have conflicting intuitions about which variable dominates. (The problem illustrated in Figure 1 is a conflict-distance problem: there is more weight on the left side, the weight is farther from the fulcrum on the right side, and the right side goes down.)

These six possibilities cover all possible cases for how weight and distance influence the action of the scale. The six cases provide a complete theory, or task analysis, of the balance scale. Notice that the six problem types place varying demands on the solver. For a balance problem or a weight problem, a solver need only consider weight. For the conflict problems, a solver has to pay attention to weight, distance, and the ways in which weight and distance interact.

Siegler formulated some psychological hypotheses about how people might solve balance-scale problems. Using the information from the task analysis, he could test his hypotheses by giving subjects problems and observing their performance. Siegler called his hypotheses "rules" and formulated them as four production-system programs (see Figure 1).

The rules make different assumptions about how and when people use weight or distance information to solve the problems. Rule I considers only weight. Rule II considers distance, but only when the weights on the two sides are equal (P3). Rule III attempts to integrate weight and distance information (P4 and P5). Rule IV introduces the law of torques (P4) when one side has more weight but less distance.

If children use Siegler's rules, then the pattern of a child's responses to a set of balance-scale problems that contains all six types will reveal what rule that child uses. Children's responses will tell us what they know about the balance-scale task, including what information—weight, distance, or both—they use to solve the problem. Siegler tested his hypotheses and predictions by giving a battery of 30 balance-scale problems (five of each of the six kinds) to a group of 40 children that included equal numbers of 5-year-olds, 9-year-olds, 13-year-olds, and 17-year-olds. He showed each child a balance scale that had weights placed on it and asked the child to predict what the scale would do. As soon as the child made a prediction, Siegler rearranged the weights for the next problem. He did not let the children see if their predictions were correct, because he wanted to find out what they knew initially. He wanted to avoid giving the students feedback on their performance so he could be sure they weren't learning about the task during the experiment. He wanted to look at their learning, but only after he assessed their initial understanding.

The children's performance confirmed Siegler's hypotheses. Ninety percent of them made predictions that followed the pattern associated with one of the four rules.

WILL THE SCALE TIP LEFT, TIP RIGHT, OR BALANCE?

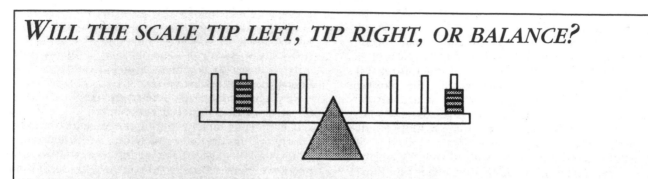

The 5-year-old—who considers only weight—says the left side will go down. The 13-year-old—who understands there's a conflict here but doesn't know how to figure it out—makes an educated guess. The expert, invoking the law of torques, says the right side will go down.

This is a classic example of novice-to-expert progression. Young children develop simple rules that will work with simple problems. Some children modify those rules when they encounter problems their current rules can't solve. Other children don't. By knowing in some detail what stages children typically pass through on their mental journeys from novice to expert—including the roadblocks and deadends—we can help them progress along the path.

RULE I

P1   **IF** weight is the same
THEN say "balance."

P2   **IF** side X has more weight
THEN say "X down."

> This is the rule that 5-year-olds most often use—for *all* problems. They only consider weight; they don't really notice the distance the weight is from the fulcrum.

RULE II

P1   **IF** weight is the same
THEN say "balance."

P2   **IF** side X has more weight
THEN say "X down."

P3   **IF** weight is the same **AND** side X has more distance
THEN say "X down."

> As children progress, they begin to consider distance, but only when the weights on the two sides are equal.

RULE III

P1   **IF** weight is the same
THEN say "balance."

P2   **IF** side X has more weight
THEN say "X down."

P3   **IF** weight is the same **AND** side X has more distance
THEN say "X down."

P4   **IF** side X has more weight **AND** side X has less distance
THEN make an educated guess.

P5   **IF** side X has more weight **AND** side X has more distance
THEN say "X down."

> By age 13, almost all are using this rule, and—with the proper kind of instruction—5 and 8-year olds can be taught to use it. Notice in P4 that the Rule III user can only make an educated guess when it comes to solving problems where one side has more weight but less distance.

RULE IV

P1   **IF** weight is the same
THEN say "balance."

P2   **IF** side X has more weight
THEN say "X down."

P3   **IF** weight is the same **AND** side X has more distance
THEN say "X down."

P4   **IF** side X has more weight **AND** side X has less distance
THEN compute torques: $t_1 = w_1 \times d_1$; $t_2 = w_2 \times d_2$.

P5   **IF** side X has more weight **AND** side X has more distance
THEN say "X down."

P6   **IF** the torques are equal
THEN say "balance."

P7   **IF** side X has more torque
THEN say "X down."

> This is the set of rules an expert might use. Now P4 has progressed from an educated guess to the law of torques: Multiply weight by distance on each arm to find the torque; the side with the larger torque goes down. The expert doesn't always use P4; only when the easier rules won't suffice. Almost no one progresses to Rule IV spontaneously, that is, without being taught.

Figure 1

Siegler's rules I-IV for the balance-scale task. (From Siegler and Klahr 1982, p. 198. Used with permission of Lawrence Erlbaum Associates.) Commentary by John T. Bruer.

There was also a strong developmental trend. The 5-year-olds most often used rule I. The 9-year-olds used rule II or rule III. The 13- and 17-year-olds used rule III. Only two children, a 9-year-old and a 17-year-old, used rule IV.

Taken together, Siegler's four rules constitute a developmental theory that explains development in terms of changes in children's knowledge structures and how they initially encode, or as cognitive psychologists say, *represent* problems. By age 5, most children are using rule I. By age 13, almost all are using rule III. Few children spontaneously progress to rule IV, the expert-level rule for the balance scale. Thus, the rules chart a course of normal development on the task, from novice to expert performance.

Siegler's rules also tell us what cognitive changes underlie the transition from novice to expert. On tasks like the balance scale, children progress through a series of partial understandings that gradually approach mastery. Performance improves, or learning occurs, when children add more effective production rules to the theories they have stored in their long-term memories. If we know what the developmental stages are and how they differ at the level of detail provided by a cognitive theory, we ought to be able to design instruction to help children advance from one stage to the next.

To investigate how children learn about the balance scale, Siegler conducted a training study. Working with 5-year-olds and 8-year-olds, all of whom used rule I, he had each child make predictions for 16 problems. After each prediction, Siegler released the lock on the balance scale and let the child see if his or her prediction was correct. This feedback experience gave the children an opportunity to learn about the balance scale. Two days later, the children had a retest with no feedback to see if they had learned anything from the training.

In this experiment, there were three training groups. One group of 5- and 8-year-olds served as a control group. Their training session consisted only of balance and weight problems—problems they could solve using rule I. A second group had training on distance problems, where rule II, but not rule I, would work. A third group had training on conflict problems, which require at least rule III for performance even at chance levels. With this training, would the children learn anything? Would they progress from rule I to a more advanced rule?

As expected, the children in the control group made no progress. They learned nothing from training on problems they already knew how to solve. The children in the second group, both 5- and 8-year-olds trained on distance problems, did learn something. Feedback from 16 problems was enough for these children to advance from rule I to rule II. The surprise came with the third group, the children who had training on conflict problems. The 8-year-olds in this group advanced two levels in their mastery of the balance scale, from rule I to rule III. *The 5-year-olds in this group either stayed at rule I or became so confused and erratic that it appeared they were no longer using a rule.*

To find out why the 8-year-olds learned and the 5-year-olds didn't, Siegler and his collaborators selected several children between 5 and 10 years old for in-depth study (Klahr and Siegler 1978). Each child had a training ses-sion with the balance scale that included conflict problems. In the training session the child was asked to make a prediction for each problem and to state his or her reasons for the prediction. The experimenter then unlocked the scale's arm and the child observed the result. If the prediction was not borne out, the experimenter asked "Why do you think that happened?" The researchers videotaped the entire session with each child and transcribed all the children's verbal responses, which provided data for protocol analysis.

Lisa, a typical 5-year-old, took 30 minutes to do 16 problems. Protocols like Lisa's suggested that the younger children were not encoding or representing distance in their initial interpretations of balance-scale problems. For example, when Lisa was given a distance problem (on the left side, one weight on peg 3; on the right side, one weight on peg 1), she predicted the scale would balance—"They would both stay up," she said. Asked why she thought this she answered "'Cause they are both the same." When she saw the left side tip down, she was genuinely puzzled: "Well, why are they both the same thing and one's up and one's down?" Lisa did not see any difference between the two sides. She was not including distance information in her initial representation of the problem. She simply did not notice and encode distance information.

An 8-year-old's protocol gave very different data. Jan was given a conflict-distance problem: on the left side, three weights on the first peg; on the right side, two weights on the third peg. She predicted incorrectly that the left side would go down. When shown what really happens (right side down) and asked for an explanation, she gave one involving both weight and distance. For her, pegs 1 and 2 on each side were "near" the fulcrum and pegs 3 and 4 were "far" from the fulcrum. She stated a rule: "If far pegs have weights, then that side will go down." She then pointed out that in this problem the far pegs on the right side had weights but the far pegs on the left had none, so the right side would go down. Jan's is not a perfect explanation, nor is her rule always true. Her protocol shows, though, that she, unlike Lisa, had noticed and encoded both weight and distance information in her representation of the problem.

On the basis of the protocols, the difference between 5-year-olds and 8-year-olds seemed to be that the younger children saw the problems in terms of weight only, whereas the older children could see the problems in terms of weight at a distance from the fulcrum. If the younger children were not encoding distance, they could not learn from training on conflict problems that differences in distance sometimes overcome differences in weight. They could not develop the concepts or—similar to the chess expert—build the chunks they needed for the conditions of P4 and P5 in rule III. On the other hand, the older children, even if they were using rule I, appeared to encode distance. They could learn from training on conflict problems how to use that information to build new productions and progress to rule III.

Can 5-year-olds learn to encode both weight and distance, or is it beyond their level of cognitive development? Siegler found that giving 5-year-olds more time to study the configurations or giving them more explicit instructions ("See how the weights are on the pegs? See how many are on each side and how far they are from the center on each side?") made no difference in their ability to reproduce the configurations from memory.

Only one intervention seemed to work. *The 5-year-olds had to be told explicitly what to encode and how to encode it.* The instructor had to tell them what was important and teach them a strategy for remembering it. The instructor taught the children to count the disks on the left side, count the pegs on the left side, and then rehearse the result (i.e., say aloud "three weights on peg 4"); to repeat this process for the right side; and then to rehearse both results together ("three weights on peg 4 and two weights on peg 3"). The instructor then told the children to try to reproduce the pattern their statement described. The instructor guided each child through this strategy on seven problems. With each problem, the children took more responsibility for executing the strategy.

After this training, the 5-year-olds' performance on reconstructing distance information from memory improved. They now correctly reproduced weight information 52 percent of the time, and distance information 51 percent of the time. Although they now apparently encoded the information, they, like the 8-year-old rule I users, did not spontaneously start using it. They continued to use rule I. However, when these 5-year-olds were given training on conflict problems, they too progressed from rule I to rule III. They had to be taught explicitly what representation, or encoding, to use in order to learn from the training experience.

The results of this study exemplify features of learning that are common to almost all school subjects. Students learn by modifying long-term memory structures, here called production systems. They modify their structures when they encounter problems their current rules can't solve. Some children modify their structures spontaneously; that is how children normally develop through Siegler's four rules. But by giving appropriate training we can facilitate children's development. For some children, presenting anomalous problems is enough. Like the 8-year-olds confronted with conflict problems, some children can build better rules when challenged with hard problems. Other children can't. Some children have inadequate initial representations of the problem. Children have to notice the information they need and encode it if they are to build better rules.

Poor readers executed a 'once-over, desperate, nonfocused read.'

Students who can't learn spontaneously from new experiences need direct instruction about the relevant facts *and* about the strategies to use. Teaching just facts or teaching strategies in isolation from the facts won't work. To know when and how to intervene, we have to understand, in some detail, what stages children pass through on their mental journeys from novice to expert. Cognitive science tells us how we can then help children progress from relative naivete through a series of partial understandings to eventual subject mastery.

The difficulties children have in learning about the balance scale are highly similar to the difficulties they encounter in learning mathematics, science, and literacy skills. The tasks, representations, and production systems will become more complex—the progression from novice to expert can't be captured by four rules in every domain. However, our innate cognitive architecture remains the same no matter what domain we try to master, and the methods of cognitive science yield detailed information about how we think and learn. The lessons learned on the simple balance scale apply across the curriculum.

III.

What Does Expertise Consist Of?

Imagine that a small, peaceful country is being threatened by a large, belligerent neighbor. The small country is unprepared historically, temperamentally, and militarily to defend itself; however, it has among its citizens the world's reigning chess champion. The prime minister decides that his country's only chance is to outwit its aggressive neighbor. Reasoning that the chess champion is a formidable strategic thinker and a deft tactician—a highly intelligent, highly skilled problem solver—the prime minister asks him to assume responsibility for defending the country. Can the chess champion save his country from invasion?

This scenario is not a plot from a Franz Lehar operetta, but a thought experiment devised by David Perkins and Gavriel Salomon (1989). As they point out, our predictions about the chess champion's performance as national security chief depend on what we believe intelligence and expertise are. If the goal of education is to develop our children into intelligent subject-matter experts, our predictions about the chess champion, based on what we believe about intelligence and expertise, have implications for what we should do in our schools.

Since the mid 1950s cognitive science has contributed to the formulation and evolution of theories of intelligence, and so to our understanding of what causes skilled cognitive performance and what should be taught in schools. In this section, we will review how our understanding of intelligence and expertise has evolved over the past two decades and see how these theories have influenced educational policy and practice.

Four theories will figure in this story.

The oldest theory maintains that a student builds up his or her intellect by mastering formal disciplines, such as Latin, Greek, logic, and maybe chess. These subjects build minds as barbells build muscles. On this theory the chess champion might succeed in the national security field. If this theory is correct, these formal disciplines should figure centrally in school instruction.

At the turn of the twentieth century, when Edward Thorndike did his work, this was the prevailing view. Thorndike, however, noted that no one had presented scientific evidence to support this view. Thorndike reasoned that if learning Latin strengthens general mental functioning, then students who had learned Latin should be able to learn other subjects more quickly. He found no evidence of this. Having learned one formal discipline did not result in more efficient learning in other domains. Mental "strength" in one domain didn't transfer to mental strength in others. Thorndike's results contributed to the demise of this ancient theory of intelligence and to a decline in the teaching of formal disciplines as mental calisthenics.

In the early years of the cognitive revolution, it appeared that general skills and reasoning abilities might be at the heart of human intelligence and skilled performance. If this is so, again the chess champion might succeed, and schools should teach these general thinking and problem-solving skills—maybe even in separate critical-thinking and study-skills classes.

But by the mid 1970s, cognitive research suggested that general domain-independent skills couldn't adequately account for human expertise. Research shows that either the teaching of traditional study skills has no impact on learning or else the skills fail to transfer from the learning context to other situations. Either way, teaching these general skills is not the path to expertise and enhanced academic performance.

A wide variety of books and commercially available courses attempt to teach general cognitive and thinking skills. (For reviews and evaluations see Nickerson et al. 1985, Segal et al. 1985, and Chipman et al. 1985.) Analysis and evaluation of these programs again fail to support the belief that the teaching of general skills enhances students' overall performance.

Most of these programs teach general skills in standalone courses, separate from subject-matter instruction. The assumption is that students would find it too difficult to learn how to think and to learn subject content simultaneously. Like the early artificial intelligence and cognitive science that inspire them, the courses contain many formal problems, logical puzzles, and games. The assumption is that the general methods that work on these problems will work on problems in all subject domains.

A few of these programs, such as the Productive Thinking Program (Covington 1985) and Instrumental Enrichment (Feuerstein et al. 1985), have undergone extensive evaluation. The evaluations consistently report that students improve on problems like those contained in the course materials but show only limited improvement on novel problems or problems unlike those in the materials (Mansfield et al. 1978; Savell et al. 1986). The programs provide extensive practice on the specific kinds of problems that their designers want children to master. Children do improve on those problems, but this is different from developing *general* cognitive skills. After reviewing the effectiveness of several thinking-skills programs, one group of psychologists concluded that "there is no strong evidence that students in any of these thinking-skills programs improved in tasks that were dissimilar to those already explicitly practiced" (Bransford et al. 1985, p. 202). Students in the programs don't become more intelligent generally; the general problem-solving

and thinking skills they learn do not transfer to novel problems. Rather, the programs help students become experts in the domain of puzzle problems.

Researchers then began to think that the key to intelligence in a domain was extensive experience with and knowledge about that domain.

One of the most influential experiments supporting this theory was William Chase and Herb Simon's (1973) study of novice and expert chess players, which followed on earlier work by A.D. De Groot (1965). Chase and Simon showed positions from *actual* chess games to subjects for 5 to 10 seconds and asked the subjects to reproduce the positions from memory. Each position contained 25 chess pieces. Expert players could accurately place 90 percent of the pieces, novices only 20 percent. Chase and Simon then had the subjects repeat the experiment, but this time the "positions" consisted of 25 pieces placed randomly on the board. These were generally not positions that would occur in an actual game. The experts were no better than the novices at reproducing the random positions: both experts and novices could place only five or six pieces correctly.

Other researchers replicated the Chase-Simon experiment in a variety of domains, using children, college students, and adults. The results were always the same: Experts had better memories for items in their area of expertise, but not for items in general. This shows, first, that mastering a mentally demanding game does not improve mental strength in general. The improved memory performance is domain specific. Chess isn't analogous to a barbell for the mind. Second, it shows that if memory *strategies* account for the expert's improved memory capacity, the strategies aren't general strategies applicable across all problem-solving domains. Chess experts have better memories for genuine chess positions, but not for random patterns of chess pieces or for strings of words or digits. Thus, experts aren't using some general memory strategy that transfers from chess positions to random patterns of pieces or to digit strings.

From long experience at the game, chess experts have developed an extensive knowledge base of perceptual patterns, or chunks. Cognitive scientists estimate that chess experts learn about 50,000 chunks, and that it takes about 10 years to learn them. Chunking explains the difference between novice and expert performance. When doing this task, novices see the chessboard in terms of individual pieces. They can store only the positions of five or six pieces in their short-term, or working, memory—numbers close to what research has shown our working memory spans to be. Experts see "chunks," or patterns, of several pieces. If each chunk contains four or five pieces and if the expert can hold five such chunks in working memory, then the expert can reproduce accurately the positions of 20 to 25 individual pieces. Chase and Simon even found that when experts reproduced the positions on the board, they did it in chunks. They rapidly placed four or five pieces, then paused before reproducing the next chunk.

Expertise, these studies suggest, depends on highly organized, domain-specific knowledge that can arise only after extensive experience and practice in the domain. Strategies can help us process knowledge, but first we have to have the knowledge to process. This suggested that our chess expert might be doomed to failure, and that schools should teach the knowledge, skills, and representations needed to solve problems within specific domains.

In the early 1980s researchers turned their attention to other apparent features of expert performance. They noticed that there were intelligent novices—people who learned new fields and solved novel problems more expertly than most, regardless of how much domain-specific knowledge they possessed. Among other things, intelligent novices seemed to control and monitor their thought processes. This suggested that there was more to expert performance than just domain-specific knowledge and skills.

Cognitive scientists called this new element of expert performance *metacognition*—the ability to think about thinking, to be consciously aware of oneself as a problem solver, and to monitor and control one's mental processing.

As part of an experiment to see which metacognitive skills might be most helpful when learning something new, John Bransford, an expert cognitive psychologist, tried to learn physics from a textbook with the help of an expert physicist. He kept a diary of his learning experiences and recorded the skills and strategies most useful to him (Brown et al. 1983). Among the things he listed were (1) awareness of the difference between understanding and memorizing material and knowledge of which mental strategies to use in each case; (2) ability to recognize which parts of the text were difficult, which dictated where to start reading and how much time to spend; (3) awareness of the need to take problems and examples from the text, order them randomly, and then try to solve them; (4) knowing when he didn't understand, so he could seek help from the expert; and (5) knowing when the expert's explanations solved his immediate learning problem. These are all metacognitive skills; they all involve awareness and control of the learning problem that Bransford was trying to solve. Bransford might have learned these skills originally in one domain (cognitive psychology), but he could apply them as a novice when trying to learn a second domain (physics).

This self-experiment led Bransford and his colleagues to examine in a more controlled way the differences between expert and less-skilled learners. They found that the behavior of intelligent novices contrasted markedly with that of the less skilled. Intelligent novices used many of the same strategies Bransford had used to learn physics. Less-skilled learners used few, if any, of them. The less-skilled did not always appreciate the difference between memorization and comprehension and seemed to be unaware that different learning strategies should be used in each case (Bransford et al. 1986; Bransford and Stein 1984). These students were less likely to notice whether texts were easy or difficult, and thus were less able to adjust their strategies and their study time accordingly (Bransford et al. 1982). Less-able learners were unlikely to use self-tests and self-questioning as sources of feedback to correct misconceptions and inappropriate learning strategies (Brown et al. 1983; Stein et al. 1982).

The importance of metacognition for education is that a child is, in effect, a universal novice, constantly confronted with novel learning tasks. In such a situation it would be most beneficial to be an intelligent novice. What is encouraging is that the research also shows that it is possible to teach children metacognitive skills and when to use them. If we can do this, we will be able to help children become intelligent novices; we will be able to teach them how to learn.

We are just beginning to see what this new understanding of expertise and intelligence might mean for educational practice. The most important implication of the theory is that how we teach is as important as what we teach. Domain-specific knowledge and skills are essential to expertise; however, school instruction must also be metacognitively aware, informed, and explicit. In the next section, we will see a vivid example of this in the teaching of reading comprehension.

IV.

Reading Comprehension: Teaching Children the Strategies Experts Use

Reciprocal teaching, the method mentioned in the introduction to this article, improved Charles' classroom reading comprehension by four grade levels in 20 days. This method illustrates how instruction designed on cognitive principles can help children to apply language-comprehension skills in their reading and to acquire the metacognitive strategies essential to skilled reading.

Reciprocal teaching also shows how researchers, administrators, and teachers can collaborate to apply the results of research in the classroom. Annemarie Palincsar, Ann Brown, and Kathryn Ransom—a graduate student, a professor, and a school administrator—shared the belief that cognitive research could improve classroom practice and that classroom practice can improve research.

After five years working as a special education teacher and administrator, Palincsar returned to the University of Illinois as a doctoral student. She felt her previous training in psychodiagnostics—training based on a medical model of learning disabilities—was not meeting the needs of her students. She decided to broaden her academic background and to study how sociocultural factors might influence students' experience in school.

The cognitive revolution was spreading through academic circles, but had not yet reached teacher-practitioners. Palincsar's classroom experience influenced her choice of a thesis project. In her words: "As a teacher, one of the situations I found most baffling was having children who were fairly strong decoders but had little comprehension or recall of what they had read." She was baffled by students like Charles, students who can adequately comprehend spoken, but not written, language.

At first, Palincsar was interested in how self-verbalization might be used to help children regulate their cognitive processing. Donald Meichenbaum (1985) had developed techniques based on self-verbalization to help impulsive children—children who mentally fail to stop, look, and listen—pace their actions and develop self-control. At the time, most of the work on self-verbalization had explored how it could be used to regulate social behavior. Palincsar wondered how it might be used to regulate *cognitive* behavior—specifically, how it might be used to improve reading comprehension. She wrote to Meichenbaum, who suggested that the application of his ideas to academic subjects might be strengthened by incorporating ideas from research on metacognition. He told Palincsar to discuss her idea with Ann Brown, an authority on metacognition who at that time was also at Illinois.

At their initial meeting, Palincsar showed Brown a design for the pilot study that was to evolve into reciprocal teaching. Brown offered her a quarter-time research appointment to do the study. When it proved successful (Brown and Palincsar 1982), Brown gave Palincsar a full-time research assistantship and supervised her thesis research.

Palincsar and Brown developed reciprocal teaching from the pilot study on a sound theoretical basis. (See Brown and Palincsar 1987). They analyzed the task's demands, developed a theory of task performance based on expert-novice studies, and formulated a theory of instruction that might improve task performance. This is the same sequence Bob Siegler followed with the balance-scale task. A major difference, of course, is that reading comprehension presents a more complex problem than the balance scale.

From their analysis and a review of previous research, Palincsar and Brown (1984) identified six functions that most researchers agreed were essential to expert reading comprehension: The competent reader *understands* that the goal in reading is to construct meaning, *activates* relevant background knowledge, *allocates* attention or cognitive resources to concentrate on major content ideas, *evaluates* the constructed meaning (the gist) for internal consistency and compatibility with prior knowledge and common sense, *draws* and *tests* inferences (including interpretations, predictions, and conclusions), and *monitors* all the above to see if comprehension is occurring.

Palincsar and Brown then identified four simple strategies that would together tap all six functions needed for comprehension: *summarizing, questioning, clarifying,* and *predicting.* They explained the relation between the four strategies and the six functions as follows (Palincsar and Brown 1986): Summarizing a passage requires that the reader recall and state the gist he or she has constructed. Thus, a reader who can summarize has activated background knowledge to integrate information appearing in the text, allocated attention to the main points, and evaluated the gist for consistency. Formulating a question about a text likewise depends on the gist and the functions needed for summarizing, but with the additional demand that the reader monitor the gist to pick out important points. When clarifying, a reader must allocate attention to difficult points and engage in critical evaluation of the gist. Making predictions involves drawing and testing inferences on the basis of

what is in the text together with activated background knowledge. A reader who self-consciously uses all four strategies would certainly appreciate that the goal of reading is to construct meaning.

Expert-novice studies supported the hypothesized connection between comprehension functions and strategies. After completing a comprehension task, expert readers reported that they spent a lot of time summarizing, questioning, clarifying, and predicting. Experts' "comprehend-aloud" protocols substantiated these self-reports. Poor readers did not report using the strategies and showed no evidence of using them in their comprehension protocols. As Palincsar and Brown characterize it, novices executed a "once-over, desperate, nonfocused read."

But can you teach the strategies to novices? And if you can, will it improve their comprehension? To answer these questions, Palincsar and Brown designed a prototype instructional intervention to teach nonexperts how to use the strategies. As with all instruction, the primary problem is transfer. How should one teach the strategies to get novices to use them spontaneously? Here Palincsar based her strategy instruction on Brown's work on teaching metacognitive skills. Brown's research had shown that successful strategy instruction must include practice on specific task-appropriate skills (the cognitive aspect), explicit instruction on how to supervise and monitor these skills (the metacognitive aspect), and explanations of why the skills work (the informed instruction aspect).

The research suggests what teachers should do to help students master strategies. First, teachers have to make the strategies overt, explicit and concrete. Teachers can best do this by modeling the strategies for the students.

Second, to ensure that students will spontaneously use the strategies where needed, teachers should link the strategies to the contexts in which they are to be used and teach the strategies as a functioning group, not in iso-

Strategies can help us process knowledge, but first we have to have the knowledge to process.

lation. This suggests that reading-strategy instruction should take place during reading-comprehension tasks, where the explicit goal is to construct meaning from written symbols.

Third, instruction must be informed. The students should be fully aware of why the strategies work and where they should use particular strategies. Thus, instruction should involve discussion of a text's content and students' understanding of why the strategies are useful in that situation.

Fourth, students have to realize the strategies work no matter what their current level of performance. Thus, instruction should include feedback from the teacher about the students' success relative to their individual abilities and encouragement to persist even if a student is not yet fully competent.

Finally, if students are to become spontaneous strategy users, responsibility for comprehension must be transferred from the teacher to the students gradually, but as soon as possible. This suggests that the teacher should slowly raise the demands made on the students and then fade into the background, becoming less an active modeler and more a sympathetic coach. Students should gradually take charge of their learning.

Palincsar designed reciprocal teaching to satisfy all five of these requirements. Reciprocal teaching takes the form of a dialogue. Dialogue is a language game children understand, and it is a game that allows control of a learning session to alternate between teacher and student. Most important, when engaged in dialogue students are *using* their language-comprehension skills and *sharing* any relevant background knowledge they have individually with the group. In reciprocal teaching, dialogue directs these skills and knowledge toward reading.

The dialogue becomes a form of cooperative learning, in which teachers model the strategies for the students and then give students guided practice in applying them to a group task of constructing a text's meaning. Teacher and students take turns leading a dialogue about the portion of text they are jointly trying to understand. The dialogue includes spontaneous discussion and argument emphasizing the four strategies.

In reciprocal teaching, the teacher assigns the reading group a portion of a text and designates one student to be the leader for that segment. Initially, the teacher might be the leader. The group reads the passage silently. Then the assigned leader summarizes the passage, formulates a question that might be asked on a test, discusses and clarifies difficult points, and finally makes a prediction about what might happen next in the story. The teacher provides help and feedback tailored to the needs and abilities of the current leader. The student-listeners act as supportive critics who encourage the leader to explain and clarify the text. Each student takes a turn as leader. The group's public goal is collaborative construction of the text's meaning. The teacher provides a model of expert performance. As the students improve, the teacher fades into the background.

In the first test of reciprocal teaching, Palincsar served as the teacher and worked with one student at a time. The students were seventh-graders in a remedial reading program who had adequate decoding skills but who were at least three grades behind in reading comprehension. At first, students found it difficult to be the leader, and Palincsar had to do a lot of modeling and prompting, but gradually the students' performance improved. In the initial sessions, over half the questions students formulated were inadequate. Only 11 percent of the questions addressed main ideas, and only 11 percent of the summaries captured the gist of the passage. After ten tutoring sessions, however, students could generate reasonably sophisticated questions and summaries. By the end of training, 96 percent of the students' questions were appropriate, 64 percent of the questions addressed main ideas, and 60 percent of their summaries captured the gists of the passages.

Students' reading comprehension improved along with their performance in reciprocal teaching. On daily comprehension tests, scores improved from 10 percent to 85 percent correct and stayed at this level for at least 6 months after reciprocal teaching ended. Back in the classroom, reciprocal-teaching students improved their performance on other reading tasks from the seventh percentile before reciprocal teaching to the fiftieth percentile after. Palincsar repeated the study working with two children simultaneously and obtained the same results. (Charles, mentioned above, was one of the students in this second study.)

Palincsar and Brown wanted to know if reciprocal teaching was the most efficient way to achieve these gains before they asked teachers to try it in classrooms. Reciprocal teaching demands a great deal of the teacher's time and requires intensive interaction with small groups of students. Both are valuable classroom commodities. Could the same results be achieved more efficiently by a different method? Reciprocal teaching turned out to be superior to all the alternatives tested (Brown and Palincsar 1987, 1989). In all the comparison studies, reciprocal teaching improved remedial seventh-graders' performance on comprehension tests from less than 40 percent before instruction to between 70 and 80 percent after instruction, a level typically achieved by average seventh-graders. The best of the alternative methods—explicit strategy instruction, where the teacher demonstrated and discussed each strategy and the students then completed worksheets on the strategies—raised scores from around 40 percent to between 55 and 60 percent (Brown and Palincsar 1987). These studies showed that the intense and prolonged student-teacher interaction characteristic of reciprocal teaching is crucial to its success (Palincsar et al. 1988). This is the investment teachers have to make to cash in on reciprocal teaching's dividends.

INTO THE CLASSROOM

Can reciprocal teaching work in a real classroom? Here Kathryn Ransom, Coordinator for Reading and Secondary Education in District 186, Springfield, Illinois, enters the story. Ransom—a former teacher—is a veteran professional educator. She makes it clear she has seen many trends come and go, and realizes that neither she nor the schools will please all the people all the time. Nonetheless, Ransom devotes time and effort to get new things happening in the Springfield schools. She has become adept at, as she puts it, "making deals" with research groups. "We can bring in people who have exciting ideas that need to become practical, and as the researchers work with Springfield teachers they can provide staff development experiences I never could."

Springfield's District 186 serves a population of 15,000 students, from kindergarten through high school. The system is 25 to 28 percent minority. On standardized tests, classes at all grade levels score at or above grade level in all subjects. This is a solid achievement, Ransom points out, because the majority of special education children in the district receive instruction in regular classrooms. When it was time for the classroom testing of reciprocal teaching, Palincsar approached Ransom. Ransom saw the potential of reciprocal teaching and recognized in Palincsar a researcher who could make cognitive science meaningful to administrators and teachers. The researcher and the administrator struck a deal advantageous to both.

Together, they decided to approach Springfield's middle school remedial reading teachers. These teachers worked daily with children who had adequate decoding skills but no functional comprehension skills. Ransom and Palincsar collaborated to design a staff development program that would encourage the teachers to think about instructional goals and methods and that would allow the researchers to introduce reciprocal teaching and the theory behind it. The teachers first watched videos of Palincsar conducting reciprocal teaching sessions. Later the teachers took part in reciprocal teaching sessions, playing the roles of teacher and student. Next a teacher and a researcher jointly conducted a reciprocal teaching lesson. The final training consisted of three formal sessions on the method over a three-day period.

In the first classroom study of reciprocal teaching, four volunteer remedial reading teachers used the method with their classes (Palincsar et al. 1988). Class size varied from four to seven students. Before reciprocal teaching, the baseline on daily reading-assessment tests for the students was 40 percent. After 20 days of reciprocal teaching their performance rose to between 70 and 80 percent, just as in Palincsar's initial laboratory studies. Students maintained this level of performance after reciprocal teaching and also improved their performance on other classroom comprehension tasks, including science and social studies reading. Reciprocal teaching worked in the classroom! Experienced volunteer teachers, after limited training, could replicate the laboratory results in classroom settings.

Palincsar and Ransom obtained similar results in a study that used conscripted teachers, who varied greatly in experience and expertise. The students also were more diverse in their reading deficiencies than the students in the first study. Class size varied from 7 to 15, with an average size of 12. Each teacher taught one reciprocal teaching group and one control group; the latter received standard reading-skills instruction. Again, after 20 days of reciprocal instruction, scores on daily comprehension tests improved to 72 percent for the reciprocal teaching group, versus 58 percent for the control group. Thus, average classroom teachers, working in less-than-ideal circumstances and teaching groups of seven or more students, replicated the original laboratory results. As the ultimate test, the Springfield team ran an experiment in which the strongest student in a remedial group served as the teacher. In this study, the student-teachers improved their scores on comprehension tests from 72 percent to 85 percent correct. The other students in the group improved their scores from 50 percent to 70 percent correct.

Since the study ended, in 1989, reciprocal teaching has become a mainstay in the Springfield schools. It is now used in all remedial reading classes, and its methods have been incorporated in some form into all regular classroom reading programs. Even more encouraging, Springfield teachers exposed to reciprocal teaching and to the importance of strategic thinking attempt to integrate these elements into their teaching of other subjects.

One benefit of reciprocal teaching, and of similar projects in the Springfield system, has been the teachers' participation in extended applied research. This was part of Ransom's original agenda. A project running over 5 years, as reciprocal teaching did, provides a powerful way to change teachers' behavior. Most in-service training for teachers lasts only a day or two and at best can have only a minor impact on their thinking and their performance. Ransom sees collaboration in classroom research as a way for teachers and researchers to interact in a dignified, mutually beneficial way. The teachers gain meaningful in-service experience that is intellectually satisfying. Working closely with fellow teachers and other education professionals helps them overcome the isolation of seven-hour days as the only adult in the classroom. The research team also gains, as the reciprocal teaching researchers will attest. The teachers initially helped refine reciprocal teaching for classroom use, providing important insights into how to make an instructional prototype work in a school. Later, they helped identify new research questions and helped the researchers design ways to test the method's classroom effectiveness. Because of her Springfield experience, Palincsar decided that all her subsequent educational research would be done in close collaboration with classroom professionals.

Interest in reciprocal teaching continues within District 186 through instructional chaining. A network has developed in which teachers who have used reciprocal teaching conduct in-service sessions for other teachers. By the 1987-88 school year, 150 teachers in 23 buildings had taken part in these sessions. Teachers formed peer support groups so they could discuss progress and problems associated with daily use of reciprocal teaching and other strategy instruction. The remedial teachers also helped the district design new reading tests to assess students' use of comprehension strategies. The Springfield experience contributed to ongoing efforts at the state level to revamp reading instruction and to develop reading tests that can measure the skills that methods such as reciprocal teaching try to impart. Veterans of the Springfield experiment now work in other schools and with national educational organizations to improve reading instruction.

In the Springfield schools and in others that have used reciprocal teaching, teachers have a better understanding of what reading is about. As Palincsar and Brown (1986, p. 770) observe, "There was a time not long ago when successful reading was thought to be execution of a series of component subskills." To teach reading one taught the subskills, from word recognition through finding the main idea, often in isolation and in a fixed sequence. Charles and the approximately 60 percent of American 17-year-olds who fail to reach the fourth reading proficiency level of the National Assessment of Educational Progress—who fail to become adept readers (Mullis and Jenkins 1990)—show the inadequacy of this approach. Reciprocal teaching works. The strategies it teaches enable students to apply their language-comprehension skills to reading so that they can read for meaning. Reading is more than decoding and more than the mastery of a series of small, isolated subskills.

V.

High School Physics: Confronting the Misconceptions of Novices

One of the best places to see a cognitive science approach to teaching is in Jim Minstrell's physics classes at Mercer Island High School. (See Minstrell 1989; Minstrell 1984; Minstrell and Stimpson 1990.)

Mercer Island is an upper-middle-class suburb of Seattle. The high school serves just over 1,000 students in four grades. Jim Minstrell has been teaching there since 1962. He holds bachelors', master's, and doctoral degrees from the Universities of Washington and Pennsylvania, and during his career he has worked on several national programs to improve high school physics instruction. Although deeply committed to educational research, he prefers the classroom to a university department or a school of education. "I have one of the best laboratories in the world right here," he observes. He adopted what he calls "a cognitive orientation to teaching" for practical, not theoretical, reasons. The cognitive approach addresses a fundamental classroom problem that confronts science teachers: Students' preconceptions influence how they understand classroom material.

In the early 1970s, after a decade of outstanding teaching (as measured both by students' test scores and by supervisors' evaluations), Minstrell became concerned about his effectiveness. His students couldn't transfer their formal book and lecture learning to the physics of everyday situations, and they showed little understanding of basic physical concepts, such as force, motion, and gravity. At first he thought, following Jean Piaget's theory of cognitive development, that his students lacked logical, or formal operational, skills. However, when he tested this hypothesis, he found otherwise.

Minstrell describes a task of Piaget's in which students are given two clay balls of equal size. Students agree that the two balls weigh the same. But if one ball is then flattened into a pancake, many students will then say that the pancake weighs more than the ball. They reason that the pancake weighs more because it has a larger upper surface on which air can press down. This is not a logical error but a conceptual one. Students believe that air pressure contributes to an object's weight.

"Students were bringing content ideas to the situation, ideas that were greatly affecting their performance on questions that were supposed to be testing their reasoning," Minstrell recalls.

Minstrell became actively involved in research on students' misconceptions, and he tried to apply the research in his classroom. First he expanded his classroom agenda. A teacher's primary goals are to control the students and to provide explanations that allow the students to solve textbook problems. A third goal, in the current climate of accountability, is to prepare the students to pass standardized tests of low-level skills. Minstrell maintains the first two goals, minimizes the third, and adds two goals of his own, based on cognitive research: to establish explicit instructional targets for understanding and to help the students actively reconstruct their knowledge to reach that understanding.

Minstrell attempts to diagnose students' misconceptions and to remedy them by instruction. Most teachers aren't trained to recognize and fix misconceptions. How does Minstrell do it?

FACETS

Minstrell assumes from the first day of school that his students have some knowledge of physics and that they have adequate reasoning ability. Unlike expert scientists who want to explain phenomena with a minimum of assumptions and laws, students are not driven by a desire for conceptual economy. Their knowledge works well enough in daily life, but it is fragmentary and local. Minstrell calls pieces of knowledge that are used in physics reasoning *facets*. Facets are schemas and parts of schemas that are used to reason about the physical world.

Students typically choose and apply facets on the basis of the most striking *surface* features of a problem. They derive their naive facets from everyday experience. Such facets are useful in particular situations; however, they are most likely false in general, and for the most part they are only loosely interrelated. Thus, students can quickly fall into contradictions. Two facets Minstrell typically finds students using when reasoning about objects are (1) that larger objects exert more force than smaller objects and (2) that only moving objects exert force. The first facet explains why the smart money was on Goliath and not David; the second explains why a football can "force" its way through a window. But how do you explain what happens when you throw a ball against the side of a building? The first facet suggests that the wall must exert a larger force on the ball than the ball does on the wall, but the second facet says that only the ball can exert a force, not the wall. So how is it that the ball bounces off the wall? As Minstrell sees it, the trick is to identify the students' correct intuitions—their facets that are consistent with formal science—and then build on these. As Minstrell says, "Some facets are anchors for instruction; others are targets for change."

BENCHMARK LESSONS: WHAT ARE YOUR IDEAS RIGHT NOW?

At the outset, Minstrell's students are not different from other high school juniors and seniors. Early in each course unit he administers a diagnostic test to assess qualitative, not quantitative, physical reasoning.

Between 50 percent and 75 percent of the students believe that when a heavy object and a light object are dropped or thrown horizontally, the heavier one hits the ground first. As many as half believe that when two moving objects are at the same position they are traveling at the same speed; yet they all know that to pass a car on the highway the overtaking car must be going faster, even when the two cars are side by side. Nearly half believe that air pressure affects an object's weight. Almost all believe that a constant, unbalanced force causes constant velocity. The results of the diagnostic tests give Minstrell a profile of which facets are prevalent, which ones might be anchors, and which ones are targets for change.

Minstrell organizes his course into units, such as measurement, kinematics, gravity, and electromagnetism. Some lessons, usually presented early in a unit, are particularly important in helping students change their reasoning. Minstrell calls these *benchmark lessons.*

In a benchmark lesson, the teacher and the students dissect their qualitative reasoning about vivid, everyday physics problems into facets. They become aware of the limitations of each facet, and they identify which facets are useful for understanding a particular phenomenon. They can explore how appropriate facets can be combined into powerful explanations that can be used to solve other problems.

The benchmark lesson on gravity begins 6 weeks into the course. By this time Minstrell has established a rapport with his class. He has created an environment conducive to developing understanding, a climate where questioning and respect for diverse opinions prevail, a climate where the process of scientific reasoning can be made explicit and self-conscious. Even veteran teachers marvel at how uninhibited Minstrell's students are in expressing ideas, suggesting hypotheses, and arguing positions.

Minstrell explains to the students that the unit will begin with a three-problem diagnostic quiz, and that their answers will be the subject of discussion for the next two days. He reassures them that the quiz is not intended to embarrass them or show how little they know. He wants to find out what they already know, and he wants them to be aware of what they already know. (Two of the problems from the quiz are reproduced in Figure 2.)

As the students work, Minstrell moves among them and observes their answers and explanations. After 15 minutes he collects the quizzes and goes to the board at the front of the classroom. He reports that on the first question, the scale problem, he saw several answers, and he writes them on the board: 15-20 pounds, a little over 10 pounds, exactly 10 pounds, a little less than 10 pounds, and about 0 pounds. "Now let's hold off on attacking these answers. Rather, let's defend one or more of them," he suggests.

Ethan explains why he thinks the object in the vacuum weighs nothing: "I felt it was zero, because when you're in space you float. It would be related to that." Minstrell helps fill in the argument: "When you're in space things seem weightless. Space is essentially an airless environment, so the object would weigh nothing."

A few students argue that the object weighs the same in the vacuum as in air. One says that when air is present the air above and the air below the scale balance out; some air pushes down and some pushes up, with no net effect. Chris, baseball cap on the back of his head and arms crossed, offers: "Ten pounds. The vacuum inside only has a relation to air pressure, not a relation to mass."

Two students argue that the object in a vacuum weighs slightly more than 10 pounds, because under normal

conditions air helps hold up the scale. When you remove the air, the object will weigh more because there is no air supporting the scale.

The most popular student response is that the scale would read slightly less than 10 pounds. These arguments invoke facets involving density and buoyancy. John presents the rationale: "It's gonna be a little less than 10. You remember Bob Beamon. He set a world record in the long jump at the Mexico City Olympics. He jumped really far there because there is less air and it is lighter and so everything weighs less."

In the class period devoted to discussion, over half the students offer explanations for one of the answers. Minstrell is strictly a facilitator, offering no facts, opinions, or arguments himself. He then encourages students to present counterarguments. When the counterarguments and the responses have run their course, Minstrell signals the start of the next lesson segment: "Sounds like there are some pretty good arguments here across the spectrum. So what do we do?" The students urge him to run an experiment. He says, "Luckily, I happen to have a scale, a bell jar, and a vacuum pump here."

Minstrell calls two students to the front to help conduct the crucial experiment. Such demonstrations are dramatic and exciting for the students and allow them to

Problem 1. Under normal atmospheric conditions, an object is placed on a scale and the scale reads 10 pounds. If the scale and the object were placed under a glass dome and all the air were removed from under the dome, what would the scale read?

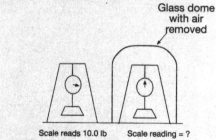

Problem 2. An object weighing 1 kilogram in normal air takes 1 second to fall a distance *d*. How long will it take an object the same size but weighing 5 kilograms to fall the same distance?

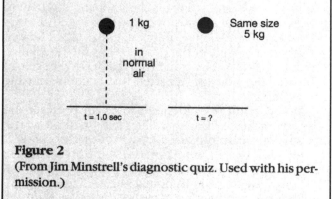

Figure 2
(From Jim Minstrell's diagnostic quiz. Used with his permission.)

see which prediction is correct. Research also suggests that such experiences have an important cognitive role in inducing conceptual change. They provide an initial experience that places naive and expert theories in conflict. As the students try to resolve the conflict, the dramatic demonstration serves as an organizing structure in long-term memory (an anchor) around which schemas can be changed and reorganized (Hunt 1993).

The first student reports that the object on the scale weighs 1.2 newtons under normal circumstances. Minstrell starts the vacuum pump, and the students watch the gauge as the pressure drops inside the bell jar. The pump stops when the pressure gauge reads nearly zero.

"Did the weight go to zero?" Minstrell asks. Somewhat amazed, the students respond that the weight stayed the same. Minstrell suggests that they see what happens when the air rushes back into the jar. He opens the valve and the air whistles in. A student exclaims, "Air or no air in there, there's not much difference either way!"

Minstrell asks "What does this tell us about gravity and air pressure?" "Air pressure doesn't affect weight," the students respond. They have started to correct a major misconception. Other experiences in the unit and throughout the course reinforce this benchmark discovery that air pressure and gravity are distinct physical phenomena.

DON'T FEEL DUMB!

A few days later, Minstrell and the class analyze their reasoning about the time it would take a 1-kilogram and a 5-kilogram object to fall the same distance (problem 2 above). They run the crucial experiment—a miniature replay of Galileo's apocryphal experiment at Pisa. After both balls hit the floor simultaneously, Minstrell returns to the board where he had written the quiz answers. "Some of you were probably feeling pretty dumb with these kinds of answers. Don't feel dumb," he counsels. "Let's see what's valuable about each of these answers, because each one is valuable. Why would you think that heavier things fall faster?"

A student suggests that heavy things (such as barbells) are harder to pull up, so it seems they would fall back to the ground more quickly too. "Right," Minstrell says. "When you lift something heavy, that sucker is heavy. Gravity is really pulling down. 'Aha,' you think, 'big effect there.' A useful rule of daily life is the more of X, the more of Z."

Why would anyone think a heavier object falls more slowly? A student argues that heavier objects are harder to push horizontally than light ones, and that because they are harder to push, one moves them more slowly; thus, when a heavier object is dropped, it must fall more slowly. Minstrell reinforces what is correct about this intuition. He points out that the first argument uses the facet of direct proportional reasoning and the second argument the facet of indirect proportional reasoning. Minstrell and the class will revisit these facets when they grapple with Newton's Second Law, $F = ma$ (i.e., when a force acts on an object the acceleration is directly proportional to the force and inversely proportional to the object's mass).

Minstrell concludes: "So, there are some good rationales behind these answers. Part of what I'm saying is that the rationales you have—the physics you've cooked up in the past 16 to 19 years of living—are valuable. But they are valuable only in certain contexts." The trick to becoming a competent physicist is knowing when to use which facet. It's not just a matter of having the pieces of knowledge; what counts is knowing when to use them—linking *conditions* of applicability to cognitive *actions*.

The unit on gravity continues with students doing experiments in the classroom and around the school building. It ends with seven problems, all taken from standard high school texts, which allow the students to assess their mastery of the unit's central facets and concepts.

Throughout the unit, Minstrell has not lectured, expounded, or "taught" in the traditional sense. He has identified students' initial intuitions, made their reasoning explicit by eliciting and debating their positions, provided vivid benchmark experiences to help trigger conceptual change, and encouraged them to reason about these views and experiences. He has taught physics from a cognitive perspective.

DOES IT WORK? WHY?

In 1986 Minstrell initiated a collaboration with Earl Hunt, a cognitive psychologist at the University of Washington, to assess and refine his classroom method. Hunt, a "basic" cognitive scientist who has developed an interest in an applied science of learning, describes himself as the "wet blanket" of the project. "I'm the professional skeptic who must be convinced that it is the cognitive approach and not just Minstrell that accounts for the effects," he says.

A comparison of students' scores on pretests and posttests makes it clear that Minstrell's method works. The students learn physics. But why does it work?

One concern is whether the method's success depends entirely on Jim Minstrell's pedagogical talents. This was the first issue Hunt and Minstrell investigated. Could someone other than Minstrell use the method successfully?

Minstrell trained Virginia Stimpson and Dorothy Simpson, two math teachers at Mercer Island High who had never taught physics, to use his method. At Mercer Island, as at most high schools, which students end up in which physics sections is due more to scheduling than to student choice or teacher selection. Thus, students of varying abilities are likely to end up in each section. This allowed Minstrell and Hunt to make reliable comparisons between the performances of Minstrell's students and the performances of Stimpson's and Simpson's. Gini's and Dottie's students did at least as well as Jim's, so the effect (at least at Mercer Island High) is not due to Minstrell himself.

Is Minstrell's method better than other instructional methods currently in use? Minstrell himself has shown at Mercer Island High that his method is superior to traditional methods. His students have fewer misconceptions at course's end than do students taught traditionally. For example, on the pretest 3 percent of Minstrell's students showed correct understanding of both Newton's First and Second Laws. When he used the traditional methods and curriculum, Minstrell observed that after instruction 36 percent understood the First Law and 62 percent the Second Law. When he used his cognitive approach, 95 percent of the students ended up with a correct understanding of the First Law and 81 percent with a correct understanding of the Second Law (Minstrell 1984).

Minstrell and Hunt compared Mercer Island students with students at a neighboring, comparable high school that Hunt calls "Twin Peaks." The physics instructor there also uses a conceptual, non-quantitative approach in his course. Performance on standardized math tests is the best predictor of high school physics performance. On this measure, Mercer Island and Twin Peaks students were not significantly different. So, in physics one would expect similar outcomes at the two schools. However, on the same final exam in mechanics, taken after 3 months of studying that topic, the Mercer Island students scored about 20 percent higher than the Twin Peaks students across the entire range of math scores. "This is an important result," skeptic Hunt emphasizes, "because it shows that the method does not selectively appeal to brighter students as measured by math achievement."

For good measure, Minstrell and Hunt also compared Mercer Island students with students in a "nationally known experimental, physics teaching, research and development program." The Mercer Island students consistently outperformed the other experimental group on all topics tested. Hunt adds: "We regard these data as particularly important because the questions we used in this comparison were developed by the other experimental group."

These results have allayed some of Hunt's initial skepticism, but Hunt and Minstrell realize that much remains to be done. The success of Minstrell's theory-based curriculum vindicates the cognitive approach, but for Hunt success raises further theoretical questions. He has begun a research program back in his laboratory to refine the theory underlying Minstrell's method. Why are benchmark lessons so important? How does transfer occur? How do students develop deep representations and make appropriate generalizations? Minstrell's classroom is a good laboratory, but a teacher who is responsible for seeing that his students learn physics is limited in the experiments he can conduct. No doubt, in a few years results from Hunt's basic research will feed back into Minstrell's applied research at Mercer Island High.

The next challenge for Minstrell and Hunt will be to test the method elsewhere. What will happen when teachers who are not under the innovators' direct supervision try to use the method? Instructional materials, including videotapes of benchmark lessons for each unit, will soon be ready for dissemination. The next step will be to assemble an implementation network and conduct applied research in a variety of classroom situations.

TEACHING FOR UNDERSTANDING

Jim Minstrell's students end up with a better understanding of physics, in part, because they learn more expert-like representations and concepts, as well as how to reason with them. There is a price to pay for this deeper understanding. As Earl Hunt points out, "From a traditional perspective one might argue that Minstrell's classes fail, because often students don't get through the standard curriculum. Last year, they did not complete electricity, and atomic physics and waves were barely mentioned." Hunt thinks that changes in curricular time and course coverage will be crucial in making science instruction more effective. Hunt is quick to add that in other countries curricula sometimes allow two to three years to teach what we cram into one.

The applied work of Minstrell and others shows that we can teach in such a way as to make a significant impact on students' scientific understanding. All who have attempted to teach for understanding, though, emphasize that doing so takes time. Minstrell spends over a week developing Newton's laws, not one or two days as in most traditional courses. Reflecting on his classroom experiences, Minstrell (1989, p. 147) advises: "We must provide the time students need for mental restructuring. Hurrying on to the next lesson or the next topic does not allow for sufficient reflection on the implications of the present lesson."

Results from cognitive research indicate that if we want more students to understand science, the instruction should start early in school, and that throughout the curriculum instruction should build on students' correct intuitions and prior understanding. We should try to teach experts' conceptual understandings, not just formulas and equations, and along with this content we should teach students how to reason scientifically. Better science instruction along these lines may require a "less is more" (or at least a "longer is better") approach to the science curriculum.

Conclusion

Learning is the process whereby novices become more expert. Teaching is the profession dedicated to helping students learn, helping them become more expert. Cognitive research has matured to where it can now tell us what is involved in the mental journey from novice to expert not just in reading and physics, but across a variety of school subject domains. The research can now describe these journeys in sufficient detail— recall Siegler's exacting, fine-grained analysis of learning the balance scale—that it can serve as a map and guide for improved learning and teaching. We have at our disposal the basis for an applied science of learning that can inform the design of new materials, teaching methods and curricula. These are the tools students and teachers must have, if, as a nation, we are serious about becoming more productive and helping all students develop their intelligence as fully as possible.

Developing these tools and restructuring our schools to use them won't be easy. We will have to start in the classroom, where teachers interact with students. We will need teachers who can create and maintain learning environments where students have the smoothest possible journey from novice to expert and where they can learn to become intelligent novices. To do this, we will have to rethink, or at least re-evaluate, much of our received wisdom about educational policy, classroom practices, national standards, and teacher training.

Admittedly, there is much we still don't know about how our minds work, how children best learn, and how to design better schools. On the other hand, we already know a great deal that we can apply to improve our schools and our children's futures.

REFERENCES

Bransford, J.D., Sherwood, R., Vye, N., and Rieser, J. 1986. Teaching thinking and problem solving. *American Psychologist* 41(10): 1078-1089.

Bransford, J.D., and Stein, B.S. 1984. *The IDEAL problem solver.* Freeman.

Bransford, J.D., Stein, B.S., Arbitman-Smith, R., and Vye, N.J. 1985. Improved thinking and learning skills: An analysis of three approaches. In J.W. Segal, S.F. Chipman, and R. Glaser, eds., *Thinking and Learning Skills,* volume 1: *Relating Instruction to Research.* Erlbaum.

Bransford, J.D., Stein, B.S., Vye, N.J., Franks, J.J., Auble, P.M., Mezynski, K.J., and Perfetto, G.A. 1982. Differences in approaches to learning: An overview. *Journal of Experimental Psychology: General* 111: 390-398.

Brown, A.L., Bransford, J.D., Ferrara, R.A., and Campione, J.C. 1983. Learning, remembering, and understanding. In P.H. Mussen, ed., *Handbook of Child Psychology,* volume 3: *Cognitive Development.* Wiley.

Brown, A.L., and Palincsar, A.S. 1982. Inducing strategic learning from text by means of informed, self-control training. *Topics in Learning and Learning Disabilities* 2: 1-17.

Brown, A.L., and Palincsar, A.S. 1987. Reciprocal teaching of comprehension strategies: A natural history of one program for enhancing learning. In J.D. Day and J.G. Borkowski, eds., *Intelligence and Exceptionality: New Directions for Theory, Assessment, and Instructional Practices.* Ablex.

Brown, A.L., and Palincsar, A.S. 1989: Guided, cooperative learning and individual knowledge acquisition. In L.B. Resnick, ed., *Knowing, Learning, and Instruction: Essays in Honor of Robert Glaser.* Erlbaum.

Chase, W.G., and Simon, H.A. 1973. Perception in chess. *Cognitive Psychology* 4: 55-81.

Chipman, S.F., Segal, J.W., and Glaser, R. 1985. *Thinking and Learning Skills,* volume 2: *Research and Open Questions.* Erlbaum.

Covington, M.V. 1985. Strategic thinking and the fear of failure. In J.W. Segal, S.F. Chipman, and R. Glaser, eds., *Thinking and Learning Skills,* volume 1: *Relating Instruction to Research.* Erlbaum.

De Groot, A.D. 1965. *Thought and Choice in Chess.* Mouton.

Feuerstein, R., Hoffman, M.B., Jensen, M.R., and Rand, Y. 1985. Instrumental enrichment, an intervention program for structural cognitive modifiability: Theory and practice. In J.W. Segal, S.F. Chipman, and R. Glaser, eds., *Thinking and Learning Skills,* volume 1: *Relating Instruction to Research.* Erlbaum.

Gardner, H. 1985. *The Mind's New Science.* Basic Books.

Hunt, E. 1993. *Thoughts on Thought: An Analysis of Formal Models of Cognition.* Erlbaum.

Klahr, D., and Siegler, R.S. 1978. The representation of children's knowledge. In H. Reese and L.P. Lipsett, eds., *Advances in Child Development and Behavior,* volume 12. Academic Press.

Mansfield, R.S., Busse, T.V., and Krepelka, E.J. 1978. The effectiveness of creativity training. *Review of Educational Research* 48(4): 517-536.

Meichenbaum, D. 1985. Teaching thinking: A cognitive-behavioral perspective. In S. F. Chipman, J. W. Segal, and R. Glaser, eds., *Thinking and Learning Skills*, volume 2: *Research and Open Questions.* Erlbaum.

Minstrell, J. 1984. Teaching for the development of understanding of ideas: Forces on moving objects. In *Observing Classrooms: Perspectives from Research and Practice.* Ohio State University.

Minstrell, J. 1989. Teaching science for understanding. In L.B. Resnick and L.E. Klopfer, eds., *Toward the Thinking Curriculum.* Association for Supervision and Curriculum Development.

Minstrell, J., and Stimpson, V.C. 1990. A teaching system for diagnosing student conceptions and prescribing relevant instruction. Paper prepared for AERA session "Classroom Perspectives on Conceptual Change Teaching," Boston.

Mullis, I.V.S., and Jenkins, L.B. 1990. *The Reading Report Card, 1971-88: Trends from the Nation's Report Card.* Office of Educational Research and Improvement, U.S. Department of Education.

Newell, A., and Simon, H.A. 1972. *Human Problem Solving.* Prentice-Hall.

Nickerson, R.S., Perkins, D.N., and Smith, E.E. 1985. *The Teaching of Thinking.* Erlbaum.

Palincsar, A.S., and Brown, A.L. 1984. Reciprocal teaching of comprehension-fostering and comprehension-monitoring activities. *Cognition and Instruction* 1(2): 117-175.

Palincsar, A.S., and Brown, A.L. 1986. Interactive teaching to promote independent learning from text. *Reading Teacher* 39: 771-777.

Palincsar, A.S., Ransom, K., and Derber, S. 1988. Collaborative research and the development of reciprocal teaching. *Educational Leadership* 46: 37-40.

Perkins, D.N., and Salomon, G. 1989. Are cognitive skills context-bound? *Educational Researcher* 18: 16-25.

Savell, J.M., Wohig, P.T., and Rachford, D.L. 1986. Empirical status of Feuerstein's "Instrumental Enrichment" (FIE) technique as a method of teaching thinking skills. *Review of Educational Research* 56(4): 381-409.

Segal, J.W., Chipman, S.F., and Glaser, R. 1985. *Thinking and Learning Skills,* volume 1: *Relating Instruction to Research.* Erlbaum.

Siegler, R.S. 1976. Three aspects of cognitive development. *Cognitive Psychology* 8: 481-520.

Siegler, R.S., and Klahr, D. 1982. When do children learn? The relationship between existing knowledge and the acquisition of new knowledge. In R. Glaser, ed., *Advances in Instructional Psychology*, volume 2. Erlbaum.

Simon, H. A., and Chase, W. G. 1973. Skill in chess. *American Scientist* 61:394-403.

Stein, B.S., Bransford, J.D., Franks, J.J., Vye, N.J., and Perfetto, G.A. 1982. Differences in judgments of learning difficulty. *Journal of Experimental Psychology (General)* 111: 406-413.

The Rewards of Learning

To teach without using extrinsic rewards is analogous to asking our students to learn to draw with their eyes closed, Mr. Chance maintains. Before we do that, we should open our own eyes.

Paul Chance

Paul Chance (Eastern Shore Maryland Chapter) is a psychologist, writer, and teacher. He is the author of Thinking in the Classroom *(Teachers College Press, 1986) and teaches at James H. Groves Adult High School in Georgetown, Del.*

A man is seated at a desk. Before him lie a pencil and a large stack of blank paper. He picks up the pencil, closes his eyes, and attempts to draw a four-inch line. He makes a second attempt, a third, a fourth, and so on, until he has made well over a hundred attempts at drawing a four-inch line, all without ever opening his eyes. He repeats the exercise for several days, until he has drawn some 3,000 lines, all with his eyes closed. On the last day, he examines his work. The question is, How much improvement has there been in his ability to draw a four-inch line? How much has he learned from his effort?

E. L. Thorndike, the founder of educational psychology and a major figure in the scientific analysis of learning, performed this experiment years ago, using himself as subject.[1] He found no evidence of learning. His ability to draw a four-inch line was no better on the last day than it had been on the first.

The outcome of this experiment may seem obvious to us today, but it was an effective way of challenging a belief widely held earlier in this century, a belief that formed the very foundation of education at the time: the idea that "practice makes perfect."

It was this blind faith in practice that justified countless hours of rote drill as a standard teaching technique. Thorndike's experiment demonstrated that practice in and of itself is not sufficient for learning. Based on this and other, more formal studies, Thorndike concluded that practice is important only insofar as it provides the opportunity for reinforcement.

To reinforce means to strengthen, and among learning researchers *reinforcement* refers to a procedure for strengthening behavior (that is, making it likely to be repeated) by providing certain kinds of consequences.[2] These consequences, called *reinforcers,* are usually events or things a person willingly seeks out. For instance, we might teach a person to draw a four-inch line with his eyes closed merely by saying "good" each time the effort is within half an inch of the goal. Most people like to succeed, so this positive feedback should be an effective way of reinforcing the appropriate behavior.

Hundreds of experimental studies have demonstrated that systematic use of reinforcement can improve both classroom conduct and the rate of learning. Yet the systematic use of reinforcement has never been widespread in American schools. In *A Place Called School*, John Goodlad reports that, in the elementary grades, an average of only 2% of class time is devoted to reinforcement; in the high schools, the figure falls to 1%.[3]

THE COSTS OF REWARD

There are probably many reasons for our failure to make the most of reinforcement. For one thing, few schools of education provide more than cursory instruction in its use. Given Thorndike's finding about the role of practice in learning, it is ironic that many teachers actually use the term *reinforcement* as a synonym for *practice*. ("We assign workbook exercises for reinforcement.") If schools of education do not teach future teachers the nature of reinforcement and how to use it effectively, teachers can hardly be blamed for not using it.

The unwanted effects of misused reinforcement have led some teachers to shy away from it. The teacher who sometimes lets a noisy class go to recess early will find the class getting noisier before recess. If high praise is reserved for long-winded essays, students will develop wordy and redundant writing styles. And it should surprise no one if students are seldom original in classrooms where only conventional work is admired or if they are uncooperative in classrooms where one can earn recognition only through competition. Reinforcement is powerful stuff, and its misuse can cause problems.

Another difficulty is that the optimal use of reinforcement would mean teaching in a new way. Some studies suggest that maximum learning in elementary and middle schools might require very high rates of reinforcement, perhaps with teachers praising someone in the class an average of once every 15 seconds.[4] Such a requirement is clearly incompatible with traditional teaching practices.

Systematic reinforcement can also mean more work for the teacher. Reinforcing behavior once every 15 seconds means 200 reinforcements in a 50 minute period — 1,000 reinforcements in a typical school day. It also implies that, in order to spot behavior to reinforce, the teacher must be moving about the room, not sitting at a desk marking papers. That may be too much to ask. Some studies have found that teachers who have been taught how to make good use of reinforcement often revert to their old style of teaching. This is so even though the teachers acknowledge that increased use of reinforcement means fewer discipline problems and a much faster rate of learning.[5]

Reinforcement also runs counter to our Puritan traditions. Most Americans have

Paul Chance, "The Rewards of Learning," from *Phi Delta Kappan*, November 1992, pp. 200-207. Reprinted with permission of *Phi Delta Kappan* and the author.

always assumed — occasional protestations to the contrary notwithstanding — that learning should be hard work and at least slightly unpleasant. Often the object of education seems to be not so much to teach academic and social skills as to "build character" through exposure to adversity. When teachers reinforce students at a high rate, the students experience a minimum of adversity and actually enjoy learning. Thus some people think that reinforcement is bad for character development.

All of these arguments against reinforcement can be countered effectively. Schools of education do not provide much instruction in the practical use of reinforcement, but there is no reason why they cannot do so. Reinforcement can be used incorrectly and with disastrous results, but the same might be said of other powerful tools. Systematic use of reinforcement means teaching in a new way, but teachers can learn to do so.[6] A great deal of reinforcement is needed for optimum learning, but not all of the reinforcement needs to come from the teacher. (Reinforcement can be provided by computers and other teaching devices, by teacher aides, by parents, and by students during peer teaching and cooperative learning.) No doubt people do sometimes benefit from adversity, but the case for the character-building properties of adversity is very weak.[7]

However, there is one argument against reinforcement that cannot be dismissed so readily. For some 20 years, the claim has been made that systematic reinforcement actually undermines student learning. Those few teachers who make extensive use of reinforcement, it is claimed, do their students a disservice because reinforcement reduces interest in the reinforced activity.

Not all forms of reinforcement are considered detrimental. A distinction is made between reinforcement involving intrinsic reinforcers — or rewards, as they are often called — and reinforcement involving extrinsic rewards.[8] Only extrinsic rewards are said to be harmful. An *intrinsic reward* is ordinarily the natural consequence of behavior, hence the name. We learn to throw darts by seeing how close the dart is to the target; learn to type by seeing the right letters appear on the computer screen; learn to cook from the pleasant sights, fragrances, and flavors that result from our culinary efforts; learn to read from the understanding we get from the printed word; and

learn to solve puzzles by finding solutions. The Japanese say, "The bow teaches the archer." They are talking about intrinsic rewards, and they are right.

Extrinsic rewards come from an outside source, such as a teacher. Probably the most ubiquitous extrinsic reward (and one of the most effective) is praise. The teacher reinforces behavior by saying "good," "right," "correct," or "excellent" when the desired behavior occurs. Other extrinsic rewards involve nonverbal behavior such as smiles, winks, thumbs-up signs, hugs, congratulatory handshakes, pats on the back, or applause. Gold stars, certificates, candy, prizes, and even money have been used as rewards, but they are usually less important in teaching — and even in the maintenance of good discipline — than those mentioned earlier.

The distinction between intrinsic and extrinsic rewards is somewhat artificial. Consider the following example. You put money into a vending machine and retrieve a candy bar. The behavior of inserting money into a vending machine has been reinforced, as has the more general behavior of interacting with machines. But is the food you receive an intrinsic or an extrinsic reward? On the one hand, the food is the automatic consequence of inserting money and pressing buttons, so it would appear to be an intrinsic reward. On the other hand, the food is a consequence that was arranged by the designer of the machine, so it would seem to be an extrinsic reward.[9]

Though somewhat contrived, the distinction between intrinsic and extrinsic rewards has been maintained partly because extrinsic rewards are said to be damaging.[10] Are they? First, let us be clear about the charge. The idea is that — if teachers smile, praise, congratulate, say "thank you" or "right," shake hands, hug, give a pat on the back, applaud, provide a certificate of achievement or attendance, *or in any way provide a positive consequence (a reward) for student behavior* — the student will be less inclined to engage in that behavior when the reward is no longer available.

For example, teachers who offer prizes to students for reading books will, it is said, make the children less likely to read when prizes are no longer available. The teacher who reads a student's story aloud to the class as an example of excellent story writing actually makes the student less likely to write stories in the future, when such public approval is not forth-

coming. When teachers (and students) applaud a youngster who has given an excellent talk, they make that student disinclined to give talks in the future. The teacher who comments favorably on the originality of a painting steers the young artist away from painting. And so on. This is the charge against extrinsic rewards.

No one disputes the effectiveness of extrinsic rewards in teaching or in maintaining good discipline. Some might therefore argue that extrinsic rewards should be used, even if they reduce interest in learning. Better to have students who read only when required to do so, some might say, than to have students who cannot read at all.

But if rewards do reduce interest, that fact is of tremendous importance. "The teacher may count himself successful," wrote B. F. Skinner, "when his students become engrossed in his field, study conscientiously, and do more than is required of them, but *the important thing is what they do when they are no longer being taught*" (emphasis added).[11] It is not enough for students to learn the three R's and a little science and geography; they must be prepared for a lifetime of learning. To reduce their interest in learning would be a terrible thing — even if it were done in the interest of teaching them effectively.

The question of whether rewards adversely affect motivation is not, then, of merely academic or theoretical importance. It is of great practical importance to the classroom teacher.

Extrinsic rewards are said to be damaging. Are they? First, let us be clear about the charge.

More than 100 studies have examined this question.[12] In a typical experiment, Mark Lepper and his colleagues observed 3- to 5-year-old nursery school children playing with various kinds of toys.[13] The toys available included felt tip pens of various colors and paper to draw on. The researchers noted the children's inclination to draw during this period. Next the researchers took the children aside and asked them to draw with the felt tip pens. The researchers promised some children a "Good Player Award" for drawing. Other children drew pictures without receiving an award.

Two weeks later, the researchers returned to the school, provided felt tip pens and paper, and observed the children's inclination to draw. They found that children who had been promised an award spent only half as much time drawing as they had originally. Those students who had received no award showed no such decline in interest.

Most studies in this area follow the same general outline: 1) students are given the opportunity to participate in an activity without rewards; 2) they are given extrinsic rewards for participating in the activity; and 3) they are again given the opportunity to participate in the activity without rewards.

The outcomes of the studies are also fairly consistent. Not surprisingly, there is usually a substantial increase in the activity during the second stage, when extrinsic rewards are available. And, as expected, participation in the activity declines sharply when rewards are no longer available. However, interest sometimes falls below the initial level, so that students are less interested in the activity than they had been before receiving rewards. It is this net loss of motivation that is of concern.

Researchers have studied this decline in motivation and found that it occurs only under certain circumstances. For example, the effect is most likely to occur when the initial interest in the activity is very high, when the rewards used are *not* reinforcers, and when the rewards are held out in advance as incentives.[14]

But perhaps the best predictor of negative effects is the nature of the "reward contingency" involved. (The term *reward contingency* has to do with the nature of the relationship between behavior and its reward.) Alyce Dickinson reviewed the research literature in this area and identified three kinds of reward contingency:[15]

Task-contingent rewards are available for merely participating in an activity, without regard to any standard of performance. Most studies that find a decline in interest in a rewarded activity involve task-contingent rewards. In the Lepper study described above, for instance, children received an award for drawing *regardless of how they drew*. The reward was task-contingent.

Performance-contingent rewards are available only when the student achieves a certain standard. Performance-contingent rewards sometimes produce negative results. For instance, Edward Deci offered college students money for solving puzzles, $1 for each puzzle solved. The rewarded students were later less inclined to work on the puzzles than were students who had not been paid. Unfortunately, these results are difficult to interpret because the students sometimes failed to meet the reward standard, and failure itself is known to reduce interest in an activity.[16]

Success-contingent rewards are given for good performance and might reflect either success or progress toward a goal. Success-contingent rewards do not have negative effects; in fact, they typically *increase* interest in the rewarded activity. For example, Ross Vasta and Louise Stirpe awarded gold stars to third- and fourth-graders each time they completed a kind of math exercise they enjoyed. After seven days of awards, the gold stars stopped. Not only was there no evidence of a loss in interest, but time spent on the math activity actually increased. Nor was there any decline in the quality of the work produced.[17]

Dickinson concludes that the danger of undermining student motivation stems not from extrinsic rewards, but from the use of inappropriate reward contingencies. Rewards reduce motivation when they are given without regard to performance or when the performance standard is so high that students frequently fail. When students have a high rate of success and when those successes are rewarded, the rewards *do not have negative effects*. Indeed, success-contingent rewards tend to increase interest in the activity. This finding, writes Dickinson, "is robust and consistent." She adds that "even strong opponents of contingent rewards recognize that success-based rewards do not have harmful effects."[18]

The evidence, then, shows that extrinsic rewards can either enhance or reduce interest in an activity, depending on how they are used. Still, it might be argued that, because extrinsic rewards *sometimes* cause problems, we might be wise to avoid their use altogether. The decision not to use extrinsic rewards amounts to a decision to rely on alternatives. What are those alternatives? And are they better than extrinsic rewards?

ALTERNATIVES TO REWARDS

Punishment and the threat of punishment are — and probably always have been — the most popular alternatives to extrinsic rewards. Not so long ago, lessons were "taught to the tune of a hickory stick," but the tune was not merely tapped on a desk. Students who did not learn their lessons were not only beaten; they were also humiliated: they sat on a stool (up high, so everyone could see) and wore a silly hat.

Gradually, more subtle forms of punishment were used. "The child at his desk," wrote Skinner, "filling in his workbook, is behaving primarily to escape from the threat of a series of minor aversive events — the teacher's displeasure, the criticism or ridicule of his classmates, an ignominious showing in a competition, low marks, a trip to the office 'to be talked to' by the principal, or a word to the parent who may still resort to the birch rod."[19] Skinner spent a lifetime inveighing against the use of such "aversives," but his efforts were largely ineffective. While extrinsic rewards have been condemned, punishment and the threat of punishment are widely sanctioned.

Punishment is popular because, in the short run at least, it gets results. This is illustrated by an experiment in which Deci and Wayne Cascio told students that, if they did not solve problems correctly within a time limit, they would be exposed to a loud, unpleasant sound. The threat worked: all the students solved all the problems within the time limit, so the threat never had to be fulfilled. Students who were merely rewarded for correct solutions did not do nearly as well.[20]

But there are serious drawbacks to the use of punishment. For one thing, although punishment motivates students to learn, it does not teach them. Or, rather, it teaches them only what *not* to do, not what *to* do. "We do not teach [a student] to learn quickly," Skinner observed, "by punishing him when he learns slowly, or to recall what he has learned by punishing him when he forgets, or to think logically by punishing him when he is illogical."[21]

Punishment also has certain undesirable side effects.[22] To the extent that punishment works, it works by making students anxious. Students get nervous before a test because they fear a poor grade, and they are relieved or anxious when they receive their report card depending on whether or not the grades received will result in punishment from their parents.[23] Students can and do avoid the anxiety caused by such punishment by cutting classes and dropping out of school. We do the same thing when we cancel or "forget" a dental appointment.

Another response to punishment is aggression. Students who do not learn easily — and who therefore cannot readily avoid punishment — are especially apt to become aggressive. Their aggression often takes the form of lying, cheating, stealing, and refusing to cooperate. Students also act out by cursing, by being rude and insulting, by destroying property, and by hitting people. Increasingly, teachers are the objects of these aggressive acts.

Finally, it should be noted that punishment has the same negative impact on intrinsic motivation as extrinsic rewards are alleged to have. In the Deci and Cascio study just described, for example, when students were given the chance to work on puzzles with the threat of punishment removed, they were less likely to do so than were students who had never worked under the threat of punishment.[24] Punishment in the form of criticism of performance also reduces interest in an activity.[25]

Punishment is not the only alternative to the use of extrinsic rewards. Teachers can also encourage students. Encouragement consists of various forms of behavior intended to induce students to perform. We encourage students when we urge them to try, express confidence in their ability to do assignments, and recite such platitudes as "A winner never quits and a quitter never wins."[26]

In encouraging students, we are not merely urging them to perform, however; we are implicitly suggesting a relationship between continued performance and certain consequences. "Come on, Billy — you can do it" means, "If you persist at this task, you will be rewarded with success." The power of encouragement is ultimately dependent on the occurrence of the implied consequences. If the teacher tells Billy he can do it and if he tries

and fails, future urging by the teacher will be less effective.

Another problem with encouragement is that, like punishment, it motivates but does not teach. The student who is urged to perform a task is not thereby taught how to perform it. Encouragement is a safer procedure than punishment, since it is less likely to provoke anxiety or aggression. Students who are repeatedly urged to do things at which they ultimately fail do, however, come to distrust the judgment of the teacher. They also come to believe that they cannot live up to the expectations of teachers — and therefore must be hopelessly stupid.

Intrinsic rewards present the most promising alternative to extrinsic rewards. Experts on reinforcement, including defenders of extrinsic rewards, universally sing the praises of intrinsic rewards. Unlike punishment and encouragement, intrinsic rewards actually teach. Students who can see that they have solved a problem correctly know how to solve other problems of that sort. And, unlike extrinsic rewards, intrinsic rewards do not depend on the teacher or some other person.

But there are problems with intrinsic rewards, just as there are with extrinsic ones. Sometimes students lack the necessary skills to obtain intrinsic rewards. Knowledge, understanding, and the aesthetic pleasures of language are all intrinsic rewards for reading, but they are not available to those for whom reading is a difficult and painful activity.

Often, intrinsic rewards are too remote to be effective. If a student is asked to add 3 + 7, what is the intrinsic reward for answering correctly? The student who learns to add will one day experience the satisfaction of checking the accuracy of a restaurant bill, but this future reward is of no value to the youngster just learning to add. Though important in maintaining what has been learned, intrinsic rewards are often too remote to be effective reinforcers in the early stages of learning.

One problem that often goes unnoticed is that the intrinsic rewards for academic work are often weaker than the rewards available for other behavior. Students are rewarded for looking out the window, daydreaming, reading comic books, taking things from other students, passing notes, telling and listening to jokes, moving about the room, fighting, talking back to the teacher, and for all sorts of activities that are incompatible

with academic learning. Getting the right answer to a grammar question might be intrinsically rewarding, but for many students it is considerably less rewarding than the laughter of one's peers in response to a witty remark.

While intrinsic rewards are important, then, they are insufficient for efficient learning.[27] Nor will encouragement and punishment fill the gap. The teacher must supplement intrinsic rewards with extrinsic rewards. This means not only telling the student when he or she has succeeded, but also praising, complimenting, applauding, and providing other forms of recognition for good work. Some students may need even stronger reinforcers, such as special privileges, certificates, and prizes.

REWARD GUIDELINES

Yet we cannot ignore the fact that extrinsic rewards can have adverse effects on student motivation. While there seems to be little chance of serious harm, it behooves us to use care. Various experts have suggested guidelines to follow in using extrinsic rewards.[28] Here is a digest of their recommendations:

1. Use the weakest reward required to strengthen a behavior. Don't use money if a piece of candy will do; don't use candy if praise will do. The good effects of reinforcement come not so much from the reward itself as from the reward contingency: the relationship between the reward and the behavior.

2. When possible, avoid using rewards as incentives. For example, don't say, "If you do X, I'll give you Y." Instead, ask the student to perform a task and then provide a reward for having completed it. In most cases, rewards work best if they are pleasant surprises.

3. Reward at a high rate in the early stages of learning, and reduce the frequency of rewards as learning progresses. Once students have the alphabet down pat, there is no need to compliment them each time they print a letter correctly. Nor is there much need to reward behavior that is already occurring at a high rate.

4. Reward only the behavior you want repeated. If students who whine and complain get their way, expect to see a lot of whining and complaining. Similarly, if you provide gold stars only for the three best papers in the class, you are rewarding competition and should not be surprised if students do not cooperate

with one another. And if "spelling doesn't count," don't expect to see excellent spelling.

5. Remember that what is an effective reward for one student may not work well with another. Some students respond rapidly to teacher attention; others do not. Some work well for gold stars; others don't. Effective rewards are ordinarily things that students seek — positive feedback, praise, approval, recognition, toys — but ultimately a reward's value is to be judged by its effect on behavior.

6. Reward success, and set standards so that success is within the student's grasp. In today's heterogeneous classrooms, that means setting standards for each student. A good way to do this is to reward improvement or progress toward a goal. Avoid rewarding students merely for participating in an activity, without regard for the quality of their performance.

7. Bring attention to the rewards (both intrinsic and extrinsic) that are available for behavior from sources *other than the teacher.* Point out, for example, the fun to be had from the word play in poetry or from sharing a poem with another person. Show students who are learning computer programming the pleasure in "making the computer do things." Let students know that it's okay to applaud those who make good presentations so that they can enjoy the approval of their peers for a job well done. Ask parents to talk with their children about school and to praise them for learning. The goal is to shift the emphasis from rewards provided by the teacher to those that will occur even when the teacher is not present.[29]

Following these rules is harder in practice than it might seem, and most teachers will need training in their implementation. But reinforcement is probably the most powerful tool available to teachers, and extrinsic rewards are powerful reinforcers. To teach without using extrinsic rewards is analogous to asking our students to learn to draw with their eyes closed. Before we do that, we should open our own eyes.

1. The study is described in E. L. Thorndike, *Human Learning* (1931; reprint ed., Cambridge, Mass.: MIT Press, 1966).

2. There are various theories (cognitive, neurological, and psychosocial) about why certain consequences reinforce or strengthen behavior. The important thing for our purposes is that they do.

3. John I. Goodlad, *A Place Called School: Prospects for the Future* (New York: McGraw-Hill, 1984). Goodlad complains about the "paucity of praise" in schools. In doing so, he echoes B. F. Skinner, who wrote that "perhaps the most serious criticism of the current classroom is the relative infrequency of reinforcement." See B. F. Skinner, *The Technology of Teaching* (Englewood Cliffs, N.J.: Prentice-Hall, 1968), p. 17.

4. Bill L. Hopkins and R. J. Conard, "Putting It All Together: Superschool," in Norris G. Haring and Richard L. Schiefelbusch, eds., *Teaching Special Children* (New York: McGraw-Hill, 1975), pp. 342-85. Skinner suggests that mastering the first four years of arithmetic instruction efficiently would require something on the order of 25,000 reinforcements. See Skinner, op. cit.

5. See, for example, Bill L. Hopkins, "Comments on the Future of Applied Behavior Analysis," *Journal of Applied Behavior Analysis*, vol. 20, 1987, pp. 339-46. In some studies, students learned at double the normal rate, yet most teachers did not continue reinforcing behavior at high rates after the study ended.

6. See, for example, Hopkins and Conard, op. cit.

7. For example, Mihaly Csikszentmihalyi found that adults who are successful and happy tend to have had happy childhoods. See Tina Adler, "Support and Challenge: Both Key for Smart Kids," *APA Monitor*, September 1991, pp. 10-11.

8. The terms *reinforcer* and *reward* are often used interchangeably, but they are not really synonyms. A reinforcer is defined by its effects: an event that strengthens the behavior it follows is a reinforcer, regardless of what it was intended to do. A reward is defined by social convention as something desirable; it may or may not strengthen the behavior it follows. The distinction is important since some studies that show negative effects from extrinsic rewards use rewards that are *not* reinforcers. See Alyce M. Dickinson, "The Detrimental Effects of Extrinsic Reinforcement on 'Intrinsic Motivation,'" *The Behavior Analyst*, vol. 12, 1989, pp. 1-15.

9. John Dewey distrusted the distinction between extrinsic and intrinsic rewards. He wrote that "what others do to us when we act is as natural a consequence of our action as what the fire does to us when we plunge our hands in it." Quoted in Samuel M. Deitz, "What Is Unnatural About 'Extrinsic Reinforcement'?," *The Behavior Analyst*, vol. 12, 1989, p. 255.

10. Dickinson writes that "several individuals have demanded that schools abandon reinforcement procedures for fear that they may permanently destroy a child's 'love of learning.'" See Alyce M. Dickinson, "Exploring New Vistas," *Performance Management Magazine*, vol. 9, 1991, p. 28. It is interesting to note that no one worries that earning a school letter will destroy a student's interest in sports. Nor does there seem to be much fear that people who win teaching awards will suddenly become poor teachers. For the most part, only the academic work of students is said to be put at risk by extrinsic rewards.

11. Skinner, p. 162.

12. For reviews of this literature, see Edward L. Deci and Richard M. Ryan, *Intrinsic Motivation and Self-Determination in Human Behavior* (New York: Plenum, 1985); Dickinson, "The Detrimental Effects"; and Mark R. Lepper and David Greene, eds., *The Hidden Costs of Reward: New Perspectives on the Psychology of Human Motivation* (Hillsdale, N.J.: Erlbaum, 1978).

13. Mark R. Lepper, David Greene, and Richard E. Nisbett, "Undermining Children's Intrinsic In-terest with Extrinsic Rewards," *Journal of Personality and Social Psychology*, vol. 28, 1973, pp. 129-37.

14. See, for example, Dickinson, "The Detrimental Effects"; and Mark Morgan, "Reward-Induced Decrements and Increments in Intrinsic Motivation," *Review of Educational Research*, vol. 54, 1984, pp. 5-30. Dickinson notes that studies producing negative effects are often hard to interpret since other variables (failure, deadlines, competition, and so on) could account for the findings. By way of example, she cites a study in which researchers offered a $5 reward to top performers. The study was thus contaminated by the effects of competition, yet the negative results were attributed to extrinsic rewards.

15. Dickinson, "The Detrimental Effects."

16. Edward L. Deci, "Effects of Externally Mediated Rewards on Intrinsic Motivation," *Journal of Personality and Social Psychology*, vol. 18, 1971, pp. 105-15.

17. Ross Vasta and Louise A. Stirpe, "Reinforcement Effects on Three Measures of Children's Interest in Math," *Behavior Modification*, vol. 3, 1979, pp. 223-44.

18. Dickinson, "The Detrimental Effects," p. 9. See also Morgan, op. cit.

19. Skinner, p. 15.

20. Edward L. Deci and Wayne F. Cascio, "Changes in Intrinsic Motivation as a Function of Negative Feedback and Threats," paper presented at the annual meeting of the Eastern Psychological Association, Boston, May 1972. This paper is summarized in Edward L. Deci and Joseph Porac, "Cognitive Evaluation Theory and the Study of Human Motivation," in Lepper and Greene, pp. 149-76.

21. Skinner, p. 149.

22. For more on the problems associated with punishment, see Murray Sidman, *Coercion and Its Fallout* (Boston: Authors Cooperative, Inc., 1989).

23. Grades are often referred to as rewards, but they are more often punishments. Students study not so much to receive high grades as to avoid receiving low ones.

24. Deci and Cascio, op. cit.

25. See, for example, Edward L. Deci, Wayne F. Cascio, and Judy Krusell, "Sex Differences, Positive Feedback, and Intrinsic Motivation," paper presented at the annual meeting of the Eastern Psychological Association, Washington, D.C., May 1973. This paper is summarized in Deci and Porac, op. cit.

26. It should be noted that encouragement often closely resembles reinforcement in form. One teacher may say, "I know you can do it, Mary," as Mary struggles to answer a question; another teacher may say, "I knew you could do it, Mary!" when Mary answers the question correctly. The first teacher is encouraging; the second is reinforcing. The difference is subtle but important.

27. Intrinsic rewards are more important to the maintenance of skills once learned. An adult's skill at addition and subtraction is not ordinarily maintained by the approval of peers but by the satisfaction that comes from balancing a checkbook.

28. See, for example, Jere Brophy, "Teacher Praise: A Functional Analysis," *Review of Educational Research*, vol. 51, 1981, pp. 5-32; Hopkins and Conard, op. cit.; and Dickinson, "The Detrimental Effects."

29. "Instructional contingencies," writes Skinner, "are usually contrived and should always be temporary. If instruction is to have any point, the behavior it generates will be taken over and maintained by contingencies in the world at large." See Skinner, p. 144.

Rewards Versus Learning:
A Response to Paul Chance

Mr. Kohn raises some questions about Paul Chance's article in the November 1992 Kappan *and suggests that an engaging curriculum — not manipulating children with artificial incentives — offers a genuine alternative to boredom in school and to diminished motivation when school lets out.*

....

ALFIE KOHN

ALFIE KOHN is an independent scholar living in Cambridge, Mass., who writes and lectures widely on human behavior and education. His newest book is Punished by Rewards: The Trouble with Gold Stars, Incentive Plans, A's, Praise, and Other Bribes *(Houghton Mifflin, October 1993). ©1993, Alfie Kohn.*

IN THE COURSE of offering some suggestions for how educators can help children become more generous and empathic ("Caring Kids: The Role of the Schools," March 1991), I argued that manipulating student behavior with either punishments or rewards is not only unnecessary but counterproductive. Paul Chance, taking exception to this passage, wrote to defend the use of rewards (Backtalk, June 1991). Now, following the publication of his longer brief for behaviorism ("The Rewards of Learning," November 1992), it is my turn to raise some questions — and to continue what I hope is a constructive dialogue between us (not to mention a long overdue examination of classroom practices too often taken for granted).

To begin, I should mention two points where our perspectives converge. Neither of us favors the use of punishment, and both of us think that rewards, like other strategies, must be judged by their long-term effects, including what they do for (or to) children's motivation. Chance and I disagree, however, on the nature of those effects.

Rewards, like punishments, can usually get people to do what we want for a while. In that sense, they "work." But my reading of the research, corroborated by real-world observation, is that rewards can never buy us anything more than short-term compliance. Moreover, we — or, more accurately, the people we are rewarding — pay a steep price over time for our reliance on extrinsic motivators.

REWARDS ARE INHERENTLY CONTROLLING

Applied behaviorism, which amounts to saying, "Do this and you'll get that," is essentially a technique for controlling people. In the classroom, it is a way of doing things *to* children rather than working *with* them. Chance focuses on the empirical effects of rewards, but I feel obliged to pause at least long enough to stress that moral issues are involved here regardless of whether we ultimately endorse or oppose the use of rewards.

By now it is not news that reinforcement strategies were developed and refined through experiments on laboratory animals. Many readers also realize that underlying the practice of reinforcement is a theory — specifically, the assumption that humans, like all organisms, are basically inert beings whose behavior must be elicited by external motivation in the form of carrots or sticks. For example, Alyce Dickinson, the author Chance cites six times and from whom he borrows the gist of his defense of rewards, plainly acknowledges the central premise of the perspective she and Chance share, which is that "all behavior is ultimately initiated by the external environment."[1] Anyone who recoils from this theoretical foundation ought to take a fresh look at the real-world practices that rest on it.

I am troubled by a model of human relationship or learning that is defined by control rather than, say, persuasion or mutual problem solving. Because the reinforcements themselves are desired by their recipients, it is easy to miss the fact that using them is simply a matter of "control[ling] through seduction rather than force."[2] Rewards and punishments (bribes and threats, positive reinforcements and "consequences" — call them what you will) are not really opposites at all. They are two sides of the same coin. The good news is that our options are not limited to variations on the theme of behavioral manipulation.[3]

REWARDS ARE INEFFECTIVE

The question of how well rewards *work*, apart from what they do to children's long-term motivation, is dispatched by Chance in a single sentence: "No one disputes the effectiveness of extrinsic rewards in teaching or in maintaining good discipline" (p. 203). I found myself rereading the paragraph in which this extraordinary claim appears, searching for signs that Chance was being ironic.

In point of fact, the evidence overwhelmingly demonstrates that extrinsic rewards are ineffective at producing lasting change in attitudes or even behaviors. Moreover, they typically do not enhance — and often actually impede — performance on tasks that are any more complex than pressing a bar. This evidence, which I have been sorting through recently for a book-length treatment of these issues (*Punished by Rewards*, scheduled for publication this fall), is piled so high on my desk that I fear it will topple over. I cannot review all of it here; a few samples will have to do.

Consider first the matter of behavior change. Even behaviorists have had to concede that the token economy, a form of behavior modification once (but, mercifully, no longer) popular for controlling people in institutions, doesn't work. When the goodies stop, people go right back to acting the way they did before the program began.[4] Studies have found that rewarding people for losing weight,[5] quitting smoking,[6] or using seat belts[7] is typically less effective than using other strategies — and often proves worse than doing nothing at all.

Children whose parents make frequent use of rewards or praise are likely to be less generous than their peers.[8] On reflection, this makes perfect sense: a child promised a treat for acting responsibly has been given no reason to keep behaving that way when there is no longer a reward to be gained for doing so. The implications for behavioristic classroom management programs such as Assertive Discipline, in which children are essentially bribed or threatened to conform to rules that the teacher alone devises, are painfully clear.

Rewards (like punishments) can get people to do what we want in the short term: buckle up, share a toy, read a book. In that sense, Chance is right that their effectiveness is indisputable. But they rarely produce effects that survive the rewards themselves, which is why behaviorists are placed in the position of having to argue that we need to keep the goodies coming or replace one kind of reward with another (e.g., candy bars with grades). The fact is that extrinsic motivators do not alter the attitudes that underlie our behaviors. They do not create an enduring *commitment* to a set of values or to learning; they merely, and temporarily, change what we do. If, like Skinner, you think there is nothing to humans other than what we do, then this criticism will not trouble you. If, on the

> The good news is that our options are not limited to variations on the theme of behavioral manipulation.

other hand, you think that our actions reflect and emerge from who we *are* (what we think and feel, expect and will), then you have no reason to expect interventions that merely control actions to work in the long run.

As for the effect on performance, I know of at least two dozen studies showing that people expecting to receive a reward for completing a task (or for doing it successfully) don't perform as well as those who expect nothing. The effect is robust for young children, older children, and adults; for males and females; for rewards of all kinds (including money, grades, toys, food, and special privileges). The tasks in these studies range from memorizing facts to engaging in creative problem solving, from discriminating between similar drawings to designing collages. In general, the more cognitive sophistication and open-ended thinking required, the worse people do when they are working for a reward.[9]

At first researchers didn't know what to make of these findings. (A good sign that one has stumbled onto something important is the phrase "contrary to hypothesis" in a research report.) "The clear inferiority of the reward groups was an unexpected result, unaccountable for by theory or previous empirical evidence," a pair of experimenters confessed in 1961.[10] Rewards "have effects that interfere with performance in ways that we are only beginning to understand," said Janet Spence (later president of the American Psychological Association) in 1971.[11] Since then, most researchers — with the exception of a small cadre of un-

reconstructed behaviorists — have gotten the message that, on most tasks, a Skinnerian strategy is worse than useless: it is counterproductive.

REWARDS MAKE LEARNING LESS APPEALING

Even more research indicates that rewards also undermine *interest* — a finding with obvious and disturbing implications for the use of grades, stickers, and even praise. Here Chance concedes there may be a problem but, borrowing Dickinson's analysis, assures us that the damage is limited. Dickinson grants that motivation tends to decline when people are rewarded just for engaging in a task and also when they receive performance-contingent rewards — those "based on performance standards" (Dickinson) or "available only when the student achieves a certain standard" (Chance).

But Dickinson then proceeds to invent a new category, "success-contingent" rewards, and calls these innocuous. The term means that, when rewards are given out, "subjects are told they have received the rewards because of good performance." For Chance, though, a "success-contingent" reward is "given for good performance and might reflect either success or progress toward a goal" — a definition that appears to diverge from Dickinson's and that sounds quite similar to what is meant by "performance-contingent." As near as I can figure, the claim both Dickinson and Chance are making is that, when people come away thinking that they have done well, a reward for what they have achieved doesn't hurt. On this single claim rests the entire defense against the devastating charge that by rewarding students for their achievement we are leading them to see learning as a chore. But what does the research really say?

Someone who simply glances at the list of studies Dickinson offers to support her assertion might come away impressed. Someone who takes the time to read those studies will come away with a renewed sense of the importance of going straight to the primary source. It turns out that two of the studies don't even deal with rewards for successful performance.[12] Another one actually *disproves* the contention that success-contingent rewards are harmless: it finds that this kind of reward not only undermines intrinsic motivation but is more destructive than rewards given just for engaging in the task![13]

The rest of the studies cited by Dickinson indicate that some subjects in laboratory experiments who receive success-contingent rewards are neither more nor less interested in the task than those who get nothing at all. But Dickinson curiously omits a number of *other* studies that are also set up so that some subjects succeed (or think they succeed) at a task and are presented with a reward. These studies have found that such rewards *do* reduce interest.[14]

Such a result really shouldn't be surprising. As Edward Deci and his colleagues have been pointing out for years, adults and children alike chafe at being deprived of a sense of self-determination. Rewards usually feel controlling, and rewards contingent on performance ("If you do a good job, here's what I'll give you") are the most controlling of all. Even the good feeling produced by doing well often isn't enough to overcome that fact. To the extent that information about how well we have done *is* interest-enhancing, this is not an argument for Skinnerian tactics. In fact, when researchers have specifically compared the effects of straightforward performance feedback ("Here's how you did") and performance-contingent rewards ("Here's a goody for doing well"), the latter undermined intrinsic motivation more than the former.[15]

Finally, even if all the research really did show what Dickinson and Chance claim it does, remember that outside of the laboratory people often fail. That result is more likely to be de-motivating when it means losing out on a reward, such as an A or a bonus. This Chance implicitly concedes, although the force of the point gets lost: students do not turn off from failing per se but from failing when a reward is at stake. In learning contexts free of extrinsic motivators, students are more likely to persist at a task and to remain interested in it even when they don't do it well.

All of this means that getting children to think about learning as a way to receive a sticker, a gold star, or a grade — or, even worse, to get money or a toy *for* a grade, which amounts to an extrinsic motivator for an extrinsic motivator — is likely to turn learning from an end into a means. Learning becomes something that must be gotten through in order to receive the reward. Take the depressingly pervasive program by which children receive certificates for free pizza when they have read a certain number of books. John Nicholls of the University of Illinois comments, only half in jest, that the likely consequence of this program is "a lot of fat kids who don't like to read."

Educational psychologists such as Nicholls, Carol Dweck, and Carole Ames keep finding that when children are led to concentrate on their performance, on how well they are doing — an inevitable consequence of the use of rewards or punishments — they become less interested in *what* they are doing. ("Do we have to know this? Will it be on the test?") I am convinced that one of the primary obligations of educators and parents who want to promote a lasting commitment to learning is to do everything in their power to help students forget that grades exist.

REWARDS IGNORE CURRICULAR QUESTIONS

One last point. Chance's defense of the Skinnerian status quo might more properly have been titled "The Rewards *for* Learning." My interest is in the rewards *of* learning, a concern that requires us to ask whether we are teaching something *worth* learning. This is a question that behaviorists do not need to ask; it is enough to devise an efficient technique to reinforce the acquisition of whatever happens to be in someone's lesson plan.

Chance addresses the matter of intrinsic motivation just long enough to dismiss it as "too remote to be effective." He sets up a false dichotomy, with an abstract math problem on one side (Why would a child be motivated to learn that 7 + 3 = 10? he wants to know) and reinforcements (the solution to this problem) on the other. Indeed, if children are required to fill in an endless series of blanks on worksheets or to memorize meaningless, disconnected facts, they may *have* to be bribed to do so. But Chance seems oblivious to exciting developments in the field of education: the whole-language movement, the emphasis on "learner-centered" learning, and the entire constructivist tradition (in which teaching takes its cue from the way each child actively constructs meaning and makes sense of the world rather than treating students as passive responders to environmental stimuli).

I invite Chance to join the campaign for an engaging curriculum that is connected to children's lives and interests, for an approach to pedagogy in which students are given real choices about their studies, and for classrooms in which they are allowed and helped to work with one another. Pursuing these approaches, not manipulating children with artificial incentives, offers a *real* alternative to boredom in school and to diminished motivation when school lets out.

1. Alyce M. Dickinson, "The Detrimental Effects of Extrinsic Reinforcement on 'Intrinsic Motivation,'" *The Behavior Analyst*, vol. 12, 1989, p. 12. Notice the quotation marks around "intrinsic motivation," as if to question the very existence of the phenomenon — a telltale sign of Skinnerian orthodoxy.

2. Edward L. Deci and Richard M. Ryan, *Intrinsic Motivation and Self-Determination in Human Behavior* (New York: Plenum, 1985), p. 70.

3. Behaviorists are apt to rejoin that control is an unavoidable feature of all relationships. In response I would point out that there is an enormous difference between saying that even subtle reinforcements can be controlling and asserting that all human interaction is best described as an exercise in control. The latter takes on faith that selfhood and choice are illusions and that we do only what we have been reinforced for doing. A far more defensible position, it seems to me, is that some forms of human interaction are controlling and some are not. The line might not be easy to draw in practice, but the distinction is still meaningful and important.

4. "Generally, removal of token reinforcement results in decrements in desirable responses and a return to baseline or near-baseline levels of performance," as the first major review of token economies concluded. In fact, not only does the behavior fail "to generalize to conditions in which [reinforcements] are not in effect" — such as the world outside the hospital — but reinforcement programs used each morning generally don't even have much effect on patients' behavior during the afternoon! See Alan E. Kazdin and Richard R. Bootzin, "The Token Economy: An Evaluative Review," *Journal of Applied Behavior Analysis*, vol. 5, 1972, pp. 359-60. Ten years later, one of these authors — an enthusiastic proponent of behavior modification, incidentally — checked back to see if anything had changed. "As a general rule," he wrote, with an almost audible sigh, "it is still prudent to assume that behavioral gains are likely to be lost in varying degrees once the client leaves the program." See Alan E. Kazdin, "The Token Economy: A Decade Later," *Journal of Applied Behavior Analysis*, vol. 15, 1982, pp. 435-37. Others reviewing the research on token economies have come to more or less the same conclusion.

5. The only two studies I am aware of that looked at weight loss programs to see what happened when people were paid for getting slimmer found that the incentives either had no effect or were actually counterproductive. See Richard A. Dienstbier and Gary K. Leak, "Overjustification and Weight Loss: The Effects of Monetary Reward," paper presented at the annual meeting of the American Psychological Association, Washington, D.C., September 1976; and F. Matthew Kramer et al., "Maintenance of Successful Weight Loss Over 1 Year: Effects of Financial Contracts for Weight Maintenance or Participation in Skills Training," *Behavior Therapy*, vol. 17, 1986, pp. 295-301.

6. A very large study, published in 1991, recruited subjects for a self-help program designed to help people quit smoking. Three months later, those who had been offered a prize for turning in weekly prog-

ress reports were lighting up again more often than were those who had received a no-reward treatment — and even more than those who didn't take part in any program at all. In fact, for people who received both treatments, "the financial incentive somehow diminished the positive impact of the personalized feedback." See Susan J. Curry et al., "Evaluation of Intrinsic and Extrinsic Motivation Interventions with a Self-Help Smoking Cessation Program," *Journal of Consulting and Clinical Psychology*, vol. 59, 1991, p. 323.

7. A committed behaviorist and his colleagues reviewed the effects of 28 programs used by nine different companies to get their employees to use seat belts. Nearly half a million vehicle observations were made over six years in the course of this research. The result: programs that rewarded people for wearing their seat belts were the least effective over the long haul. The author had to confess that "the greater impact of the no-reward strategies from both an immediate and [a] long-term perspective . . . [was] not predicted and [is] inconsistent with basic reinforcement theory." See E. Scott Geller et al., "Employer-Based Programs to Motivate Safety Belt Use: A Review of Short-Term and Long-Term Effects," *Journal of Safety Research*, vol. 18, 1987, pp. 1-17.

8. Richard A. Fabes et al., "Effects of Rewards on Children's Prosocial Motivation: A Socialization Study," *Developmental Psychology*, vol. 25, 1989, pp. 509-15. Praise appears to have a similar detrimental effect; see Joan E. Grusec, "Socializing Concern for Others in the Home," *Developmental Psychology*, vol. 27, 1991, pp. 338-42. See also the studies reviewed in Alfie Kohn, *The Brighter Side of Human Nature: Altruism and Empathy in Everyday Life* (New York: Basic Books, 1990), pp. 201-4.

9. A complete bibliography will be available in my forthcoming book, *Punished by Rewards*. Readers unwilling to wait might wish to begin by reading Mark R. Lepper and David Greene, eds., *The Hidden Costs of Rewards* (Hillsdale, N.J.: Erlbaum, 1978), and some of Teresa Amabile's work from the 1980s documenting how rewards kill creativity.

10. Louise Brightwell Miller and Betsy Worth Estes, "Monetary Reward and Motivation in Discrimination Learning," *Journal of Experimental Psychology*, vol. 61, 1961, p. 503.

11. Janet Taylor Spence, "Do Material Rewards Enhance the Performance of Lower-Class Children?," *Child Development*, vol. 42, 1971, p. 1469.

12. In one of the studies, either money or an award was given to children just for taking part in the experiment — and both caused interest in the task to decline. See Rosemarie Anderson et al., "The Undermining and Enhancing of Intrinsic Motivation in Preschool Children," *Journal of Personality and Social Psychology*, vol. 34, 1976, pp. 915-22. In the other, a total of three children were simply praised ("good," "nice going") whenever they engaged in a task; no mention was made of how well they were performing. See Jerry A. Martin, "Effects of Positive and Negative Adult-Child Interactions on Children's Task Performance and Task Preferences," *Journal of Experimental Child Psychology*, vol. 23, 1977, pp. 493-502.

13. Michael Jay Weiner and Anthony M. Mander, "The Effects of Reward and Perception of Competency upon Intrinsic Motivation," *Motivation and Emotion*, vol. 2, 1978, pp. 67-73.

14. Chance doesn't like Deci's 1971 study, but there are plenty of others. In David Greene and Mark R. Lepper, "Effects of Extrinsic Rewards on Children's Subsequent Intrinsic Interest," *Child Development*, vol. 45, 1974, pp. 1141-45, children who were promised a reward if they drew very good pictures — and then did receive the reward, along with a reminder of the accomplishment it represented — were less interested in drawing later than were children who got nothing. See also James Garbarino, "The Impact of Anticipated Reward upon Cross-Age Tutoring," *Journal of Personality and Social Psychology*, vol. 32, 1975, pp. 421-28; Terry D. Orlick and Richard Mosher, "Extrinsic Awards and Participant Motivation in a Sport Related Task," *International Journal of Sport Psychology*, vol. 9, 1978, pp. 27-39; Judith M. Harackiewicz, "The Effects of Reward Contingency and Performance Feedback on Intrinsic Motivation," *Journal of Personality and Social Psychology*, vol. 37, 1979, pp. 1352-63; and Richard A. Fabes, "Effects of Reward Contexts on Young Children's Task Interest," *Journal of Psychology*, vol. 121, 1987, pp. 5-19. See too the studies cited in, and conclusions offered by, Kenneth O. McGraw, "The Detrimental Effects of Reward on Performance: A Literature Review and a Prediction Model," in Lepper and Greene, eds., p. 40; Mark R. Lepper, "Extrinsic Reward and Intrinsic Motivation," in John M. Levine and Margaret C. Wang, eds., *Teacher and Student Perceptions: Implications for Learning* (Hillsdale, N.J.: Erlbaum, 1983), pp. 304-5; and Deci and Ryan, p. 78.

15. Richard M. Ryan et al., "Relation of Reward Contingency and Interpersonal Context to Intrinsic Motivation: A Review and Test Using Cognitive Evaluation Theory," *Journal of Personality and Social Psychology*, vol. 45, 1983, pp. 736-50. "Rewards in general appear to have a controlling significance to some extent and thus in general run the risk of undermining intrinsic motivation," the authors wrote (p. 748).

Sticking Up for Rewards

It is ironic that honest feedback or a straightforward contingency between work and rewards should be called manipulative, while "persuasion" and "mutual problem solving" should not, Mr. Chance retorts.

....

PAUL CHANCE

PAUL CHANCE (Eastern Shore Maryland Chapter) is a psychologist, writer, and former teacher. He is the author of Thinking in the Classroom *(Teachers College Press, 1986).*

I T IS DIFFICULT to know how to respond to Alfie Kohn's critique.* It is so disjointed and so full of misrepresentations of fact and theory that it is like a greased pig: one can scarcely get a grip on it, let alone wrestle it to the ground. I will illustrate what I mean with a few examples and then reply to what I believe to be Kohn's major objections.

Item: To reward, Kohn says, is to say to a student, "Do this and you'll get that." But this is only one kind of reward — and one that I specifically advised readers to avoid when possible. It is these "contractual rewards" (or incentives) that are apt to be problematic.[1] My article focused on rewards that provide feedback about performance. Such "informational rewards" reflect effort or the quality of performance (e.g., "Good try, Janet"; "Great job, Billy"). As we shall see, even researchers who criticize contractual rewards do not normally object to informational rewards.

[*See *Phi Delta Kappan*, June 1993. Ed.]

Item: Kohn says that I ask, Why would a child be motivated to learn that 7 + 3 = 10? But my question was, *How* can a child learn that 7 + 3 = 10 without some sort of response from the environment? A teacher, a peer tutor, or a computer program may provide the necessary feedback, but the natural environment rarely does. This was the point of E. L. Thorndike's line experiment, described in my article.

Item: Kohn suggests that the use of rewards is manipulative and controlling. It is ironic that honest feedback or a straightforward contingency between work and rewards should be called manipulative, while "persuasion" and "mutual problem solving" should not. Students, I suspect, know the truth of the matter. As for control: a parent rewards a baby's crying when he or she offers a bottle, and the baby rewards the parent's action by ceasing to cry. Each controls the other. Students and teachers exert the same sort of reciprocal control in the classroom.[2]

Item: Nowhere do I suggest that students must "fill in an endless series of blanks on worksheets or memorize meaningless, disconnected facts," nor is there any reason to assume that the use of rewards implies such practices. The truth is that rewards are useful whether the student is memorizing dates, mastering algebra word problems, or learning to think.[3] Some sort of extrinsic reinforcement (informational reward) is usually necessary, in the early stages at least, for learning to occur efficiently.

Item: Kohn refers to "practices too often taken for granted." Evidently he believes the mythology that rewards are widely used in our schools. Yet I noted in my article that John Goodlad found that only 2% of class time is devoted to reinforcement in elementary school — and only 1% in high school.[4] Other research consistently shows that reinforcement is notable by its absence. Harold Stevenson, for example, compared elementary classrooms in America and Asia. He found pronounced differences in the activities of teachers when students were engaged in seatwork. In half of the classes observed in the Chicago area, the teachers provided no feedback about student performance; this seldom happened in Taiwan and almost never happened in Japan.[5]

Item: I do not assume, as suggested, that "humans, like all organisms, are basically inert beings." Nor do I know any psychologist who would embrace this view. Behavioral psychologists in particular emphasize that we learn by *acting on* our environment. As B. F. Skinner put it: "[People] act on the world, and change it, and are changed in turn by the consequences of their actions."[6] Skinner, unlike Kohn, understood that people learn best in a responsive environment. Teachers who praise or otherwise reward student performance provide such an environment.

Item: Kohn implies that I consider grades a reward. In fact, I noted (as Skinner and others had before me) that grades are more often a form of punishment. Incidentally, F. S. Keller, a behaviorist, proposed a system of education that could eliminate grades. In the Keller plan, students are required to demonstrate mastery of each skill before moving to the next. Mastery of each unit in the curriculum is recorded, so grades become superfluous.[7]

Item: Kohn says that "moral issues are involved." The implication is that I and other teachers who use rewards are immoral. If it is immoral to let students know they have answered questions correctly, to pat a student on the back for a good effort, to show joy at a student's understanding of a concept, or to recognize the achievement of a goal by providing a gold star or a certificate — if this is immoral, then count me a sinner.

The above points illustrate, I think, the slippery nature of Kohn's critique and may lead the reader to question his scholarship and his motives for writing. I now turn to what seem to be his major criticisms of rewards.

▰ Kohn insists that rewards undermine interest in rewarded activities.[8] Notice that Kohn does not argue that *some* rewards — or *some uses of* rewards — undermine interest. There is, in his view, no such thing as a good reward. Simple feedback, praise, smiles, hugs, pats on the back, gold stars, applause, certificates of completion, public and private commendations, prizes, special privileges, money, informational rewards, and contractual rewards — they are all one to Kohn, and they are all bad.

The best-known researchers who have found rewards sometimes troublesome are Edward Deci, Richard Ryan, Mark Lepper, and David Greene. Kohn cites all four in making his case. What he does not tell us (though he must surely know it) is that all of these researchers reject his view.[9]

Deci and Ryan believe that rewards can undermine motivation if used in a controlling way. But they add, "When used to convey to people a sense of appreciation for work well done, [rewards] will tend to be experienced informationally and will *maintain or enhance intrinsic motivation*" (emphasis added).[10]

Lepper and Greene take a similar stand. They note, "If rewards provide [a student] with new information about his ability at a particular task, this may *bolster his feelings of competence and his desire to engage in that task for its own sake*" (emphasis added).[11] They add, "If a child does not possess the basic skills to discover the intrinsic satisfaction of complex activities such as reading, the use of extrinsic rewards may be required to equip him with these skills."[12]

The position taken by Deci, Ryan, Lepper, and Greene reflects the consensus among researchers who are concerned about the possible negative effects of rewards. Mark Morgan, for example, reviewed the research and wrote that "the central finding emerging from the present review is that rewards can have either undermining or enhancing effects depending on circumstances."[13] He concludes that "the evidence seems to support strongly the hypothesis that rewards that emphasize success or competence on a task enhance intrinsic motivation."[14]

▰ Kohn claims that rewards do not work. It is true that not all rewards are

> Certain rewards (e.g., attention, positive feedback, praise) are almost always effective reinforcers when used properly.

reinforcing. Teachers must not assume that a reward will strengthen behavior merely because that is the teacher's intention. What is reinforcing for one student may not be for another. But there is overwhelming evidence that certain rewards (e.g., attention, positive feedback, praise) are almost always effective reinforcers when used properly.

In a study by Bill Hopkins and R. J. Conard, cited in my article, teachers who provided frequent feedback, praise, and other rewards saw much faster learning.[15] Students in these classes advanced at the normal rate in spelling, at nearly twice the normal rate in mathematics, and at more than double the usual rate in reading.[16] Studies showing similar gains, due at least partly to frequent use of rewards (especially feedback and praise), are easily found by those who seek them.[17]

Even contractual rewards may be useful in some circumstances. In one program, high-risk, low-income adolescents and young adults in Lafayette Parish, Louisiana, were paid $3.40 an hour to participate in a summer program of academic instruction and job training. Students gained an average of 1.2 grade levels in reading and 1.5 grade levels in math in just eight weeks.[18]

It may be the case that the Lafayette Parish students stopped reading when money was no longer available. It probably cannot be said, however, that they read less than they did before participating in the program. If students show little or no interest in an activity, it is silly to refuse to provide rewards for fear of undermining their interest in the activity — a point made by Greene and Lepper.[19]

Kohn ignores such evidence and instead cites studies on the use of contractual rewards in weight control, smoking, and seat belt programs.[20] I am (understandably, I think) reluctant to take Kohn's assessment of these programs at face value.[21] But let us assume for the sake of argument that he is right. Note that none of these programs has anything to do with the value of rewards in classroom learning. Kohn's logic is, "If rewards do not help people stop smoking, they cannot help students learn to write." By the same logic, we would have to conclude that since aspirin is of no use in treating cancer, it must not be effective in treating headache. It is a bizarre logic.

▰ The benefits of rewards, says Kohn, are only temporary. Obviously this is not true if we are speaking of academic learning: the child who learns the Pythagorean theorem at the hands of a teacher who provides frequent feedback and praise does not suddenly forget Pythagoras because his next teacher no longer pays attention to his efforts. Nor is there any reason to think that students who are paid to read become illiterate when the money runs out.

But perhaps Kohn has other kinds of learning in mind. Teachers who praise and attend to students when they are on-task will find those students spending less time staring out the window or doodling in their notebooks.[22] If the teacher abruptly stops rewarding on-task behavior, the rate of window staring and doodling will return to its previous level.[23] To conclude from this that teachers should not reward behavior is ridiculous. It is like saying that regular exercise is pointless because your muscles get flabby again when you stop exercising. The point is not to stop.

It should be noted, moreover, that one of the things we can strengthen with rewards is persistence. Once our students are on-task for short periods, we can then begin rewarding longer periods of on-task behavior. We must be careful not to raise the standard too quickly, but we can *gradually* require more from our students. Persistence at other kinds of activities can also be built up by systematically providing rewards (especially praise) for meeting successively higher standards. Many teachers do this over the course of a school year, often without realizing it.

When behavior is rewarded intermittently in this way, it tends to become stronger. That is, it becomes *less* likely to fall off when rewards are no longer available. This is a well-established phenomenon called the partial reinforcement effect (PRE). The PRE reflects the fact that, in an uncertain world, persistence often pays off.

ONE FINAL comment: I realize that this reply to Kohn's remarks will have little impact on most readers. Kohn is selling what educators want to buy — and what many of them have been buying for several decades. It is the philosophy of education that says that students must teach themselves, that the teacher's job is to let students explore and discover on their own, and that teachers can, at most, "facilitate learning."[24]

This philosophy renders the teacher essentially impotent and leads ultimately to the conclusion that, when students fail, it is their own fault.[25] If students do not learn, it is because of some deficiency in them: lack of ability, lack of motivation, hyperactivity, attention deficit disorder — we have lots of choices. The failure is never due to inadequate teaching. Learning depends, after all, on things inside the student, well out of the teacher's reach.

I reject this view. I believe that a fair reading of the research on classroom learning points to a better way. That better way includes a teacher who is actively engaged in the educational process. Such a teacher recognizes the importance of, among other things, providing students with opportunities to perform and providing consequences for that performance. Those consequences include feedback, praise, smiles, and other forms of informational reward. In certain circumstances, they may include contractual rewards. This view of education places responsibility for learning squarely on the teacher's shoulders. Perhaps that is why there is so much opposition to it.

1. B. F. Skinner was not fond of contractual rewards himself, but he agreed that they may sometimes be necessary. See B. F. Skinner, "The Contrived Reinforcer," *The Behavior Analyst*, Spring 1982, pp. 3-8.

2. In an *Industry Week* survey, about one in three employees complained about a lack of praise for their work, a fact reported in Randall Poe and Carol L. Courter, "Fast Forward," *Across the Board*, September 1991, p. 5. Would workers want more praise if they considered it manipulative and controlling?

3. For instance. students can learn to find logical errors in a text by reading texts containing such errors and receiving feedback and praise for their efforts. See Kent R. Johnson and T. V. Joe Layng, "Breaking the Structuralist Barrier: Literacy and Numeracy with Fluency," *American Psychologist*, vol. 47, 1992, pp. 1475-90. For more on the use of rewards to teach thinking, see Paul Chance, *Thinking in the Classroom* (New York: Teachers College Press, 1986), Ch. 9.

4. John I. Goodlad, *A Place Called School: Prospects for the Future* (New York: McGraw-Hill, 1984), p. 112. Goodlad argues that teachers should be taught the skills of "providing students with knowledge of their performance, and giving praise for good work" (p. 127). For the most part they are not taught these skills. Ernest Vargas notes that, "with the exception of a stray course here or there," the 1,200 colleges of education in this country offer little instruction in reinforcement and related techniques. See Ernest A. Vargas, "Teachers in the Classroom: Behaviorological Science and an Effective Instructional Technology," *Youth Policy*, July/August 1988, p. 35.

5. Harold W. Stevenson, "Learning from Asian Schools," *Scientific American*, December 1992, pp. 70-76. Stevenson suggests that the American preference for seatwork and the failure to provide feedback may be due partly to the fact that Americans teach longer hours than their Asian counterparts.

6. Quoted in James G. Holland, "B. F. Skinner (1904-1990)," *American Psychologist*, vol. 47, 1992, p. 667.

7. F. S. Keller, "Goodbye, Teacher . . . ," *Journal of Applied Behavior Analysis*, Spring 1968, pp. 79-89. See also Paul Chance, "The Revolutionary Gentleman," *Psychology Today*, September 1984, pp. 42-48.

8. Studies reporting a loss of interest following rewards typically involve 1) contractual rewards and 2) behavior that is already occurring at a high rate. This is, of course, a misuse of contractual rewards, since the purpose of such rewards is to boost the rate of behavior that occurs *infrequently*.

9. In my article, I provided guidelines for the effective use of rewards. These guidelines were drawn, in part, from the recommendations of Deci, Ryan, Lepper, and Greene.

10. Edward L. Deci and Richard M. Ryan, *Intrinsic Motivation and Self-Determination in Human Behavior* (New York: Plenum, 1985), p. 300.

11. David Greene and Mark R. Lepper, "Intrinsic Motivation: How to Turn Play into Work," *Psychology Today*, September 1974, p. 54. Elsewhere they write that "the effects of rewards depend upon the manner and context in which they are delivered." See Mark R. Lepper and David Greene, "Divergent Approaches," in idem, eds., *The Hidden Costs of Reward* (New York: Erlbaum, 1978), p. 208.

12. Greene and Lepper, p. 54.

13. Mark Morgan, "Reward-Induced Decrements and Increments in Intrinsic Motivation," *Review of Educational Research*, Spring 1984, p. 13.

14. Ibid., p. 9. Another of Kohn's sources, Teresa Amabile, also specifically defends the use of informational rewards. See Teresa Amabile, "Cashing in on Good Grades," *Psychology Today*, October 1989, p. 80. See also idem, *The Social Psychology of Creativity* (New York: Springer-Verlag, 1983).

15. Bill L. Hopkins and R. J. Conard, "Putting It All Together: Superschool," in Norris G. Haring and Richard L. Schiefelbusch, eds., *Teaching Special Children* (New York: McGraw-Hill, 1975), pp. 342-85.

16. The students also enjoyed school more and were better behaved.

17. See, for example, Charles R. Greenwood et al., "Out of the Laboratory and into the Community," *American Psychologist*, vol. 47, 1992, pp. 1464-74; R. Douglas Greer, "L'Enfant Terrible Meets the Educational Crisis," *Journal of Applied Behavior Analysis*, Spring 1992, pp. 65-69; and Johnson and Layng, op. cit.

18. Steven Hotard and Marion J. Cortez, "Evaluation of Lafayette Parish Job Training Summer Remedial Program: Report Presented to the Lafayette Parish School Board and Lafayette Parish Job Training Department of Lafayette Parish Government," August 1987. Note that this research may not represent the best use of contractual rewards, since payment was only loosely contingent on performance.

19. "Clearly," they write, "if a child begins with no intrinsic interest in an activity, there will be no intrinsic motivation to lose." See Greene and Lepper, p. 54.

20. Note that Kohn cites no evidence that his own preferred techniques — persuasion and mutual problem solving — are effective in helping people lose weight, quit smoking, or use seat belts. Indeed, reward programs have been used to treat these problems precisely because persuasion and education have proved ineffective.

21. For instance, in the study on smoking that Kohn cites, the researchers note that "the incentive was not linked directly to smoking cessation." See Susan J. Curry et al., "Evaluation of Intrinsic and Extrinsic Motivation Interventions with a Self-Help Smoking Cessation Program," *Journal of Consulting and Clinical Psychology*, vol. 59, 1991, p. 309. The researchers rewarded participants for completing progress reports, *not* for refraining from smoking.

22. Teacher attention can be an effective reward for on-task behavior. See R. Vance Hall, Diane Lund, and Deloris Jackson, "Effects of Teacher Attention on Study Behavior," *Journal of Applied Behavior Analysis*, Spring 1968, pp. 1-12.

23. Some might argue that we should merely provide students with more interesting (i.e., intrinsically rewarding) material. While interesting learning materials are certainly desirable, it is probably unrealistic to expect that students will always have interesting material with which to work. It may therefore be desirable for them to learn to concentrate on work even when it is not particularly agreeable.

24. The roots of today's constructivist "revolution" are described in Lawrence A. Cremin, "The Free School Movement," *Today's Education*, September/October 1974, pp. 71-74; and in B. F. Skinner, "The Free and Happy Student," *New York University Education Quarterly*, Winter 1973, pp. 2-6.

25. This is apparently the prevailing view. Galen Alessi has found that school psychologists, for instance, rarely consider poor instruction the source of a student's difficulties. Instead, the student and, in a few cases, the student's parents are said to be at fault. Galen Alessi, "Diagnosis Diagnosed: A Systematic Reaction," *Professional School Psychology*, vol. 3, 1988, pp. 145-51.

The Return of Character Education

Concern over the moral condition of American society is prompting a reevaluation of the schools' role in teaching values.

Thomas Lickona

Thomas Lickona is a developmental psychologist and Professor, Education Department, State University of New York at Cortland, Cortland, NY 13045. He is author of *Educating for Character: How Our Schools Can Teach Respect and Responsibility* (New York: Bantam Books, 1991.)

To educate a person in mind and not in morals is to educate a menace to society.
—*Theodore Roosevelt*

Increasing numbers of people across the ideological spectrum believe that our society is in deep moral trouble. The disheartening signs are everywhere: the breakdown of the family; the deterioration of civility in everyday life; rampant greed at a time when one in five children is poor; an omnipresent sexual culture that fills our television and movie screens with sleaze, beckoning the young toward sexual activity at ever earlier ages; the enormous betrayal of children through sexual abuse; and the 1992 report of the National Research Council that says the United States is now *the* most violent of all industrialized nations.

As we become more aware of this societal crisis, the feeling grows that schools cannot be ethical bystanders. As a result, character education is making a comeback in American schools.

Early Character Education

Character Education is as old as education itself. Down through history, education has had two great goals: to help people become smart and to help them become good.

Acting on that belief, schools in the earliest days of our republic tackled character education head on—through discipline, the teacher's example, and the daily school curriculum. The Bible was the public schools' sourcebook for both moral and religious instruction. When struggles eventually arose over whose Bible to use and which doctrines to teach, William McGuffey stepped onto the stage in 1836 to offer his McGuffey Readers, ultimately to sell more than 100 million copies.

McGuffey retained many favorite Biblical stories but added poems, exhortations, and heroic tales. While children practiced their reading or arithmetic, they also learned lessons about honesty, love of neighbor, kindness to animals, hard work, thriftiness, patriotism, and courage.

Why Character Education Declined

In the 20th century, the consensus supporting character education began to crumble under the blows of several powerful forces.

Darwinism introduced a new metaphor—evolution—that led people to see all things, including morality, as being in flux.

The philosophy of logical positivism, arriving at American universities from Europe, asserted a radical distinction between *facts* (which could be scientifically proven) and *values* (which positivism held were mere expressions of feeling, not objective truth). As a result of positivism, morality was relativized and privatized—made to seem a matter of personal "value judgment," not a subject for public debate and transmission through the schools.

In the 1960s, a worldwide rise in personalism celebrated the worth, autonomy, and subjectivity of the person, emphasizing individual rights and freedom over responsibility. Personalism rightly protested societal oppression and injustice, but it also delegitimized moral authority, eroded belief in objective moral norms, turned people inward toward self-fulfillment, weakened social commitments (for example, to marriage and parenting), and fueled the socially destabilizing sexual revolution.

Finally, the rapidly intensifying pluralism of American society (Whose values should we teach?) and the increasing secularization of the public arena (Won't moral education violate the separation of church and state?), became two more barriers to achieving the moral consensus indispensable for character education in the public schools. Public schools retreated from their once central role as moral and character educators.

The 1970s saw a return of values education, but in new forms: values clarification and Kohlberg's moral dilemma discussions. In different ways, both expressed the individualist spirit of the age. Values clarification said, don't impose values; help students choose

Thomas Lickona, "The Return of Character Education," *Educational Leadership*, Vol. 51, No. 3, November 1993, pp. 6-11.

their values freely. Kohlberg said, develop students' powers of moral reasoning so they can judge which values are better than others.

Each approach made contributions, but each had problems. Values clarification, though rich in methodology, failed to distinguish between personal preferences (truly a matter of free choice) and moral values (a matter of obligation). Kohlberg focused on moral reasoning, which is necessary but not sufficient for good character, and underestimated the school's role as a moral socializer.

The New Character Education

In the 1990s we are seeing the beginnings of a new character education movement, one which restores "good character" to his historical place as the central desirable outcome of the schools' moral enterprise. No one knows yet how broad or deep this movement is; we have no studies to tell us what percentage of schools are making what kind of effort. But something significant is afoot.

In July 1992, the Josephson Institute of Ethics called together more than 30 educational leaders representing state school boards, teachers' unions, universities, ethics centers, youth organizations, and religious groups. This diverse assemblage drafted the Aspen Declaration on Character Education, setting forth eight principles of character education.[1]

The Character Education Partnership was launched in March 1993, as a national coalition committed to putting character development at the top of the nation's educational agenda. Members include representatives from business, labor, government, youth, parents, faith communities, and the media.

The last two years have seen the publication of a spate of books—such as *Moral, Character, and Civic Education in the Elementary School, Why Johnny Can't Tell Right From Wrong,* and *Reclaiming Our Schools: A Handbook on Teaching Character, Academics, and Discipline*—that make the case for character education and describe promising programs around the country. A new periodical,

the *Journal of Character Education,* is devoted entirely to covering the field.[2]

Why Character Education Now?

Why this groundswell of interest in character education? There are at least three causes:

1. *The decline of the family.* The family, traditionally a child's primary moral teacher, is for vast numbers of children today failing to perform that role, thus creating a moral vacuum. In her recent book *When the Bough Breaks: The Cost of Neglecting Our Children,* economist Sylvia Hewlett documents that American children, rich and poor, suffer a level of neglect unique among developed nations (1991). Overall, child well-being has declined despite a decrease in the number of children per family, an increase in the educational level of parents, and historically high levels of public spending in education.

In "Dan Quayle Was Right," (April 1993) Barbara Dafoe Whitehead synthesizes the social science research on the decline of the two biological-parent family in America:

> If current trends continue, less than half of children born today will live continuously with their own mother and father throughout childhood.... An increasing number of children will experience family break-up two or even three times during childhood.

Children of marriages that end in divorce and children of single mothers are more likely to be poor, have emotional and behavioral problems, fail to achieve academically, get pregnant, abuse drugs and alcohol, get in trouble with the law, and be sexually and physically abused. Children in stepfamilies are generally worse off (more likely to be sexually abused, for example) than children in single-parent homes.

No one has felt the impact of family disruption more than schools. Whitehead writes:

> Across the nation, principals report a dramatic rise in the aggressive, acting-out behavior characteristic of children, especially boys, who are living in

single-parent families. Moreover, teachers find that many children are so upset and preoccupied by the explosive drama of their own family lives that they are unable to concentrate on such mundane matters as multiplication tables.

Family disintegration, then, drives the character education movement in two ways: schools have to teach the values kids aren't learning at home; and schools, in order to conduct teaching and learning, must become caring moral communities that help children from unhappy homes focus on their work, control their anger, feel cared about, and become responsible students.

2. *Troubling trends in youth character.* A second impetus for renewed character education is the sense that young people in general, not just those from fractured families, have been adversely affected by poor parenting (in intact as well as broken families); the wrong kind of adult role models; the sex, violence, and materialism portrayed in the mass media; and the pressures of the peer group. Evidence that this hostile moral environment is taking a toll on youth character can be found in 10 troubling trends: rising youth violence; increasing dishonesty (lying, cheating, and stealing); growing disrespect for authority; peer cruelty; a resurgence of bigotry on school campuses, from preschool through higher education; a decline in the work ethic; sexual precocity; a growing self-centeredness and declining civic responsibility; an increase in self-destructive behavior; and ethical illiteracy.

The statistics supporting these trends are overwhelming.[3] For example, the U.S. homicide rate for 15- to 24-year-old males is 7 times higher than Canada's and 40 times higher than Japan's. The U.S. has one of the highest teenage pregnancy rates, the highest teen abortion rate, and the highest level of drug use among young people in the developed world. Youth suicide has tripled in the past 25 years, and a survey of more than 2,000 Rhode Island students, grades six through nine, found that two out of three boys and one of two girls thought it "acceptable for a man to force sex on a woman" if they had been dating for six months or more (Kikuchi 1988).

3. *A recovery of shared, objectively important ethical values.* Moral decline in society has gotten bad enough to jolt us out of the privatism and relativism dominant in recent decades. We are recovering the wisdom that we do share a basic morality, essential for our survival; that adults must promote this morality by teaching the young, directly and indirectly, such values as respect, responsibility, trustworthiness, fairness, caring, and civic virtue; and that these values are not merely subjective preferences but that they have objective worth and a claim on our collective conscience.

Such values affirm our human dignity, promote the good of the individual and the common good, and protect our human rights. They meet the classic ethical tests of reversibility (Would you want to be treated this way?) and universalizability (Would you want all persons to act this way in a similar situation?). They define our responsibilities in a democracy, and they are recognized by all civilized people and taught by all enlightened creeds. *Not* to teach children these core ethical values is a grave moral failure.

What Character Education Must Do

In the face of a deteriorating social fabric, what must character education do to develop good character in the young?

First, it must have an adequate theory of what good character is, one which gives schools a clear idea of their goals. Character must be broadly conceived to encompass the cognitive, affective, and behavioral aspects of morality. Good character consists of knowing the good, desiring the good, and doing the good. Schools must help children *understand* the core values, *adopt* or commit to them, and then *act upon* them in their own lives.

The cognitive side of character includes at least six specific moral qualities: awareness of the moral dimensions of the situation at hand, knowing moral values and what they require of us in concrete cases, perspective-taking, moral reasoning, thoughtful decision-making, and moral self-knowledge. All these powers of rational moral thought are required for full moral maturity and citizenship in a democratic society.

People can be very smart about matters of right and wrong, however, and still choose the wrong. Moral education that is merely intellectual misses the crucial emotional side of character, which serves as the bridge between judgment and action. The emotional side includes at least the following qualities: conscience (the felt obligation to do what one judges to be right), self-respect, empathy, loving the good, self-control, and humility (a willingness to both recognize and correct our moral failings).

At times, we know what we should do, feel strongly that we should do it, yet still fail to translate moral judgment and feeling into effective moral behavior. Moral action, the third part of character, draws upon three additional moral qualities: competence (skills such as listening, communicating, and cooperating), will (which mobilizes our judgment and energy), and moral habit (a reliable inner disposition to respond to situations in a morally good way).

Developing Character

Once we have a comprehensive concept of character, we need a comprehensive approach to developing it. This approach tells schools to look at themselves through a moral lens and consider how virtually everything that goes on there affects the values and character of students. Then, plan how to use all phases of classroom and school life as deliberate tools of character development.

If schools wish to maximize their moral clout, make a lasting difference in students' character, and engage and develop all three parts of character

(knowing, feeling, and behavior), they need a comprehensive, holistic approach. Having a comprehensive approach includes asking, Do present school practices support, neglect, or contradict the school's professed values and character education aims?

In classroom practice, a comprehensive approach to character education calls upon the individual teacher to:

■ *Act as caregiver, model, and mentor,* treating students with love and respect, setting a good example, supporting positive social behavior, and correcting hurtful actions through one-on-one guidance and whole-class discussion;

■ *Create a moral community,* helping students know one another as persons, respect and care about one another, and feel valued membership in, and responsibility to, the group;

■ *Practice moral discipline,* using the creation and enforcement of rules as opportunities to foster moral reasoning, voluntary compliance with rules, and a respect for others;

■ *Create a democratic classroom environment,* involving students in decision making and the responsibility for making the classroom a good place to be and learn;

■ *Teach values through the curriculum,* using the ethically rich content of academic subjects (such as literature, history, and science), as well as outstanding programs (such as *Facing History and Ourselves*[4] and *The Heartwood Ethics Curriculum for Children*[5]), as vehicles for teaching values and examining moral questions;

■ *Use cooperative learning* to develop students' appreciation of others, perspective taking, and ability to work with others toward common goals;

■ *Develop the "conscience of craft"* by fostering students' appreciation of learning, capacity for hard work, commitment to excellence, and sense of work as affecting the lives of others;

■ *Encourage moral reflection* through reading, research, essay writing, journal keeping, discussion, and debate;

■ *Teach conflict resolution,* so that students acquire the essential moral skills of solving conflicts fairly and without force.

Besides making full use of the moral life of classrooms, a comprehensive approach calls upon the school *as a whole* to:

■ *Foster caring beyond the classroom,* using positive role models to inspire altruistic behavior and providing opportunities at every grade level to perform school and community service;

■ *Create a positive moral culture in the school,* developing a schoolwide ethos (through the leadership of the principal, discipline, a schoolwide sense of community, meaningful student government, a moral community among adults, and making time for moral concerns) that supports and amplifies the values taught in classrooms;

■ *Recruit parents and the community as partners in character education,* letting parents know that the school considers them their child's first and most important moral teacher, giving parents specific ways they can reinforce the values the school is trying to teach, and seeking the help of the community, churches, businesses, local government, and the media in promoting the core ethical values.

The Challenges Ahead

Whether character education will take hold in American schools remains to be seen. Among the factors that will determine the movement's long-range success are:

■ *Support for schools.* Can schools recruit the help they need from the other key formative institutions that shape the values of the young—including families, faith communities, and the media? Will public policy act

to strengthen and support families, and will parents make the stability of their families and the needs of their children their highest priority?

■ *The role of religion.* Both liberal and conservative groups are asking, How can students be sensitively engaged in considering the role of religion in the origins and moral development of our nation? How can students be encouraged to use their intellectual and moral resources, including their faith traditions, when confronting social issues (For example, what is my obligation to the poor?) and making personal moral decisions (For example, should I have sex before marriage?)?

■ *Moral leadership.* Many schools lack a positive, cohesive moral culture. Especially at the building level, it is absolutely essential to have moral leadership that sets, models, and consistently enforces high standards of respect and responsibility. Without a positive schoolwide ethos, teachers will feel demoralized in their individual efforts to teach good values.

■ *Teacher education.* Character education is far more complex than teaching math or reading; it requires personal growth as well as skills development. Yet teachers typically receive almost no preservice or inservice training in the moral aspects of their craft. Many teachers do not feel comfortable or competent in the values domain. How will teacher education colleges and school staff development programs meet this need?

"Character is destiny," wrote the ancient Greek philosopher Heraclitus. As we confront the causes of our deepest societal problems, whether in our intimate relationships or public institutions, questions of character loom large. As we close out a turbulent century and ready our schools for the next, educating for character

is a moral imperative if we care about the future of our society and our children.

---

[1]For a copy of the Aspen Declaration and the issue of *Ethics* magazine reporting on the conference, write the Josephson Institute of Ethics, 310 Washington Blvd., Suite 104, Marina del Rey, CA 90292.
[2]For information write Mark Kann, Editor, *The Journal of Character Education,* Jefferson Center for Character Education, 202 S. Lake Ave., Suite 240, Pasadena, CA 91101.
[3]For documentation of these youth trends, see T. Lickona, (1991), *Educating for Character:How Our Schools Can Teach Respect and Responsibility* (New York: Bantam Books).
[4]*Facing History and Ourselves* is an 8-week Holocaust curriculum for 8th graders. Write Facing History and Ourselves National Foundation, 25 Kennard Rd., Brookline, MA 02146.
[5]*The Heartwood Ethics Curriculum for Children* uses multicultural children's literature to teach universal values. Write The Heartwood Institute, 12300 Perry Highway, Wexford, PA 15090.

References

Benninga, J.S., ed. (1991). *Moral, Character, and Civic Education in the Elementary School.* New York: Teachers College Press.
Hewlett, S. (1991). *When the Bough Breaks: The Cost of Neglecting Our Children.* New York: Basic Books.
Kikuchi, J. (Fall 1988). "Rhode Island Develops Successful Intervention Program for Adolescents." *National Coalition Against Sexual Assault Newsletter.*
National Research Council. (1992). *Understanding and Preventing Violence.* Washington, D.C.: National Research Council.
Whitehead, B. D. (April 1993) "Dan Quayle Was Right." *The Atlantic* 271: 47-84.
Wynne, E. A., and K. Ryan. (1992). *Reclaiming Our Schools: A Handbook on Teaching Character, Academics, and Discipline.* New York: Merrill.

Synthesis of Research on Cooperative Learning

The use of cooperative learning strategies results in improvements both in the achievement of students and in the quality of their interpersonal relationships.

ROBERT E. SLAVIN

Robert E. Slavin is Director of the Elementary School Program, Center for Research on Effective Schooling for Disadvantaged Students, The Johns Hopkins University, 3505 N. Charles St., Baltimore, MD 21218.

There was once a time when it was taken for granted that a quiet class was a learning class, when principals walked down the hall expecting to be able to hear a pin drop. Today, however, many schools are using programs that foster the hum of voices in classrooms. These programs, called *cooperative learning*, encourage students to discuss, debate, disagree, and ultimately to teach one another.

Cooperative learning has been suggested as the solution for an astonishing array of educational problems: it is often cited as a means of emphasizing thinking skills and increasing higher-order learning; as an alternative to ability grouping, remediation, or special education; as a means of improving race relations and acceptance of mainstreamed students; and as a way to prepare students for an increasingly collaborative work force. How many of these claims are justified? What effects do the various cooperative learning methods have on student achievement and other outcomes? Which forms of cooperative learning are most effective, and what components must be in place for cooperative learning to work?

To answer these questions, I've synthesized in this article the findings of studies of cooperative learning in elementary and secondary schools that have compared cooperative learning to traditionally taught control groups studying the same objectives over a period of at least four weeks (and up to a full school year or more). Here I present a brief summary of the effects of cooperative learning on achieve-

---

Highlights of Research on Cooperative Learning

In cooperative learning, students work in small groups to help one another master academic material. There are many quite different forms of cooperative learning, and the effectiveness of cooperative learning (particularly for achievement outcomes) depends on the particular approach used.

- For enhancing student achievement, the most successful approaches have incorporated two key elements: group goals and individual accountability. That is, groups are rewarded based on the individual learning of all group members.
- When group goals and individual accountability are used, achievement effects of cooperative learning are consistently positive; 37 of 44 experimental/control comparisons of at least four weeks' duration have found significantly positive effects, and none have favored traditional methods.
- Achievement effects of cooperative learning have been found to about the same degree at all grade levels (2–12), in all major subjects, and in urban, rural, and suburban schools. Effects are equally positive for high, average, and low achievers.
- Positive effects of cooperative learning have been consistently found on such diverse outcomes as self-esteem, intergroup relations, acceptance of academically handicapped students, attitudes toward school, and ability to work cooperatively.

—Robert E. Slavin

---

ment and noncognitive outcomes; for a more extensive review, see *Cooperative Learning: Theory, Research, and Practice* (Slavin 1990).

Cooperative Learning Methods

There are many quite different forms of cooperative learning, but all of them involve having students work in small groups or teams to help one another learn academic material. Cooperative learning usually supplements the teacher's instruction by giving students an opportunity to discuss information or practice skills originally presented by the teacher; sometimes cooperative methods require students to find or discover information on their own. Cooperative learning has been used—and investigated—in every imaginable subject in grades 2–12, and is increasingly used in college.

Small-scale laboratory research on cooperation dates back to the 1920s (see Deutsch 1949; Slavin 1977a); research on specific applications of cooperative learning to the classroom began in the early 1970s. At that time, four research groups, one in Israel and three in the U.S., began independently to develop and study cooperative learning methods in classroom settings.

Now researchers all over the world are studying practical applications of cooperative learning principles, and many cooperative learning methods have been evaluated in one or more experimental/control comparisons. The best evaluated of the cooperative models are described below (adapted from Slavin 1990). These include four Student Team Learning variations, Jigsaw, Learning Together, and Group Investigation.

Student Team Learning

Student Team Learning (STL) techniques were developed and researched at Johns Hopkins University. More than half of all experimental studies of practical cooperative learning methods involve STL methods.

All cooperative learning methods share the idea that students work together to learn and are responsible for one another's learning as well as their own. STL methods, in addition to this idea, emphasize the use of team goals and team success, which can only be achieved if all members of the team learn the objectives being

Cooperative learning has been suggested as the solution for an astonishing array of educational problems.

taught. That is, in Student Team Learning the students' tasks are not to *do* something as a team but to *learn* something as a team.

Three concepts are central to all Student Team Learning methods: *team rewards, individual accountability,* and *equal opportunities for success.* Using STL techniques, teams earn certificates or other team rewards if they achieve above a designated criterion. The teams are not in competition to earn scarce rewards; all (or none) of the teams may achieve the criterion in a given week. *Individual accountability* means that the team's success depends on the individual learning of all team members. This focuses the activity of the team members on explaining concepts to one another and making sure that everyone on the team is ready for a quiz or other assessment that they will take without teammate help. *Equal opportunities for success* means that students contribute to their teams by improving over their own past performances. This ensures that high, average, and low achievers are equally challenged to do their best and that the contributions of all team members will be valued.

The findings of these experimental studies (summarized in this section) indicate that team rewards and individual accountability are essential elements for producing basic skills achievement (Slavin 1983a, 1983b,

Cooperative learning usually supplements the teacher's instruction by giving students an opportunity to discuss information or practice skills originally presented by the teacher.

1990). It is not enough to simply tell students to work together. They must have a reason to take one another's achievement seriously. Further, if students are rewarded for doing better than they have in the past, they will be more motivated to achieve than if they are rewarded based on their performance in comparison to others, because rewards for improvement make success neither too difficult nor too easy for students to achieve (Slavin 1980).

Four principal Student Team Learning methods have been extensively developed and researched. Two are general cooperative learning methods adaptable to most subjects and grade levels: Student Teams-Achievement Divisions (STAD) and Teams-Games-Tournament (TGT). The remaining two are comprehensive curriculums designed for use in particular subjects at particular grade levels: Team Assisted Individualization (TAI) for mathematics in grades 3–6 and Cooperative Integrated Reading and Composition (CIRC) for reading and writing instruction in grades 3–5.

Student Teams-Achievement Divisions (STAD)

In STAD (Slavin 1978, 1986), students are assigned to four-member learning teams mixed in performance level, sex, and ethnicity. The teacher presents a lesson, and then students work within their teams to make sure that all team members have mastered the lesson. Finally, all students take individual quizzes on the material, at which time they may *not* help one another.

Students' quiz scores are compared to their own past averages, and points are awarded based on the degree to which students can meet or exceed their own earlier performances. These points are then summed to form team scores, and teams that meet certain criteria earn certificates or other rewards. The whole cycle of activities, from teacher presentation to team practice to quiz, usually takes three to five class periods.

STAD has been used in a wide variety of subjects, from mathematics to language arts and social studies. It has been used from grade 2 through college. STAD is most appropriate for teaching well-defined objectives with single right answers, such as mathematical computations and applications, language usage and mechanics, geography and map skills, and science facts and concepts.

Teams-Games-Tournament (TGT)
Teams-Games-Tournament (DeVries and Slavin 1978; Slavin 1986) was the first of the Johns Hopkins cooperative learning methods. It uses the same teacher presentations and teamwork as in STAD, but replaces the quizzes with weekly tournaments. In these, students compete with members of other teams to contribute points to their team scores. Students compete at three-person "tournament tables" against others with similar past records in mathematics. A "bumping" procedure changes table assignments to keep the competition fair. The winner at each tournament table brings the same number of points to his or her team, regardless of which table it is; this means that low achievers (competing with other low achievers) and high achievers (competing with other high achievers) have equal opportunities for success. As in STAD, high-performing teams earn certificates or other forms of team rewards. TGT is appropriate for the same types of objectives as STAD.

Team Assisted Individualization (TAI)
Team Assisted Individualization (TAI; Slavin et al. 1986) shares with STAD and TGT the use of four-member mixed ability learning teams and certificates for high-performing teams. But where STAD and TGT use a single pace of instruction for the class, TAI combines cooperative learning with individualized instruction. Also, where STAD and TGT apply to most subjects and grade levels, TAI is specifically designed to teach mathematics to students in grades 3–6 (or older students not ready for a full algebra course).

In TAI, students enter an individualized sequence according to a placement test and then proceed at their own rates. In general, team members work on different units. Teammates check each others' work against answer sheets and help one another with any problems. Final unit tests are taken without teammate help and are scored by student monitors. Each week, teachers total the number of units completed by all team members and give certificates or other team rewards to teams that exceed a criterion score based on the number of

All cooperative learning methods share the idea that students work together to learn and are responsible for one another's learning as well as their own.

final tests passed, with extra points for perfect papers and completed homework.

Because students take responsibility for checking each others' work and managing the flow of materials, the teacher can spend most of the class time presenting lessons to small groups of students drawn from the various teams who are working at the same point in the mathematics sequence. For example, the teacher might call up a decimals group, present a lesson, and then send the students back to their teams to work on problems. Then the teacher might call the fractions group, and so on.

Cooperative Integrated Reading and Composition (CIRC)
The newest of the Student Team Learning methods is a comprehensive program for teaching reading and writing in the upper elementary grades called Cooperative Integrated Reading and Composition (CIRC) (Stevens et al. 1987). In CIRC, teachers use basal or literature-based readers and reading groups, much as in traditional reading programs. However, all students are assigned to teams composed of two pairs from two different reading groups. For example, a team might have two "Bluebirds" and two "Redbirds." While the teacher is working with one reading group, the paired students in the other groups are working on a series of cognitively engaging activities, including reading to one another, making predictions about how narrative stories will come out, summarizing stories to one another, writing responses to stories, and practicing spelling, decoding, and vocabulary. If the reading class is not divided into homogeneous reading groups, all students in the teams work with one another. Students

work as a total team to master "main idea" and other comprehension skills. During language arts periods, students engage in writing drafts, revising and editing one another's work, and preparing for "publication" of team books.

In most CIRC activities, students follow a sequence of teacher instruction, team practice, team pre-assessments, and quizzes. That is, students do not take the quiz until their teammates have determined that they are ready. Certificates are given to teams based on the average performance of all team members on all reading and writing activities.

Other Cooperative Learning Methods
Jigsaw
Jigsaw was originally designed by Elliot Aronson and his colleagues (1978). In Aronson's Jigsaw method, students are assigned to six-member teams to work on academic material that has been broken down into sections. For example, a biography might be divided into early life, first accomplishments, major setbacks, later life, and impact on history. Each team member reads his or her section. Next, members of different teams who have studied the same sections meet in "expert groups" to discuss their sections. Then the students return to their teams and take turns teaching their teammates about their sections. Since the only way students can learn sections other than their own is to listen carefully to their teammates, they are motivated to support and show interest in one another's work.

Slavin (1986) developed a modification of Jigsaw at Johns Hopkins University and then incorporated it in the Student Team Learning program. In this method, called Jigsaw II, students work in four- or five-member teams as in TGT and STAD. Instead of each student's being assigned a particular section of text, all students read a common narrative, such as a book chapter, a short story, or a biography. However, each student receives a topic (such as "climate" in a unit on France) on which to become an expert. Students with the same topics meet in expert groups to discuss them, after which they return to their teams to teach what they have learned to their teammates. Then students take individual quizzes, which result in team scores based on the improvement score system of STAD. Teams that meet preset standards earn certificates. Jigsaw is primarily used in social studies and other subjects where learning from text is important.

Learning Together
David Johnson and Roger Johnson at the University of Minnesota developed the Learning Together models of cooperative learning (Johnson and Johnson 1987). The methods they have researched involve students working on assignment sheets in four- or five-member heterogeneous groups. The groups hand in a single sheet and receive praise and rewards based on the group product. Their methods emphasize team-building activities before students begin working together and regular discussions within groups about how well they are working together.

Group Investigation
Group Investigation, developed by Shlomo Sharan and Yael Sharan at the University of Tel-Aviv, is a general classroom organization plan in which students work in small groups using cooperative inquiry, group discussion, and cooperative planning and projects (Sharan and Sharan 1976). In this method, students form their own two- to six-member groups. After choosing subtopics from a unit being studied by the entire class, the groups further break their subtopics into individual tasks and carry out the activities necessary to prepare group reports. Each group then makes a presentation or display to communicate its findings to the entire class.

Research on Cooperative Learning
Cooperative learning methods are among the most extensively evaluated alternatives to traditional instruction in use today. Outcome evaluations include:
- academic achievement,
- intergroup relations,
- mainstreaming,
- self-esteem,
- others.

Academic Achievement
More than 70 high-quality studies have evaluated various cooperative learning methods over periods of at least four

Cooperative learning methods have been equally successful in urban, rural, and suburban schools and with students of different ethnic groups.

weeks in regular elementary and secondary schools; 67 of these have measured effects on student achievement (see Slavin 1990). All these studies compared the effects of cooperative learning to those of traditionally taught control groups on measures of the same objectives pursued in all classes. Teachers and classes were either randomly assigned to cooperative or control conditions or matched on pretest achievement level and other factors.

Overall, of 67 studies of the achievement effects of cooperative learning, 41 (61 percent) found significantly greater achievement in cooperative than in control classes. Twenty-five (37 percent) found no differences, and in only one study did the control group outperform the experimental group. However, the effects of cooperative learning vary considerably according to the particular methods used. As noted earlier, two elements must be present if cooperative learning is to be effective: *group goals* and *individual accountability* (Slavin 1983a, 1983b, 1990). That is, groups must be working to achieve some goal or to earn rewards or recognition, and the success of the group must depend on the individual learning of every group member.

In studies of methods such as STAD, TGT, TAI, and CIRC, effects on achievement have been consistently positive;

Cooperative learning methods are among the most extensively evaluated alternatives to traditional instruction in use in schools today.

37 out of 44 such studies (84 percent) found significant positive achievement effects. In contrast, only 4 of 23 studies (17 percent) lacking group goals and individual accountability found positive effects on student achievement. Two of these positive effects were found in studies of Group Investigation in Israel (Sharan et al. 1984; Sharan and Shachar 1988). In Group Investigation, students in each group are responsible for one unique part of the group's overall task, ensuring individual accountability. Then the group's overall performance is evaluated. Even though there are no specific group rewards, the group evaluation probably serves the same purpose.

Why are group goals and individual accountability so important? To understand this, consider the alternatives. In some forms of cooperative learning, students work together to complete a single worksheet or to solve one problem together. In such methods, there is little reason for more able students to take time to explain what is going on to their less able groupmates or to ask their opinions. When the group task is to *do* something, rather than to *learn* something, the participation of less able students may be seen as interference rather than help. It may be easier in this circumstance for students to give each other answers than to explain concepts or skills to one another.

In contrast, when the group's task is to ensure that every group member *learns* something, it is in the interests of every group member to spend time explaining concepts to his or her groupmates. Studies of students' behaviors within cooperative groups have consistently found that the students who gain most from cooperative work are those who give and receive elaborated explanations (Webb 1985). In contrast, Webb found that giving and receiving answers without explanations were *negatively* related to achievement gain. What group goals and individual accountability do is to motivate students to give explanations and to take one another's learning seriously, instead of simply giving answers.

Cooperative learning methods generally work equally well for all types of students. While occasional studies find particular advantages for high or low achievers, boys or girls, and so on, the great majority find equal benefits for all types of students. Sometimes teachers or parents worry that cooperative learning will hold back high achievers. The research provides absolutely no support for this claim; high achievers gain from cooperative learning (relative to high achievers in traditional classes) just as much as do low and average achievers.

Research on the achievement effects of cooperative learning has more often taken place in grades 3–9 than 10–12. Studies at the senior high school level are about as positive as those at earlier grade levels, but there is a need for more research at that level. Cooperative learning methods have been equally successful in urban, rural, and suburban schools and with students of different ethnic groups (although a few studies have found particularly positive effects for black students; see Slavin and Oickle 1981).

Among the cooperative learning methods, the Student Team Learning programs have been most extensively researched and most often found instructionally effective. Of 14 studies of STAD and closely related methods, 11 found significantly higher achievement for this method than for traditional instruction, and two found no differences. For example, Slavin and Karweit (1984) evaluated STAD over an entire school year in inner-city Philadelphia 9th grade mathematics classes. Student performance on a standardized mathematics test increased significantly more than in either a mastery learning group or a control group using the same materials. Substantial differences favoring STAD have been found in such diverse subjects as social studies (e.g., Allen and Van Sickle 1984), language arts (Slavin and Karweit 1981), reading comprehension (Stevens, Slavin, Farnish, and Madden 1988), mathematics (Sherman and Thomas 1986), and science (Okebukola 1985). Nine of 11 studies of TGT found similar results (DeVries and Slavin 1978).

The largest effects of Student Team Learning methods have been found in studies of TAI. Five of six studies found substantially greater learning of mathematics computations in TAI than in control classes, while one study found no differences (see Slavin 1985b). Experimental control differences were

In the laboratory research on cooperation, one of the earliest and strongest findings was that people who cooperate learn to like one another.

still substantial (though smaller) a year after the students were in TAI (Slavin and Karweit 1985). In mathematics concepts and applications, one of three studies (Slavin et al. 1984) found significantly greater gains in TAI than control methods, while two found no significant differences (Slavin and Karweit 1985).

In comparison with traditional control groups, three experimental studies of CIRC have found substantial positive effects on scores from standardized tests of reading comprehension, reading vocabulary, language expression, language mechanics, and spelling (Madden et al. 1986, Stevens et al. 1987, Stevens et al. 1990). Significantly greater achievement on writing samples was also found favoring the CIRC students in the two studies which assessed writing.

Other than STL methods, the most consistently successful model for increasing student achievement is Group Investigation (Sharan and Sharan 1976). One study of this method (Sharan et al. 1984) found that it increased the learning of English as a foreign language, while Sharan and Shachar (1988) found positive effects of Group Investigation on the learning of history and geography. A third study of only three weeks' duration (Sharan et al. 1980) also found positive effects on social studies achievement, particularly on higher-level concepts. The Learning Together methods (Johnson and Johnson 1987) have been found

We now see the usefulness of cooperative learning strategies . . . at a variety of grade levels and in many subjects.

instructionally effective when they include the assignment of group grades based on the average of group members' individual quiz scores (e.g., Humphreys et al. 1982, Yager et al. 1985). Studies of the original Jigsaw method have not generally supported this approach (e.g., Moskowitz et al. 1983); but studies of Jigsaw II, which uses group goals and individual accountability, have shown positive effects (Mattingly and VanSickle 1990, Ziegler 1981).

Intergroup Relations
In the laboratory research on cooperation, one of the earliest and strongest findings was that people who cooperate learn to like one another (Slavin 1977b). Not surprisingly, the cooperative learning classroom studies have found quite consistently that students express greater liking for their classmates in general as a result of participating in a cooperative learning method (see Slavin 1983a, 1990). This is important in itself and even more important when the students have different ethnic backgrounds. After all, there is substantial evidence that, left alone, ethnic separateness in schools does not naturally diminish over time (Gerard and Miller 1975).

Social scientists have long advocated interethnic cooperation as a means of ensuring positive intergroup relations in desegregated settings. Contact Theory (Allport 1954), which is in the U.S. the dominant theory of intergroup relations, predicted that positive intergroup relations would arise from school desegregation if and only if students participated in cooperative, equal-status interaction sanctioned by the school. Research on cooperative learning methods has borne out the predictions of Contact Theory. These techniques emphasize cooperative, equal-status interaction between students of different ethnic backgrounds sanctioned by the school (Slavin 1985a).

In most of the research on intergroup relations, students were asked to list their best friends at the beginning of the study and again at the end. The number of friendship choices students made outside their own ethnic groups was the measure of intergroup relations.

Positive effects on intergroup relations have been found for STAD, TGT,

TAI, Jigsaw, Learning Together, and Group Investigation models (Slavin 1985b). Two of these studies, one on STAD (Slavin 1979) and one on Jigsaw II (Ziegler 1981), included follow-ups of intergroup friendships several months after the end of the studies. Both found that students who had been in cooperative learning classes still named significantly more friends outside their own ethnic groups than did students who had been in control classes. Two studies of Group Investigation (Sharan et al. 1984, Sharan and Shachar 1988) found that students' improved attitudes and behaviors toward classmates of different ethnic backgrounds extended to classmates who had never been in the same groups, and a study of TAI (Oishi 1983) found positive effects of this method on cross-ethnic interactions outside as well as in class. The U.S. studies of cooperative learning and intergroup relations involved black, white, and (in a few cases) Mexican-American students. A study of Jigsaw II by Ziegler (1981) took place in Toronto, where the major ethnic groups were Anglo-Canadians and children of recent European immigrants. The Sharan (Sharan et al. 1984, Sharan and Shachar 1988) studies of Group Investigation took place in Israel and involved friendships between Jews of both European and Middle Eastern backgrounds.

Mainstreaming
Although ethnicity is a major barrier to friendship, it is not so large as the one between physically or mentally handicapped children and their normal-progress peers. Mainstreaming, an unprecedented opportunity for handicapped children to take their place in the school and society, has created enormous practical problems for classroom teachers, and it often leads to social rejection of the handicapped children. Because cooperative learning methods have been successful in improving relationships across the ethnicity barrier—which somewhat resembles the barrier between mainstreamed and normal-progress students—these methods have also been applied to increase the acceptance of the mainstreamed student.

The research on cooperative learning and mainstreaming has focused on the academically handicapped child. In

What group goals and individual accountability do is to motivate students to give explanations and to take one another's learning seriously, instead of simply giving answers.

one study, STAD was used to attempt to integrate students performing two years or more below the level of their peers into the social structure of the classroom. The use of STAD significantly reduced the degree to which the normal-progress students rejected their mainstreamed classmates and increased the academic achievement and self-esteem of all students, mainstreamed as well as normal-progress (Madden and Slavin 1983). Similar effects have been found for TAI (Slavin et al. 1984), and other research using cooperative teams has also shown significant improvements in relationships between mainstreamed academically handicapped students and their normal-progress peers (Ballard et al. 1977, Cooper et al. 1980).

In addition, one study in a self-contained school for emotionally disturbed adolescents found that the use of TGT increased positive interactions and friendships among students (Slavin 1977a). Five months after the study ended, these positive interactions were still found more often in the former TGT classes than in the control classes. In a study in a similar setting, Janke (1978) found that the emotionally disturbed students were more on-task, were better behaved, and had better attendance in TGT classes than in control classes.

Self-Esteem
One of the most important aspects of a child's personality is his or her self-esteem. Several researchers working on cooperative learning techniques have found that these methods do increase students' self-esteem. These improvements in self-esteem have been found for TGT and STAD (Slavin 1990), for Jigsaw (Blaney et al. 1977), and for the three methods combined (Slavin and

Karweit 1981). Improvements in student self-concepts have also been found for TAI (Slavin et al. 1984).

Other Outcomes
In addition to effects on achievement, positive intergroup relations, greater acceptance of mainstreamed students, and self-esteem, effects of cooperative learning have been found on a variety of other important educational outcomes. These include liking school, development of peer norms in favor of doing well academically, feelings of individual control over the student's own fate in school, and cooperativeness and altruism (see Slavin 1983a, 1990). TGT (DeVries and Slavin 1978) and STAD (Slavin 1978, Janke 1978) have been found to have positive effects on students' time-on-task. One study found that lower socioeconomic status students at risk of becoming delinquent who worked in cooperative groups in 6th grade had better attendance, fewer contacts with the police, and higher behavioral ratings by teachers in grades 7–11 than did control students (Hartley 1976). Another study implemented forms of cooperative learning beginning in kindergarten and continuing through the 4th grade (Solomon et al. 1990). This study found that the students who had been taught cooperatively were significantly higher than control students on measures of supportive, friendly, and prosocial behavior; were better at resolving conflicts; and expressed more support for democratic values.

Useful Strategies
Returning to the questions at the beginning of this article, we now see the usefulness of cooperative learning strategies for improving such diverse outcomes as student achievement at a variety of grade levels and in many subjects, intergroup relations, relationships between mainstreamed and normal-progress students, and student self-esteem. Further, their widespread and growing use demonstrates that cooperative learning methods are practical and attractive to teachers. The history of the development, evaluation, and dissemination of cooperative learning is an outstanding example of the use of educational research to create programs that have improved the educational experience of thou-

sands of students and will continue to affect thousands more.

Author's note. This article was written under funding from the Office of Educational Research and Improvement, U.S. Department of Education (Grant No. OERI-R-117-R90002). However, any opinions expressed are mine and do not represent OERI positions or policy.

References

Allen, W.H., and R.L. Van Sickle. (1984). "Learning Teams and Low Achievers." *Social Education*: 60–64.

Allport, G. (1954). *The Nature of Prejudice*. Cambridge, Mass.: Addison-Wesley.

Aronson, E., N. Blaney, C. Stephan, J. Sikes, and M. Snapp. (1978). *The Jigsaw Classroom*. Beverly Hills, Calif.: Sage.

Ballard, M., L. Corman, J. Gottlieb, and M. Kauffman. (1977). "Improving the Social Status of Mainstreamed Retarded Children." *Journal of Educational Psychology* 69: 605–611.

Blaney, N.T., S. Stephan, D. Rosenfeld, E. Aronson, and J. Sikes. (1977). "Interdependence in the Classroom: A Field Study." *Journal of Educational Psychology* 69: 121–128.

Cooper, L., D.W. Johnson, R. Johnson, and F. Wilderson. (1980). "Effects of Cooperative, Competitive, and Individualistic Experiences on Interpersonal Attraction Among Heterogeneous Peers." *Journal of Social Psychology* 111: 243–252.

Deutsch, M. (1949). "A Theory of Cooperation and Competition." *Human Relations* 2: 129–152.

DeVries, D.L., and R.E. Slavin. (1978). "Teams-Games-Tournament (TGT): Review of Ten Classroom Experiments." *Journal of Research and Development in Education* 12: 28–38.

Gerard, H.B., and N. Miller. (1975). *School Desegregation: A Long-Range Study*. New York: Plenum.

Hartley, W. (1976). *Prevention Outcomes of Small Group Education with School Children: An Epidemiologic Follow-Up of the Kansas City School Behavior Project*. Kansas City: University of Kansas Medical Center.

Humphreys, B., R. Johnson, and D.W. Johnson. (1982). "Effects of Cooperative, Competitive, and Individualistic Learning on Students' Achievement in Science Class." *Journal of Research in Science Teaching* 19: 351–356.

Janke, R. (April 1978). "The Teams-Games-Tournament (TGT) Method and the Behavioral Adjustment and Academic Achievement of Emotionally Impaired Adolescents." Paper presented at the annual convention of the American Educational Research Association, Toronto.

Johnson, D.W., and R.T. Johnson. (1987). *Learning Together and Alone*. 2nd ed. Englewood Cliffs, N.J.: Prentice-Hall.

Madden, N.A., and R.E. Slavin. (1983). "Cooperative Learning and Social Acceptance of Mainstreamed Academically Handicapped Students." *Journal of Special Education* 17: 171–182.

Madden, N.A., R.J. Stevens, and R.E. Slavin. (1986). *A Comprehensive Cooperative Learning Approach to Elementary Reading and Writing: Effects on Student Achievement*. Report No. 2. Baltimore, Md.: Center for Research on Elementary and Middle Schools, Johns Hopkins University.

Mattingly, R.M., and R.L. VanSickle. (1990). *Jigsaw II in Secondary Social Studies: An Experiment*. Athens, Ga.: University of Georgia.

Moskowitz, J.M., J.H. Malvin, G.A. Schaeffer, and E. Schaps. (1983). "Evaluation of a Cooperative Learning Strategy." *American Educational Research Journal* 20: 687–696.

Oishi, S. (1983). "Effects of Team-Assisted Individualization in Mathematics on Cross-Race Interactions of Elementary School Children." Doctoral diss., University of Maryland.

Okebukola, P.A. (1985). "The Relative Effectiveness of Cooperative and Competitive Interaction Techniques in Strengthening Students' Performance in Science Classes." *Science Education* 69: 501–509.

Sharan, S., and C. Shachar. (1988). *Language and Learning in the Cooperative Classroom*. New York: Springer.

Sharan, S., and Y. Sharan. (1976). *Small-group Teaching*. Englewood Cliffs, N.J.: Educational Technology Publications.

Sharan, S., R. Hertz-Lazarowitz, and Z. Ackerman. (1980). "Academic Achievement of Elementary School Children in Small-group vs. Whole Class Instruction." *Journal of Experimental Education* 48: 125–129.

Sharan, S., P. Kussell, R. Hertz-Lazarowitz, Y. Bejarano, S. Raviv, and Y. Sharan. (1984). *Cooperative Learning in the Classroom: Research in Desegregated Schools*. Hillsdale, N.J.: Erlbaum.

Sherman, L.W., and M. Thomas. (1986). "Mathematics Achievement in Cooperative Versus Individualistic Goal-structured High School Classrooms." *Journal of Educational Research* 79: 169–172.

Slavin, R.E. (1977a). "A Student Team Approach to Teaching Adolescents with Special Emotional and Behavioral Needs." *Psychology in the Schools* 14: 77–84.

Slavin, R.E. (1977b). "Classroom Reward Structure: An Analytical and Practical Review." *Review of Educational Research* 47: 633–650.

Slavin, R.E. (1978). "Student Teams and Achievement Divisions." *Journal of Research and Development in Education* 12: 39–49.

Slavin, R.E. (1979). "Effects of Biracial Learning Teams on Cross-Racial Friendships." *Journal of Educational Psychology* 71: 381–387.

Slavin, R.E. (1983a). *Cooperative Learning*. New York: Longman.

Slavin, R.E. (1983b). "When Does Cooperative Learning Increase Student Achievement?" *Psychological Bulletin* 94: 429–445.

Slavin, R.E. (March 1985a). "Cooperative Learning: Applying Contact Theory in Desegregated Schools." *Journal of Social Issues* 41: 45–62.

Slavin, R.E. (1985b). "Team Assisted Individualization: A Cooperative Learning Solution for Adaptive Instruction in Mathematics." In *Adapting Instruction to Individual Differences*, edited by M.Wang and H. Walberg. Berkeley, Calif.: McCutchan.

Slavin, R.E. (1986). *Using Student Team Learning*. 3rd ed. Baltimore, Md.: Center for Research on Elementary and Middle Schools, Johns Hopkins University.

Slavin, R.E. (1990). *Cooperative Learning: Theory, Research, and Practice*. Englewood Cliffs, N.J.: Prentice-Hall.

Slavin, R.E. (February 1991). "Are Cooperative Learning and 'Untracking' Harmful to the Gifted?" *Educational Leadership* 48: 63–74.

Slavin, R.E., and N. Karweit. (1981). "Cognitive and Affective Outcomes of an Intensive Student Team Learning Experience." *Journal of Experimental Education* 50: 29–35.

Slavin, R.E., and N. Karweit. (1984). "Mastery Learning and Student Teams: A Factorial Experiment in Urban General Mathematics Classes." *American Educational Research Journal* 21: 725–736.

Slavin, R.E., and N.L. Karweit. (1985). "Effects of Whole-Class, Ability Grouped, and Individualized Instruction on Mathematics Achievement." *American Educational Research Journal* 22: 351–367.

Slavin, R.E., M. Leavey, and N.A. Madden. (1984). "Combining Cooperative Learning and Individualized Instruction: Effects on Student Mathematics Achievement Attitudes and Behaviors." *Elementary School Journal* 84: 409–422.

Slavin, R.E., M.B. Leavey, and N.A. Madden. (1986). *Team Accelerated Instruction-Mathematics*. Watertown, Mass.: Mastery Education Corporation.

Slavin, R.E., N.A. Madden, and M.B. Leavey. (1984). "Effects of Team Assisted Individualization on the Mathematics Achievement of Academically Handicapped and Nonhandicapped Students." *Journal of Educational Psychology* 76: 813–819.

Slavin, R.E., and E. Oickle. (1981). "Effects of Cooperative Learning Teams on Student Achievement and Race Relations: Treatment x Race Interactions." *Sociology of Education* 54: 174–180.

Solomon, D., M. Watson, E. Schaps, V. Battistich, and J. Solomon. (1990). "Cooperative Learning as Part of a Comprehensive Classroom Program Designed to Promote Prosocial Development." In *Current Research on Cooperative Learning*, edited by S. Sharan, New York: Praeger.

Stevens, R.J., N.A. Madden, R.E. Slavin, and A.M. Farnish. (1987). "Cooperative Integrated Reading and Composition: Two Field Experiments." *Reading Research Quarterly* 22: 433–454.

Stevens, R.J., R.E. Slavin, and A.M. Farnish. (April 1990). "A Cooperative Learning Approach to Elementary Reading and Writing Instruction: Long-Term Effects." Paper presented at the annual convention of the American Educational Research Association, Boston.

Stevens, R.J., R.E. Slavin, A.M. Farnish, and N.A. Madden. (April 1988). "The Effects of Cooperative Learning and Direct Instruction in Reading Comprehension Strategies on Main Idea Identification." Paper presented at the annual convention of the American Educational Research Association, New Orleans.

Webb, N. (1985). "Student Interaction and Learning in Small Groups: A Research Summary." In *Learning to Cooperate, Cooperating to Learn*, edited by R. Slavin, S. Sharan, S. Kagan, R. Hertz-Lazarowitz, C. Webb, and R. Schmuck. New York: Plenum.

Yager, S., D.W. Johnson, and R.T. Johnson. (1985). "Oral Discussion, Group-to-Individual Transfer, and Achievement in Cooperative Learning Groups." *Journal of Educational Psychology* 77: 60–66.

Ziegler, S. (1981). "The Effectiveness of Cooperative Learning Teams for Increasing Cross-Ethnic Friendship: Additional Evidence." *Human Organization* 40: 264–268.

Five Standards of Authentic Instruction

What types of instruction engage students in using their minds well? A framework developed at Wisconsin's Center on Organization and Restructuring of Schools may be a valuable tool for teachers and researchers attempting to answer this complex question.

Fred M. Newmann and
Gary G. Wehlage

Fred M. Newmann is Director of the Center on Organization and Restructuring of Schools and Professor of Curriculum and Instruction, University of Wisconsin-Madison, Wisconsin Center for Education Research, 1025 W. Johnson St., Madison, WI 53706. **Gary G. Wehlage** is Associate Director of the Center on Organization and Restructuring of Schools and Professor of Curriculum and Instruction, University of Wisconsin-Madison, same address.

W hy do many innovations fail to improve the quality of instruction or student achievement? In 1990, we began to explore this question by studying schools that have tried to restructure. Unfortunately, even the most innovative activities—from school councils and shared decision making to cooperative learning and assessment by portfolio—can be implemented in ways that undermine meaningful learning, unless they are guided by substantive, worthwhile educational ends. We contend that innovations should aim toward a vision of authentic student achievement, and we are examining the extent to which instruction in restructured schools is directed toward

authentic forms of student achievement. We use the word *authentic* to distinguish between achievement that is significant and meaningful and that which is trivial and useless.

To define authentic achievement more precisely, we rely on three criteria that are consistent with major proposals in the restructuring movement:[1] (1) students construct meaning and produce knowledge, (2) students use disciplined inquiry to construct meaning, and (3) students aim their work toward production of discourse, products, and performances that have value or meaning beyond success in school.[2]

The Need for Standards for Instruction

While there has been much recent attention to standards for curriculum and for assessment,[3] public and professional discussion of standards for instruction tends to focus on procedural and technical aspects, with little attention to more fundamental standards of quality. Is achievement more likely to be authentic when the length of class periods varies, when teachers teach in teams, when students participate in hands-on activities, or when students spend time in cooperative groups, museums, or on-the-job apprenticeships?

We were cautious not to assume that technical processes or specific sites for learning, however innovative, necessarily produce experiences of high intellectual quality. Even activities that place students in the role of a more active, cooperative learner and that seem to respect student voices can be implemented in ways that do not produce authentic achievement. The challenge is not simply to adopt innovative teaching techniques or to find new locations for learning, but deliberately to counteract two persistent maladies that make conventional schooling inauthentic:

1. Often the work students do does not allow them to use their minds well.

2. The work has no intrinsic meaning or value to students beyond achieving success in school.

To face these problems head-on, we articulated standards for instruction that represented the quality of intellectual work but that were not tied to any specific learning activity (for example, lecture or small-group discussion). Indeed, the point was to assess the extent to which any given activity— traditional or innovative, in or out of school—engages students in using their minds well.

Instruction is complex, and quantification in education can often be as misleading as informative. To guard against oversimplification, we formulated several standards, rather than only one or two, and we conceptualized each standard as a continuous construct from "less" to "more" of a quality, rather than as a categorical (yes or no) variable. We expressed each standard as a dimensional construct on a five-point scale. Instructions for rating lessons include specific criteria for each score—1 to 5—on each standard. Space does not permit us to present criteria for every possible rating, but for each standard we first distinguish between high and low scoring lessons and then offer examples of criteria for some specific ratings. Raters consider both the number of students to which the criterion applies and the proportion of class time during which it applies.[4] The five standards are: higher-order thinking, depth of knowledge, connectedness to the world beyond the classroom, substantive conversation, and social support for student achievement (see fig. 1).

Higher-Order Thinking

The first scale measures the degree to

Fred M. Newmann and Gary G. Wehlage, "Five Standards of Authentic Instruction," *Educational Leadership,* Vol. 50, No. 7, April 1993, pp. 8-12. Reprinted with permission of the Association for Supervision and Curriculum Development. © 1991 by ASCD. All rights reserved.

which students use higher-order thinking.

Lower-order thinking (LOT) occurs when students are asked to receive or recite factual information or to employ rules and algorithms through repetitive routines. As information-receivers, students are given pre-specified knowledge ranging from simple facts and information to more complex concepts. Students are in this role when they recite previously acquired knowledge by responding to questions that require recall of pre-specified knowledge.

Higher-order thinking (HOT) requires students to manipulate information and ideas in ways that transform their meaning and implications, such as when students combine facts and ideas in order to synthesize, generalize, explain, hypothesize, or arrive at some conclusion or interpretation. Manipulating information and ideas through these processes allows students to solve problems and discover new (for them) meanings and understandings. When students engage in HOT, an element of uncertainty is introduced, and instructional outcomes are not always predictable.

Criteria for higher-order thinking:
3 = Students primarily engage in routine LOT operations a good share of the lesson. There is at least one significant question or activity in which some students perform some HOT operations.
4 = Students engage in an at least one major activity during the lesson in which they perform HOT operations. This activity occupies a substantial portion of the lesson, and many students perform HOT.

Depth of Knowledge

From "knowledge is shallow" (1) to "knowledge is deep" (5), the next scale assesses students' depth of knowledge and understanding. This term refers to the substantive character of the ideas in a lesson and to the level of understanding that students demonstrate as they consider these ideas.

Knowledge is thin or superficial when it does not deal with significant concepts of a topic or discipline—for example, when students have a trivial

> We wanted to assess the extent to which any given activity—traditional or innovative, in or out of school—engages students in using their minds well.

understanding of important concepts or when they have only a surface acquaintance with their meaning. Superficiality can be due, in part, to instructional strategies that emphasize coverage of large quantities of fragmented information.

Knowledge is deep or thick when it concerns the central ideas of a topic or discipline. For students, knowledge is deep when they make clear distinctions, develop arguments, solve problems, construct explanations, and otherwise work with relatively complex understandings. Depth is produced, in part, by covering fewer topics in systematic and connected ways.

Criteria for depth of knowledge:
2 = Knowledge remains superficial and fragmented; while some key concepts and ideas are mentioned or covered, only a superficial acquaintance or trivialized understanding of these complex ideas is evident.
3 = Knowledge is treated unevenly during instruction; that is, deep understanding of something is countered by superficial understanding of other ideas. At least one significant idea may be presented in depth and its significance grasped, but in general the focus is not sustained.

Connectedness to the World

The third scale measures the extent to which the class has value and meaning

beyond the instructional context. In a class with little or no value beyond, activities are deemed important for success only in school (now or later). Students' work has no impact on others and serves only to certify their level of compliance with the norms of formal schooling.

A lesson gains in authenticity the more there is a connection to the larger social context within which students live. Instruction can exhibit some degree of connectedness when (1) students address real-world public problems (for example, clarifying a contemporary issue by applying statistical analysis in a report to the city council on the homeless); or (2) students use personal experiences as a context for applying knowledge (such as using conflict resolution techniques in their own school).

Criteria for connectedness:
1 = Lesson topic and activities have no clear connection to issues or experience beyond the classroom. The teacher offers no justification for the work beyond the need to perform well in class.
5 = Students work on a problem or issue that the teacher and students see as connected to their personal experiences or contemporary public situations. They explore these connections in ways that create personal meaning. Students are involved in an effort to influence an audience beyond their classroom; for example, by communicating knowledge to others, advocating solutions to social problems, providing assistance to people, or creating performances or products with utilitarian or aesthetic value.

Substantive Conversation

From "no substantive conversation" (1) to "high-level substantive conversation" (5), the fourth scale assesses the extent of talking to learn and understand the substance of a subject. In classes with little or no substantive conversation, interaction typically consists of a lecture with recitation in which the teacher deviates very little from delivering a preplanned body of information and set of questions; students routinely give very short answers. Teachers' list of questions, facts, and concepts tend to make the discourse choppy, rather than coherent; there is often little or no follow-up of student responses. Such discourse is the oral equivalent of fill-in-the-blank or short-answer study questions.

High levels of substantive conversation are indicated by three features:

1. There is considerable interaction about the ideas of a topic (the talk is about disciplined subject matter and includes indicators of higher-order thinking such as making distinctions, applying ideas, forming generalizations, raising questions, and not just reporting experiences, facts, definitions, or procedures).

2. Sharing of ideas is evident in exchanges that are not completely scripted or controlled (as in a teacher-led recitation). Sharing is best illustrated when participants explain themselves or ask questions in complete sentences and when they respond directly to comments of previous speakers.

3. The dialogue builds coherently on participants' ideas to promote improved collective understanding of a theme or topic.

Criteria for substantive conversation:
To score 2 or above, conversation must focus on subject matter as in feature (1) above.
2 = Sharing (2) and/or coherent promotion of collective understanding (3) occurs briefly and involves at least one example of two consecutive interchanges.
4 = All three features of substantive conversation occur, with at least one example of sustained conversation (that is, at least three consecutive interchanges), and many students participate.

Social Support for Student Achievement

The social support scale involves high expectations, respect, and inclusion of all students in the learning process. Social support is low when teacher or student behavior, comments, and actions tend to discourage effort, participation, or willingness to express one's views. Support can also be low if no overt acts like the above occur, but when the overall atmosphere of the class is negative as a result of previous behavior. Token acknowledg-

Figure 1

Five Standards of Authentic Instruction

1. Higher-Order Thinking
lower-order thinking only 1...2...3...4...5 higher-order thinking is central

2. Depth of Knowledge
knowledge is shallow 1...2...3...4...5 knowledge is deep

3. Connectedness to the World Beyond the Classroom
no connection 1...2...3...4...5 connected

4. Substantive Conversation
no substantive conversation 1...2...3...4...5 high-level substantive conversation

5. Social Support for Student Achievement
negative social support 1...2...3...4...5 positive social support

ments, even praise, by the teacher of student actions or responses do not necessarily constitute evidence of social support.

Social support is high in classes when the teacher conveys high expectations for all students, including that it is necessary to take risks and try hard to master challenging academic work, that all members of the class can learn important knowledge and skills, and that a climate of mutual respect among all members of the class contributes to achievement by all. "Mutual respect" means that students with less skill or proficiency in a subject are treated in ways that encourage their efforts and value their contributions.

Criteria for social support:
2 = Social support is mixed. Both negative and positive behaviors or comments are observed.
5 = Social support is strong. The class is characterized by high expectations, challenging work, strong effort, mutual respect, and assistance in achievement for almost all students. Both teacher and students demonstrate a number of these attitudes by soliciting and welcoming contributions from all students. Broad student participation may indicate that low-achieving students receive social support for learning.

Using the Framework to Observe Instruction

We are now using the five standards to estimate levels of authentic instruction in social studies and mathematics in elementary, middle, and high schools

that have restructured in various ways. Our purpose is not to evaluate schools or teachers, but to learn how authentic instruction and student achievement are facilitated or impeded by:

■ organizational features of schools (teacher workload, scheduling of instruction, governance structure);
■ the content of particular programs aimed at curriculum, assessment, or staff development;
■ the quality of school leadership;
■ school and community culture.

We are also examining how actions of districts, states, and regional or national reform projects influence instruction. The findings will describe the conditions under which "restructuring" improves instruction for students and suggest implications for policy and practice.

Apart from its value as a research tool, the framework should also help teachers reflect upon their teaching. The framework provides a set of standards through which to view assignments, instructional activities, and the dialogue between teacher and students and students with one another. Teachers, either alone or with peers, can use the framework to generate questions, clarify goals, and critique their teaching. For example, students may seem more engaged in activities such as cooperative learning or long-term projects, but heightened participation alone is not sufficient. The standards provide further criteria for examining the extent to which such activities actually put students' minds to work on authentic questions.

In using the framework, either for reflective critiques of teaching or for research, it is important to recognize its limitations. First, the framework does not try to capture in an exhaustive way all that teachers may be trying to accomplish with students. The standards attempt only to represent in a quantitative sense the degree of authentic instruction observed within discrete class periods. Numerical ratings alone cannot portray how lessons relate to one another or how multiple lessons might accumulate into experiences more complex than the sum of individual lessons. Second, the relative importance of the different standards remains open for discussion. Each suggests a distinct ideal, but it is probably not possible for most teachers to show high performance on all standards in most of their lessons. Instead, it may be important to ask, "Which standards should receive higher priority and under what circumstances?"[5]

Finally, although previous research indicates that teaching for thinking, problem solving, and understanding often has more positive effects on student achievement than traditional teaching, the effects of this specific framework for authentic instruction on student achievement have not been examined.[6] Many educators insist that there are appropriate times for traditional, less authentic instruction—emphasizing memorization, repetitive practice, silent study without conversation, and brief exposure—as well as teaching for in-depth understanding.

Rather than choosing rigidly and exclusively between traditional and authentic forms of instruction, it seems more reasonable to focus on how to move instruction toward more authentic accomplishments for students. Without promising to resolve all the dilemmas faced by thoughtful teachers, we hope the standards will offer some help in this venture.

[1]See Carnegie Corporation of New York (1989), Elmore and Associates (1990), and Murphy (1991).

[2]See Archbald and Newmann 1988, Newmann 1991, Newmann and Archbald 1992, Newmann et al. 1992, and Wehlage et al. 1989.

[3]For example, see the arguments for standards in National Council on Education Standards and Testing (1992), and Smith and O'Day (1991).

[4]In three semesters of data collection, correlations between raters were .7 or higher, and precise agreement between raters was about 60 percent or higher for each of the dimensions. A detailed scoring manual will be available to the public following completion of data collection in 1994.

[5]The standards may be conceptually distinct, but initial findings indicate that they cluster together statistically as a single construct. That is, lessons rated high or low on some dimensions tend to be rated in the same direction on others.

[6]Evidence for positive achievement effects of teaching for thinking is provided in diverse sources such as Brown and Palinscar (1989), Carpenter and Fennema (1992), Knapp et al. (1992), and Resnick (1987). However, no significant body of research to date has clarified key dimensions of instruction that produce *authentic* forms of student achievement as defined here.

References

Archbald, D., and F.M. Newmann. (1988). *Beyond Standardized Testing: Assessing Authentic Academic Achievement in the Secondary School*. Reston, Va.: National Association of Secondary School Principals.

Brown, A., and A. Palinscar. (March 1989). "Coherence and Causality in Science Readings." Paper presented at the annual meeting of the American Educational Research Association, San Francisco.

Carnegie Corporation of New York. (1989). *Turning Points: Preparing American Youth for the 21st Century*. Report on the Carnegie Task Force on the Education of Young Adolescents. New York: Carnegie Council on Adolescent Development.

Carpenter, T. P., and E. Fennema. (1992). "Cognitively Guided Instruction: Building on the Knowledge of Students and Teachers." In *Curriculum Reform: The Case of Mathematics in the United States*. Special issue of *International Journal of Educational Research*, edited by W. Secada, pp. 457-470. Elmsford, N.Y.: Pergamon Press, Inc.

Elmore, R. F., and Associates. (1990). *Restructuring Schools: The Next Generation of Educational Reform*. San Francisco: Jossey-Bass.

Knapp, M. S., P.M. Shields, and B.J. Turnbull. (1992). *Academic Challenge for the Children of Poverty: Summary Report*. Washington, D.C.: U.S. Department of Education, Office of Policy and Planning.

Murphy, J. (1991). *Restructuring Schools: Capturing and Assessing the Phenomena*. Nashville, Tenn.: National Center for Educational Leadership, Vanderbilt University.

National Council on Education Standards and Testing. (1992). *Raising Standards for American Education*. A Report to Congress, the Secretary of Education, the National Education Goals Panel, and the American People. Washington, D.C.: U.S. Government Printing Office, Superintendent of Documents, Mail Stop SSOP.

Newmann, F. M. (1991). "Linking Restructuring to Authentic Student Achievement." *Phi Delta Kappan* 72, 6: 458-463.

Newmann, F.M., and D. Archbald. (1992). "The Nature of Authentic Academic Achievement." In *Toward a New Science of Educational Testing and Assessment*, edited by H. Berlak, F.M. Newmann, E. Adams, D.A. Archbald, T. Burgess, J. Raven, and T.A. Romberg, pp. 71-84. Albany, N.Y.: SUNY Press.

Newmann, F. M., G.G. Wehlage, and S.D. Lamborn. (1992). "The Significance and Sources of Student Engagement." In *Student Engagement and Achievement in American Secondary Schools*, edited by F.M. Newmann, pp. 11-30. New York: Teachers College Press.

Resnick, L. (1987). *Education and Learning to Think*. Washington, D.C.: National Academy Press.

Smith, M. S., and J. O'Day. (1991). "Systemic School Reform." In *The Politics of Curriculum and Testing: The 1990 Yearbook of the Politics of Education Association*, edited by S.H. Fuhrman and B. Malen, pp. 233-267. Philadelphia: Falmer Press.

Wehlage, G. G., R.A. Rutter, G.A. Smith, N. Lesko, and R.R. Fernandez. (1989). *Reducing the Risk: Schools as Communities of Support*. Philadelphia: Falmer Press.

Authors' note: This paper was prepared at the Center on Organization and Restructuring of Schools, supported by the U.S. Department of Education, Office of Educational Research and Improvement (Grant No. R117Q0005-92) and by the Wisconsin Center for Education Research, School of Education, University of Wisconsin-Madison. Major contributions to the development of these standards have been made by Center staff members. The opinions expressed here are those of the authors and do not necessarily reflect the views of the supporting agencies.

Optimizing the Instructional Moment:
A Guide to Using Socratic, Didactic, Inquiry, and Discovery Methods

Mark Keegan

Mark Keegan is an Instructor at Columbia University Teachers College, a Teacher of Life Sciences at Asa Philip Randolph High School in Harlem, and a software designer and programmer with Scenario Educational Software in New York.

Sound bites overheard from American high school teachers:

- "I *taught* cell respiration, but they didn't learn it."
- "We *covered* flower parts but students failed the test."
- "We'd *gone over* supply-and-demand about four times but they acted like they didn't know it."
- "I *told* them about colonialism, they ought to know it."
- "No one is learning anything, so I *declared martial law*."

The students aren't learning, apparently. But why? What are the teachers doing? From these statements, one would think the teachers' repertoire includes just five methods: "*teaching*," "*covering*," "*going over*," "*telling*," and "*declaring martial law*." Not very exact, these terms. (And, anyway, how can one "teach," if no one learns?)

Having precise terms for something facilitates its use. Having precise terms for what teachers do in their classrooms will help improve what it is that they do. How much better these statements begin:

- "Demonstrating cell respiration, I encouraged *Inquiry*..."

- "The students *Discovered* the flower parts..."
- "I used a *Socratic* dialog on supply-and-demand..."
- "*Didactically*, I presented colonialism, using lecture and maps..."

Still, some of the students may not have achieved the instructional objective(s). But at least the teacher, alone or with colleagues, can plan what to do differently next time. How much more *professional* teachers would be—how much more like physicians, attorneys, and engineers—if they could sharpen their introspection, make reasoned improvements, and pass those improvements onto other teachers by using precisely understood terms.

"Eventually," say Postman and Weingartner (1969, p. 26), "the profession will have to get its names straight so that intelligent discussions can go forward."

Of course, instruction can change from minute to minute. And, with thirty students in a classroom, not all will be on task every moment. But a teacher should be able to contemplate his or her instructional objectives and think which of several basic strategies to use, best suited for achieving each objective. A typology of instructional methods is needed, a typology sensitive enough to be meaningful, but simple enough not to be unwieldy.

So what are the basic instructional methods?

Four "Kingdoms" of Instructional Methods
Much of the literature on intructional design employs a "cognitive paradigm," viewing the learner as an information processor (Winn, 1989); and a vital voice in instructional design insists that

the affective domain be included in any model of learning (Tennyson, 1992). Though we can generalize that every learner in every learning environment simply "interfaces with the environment at his sensory receptors," it certainly matters what that environment is. That is, it certainly matters how the educator creates that environment. So, though we need to improve our model of how the learner learns, we also need to improve our view of how the educator creates the appropriate learning environment.

There are many typologies of instructional methods. One dichotomy is whether or not the student is actively exercising his or her volition and imagination, or whether the student is subject to the will and imagination of others. One could dub this a "discovery versus didactic" dichotomy, or "active versus passive." Then there is the "inductive" versus "deductive" dichotomy: *inductus*, to lead in or toward, proceeds from specific experiences toward general rules; *deductus*, to lead from or away, proceeds from general rules toward specific experiences. Then there's Ausubel (1963), categorizing learning as discovery or reception. And Schmalholfer *et al.* (1990) categorize learning as exploratory versus receptive.

Here's another typology, a bit more sensitive than the dichotomies described above. Consider that both expert and learner are involved in the instructional process, and that the instructional moment, in essence, is a stimulus followed by a response (though not necessarily in "behavioral" terms). Questions beg answers, desires want fulfillment, and necessities are the mothers of invention. We can thus delineate four "kingdoms" of instructional methods (see Table 1), based on who generates the stimulus and who generates the response, with the instructional moment. **These four "Kingdoms" of instructional methods are Didactic, Socratic, Inquiry, and Discovery.**

When the expert generates both stimulus and response, as in an uninterrupted lecture, the instruction can be said to be **Didactic**. When the expert generates the stimulus, and the learner responds, the method is **Socratic**, as in a teacher-led discussion. When the learner generates the stimulus—for example, a question—and a book or an expert or an expert system produces a processed, finished response, then the **Inquiry** method is taking place. And, finally, when the learner generates both stimulus and response, the instructional moment is one of **Discovery** method, as in an interactive laboratory environment.

Examples and Descriptions of Each Method

At the two ends of the "learner passive-learner active" continuum are the Didactic and the Discovery methods. The Didactic method is also known as "teaching (or learning) by example"; the Discovery method is also known as "teaching (or learning) by doing" (see Figure 1).

Figure 1. Hypothetical amount of activity *during* instruction. Amount of activity *prior to* instruction is not shown.

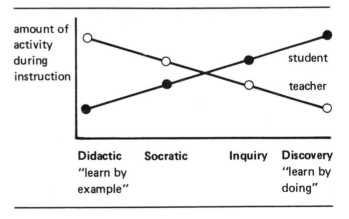

Table 1. Four general instructional methods, for an instructional moment of stimulus followed by response.

generates stimulus	generates response	name of method	activities containing high amounts of method
expert	expert	Didactic	lecture, text, film
expert	learner	Socratic	recitation, discussion
learner	expert	Inquiry	library search
learner	learner	Discovery	lab, field work

For a given illness, a physician can prescribe most any medicine, though one type of medicine is more appropriate for the illness than are other medicines. Likewise, most instructional objectives can be attempted by any of the four instructional methods, though it stands to reason that, for a given student or group of students and the objective at hand, one method will be superior to the others. Let us look at the use of the four methods on a few instructional objectives. (For purposes of simplicity, in the textual mode of this article, I must use objectives that can be textually represented.)

Table 2. OBJECTIVE: Student will be able to declare that 2 + 2 is 4.

DIDACTIC METHOD:
Teacher: "2 + 2 is ... 4."
Student: "..."

SOCRATIC METHOD:
Teacher: "2 + 2 is ...?"
Student: "4."

INQUIRY METHOD:
Student: "2 + 2 is ... ?"
Teacher: "4."

DISCOVERY METHOD:
Student: "2 + 2 is ... 4."
Teacher: "..."

Table 3. OBJECTIVE: Student will be able to state one of the first symptoms of acute MI.

DIDACTIC METHOD:
Teacher: "Deep, substernal, visceral pain is a first symptom of acute myocardial infarction."
Student: "..."

SOCRATIC METHOD:
Teacher: "Deep, substernal, visceral pain. Use your understanding of thoracic anatomy and innervation. What do you think such pain is a symptom of?"
Student: "Hmm ... Acute myocardial infarction."

INQUIRY METHOD:
Student: "If a patient has deep, substernal, visceral pain, what might that be a symptom of?"
Teacher: "Acute myocardial infarction should be suspected."

DISCOVERY METHOD:
Student: "Deep, substernal, visceral pain is ... oh, no! A first symptom of acute myocardial infarction."
Teacher: "..."

In Table 2, we suspect that most people initially learn that "2 + 2 = 4" via the Didactic method, and later reinforce the learning via other methods. It is conceivable, however, that a student could *discover* "2 + 2 = 4," using concrete objects.

Table 4. OBJECTIVE: Student will be able to point out the location, texture, and function of trachea. (Didactic moment taken from class observation notes, American Peace Corps teacher in Fiji, 1990.)

DIDACTIC METHOD:
Teacher: (Points to own neck.)
"The trachea is in front and you can feel it is stiff and hollow; it carries air to the lungs."
Student: (Writes in notebook.)

SOCRATIC METHOD:
Teacher: (Points to own neck.)
"This is called the trachea, and it carries air to the lungs. Describe on paper its location and how it feels to your hand."
Student: (Feels own neck. Writes or responds:)
"Trachea. In front of neck. Feels stiff and hollow."

INQUIRY METHOD:
Student: "What is the name of this stiff tube right here in front of my neck?"
Teacher: "That's the trachea. It is hollow, and lets air go to and from the lungs."

DISCOVERY METHOD:
Teacher: (Creating the learning environment)
"Air needs to get from the nose or mouth, down to the lungs, through a tube called the trachea. Find it, on your own body, and then describe on paper where it is and how it feels."
Student: (Feels neck, feels neighbor's neck.)
"The trachea? Aha! It is right here, in front. I can feel it! It is stiff and hollow."

In Table 3, I suspect that the medical student would learn the symptoms of MI permanently via the Discovery method, when attending to an emergency room case. She might interview the victim, who gasps about the symptom. Then moments later, the infarction worsens, and the medical student saves the day (calling for 5 mg morphine intravenously, establishment of a 12-lead ECG, drawing of blood for enzyme analysis, and employment of β-adrenergic blockers to restrict the area of infarction).

Table 4 presents a moment from a high school classroom in the South Pacific in 1990, with a United States Peace Corps Volunteer teaching biology. The teacher attempted a Didactic approach; I have speculated how the instructional moment might have transpired if alternative approaches were employed.

Note that even within this one moment, there are many possible paths the teacher or students could take. Also, the sharp boundary blurs between the four methods. Still, the typology facilitates communication. Here, the Discovery method again sounds memorable; but it would consume more time, and probably not all students would succeed in the Discovery. (How is one sure, from the outside, that the trachea is hollow or indeed travels all the way to the lungs?) And the Inquiry method depends on an already curious student. Perhaps, then, the Socratic method would be most effective here.

If we analyzed dozens of instructional moments, we would find that, generally, the various classroom activities tend to have more of one type of instructional moment than another. Table 5 shows more examples of each method.

Table 5. Common examples of four instructional methods. Four basic types of instructional computer software are also named and classified.

method	typical examples
Didactic	lectures, textbook, film, tutorial software
Socratic	recitation, q/a, discussion, drill software
Inquiry	library research, simulation software
Discovery	lab, field work, scenario software

How the Moment Can Change

Though the teacher may attempt an instructional objective by one of the four methods, the attempt might fail for some students. The teacher can quickly and naturally shift methods, and also use different methods for different students. Table 6 paraphrases an occurrence I've seen many times as a high school biology teacher.

Unlike professional athletes or actors, teachers rarely have time or facilities to analyze their work. But analysis of this example is instructive. Student A, of course, learned by Discovery, and then used Inquiry to obtain nomenclature from a textbook. Student B employed Inquiry: he chose a stimulus—the parts of the flower he uniquely dissected—and then sought a response from the teacher. The teacher found it necessary to engage Student C in a Socratic dialog, and then launched student C, hopefully, off into a few minutes of Discovery. Student D, either for lack of materials, interest, or skills, was left with no alternative but to attempt

learning by the Didactic method. So, in the space of a few minutes, all four methods were employed; different students responded to different methods; and, for most students, the method changed, from one instructional moment to the next.

Table 6. Use of all four instructional methods to achieve one objective: students will be able to describe parts of a flower.

Teacher: "Okay, get busy. See what you discover! We'll talk about it in ten minutes."

(Students begin dissecting flowers. Teacher circulates, observes. After 5 minutes:)

Student A: "I'm done. Here, I've taped the parts to my lab sheet and put the names beside them. Is that what you want? I got the names from the book. Page 340 and 341."

(Teacher assigns Student A to a more complex task.)

Student B: "Teacher, I think there are two types of, I don't know what they're called, these colored parts. But is this inside stuff all one part?"
Teacher: "No. These outer filaments are a separate part from this inner core. Dissect them apart."
Student B: (Resumes dissection.)

Student C: "I don't get what to do."
Teacher: "Just dissect it."
Student C: "I did. I still don't get it."
Teacher: "Okay, take a new flower. Now, suppose this was some rare rain forest flower that may be a cure for juvenile lymphocytic leukemia. Should you just chop it all up, or proceed carefully?"
Student C: "Go carefully."
Teacher: "And proceed from inside out, or outside in?"
Student C: "Either way. Maybe outside in."
Teacher: "Okay, now what happens if you start pulling the outermost parts?"
Student C: (Does it.) "They come off. They're separate."
Teacher: "Okay. Keep going like that. Record data."
Student C: (Resumes dissection.)

Student D: "This is boring."
Teacher: "You must learn it. Quiz at the end of the period."
Student D: "Can't I just read about it? Or wait for you to tell me? Anyway, there's no more flowers."
Teacher: "Okay. Read 340 to 341."
Student D: (Begins reading.)

Again the typology is valuable. Here we are, able to intelligently discuss a teacher's work using agreed-upon terms, and avoid the vagaries of "I taught it" and "They had it" and "We covered it." (Hopefully, skillful use of methods can also help alleviate the need to *declare martial law*!)

What Each Method May Be Best Suited For, and Why

Optimizing the instructional moment shouldn't depend only upon making mistakes and then improving one's methods the following year. A teacher must be able to more intelligently plan the achievement of new objectives, getting it right the first time. What heuristic do teachers use? Many teachers seem to opt "automatically" for Didactic methods—lectures and textbooks—rarely if ever employing the other three "medicines" in the doctor's bag. Other teachers usually attempt Discovery first, like the biology teacher in Table 6, falling back on Socratic, Inquiry, or Didactic methods as needed. (Keegan, 1992, presents a detailed survey of the empirical research supporting Discovery and Didactic methods.) Didactic methods tend to require less time, less preparation, and fewer materials, and they tend to convey a sense of power to the teacher. Discovery methods have a plethora of neurological and affective advantages, and a body of research (Ray, 1961, among others) supporting their superiority in producing long-term transfer of learning.

It may seem presumptuous that I am talking about something so fuzzy and subjective as learning styles, teaching methods, and instructional objectives as though they were chemical reactants, catalysts, and chemical products. Let's see just how much or how little ambiguity exists, for a few choices of instructional method. Right now, before looking at it, cover the right-hand column of Table 7. Study the left-hand column. Then for each of the instructional objectives, consider which of the four instructional methods—Didactic, Socratic, Inquiry, or Discovery—might be best, initially, for a typical secondary school classroom.

Did we agree on more than one-fourth of these? The taste of harmless phenylthiocarbamide paper, and life in Nicaragua, are both experiences a novice can explore and interpret for himself. Running red lights is too dangerous to do via Discovery; it is best to simply be told. The learning and use of a viable language must, by definition, be something many people can "learn on their own" from people who already know it. This calls for a Socratic method: expert speaks, learner responds.

Table 7. Recommended methods for various instructional objectives for a secondary school.

instructional objective	recommended method
avoid running red lights	Didactic
speak French	Socratic
list the six most populous nations	Inquiry
describe taste of harmless PTC paper . .	Discovery
describe how periodic table works	Didactic
program a computer	Socratic
describe effects of economic variables . .	Inquiry
describe life in Nicaragua	Discovery

(It can later call for an Inquiry method: learner speaks, expert responds.) The rules and trends of the periodic table are too complex and hidden for the average learner to inquire about, much less to discover on his own; the Didactic method is called for.

So it would seem each method has a "niche" in education (see Table 8 for speculation), and further research needs to better delineate these niches. A child is not likely to learn how to read on his own. His mind can neither frame the proper questions ("Teacher, what is 'A'?") nor can he interpret the answer. He must learn the alphabet and sight words from Didactic instruction. On the other hand, a child can well learn the sight or sound or taste or smell or touch of something (something safe, that is) by Discovery. The child knows how to put it in his mouth, and how to interpret the results. In fact, it would be hard for an expert to convey, Didactically, what chocolate tastes like.

Table 8. Hypothesized general use of four instructional methods, very tentatively described.

method	general use
Didactic	introducing nomenclature, abstractions
Socratic	ingraining nomenclature, rules, habits
Inquiry	learning to use complex systems
Discovery	learning to use simple systems

Table 9 presents a more general key to the methods, based upon the likelihood that a learner can effectively produce the learning stimulus or the learning response for a given objective.

Table 9. General use of instructional methods, very tentatively described.

---

likelihood learner could ...

ask the question	interpret the answer	indicate method
low	low	Didactic
low	high	Socratic
high	low	Inquiry
high	high	Discovery

What Teachers Can Do

In the final analysis, reality is not quite so neatly packaged as our tables suggest. Treatment of a human patient is not so clear-cut as medical textbooks suggest, either. Many objectives call for combinations of strategies, or strategies intermediate among the four extremes. And, more importantly, there are trade-offs among the methods. P. K. Smith (1982, p. 153) suggests:

> There is a trade-off between the self-motivated but not optimally focused activities of play, and the potentially more optimally focused but probably less motivating activities in training and instruction.

Smith's "play" suggests the Discovery method; his "training and instruction" implies a more Didactic approach.

The more clearly that teachers know the strengths of the various instructional methods, the more optimal will their choices of method be. And the more skilled the teachers of the 21st century are, the better students will emerge from our schools.

References

Ausubel, D. P. *The Psychology of Meaningful Verbal Learning.* New York: Grune and Stratton, 1963.

Keegan, M. D. *The Design and Effects of Scenario Educational Software.* Doctoral thesis. Columbia University Teachers College, 1992.

Postman, N., & Weingartner, C. *Teaching as a Subversive Activity.* New York: Dell Publishing Company, 1969.

Ray, W. E. Pupil Discovery vs. Direct Instruction. *Journal of Experimental Education,* 1961, *29,* 271–280.

Schmalhofer, F., Kuhn, O., Messamer, P., & Charron, R. An Experimental Evaluation of Different Amounts of Receptive and Exploratory Learning in a Tutoring System. *Computers in Human Behavior,* 1990, *6,* 51–68.

Smith, P. K. Does Play Matter? Functional and Evolutionary Aspects of Animal and Human Play. *The Behavioral and Brain Sciences,* 1982, *5,* 139–184.

Tennyson, R. D. An Educational Learning Theory for Instructional Design. *Educational Technology,* January 1992, *32*(1), 36–41.

Winn, W. D. Towards a Rationale and Theoretical Basis for Educational Technology. *ETR&D,* 1989, *37,* 35–46.

The Culture/Learning Style Connection

Cultures do have distinctive learning style patterns, but the great variation among individuals within groups means that educators must use diverse teaching strategies with all students.

Pat Guild

Pat Guild is owner of Pat Guild Associates, P. O. Box 99131, Seattle, WA 98199.

Our ability to give every child a chance to succeed in school depends upon a full understanding of culture and learning styles. After all, effective educational decisions and practices must emanate from an understanding of the ways that individuals learn. Consequently, knowing each student, especially his or her culture, is essential preparation for facilitating, structuring, and validating successful learning for all students.

This imperative leads to three critical questions. Do students of the same culture have common learning style patterns and characteristics? If they do, how would we know it? And most important, what are the implications for educators?

These questions are both important and controversial. They are important because we need all the information we can get to help every learner succeed in school and because our understanding of the learning process is the basis for decisions about curriculum and instruction. They are important because success for the diverse populations that schools serve calls for continual reexamination of educators' assumptions, expectations, and biases. And they are important because, ultimately, every educational decision is evaluated according to its impact on individual students' learning.

One reason that the linkage between culture and learning styles is controversial is that generalizations about a *group* of people have often led to naive inferences about *individuals* within that group. Although people connected by culture do exhibit a characteristic pattern of style preferences, it is a serious error to conclude that all members of the group have the same style traits as the group taken as a whole.

A second source of controversy is the understandable sensitivity surrounding attempts to explain the persistent achievement differences between minority and nonminority students—it is all too easy to confuse descriptions of differences with explanations for deficits. Finally, the relationship between culture and learning styles is controversial because it brings us face to face with philosophical issues that involve deeply held beliefs. Debaters in the uniformity versus diversity dispute, for instance, differ over whether instructional equality is synonymous with educational equity. Another debate concerns the ultimate purpose of schooling.

Is it "cultural pluralism" or the "melting pot"?

A highly public example of how sensitive these issues are occurred in 1987 when the state of New York published a booklet to help decrease the student dropout rate. A small section of the booklet described the learning styles typical of minority students and identified certain patterns associated with African-American students.

These descriptions became the subject of intense scrutiny and animated debate. Eventually, the descriptions were deleted from the booklet. Nonetheless, in the *New York State Regent's Report,* a review panel reiterated that:

> learning style and behavioral tendency do exist, and students from particular socialization and cultural experiences often possess approaches to knowledge that are highly functional in the indige-

nous home environment and can be capitalized upon to facilitate performance in academic settings (Claxton 1990).

How We Know That Culture and Ways of Learning Are Linked

There is very little disagreement that a relationship does exist between the culture in which children live (or from which they are descended) and their preferred ways of learning. This relationship, further, is directly related to academic, social, and emotional success in school.

These conclusions are not as simple or definite as they seem, however. Though many syntheses and surveys have discussed the interdynamics of different cultures and ways of learning, each comes from a very distinctive approach, focusing either on a specific learning style model or a particular cultural group. No work, to my knowledge, claims to be comprehensive on the topic of culture and learning styles.

In general, researchers have reported three kinds of information about culture and learning styles.

The first is the set of *observation-based descriptions of cultural groups of learners.* For the most part, people who are familiar with each group have written these descriptions to sensitize people outside the culture to the experiences of children inside the culture. They have often contrasted minority students' learning patterns with European-American students' ways of learning and the school practices designed for such students.

Researchers have identified typical learning patterns among African Americans (Hale-Benson 1986, Shade 1989, Hilliard 1989), Mexican Americans (Ramirez 1989, Vasquez 1991, Berry 1979, Cox and Ramirez 1981), and Native Americans (Bert and Bert 1992, More 1990, Shade 1989).

The reports conclude that Mexican Americans regard family and personal relationships as important and are comfortable with cognitive generalities and patterns (Cox and Ramirez 1981, Vasquez 1991). Such traits explain why Mexican-American

students often seek a personal relationship with a teacher and are more

Generalizations about a *group* of people often lead to naive inferences about *individual* members of that group.

comfortable with broad concepts than component facts and specifics.

Research about the African-American culture shows that students often value oral experiences, physical activity, and loyalty in interpersonal relationships (Shade 1989, Hilliard 1989). These traits call for classroom activities that include approaches like discussion, active projects, and collaborative work.

Descriptions indicate that Native-American people generally value and develop acute visual discrimination and skills in the use of imagery, perceive globally, have reflective thinking patterns, and generally value and develop acute visual discrimination and skills in the use of imagery (Shade 1989, More 1990, Bert and Bert 1992). Thus, schooling should establish a context for new information, provide quiet times for thinking, and emphasize visual stimuli.

In contrast, the observers describe mainstream white Americans as valuing independence, analytic thinking, objectivity, and accuracy. These values translate into learning experiences that focus on competition, information, tests and grades, and linear logic. These patterns are prevalent in most American schools.

A second way that we know about the links between culture and learning styles is *data-based descriptions of*

specific groups. In this class of inquiry, researchers administer learning style/cognitive style instruments to produce a profile of a cultural group, compare this group with another previously studied one (usually white Americans), or validate a particular instrument for cross-cultural use.

The various formal assessment instruments that purport to measure learning styles detect differences in two general ways. In the category of instruments that looks for style *preferences,* respondents usually self-report their favored approaches to learning. The best known instrument of this kind is probably the Myers-Briggs Type Indicator. It infers learning style patterns from basic perceptual and judging traits.

Another type of assessment instrument tests style *strengths,* that is, the ability to do tasks with a certain approach. The Swassing-Barbe Modality Index, for example, asks test takers to repeat patterns given auditorily, visually, and tactilely. Another example is the well-known series of assessments that distinguishes between field-dependence and independence. In this series, the test taker tries to find a simple figure embedded in a more complex one. The results show differences in cognitive strengths, such as global, holistic learning in contrast to analytic, part-to-whole approaches.

Formal assessment data should be interpreted (though often, it is not) in the light of the kind of assessment used. An important fact about self-report instruments, for instance, is that they are language- and culture-specific. In other words, when test takers respond to specific words, they interpret the words through their cultural experiences.

Further, different assessments may yield conflicting results. For instance, someone might self-report a preference for learning something in a certain way and yet test out in a different way on a task involving strengths. It is equally possible for descriptions based on observations to conflict with self-reported preferences.

These inconsistencies do not invalidate the usefulness of each of the ways of assessing learning styles. They do point out, however, that understanding learning patterns is a complex task and that the scope of the diagnostic tool used imposes limits on generalizations that can be drawn on the basis of it. Further, the characteristics of the assessment instruments used often account for the seemingly contradictory information reported about groups of learners.

The third way we know about the relationship of learning and culture is through *direct discussion*. Shade (1989), for instance, comments that:

> perceptual development differs within various ethnocultural groups. It is [therefore] an erroneous assumption in the teaching-learning process to assume children "see" the same event, idea, or object in the same way.

Cognitive styles research, Ramirez (1989) believes, could help accommodate children who see things differently. The research findings, he notes, provide "a framework to look at and be responsive to diversity within and between cultures."

Bennett (1986) warns that ignoring the effects of culture and learning styles would depress learning among nonmainstream students:

> If classroom expectations are limited by our own cultural orientations, we impede successful learners guided by another cultural orientation. If we only teach according to the ways we ourselves learn best, we are also likely to thwart successful learners who may share our cultural background but whose learning styles deviate from our own.

Accepted Conclusions About Culture and Learning Styles

Those who study culture and those who study learning styles generally agree on at least five points.

1. Educators concur that *students of any particular age will differ in their ways of learning.* (Guild and Garger 1985). Both empirical research and experiences validate these learning style differences, which in their cognitive, affective, and behavioral dimen-

sions, help us to understand and talk about individual learning processes.

2. Most researchers believe that *learning styles are a function of both nature and nurture.* Myers (1990) asserts that:

> Type development starts at a very early age. The hypothesis is that *type* is inborn, an innate predisposition like right- or left-handedness, but the *successful development* of type can be greatly helped or hindered by environment.

Some researchers downplay the innate aspects of learning style, preferring to focus on the impact of environment. Many place great importance on the early socialization that occurs within the family, immediate culture, and wider culture.

3. Most researchers also believe that *learning styles are neutral* (Guild and Garger 1985). Every learning style approach can be used successfully, but can also become a stumbling block if applied inappropriately or overused.

This concept in the learning styles literature says a great deal about the effects of different learning approaches with different school tasks. Without question, for example, an active, kinesthetic learner has a more difficult time in school because of the limited opportunities to use that approach, especially for the development of basic skills. Nonetheless, the kinesthetic approach is a successful way to learn, and many adults, including teachers and administrators, use this approach quite effectively. Howard Gardner's (1983, 1991) identification of various intelligences has helped people appreciate the strengths of various approaches to learning.

4. In both observational and data-based research on cultures, one consistent finding is that, *within a group, the variations among individuals are as great as their commonalities.* Therefore, no one should automatically attribute a particular learning style to all individuals within a group (Griggs and Dunn 1989).

This subtle point is often verbally acknowledged, but ignored in practice. Cox and Ramirez (1981) explain the result:

> Recognition and identification of ... average differences have had both positive and negative effects in education. The positive effect has been the development of an awareness of the types of learning that our public schools tend to foster.... The negative effect ... is [that] the great diversity within a culture is ignored and a construct that should be used as a tool for individualization becomes yet another label for categorizing and evaluating.

5. Finally, many *authors acknowledge the cultural conflict between some students and the typical learning experiences in schools.* When a child is socialized in ways that are inconsis-

When people are asked to respond to specific words, they will interpret the words through their cultural experiences.

tent with school expectations and patterns, the child needs to make a difficult daily adjustment to the culture of the school and his or her teachers. Hale-Benson (1986) points out the added burden this adjustment places on black youngsters:

> Black children have to be prepared to imitate the "hip," "cool" behavior of the culture in which they live and at the same time take on those behaviors that are necessary to be upwardly mobile.

Debates About Applying Theory on Culture and Learning Styles

The published literature recommends caution in applying knowledge about culture and learning styles to the classroom. This prudence seems advisable because, despite the accepted ideas, at least five differences of opinion persist.

1. People differ, for instance, on *whether educators should acquire more explicit knowledge about particular cultural values and expectations.* Proponents say that such knowledge would enable educators to be more sensitive and effective with students of particular cultures. Certain states even mandate such information as part of their goals for multiculturalism.

Other authors argue, however, that describing cultures has resulted in more stereotyping and may well lead to a differentiated, segregated approach to curriculum. For example, Cox and Ramirez (1981) note that "the concept of cognitive or learning styles of minority and other students is one easily oversimplified, misunderstood, or misinterpreted." The authors go on to say that misuse of the concept has led to stereotyping and labeling rather than the identification of educationally meaningful differences among individuals.

2. Authors also debate the *proper response to the fact that the culture-learning styles relationship affects student achievement.* Evidence suggests that students with particular learning style traits (field-dependent, sensing, extraversion) are underachievers in school, irrespective of their cultural group. Students with such dominant learning style patterns have limited opportunities to use their style strengths in the classroom.

Even more disheartening is the practice of remediating problems so that the learner conforms to school expectations, rather than structuring school tasks in ways that respond to students' strengths. With the current emphasis on the inclusion of all learners in classrooms, it seems essential to change that practice.

Another achievement problem is the serious inequity that results when certain cultures value behaviors that are undervalued in school. Will increased attention to culture and learning styles eradicate this problem? Hilliard (1989) thinks not:

> I remain unconvinced that the explanation for the low performance of culturally different "minority group" students will be found by pursuing questions of behavioral style.... Children, no matter what their style, are failing primarily because of systemic inequities in the delivery of whatever pedagogical approach the teachers claim to master—not because students cannot learn from teachers whose styles do not match their own.

Bennett (1986) agrees that accommodating learning styles won't solve all problems:

> We must be careful ... not to view learning styles as the panacea that will eliminate failure in the schools. To address learning styles is often a necessary, but never sufficient, condition of teaching.

3. Another unresolved issue is *how teachers working from their own cultures and teaching styles can successfully reach diverse populations.* Bennett (1986) sums up the problem this way:

> To the extent that teachers teach as they have been taught to learn, and to the extent that culture shapes learning style, students who share a teacher's ethnic background will be favored in class.

Some argue, though, that teachers properly play a special role in representing their own culture. Hale-Benson (1986), for example, says:

> It is incumbent upon black professionals to identify the intelligences found especially in black children and to support the pursuit of their strengths.

Yes, that seems sensible. But we have all learned successfully from teachers who were neither like us in learning style or in culture. Often, these were masterful, caring teachers. Sometimes our own motivation helped us learn in spite of a teacher. Clearly, neither culture nor style is destiny. Just as clearly, though, teachers of all cultures and styles will have to work conscientiously to provide equitable opportunities for all students.

4. *How cultural identity and self-esteem are related* remains an open question, too. Many large city school systems are wrestling with the appropriateness of ethnically identified schools, such as an African-American academy. Bilingual programs continue to debate the value of instruction in the students' first language.

I would add to this discussion a remark of Carl Jung's: "If a plant is to unfold its specific nature to the full, it must first be able to grow in the soil in which it is planted" (Barger and Kirby 1993). This comment has led me to argue against the approach to learning so prevalent in our schools (especially in special education programs), which emphasizes the identification and remediation of deficiencies.

An acceptance of learning styles demands an approach that develops skills through strengths. Should the same not be said of cultural identity?

5. Perhaps the most weighty of the application issues has to do with *ways to counteract our tendency toward instructional pendulum swings.* This oscillation has become so predictable in schooling in our country. Today it's phonics. Tomorrow whole language. The day after that, phonics again. We are always seeking one right way to teach, and when we accumulate evidence that a strategy is effective with some students, we try to apply it to every student in every school.

A deep understanding of culture and learning styles makes this behavior seem naive. If instructional decisions were based on an understanding of each individual's culture and ways of learning, we would never assume that uniform practices would be effective for all. We would recognize that the only way to meet diverse learning needs would be to intentionally apply diverse strategies. As Bennett (1986) says, equitable opportunities for success demand "unequal teaching methods that respond to relevant differences among students."

Ideas about culture and learning styles can be of great help to teachers as they pursue such intentional instructional diversity. A teacher who truly understands culture and learning styles and who believes that all students

When a child is socialized in ways that are inconsistent with school expectations and patterns, the child needs to make a difficult daily adjustment.

can learn, one way or another, can offer opportunities for success to all students.

Not Easy, but Crucial

While the culture/learning styles relationship is deceptively simple and the issues surrounding it are complex, it is a crucially important idea to contemplate. We should not be reluctant to do so for fear of repeating past mistakes. With a better understanding of these missteps, we can avoid them in the future. As Hilliard (1989) assures us:

Educators need not avoid addressing the question of style for fear they may be guilty of stereotyping students. Empirical observations are not the same

as stereotyping, but the observations must be empirical and must be interpreted properly for each student.

As we try to accommodate students' cultural and learning differences, it is most important to deeply value each person's individuality. If we believe that people do learn—and have the right to learn—in a variety of ways, then we will see learning styles as a comprehensive approach guiding all educational decisions and practices. The ideas will not become ends in themselves, which would merely support the uniformity found in most schools.

Using information about culture and learning styles in sensitive and positive ways will help educators value and promote diversity in all aspects of the school. This task will not be easy, but then teaching is not a profession for the faint of heart. It requires courage and a willingness to grapple with real questions about people and their learning. Many students stand to benefit from that effort.

References

Barger, N. J., and L. K. Kirby. (Fall 1993). "The Interaction of Cultural Values and Type Development: INTP Women Across Cultures." *Bulletin of Psychological Type* 16: 14-16.

Bennett, C. (1986). *Comprehensive Multicultural Education, Theory and Practice.* Boston: Allyn and Bacon.

Berry, J. W. (1979). "Culture and Cognitive Style." In *Perspectives on Cross-Cultural Psychology,* edited by A. Marsella, R. Tharp, and T. Ciborowski. San Francisco: Academic Press.

Bert, C. R. G., and M. Bert. (1992). The Native American: An Exceptionality in Education and Counseling. (ERIC Document Reproduction Service No. ED 351 168).

Claxton, C. S. (Fall 1990) "Learning Styles, Minority Students, and Effective Education." *Journal of Developmental Education* 14: 6-8, 35.

Cox, B., and M. Ramirez III. (1981). "Cognitive Styles: Implications for Multiethnic Education." In *Education in the '80s,* edited by J. Banks. Washington, D. C.: National Education Association.

Gardner, H. (1983) *Frames of Mind.* New York: Basic Books.

Gardner, H. (1991) *The Unschooled Mind: How Children Think and How Schools Should Teach.* New York: Basic Books.

Griggs, S. A., and R. Dunn. (1989). "The Learning Styles of Multicultural Groups and Counseling Implications." *Journal of Multicultural Counseling and Development* 17: 146-155.

Guild, P., and S. Garger. (1985). *Marching to Different Drummers.* Alexandria, Va.: Association for Supervision and Curriculum Development.

Hale-Benson, J. E. (1986). *Black Children: Their Roots, Culture, and Learning Styles.* Rev. ed. Baltimore: Johns Hopkins University Press.

Hilliard, A. G., III. (January 1989). "Teachers and Cultural Styles in a Pluralistic Society." *NEA Today*: 65-69.

More, A. J. (1990). "Learning Styles of Native Americans and Asians." Paper presented at the Annual Meeting of the American Psychological Association, Boston. (ERIC Document Reproduction Service No. ED 330 535)

Myers, I. B. (1990). *Gifts Differing.* 2nd ed. Palo Alto, Calif.: Consulting Psychologists Press.

Ramirez, M., III. (1989). "Pluralistic Education: A Bicognitive-Multicultural Model." *The Clearinghouse Bulletin* 3: 4-5.

Shade, B. J. (October 1989) "The Influence of Perceptual Development on Cognitive Style: Cross Ethnic Comparisons." *Early Child Development and Care* 51: 137-155.

Vasquez, J. A. (1991). Cognitive Style and Academic Achievement. In *Cultural Diversity and the Schools: Consensus and Controversy,* edited by J. Lynch, C. Modgil, and S. Modgil. London: Falconer Press.

Paradigm Shifts in Designed Instruction:
From Behaviorism to Cognitivism to Constructivism

Peter A. Cooper

Peter A. Cooper teaches at Southwest Baptist University, Bolivar, Missouri.

Introduction

Designed instruction has moved through a series of development phases since its reliance on the early behaviorist work of Skinner and Pressey and their followers. The move from instructional theory emphasis on the environmental to emphasis on the internal has been accompanied by similar changes in three technologies: instructional design methodology, the physical technology with which the instruction is implemented or mediated, and the programming mechanism(s) used to develop the instructional software conveying the subject content. The purpose of this article is to chart the development of designed instruction in relation to these factors and to look beyond, to the possibility of further changes. Such changes are of such a dramatic nature that they can be considered paradigm shifts. A relationship exists between instructional theory and its dependent technologies, and it is suggested that implementation of designed instruction, grounded in theory, is limited by the available technology paradigms.

This article examines the history, characteristics, and value of designed instruction, grounded in behaviorist, cognitive science, and constructivist theory. The article attempts to connect the theories to the prevailing technology paradigms.

Behaviorism

Bullock (1982) identifies the basic assumptions of the behaviorist: *objectivism*, where the key to analyzing human behavior lies in the observation of external events; *environmentalism*, in which the environment is the significant factor in determining human behavior; and *reinforcement*, where the consequences of our actions affect subsequent behavior.

Lamos (1984) describes the beginnings of the instructional design movement as centering around B. F. Skinner and programmed instruction (PI). Programmed instruction was behaviorally based and was characterized as having three stages: analysis, design, and evaluation. The stages map to the general scientific approach (hypothesis generation, experimental design, and hypothesis testing). The analysis of requirements—constructed as behavioral objectives with criterion-referenced tests as a means of assessing performance—lead to concentration on the required *performance* and the elimination of peripheral knowledge acquisition.

Reinforcement and the concepts that are developed from reinforcement—stimulus control, chaining, shaping, competing and enhancing repertoires, and interpersonal and intrapersonal behaviors—are central to behaviorism. A simplistic early view of knowledge-of-results feedback as being reinforcement gave way to a more complex notion that while learning increases the likelihood of the emergence of target behaviors, the primary reinforcers are considered to be learner generated ("intrinsic") and that external feedback ("extrinsic") is most effective as either correctional or motivational feedback (Bullock, 1982). Behaviorists now consider that the potential for behavioral change is heavily influenced by the current behavior of the learner and the way in which that behavior either competes with or enhances the development of new behaviors.

Feedback as reinforcement has been subjected to some criticism, as research has emerged demonstrating that under certain circumstances, delayed feedback is more effective than immediate feedback. Students, it appears, spend more time studying feedback if it is delayed than if it is provided immediately after difficult material has been presented. The issue of who maintains control of feedback is also important. Student control of feedback can lead to students not interacting with the material, if they can obtain the feedback without doing so. The feedback then lacks value.

The first technology-based instructional programs derived from behaviorally oriented programmed instruction, which was task-based and developed stimulus-response chains of behavior, which were shaped toward a desired terminal or final behavior. Experimental research concluded that, while feedback (reinforcement) is an effective tool, the quality of feedback is dependent upon the quality of information that it imparts to the learner; which, in turn, is a function of the diagnostic ability of the program. Feedback mechanisms which only provide a bare-bones indication of correct or incorrect response perform relatively poorly.

Jelden (1984) discusses two mechanisms for achieving stimulus control: *behavior modelling*, which can be job-relevant and achieves successive approximations to the desired behavior, and *algorithms and other job aids*, which provide procedural cues. He then identifies a set of procedures for implementing a behaviorally based instructional unit which allows a degree of learner control. He describes the system as "a computer-based, multimedia, computer-managed instructional approach which emphasizes self-paced individualized learning" (p. 2). He identifies four major components of the system:

(1) a *student information* module, which performs learner characteristic and capability assessment;

(2) an *instructional analysis* module to analyze and order the instructional content;
(3) a *learning activity* module, which identifies the support mechanisms and media required, and suggests a learning sequence for each student; and
(4) a *system evaluation* module, which performs a statistical analysis of the effectiveness of the overall system.

Jelden summarizes his approach by providing a procedure to aid in the development or revision of instructional materials.

Chase (1985) attempts to address some of the criticisms levelled at the application of behavioral principles to instructional design, identifying two major negative reactions to behaviorism. First, technological developments have not been utilized effectively by behaviorists, in particular, the use of computers and interactive media; as a result, few realistic educational applications have been developed. Second, and perhaps more damaging, the application of behaviorist principles leads to a reductionist and fragmented program, which concentrates on low-level skills at the expense of "complex, conceptual behavior" (p. 65). Golub (1983) criticizes the use of microcomputers in schools and at home as automated page turners, which leave the learner as an almost passive bystander, required only to press the RETURN key. Although the criticism is often directed at the behaviorist foundation of such software, he notes that the criticism should be of poorly developed software rather than the underlying theoretical approach.

To combat these criticisms, Chase offers an approach to instructional design which includes the use of authoring systems and the strict application of behaviorist principles. He cites Scandura (1981), who suggested that the courseware developer requires three skills: content expertise, computer expertise, and design expertise. The confluence of all three skills is rare, so the courseware author might have to collaborate with a subject matter expert or a computer expert. Chase identifies a series of practical questions that the prospective author might reasonably ask of himself/herself, including hardware/software compatibility and an assessment of the utility of the authoring system. An approach to instructional analysis follows, which includes specification of the goals, objectives, and tasks; the development of a continuum of tasks from elementary to conceptual relationships; and analysis of the content. He provides a checklist for conducting a content analysis. The final element in the development process concerns evaluation. Evaluation should comprise the assessment of the learners' entering skills, the changes that occur as a result of the instruction, and the calibration of the collected data. Again, a checklist of steps is provided.

Behaviorist attributes are found in most technology-based instructional applications in the learning of small chunks of material related to a single skill and the use of reinforcement through reward. Golub (1983) suggests that behaviorally based instruction seems most useful for clearly delineated content where the branching is constrained and learner responses are categorized as right or wrong.

Numerous studies have been conducted demonstrating the effectiveness of behaviorally-based instructional software in general, and on the utility of feedback in particular. McGowan and Clark (1985), citing Snow (1977) and Snow and Lohman (1984), identify a relationship between the underlying theoretical rationale of computer-based instruction and the effectiveness of that instruction at different learner-ability levels. There is evidence to suggest that lower-ability learners perform better in well-structured, behaviorally oriented instructional environments, whereas higher-ability learners perform better in less-structured environments. They argue against learner-controlled support, as higher-ability students have tended, despite their abilities, to select high-support mechanisms, and lower-ability learners have tended to select low-support mechanisms. Poppen and Poppen (1988), evaluating six widely-used computer-based instruction (CBI) applications, noted that many of the characteristics of a behavioral approach were missing, including lack of assessment of the target population and its capabilities, lack of intermittent reinforcement, lack of prompting or fading, and little evaluation based on student-response data. They conclude that even the "best" software is not very good from a theoretical view, and they urge designers to more closely follow a theoretical framework.

Behaviorist learner principles were first applied to instruction using relatively low-level physical technology, employing relatively simple "programming" principles. The introduction of electronic rather than electromechanical devices was a technological enhancement. The programming paradigm requires the use of sequencing and iteration. In some ways this parallels the behaviorist design view. The input and output components are of importance, but the internal processing is underdeveloped. Information is presented in "frames" and the responses elicited from the learner are evaluated and used to generate some form of feedback.

Cognitivism

Although Skinner effectively applied Pressey's physical technology to a behaviorist approach, Pressey "in addition to providing the necessary technology implement, anticipated ... the present cognitive perspective and its importance for the instructional technology of the present and the future—the computer" (Lamos, 1984, p. 169).

Hartley (1985) charts the development of the cognitive approach from the initial conception of short- and long-term memory (Hebb, 1949) through the notions of automatic and controlled processing to our current understanding of the cognitive structure model. Tennyson (1992) provides a model of the cognitive system which relates the main areas of cognition (sensory receptors, executive control, working memory, and long-term memory) to their purposes and instructional needs. Long-term memory, for example, holds the knowledge base, which comprises content, skills, and strategies. Tennyson suggests that the model gives rise to a "dynamic, interactive system that assumes constant integration of the various components" (p. 36).

As the behaviorist ground gave way in the past two to three decades, the need to encompass individual differences emerged and brought with it an increased complexity in the technology required. Programmed instruction was forced "toward the handling of the complexity of individual differences" but the "technology of programmed texts and of electromechanical 'teaching machines' proved to be the limiting factor to the instructional accommodation of such individual differences" (Lamos, p. 171).

The analysis phase of PI now had to accommodate the evaluation of individual learner requirements and capabilities, among them cognitive styles and the ability to apply cognitive strategies. Some mechanism for determining the task in terms of cognitive analysis rather than procedural decomposition had to be developed. Central to the notion of cognitive analysis is a model of the internal workings of the mind, the identification of functional components to handle information filtering, storage in short-term memory, semantic encoding for storage in long-term memory, and retrieval when required.

Lamos suggests that there had been a progressive shift from the behavioral to the cognitive, which "has been matched by a corresponding shift in the research and implementation of instructional technology supporting individualized instruction" (p. 169) Robinson (1979) takes this notion of increased complexity one stage further, and theorizes that complexity in the learners' actions has to be matched by a similar level of complexity in the instructor's actions. The instructor employs constraining mechanisms to match the level of complexity appropriately to obtain a form of equilibrium. "One form of constraint is to reduce variety by such means, for example, as ignoring individual differences in a set of learners. The other form of constraint is to reduce variety by absorbing it. It is in this latter form of constraint that the technology becomes important" (p. 173). Lamos distinguished between computer-managed instruction (CMI), which provides a mechanism for evaluating individual aptitudes so that individualized instruction can be applied, and computer-assisted instruction (CAI), the use of computer technology to instruct a learner on a one-to-one basis with interaction, and giving the appearance of being able to make intelligent judgments based on learner interaction as the primary features.

The first attempts at technology-based instruction in the form of CAI betrayed a PI foundation with a linear "frame based" approach, followed by the use of branching mechanisms to anticipate different responses. These approaches, however, lacked the sophistication required to truly compensate for learner differences. Lamos suggests that we are currently in a transition state toward a more complex CAI paradigm, which is exemplified in experimental mechanisms such as Brown's SOPHIE, based on Pask's "conversational theory." Lamos concludes that increasing the complexity of the technology to accommodate individual differerences moves us closer to Pressey's conception of the purpose of his original teaching machine.

Orey (1991) identifies problems that designers of computer-based instruction have experienced in implementing cognitive theory into instruction. While developments in describing the processes and structures of cognition have made significant progress through the work of Merrill (1983, 1990), Hannafin and Reiber (1989), Salomon (1983), and others, the problem of integrating cognitive theory into the design of computer-based instruction remains. The instructional design models available do not currently support cognitively based activities. The ability to capture more data than just the learner response is crucial to the cognitive model. Understanding of the preferred style of the learner and data concerning the predictability of behavior can provide valuable information in manipulating the knowledge base. Hartley (1985) proposes that the use of an intelligent tutoring model as a paradigm can overcome such integration problems. Orey (1991) distinguishes between current computer-based design methods and an

intelligent tutoring mechanism, citing Wenger (1987), who states that "intelligent tutoring systems encode knowledge, while computer-based instruction encodes instructional decisions based on knowledge" (p. 3).

The intelligent tutoring model comprises four components:

(1) an *interface*, which is the means by which the system interacts with the learner;
(2) the *expert* module, typically a database of correct responses with which the learner responses are compared;
(3) a *learner* module, which is a "representation of the errors or misconceptions" that typically occur when a learner is presented with new content; and
(4) a *pedagogical* module, which evaluates what is known about the learner and the learner responses and makes decisions about how information is to be presented to the learner.

The learner may not only be learning the content but also how to manipulate the programmed environment. Ease of use and interface consistency are of significance in that they can allow a greater degree of concentration on the content, if well designed. The interaction style can also influence learning. Appropriate style in relation to the preferred learning style of the learner should be a goal. Orey discusses the use of metaphor, such as a windows environment and the mapping of a physical device such as a mouse, to application interaction. "The goal of instruction from a cognitive perspective, then, should be to replicate the knowledge structures and processes of the expert in the mind of the learner" (Orey, p. 6, citing Wildman and Burton, 1981).

Although a number of pedagogical models have been used in different systems, most systems only implement a single pedagogical model. Three general groups of models emerge, those that monitor activity in a problem-solving domain, those that use dialogue between learner and system, and those that use guided discovery. Orey advocates the use of multiple pedagogical strategies and tactics within the same application.

He concludes that some of the characteristics of intelligent tutoring devices are present in CBI that has been designed from a cognitive perspective and that, rather than there being a dichotomy between CBI and intelligent tutoring devices, there appears to be some continuum "anchored at one end by traditional computer-based instruction developed from an instructional systems design perspective (such as that found in many training settings) and at the other end by the 'ideal' intelligent tutoring system" (Orey, p. 10).

Hartley (1985) examines the likely value of artificial intelligence as a modelling device for more intelligent CAI. He notes three main problems that arise from the use of computers in the classroom: the unevenness of the quality of instructional software, the difficulties involved in integrating CAI into conventional classroom teaching, and the difficulty of developing software given current tools. Although there has been some interest in the development of programming tools for the learner (e.g., Logo) there is little documented evidence of the use of the tools in the classroom or of the effect of such tools on cognitive processes.

Current behaviorally oriented and cognitively oriented applications contain relatively little knowledge about the learning topic. Hartley suggests that this needs to be remedied, that the programs must contain an extensive knowledge base, somewhat like expert systems such as MYCIN. The learner's knowledge must be represented in the form of rules and mal-rules representing learner misconceptions. Expressing misconceptions in the form of rules not only provides guidance as to what must be corrected, but also offers a mechanism for correcting them. It has been shown (Newell and Simon, 1972) that learners are not erratic in their responses but consistently apply mal-rules to problems.

Behaviorism Versus Cognitivism

Skinner (1985) criticizes the claims of cognitive scientists in the use of computer simulations of mental models and the implication that behavior is internally initiated. He argues that the cognitive scientists have misused the metaphor of storage and retrieval, replaced experimentation and evaluation with descriptions of experiments and assessment of expectations, and have raised feelings and mental states to the status of *causes* of behavior.

The construction of the notion of "meaningful structures" is also criticized. Cognitivists assume a structure without necessarily any experimental validation. Skinner argues that the behavioral view of perception causing a response explains behavior as well as the cognitivists' abstraction of structure, and suggests that the identification of the internal mechanism is more likely to occur within neurology than cognitive science.

The third area of criticism concerns the learning of rules. When an organism learns a rule, the cognitivist concludes that the organism *knows* the rule. Skinner suggests that there is no evidence to suggest that the organism necessarily knows anything and, with repeated practice and the development of automaticity, the rule becomes unnecessary anyway.

Bourne (1990) examines the development of CAI in library instruction, beginning with a caution that "CAI should not be a gratuitous 'techtronic' exercise but a superior way of learning" (p. 160). She characterizes cognitive theory in contrast to behaviorist theory as "less reductionist, more holistic, and concerned with the developing mind and its organizing cognitive structure" (p. 162). She comments on the usage of hypertext mechanisms, where webs of connections exist between frames, rather than a linear progression between frames. Hypertext and hypermedia have been shown to be effective, although she cites authors commenting on the dangers of the learner becoming overwhelmed as the complexity of the linkage between frames becomes more complex. Navigation through the hyper system becomes problematic, and the *purpose* becomes lost in the process.

In summary, the early attempts to develop cognitively oriented designed instruction used a technological tool set inappropriate for the task. Only later did the programming and instructional design technology allow for the development of useful tools. The increasing complexity of the task resulting from the need to account for individual differences has necessitated increased hardware sophistication. The interface must be intuitive, almost forcing a graphical user interface. The complexity of the software has resulted in the need for mass storage and increased hardware speed and capacity.

The programming paradigm needed to change. The use of modularity and functional decomposition represented a means of reducing the complexity of software development. Even so, that development required the greater application of development resources, particularly time and programming expertise. Of particular interest is the idea that the programming paradigm mirrors learning theory, with additional emphasis on the need to structure and partition internally to make sense of the external.

The paradigm shift, then, has involved more than a tendency toward acceptance of the cognitive view. The development of cognitively oriented computer-based learning, for example, relies on a level of hardware previously unavailable; implementation mechanisms such as intelligent tutoring, hypertext, hypermedia, and expert systems; and a design mechanism that emphasizes content structure.

Constructivism

Jonassen (1991) distinguishes between the assumptions in objectivism (both behaviorism and cognitivism) and constructivism. The objectivist sees reality as external to the knower with the mind acting as a processor of input from reality. Meaning is derived from the structure of reality, with the mind processing symbolic representations of reality. The constructivist, on the other hand, sees reality as determined by the *experiences of the knower*. The move from behaviorism through cognitivism to constructivism represents shifts in emphasis away from an external view to an internal view. To the behaviorist, the internal processing is of no interest; to the cognitivist, the internal processing is only of importance to the extent to which it explains how external reality is understood. In contrast, the constructivist views the mind as a builder of symbols—the tools used to represent the knower's reality. External phenomena are meaningless except as the mind perceives them. Von Glasersfeld (1977) argues that the objectivist view is based on two illogical premises: "that what we learn is a replica of some independent, well-structured world and that this independent ontological reality determines our experiences" (p. 34). Constructivists view reality as personally constructed, and state that personal experiences determine reality, and not the other way round.

Chomsky's (1973) review of Skinner's *Verbal Learning* (1957) began the revolution in thinking that was the beginning of the transition to cognitive learning theory. The first real use of learning technology was applied behaviorally. With the application of systems theory, instructional design accommodated cognitive psychology somewhat. Jonassen (1990) argues that the accommodation is theoretical rather than practical. The reason, Jonassen suggests, is that instructional systems theory is an "objectivist epistemology" (p. 32), holding that knowledge is based somehow in reality and that reality is what the learners learn. In a cognitive frame, what is learned has to be based upon external, observable actions; therefore, the behaviorist view actually is always going to be significant in theory, despite the cognitivist's stated disdain for behaviorism. How ironic!

For the constructivist, learning is problem solving based on personal discovery, and the learner is intrinsically motivated. The learner needs a responsive environment in which consideration has been given to the learner's individual style as an "active, self-regulating, reflective learner" (Seels, 1989, p. 14). Designing instruction that accommodates individual motivations and goals represents a problem for current instructional design theory. Jonassen (1991) notes that the instructional goals and objectives would have to be negotiated rather than set, with no one best way of sequencing instruction. The goal of instructional systems theory would then concern itself more with developing "mental construction 'toolkits' embedded in relevant learning environments that facilitate knowledge construction by learners" (p. 12), rather than specific instructional strategies.

A number of issues arise from this view. The design tools in current use are founded on an objectivist view. Constructivists would argue that there is no such thing as content-independent knowledge or skill; yet the design mechanism are supposed to be domain-independent. Current forms of presentation and learning environments may well be suboptimal if learners are not converging to a single objective. Jonassen (1990) argues for the use of cognitive and constructive 'mindtools' such as databases, hypermedia, and expert systems. Sawyer (1992) envisions a virtual computer where the computer represents an access point to global resources for education. Alternative forms of evaluation must be designed to account for multiple goals. As a result, evaluation would be less founded upon criterion-referenced tests. Gill, Dick, Reiser, and Zahner (1992) propose a model for evaluating educational software which includes both objective and subjective components. If this can be developed for educational software, then a parallel approach might also be used for performance evaluation. Changing the learning environment to incorporate a constructivist view adds complexity. Robinson's (1979) notion of using technology to absorb that complexity becomes more significant as other forms of managing complexity become overloaded.

The technology on the desktop is not the major hardware issue of importance in supporting the implementation of a constructivist approach. While the hardware has to be powerful enough to support large and complex software, it is becoming increasingly clear that replicating resources locally is not feasible from a cost viewpoint. In consequence, providing access to remote resources is of vital importance. Those resources might not be only hardware and software but also instructional resources, evaluation resources, and communication with other learners.

One key goal is making access to those resources seamless and transparent to the user. Sawyer (1992) goes some way to identifying the major issues and places networking in the center of the arena. Although he does not explicitly make the point, adherence to *standards*, both programming and communication, is an important ingredient of his argument.

The development of instructional software is also undergoing a shift in emphasis. The basic building blocks used to construct a program are relatively well established. Although new approaches such as object oriented analysis and design allow for easier development, the building process, especially in such areas as user interface, has been semi-automated, and it is the analysis design aspects of software development that pose the greatest challenges.

There is a much stronger emphasis on applications that allow exploration, such as database management systems and expert systems, where the learner can interactively query the database; simulations where a model reality is explored; and 'virtual reality,' an extension of the simulation idea which allows the user to physically interact with the application. Once again we see the programming paradigm running in parallel with the theoretical framework.

The issue is no longer simply whether the software can manage the complexity required, but does it fit and can it work with other software and across a complex computer network? Sawyer, for example, notes that "As a general principle it will make more and more sense over time to put the computing element of a personal computer close to its source of data, and use the network to deliver the [rest] to the user. This is potentially the next paradigm of personal computing" (p. 14). When the applications require very powerful processing capabilities, it may make more sense to place just the user interface close to the user and utilize the network to deliver both data and processing resources. The network infrastructure is developing, indeed is viewed as a significant political and economic issue by some, and the basic mechanisms required to distribute applications across that network, e.g., HP/Apollo's "Network Computing System," are already in place.

Conclusion

There is evidence in the shift from behaviorism to cognitivism in designed instruction that the theory had to be accompanied by adequate physical technology, a change in the instructional design methodology, and appropriate programming tools to implement the new theory. It is becoming increasingly clear that a second paradigm shift is occurring; indeed Jonassen (1990) might consider it a *fait accompli*. Certainly the theory and the physical and programming mechanisms exist, even if they are not properly in place. The instructional design mechanism appears to be lacking, and there needs to be a greater effort in addressing that issue.

The first shift changed the way in which designed learning took place. The second shift may well have a more dramatic effect. It represents not just a change in approach but a significant *expansion of the dimensions of the learning*

setting, where the limits are expressed in terms of the desires and goals of the learner and not the designs (whether behavioral or cognitive) of the instructor.

References and Suggested Readings

Bourne, D. E. Computer Assisted Instruction, Learning Theory, and Hypermedia: An Associative Linkage. *Research Strategies*, 1990, *8*(4), 160-171.

Bagley, C., and Hunter, B. Restructuring, Constructivism, and Technology: Forging a New Relationship. *Educational Technology*, 1992, *32*(7), 22-27.

Bullock, D. H. Behaviorism and NSPI: The Erratically Applied Discipline. *Performance & Instruction*, 1982, *21*(3), 4-8, 11.

Chase, P. N. Designing Courseware: Prompts from Behavioral Instruction. *The Behavior Analyst*, 1985, *8*(1), 65-76.

Chomsky, A. N. *For Reasons of State*. New York: Pantheon, 1973.

Cole, P. Constructivism Revisited: A Search for Common Ground. *Educational Technology*, 1992, *32*(2), 27-34.

Gill, B. J., Dick, W. Resier, R. A., and Zahner, J. E. A New Model for Evaluating Instructional Software. *Educational Technology*, 1992, *32*(3), 39-43.

Golub, L. S. *With the Microcomputer, Behaviorism Returns to Early Childhood Education*. Paper presented at the 68th Annual Meeting of the American Educational Research Association, New Orleans, LA, 1983.

Hannafin, M. J., and Reiber, L. P. Psychological Foundations of Instructional Design for Emerging Computer-Based Instructional Technologies: Part I. *Educational Technology Research & Development*, 1989, *32*(2), 91-101.

Hartley, J. R. Some Psychological Aspects of Computer-Assisted Learning and Technology. *Programmed Learning and Educational Technology*, 1985, *22*(2), 140-149.

Hebb, D. O. *The Organization of Behavior*. New York: John Wiley & Sons, 1949.

Jelden, D. L. *Operationalizing Learner-Controlled Education*. Paper presented at the International Conference on Systems Research and Cybernetics, Baden-Baden, West Germany, 1984.

Jonassen, D. H. Thinking Technology: Toward a Constructivist View of Instructional Design. *Educational Technology*, 1990, *30*(9), 32-34.

Jonassen, D. H. Objectivism Versus Constructivism: Do We Need a New Philosophical Paradigm? *Educational Technology Research and Development*, 1991, *39*(3), 5-14.

Lamos, J. P. Programmed Instruction to Computer-Based Instruction: The Evolution of an Instructional Technology. In R. K. Bass and D. B. Lumsden (Eds.) *Instructional Development: The State of the Art*. McAlester, OK: Best Books, 1984.

McGowan, J., and Clark, R. E. Instructional Software Features that Support Learning for Students with Widely Different Ability Levels. *Performance &*

Instruction, 1985, *24*(4), 14, 17.

Merrill, M. D. Component Display Theory. In C. M. Reigeluth (Ed.), *Instructional-Design Theories and Models: An Overview of Their Current Status.* Hillsdale, NJ: Lawrence Erlbaum Associates, 1983.

Merrill, M. D., Li, Z., and Jones, M. K. Limitations of First-Generation Instructional Design. *Educational Technology*, 1990, *30*(1), 7–11.

Orey, M. A. *Using Intelligent Tutoring Design Principles to Integrate Cognitive Theory into Computer-Based Instruction.* Proceedings of Selected Research Presentations at the Annual Convention of the Association for Educational Communications and Technology, 1991.

Poppen, L., and Poppen, R. The Use of Behavioral Principles in Educational Software. *Educational Technology*, 1988, *28*(2), 37–41.

Reed, W. M. *A Combined Behavioral-Cognitive Orientation to an Instructional Design on Writing*, unpublished paper, 1981.

Robinson, M. Classroom Control: Some Cybernetic Comments on the Possible and the Impossible. *Instructional Science*, 1979, *8*, 369–392.

Salomon, G. The Differential Investment of Mental Effort in Different Sources of Learning Material. *Educational Psychologist*, 1983, *18*, 42–50.

Sawyer, W. D. M. The Virtual Computer: A New Paradigm for Educational Computing. *Educational Technology*, 1992, *32*(1), 7–14.

Scandura, J. M. Microcomputer Systems for Authoring, Diagnosis, and Instruction in Rule-Based Subject Matter. *Educational Technology*, 1981, *21*(9), 13–19.

Schack, E. O. *The Application of Encephalography to Computer Assisted Instruction.* Paper presented at The Annual Regional Conference of the Growth and Research Organization for Women, Morehead, New York, 1988.

Seels, B., The Instructional Design Movement in Educational Technology. *Educational Technology*, 1989, *29*(5), 11–15.

Skinner, B. F. Cognitive Science and Behaviorism. *British Journal of Psychology*, 1985, *76*(3), 291–301.

Snow, R. E. Individual Differences and Instructional Theory. *Educational Researcher*, 1977, *6*(10), 11–15.

Snow, R. E., and Lohman, D. F. Toward a Theory of Cognitive Aptitude for Learning from Instruction. *Journal of Educational Psychology*, 1984, *76*(3) 347–377.

Tennyson, R. D. An Educational Learning Theory for Instructional Design. *Educational Technology*, 1992, *32*(1), 36–41.

von Glasersfeld, E. A Radical Constructivist View of Knowledge. Symposium on Constructivism and Cognitive Development, AERA, New York, 1977.

Warren B., and Rosebery, A. S. Theory and Practice: Use of the Computer in Reading. *Remedial and Special Education*, 1988, *9*(2), 29–38.

Wenger, E. *Artificial Intelligence and Tutoring Systems.* Los Altos, CA: Morgan Kaufmann, 1987.

Wildman, T. M., and Burton, J. K. Integrating Learning Theory with Instructional Design. *Journal of Instructional Development*, 1981, *4*(3) 5–14.

Zahn, L. *Network Computing Architecture.* Englewood Cliffs, NJ: Prentice-Hall, 1989.

The Link Between Technology and Authentic Learning

Barbara Means and Kerry Olson

Barbara Means heads the Learning and Technology Program at SRI International, 333 Ravenswood Ave., Menlo Park, CA 94025. **Kerry Olson** is a Research Social Scientist with the Learning and Technology Program.

A new climate in school reform welcomes technology as never before. Case studies show that as a tool for complex, authentic tasks, technology will be a powerful performer.

Television in the 1960s, computers in the 1970s, videodiscs and artificial intelligence in the 1980s—all were predicted to transform America's classrooms. As we know, they did not.

Certain technologies have definitely found niches in education, but the technology of the last two decades has changed schools far less than it has the worlds of work, entertainment, and communication. On the whole, teachers have simply closed their classroom doors and gone right on teaching just as they were taught (Smith and O'Day 1990).

Why Earlier Efforts Failed

Despite its disappointing record, technology now has the potential to exert a much stronger impact on learning in schools. The greater potential is not due solely to technological advances per se—the exciting new capabilities like multimedia and wireless communication, the increasing accessibility of technology, and the beginnings of a national information infrastructure. A more important basis for optimism is progress in *education reform*.

In our view, early efforts to introduce technology in schools failed to have profound effects because the attempts were based on the wrong model of teaching with technology. Product developers believed in their content knowledge, pedagogical techniques, and in the power of technology to transmit knowledge to students. With satisfaction, the developers touted the so-called "teacher-proof" instructional programs.

How surprised they must have been that most of their applications were never used for very long. The applications had, as it turned out, a primary problem. They were an imperfect and incomplete match with the bulk of the core curriculum.

Two types of software were common. The dominator of the software market, computer-assisted instruction, tended to focus narrowly on drill and practice in very basic skills. Thus, CAI was used extensively among students with disadvantaged backgrounds. At the other end of the software spectrum, instructional games, simulations, and intelligent tutoring systems generally conveyed more challenging material, but only covered a very narrow slice of a subject domain and were often a poor match with state curriculum guidelines or teacher preferences. This genre of software, too, was commonly reserved for limited populations: gifted students, those who finished their work early, or students in innovative schools serving affluent neighborhoods.

Because of their narrow applicability, these two classes of software had little effect on what most teachers did with the bulk of their students for the majority of the school day (Cohen 1988). In contrast, today's applications software is likely to fare much better because of a new climate in school reform.

In the 1980s, reform efforts tried to improve student performance by increasing course requirements. Reformers did not, however, examine the way that teaching and learning unfold. Today's reform efforts, in contrast, strive to change the education system by fostering a different style of learning (David and Shields 1991). The efforts seek to move classrooms away from conventional didactic instructional approaches, in which teachers do most of the talking and students listen and complete short exercises on well-defined, subject-area-specific material. Instead, students are challenged with complex, authentic tasks, and reformers are pushing for lengthy multidisciplinary projects, cooperative learning groups, flexible scheduling, and authentic assessments.

In such a setting, technology is a valuable tool. It has the power to support students and teachers in obtaining, organizing, manipulating, and displaying information. These uses of technology will, we believe, become an integral feature of schooling.

When technology is used as a tool for accomplishing complex tasks, the issue of mismatch between technology content and curriculum disappears altogether. Technological tools can be used to organize and present any kind of information. Moreover, it is not necessary for the teacher to know everything about the tools that students use; students and teachers can acquire whatever technology skills they need for specific projects. In fact, one of the best things that teachers can do with respect to technology is to model what to do when one doesn't know what to do.

Technology in the Hands of a Skilled Teacher

As part of an ongoing project[1] funded by the Office of Educational Research and Improvement, we are conducting case studies[2] in schools that are using technology as part of a concentrated program of school reform. On one of our initial site visits to a school in our study, we found a 5th grade classroom that illustrated how a skilled teacher can use technology to help orchestrate a project.

Frank Paul Elementary School is located in an agricultural area of California, which is troubled by poverty, crime, drugs, and gangs. The student population is 86 percent Hispanic, 7 percent African American, 4 percent Anglo, and 3 percent Asian American. A third of the students qualify for migrant education. Nearly two-thirds are limited-English-proficient.

One of the school's goals is to produce students who are literate in both English and Spanish, so some students do their content reading in English, while others use comparable materials in Spanish. The school's philosophy shows up in three other concrete ways as well: an ethic of respect for everyone's contributions; the extensive use of collaborative learning and small-group work; and an attempt to provide a homelike atmosphere (lighting is soft, and in classroom reading corners, kids can lounge on pillows as they read).

The 5th grade teacher, Cliff Gilkey, has 12 years of teaching experience, 9 of them at his current school. In his prior teaching experience, Gilkey used computers with primary school students. Accordingly, when the opportunity arose to obtain 4 computers for his 31 current students, Gilkey welcomed it. He shared the school's commitment to thematic instruction and collaborative learning, so he did not necessarily need enough computers for the whole class to use at once.

At first, the class used computers primarily for word processing and telecommunications with distant class-

Authentic tasks are completed for reasons beyond earning a grade.

rooms through the National Geographic Society *Kids' Network*. At the time of our visit, the students were involved in a long-term project employing technology to develop curriculum materials on local minority leaders. The particulars of the project illustrate five features of reformed classrooms:

1. *An authentic, challenging task is the starting point.* Authentic tasks are completed for reasons beyond earning a grade. Students also see the activity as worthwhile in its own right.

The Local Heroes Project grew out of two genuine needs. In the past, students had participated in a popular, week-long science camp during their 6th grade year. In 1992-93, funding cuts led to suspension of the camp activity, and the 5th graders did not expect it to be funded in the next year either. The trip was important to them, so they were interested in raising money.

The second need was for appropriate curriculum materials about contemporary Hispanic leaders. Materials in textbooks and libraries were limited, and when the material did exist, the reading level was too high for students just learning to read

English. Furthermore, the Hispanic leaders featured were generally entertainers or people who are no longer well known.

The class not only wanted to find better materials for its own use, but also became convinced that there was a market for such materials in other schools. The students got an idea, a multimedia project on local heroes. The project would involve:

■ identifying local Hispanic, African American, and Vietnamese leaders (including politicians, businessmen, researchers, and educators);

■ conducting and videotaping interviews; and

■ composing written highlights from the interviews.

In this undertaking, technology would be important. Students needed it to assemble their materials and produce many copies of salable quality.

2. *All students practice advanced skills.* Complex tasks involve both basic and advanced skills. In this regard, the heroes project was typical. It involved students in a wide range of tasks, some of which called for high-level thinking.

For example, the students prepared to conduct their interviews by analyzing interviews with famous people. From these, they developed a set of questions that would elicit certain information and generate interesting responses.

Through this process, students learned concepts (such as the difference between open- and close-ended questions) and presentation techniques (like maintaining eye contact during

Coaching does not mean fading into the background.

an interview). Further, as the class organized its activities, selected appropriate local leaders, and carried out the videorecording and editing, the students learned and practiced complex skills in a variety of domains (cognitive, social, and technical).

3. *Work takes place in heterogeneous, collaborative groups.* Initial practice convinced students that it is hard to conduct a good interview and take notes at the same time, so three-student teams went out to conduct each interview. One student asked the questions, a second videotaped, and a third recorded notes.

After completing the fieldwork, each team of students reviewed and critiqued its videotaped interviews. In their groups, students discussed ways to improve their technique and considered additional questions that should have been asked. Students also prepared a written transcript and summary of the key points in the videotape and recorder's notes. While entering text onto the computer for later editing and formatting, the individuals on a team each took responsibility for aspects of the task (such as typing, spelling, or remembering and repeating what was said on the videotape).

4. *The teacher is a coach.* Coaching, as Cliff Gilkey practices it, does not mean fading into the background. It means providing structure and actively supporting students' performances and reflections.

As we observed the classroom, small groups of students were working on a range of project activities—creating a large mural of famous minority leaders, telephoning local leaders to schedule interviews, transcribing videotapes, and practicing interviewing skills. Gilkey moved from group to group, checking on progress, monitoring students' practice, and suggesting questions to explore.

At the video monitor, Gilkey helped a group improve its interviewing technique. He asked, "What could you have asked when she mentioned that she had dropped out of school? What will the listener want to know?" Moving on to another group, Gilkey sat on the floor with students as they practiced opening an interview with a simulated microphone and camera (for

5th graders, simply introducing themselves and asking the first question brings on waves of self-consciousness). Gilkey had students work on maintaining eye contact and posing the initial question without looking down at the prompt sheet.

5. *Work occurs over extended blocks of time.* Serious intellectual activity doesn't usually fall neatly into 50-minute periods for a set number of days. Thus, complex tasks put pressure on the conventional small blocks of instructional time.

Gilkey's project began in January 1993 and was expected to continue through the rest of the school year. In fact, at the time of our visit, Gilkey was contemplating extending the project into the next year by teaching a mixed 5th and 6th grade class, allowing him to continue working with a core of students from the first year of the project.

The Contributions of Technology

In the Local Heroes Project, technology itself is not the driving force behind the learning. Nevertheless, our observations in settings that couple technology with education reform suggest that the technology certainly amplifies what teachers are able to do and what they expect from students.

One reason that technology has this positive effect is that teachers see complex assignments as feasible. For example, in some case-study schools, the availability of database programs and graphing capacities is leading teachers to think in terms of extensive data collection and analysis projects.

Technology also appears to provide an entry point to content areas and inquiries that might otherwise be inaccessible until much later in an academic career. For instance, when we start assuming that 1st graders will have access to word processing programs, it becomes much more sensible to think about asking them to write before they are fluent readers.

A third benefit from technology is that it can extend and enhance what students are able to produce, whether the task at hand is writing a report or graphing data. The selection and manipulation of appropriate tools for such purposes also appear to stimulate problem solving and other thinking skills.

The introduction of technology has given teachers the opportunity to become learners again.

In addition, technology lends authenticity to school tasks. Because the products of student efforts are more polished, schoolwork seems real and important. Students take great pride in using the same tools as practicing professionals. At one school we visited, a student informed us with glee that "I know musicians who would die for the technology we have in our music class." Technology also supports collaborative efforts (like Gilkey's interview teams).

Finally, in many of the classrooms we visited, the introduction of technology has given teachers the opportunity to become learners again. The challenge of planning and implementing technology-supported activities has provided a context in which an initial lack of knowledge is not regarded as cause for embarrassment. As a result, teachers are eager to share their developing expertise and to learn from one another. As they search out the links among their instructional goals, the curriculum, and technology's possibilities, they collaborate more, reflect more, and engage in more dialogue.

What technology will not do is make the teacher's life simple. The kind of teaching and learning that we have described requires teachers with multiple skills. The subject matter is inherently challenging, and because it is evolving and open-ended, it can never be totally mastered. Especially at first, the technology itself poses challenges, like learning to set up equipment, remembering software commands, and troubleshooting system problems. New roles pose many challenges, too. The teacher must be able to launch and orchestrate multiple groups of students, intervene at critical points, diagnose individual learning problems, and provide feedback.

Nevertheless, in classrooms where teachers have risen to this challenge, a profound change is occurring in the learning environment. Technology plays an important role, but it is a supporting role. The students are the stars. The playwright and director—and the power behind the scene—is, as always, the teacher.

[1]This article is based on work conducted as part of the Studies of Education Reform program, which is supported by the U.S. Department of Education, Office of Educational Research and Improvement, Office of Research, under contract RR 91-1720-2010. The opinions expressed in this article do not necessarily reflect the position or policy of the U.S. Department of Education, and no official endorsement should be inferred.

[2]Several of these cases are described more fully in "Tomorrow's Schools: Technology and Reform in Partnership" (Means and Olson 1994).

References

Cohen, D. K. (1988). "Educational Technology and School Organization." In *Technology in Education: Looking Toward 2020.* Hillsdale, N. J.: Erlbaum.

David, J. K., and P. M. Shields. (1991). *From Effective Schools to Restructuring: A Literature Review.* Menlo Park, Calif.: SRI International.

Means, B., and K. Olson. (1994). "Tomorrow's Schools: Technology and Reform in Partnership." In *Technology and Education Reform: The Reality Behind the Promise,* edited by B. Means. San Francisco: Jossey-Bass.

Smith, M. S., and J. O'Day. (1990). "Systemic School Reform." In *Politics of Education Association Yearbook,* edited by R. S. Nickerson and P. P. Zodhiates. London: Taylor and Francis.

Motivation and Classroom Management

- Motivation (Articles 29–31)
- Classroom Management and Discipline (Articles 32–35)

The term *motivation* is used by educators to describe the processes of initiating, directing, and sustaining goal-oriented behavior. Motivation is a complex phenomenon, involving many factors that affect an individual's choice of action and perseverance in completing tasks. Furthermore, the reasons why people engage in particular behaviors can only be inferred; motivation cannot be directly measured.

Several theories of motivation, each highlighting different reasons for sustained goal-oriented behavior, have been proposed. We will discuss three of them: behavioral, humanistic, and cognitive. The behavioral theory of motivation suggests that an important reason for engaging in behavior is that reinforcement follows the action. If the reinforcement is controlled by someone else and is arbitrarily related to the behavior (such as money, a token, or a smile), then the motivation is extrinsic. In contrast, behavior may also be initiated and sustained for intrinsic reasons such as curiosity or mastery.

Humanistic approaches to motivation are concerned with the social and psychological needs of individuals. Humans are motivated to engage in behavior to meet these needs. Abraham Maslow, a founder of humanistic psychology, proposes that there is a hierarchy of needs that directs behavior, beginning with physiological and safety needs and progressing to self-actualization. Some other important needs that influence motivation are affiliation and belonging with others, love, self-esteem, influence with others, recognition, status, competence, achievement, and autonomy.

The dominant view of motivation in the educational psychology literature is the cognitive approach. This set of theories proposes that our beliefs about our success and failure affect our expectations concerning future performance. Students who believe that their success is due to their ability and effort are motivated toward mastery of skills. Students who blame their failures on inadequate abilities have low self-efficacy and tend to be discouraged and at risk for dropping out. Alfie Kohn, in the first selection, argues that one important way to help eliminate student apathy is to allow students to make decisions about their own learning. His article provides a rationale for incorporating more opportunities for student choice in the classroom. Next, Deborah Stipek echoes the importance of allowing children to set their own goals. She also discusses other techniques to encourage more effort on academic tasks. Finally, Antoine Garibaldi discusses the needs of a special group of students, African American males. He proposes motivational techniques that he believes will work with African American males as well as other students.

No matter how effectively students are motivated, teachers always need to exercise management of behavior in the classroom. As Edwin Ralph points out in his selection, classroom management is more than controlling student behavior. Instead, teachers need to initiate and maintain a classroom environment that supports successful teaching and learning. The skills that effective teachers use include preplanning, deliberate introduction of rules and procedures, immediate assertiveness, continual monitoring, consistent feedback to students, and specific consequences.

Kathryn Castle and Karen Rogers argue that when students are involved in creating classroom rules they often make the same rules as adults. They describe how teachers can establish classroom rules, and at the same time, encourage student autonomy and responsibility. In the next selection, Wanda Lincoln proposes additional techniques to enable students to take responsibility for their own behavior. Effective teachers also have a plan for responding to students who do misbehave. In the final selection, Don Fuhr argues that students appreciate teachers who know how to discipline. He discusses basic procedures that effective teachers routinely follow.

Looking Ahead: Challenge Questions

Discuss several ways to motivate both at-risk students and typical students. Is there a difference?

How are motivation and classroom management related?

How are classroom management and discipline different? Can discipline be developed within students, or must it be imposed by teachers? Support your position with data derived from your reading.

Choices for Children:

Why and How to Let Students Decide

*The key to transforming
student apathy into student
engagement, Mr. Kohn sug-
gests, may be as simple as
allowing students to make
decisions about their learning.*

....

ALFIE KOHN

*ALFIE KOHN, who writes and lectures
widely on education and human behavior,
lives in Cambridge, Mass. His books include*
Punished by Rewards: The Trouble with
Gold Stars, Incentive Plans, A's, Praise, and
Other Bribes *(Houghton Mifflin, 1993), a
newly revised edition of* No Contest: The
Case Against Competition *(Houghton Mifflin,
1992), and* The Brighter Side of Human Nature *(Basic Books, 1990).*

---

*The essence of the demand for freedom
is the need of conditions which will enable an individual to make his own special contribution to a group interest,
and to partake of its activities in such
ways that social guidance shall be a
matter of his own mental attitude, and
not a mere authoritative dictation of his
acts.*

> — John Dewey
> *Democracy and Education*

EDUCATORS ARE painfully
well acquainted with the phenomenon known as "burnout."
Some days it seems that the
bulbs have gone out in most
faculty lounges and administration buildings. But what if, hypothetically speaking, this syndrome also affected students?
How would *they* talk and act? Teachers
around the country to whom I have put
this question immediately suggest such
symptoms as disengagement and apathy
— or, conversely, thoughtlessness and
aggression. Either tuning out or acting
out might signal that a student was burn-
ing out. In both cases, he or she would
presumably just go through the motions
of learning, handing in uninspired work
and counting the minutes or days until
freedom.

Of course, no sooner is this sketch of
a hypothetical student begun than we
recognize it as a depiction of real life.
The fact is that students act this way
every day. But now let us ask what we
know from research and experience in the
workplace about the cause of burnout.
The best predictor, it turns out, is not too
much work, too little time, or too little
compensation. Rather, it is powerlessness
— a lack of control over what one is doing.

Combine that fact with the premise that
there is no minimum age for burnout, and
the conclusion that emerges is this: much
of what is disturbing about students' attitudes and behavior may be a function of
the fact that they have little to say about

what happens to them all day. They are
compelled to follow someone else's rules,
study someone else's curriculum, and submit continually to someone else's evaluation. The mystery, really, is not that so
many students are indifferent about what
they have to do in school but that any of
them are not.

To be sure, there is nothing new about
the idea that students should be able to
participate, individually and collectively, in making decisions. This conviction
has long played a role in schools designated as progressive, democratic, open,
free, experimental, or alternative; in educational philosophies called developmental, constructivist, holistic, or learner-
centered; in specific innovations such
as whole-language learning, discovery-
based science, or authentic assessment;
and in the daily practice of teachers
whose natural instinct is to treat children
with respect.

But if the concept is not exactly novel,
neither do we usually take the time to
tease this element out of various traditions and examine it in its own right. Why
is it so important that children have a
chance to make decisions about their
learning? How might this opportunity be

 From *Phi Delta Kappan*, September 1993, pp. 8-20.

provided with regard to academic matters as well as other aspects of school life? What limits on students' right to choose are necessary, and what restrictions compromise the idea too deeply? Finally, what barriers might account for the fact that students so rarely feel a sense of self-determination today? A close inspection of these issues will reveal that the question of choice is both more complex and more compelling than many educators seem to assume.

SEVERAL years ago, a group of teachers from Florida traveled to what was then the USSR to exchange information and ideas with their Russian-speaking counterparts. What the Soviet teachers most wanted from their guests was guidance on setting up and running democratic schools. Their questions on this topic were based on the assumption that a country like the United States, so committed to the idea of democracy, surely must involve children in decision-making processes from their earliest years.

The irony is enough to make us wince. As one survey of American schools after another has confirmed, students are rarely invited to become active participants in their own education.[1] Schooling is typically about doing things *to* children, not working *with* them. An array of punishments and rewards is used to enforce compliance with an agenda that students rarely have any opportunity to influence.

Think about the rules posted on the wall of an elementary school classroom, or the "rights and responsibilities" pamphlet distributed in high schools, or the moral precepts that form the basis of a values or character education program. In each case, students are almost never involved in deliberating about such ideas; their job is basically to do as they are told.

Moreover, consider the conventional response when something goes wrong (as determined, of course, by the adults). Are two children creating a commotion instead of sitting quietly? Separate them. Have the desks become repositories for used chewing gum? Ban the stuff. Do students come to class without having done the reading? Hit them with a pop quiz. Again and again, the favorite motto of teachers and administrators seems to be "Reach for the coercion" rather than engaging children in a conversation about the underlying causes of what is happen-

ing and working together to negotiate a solution.

Earlier this year, the principal of a Brooklyn high school told a *New York Times* reporter that he lived by "a simple proposition: This is my house, I'm 46 years old. A 15-year-old is not going to dictate to me how this school is run."[2] But even educators who recoil from such a frank endorsement of autocracy may end up acting in accordance with the same basic principle. I have met many elementary teachers, for example, who make a point of assuring students that "this is *our* classroom" — but proceed to decide unilaterally on almost everything that goes on in it, from grading policy to room decor.

As for the content of instruction, the educators who shape the curriculum rarely bother to consult those who are to be educated. There is plenty of enthusiasm about reforms such as outcome-based education but little concern about bringing students into the process of formulating the outcomes. There is spirited debate about "school choice" — an arrangement in which districts are compelled to compete for the business of parent-consumers — but much less talk about how much choice students have concerning what happens in their classrooms. Indeed, spontaneous, animated conversations about topics of interest to children, when they are allowed to occur at all, are soon snuffed out in order that the class can return to the prescribed lesson plan.

THE RATIONALE

To talk about the destructive effects of keeping students powerless is to describe the benefits of having a sense of self-determination.[3] Five such benefits seem particularly compelling.

1. *Effects on general well-being.* Many different fields of research have converged on the finding that it is desirable for people to experience a sense of control over their lives. These benefits reach into every corner of human existence, starting with our physical health and survival. One series of studies has shown that people who rarely become ill despite having to deal with considerable stress tend to be those who feel more control over what happens to them.[4] In another well-known experiment, nursing home residents who were able to make decisions about their environment not only became happier and more active but were

> *Those who feel more control over what happens to them rarely become ill despite high levels of stress.*

also more likely to be alive a year and a half later than were other residents.[5]

The psychological benefits of control are, if anything, even more pronounced. All else being equal, emotional adjustment is better over time for people who experience a sense of self-determination; by contrast, few things lead more reliably to depression and other forms of psychological distress than a feeling of helplessness.[6] (One recent study showed this was true in an educational setting: distress was inversely related to how much influence and autonomy teachers said they had with respect to school policy.[7]) Whereas rewards and punishments are notably ineffective at maintaining behavior change,[8] people are likely to persist at doing constructive things, like exercising, quitting smoking, or fighting cavities, when they have some choice about the specifics of such programs.[9] Laboratory experiments have also shown that individuals are better able to tolerate unpleasant sensations like noise, cold, or electric shock when they know they have the power to end them.[10]

Children are no exception to these rules, the studies show. One-year-old infants had fun with a noisy mechanical toy if they could make it start; it was less interesting, and sometimes even frightening, if they had no control over its action.[11] Elementary students had higher self-esteem and a greater feeling of academic competence when their teachers bolstered their sense of self-determination in the classroom.[12]

2. *Effects on behavior and values.* One is repeatedly struck by the absurd spectacle of adults insisting that children need to become self-disciplined or lamenting

that "kids just don't take responsibility for their own behavior" — while spending their days ordering children around. The truth is that, if we want children to *take* responsibility for their own behavior, we must first *give* them responsibility, and plenty of it. The way a child learns how to make decisions is by making decisions, not by following directions. As Constance Kamii has written,

> We cannot expect children to accept ready-made values and truths all the way through school, and then suddenly make choices in adulthood. Likewise, we cannot expect them to be manipulated with reward and punishment in school, and to have the courage of a Martin Luther King in adulthood.[13]

In fact, an emphasis on following instructions, respecting authority (regardless of whether that respect has been earned), and obeying the rules (regardless of whether they are reasonable) teaches a disturbing lesson. Stanley Milgram's famous experiment, in which ordinary people gave what they thought were terribly painful shocks to hapless strangers merely because they were told to do so, is not just a comment about "society" or "human nature." It is a cautionary tale about certain ways of teaching children. Indeed, an emphasis on obedience, with all the trappings of control that must be used for enforcing it, typically fails even on its own terms: children are less likely to comply with a rule when they have had no role in inventing or even discussing it. And if our goals are more ambitious — if we want children to make good values their own over the long haul — then there is no substitute for giving them the chance to become actively involved in deciding what kind of people they want to be and what kind of classroom or school they want to have.

To talk about the importance of choice is also to talk about democracy. At present, as Shelley Berman of Educators for Social Responsibility has drily noted, "We teach reading, writing, and math by [having students do] them, but we teach democracy by lecture."[14] I believe it is time to call the bluff of every educator who claims to prize democratic principles. Anyone who truly values democracy ought to be thinking about preparing students to participate in a democratic culture — or to transform a culture *into* a democracy, as the case may be. The only way this can happen, the only way children can acquire both the skills of decision mak-

ing and the inclination to use them, is if we maximize their experiences with choice and negotiation.[15]

Ultimately, even virtues that appear to be quite different from an orientation toward participation or a capacity to make intelligent decisions turn out to depend on these things. For example, like many others, I am concerned about how we can help children to become generous, caring people who see themselves as part of a community.[16] But these values simply cannot be successfully promoted in the absence of choice. A jarring reminder of that fact was provided by a man who recalled being "taught that my highest duty was to help those in need" but added that he learned this lesson in the context of how important it was to "obey promptly the wishes and commands of my parents, teachers, and priests, and indeed of all adults. . . . Whatever they said was always right." The man who said that was Rudolf Höss, the commandant of Auschwitz.[17] A commitment to helping is important, but if the environment in which such values are taught emphasizes obedience rather than autonomy, all may be lost.

3. *Effects on academic achievement.* Every teacher who is told what material to cover, when to cover it, and how to evaluate children's performance is a teacher who knows that enthusiasm for one's work quickly evaporates in the face of being controlled. Not every teacher, however, realizes that exactly the same thing holds true for students: deprive them of self-determination and you have likely deprived them of motivation. If learning is a matter of following orders, students simply will not take to it in the way they would if they had some say about what they were doing. Not long ago, in a 10th-grade geometry class whose teacher collaborates with students to decide about curriculum and grades, a student explained to me that being able to make such choices "leads to learning rather than just remembering."

The evidence to support that view is so compelling that it is frankly difficult to understand how anyone can talk about school reform without immediately addressing the question of how students can be given more say about what goes on in their classes. The classic Eight-Year Study, which should be required reading for everyone with an interest in education, provided data on this point more than half a century ago. After 30 high schools were encouraged to develop in-

novative programs whose "essential value was democracy,"[18] researchers found that the graduates of those schools did better in college than a matched comparison group from traditional schools. In fact, the students who were most successful tended to come from the schools that had departed most significantly from the conventional college-prep approach — the approach currently lauded by those calling for higher standards, more accountability, and getting back to basics.

Subsequent research has confirmed the conclusion:

• When second-graders in Pittsburgh were given some choice about their learning, including the chance to decide which tasks they would work on at any given moment, they tended to "complete more learning tasks in less time."[19]

• When high school seniors in Minneapolis worked on chemistry problems without clear-cut instructions — that is, with the opportunity to decide for themselves how to find solutions — they "consistently produced better write-ups of experiments" and remembered the material better than those who had been told exactly what to do. They put in more time than they had to, spending "extra laboratory periods checking results that could have been accepted without extra work." Some of the students initially resisted having to make decisions about how to proceed, but these grumblers later "took great pride in being able to carry through an experiment on their own."[20]

• When preschoolers in Massachusetts were allowed to select the materials they used for making a collage, their work was judged more creative than the work of children who used exactly the same materials but did not get to choose them.[21]

• When college students in New York State had the chance to decide which of several puzzles they wanted to work on and how to allot their time to each of them, they were a lot more interested in working on such puzzles later than were students who were told what to do.[22]

• When teachers of inner-city black children were trained in a program designed to promote a sense of self-determination, the students in these classes missed less school and scored better on a national test of basic skills than those in conventional classrooms.[23]

• When second-graders spent the year in a math classroom where textbooks and rewards were discarded in favor of an emphasis on "intellectual autonomy"

— that is, where children, working in groups, took an active role in figuring out their own solutions to problems and were free to move around the classroom on their own initiative to get the materials they needed — they developed more sophisticated reasoning skills without falling behind on basic conceptual tasks.[24]

The evidence goes on and on. At least one recent study has found that children given more "opportunity to participate in decisions about schoolwork" score higher on standardized tests;[25] other research shows that they are more likely than those deprived of autonomy to continue working even on relatively uninteresting tasks.[26] There is no question about it: even if our only criterion is academic performance, choice works.

In a way, this conclusion shouldn't be surprising. Putting aside the value of particular programs that give students more discretion about what they are doing, the irrefutable fact is that students always have a choice about whether they will learn. We may be able to force them to complete an assignment, but we can't compel them to learn effectively or to care about what they are doing. The bottom line is that "teaching requires the consent of students, and discontent will not be chased away by the exercise of power."[27] No wonder that expanding the realm in which the learner's consent is sought tends to enhance learning.

4. *Effects on teachers.* Despite attitudinal barriers to creating democratic classrooms and schools, which I will discuss later, educators who are willing to share power may well find that they benefit directly from doing so. One's job becomes a good deal more interesting when it involves collaborating with students to decide what is going to happen. As one fifth-grade teacher in upstate New York explained,

I've been teaching for more than 30 years, and I would have been burned out long ago but for the fact that I involve my kids in designing the curriculum. I'll say to them, "What's the *most* exciting way we could study this next unit?" If we decide their first suggestion isn't feasible, I'll say, "Okay, what's the *next* most exciting way we could study this?" They always come up with good proposals, they're motivated because I'm using their ideas, and I never do the unit in the same way twice.[28]

Teachers also benefit in other ways from allowing students to be active participants in their learning. In such a classroom, according to the researchers involved in the second-grade math project described above, the teacher is "freed from the chore of constantly monitoring and supervising the children's activity and [is] able to give her full attention to . . . interacting with the children" as they work.[29]

5. *Intrinsic value.* Finally, it needs to be said that allowing people to make decisions about what happens to them is inherently preferable to controlling them. It is more respectful and consistent with basic values to which most of us claim to subscribe. Apart from the skills that will be useful for students to have in the future, they ought to have a chance to choose in the present. Children, after all, are not just adults-in-the-making. They are people whose current needs and rights and experiences must be taken seriously. Put it this way: students should not only be trained to live in a democracy when they grow up; they should have the chance to live in one today.[30]

CHOOSING IN PRACTICE

Because quite a few programs and practices in which children can make meaningful choices have been described elsewhere, I will offer only a sampling of the ways this basic idea can be implemented. These suggestions can be grouped according to whether they are primarily concerned with academic decisions or with social and behavioral ones.

Academic issues. The four key realms in which students can make academic decisions are what, how, how well, and why they learn. *What* they learn is the most straightforward of these. Student participation here can range from choosing where in an assigned text to start reading to deciding what course to take. In between these examples is the question of what is to be read, not only by individual students but by the class as a whole. "Here are five books that the supply store has in stock," a fourth-grade teacher may say to the class. "Why don't you flip through them during your free time this week, and we'll decide together on Friday which one to read next." (Of course, if students are not reading stories at all but making their way through worksheets and workbooks, basals and primers and dittos, then their capacity to par-

Every day ought to include at least one block of time in which children can decide what to do.

ticipate in their education has been significantly curtailed from the start.)

Teachers may not always have the discretion to let students participate in deciding what topic to study. But even when compelled to teach a certain lesson, a teacher might open up a discussion in which members of the class try to figure out together why someone apparently thought the subject was important enough to be required. The next step would be to connect that topic to students' real-world concerns and interests. When teachers have themselves decided for one reason or another to exclude students from the selection of the subject matter, there is still room to give them choices about the specific questions within a general topic to be explored. A teacher might begin any unit, for example, by inviting children to discuss what they already know about the subject and what they would like to know.

The question of *how* students learn embraces a great many issues — beginning with whether to work alone, in small groups, or as a class — and including such incidental matters as where students will sit (or lie) while they work. (One teacher swears that achievement in her class improved markedly as soon as she gave students the right to find a favorite reading place and position.) And there are other choices as well: if a student has written a story, she ought to be able to decide whether or not to read it aloud and, if so, whether to answer her classmates' questions about it afterward and, if so, whom to call on.

Every day ought to include at least one block of time in which children can decide individually what to do: get a head start on homework, write in one's journal, work on an art project, or read a library book. Creative writing assignments offer plenty of opportunity for decisions to be made by the writers themselves. In expressing an idea or responding to a lesson, children sometimes can be allowed to decide what medium or genre they will use — whether they want to write a poem, an essay, or a play or do a collage, painting, or sculpture. Mathematics lessons can be guided by quantitative issues of interest to students.

The entire constructivist tradition is predicated on the idea of student autonomy, which is to say, the chance for students to view learning as something "under their control rather than as disembodied, objectified, subject matter."[31] The same can be said about some (but not all) models of cooperative learning. One version, devised by Shlomo Sharan and his colleagues and known as Group Investigation, is based on the idea of active participation throughout the process. Students break a subject into specific questions, sort themselves into groups to explore these questions, plan and conduct an investigation, and figure out how to share what they have learned with the rest of the class.[32]

To talk about *how well* a student is doing is to raise the complicated issues of assessment and evaluation, the improvement of which has lately been of increasing concern to educators. But a key consideration in changing these systems, beyond whether judgments are based on sufficiently rich measures of student achievement, is the extent to which students themselves are involved in the process. Obviously, the chance to pick one of three possible essay questions for one's final paper does not begin to get at what is important here. Students ought to help determine the criteria by which their work will be judged and then play a role in weighing their work against those criteria. This achieves several things at once: it gives students more control over their education, it makes evaluation feel less punitive, and it provides an important learning experience in itself. Students can derive enormous intellectual benefits from thinking about what makes a story interesting, a mathematical proof elegant, or an argument convincing. More traditional approaches to testing can also be improved if students are consulted

about what the test ought to cover and when it ought to be given; there is no need for teachers to decide these things on their own.

Last, and most frequently overlooked, is the need to involve students in talking about *why* they are learning. Few aspects of education are more important than the "participation of the learner in the formation of the purposes which direct his activities in the learning process," as Dewey put it.[33] Children should be given a voice not only about the means of learning but also the ends, the why as well as the what. Even very young children are "curriculum theorists," according to John Nicholls, and there may be no better use of classroom time than a sustained conversation following someone's challenge: "Why do we gotta do this stuff?"[34]

Social and behavioral issues. School is about more than intellectual development; it is about learning to become a responsible, caring person who can make good choices and solve problems effectively. Thus educators must think about ways of helping students to take an active part in decisions that are only indirectly related to academics.

Is it necessary to raise one's hand before talking or to line up before walking through the school? How much noise is too much? How should the furniture be arranged in our room? Where might we take a field trip? These are the sorts of questions that children should be encouraged to ponder and argue about. In considering what kind of classroom or school each person wants to have, the point is to reach consensus on general guidelines or principles, not to formulate a list of rules. (Specific admonitions tend to invite legalistic thinking about their application and a preoccupation with enforcement that emphasizes punishment over problem solving.) Moreover, this process goes well beyond, and may even exclude, the practice of voting. What we want to promote are talking and listening, looking for alternatives and trying to reach agreement, solving problems together and making meaningful choices. Voting, which is an exercise in adversarial majoritarianism, often involves none of these acts. It may be the least objectionable method when a quarter of a billion people must govern themselves, but classroom teachers can do better.[35]

A structured opportunity for members of a class or school to meet and make decisions provides several advantages: it helps children feel respected by making

it clear that their opinions matter; it builds a sense of belongingness and community; and it contributes to the development of social and cognitive skills such as perspective taking (imagining how the world looks to someone else), conflict resolution, and rational analysis.[36] Few contrasts in education are as striking as that between students participating in such meetings, taking responsibility for deciding how they want their classroom to be, and students sitting in rows, having been bribed or threatened into complying with an adult's rules.

Thus, when problems develop, the adage for teachers to keep in mind is "Bring the kids in on it." This approach may call for a class meeting in the case of a conflict involving a number of students, or, when only one or two are directly concerned, it could mean a conversation just with them. If a child is daydreaming and failing to complete assignments, or if two children cannot seem to be anywhere near each other without becoming nasty, the most successful (and respectful)[37] solutions are those that emerge after the teacher asks, "What do you think we can do about this?"

REASONABLE LIMITS

A number of writers and teachers who resist giving children the chance to make decisions have justified their opposition by erecting an enormous straw man called "absolute freedom" and counterposing it to the status quo. Since most of us do not relish the idea of children spending their time at school doing anything they please, deprived of structure or adult guidance, we are encouraged to settle for the controlling practices that now exist.

Not only is this a classic false dichotomy, but virtually every influential proponent of choice for students — as well as the programs that have put the idea into effect — proceeds from the assumption that there are indeed limits on the capacity and right of children to decide. The scary specter of laissez-faire liberty that shows up in the rhetoric of traditionalists is not easy to locate in the real world. Nearly every essay on education by John Dewey, the father of progressive schooling, stresses the importance of adult guidance and derides the idea of "leaving a child to his own unguided fancies."[38] Even A. S. Neill, whose Summerhill school and philosophy lie at the outer edges of serious discussion about the issue, distinguished sharply between freedom and license, emphasizing repeatedly that "a child should not be permitted to violate the personal rights of others."[39] All reasonable adults, meanwhile, acknowledge that safety concerns will necessitate placing constraints on certain kinds of actions.

While agreement exists at a general level about the need to restrict students' choice, however, there is far less consensus about when and how to do so. The issues most frequently raised in support of such restrictions are not as simple as they first appear. Take the question of *age*. It goes without saying that a 16-year-old can approach a decision in a more sophisticated way than a 6-year-old and therefore can usually be entrusted with more responsibility. But this fact is sometimes used to justify preventing younger children from making choices that are well within their capabilities. Moreover, the idea that we must wait until children are mature enough to handle responsibilities may set up a vicious circle: after all, it is experience with decisions that helps children become capable of handling them.[40]

A second rationale for restricting choice is *time*: if students were entitled to make decisions about, and had to agree on, everything they did, there would be no time to do anything else. True enough, and yet the heuristic value of such discussions is often overlooked in the rush to get on with the "real" lesson. In class meetings, for example, teachers would do well to remember that, at least to some extent, *the process is the point*. The idea isn't just to make a choice, reach a decision, and move on.

Of course, it is still true that there won't be time to hash out every matter; sometimes a teacher will need to request that students just do something. But a democratic approach doesn't demand that everything *is* actively chosen, only that it *can* be. As Deborah Meier has said, what matters is not whether a given issue is discussed but that it is discussable. Unavoidable time constraints should not be used to rationalize avoidable authoritarian practices.

Third, the importance of choice is often weighed against the fact that children need some *structure or limits* for their behavior, if not for their learning. Once again, this point may be accurate but does not justify much of what educators actually do. "The critical question," as Thomas Gordon has put it, "is not *wheth-*

er limits and rules are needed . . . but rather *who* sets them: the adults alone or the adults and kids — together."[41] Before depriving children of choice, then, an educator is obliged to demonstrate not that they need some structure but that there is some reason to exclude them from helping to shape that structure. The crucial difference between structures and limits, on the one hand, and control and coercion, on the other, has generally gone unrecognized.[42]

Fourth, and possibly most compelling, is the caution that the right to choose must give way to the needs and preferences of *other people*. Even the minimalist sort of liberalism articulated by Neill (in which one's connection to others is limited to not violating their rights) implies that people cannot do whatever they want. A more ambitious commitment to the value of community would seem to restrict choice even more severely. While each child ought to have more opportunity to make decisions than is typically allowed in American classrooms, such decisions must take into account their impact on the other people in the room. This may not feel like a burdensome restriction once a child has internalized a concern about others' well-being — but, strictly speaking, one person's freedom to choose is always compromised by a set of obligations to others. At a recent town meeting of the long-standing experimental school-within-a-school program at Brookline (Massachusetts) High School, one student remarked that someone's choice to show up in class without having done the reading assignment adversely affects the quality of discussion for everyone. "It's not just 'You get out what you put into it,' " another girl added. "It's 'You get out what the class puts into it' " — and vice versa.

On closer examination, however, it seems clear that what must occasionally be restricted is not choice but *individual* choice. (It is an interesting reflection on our culture that we tend to see these as interchangeable.) To affirm the importance of community does not at all compromise the right to make decisions, per se, or the importance of involving everyone in a class or school in such a process. In fact, we might say that it is the integration of these two values, community and choice, that defines democracy.

I THINK we can conclude that, while some legitimate limits to the right to choose can be identified, the most commonly cited reasons for those

limits may not automatically justify restrictions. But this discussion also raises questions about a conventional response to the matter of appropriate limits. Many people, understandably impatient with an either/or choice in which the possibilities are limited to freedom and its absence, assert that we need to find a happy medium between these two poles. This seems facile. For one thing, such a pronouncement offers no guidance about where on that continuum we should set up camp. For another, it overlooks the fact that the sensible alternative to two extremes may not be an intermediate point but a different way of thinking about the issue altogether. The interesting question here, for example, is not how *much* adults should limit the power of children to make decisions, but *how* they should get involved.

In a broad sense, that involvement may consist of suggesting the tasks, teaching the skills, supplying the resources — in short, providing the conditions under which students can choose productively and learn effectively. The teacher's role is to be a facilitator, but, as Carolyn Edwards points out, this doesn't mean to " 'mak[e] smooth or easy,' but rather to 'stimulate' [learning] by making problems more complex, involving, and arousing."[43] Notice the implication here: a democratic classroom is not one where the teacher has less work to do. There is no zero-sum game in which more responsibility for the children means less for the adults. Helping students to participate effectively takes talent and patience and hard work. "I'm in control of putting students in control," one teacher told me — a responsibility that demands more of an educator than simply telling students what to do.

Notice also that this role for the teacher does not always amount to being a voice for moderation or mainstream values — a conservative counterweight to students' reckless impulses. If, for example, children have been raised to assume that anyone who does something wrong must be forced to suffer a punitive consequence, they will be likely, left to their own devices, to spend their time deciding what should be done to a rule breaker. Here, the teacher might intervene to guide the discussion away from "Which punishment?" and toward the more radical question of whether an entirely different response — "Something has gone wrong; how can we solve this problem?" — might be more productive.

On a range of issues, adults can participate — and circumscribe children's choices — in fundamentally different ways. To wit:

• The teacher and the students may take turns at deciding something, each choosing on alternate weeks, for example, which book to read next. Or the responsibility can rotate between individual students, cooperative learning groups, the whole class, and the teacher.

• The teacher may offer suggestions and guidance, questions and criticism, but leave the final choice to students. Thus I have heard a third-grade teacher advise her students that it might not be a good idea to go outside for recess on a day when there is slush on the ground but then make it clear that it is up to each child to make the final decision for him- or herself. A high school teacher, meanwhile, suggests that it might make sense for the whole class to talk about the homework together but offers them the option of discussing it in small groups if they prefer.

• The teacher can narrow the number of possibilities from which students are permitted to choose. He or she may want to do this to make sure that any material or text a student works with is likely to be of educational value and of approximately the right level of challenge. (On the other hand, neither of these goals always requires restricting children's choice.[44] And even when the teacher does decide to limit their options, she should explain her rationale for doing so and remain open to reasonable additions to her list. As a general rule, it is more important for children to have the chance to *generate* different possibilities than merely to select one possibility from among those that have been set before them.[45])

• The teacher may provide the parameters according to which decisions can be made, perhaps specifying the goal that has to be reached but inviting students to figure out how they want to get there. For example, "It's important to me that no one in here feels scared that other people will laugh at him for saying something stupid. How do you think we can prevent that from happening?" Or, "I need some way at the end of this unit to see how much you understand. Think of a way you might be able to demonstrate what you've learned."

• A decision does not have to be thought of as something that teachers either make or turn over to students. Instead, it can be negotiated together. The emphasis here is on shared responsibility for deciding what gets learned and how the learning takes place. This process can become a lesson in itself — an opportunity to make arguments, solve problems, anticipate consequences, and take other people's needs into account — as well as a powerful contribution to motivation.

WHILE well-meaning educators may offer very different prescriptions regarding the nature and scope of students' participation in decision making, I believe that certain ways of limiting participation are basically deceptive and best described as "pseudochoice." It is disturbing to find these tactics recommended not only by proponents of blatantly controlling classroom management programs, such as Assertive Discipline, but also by critics of such programs who purport to offer an enlightened alternative.

In the first version of pseudochoice, a student is offered a choice that is obviously loaded. "You can finish your math problems now or you can stay in during recess. Which would you prefer?" The problem here is not just that the number of options has been reduced to two, but that the second one is obviously something no student would select. The teacher is really saying, "Do what I tell you or you'll be punished," but he is attempting to camouflage this conventional use of coercion by pretending to offer the student a choice.

In a variation of this gambit, the student is punished after disobeying the teacher's command, but the punishment is presented as something the student asked for: "I see you've chosen to miss recess today." The appeal of this tactic is no mystery: it appears to relieve the teacher of responsibility for what she is about to do to the child. But it is a fundamentally dishonest attribution. Children may choose not to complete a math assignment,* but they certainly do not

choose to miss recess; teachers do that *to* them. To the injury of punishment is added the insult of a kind of mind game whereby reality is redefined and children are told, in effect, that they chose to be punished. This gimmick uses the word *choice* as a bludgeon rather than giving children what they need, which is the opportunity to participate in making real decisions about what happens to them.[46]

Another kind of pseudochoice purports to let a student or a class make a decision even though there is only one choice that will be accepted. I recently heard a well-known educator and advocate for children reminisce about her experiences as a teacher. Recalling a student of hers who frequently and articulately challenged her authority, she commented with a smile, "I had to be a better negotiator than she was." This remark suggests that what had taken place was not negotiation at all but thinly disguised manipulation. As Nel Noddings has written, "We cannot enter into dialogue with children when we know that our decision is already made."[47]

If students are informed that they have made the "wrong" decision and must try again, they will realize they were not truly free to choose in the first place. But the last, and most insidious, variety of pseudochoice tries to prevent students from figuring this out by encouraging them to think they had a say when the game was actually rigged. The "engineering of consent," as it has been called, seems to offer autonomy while providing "the assurance of order and conformity — a most seductive combination. Yet its appearance and its means should be understood for what they really are: a method of securing and solidifying the interests of those in power."[48] This description by educator James Beane might have been inspired by the behavior of politicians, but it is no less applicable to what goes on in schools. If we want students to learn how to choose, they must have the opportunity to make *real* choices.

---

*Even this assumption needs to be questioned, since a young child may lack the capacity for rational decision making or impulse control that is implicit in the suggestion that he made a choice. If so, the child needs help in developing these faculties, not punishment accompanied by blame. I have heard some teachers reply to this point by insisting that, if students are permitted to make choices, they must "take responsibility" for making a bad one. This approach, however, assumes that "taking responsibility" for a poor decision means being made to suffer for it rather than being part of a nonpunitive problem-solving process.

BARRIERS

If we are to act on the arguments and evidence supporting the value of making students active participants in their education, we need to understand why more educators haven't already done so. I think the barriers to giving students more choice fall into three categories: structural impediments, resistance by teachers, and resistance by the students themselves.

Structural impediments. Classroom teachers frequently protest that they would love to open up the decision-making process but for the fact that a significant number of decisions are not theirs to give away or even to make themselves. Highly controlling schools and school districts may leave teachers very little discretion about either curricular or disciplinary issues. As Dewey noted, classrooms characterized by demands for "sheer obedience to the will of an adult" may sometimes imply a "situation [that] almost forced [that arrangement] upon the teacher," such as an absence of democracy or community among the educators themselves.[49] Even if controlling structures do not literally remove options from teachers, they may create a climate in which teachers do to children what is done to them. Often, teachers subject to rigid directives from above may find it easier not "to resist administrators but to increase controls on their students."[50]

Resistance by teachers. While structural constraints are sometimes very real, they can also be used as excuses to with-

> *Parting with power is not easy, if only because the results are less predictable without control.*

hold power from students that teachers in any case are not inclined to share. The traditional instructional model sees the teacher as the king or queen of the classroom, and the fact is that monarchs do not always abdicate gracefully. On the basis of my own years as a teacher as well as my conversations with scores of others in the profession, I would argue that there is a certain reassurance and satisfaction to be taken from making unilateral decisions. No wonder many teachers who express relief at having "a good class this year" use the word *good* as parents of a newborn might talk about having "a good

baby" — that is, one who is quiet, docile, and little trouble to manage.

Popular books about classroom life, as well as workshops and other forms of guidance offered to educators, typically take for granted that a teacher must secure control of the class. Hence the use of curricular materials, including basals and worksheets, that have the effect of keeping order.[51] And hence the popularity of manipulative measures such as punishments and rewards: their use can be traced back to the belief that there are exactly two possibilities: control or chaos. When students are allowed to make decisions, it is therefore only about matters that don't threaten the teacher's reign. More than once I have heard teachers pride themselves on letting students choose "when I don't really care what they end up with" — which is, of course, a far cry from a democratic process that helps students to become responsible decision makers.

If challenged, defenders of classroom autocracy may insist that a teacher must get control of the class *first* in order that students can be helped to become good learners and good people. Whether this is a sincerely held belief or just a rationalization for holding on to power, it is simply wrong. Control not only is unnecessary for fostering academic motivation; it undermines its development, substituting reluctant compliance for the excitement that comes from the experience of self-determination. Likewise for the nonacademic realm: as one group of social scientists put it, the emphasis on control "endanger[s] the long-term enterprise of socialization itself."[52]

This is no mere academic speculation. Watch what happens when a teacher concerned about maintaining control of his classroom walks away for a few minutes or is absent for a day: the class is likely to erupt, just as a child raised by parents who emphasize strict discipline is apt to misbehave when he is away from home. It is in classrooms (and families) where participation is valued above adult control that students have the chance to learn *self*-control — and are more likely to keep working when the teacher or parent isn't around.

There is nothing surprising about the fact that teachers resist being told what they can teach and how they must manage their classrooms. The astonishing fact is that so many of these teachers treat their students in exactly the way they themselves find so offensive. Whatever

the reason for this discrepancy, though, students must be permitted to make substantive decisions about learning and living together, and this will not happen until teachers and administrators understand that *control can't be the goal* — or even a technique. This recognition, in turn, may require reconsidering basic beliefs about human nature and motivation. A teacher convinced that children are egocentric little terrors who must be forced to attend to other people's needs is likely to prefer a model of tight control.[53] And control, in turn, produces exactly the sort of antisocial behavior that such a teacher expects, confirming the view that such tactics are needed.

Sometimes, however, the main barrier to giving children choices is a simple lack of gumption. Parting with power is not easy, if only because the results are less predictable than in a situation where we have control. Asking students to decide about even the simplest issues can be scary. An elementary teacher once told me how difficult it was for her to leave the classroom walls bare when her students showed up on the first day of school. If she had already decorated them, she realized, it was really *her* room they were entering. But it took several years before she found the courage to bring them into the process, a decision that ultimately made an enormous difference in how the children felt about coming to school — and also occasioned a natural and eagerly received lesson on fractions so that the students could measure and tack up the construction paper that they had chosen for *their* walls.

Student resistance. Finally, and most discouragingly, teachers sometimes find that their willingness to let students make decisions is met with an apparent reluctance on the part of the students. This is really not so surprising, given that most of them have been conditioned to accept a posture of passivity at school and sometimes at home. After a few years of being instructed to do what you're told, it is disconcerting to be invited — much less expected — to take responsibility for the way things are.[54]

This resistance takes three primary forms. The first is simply *refusing*: "That's your job to decide," students may protest. The second is *testing*: offering outrageous suggestions or responses to see if the teacher is really serious about the invitation to participate. The third is *parroting*: repeating what adults have said or guessing what this adult probably wants to hear. (Thus a fifth-grader asked to suggest a guideline for class conduct may recite, "We should keep our hands and feet to ourselves.")

The key question is how we respond to these maneuvers. It can be tempting to conclude that students are either unable to handle the responsibility of making decisions or unworthy of having it. But our challenge is to persevere. As Selma Wassermann has written,

> I have heard teachers give it up after a single attempt, saying, "Children cannot behave responsibly," then remove all further opportunity for students to practice and grow in their responsible behavior. I have also heard teachers say, "Children cannot think for themselves," and proceed thereafter to do children's thinking for them. But these same teachers would *never* say, "These children cannot read by themselves," and thereafter remove any opportunity for them to learn to read.[55]

Specifically, the comment "That's your job" provides a teachable moment, a chance to engage students in a conversation about their experiences with being controlled and about when they have found learning to be most exciting. Outlandish ideas can be met with a sense of humor but also taken seriously: a student who is asked how school could be improved and replies that all the books should be thrown away may be saying something about her experience of the curriculum that we ignore at our peril. Finally, in the case of parroting, it can be hard even to recognize this tactic as a form of resistance — or as something undesirable. Getting our ideas to come out of their mouths is a ventriloquist's trick, not a sign of successful participation and student autonomy. It represents an invitation to ask students about their experiences with saying what they knew would please an adult and how different that feels from taking the risk of making a suggestion that someone might not like — and then emphasizing that the latter is what we are looking for here.

Of course, whether the last point is true — whether we really are looking for students who take risks and make decisions — is the first question that each of us must answer. The structural and attitudinal barriers erected by educators often seem impregnable, with the result that students continue to feel powerless and, to that extent, burned out. For decades, prescriptions have been offered to en-

hance student motivation and achievement. But these ideas are unlikely to make much of a difference so long as students are controlled and silenced. It is not "utopian" or "naive" to think that learners can make responsible decisions about their own learning; those words best describe the belief that any group of people will do something effectively and enthusiastically when they are unable to make choices about what they are doing.

1. For example, see Charles E. Silberman, *Crisis in the Classroom: The Remaking of American Education* (New York: Random House, 1970); John I. Goodlad, *A Place Called School: Prospects for the Future* (New York: McGraw-Hill, 1984); Linda McNeil, *Contradictions of Control: School Structure and School Knowledge* (New York: Routledge and Kegan Paul, 1986); and the observations of William Glasser in much of his work.
2. Felicia R. Lee, "Disrespect Rules," *New York Times Education Life*, 4 April 1993, p. 16.
3. Strictly speaking, as such thinkers as Jean-Paul Sartre and Viktor Frankl have pointed out, people are never entirely powerless. Deborah Meier applies this observation to an education context: "Even devalued and disrespected people remain powerful, but they are forced to exercise their powers in odd, distorted, and limited ways. . . . Children have been exercising their powers for years, without the formal right to do so. Ditto for teachers . . . [who] sabotage reforms — the best and the worst — when they feel imposed upon and helpless." See "The Kindergarten Tradition in the High School," in Kathe Jervis and Carol Montag, eds., *Progressive Education for the 1990s: Transforming Practice* (New York: Teachers College Press, 1991), pp. 140-41.
4. Suzanne C. Kobasa and her colleagues found that control, together with a deeply felt commitment to one's activities and the tendency to perceive change as a positive challenge, contributed to a profile of "hardiness" that provides significant protection against illness. See, for example, "Stressful Life Events, Personality, and Health: An Inquiry into Hardiness," *Journal of Personality and Social Psychology*, vol. 37, 1979, pp. 1-10. See also Robert A. Karasek et al., "Job Characteristics in Relation to the Prevalence of Myocardial Infarction in the U.S. Health Examination Survey (HES) and the Health and Nutrition Examination Survey (HANES)," *American Journal of Public Health*, vol. 78, 1988, pp. 910-16.
5. Judith Rodin and Ellen J. Langer, "Long-Term Effects of a Control-Relevant Intervention with the Institutionalized Aged," *Journal of Personality and Social Psychology*, vol. 35, 1977, pp. 897-902. In another study, nursing home residents who were able to control (or at least predict) when a student would come visit them were not only happier and more hopeful but also physically healthier than those who received the same number of visits but on a random schedule. See Richard Schulz, "Effects of Control and Predictability on the Physical and Psychological Well-Being of the Institutionalized Aged," *Journal of Personality and Social Psychology*, vol. 33, 1976, pp. 563-73.
6. Martin Seligman's research on helplessness is central to this field of study. For a review of the relevant studies by him and others, see Shelley E. Taylor, *Positive Illusions: Creative Self-Deception and the Healthy Mind* (New York: Basic Books, 1989).

7. See Elizabeth Tuettemann and Keith F. Punch, "Teachers' Psychological Distress: The Ameliorating Effects of Control over the Work Environment," *Educational Review*, vol. 44, 1992, pp. 181-94.
8. See Alfie Kohn, *Punished by Rewards: The Trouble with Gold Stars, Incentive Plans, A's, Praise, and Other Bribes* (Boston: Houghton Mifflin, 1993).
9. Women who were told they could choose the particulars of an exercise program at a health club were more likely to continue attending over six weeks (and to declare their willingness to keep coming after that) than were women who were told their program was simply assigned to them — even though they, too, were actually assigned activities on the basis of the preferences they had expressed. See Carol E. Thompson and Leonard M. Wankel, "The Effects of Perceived Activity Choice upon Frequency of Exercise Behavior," *Journal of Applied Social Psychology*, vol. 10, 1980, pp. 436-43. A smoking cessation program that "focused attention on the individual's own efforts in smoking cessation" was more successful than one in which people followed a set of guidelines. See Judith M. Harackiewicz et al., "Attributional Processes in Behavior Change and Maintenance: Smoking Cessation and Continued Abstinence," *Journal of Consulting and Clinical Psychology*, vol. 55, 1987, pp. 372-78. Adolescent girls (but not boys) were more likely to continue using an anticavity fluoride rinse for nearly half a year when they were invited to make decisions about how the program was designed and monitored. See Joseph A. Burleson et al., "Effects of Decisional Control and Work Orientation on Persistence in Preventive Health Behavior," *Health Psychology*, vol. 9, 1990, pp. 1-17.
10. This research has been reviewed and evaluated by Suzanne C. Thompson, "Will It Hurt Less If I Can Control It? A Complex Answer to a Simple Question," *Psychological Bulletin*, vol. 90, 1981, pp. 89-101.
11. Megan R. Gunnar-Vongnechten, "Changing a Frightening Toy into a Pleasant Toy by Allowing the Infant to Control Its Actions," *Developmental Psychology*, vol. 14, 1978, pp. 157-62.
12. Richard M. Ryan and Wendy S. Grolnick, "Origins and Pawns in the Classroom: Self-Report and Projective Assessment of Individual Differences in Children's Perceptions," *Journal of Personality and Social Psychology*, vol. 50, 1986, pp. 550-58.
13. Constance Kamii, "Toward Autonomy: The Importance of Critical Thinking and Choice Making," *School Psychology Review*, vol. 20, 1991, p. 387. In fact, the lessons of conformity that Kamii finds troubling are those that concern academic activities (such as having to "learn mathematics through blind obedience"), not just behavior.
14. Shelley Berman, "The Real Ropes Course: The Development of Social Consciousness," *ESR Journal*, 1990, p. 2. The authors of a classic text on high school teaching comment wryly that the American motto could be: "Let's have education *for* democracy, but let's be careful about democracy *in* education!" See Jean Dresden Grambs and John C. Carr, *Modern Methods in Secondary Education*, 4th ed. (New York: Holt, Rinehart & Winston, 1979), p. 71.
15. Citing several sources, Joseph D'Amico concludes that "children who have experiences in a school where they participate in making decisions are more likely to be . . . motivated to make decisions both in and out of school." See "Reviving Student Participation," *Educational Leadership*, October 1980, pp. 44-46.
16. See Alfie Kohn, "Caring Kids: The Role of the Schools," *Phi Delta Kappan*, March 1991, pp. 496-506.
17. Höss is quoted in Alice Miller, *For Your Own Good: Hidden Cruelty in Child-Rearing and the*

Roots of Violence (New York: Farrar, Straus & Giroux, 1984), pp. 67-68.

18. Kathy Irwin, "The Eight Year Study," in Jervis and Montag, eds., p. 59. For a more comprehensive description of the study, see Wilford M. Aiken, *The Story of the Eight-Year Study* (New York: Harper, 1942); and Dean Chamberlin et al., *Did They Succeed in College?* (New York: Harper, 1942).

19. Margaret C. Wang and Billie Stiles, "An Investigation of Children's Concept of Self-Responsibility for Their School Learning," *American Educational Research Journal*, vol. 13, 1976, pp. 159-79. Unfortunately, task completion was the only outcome measured in this study.

20. Robert G. Rainey, "The Effects of Directed Versus Non-Directed Laboratory Work on High School Chemistry Achievement," *Journal of Research in Science Teaching*, vol. 3, 1965, pp. 286-92.

21. Teresa M. Amabile and Judith Gitomer, "Children's Artistic Creativity: Effects of Choice in Task Materials," *Personality and Social Psychology Bulletin*, vol. 10, 1984, pp. 209-15.

22. Miron Zuckerman et al., "On the Importance of Self-Determination for Intrinsically-Motivated Behavior," *Personality and Social Psychology Bulletin*, vol. 4, 1978, pp. 443-46. On the relation between choice and task involvement, see also John G. Nicholls, *The Competitive Ethos and Democratic Education* (Cambridge: Harvard University Press, 1989), p. 169.

23. Richard deCharms, "Personal Causation Training in the Schools," *Journal of Applied Social Psychology*, vol. 2, 1972, pp. 95-113.

24. For a description of the classroom structure in this yearlong experiment, see Erna Yackel et al., "Small-Group Interactions as a Source of Learning Opportunities in Second-Grade Mathematics," *Journal for Research in Mathematics Education*, vol. 22, 1991, pp. 390-408. For a discussion of the results, see Paul Cobb et al., "Assessment of a Problem-Centered Second-Grade Mathematics Project," *Journal for Research in Mathematics Education*, vol. 22, 1991, pp. 3-29.

25. Ann K. Boggiano et al., "Helplessness Deficits in Students: The Role of Motivational Orientation," *Motivation and Emotion*, vol. 16, 1992, pp. 278-80. Informal reports from other researchers suggest that a more typical result from an intervention of this sort is an enhancement of conceptual thinking skills (along with intrinsic motivation and other psychological and social benefits) but no change on standardized test scores, which probably is a reflection on how little these scores really mean. It should be sufficient to be able to show people who care about these scores that giving students more choice about their learning has no detrimental effect on their performance on machine-scored tests while bringing about a variety of other advantages.

26. Three studies to this effect are cited in John Condry, "Enemies of Exploration: Self-Initiated Versus Other-Initiated Learning," *Journal of Personality and Social Psychology*, vol. 35, 1977, p. 466.

27. John Nicholls and Susan P. Hazzard, *Education as Adventure: Lessons from the Second Grade* (New York: Teachers College Press, 1993), p. 76.

28. Richard Lauricella is quoted in Thomas Lickona, *Educating for Character: How Our Schools Can Teach Respect and Responsibility* (New York: Bantam, 1991), p. 148. Presumably he does not mean to suggest that every aspect of a unit must be taught differently from one year to the next, only that an element that is changed on the basis of students' suggestions within a predictable structure can be invigorating for a teacher.

29. Yackel et al., p. 401.

30. This point is made forcefully by David Char-

noff, "Democratic Schooling: Means or End?," *High School Journal*, vol. 64, 1981, pp. 170-75.

31. Paul Cobb et al., "Young Children's Emotional Acts While Engaged in Mathematical Problem Solving," in D. B. McLeod and V. M. Adams, eds., *Affect and Mathematical Problem Solving: A New Perspective* (New York: Springer-Verlag, 1989), p. 129.

32. See Yael Sharan and Shlomo Sharan, *Expanding Cooperative Learning Through Group Investigation* (New York: Teachers College Press, 1992). At its best, cooperative learning "gives students an active role in deciding about, planning, directing and controlling the content and pace of their learning activities. It changes the students' role from recipients of information to seekers, analyzers and synthesizers of information. It transforms pupils from listeners into talkers and doers, from powerless pawns into participant citizens empowered to influence decisions about what they must do in school." See Shlomo Sharan, "Cooperative Learning: Problems and Promise," *The International Association for the Study of Cooperation in Education Newsletter*, December 1986, p. 4.

33. John Dewey, *Experience and Education* (1938; reprint, New York: Collier, 1963), p. 67.

34. See Nicholls and Hazzard, esp. pp. 182-84.

35. Sometimes elementary school students are asked to put their heads down when they raise their hands to register a preference. This strikes me as an apt metaphor for the whole enterprise of voting. "Who thinks we should take our field trip to the museum? Who prefers the zoo? Okay, the zoo wins, 15 to 12." About the best that can be said for this exercise is that it didn't take very long. Children have learned precious little about how to solve a problem, accommodate other people's preferences, or rethink their initial inclinations. Moreover, 12 children are now unlikely to feel very excited about the upcoming field trip. The same analysis applies on a schoolwide basis. The usual student council apparatus is deficient on three counts: most students are excluded from direct participation in decision making, some students are turned into losers since the representatives are chosen in a contest, and the council has little real power in any case. Educators interested in democratic values will discourage voting whenever possible; as the political philosopher Benjamin Barber has cogently argued, it is "the least significant act of citizenship in a democracy." See *Strong Democracy: Participatory Politics for a New Age* (Berkeley: University of California Press, 1984), p. 187.

36. My own thinking on how class meetings might be structured has been influenced primarily by the work of the Child Development Project, whose writings on the topic have not been published. I would, however, recommend two other useful and very practical discussions of class meetings: William Glasser, *Schools Without Failure* (New York: Harper and Row, 1969), chaps. 10-12; and Lickona, chap. 8.

37. "Democracy in the classroom . . . begins simply: with respect for the child as a person, someone who has a point of view and a right and a need to express it." See Thomas Lickona and Muffy Paradise, "Democracy in the Elementary School," in Ralph Mosher, ed., *Moral Education: A First Generation of Research and Development* (New York: Praeger, 1980), p. 325.

38. The quotation is from Dewey's *The School and Society* (Chicago: University of Chicago Press, 1990), p. 130.

39. "In Summerhill, a child is *not* allowed to do as he pleases," Neill added. See *Summerhill* (New York: Hart, 1960), pp. 308, 348.

40. On this point, see Lickona and Paradise, p. 323.

41. Thomas Gordon, *Teaching Children Self-Discipline* (New York: Times Books, 1989), p. 9.

42. This distinction is offered frequently in the work

of Edward Deci and Richard Ryan. It seemed to be lost on several teachers at an alternative school program I visited recently who maintained that, because today's students come from less structured home environments or are more conservative, it is appropriate to give them fewer choices about their learning.

43. Carolyn Edwards, "Partner, Nurturer, and Guide," in Carolyn Edwards et al., eds., *The Hundred Languages of Children: The Reggio Emilia Approach to Early Childhood Education* (Norwood, N.J.: Ablex, 1993), p. 157.

44. Indeed, children whose curiosity has not been killed by the use of rewards or other extrinsic controls typically select tasks of the right difficulty level for themselves. This finding "suggests that at least part of the teacher's difficult problem of matching tasks to children can be solved by providing children with more choices than they are typically offered." See Fred W. Danner and Edward Lonky, "A Cognitive-Developmental Approach to the Effects of Rewards on Intrinsic Motivation," *Child Development*, vol. 52, 1981, p. 1050.

45. A related restriction on choice that may be employed excessively is the practice of preventing students from altering an activity once they have selected it. They can choose, in other words, only among tasks that must be performed in a rigidly prescribed manner. Some critics have argued that this is a weakness of the Montessori method.

46. A nice discussion of this misuse of the idea of choice can be found in Vincent Crockenberg, "Assertive Discipline: A Dissent," *California Journal of Teacher Education*, vol. 9, 1982, esp. pp. 65-70.

47. Nel Noddings, *The Challenge to Care in Schools* (New York: Teachers College Press, 1992), p. 23.

48. James A. Beane, *Affect in the Curriculum: Toward Democracy, Dignity, and Diversity* (New York: Teachers College Press, 1990), p. 35.

49. Dewey, *Experience and Education*, p. 55.

50. McNeil, p. 9. This phenomenon is not limited to schools, of course. There is evidence from the corporate world that the middle managers most likely to act in an autocratic fashion toward those below them in the hierarchy are those who are restricted and controlled themselves. See Rosabeth Moss Kanter, *Men and Women of the Corporation* (New York: Basic Books, 1977), pp. 189-90.

51. Despite the claim that discipline is "instrumental to mastering the content," the truth is often just the reverse: "many teachers . . . maintain discipline by the ways they present course content." The reduction of teaching to the transfer of disconnected facts and skills is the means; keeping a tight grip on student behavior is the end. See McNeil, pp. 157-58.

52. Phyllis C. Blumenfeld et al., "Teacher Talk and Student Thought," in John M. Levine and Margaret C. Wang, eds., *Teacher and Student Perceptions* (Hillsdale, N.J.: Erlbaum, 1983), p. 147.

53. A survey of more than 300 parents found that those who inclined toward a negative view of human nature were more likely to prefer an authoritarian approach to child rearing. See Lawrence O. Clayton, "The Impact upon Child-Rearing Attitudes of Parental Views of the Nature of Humankind," *Journal of Psychology and Christianity*, vol. 4, no. 3, 1985, pp. 49-55. For an argument that the data do not support this negative view of human nature, see Alfie Kohn, *The Brighter Side of Human Nature: Altruism and Empathy in Everyday Life* (New York: Basic Books, 1990).

54. On this point, see Seth Kreisberg, "Educating for Democracy and Community," *ESR Journal*, 1992, p. 72; and Rheta DeVries, *Programs of Early Education: The Constructivist View* (New York: Longman, 1987), p. 379.

55. Selma Wassermann, "Children Working in Groups? It Doesn't Work!," *Childhood Education*, Summer 1989, p. 204.

Motivating Underachievers:
Make them *want* to try

DEBORAH STIPEK

Deborah Stipek was an associate professor of education at UCLA when she wrote this article.

SOONER OR LATER, AN UNDER-achiever will challenge your teaching skill—and your patience—with unfinished assignments, complaints, and excuses. Maybe you'll try to coax the child into working harder. Maybe you'll enlist the aid of parents. Maybe you'll search for special projects to pique the child's interest. And maybe none of these tactics will succeed.

Laziness, boredom, and apathy don't explain the behavior of all underachieving students. For many smart kids who fail, *not* trying simply makes more sense than the alternative. Take Melanie and Jeff, for example.

Melanie, an intelligent 2nd grader, rarely hands in homework. And when given an in-class assignment, she invariably whines, "That's too hard" or "I can't do this" until her teacher comes to help. On tests, Melanie often "consults" her classmates' papers.

Jeff, on the other hand, would never cheat on a test or seek help from a teacher or classmate. But the 6th grader is often conspicuously inattentive in class. And "bad luck" keeps him from completing a surprising number of tasks, particularly ones dealing with new material. He leaves books necessary for doing homework at school. He loses assignments on the bus. Sometimes during a test his pen runs out of ink, and he wastes valuable time rummaging through his desk to find another.

Why try?
Both Jeff and Melanie pay a price for their lack of effort: bad grades, reprimands from their teachers, detentions. Yet both persist in their behavior. Why? The answer is deceptively simple: These kids see the benefits of not trying as outweighing the costs.

Melanie is sure she *can't* do the assigned work, regardless of how hard she tries. Since effort or apathy will lead to the same end—failure—putting forth the least effort possible is perfectly logical. So Melanie continues to rely on teachers and classmates to get her through.

Unlike Melanie, Jeff isn't convinced that he can't do his schoolwork. But he has serious doubts. Since Jeff desperately wants to believe that he's intelligent and competent, and wants others to believe this too, he's afraid to try hard and fail. So for Jeff also, *not* trying—and flaunting his lack of effort—makes sense. It allows him to hold on to a self-image of competence.

Stubborn beliefs
For students like Jeff and Melanie, beliefs about personal ability and the costs and benefits of

effort can be difficult to change. For example, when Melanie *does* do well on an assignment or test, she's likely to attribute her success to the teacher's help, an easy task, or good luck. So occasional successes won't necessarily bolster her self-confidence. What really needs to be changed is her belief that no amount of effort will improve her chances of succeeding. Similarly, Jeff needs to be persuaded that making mistakes isn't a sign of stupidity or incompetence, but a natural part of the learning process. Only then will trying make sense.

Encouraging effort

The following guidelines will help you make sure that the benefits of trying outweigh those of not trying—for *all* your students.

1. Make sure that assigned tasks are realistic, so that all students can complete them if they really try. When your class contains kids with vastly different skill levels, this isn't easy. But you can use such techniques as teaching in small, flexible groups; creating cooperative work groups or setting up a peer teaching program; and preparing different assignments for different skill levels. To alleviate the additional burden this places on you, have your students check some of their own or one anoth-er's assignments. This also gives students a sense of responsibility for their own learning.

2. Focus students' attention on their own progress, not on their classmates' performance. When students measure their success by their peers' performance, those who don't do as well are bound to feel like failures. Base grades and rewards on mastery or improvement, not on relative performance. Reward the child who reduced his spelling errors from 50 percent to 20 percent just as enthusiastically as you reward the child who invariably gets all the words right. Put papers that show improvement, not just the best papers, on the bulletin board. Consider marking workbook exercises with a check mark if they're correct but making no mark if they're not. Have the student continue to work on the exercises until all have received a check mark. This allows kids many opportunities to improve their performance without any negative evaluation.

3. Reward effort, whatever the outcome. Tell your students that in learning, as in any endeavor, setbacks are inevitable. But effort and perseverance *do* pay off. Praise kids when they make progress, not just when they get everything right. If only success is praised, some students may become demoralized when their efforts don't lead to immediate mastery—which is a likely outcome when they're studying new material. And when a student does immediately master a new skill, take care not to be overly enthusiastic. Otherwise, you'll risk sending the message that you really do value brilliance rather than diligence, and slower kids may become discouraged.

4. Give every student opportunities to demonstrate competence in class. Consider setting aside a few minutes each week for kids to demonstrate an unusual—and nonacademic—skill. For example, ask your teeny Houdini to show off some sleight of hand, or your fledgling "Bird" to play a saxophone solo. This way, even academically weak students will get a good dose of self-confidence.

5. Allow students to set their own goals. (Of course, you need to make sure that these goals are realistic but challenging.) For example, encourage a child who consistently fails the weekly math quiz to set a goal for next week's quiz (say, getting two more problems correct). Have the child record the goal and his actual performance on a chart. This will give the child a concrete picture of his own progress and will foster personal responsibility. It will also reinforce the importance of perseverance.

Educating and Motivating African American Males to Succeed

Antoine M. Garibaldi

Xavier University of Louisiana

One of the most actively discussed, and sometimes vigorously debated, issues since the late 1980s has been the declining social, economic, and educational status of young African American males in our society. The negative indicators that describe a substantial share of this group's depressing condition in unemployment statistics, homicide rates (as both victims and perpetrators), their overwhelmingly disproportionate representation in the criminal justice system, as well as their last-place ranking on many measures of educational performance and attainment have become so commonplace that it has caused many to view the majority of these young men's futures as hopeless and impossible to salvage.

Even if one doubts that a "crisis" truly exists or questions whether African American males may one day become an "endangered species," few systematic solutions have been offered to address realistically the problems that at least one-third of young Black men experience. Many conferences, symposia, and workshops have been held over the last few years (and I confess that I have been a participant in some of those meetings), but too much of our time has been devoted to discussing the plight of African American males rather than developing potential solutions to mitigate this crisis. Remedies *do* exist, and this article highlights some educational solutions developed more than four years ago which might reverse the negative trends that have become widely associated with African American males.

THE NEW ORLEANS PUBLIC SCHOOL STUDY ON BLACK MALES

My own involvement with this topic began in 1987 when I was asked by the New Orleans Public School System to chair a task force of community leaders and educators to review the status of African American males in that city's schools. The specific charge of the committee was to examine the rates of school retention, suspension, expulsion, academic achievement, grade attainment, school attendance and participation in co-curricular activities by African American male students, since it had become obvious that these young men were rarely represented among the school system's honor roll recipients and yet were disproportionately represented in almost all categories of academic failure. As typically happens when committees such as these are established, much of our initial meeting time was spent discussing "the problem" and offering possible solutions without any hard facts or data to support them. Thus, we decided that the previous school year's data on the relevant indicators should be assembled and analyzed so that we could use that information to develop our own surveys of students, teachers, parents, and the general public. Further, we agreed to have four public hearings whereby citizens could offer their own suggestions about what should be done to address these widespread educational problems. With this comprehensive information in hand we believed that we would then be in a better position to make sound recommendations based on fact rather than anecdotal and unsubstantiated perceptions. While no deadline was given for submitting a final report, the committee worked for an entire school year and developed recommendations consistent with the results of the previous school year's data, the surveys of students, teachers, parents, and the public, as well as the testimony of local citizens.[1]

---

1. The complete final report of this study, *Educating Black Male Youth: A Moral and Civic Imperative,* is available from the New Orleans Public Schools, Office of the Superintendent, 4100 Touro Street, New Orleans, Louisiana 70122, for a nominal charge of $3.00. It is also available through ERIC (ED 303 546) and on microfiche.

From *The Journal of Negro Education,* Vol. 61, No. 1, Winter 1992, pp. 4-11. © 1992 by The Journal of Negro Education, Howard University, Washington, DC. Reprinted by permission.

The analyses of the 1986–87 school year's data not only verified the committee's beliefs but the results were also quite startling. In an urban school system where 87% of the 86,000 students were African American, we found that African American males accounted for 58% of the nonpromotions, 65% of the suspensions, 80% of the expulsions, and 45% of the dropouts—even though these young men represented only 43% of the school population. The picture for African American females in the school system was somewhat less bleak, but still of concern. These young women represented 44% of the school population but accounted for 34% of the nonpromotions, 29% of the suspensions, 20% of the expulsions, and 41% of the dropouts. It was also very discomforting to find that more than 800 of the 1,470 nonpromotions in the first grade and more than 1,600 of the almost 2,800 nonpromotions in the sixth through eighth grades were African American males.

With respect to academic achievement, we also found that one-third of African American males and females in New Orleans's public schools scored in the lowest quartile on the reading and mathematics sections of the California Test of Basic Skills. Only 18% of the African American males and 20% of the females scored in the highest quartile on the mathematics component of the test, and only 16% of females and 13% of males scored in the highest quartile on the reading test. The only bright spot from the New Orleans study's analysis of the academic achievement of its African American students was that roughly one-third of the males scored at or above the mean on both sections of the test.

Since this study was conducted in 1987–88, other school systems, most notably Prince Georges County (MD) and Milwaukee (WI), have replicated the findings of poor academic performance for African American males. The results in Prince Georges County showed that the performance of Black males and females on criterion-referenced tests in both mathematics and reading was comparable to that of White students up to third grade. By grade four, however, Black males experienced a sharp decline on criterion-referenced mathematics and reading tests. Moreover, the percentage of Black males in the top reading group among 18 Prince Georges County elementary schools dropped significantly from grade four to grade six. In the first and fourth grades, 23% of the African American males were in the top reading group, but by grade six only 12% were in the top groups (Simmons & Grady, 1990).

In Milwaukee during the 1988–89 school year, the percentage of African American males scoring at or above the national average on the norm-referenced test in reading dropped from 28% in second grade to 24% in grades five and seven (African American Male Task Force, 1990). On the norm-referenced mathematics test, 45% of the Black males scored at or above the national average in second grade. That proportion dropped to 33% in grade five and to 22% in grade seven. Black females in Milwaukee also experienced the same declining score trends on norm-referenced reading and mathematics tests. In reading, the percentage of Black girls scoring at or above the national average declined from 34% in grade two to 22% in grade five, but then rose sharply, to 30%, in grade seven. In mathematics, 45% of African American girls scored at or above the national mean in the second grade, 37% did so in the fifth grade, while the percentage dropped down to 26% in grade seven.

A national decline in performance on mathematics and reading tests for African American students around grade four is clearly evident, and further study is needed to identify the critical factors that are causing this phenomenon. These adverse trends in reading performance, particularly for Black males and females, have been verified by analyses of national assessments by Winfield (1988) and Winfield and Lee (1990), who note that minority females outscore their male counterparts to a greater degree than do White females vis-à-vis White males on National Assessment of Educational Progress (NAEP) reading tests.

All the above results clearly demonstrate that the academic failure of African American males (and also females but apparently not as rapidly) begins early and eventually leads to these youths becoming disinterested in school and some even dropping out before they reach senior high school. This has become quite apparent in college enrollment rates as well: African American female undergraduates outnumbered African American males by more than 240,000 in 1988 (Carter & Wilson, 1991). Nevertheless, systematic solutions can be implemented to address these problems, but it is first important to learn what the educational expectations and interests of the school system's African American male students are and how their teachers and parents perceive them and their ambitions.

STUDENT, TEACHER, AND PARENTAL PERCEPTIONS

Contrary to public perception, African American boys *do* want to finish school and many want to be challenged academically. In our survey of more than 2,250 African American males in the New Orleans school district, 95% reported that they expected to graduate from high school. However, 40% responded that they believed their teachers did not set high enough goals for them, and 60% suggested that their teachers should push them harder. (Black females in the study responded similarly to the boys on these items.) However, when we surveyed a random sample of 500 teachers (318 of whom responded) and asked them if they believed their Black male students would go to college, almost 6 out of every 10 teachers responded in the negative. This is even more troubling because 60% of the teachers sampled taught in elementary schools, 70% of them had 10 or more years of experience, and 65% of them were Black! This disconcerting response lends added support to the teacher expectancy literature and confirms that no teachers are immune from holding negative, self-fulfilling prophecies about the children they teach.

While students' aspirations and their assessments of the education they were receiving did not coincide well with the perceptions of some teachers, parental beliefs were more similar to those of their children. Parents did not share the teachers' beliefs with respect to their sons' postsecondary interests. Eight out of every 10 of the 3,523 parents surveyed indicated that they believed their sons expected to go to college (compared to 4 out of 10 teachers who believed similarly). However, one-fourth of those parents also responded that they had never gone to their child's school for parental conferences during which report cards are usually given out and children's performance in classes is discussed. Because some parents do not (or cannot) attend parental conferences, it is very likely that some teachers may misinterpret parental absenteeism as a sign that the children of these parents are not interested in finishing school or do not have positive educational aspirations. This may further confirm teachers' skepticism regarding African American male children's futures in particular. Given the latter possibility as well as the large perception gap that apparently exists between parents' and teachers' appraisals of African American males' educational expectations and aspirations, more must be done to increase the amount and quality of communication between parents and teachers to minimize incorrect interpretations about these students' motivation and desire to succeed academically.

SOLUTIONS AND RECOMMENDATIONS

To alleviate this expanding problem, systematic solutions are needed and more must be done to motivate, encourage, and reinforce more young Black men to perform well in the classroom. While negative peer pressure tends to diminish African American males' propensity to succeed academically, that influence can be reduced, if not entirely eliminated, by verbally and materially rewarding academic achievement in the same way that society acknowledges and even extols athletic performance. When we publicly recognize the successful academic experiences of young African American men, we simultaneously raise their self-concept, self-esteem, and academic confidence. Negative peer pressure, specifically the invective that African American students are "acting White" if they strive to achieve academically (Fordham & Ogbu, 1986), is a major deterrent to many non-White students' school performance. External influences that affect children's dispositions toward learning must be addressed by schools and teachers so that students who do perform at or above average are not ostracized, ridiculed, intimidated, physically assaulted, or belittled by their peers. More must be done by parents, communities, the media, and educators to minimize the social and psychological stresses that academically talented African American students must confront on a daily basis.

Teachers have a pivotal role to play in reversing the negative academic and social behaviors of African American males; but they, too, are susceptible to internalizing and projecting the negative stereotypes and myths that are unfairly used to describe African American males as a monolithic group with little hope of surviving and being successful. Teachers who ascribe to such beliefs, therefore, must change their subjective attitudes about Black boys' ability to succeed. The fact that many African American males do succeed in schools makes this issue even more important. Teachers who hold negative perceptions can inadvertently "turn off" Black male students who have high abilities, positive self-concepts, and outstanding personal expectations, and who set achievable aspirations. Teachers, therefore, must challenge these young men intellectually and, when possible, provide them with immediate, continuous, and appropriate reinforcement as well as positive feedback for their academic accomplishments. Their encouragement can significantly enhance for all students the importance and value of education for long-term financial and personal success, but especially so for Black male youths.

Recognizing that teachers alone cannot be expected to raise the achievement and aspirations of African American male children, the parents of these young men must motivate, encourage and reinforce their sons so that they will use their talents and ability to perform successfully in the classroom. Parents must acknowledge and/or reward their sons' academic accomplishments; they must require that they do homework; they must emphasize the value of learning; and they must meet and consult with their sons' teachers to find out how they are performing in school and to be apprised of areas in which their sons need assistance. Even more importantly, parents of African American boys must monitor the courses their sons are taking and support their aspirations to go to college in the same way they encourage their female children.

Many parents, however, especially those who themselves have little education, will need help from schools, teachers, and the community to accomplish the above recommendations. Just as some students are ostracized for doing well in school by their peers, so, too, are some parents intimidated by teachers for asking questions about their sons' performance and/or behavior in the classroom. Teachers, therefore, must be taught during their undergraduate training or in staff development sessions how to communicate with these parents. For example, they should be instructed how to convey to them, *in layman's language,* the results of children's performance on standardized tests. Teacher candidates should also learn what kinds of helpful suggestions they can give to these parents to enhance their sons' academic performance or participation in school activities.

Teachers must make a serious effort to tell parents about their children's academic strengths as well as weaknesses. Such balanced evaluations give teachers the opportunity to suggest to parents ways in which their sons might develop better study skills and be more constructive in their uses of time after school. Emphasizing these children's positive characteristics, even when their abilities are below average, is a very constructive way of demonstrating to parents their role in encouraging, assisting, and monitoring more closely the academic performance of their sons (Garibaldi, 1992). The apparent perception gap that exists about Black male students' abilities among teachers, parents, and students must be reduced, and this can only be achieved through more cooperation, communication, and understanding among all three groups.

While it is not possible here to list all the more than 50 recommendations from the New Orleans Public Schools study, below are a few which the committee proposed as well as some of the suggestions obtained from citizens who testified at the public hearings. These suggestions are not listed in any order of priority but are merely illustrative of the range of strategies recommended for teachers, students, parents, the general public, and the business community. Again, they are beneficial for all youth, but special attention is given to the educational needs of African American males:

1. African American male students should be taught values, etiquette, and morality at school and in the home. They should also be taught why they should resist peer pressure and why success in school must be reinforced.

2. African American male students should be strongly encouraged to participate in more extracurricular activities that are related to academics and leadership (such as academic clubs, yearbook staffs, debate teams, student councils, safety patrols, and so forth) and not just athletics.

3. African American male students who perform well in school should also receive recognition and tangible rewards (e.g., letter jackets, sweaters, etc.) comparable to that given to athletes and band/chorus members.

4. African American male college students should perform community service at local elementary and secondary schools as tutors, teacher aides, speakers, or assistants to extracurricular sponsors. Their posi-

tive role modeling and mentoring can have a tremendous impact on young boys, both those who are succeeding as well as those who are not, and can further underscore for these youth the importance of doing well in the classroom.

5. Various segments of the community such as the media, businesspersons, religious leaders, public servants, senior citizens, retired professionals, skilled craftsmen, and members of social and civic organizations should also volunteer to assist schools on a regular and on-going basis as tutors, speakers, resource persons, and counselors. These individuals and groups can emphasize the importance of values, the work ethic, the appreciation of culture and the arts, and many other topics to which young African American males need to be exposed.

6. Teachers should strongly encourage their African American male students in the earliest grades to pursue college or postsecondary training. Visitations to colleges or vocational/trade schools, career day programs, and guest speakers representing white- and blue-collar careers are some examples of how Black male youth can be exposed to advanced educational and career opportunities.

7. More African American male elementary teachers and social workers should be hired and, where possible, assigned as counselors to elementary schools. A short-term strategy which might be utilized is the hiring and/or recruiting of African American males as teacher aides or volunteer aides in the lower grades. Peer counselors from junior and senior highs can benefit both younger as well as older African American male students.

8. Businesses should consider allowing release or compensatory time for their African American employees who are parents so they can attend schools for meetings and report card conferences. African American parents of elementary-age children should be allowed leave from their jobs to visit their children's schools at least one day during the school year.

9. Businesses might also provide rewards and incentives (e.g., summer jobs, tangible forms of recognition, etc.) to the children of their employees who maintain above-average grades, attend school daily, and participate in extracurricular activities. These kinds of reinforcement and rewards will not only help students to excel in school but they will also encourage parents to promote their children's education.

10. Teachers must help to show their African American male students the relevance and applicability of coursework to one's adult years by incorporating family living skills into social studies curricula, introducing family budgeting concepts into mathematics lessons, and emphasizing business and job-related communication and writing skills instruction into language arts and English classes.

The majority of the above recommendations are reasonable, realistic, and easy to implement. Moreover, little funding is necessary within schools and within school districts to employ many of the strategies suggested. However, these approaches can significantly boost the self-concept, self-esteem, and academic achievement of all school-aged youth and especially African American males. If we expect to substantially alleviate the adverse conditions faced by many Black males and improve their life chances, strong commitment and leadership are essential. We must begin by improving the educational performance and attainment of African American boys. When they succeed the educational performance of others will also be raised, and the adage, "a rising tide lifts all boats," will be realized.

REFERENCES

African American Male Task Force. (1990). *Educating African American males: A dream deferred.* Milwaukee, WI: Milwaukee Public Schools.

Carter, D., & Wilson, R. (1991). *Minorities in higher education: Ninth annual status report.* Washington, DC: American Council on Education.

Garibaldi, A. M. (1988). *Educating Black male youth: A moral and civic imperative.* New Orleans, LA: New Orleans Public Schools Committee to Study the Status of the Black Male Student.

Garibaldi, A. M. (1991). The educational experiences of Black males: The early years. *Challenge, 2,* 1.

Garibaldi, A. M. (In press). Preparing teachers for culturally diverse classrooms. In M. E. Dilworth (Ed.), *Restructuring schools, colleges and departments of education to accommodate diverse students in schools.* San Francisco: Jossey-Bass.

Fordham, S., & Ogbu, J. (1986). Black students' school success: Coping with the "burden of 'acting White.'" *The Urban Review, 18,* 176–206.

Simmons, W., & Grady, M. (1990). *Black male achievement: From peril to promise* (Report of the Superintendent's Advisory Committee on Black Male Achievement). Prince Georges County, MD: Prince Georges County Schools.

Winfield, L. F. (1988). *An investigation of characteristics of high versus low literacy proficient Black young adults* (Final report to the Rockefeller Foundation). Philadelphia, PA: Temple University, Center for Research in Human Development and Education.

Winfield, L. F., & Lee, V. E. (1990). *Gender differences in reading proficiency: Are they constant across racial groups?* Baltimore, MD: The Johns Hopkins University Center for Research on Effective Schooling for Disadvantaged Students.

Beginning Teachers and Classroom Management: Questions from Practice, Answers from Research

Edwin G. Ralph

Edwin G. Ralph teaches at the University of Saskatchewan, Saskatoon, Canada.

Wouldn't teaching be a wonderful career, if there were just no kids? This remark, overheard in a staffroom, reflects a recurring concern about classroom management reported by teachers at the middle years level — particularly by novices in the profession. The critical challenge is often how to deal effectively with pupils labelled as "difficult," "disruptive," or "disinterested" (Borich, 1992; Ralph, 1982).

Ryan (1992), for instance, refers to one recent survey which indicates that 83% of beginning teachers report problems with student discipline. Moreover, for the last 23 years, the annual Gallup/Phi Delta Kappa Poll of the U.S. public's views toward schooling has consistently shown that lack of pupil discipline, violence in schools, and substance abuse have been rated as the most serious problems in public schools (Elam, Rose, & Gallup, 1992).

The purpose of this article is to answer five critical questions concerning classroom management often posed by neophyte teachers. The responses to the questions form a set of useful principles supporting proactive classroom management that offers a practical framework for novice teachers to consider as they analyze and construct their own practices in the field. This framework is not intended to be a prescriptive list of routine procedures to master, but rather it is a description of research-based management practices that educators may add to their personal knowledge base. Effective teachers will reflect upon this knowledge base as they make decisions related to organizing students' learning activities for unique contexts (Darling-Hammond & Sclan, 1992).

In this discussion, the term *effective* when linked with *teaching, instruction,* or *management* is used interchangeably with other descriptors, such as: *good, veteran, experienced, successful, professional, competent, exemplary, sound, skillful, expert,* or *productive.* Some authors, however, distinguish among such adjectives when analyzing the concepts and skills involved (Brandt, 1986).

Critical questions and possible solutions

The five key questions in this review are addressed by means of a conceptual structure which analyzes classroom management according to two basic themes: (a) What do successful teachers do to initiate an effective management process? and (b) How do they maintain it? The question framework is shown in Figure 1.

How are classroom management and effective teaching related?

To ask "What is more important in teaching, classroom management or instructional skill?" is really a non-question, because both elements are closely integrated within teaching practice (Doyle, 1986). However, for purposes of analysis and reflection, one could classify teachers' work into the two essential

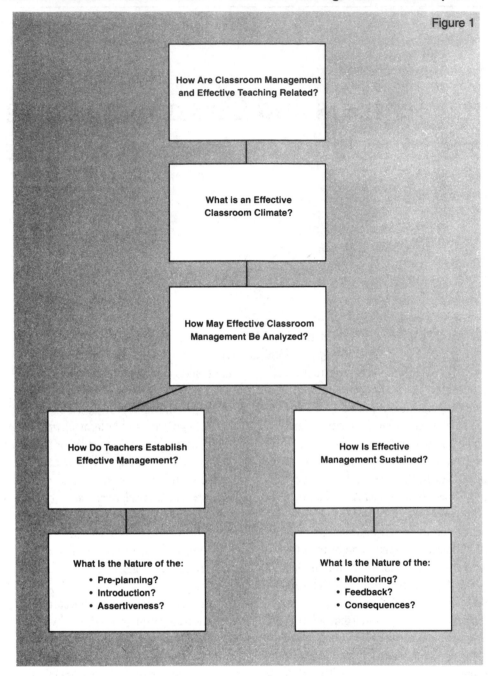

Figure 1

categories: management and instruction (Porter & Brophy, 1988). Although this discussion is limited to the former, it is obvious that teachers could not exercise good classroom management without demonstrating the following: (a) a sound grasp of their subject matter; (b) both generic and content specific pedagogical skills; and (c) competence in planning, preparing, and presenting clear and motivational learning experiences for pupils (Evertson & Harris, 1992; Nolan & Francis, 1992). Clearly, teach-

ers' use of effective instructional strategies will "prevent problems by maximizing student attention to and participation in the learning task" (McQueen, 1992, p. 197).

Because *effective teaching* has multiple definitions (Borich, 1992), the current literature conceptualizes it as a reflective orchestration and integration of a pluralism of teaching/learning activities into meaningful patterns for the purpose of meeting curricular goals (Good & Brophy, 1991). Based on this concept, proactive classroom management could be defined as a process of establishing and maintaining the conditions under which this effective teaching and learning will occur.

What is an effective classroom climate?

Before studying specific managerial aspects of successful teaching, one should note that the research indicates that the overall classroom socio-emotional climate created by effective teachers is one characterized as positive and productive (Cooper, 1982). Educational psychologists from every school of psychology agree that student morale, and often achievement level, increase when students feel accepted and respected by both the teacher and peers as being worthwhile, contributing members of the group (Watson, 1968). Expert teachers are able to vary their overall leadership style, according to the contextual situation, in order to create a friendly and business-like atmosphere (Callahan & Clark, 1988; McQueen, 1992). Hence, when middle year students possessing negative attitudes towards a course, or school in general, first enter into an effective teacher's class, they will encounter a psychosocial environment which seeks to meet their affiliation or belonging needs, despite what their previous record of low achievement and/or misbehavior may have been (Ralph, 1989).

Establishing this positive climate does not imply that teachers will be seen as "easy," "weak," or lacking authority, but it does mean that they will convey to students the perception that each person counts, and is welcome in the group (Ryan, 1992). This principle is the foundation upon which proactive management is built (Jacobsen, Eggen, & Kauchak, 1993).

How may effective classroom management be analyzed?

For analytical purposes, effective management can be categorized into two parts: what teachers do, initially, to establish basic classroom order, when they meet their students during the first day and the first week of classes, and subsequently, what is done to maintain that tone for the remainder of the school term (Figure 1).

How do teachers establish effective management?

The research demonstrates that, prior to and as soon as they meet a new group of students, experienced teachers plan and implement specific management principles by engaging in three basic processes, as shown on the left side of Figure 1 and as explained below (Doyle, 1987; Evertson, 1989). These three processes are: doing proactive pre-planning, using a deliberate introduction, and practising immediate assertiveness. These pre-planning phases form the heart of the proactive process.

Proactive pre-planning

Effective teachers reflect upon, anticipate and develop specific classroom rules (the stated expectations of student conduct) and procedures (the specific activities designed to implement the rules), prior to meeting a new class. These pre-established rules tend to have certain characteristics: they are few in number, they are stated in specific rather than general terms, and they describe the desired rather than the undesirable student behavior (University of Saskatchewan, 1992).

Deliberate introduction

During their first few meetings with new classes, professional teachers not only clearly explain the rules and procedures but they are as consistent as possible in enforcing them. The term "consistent" in much of the research on effective teaching means that exemplary teachers are able to make reliable judgments about the probable consequences of students' actions in specific situations. It does not mean that teachers always behave in a rigidly prescribed manner (Brandt, 1986; Doyle, 1986).

Furthermore, good teachers ensure that the rules and procedures are implemented in a rational and just fashion, realizing that exceptions invariably arise. During this initial phase, if an occasional student does not comply with a rule, the emphasis by the teacher seems to be reflected by the cliche, "Children are children," rather than, "They are bad." Students may forget. Thus, competent teachers reteach, review and/or rehearse the rules as required—just as explicitly as they would reteach a concept in the content area in an objective, pleasant and clear manner (Ralph, 1989).

Also, during this "break-in" period, effective teachers consistently follow up the presentation of the rules with feedback to students reinforcing students for following procedures but correcting them for non-compliance. The key factor here is that good teachers conscientiously monitor the entire learning milieu, and that they promptly deal with both appropriate and inappropriate student conduct in a straightforward yet firm manner (Calahan & Clark, 1988; McQueen, 1992).

Immediate assertiveness

Effective teachers work at establishing their authority with a new class from the very first meeting by implementing specific managerial activities (Hawkins, Doueck, & Lishner, 1988). The teachers display an assertive manner, projecting an "in charge," yet approachable, attitude towards students. For example, they commonly speak with the "I mean it" tone of voice, when required to make management statements; and after issuing such a directive, they hold eye-contact with students until the latter comply. They also routinely employ conviction and enthusiasm—conveying a feeling among students that the activity in which they are engaged is important. To further assist in establishing their authority early, successful teachers typically do not begin (or continue) conducting, or giving instructions for a learning activity until they have the attention of all students. The research has shown, in fact, that a "benevolent dictator" leadership style, rather than either a democratic or a permissive one, seems more effective in managing a new group of students, or if one "inherits a bad class" from the previous year (McCandless, 1967). Being democratic too early, with some groups, may convey a signal that the teacher is indecisive or "easy" (Jacobsen, Eggen, & Kauchak, 1993).

If an occasional student decides deliberately to challenge the teacher's authority, the expert practitioner establishes and enforces specific negative consequences for student non-compliance (Emmer, Evertson, Sanford, Clements, & Worsham, 1989)—a consequence being defined as a natural, logical extension resulting from a student's willful violation of a classroom rule. Skillful teachers, however, often defuse a potential discipline problem before it can develop into a major confrontation, and this ability is central to pro-active management (Ralph, 1982, 1989).

How is effective classroom management sustained?

Once effective middle years teachers have established the positive, productive tone for an orderly learning environment, they are consistent about maintaining it for the balance of the school term. Some of these maintenance strategies are described below.

Continual monitoring

Experienced teachers, realizing that classroom rules have exceptions, assess the effect of the procedures periodically (Hollingsworth & Hoover, 1991). It is better not to state a rule, if one does not monitor students' compliance with it. Perhaps students begin to violate a rule because it may not in fact be reasonable and/or fair, or perhaps the teacher simply does not feel strongly enough about its importance in order to consistently enforce it; or perhaps he/she is not monitoring student conduct carefully enough, and students consequently believe that the teacher is showing partiality. In these cases, exemplary teachers generally make one of three choices. They: (a) reteach/review/rehearse the rule with students in an objective, courteous manner; (b) modify the original rule; or (c) remove it completely. Students tend to respond positively to the teacher's frankness and fairness in this process, and it is at this juncture that a more democratic approach to classroom management may be implemented (McDaniel, 1986).

Consistent feedback

Successful teachers are consistent and patient in using positive reinforcement for student "approach behavior" (Borich, 1992), endeavouring to employ reinforcement which is immediate, specific and genuine.

Clearly describable student progress or positive attitude is reinforced: rewards are earned by students. However, if the reward is perceived by students as being superficial then the teacher may be viewed as being weak or insincere. Furthermore, experienced teachers avoid neutral responses when giving meaningful reinforcement to students. For instance, a teacher's overuse of certain words or actions, such as "good," "okay" or "right" will eventually lose the intended motivational impact on students. Rather, experienced teachers use a variety of positive reinforcers: assorted positive statements, nods, smiles, gestures, movements, or extrinsic rewards/activities, appropriate to age and grade, which students merit by their conduct and/or performance (University of Saskatchewan, 1992).

With respect to maintaining a consistency of consequences, effective teachers administer a specific consequence for student misbehavior in a matter-of-fact, simple manner: "If A, then B." The consequence will have been clearly described for all students beforehand, and it will be enforced in a non-threatening, impartial way (Eby, 1992).

Specific consequences

Effective teachers have their share of student discipline problems; however, they deal with them specifically and consistently (Doyle, 1986): they tend not to neglect, ignore or "miss" an infringement of a rule. They are characterized by a high degree of withitness, an awareness of all of the happenings in the classroom (Bellon, Bellon, & Blank, 1992). Competent teachers demonstrate withitness by glancing periodically around the classroom while helping an individual or small group; moving casually throughout the room while teaching and assisting, rather than sitting in one place; monitoring individual seatwork; or standing sideways (rather than with one's back toward the class) while writing at the chalkboard. Competent teachers maintain this alertness in a manner which is not necessarily seen by students as negative, threatening, or suspicious (Ralph, 1989).

Moreover, exemplary teachers make firm, consistent management statements as needed assertively, but not unpleasantly. Above all, experienced teachers tend to possess an overall calmness and composure in the face of trying management situations. Overly emotional, intimidating or sarcastic comments to or about students are rare (Good & Brophy, 1991).

Conclusion

A surprising research finding recently reported by Evertson and Harris (1992) and Weade and Evertson (1988) was that some classrooms had the air of effective organization and the indication of student engagement, but did not produce correspondingly high levels of academic achievement or student learning. Thus, good management, alone, is insufficient: it is not a substitute for motivational instruction.

In summary, classroom management is a means to an end: it is meant to establish and support successful teaching and learning. The goal is what Good and Brophy (1991, p. 295) call "proactive problem prevention." If beginning middle years teachers are able to implement reflectively the above management strategies during the initial meeting(s) with their classes and also to maintain these activities throughout the term, then one could reasonably assume that: (a) the problem of dealing with uncooperative learners would be reduced considerably, and (b) the classroom climate would be conducive to learning by *all* students and teachers—in a variety of contexts.

Note: Portions of this article appeared in an earlier draft by Ralph in the Canadian Modern Language Review, 46 (1), 135-146.

References

Bellon, J., Bellon, E., & Blank, M. (1992). *Teaching from a research knowledge base: A development and renewal process.* New York: Merrill.

Borich, G. D. (1992). *Effective teaching methods* (2nd ed.). New York: Merrill.

Brandt, R. (1986). On the expert teacher: A conversation with David Berliner. *Educational Leadership* 44(2), 4-9.

Callahan, J. F., & Clark, L. H. (1988). *Teaching in the middle and secondary schools: Planning for competence* (3rd ed.). New York: Macmillan.

Cooper, J.M. (Ed.). (1982). *Classroom teaching skills* (2nd ed.). Toronto: Heath.

Darling-Hammond, L., & Sclan, E. (1992). Policy and supervision. In C. Glickman (Ed.), *Supervision in transition* (pp. 7-29). Alexandria, VA: Association for Supervision and Curriculum Development.

Doyle, W. (1987). Research on teaching effects as a resource for improving instruction. In M. Wideen & I. Andrews (Eds.), *Staff development for school improvement: A focus on the teachers* (pp. 91-102). New York: Falmer.

Doyle, W. (1986). Classroom organization and management. In M.C. Wittrock (Ed.), *Handbook of research on teaching* (pp. 392-431). New York: Macmillan.

Eby, J. W. (1992). *Reflective planning, teaching, and evaluation for the elementary school.* New York: Merrill.

Elam, S., Rose, L., & Gallup, A. (1992). The 24th annual Gallup/Phi Delta Kappa poll of the public's attitudes toward the public schools. *Phi Delta Kappan, 74,* 41-53.

Emmer, E., Evertson, C., Sanford, J., Clements, B., & Worsham, M. (1989). *Classroom management for secondary teachers.* Englewood Cliffs, NJ: Prentice Hall.

Evertson, C. (1989). Improving classroom management: A school-based program for beginning the year. *Journal of Educational Research, 83*(2), 82-90.

Everston, C., & Harris, A. (1992). What we know about managing classrooms. *Educational Leadership, 49*(7), 74-78.

Good, T. L., & Brophy, J. (1991). *Looking in classrooms* (5th ed.). New York: Harper Collins.

Harless, J., & Linesberry, C., Jr. (1971). *Turning kids on and off.* Springfield, VA: Guild V.

Hawkins, D. J., Doueck, H. J., & Lishner, D. M. (1988). Changing teaching practices in mainstream classrooms to improve bonding and behavior of low achievers. *American Educational Research Journal* 25(1), 31-50.

Hollingsworth, P., & Hoover, K. (1991). *Elementary teaching methods* (4th ed.). Boston: Allyn and Bacon.

Jacobsen, D., Eggen, P., & Kauchak, D. (1993). *Methods for Teaching: A skills approach* (4th ed.). New York: Merrill.

McCandless, B.R. (1967). *Children: Behavior and development.* New York: Holt, Rinehart and Winston.

McDaniel, T. (1986). A primer on classroom discipline: Principles old and new. *Phi Delta Kappan, 68*(1),63-66.

McQueen, T. (1992). *Essentials of classroom management and discipline.* New York: Harper Collins.

Nolan, J., & Francis, P. (1992). Changing perspectives in curriculum and instruction. In C. Glickman (Ed.), *Supervision in transition* (pp. 44-60). Alexandria, VA: Association for Supervision and Curriculum Development.

Porter, A. C., & Brophy, J. (1988). Synthesis of research on good teaching: Insights from the work of the Institute for Research on Teaching. *Educational Leadership 45*(8), 74-83.

Ralph, E.G. (1989). Research on effective teaching: How can it help L2 teachers motivate the unmotivated learner? *The Canadian Modern Language Review, 46* (2), 135-146.

Ralph, E.G. (1982). The unmotivated second-language learner: Can students' negative attitudes be changed? *The Canadian Modern Language Review, 38,* 493-502.

Ryan, K (Ed.). (1992). *The roller coaster year.* New York: Harper Collins.

University of Saskatchewan. (1992). *The internship manual.* Saskatoon: College of Education, Center for School-Based Programs.

Weade, R., & Evertson, R. (1988). The construction of lessons in effective and less effective classrooms. *Teaching and Teacher Education 4,* 189-213.

Rule-Creating in a Constructivist Classroom Community

Kathryn Castle and Karen Rogers

Kathryn Castle is Professor, Department of Curriculum and Instruction, College of Education, Oklahoma State University, Stillwater. Karen Rogers is a classroom teacher, Orvis Risner Elementary School, Edmond, Oklahoma.

Challenging children to think about the rules that should govern the social life of the classroom is a basic way to stimulate their construction of moral knowledge. (DeVries & Kohlberg, 1987, p. 158)

Constructivist classrooms may do a better job promoting children's social, cognitive and moral development than do more teacher-centered programs (DeVries, Reese-Learned & Morgan, 1991; Kamii & Joseph, 1989). Constructivist classrooms, which focus on reasoning rather than recitation, give children greater opportunities to choose and experiment. Constructivist teachers develop reciprocal relationships with children, express understanding of children's feelings and de-

---

Constructivist classrooms. . . give children greater opportunities to choose and experiment.

---

sires, communicate ideals of fairness, emphasize logical consequences rather than punishment, and encourage children to develop

their own solutions to interpersonal problems through peer negotiations (DeVries et al., 1991). DeVries et al. (1991) report that children in constructivist classrooms view themselves as creators of classroom rules. The children give broad reasons for the rules, including consideration of natural or logical consequences, respect for others' feelings, preservation of friendships and general respect for rules.

Children in constructivist classrooms actively engage in knowledge construction, including constructing knowledge of rules and their importance in a classroom community. Constructivist teachers who foster autonomy, or self-governance, involve children in rule-creating discussions. The children share their perspectives about rules in general as they negotiate their own classroom rules. Such discussions promote advances in children's moral reasoning: "Prosocial behavior (rule making, group problem solving, co-operative work or play) leads to advances in social-moral reasoning, which in turn provides better reasons for engaging in social behavior" (Kohlberg & Lickona, 1987, p. 164).

When children create rules, as they do when they invent their own games, they feel they are playing an important role in the democratic process (Castle & Wilson,

1992). They are more likely to want to create rules that peers will view as helpful and fair to all. Rule discussions provide opportunities for children to debate the fairness of rules within the meaningful context of the classroom community. Teachers can guide these discussions without imposing adult authority. Giving children choices for establishing their own classroom rules promotes their autonomy and

---

"When children are allowed to make decisions, they often make the same rules that adults would make . . ."

---

ability to make decisions: "When children are allowed to make decisions, they often make the same rules that adults would make; however, they respect the rules that they themselves make much more than the same rules imposed by adults" (Kamii & Joseph, 1989, p. 51-52).

What Children Gain from Creating Their Own Rules
Engaging children in classroom discussions on creating rules leads to:

From *Childhood Education*, Winter 1993/94, pp. 77-80. Reprinted by permission of the authors and the Association for Childhood Education International, 11501 Georgia Avenue, Suite 315, Wheaton, MD. © 1994 by the Association.

- *Active Involvement.* Children are actively thinking and expressing their ideas to others. They compare their ideas to others' ideas.
- *Reflection.* Children reflect on their own experiences with rules and rule infractions. They share examples that have personal meaning.
- *Meaningful Connections.* As children relate one rule to another, combine rules, delete rules, and think of better overarching rules, they are connecting how one behavior relates to another.
- *Respect for Rules.* Children are more likely to respect the rules because they understand why rules are important to them personally.
- *Sense of Community.* When children discuss rules, they see the need for helping one another and working together. They develop a sense of unity as a class with mutual interests and goals.
- *Problem Solving Through Negotiation.* Debating and sharing ideas allow children to find areas of mutual agreement.
- *Cooperation.* Children who discuss the relevance of rules and question each other's thinking are more likely to engage in cooperation as they understand the need to take the other's point of view.
- *Inductive Thinking.* Moving from specific rules to general principles facilitates inductive thinking and searching for broader issues.
- *Ownership.* Children have a sense of rule ownership and are more likely to view the classroom as belonging to them. As they experience ownership, their sense of responsibility to themselves and to others grows.

Classroom Anecdote of Rule Creation

A sense of classroom community—that we are all in this together and will help one another—can be achieved early in the school year by engaging children in thinking about, discussing and agreeing on a set of classroom rules. The following narrative of an actual classroom brainstorming session illustrates the level of meaningful involvement that can be achieved when children are given a chance to establish their own classroom rules. The teacher's purpose is to give each child control of his/her behavior.

The one-hour session occurred on the second day of school in a 3rd-grade classroom of a metropolitan elementary school com-

---

*T*he teacher's purpose is to give each child control of his/her behavior.

---

posed of children from a variety of socioeconomic, ethnic and racial backgrounds. Karen Rogers, the teacher, covered the school-wide rules on the first day. She began the discussion on the second day by reviewing the school rules and asking children to come up with some rules that would be good for their specific classroom and for times when they would work in teams with the younger children in 1st and 2nd grades.

Active Involvement and Reflection. The 3rd-graders immediately became actively engaged in the discussion. Rogers wrote the rules on the board as children offered them. She did not rush through the discussion, but rather continued as long as the children remained interested. They discussed specific examples of rules and related them to situations that the children and teacher could remember. As each rule was written, the children would recall an incident in which that rule was broken and resulted in an injury to a child or to someone's property. The teacher also contributed examples of playground or classroom incidents that reinforced the value of the rule under discussion. By recalling and relating previous experiences, children see the purpose for a certain rule and can give reasons why it is a good rule. In this way, the rule discussion occurred within a personally meaningful context.

Meaningful Connections. The group also discussed the idea that some rule infractions were accidental or nonintentional, but nevertheless resulted in hurting someone or in property destruction. The children discussed the difference between intentional and accidental rule infractions. Children commented that accidental rule infractions can teach one to be more careful in the future and thus more considerate of others. Another idea that emerged was the importance of restitution and repair of damage as a way of correcting the behavior in question. Children agreed that restitution would help make things right with the offended child. Such reasoning reflects an advance from a lower stage concern with material damage to a higher level concern with consideration of intention and restitution (DeVries & Kohlberg, 1987; Piaget 1965).

Respect for Rules. The discussion was lengthy and allowed time for children to remember incidents, reflect on reasons why certain rules were necessary, and make meaningful connections between rules and behaviors. Extended time spent thinking and discussing will actually save time in the long run. Children who have had time to reflect on and debate about rules are more likely to remember the rules and understand their importance, thus preventing problems from occurring in the first place. Also, time spent early in the school year on rule discussions helps create an atmosphere of classroom community in which children feel free to express their ideas and debate important issues without fearing their ideas will be rejected or ridiculed. Children learn that helping others and being helped by others result in a more pleasant and interesting learning experience. The rule discussion in Rogers' class resulted in 27 child-created rules (see Figure 1).

Sense of Community. Before the last two rules were written, one child said there were too many rules. But two children were eager

---

Figure 1
- No Tipping Chairs
- Don't Misuse Animals (classroom pets)
- Treat Books Nicely
- Ask Teacher for Author-Signed Books
- Don't Mark in Books
- Be Quiet When Someone Is Talking
- Don't Draw on Chalkboard
- Don't Open the Door (backdoor to playground)
- Leave Stuff Alone During Team Time
- Don't Go Crazy When Firebell Rings
- Be Kind
- Keep Classroom Clean
- Don't Throw Things Across Room
- Don't Shout
- Don't Take Animals out of Cages
- Do What Teacher Asks
- Raise Your Hand To Talk
- Don't Mess with Others' Stuff
- Don't Chew Gum
- Don't Talk When People are Working and Listening
- Don't Hog Stuff
- Don't Take Others' Stuff out of Room
- Always Apologize for Accidents
- Help Other People
- Don't Fight
- Don't Take Community Stuff off Teacher's Desk
- Don't Mess with Calendar Stuff

---

to add the last two rules. The teacher allowed the brainstorming session to last long enough so that everyone had a chance to participate. Finally, the class voted on whether the list was sufficient. Through voting, children learn what it means to participate in a democratic process (DeVries & Kohlberg, 1987). They are also more likely to view themselves as contributors to the classroom community. The large number of rules may indicate that the children were attempting to cover every specific situation that came to mind. The majority of the rules were stated in negative terms—possibly due to children's previous experiences with adult restrictions and also because it is easier for children to state rules negatively than positively (DeVries & Kohlberg, 1987).

Problem Solving Through Negotiation. The second, less lengthy, part of the rule discussion involved reflecting on the list of rules and deciding which ones might be combined. The children began to think how one rule related to another; for example, how "Don't Take Others' Stuff out of Room" was related to "Don't Mess with Others' Stuff" and how "Don't Take Animals out of Cages" was related to "Don't Misuse Animals." Whenever a child had an idea of how one rule was related to another, the class discussed it and decided either to erase a rule or come up with a better rule that would cover both situations. Children openly showed excitement when they made a relevant connection.

Cooperation. During the discussion, Rogers asked the children to reconsider the rule "Do What Teacher Asks" because everyone is a teacher in her classroom. The class agreed this rule was unnecessary. Rogers' goal was to foster autonomy and the idea that each person is responsible for his/her behavior. If everyone learns, teaches and cooperates, everyone benefits.

"Democratizing the early childhood classroom does not mean less leadership or authority on the part of the teacher, but a different kind" (Kohlberg & Lickona, 1987, p. 161). When teachers reduce their adult authority and engage in reciprocity, children are allowed to become more independent learners and as-

> *When teachers reduce their adult authority . . . children are allowed to become more independent learners . . .*

sume responsibility for their own actions. Children in this environment will learn they are important and respected. They become capable decision-makers who know how to help one another and understand the importance of cooperation.

Inductive Thinking. As the children discussed the relationship of one rule to another, the idea of a general principle or overarching rule began to emerge. Children began to discuss how a more general rule could take the place of several specific ones. When thinking about how the rule "Don't Go Crazy When Firebell Rings" was related to "Be Kind," one child excitedly exclaimed, "The rule 'Be a Good Role Model' could take the place of all the rules!" The class agreed and decided to use this overarching rule to replace several others. Rogers related a personal example of a 3rd-grade child who taught her, through his example, to be a better listener. She emphasized that children could be good role models not only for each other, but also for adults.

The idea of an overarching rule or guiding principle represents an advance in reasoning from specific to classifying similar specific cases into one category—reasoning from the specific case to the general (Piaget, 1966). Younger children, for example 1st-graders, do not typically engage in this level of inductive thinking about rules. They will end their rule discussion content with a long list of rules to cover every situation they have discussed. Older children, as these 3rd-graders did, will search for a few good overarching rules that are not so situation-specific.

As the discussion continued, more rules were erased until only a few remained. Two children said

> *When children are always told exactly what to do . . . they are less likely to think for themselves.*

too many rules had been erased. After three more rules were erased, one child asked Rogers to please stop erasing. Rogers emphasized the importance of narrowing the list to a few good rules. This child's concern shows that some children feel a need for many rules that specify behaviors for every situation. When children are always told exactly what to do, however, they are less likely to think for themselves. In this example, the children were encouraged to think of how specific behaviors are connected by a unifying category or rule. Classrooms that foster autonomy help children to make better choices and to feel in control and responsible for their own behavior. They are not dependent upon a teacher to tell them what they should do.

At one point in the discussion, Rogers asked that the rule "Ask

Teacher for Author-Signed Books" be erased because it was a rule that had importance only for her. She explained her feelings about books and gave reasons why the books in her classroom were so important: she paid for them herself, many were signed by the authors, she loves books and she has read each of them. Although the class erased this rule, the children nevertheless ask her for the author-signed books. Because Rogers openly shared her feelings and honestly expressed what the books meant to her, the children follow the unwritten rule out of respect for their teacher. Children are more likely to show respect to teachers who treat them respectfully.

Four rules remained at the end of the discussion. The class then debated their order of importance and finally agreed upon the following:

1. Be Kind
2. Be a Good Role Model
3. No Tipping in Chairs
4. Don't Open the Door (backdoor to playground).

Rules 1 and 2 were the overarching rules that replaced all but rules 3 and 4. The class decided they really needed rules 3 and 4 and neither fit under the first two rules. The children also discussed their role in reminding the younger children who would be coming to their class during Team Time about the class rules.
Ownership. When the classroom discussion on rules ended, all agreed that they had established a very workable set of classroom rules. Teacher and children made a commitment to be good role models. The children's ideas had been accepted and respected.

During the course of the year, very few instances of rule infractions occurred. When they did, one

child would remind the offending child of the rule and point out how it was being broken. Rogers and the class role-played unkind behaviors and alternative behaviors that foster good will. When asked about classroom rules, the children indicated that rules were not a concern. They felt an ownership of the rules.

Conclusion
Creating classroom rules together can be a very meaningful learning experience for children and teachers and can help establish a positive sense of classroom community. Teachers who commit time and effort to the process have found it benefits children's relationships and increases understanding of what it means to participate as a constructive member of a classroom community.

References
Castle, K., & Wilson, E. (1992). Creativity is alive in outdoor play! *Dimensions, 20*(4), 11-39.
DeVries, R., & Kohlberg, L. (1987). *Programs of early education.* New York: Longman.
DeVries, R., Reese-Learned, H., & Morgan, P. (1991). Sociomoral development in direct-instruction, eclectic, and constructivist kindergartens: A study of children's enacted interpersonal understandings. *Early Childhood Research Quarterly, 6*(4), 473-511.
Kamii, C., & Joseph, L. (1989). *Young children continue to reinvent arithmetic, 2nd grade.* New York: Teachers College Press.
Kohlberg, L., & Lickona, T. (1987). Moral discussion and the class meeting. In R. DeVries & L. Kohlberg (Eds.), *Programs of early education* (pp. 143-181). New York: Longman.
Piaget, J. (1965). *The moral judgment of the child.* New York: Free Press.
Piaget, J. (1966). *Psychology of intelligence.* Totowa, NJ: Littlefield, Adams.

SELF-DISCIPLINE

HELPING STUDENTS DEVELOP

Wanda Lincoln

Wanda Lincoln is an education consultant and author with more than 20 years' experience as a classroom teacher. Her book, *Write Through the Year* (Monday Morning Books, 1992), combines classroom management and writing and is available from Evan-Moor, 18 Lower Ragsdale, Monterey, CA 93940.

IDEALLY, CLASSROOM DISCIPLINE should be based on *student* self-discipline. Helping your students learn to take responsibility for their own actions and monitor their own behavior now will give them the skills they'll need later to become responsible, reasonable adults. And this approach to classroom management will help you create a nurturing, cooperative environment. Here are some ways to get started.

Make fundamental decisions
First of all, you've got to make some decisions about your teaching style. You can't teach self-discipline part of the day, then at other times take an authoritarian or permissive stance. External methods of control don't teach self-discipline. You have to make teaching self-discipline a full-time commitment.

You also have to make a firm decision not to dole out rewards and punishments. These external factors won't help your students learn the key principle of self-discipline: Life is a do-it-yourself

project. Rather than emphasizing stickers, food, or threats of missed recess, help students focus on their own positive behavior and good decisions. Another problem with rewards is that your students soon start expecting them, so the rewards lose their value and no longer work to control behavior unless they're enhanced. For example, 5 minutes of extra recess today will have to become 10 minutes within a few weeks.

You'll need to learn the language of self-discipline. For example, the next time you observe a student clowning around when he should be working, don't lecture him about how to act. Calmly ask him, "What are you doing right now?" (You'll find that some students will have to stop and think about it.) Then ask, "And what do you think you should be doing?" He'll have to think about the appropriate behavior, then tell you what it is. You haven't told the student what he should be doing—he's figured it out for himself.

**Have students
help set the guidelines**
Every classroom needs limits that establish clear behavioral guidelines. Having your students

help you establish the guidelines encourages them to make a commitment to following them, which develops self-discipline.

One strategy for coming up with class guidelines is to hold a Classroom Constitutional Convention to create a document that encourages learning. Your students are the convention delegates and you are the chairperson. Start the discussion by asking students, "How do you like to be treated in school?" and "What helps you to learn the most?" List students' answers and then work together to compile an official class constitution. Here's how one 4th-grade class began their document: *We, the members of room 131, in order to learn a lot and get along better, have written the following rules for living together.*
● *Treat everyone as you want to be treated.*
● *Share what you know with others in the room. Share what you have too.*

All of your students (and you) should sign the class constitution, making it official.

To reinforce the principles outlined in their constitution, test delegates' knowledge of it. Create a set of cards describing typical classroom situations that have the potential to lead to problems or conflicts. Some possible examples:

● A classmate asks to use your new markers.

● A classmate sitting next to you keeps humming while you're trying to work.

● You haven't done your homework and class is ready to start.

● Your classmate is being bossy and won't let anyone else in your group talk.

Have small groups of students discuss possible reactions to the situations and then role-play one for the class. Have the other students point out which parts of the constitution are being implemented or violated. Then encourage them to suggest alternative reactions.

Another way to help students identify appropriate behaviors is to have each draw another student's name and secretly watch that student throughout the day, noting when the student acts in accord with the class constitution. At the end of the day, hold an "I noticed" session during which each student states something positive about the watched student's behavior. Later, when students are more familiar with the constitution, have them monitor and chart their own positive behavior.

Teach a problem-solving process
Problems are bound to occur. And when they do, approach the students involved with empathy. Let them know that, like every problem, this one has a solution. You and they just need to find it. Start the discussion with such phrases as "This situation seems to have made you angry" or "You look upset. Take a deep breath before we begin." Then go through a step-by-step problem-solving process with the children. (See box this page.) As your students practice it, they'll be able to internalize the

steps and eventually follow them without adult guidance.

If the students are too upset to make sense out of their feelings, try having them write about the problem. This will help make the facts clearer and lead them to solutions. (You could even create a form for students to complete as a starting point.)

Encourage "I" statements
Explain to your students that the words they choose when discussing a problem can make a big difference in working it out. Instead of starting a statement with "You," suggest they start with "I." Give an example to show how a "you" statement is frequently followed by anger and blame and doesn't include suggestions for correcting the problem: "You took my book!" But an "I" statement can encourage communication to help students work out a solution: "I left my book on my desk and now it's gone." An "I" statement may lead to a way to find the book.

Use a goal sheet
Some classroom problems take more time to solve than others. For those situations, have the student choose an achievable goal and design steps for reaching it. One 3rd-grade girl developed the following steps for making a new friend:

● *Find someone interested in Roald Dahl and ice skating.*
● *Smile more.*
● *Help classmates with their reading without being bossy.*
● *Never hit classmates as a way of getting their attention.*

Once the goal sheet is done, it's the student's responsibility to gauge progress. Your job is to encourage the student to keep working toward the goal. Ask, "Have you found anyone interested in Roald Dahl?" If the child doesn't reach the goal, you can help modify the goal sheet for another try.

Six Steps for Solving a Problem
1. Describe (or have the student describe) the problem behavior. Examine why this behavior isn't acceptable according to the class guidelines.
2. Together write a list of acceptable behavioral choices.
3. Help the student evaluate the consequences of each choice.
4. Have the student choose one option.
5. As the student goes off to try the option, be encouraging. Shake hands and say, "I have faith in you!"
6. If the problem recurs, repeat the process. Remind the student that making a mistake in behavior is no different from making a mistake in math. Sometimes what's required is practice, practice, practice!

Involve students in class meetings
Class meetings give students a chance to exercise their rights as group members. Students learn the value of their input, the art of compromise, and the ability to communicate their ideas calmly and persuasively. Encourage each student to participate in the meeting.

Meetings can focus on group problem solving, planning a special activity, or discussing a recent event. Have a sign-up board where students can suggest topics they'd like to cover. This gives them practice in raising issues and presenting them at a meeting. Model leadership at the first meeting yourself, asking students to pay attention to what makes an effective leader.

Afterward, discuss with your students what an effective leader does during a class meeting and make a list. A 5th-grade class's list included:
● *Stand in front of the class.*
● *Appoint someone to record important information.*
● *Keep the conversation moving.*
● *Let everyone have a chance to talk.*

● *Guide the group in coming to a decision.*

● *Have the recorder review the meeting.*

Once students are ready, you can draw names or set up another system for deciding when each student will have a chance to lead a meeting.

Have students evaluate themselves

Self-evaluations give students the chance to practice judging their own progress and success. The experience encourages students to understand and question themselves and practice making accurate judgments.

Get your students focused on self-evaluation by asking them to complete a sentence stem several times a day. Try these:

● A question I have about this lesson is....

● The best thing about the day so far is....

● I've done quality work in....

● An important idea from our lesson is....

● Today I learned....

Allow time for students to think about how to complete the stem, either orally or in writing. Model the procedure yourself.

Each month have your students reflect on their work and behavior by filling out a self-evaluation form. To make the form, list not only curriculum areas but also other areas you want to emphasize, such as self-control. As a guided writing activity, help students write about their successes in each area and state what their goals are. Students can learn from your example if you fill out your own form, commenting on your teaching successes and goals.

Another way to encourage self-evaluation is to give students a

Self-Discipline Starts at Home

Let your students' parents know that you've made building self-discipline a priority and suggest things they can do at home to help. For example:

● Give children a family-oriented responsibility that they aren't paid for.

● Give children chances to make choices and take the consequences.

● Set clear, reasonable limits for children.

list of behaviors you want to encourage and have them rate themselves. Here's an example: Rate yourself at 1 (tops), 2 (most of the time), 3 (some slipups), or 4 (the pits) on how you think you're doing.

_____ I express ideas calmly.

_____ I've completed my work.

_____ I've been helpful to my classmates.

_____ I'm friendly to my classmates.

_____ I don't hit other people to solve problems.

_____ I'm willing to try new activities.

_____ I try to solve a learning problem myself before asking someone else.

_____ I help make sure everyone in my group has a turn.

Be part of the process

Developing self-discipline is an ongoing process that can't be completed in a single school year. But by forming a partnership with your students, you can get them started on the path to confidence and competence.

Effective Classroom Discipline: Advice for Educators

Top performing teachers understand and practice effective discipline. They search for what is "right" in a student's behavior, and build on that strength

Don Fuhr

Don Fuhr is professor, College of Education, Clemson University, Clemson, S.C.

There is growing concern that classroom behavior in public schools is out of hand. Parents insist that many teachers are losing or have already lost control of their classes. Teachers maintain that many parents have abdicated their parental role and are sending their discipline problems to school.

Even when schools assume such responsibilities, they often encounter criticism from the very persons who need to support their efforts: the parents. It is just as important for parents to support teachers as it is for teachers to help those parents who practice effective discipline in the home.

Discipline Is Not a Negative Term

The role of the teacher is to create a climate within the classroom that promotes learning. Sometimes this must be accomplished in the face of overwhelming odds.

Students prefer teachers who know how to properly administer discipline. Students want discipline. They expect it. When required discipline is not given, students will act out in a variety of ways: assuming the role of the attention-getter, refusing to follow directions, being chronically tardy or absent, or becoming involved with the "wrong" crowd.

Keep in mind that "discipline" is not necessarily a negative word, and does not always involve punishment. For example, the administering of classroom discipline can be determined by students to be either negative or positive, based on how it is presented. Properly administered discipline involves consistency and fairness.

To illustrate, recall your favorite teacher, the one who had your respect and admiration. I submit that your favorite teacher had the following professional attributes: He or she was an effective disciplinarian (consistent and fair), and . . .

- Was always prepared
- Cared for students
- Was an effective, motivating role model
- Was knowledgeable and enthusiastic
- Believed all students could be taught.

In addition, your favorite teacher no doubt knew when to act, how to act, and why. Effective classroom disciplinarians gain the respect of students, while ineffective classroom disciplinarians lose respect.

Students Desire Discipline

The need for properly administered discipline in our classrooms is manifested in misbehaving students who desire structure in their lives. The majority want to function in an environment of established principles and regulations so they know what is expected of them.

Such students routinely reach out for structure that can reveal to them the importance of managing time; structure that is aimed at making the distinction between right and wrong; and structure that supports the notion of persevering to achieve. Students desperately want someone in authority (whom they respect) to tell them where the boundaries are so they can function within the proper behavioral limits. They eventually come to understand there is freedom in knowing boundaries.

Unfortunately, the administering of effective discipline is ignored by many educators due to either a lack of training in effective classroom management practices, a lack of self-confidence, or a need to be "liked" rather than respected. Such positions can be supported by analyzing various data as to how students perceive classroom teaching.

I have discovered that the number one area of student concern is the need for better classroom control. Research studies consistently mention that student perceptions of classroom practices yield valid and reliable data. In other words, students consistently hit the mark with regard to a particular teacher's classroom strengths and weaknesses.

From *NASSP Bulletin*, January 1993, pp. 82-86. Reprinted with permission from the National Association of Secondary School Principals.

Even students who routinely disrupt class will cite the need for effective classroom management and control. Again, such information suggests that students not only need order and control in the classroom, they want it.

Top Performing Teachers

Top performing teachers understand and practice effective discipline. They know from experience and training the importance of the well-timed verbal reprimand. They know that establishing expectations and communicating them to all students early in the school year will provide the way for better classroom climate throughout the year, and that ignoring discipline problems will only cause things to become worse.

Top performing teachers fully understand that the majority of discipline problems occur in classrooms where there is inadequate advance planning and preparation. Effective teachers will tell you that failure to plan and prepare breeds classroom disruptions; that with constant disruptions a student's productive learning time is greatly diminished; and that opportunities for students to act out increase.

Top performing teachers also understand that discipline should not be something that is used to crush a student, but rather to motivate that student to avoid negative behavior. Such teachers rarely get involved in yelling, using sarcasm, or resorting to the use of corporal punishment. The emphasis is on searching for what is right and building on a student's strengths.

Whether it's using Discipline Program A or Discipline Program B, there are certain basic classroom management procedures that top performing teachers routinely follow in their teaching. They include:
• Telling students and parents what you expect and posting these expectations when classes first begin.
• Communicating the consequences for not doing what is expected.
• Carrying out the plan in a consistent manner within the classroom as well as throughout the school.
• Planning creative teaching lessons. (A teacher should always ask, "Would I want to be a student in my class?")
• Treating all students fairly and with a positive attitude.
• Constantly searching for the gifts and talents students possess by helping them develop their particular strengths, and encouraging and praising them when they succeed.
• Being a role model.
• Being devoted.

Combining the basics of effective classroom management with some humor will go a long way toward reducing classroom discipline problems. However, even top performing teachers will encounter classroom situations where immediate discipline is required.

Effective teachers don't allow things to get out of control. Many pride themselves on the fact they rarely send a student to the office, since they possess the confidence and capability to handle discipline cases themselves. When teaching is good, classroom behavior is good. When teaching is marginal, classroom behavior is marginal.

Effectively Administered Discipline

On the other hand, what often occurs in various classrooms is that teachers, especially those who are considered marginal, back away from correcting a student's inappropriate behavior. They fail to address the issue at hand because they are concerned that students won't like them, or because they dread confrontation. Some feel if the disruption is left alone it will go away.

Nothing could be further from the truth. As we know from psychology courses, if a person has a need for something, that person will use a variety of tactics and attention-getting patterns until the need is satisfied. Students who need attention will do anything for it, including misbehaving.

Catch such students doing something right, and give them the attention they want by rewarding their good behavior. Don't reward their bad behavior by focusing attention on it. The disruptions will continue until their need is met through effectively administered discipline.

The following story appeared in a recent newspaper: Three teenagers were picked up for shoplifting in a suburban midwestern town and driven to the local jail. When questioned, the youths admitted to a number of shoplifting incidents over a six-month period. All three were from well-to-do homes where money was not a problem. Puzzled by this, authorities called in a researcher to find out why they had become involved in this kind of behavior.

What the researcher found was interesting. The youths stated they did it because they knew eventually they would be caught, and thus cause their parents social embarrassment. They felt perhaps their parents would then start spending more time with them, and give them some attention. In addition, all three implied that they wanted their parents to hold them accountable and responsible for their behavior. In other words, these youths wanted some structure to be established in their lives. They wanted boundaries to be set.

Top performers in administration and teaching fully understand that you can't motivate students to achieve by backing away from correcting their behavior problems and mistakes.

Finally, all students want effective teachers. Enthusiastic, positive teachers are not only effective classroom managers but desirable mentors for students, since they receive respect and esteem from colleagues and parents alike. Such teachers will provide everlasting positive memories for their students. They become the remembered "favorite teacher," not because they were out to win a popularity contest with each class of students, but because they earned respect by knowing when to act, how to act, and why.

Assessment

In which reading group does Jon belong? How do I construct tests? How do I know when my students have mastered the course objectives? How can I explain test results to Mary's parents? Each of these questions, and many more, are answered by applying principles of assessment. Assessment refers to procedures for measuring and recording student performance, and constructing grades from assessment that communicate to others levels of proficiency or relative standing. Assessment principles constitute a set of concepts that is integral to the teaching-learning process. Indeed, a significant amount of teacher time is spent in assessment activities, and with more accountability has come a greater emphasis on assessment.

Assessment provides a foundation for making sound evaluative judgments about students' learning and achievement. Teachers need to use fair and unbiased criteria in order to objectively and accurately assess student learning and make appropriate decisions about student placement. For example, in assigning Jon to a reading group, the teacher will use Jon's test scores as an indication of his skill level. Are the inferences from the test results valid for the school's reading program? Are his test scores consistent over several months or years? Are they consistent with his performance in class? These questions should be asked and then answered by the teacher before he or she can make intelligent decisions about Jon. On the other hand, will knowledge of the test scores affect the teacher's perception of classroom performance and create a self-fulfilling prophesy? Teachers also evaluate students in order to assign grades, and the challenge is to balance "objective" test scores with more subjective, informally gathered information. Both kinds of evaluative information are necessary, but both can be inaccurate and are frequently misused.

The first article in this section examines changes in assessment theory that effect what and how we measure student achievement. Once a sound framework is developed, teachers need to be aware of grading practices and procedures that lead to inaccurate conclusions, such as the indiscriminate use of zeros and averages, and the failure to understand the impact of measurement error in interpreting test scores. The second article explains how teachers also need to differentiate between criterion-referenced grading for minimal objectives, and using norms to evaluate achievement.

The next two articles introduce and discuss performance-based, "authentic" assessment. This form of assessment has great potential to more effectively integrate measurement procedures with instructional methods and to focus student learning on the application of thinking and problem-solving skills in real-life contexts. A related form of assessment, using portfolios, is described in the next article.

In the last article the characteristics and limitations of standardized aptitude tests are reviewed with suggestions for how to appropriately use results from such tests.

Looking Ahead: Challenge Questions

Many educators believe that schools should identify the brightest, most capable students. What are the assessment implications of this philosophy? How would low-achieving students be affected?

What is the essential difference between criterion-referenced and norm-referenced testing? What are the factors that should be considered when deciding when to use each approach?

What principles of assessment should teachers adopt for their own classroom testing? Is it necessary or feasible to develop a table of specifications for each test? How do we know if the tests teachers make are reliable and if valid inferences can be drawn from the results?

How can teachers grade thinking skills such as analysis, application, and reasoning? How should objectives for student learning and grading be integrated? What are some practices to avoid in grading students? Why?

What are appropriate teacher uses of standardized test scores? What are some common mistakes teachers make when interpreting the results of standardized tests?

Assessment Theory and Research for Classrooms: From *Taxonomies* to Constructing Meaning in Context

Carol Kehr Tittle, Deborah Hecht, and Patrick Moore
City University of New York

Carol Kehr Tittle is Executive Officer of the PhD Program in Educational Psychology in the Graduate School at the City University of New York, 33 West 42nd Street, New York, NY 10021. Her specializations are applied measurement and evaluation.

Deborah Hecht is the Associate Project Director of the Center for Advanced Study in Education at the City University of New York Graduate Center, 25 West 43rd Street, Room 620, New York, NY 10036. Her specializations are research and evaluation.

Patrick Moore is a graduate student, assessor, and adjunct professor at 23 Waverly Street, Jersey City, NJ 07306. His specializations are personnel assessment and statistical analysis.

Why should we take a broader view of assessment theory and research when constructing measures of school achievement? How might we incorporate a learner's awareness of his or her own learning strategies into the assessment process? How could an assessment developer combine the use of psychological constructs and varying contexts for learning in the assessment of competence in mathematics?

Educational measurement is the center of attention in educational reform efforts. From efforts to legislate national standards and national assessments to rapid development of performance assessments, educational measurement is caught up in efforts for change. A major result of all these efforts is that developers and users of school achievement measures are taking a much broader look at the objectives, process, and utility of measurement. Starting from the taxonomies of educational objectives, we will identify changes in perspectives on the objectives of education, a broader view of process outcomes in education, and the need to address the utility of educational measurement in more direct interactions with teachers and learners. These changes require a broader view of assessment theory and research for test developers and users.

Overview

Several generations of researchers, test developers, and teachers have been guided in developing assessments by the *Taxonomy of Educational Objectives: I. The Cognitive Domain* (Bloom, 1956). This taxonomy focuses attention on the broad processes that students might use in responding to examination questions, ranging from recall of facts, to application of knowledge, to synthesis of facts and principles. The organizing principle is that of cognitive complexity, from knowledge and comprehension to synthesis and evaluation. A second taxonomy, *The Taxonomy of Educational Objectives: II. The Affective Domain* (Krathwohl, Bloom, & Masia, 1964), attempts to focus assessment on such educational goals as art appreciation and valuing of literature. The organizing principle is that of internalization, from being

aware of art, for example, to characterization of the individual's activities around seeking out and doing art. This second taxonomy had little influence in ongoing testing and research in comparison with the taxonomy in the cognitive domain.

It has now been over 25 years since these taxonomies were developed, and there have been major changes in the educational and psychological theories that are the underpinnings of the taxonomies. The changing theory about learners in educational settings will be described. Teachers and assessment developers will necessarily have their attention focused on subject-matter assessments with this changing theory. However, to encourage thinking about other research and the development of materials for classroom assessment, we illustrate a different framework for mathematics. The framework includes psychological constructs that are concerned with the learners' awareness of their own learning strategies or self-regulatory behaviors and affective and motivation-related beliefs.[1] The framework suggests that now we have an opportunity to provide the bridge to the classroom that was intended with the earlier taxonomy for the affective domain.

The framework was used to develop an assessment tool, the *Mathematics Assessment Questionnaire* (Hecht & Tittle, 1990; Tittle & Hecht, 1990).[2] To illustrate how teachers may understand the assessment, we provide a transcript from a teacher "thinking aloud" about her students' responses to statements in the assessment, as well as a student talking about the statements. We conclude with implications of this framework and the examples for research and development on assessments for classroom use.

Then and Now in Theory

The changes in the theories between then and now can be characterized briefly:

1. Both the cognitive and affective taxonomies are based on a teaching-outcomes or objectives framework. Current psychological theories now attempt to describe student processes—thinking and beliefs—as important in themselves and as outcomes of the teaching and learning process (e.g., Confrey, 1990; Snow, 1989).

2. The taxonomies implicitly provide a view of the learner as an object for teaching, as a reactor in the learning situation, having either attained or not attained a category in the taxonomies. Current theories consider the student an active information processor, a constructor of knowledge, and as self-directed (e.g., Steffe & Cobb, 1988; von Glaserfeld, 1987, 1989; Wittrock, 1977).

3. The cognitive and affective taxonomies use broad, single, psychological organizing principles of cognitive complexity and internalization of values, respectively. Current psychological theories are more domain-specific (Chi, Feltovich, & Glaser, 1981; Confrey, 1990; Ginsberg, 1983).

The framework we propose, and discuss subsequently, is similar to the earlier taxonomies in one critical aspect—the subject matter. The framework differs from the taxonomies with the inclusion of two dimensions: one for domain-specific psychological constructs and one for the situation or classroom activity within which the subject matter and constructs of interest interact.

A Framework for Assessment: Classroom Activities and Psychological Constructs

How can the activity settings and the psychological constructs be organized into an assessment framework for classrooms? The organization is facilitated by using a dimension or facet approach within any subject matter or curriculum topic: One dimension is the activity setting, and the second is the psychological construct.

The purpose of the situation facet is to directly link assessment to teacher and learner instructional activities. Classroom activities constitute a dimension that is typically not considered in educational assessments. However, teachers use a variety of activities for instruction. Descriptive research on teaching indicates different teaching methods are used in different subject matters. For example, Stodolsky (1988) reports differences in classroom activities between social studies and mathematics classes in elementary schools. Brophy and Alleman (1991) have also argued for the importance of learning activities as units for educational research and study. They define activities as a means "of enabling students to accomplish curricular goals, and students are expected to engage in them for that purpose" (p. 9).

As another example of the importance of an activity setting, consider the Leinhardt and Putnam (1986) description of the cognitive tasks of students during whole-class direct instruction by the teacher. The student's tasks will be different in this activity than when doing independent work, such as homework. The student's tasks will also differ when participating in a problem-solving group with peers (Artzt & Armour-Thomas, 1992).

The dimension of psychological constructs involves selecting the constructs that are meaningful for the particular assessment context. Snow (1989) has provided a broad organizational scheme for a network of psychological constructs that are of interest for assessing learning, including the general categories of conceptual structures, procedural skills, learning strategies, self-regulatory functions, and motivational orientations. This set of categories indicates the large number of constructs that are of potential interest in assessment.

How Would the Assessment Framework Be Used?

The framework would be used to guide the development of assessment procedures in the following way. The major construct and activity settings within the subject matter would be identified and defined. Assessment procedures would be specified and developed. Although an assessment framework is typically used to write assessments for each cell, this is not necessary in many instances. Development of the assessment would rely upon a teacher's knowledge about the students, the classroom activities, and the assessment goals. Thus, a given assessment procedure could encompass one or a number of cells in the framework. Assessment procedures such as portfolios, for example, are likely to encompass several "cells" of a framework. A portfolio of writing samples for a student might provide a teacher indicators of the student's motivational processes.

An Example: Use of an Assessment Framework for Mathematics Classrooms

A general outline of an assessment framework for junior high school mathematics classrooms is given in Figure 1. Because we emphasize the need to embed assessment, research, and development within the classroom setting, we have drawn our illustration for a model framework from a single classroom subject area, mathematics. We selected specific constructs in research on mathematics education at the middle school level (cf. McLeod & Adams, 1989), which are also discussed in curriculum development (National Council of Teachers of Mathematics, 1989). The constructs include awareness of self-regulation and affective and motivational beliefs.

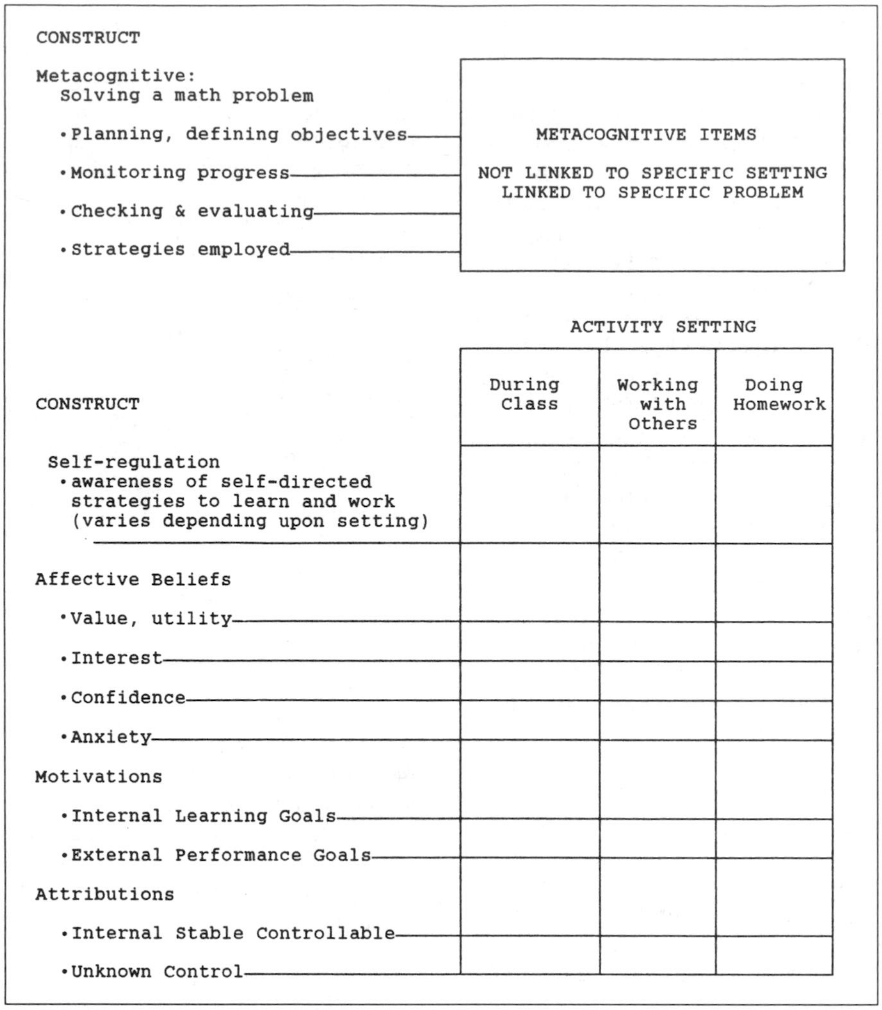

6. ASSESSMENT

In our junior high school mathematics classroom example, the activity dimension in Figure 1 has three categories: During Class, Working With Others, and Homework. *During Class* refers to the instructional setting that is teacher-directed, typically for the whole class. Teacher-directed classes typically involve review, introduction of new concepts, and working out of examples by teachers and students. *Working With Others* refers to students working together in small groups to solve mathematical problems. *Homework* refers to an instructional activity typically carried out independently by an individual student out of the classroom.

The psychological constructs dimension has two major categories: (a) self-regulatory skills and (b) affective, motivational, and attributional beliefs.

Self-Regulatory Skills

We include here the cognitive processes variously labeled metacognition and self-regulatory skills. Metacognition refers to knowledge of the cognitive processes one uses while undertaking specific cognitive tasks (Flavell, 1976; Brown, 1978; Weinert, 1987; Weinert & Kluwe, 1987). As represented in Figure 1, it encompasses awareness of one's cognitions or thoughts and strategies while working on an individual problem, such as a mathematics word problem (Schoenfeld, 1985).

The self-regulatory category also encompasses the individual's awareness of monitoring processes in working in a problem-solving group with other students, participating in a teacher lesson, and doing homework. Self-regulatory skills have received attention from several research perspectives (e.g., Meichenbaum, 1977; Bandura, 1986; Corno & Mandinach, 1983; Zimmerman & Schunk, 1989).

Affect, Motivation, and Attributions

As organized here, affective beliefs refer to four characteristics of a learner of mathematics: perceived *value* or utility of a mathematically related activity; *interest* in the task;

FIGURE 1. *Domain specifications for the Mathematics Assessment Questionnaire—Two facets: Psychological construct and setting*

confidence in doing the task; and *anxiety* about doing the mathematically related activity (Fennema & Sherman, 1976; Eccles et al., 1985). Motivations include the perceived reasons for approaching the task, whether these originate from the individual's own *internal* goals for learning or from *external* sources (Dweck, 1986). Attributions include those beliefs that describe the causes for success or failure in mathematical activities, as well as those instances in which the individual feels no sense of control for performance outcomes (Connell, 1985; Weiner, 1986).

To illustrate the use of the framework in designing a specific assessment tool for teacher use in junior high school mathematics classrooms, we provide sample statements in Table 1. Statements are intended to provide teachers with observations

of student beliefs in each cell formed by the intersection of the two dimensions in Figure 1, construct and activity setting. Students indicate their strength of agreement with a statement on a Likert-type scale from Very True to Not at All True (for me). Students' perceptions of the extent to which such statements are true for them can be examined both within and across activity settings for classroom use.

Meaning and Use of the Assessment Framework: Teacher and Student Protocols

Although much is written about assessments for classroom use, a key question is "What meaning and use do teachers make of such assessments?" (Tittle, 1989). We are beginning to develop at least a preliminary answer to this question using the assessment tool and the framework described previously. We used the *Mathematics Assessment Questionnaire* (MAQ), which students in Grades 7–9 answered on a computer.[3] Using the accompanying teacher program disk, teachers explored responses for individuals and for their classes.[4]

This teacher program provides an opportunity to have teachers "think aloud" (Ericsson & Simon, 1984) as they review and reflect on the responses of their students to the statements in the MAQ. Using the think-aloud procedures, we have asked teachers to consider student responses; in particular, which responses suggest the need for follow up and which instructional activities might be undertaken. We report here, with permission, the transcript from one such session with a teacher.

Teacher: This is what I like best about this program. This is interesting, because this kid is uncomfortable during instruction, but he doesn't show up here (pointing to the homework setting). He's very introverted, but at home I guess he can do math better than he can in school. (She reviews other students who have a need with regard to Anxiety in the During Class and Working With Others settings). If it's really true that they're anxious during instruction, I'm not sure if it has something to do with being called on to go to the board, or putting them in situations with other students where they don't feel they can either handle it or perform well, and if that were the case, I would probably try to arrange a different situation for them. Instead of just randomly calling them to the board, I may go over and work with them a little bit before the lesson starts so that they feel they have a grasp on it, so then I can call them to participate, and go to the board and get some positive feedback. I may try then to put them with other students that maybe are also anxious that need more help, where they can take charge a little bit, or something. But what happens with some of these students is because they're anxious, they're very difficult; they have a tendency to be dismissed as troublemakers because you don't have time for all of them. . . . This kid is anxious and lacks confidence, so I would try to set up a situation where he could

build some in math. He's not the weakest student, so I'd probably put him with someone who is weaker, or maybe has a language deficit, where he could try to communicate in a way where they could help each other. I think when they help somebody else start to succeed, they feel better about themselves. . . .

This kid is very withdrawn; I don't know if he could work with other students, but if it was a confidence thing, I would probably try to get to him at least once during the day to see if he can do the work, and praise him if he could, and then try to get him to work one-on-one to help another student.

The importance of considering activity setting and the meaning of student assessment is further supported by examining a transcript from a student "think aloud" while answering the MAQ. The following statements were made in response to anxiety statements in each activity setting.

Activity setting: During Class. (Statement) I am afraid when I have to ask my math teacher a question about a word problem during class.

Student response: Afraid. Well, sometimes I'm like afraid because if everyone else seems like they have gotten it and like I'm totally lost, it could be kind of embarrassing. That used to happen, but not always, so it is sort of true. . . . Sometimes if I'm just like lost I don't want to raise my hand or anything because I am afraid I'll be branded. If it is important and I don't understand it, like it is the day before a test, then I will just

raise my hand . . . so I guess it is sort of true.

Activity setting: Working With Other Students. (Statement) I dread the thought of trying to solve a math word problem with other students.

Student response: Not at all true, because you can learn more that way.

Activity setting: Homework. (Statement) I feel nervous when I think about doing hard word problems for homework.

Student response: I feel kind of nervous . . . 'cause I want to show that at least I can do good effort.

As the previous examples suggest, student reflections about anxiety are linked to the activity setting in which the possibility for anxiety occurs. Thus, the meaning of the assessment is tied not only to the psychological construct but also the activity setting. As the teacher protocol indicates, the activity setting also provides opportunities to plan different strategies for working with individual students.

Implications for Research on and Development of Assessments for Classroom Use

The broader organizing framework for classroom assessments has implications for the assessment development process itself, for the measurement analyses and research, for the communication of results, and for the integration of assessment and instruction.

Developing Assessments

With respect to the process of developing assessments, the implications

Table 1

Sample Statements From the Mathematics Assessment Questionnaire *Illustrating Constructs and Classroom Activity Settings*

Self-Regulation: During Class
When I can think of another way to solve a word problem, I volunteer to show the class.

Anxiety: Working With Others
I dread the thought of trying to solve a math word problem with other students.

Internal Learning Goals: Homework
I like to do hard homework math word problems because I learn more math by working them.

are that collaborative efforts with teachers are required. Although researchers will be knowledgeable about the empirical base for the constructs or cognitive processes, teachers have a working knowledge of students and classrooms (Schon, 1983) that is different from that of researchers, measurement specialists, and test constructors.

Expert teachers can provide judgments in the development stage as to whether information from the proposed assessments will have meaning for instructional planning and whether instructional activities can be suggested based on student responses. The development of the assessment used as an example here was based on extensive interactions with a small group of teachers. Initially, mathematics teachers judged prototype statements for their usefulness in providing information for instructional planning. Subsequently, teachers were, and still are, involved in trying out statements in their classes and evaluating all aspects of the student and teacher computer-based versions of the assessment.

Measurement Analyses

There are implications for measurement analyses and for viewing or reporting assessment information. From a statistical or test-theory perspective, alternatives to the overall proficiency or linear ordering of students are needed for classroom assessment (Mislevy, 1989; Nickerson, 1989; Snow & Mandinach, 1991). Because working models are not readily at hand, we need to draw on ideas from achievement testing. Just as domain- or objectives-referenced clusters of items have proven useful to teachers for standardized achievement tests, analyses for classroom assessment of the type we are proposing should focus on smaller units of items, seeking to provide direct meaning to the user however the information is reported, numerically, pictorially, or verbally (Yen, 1987). Based on the organizational framework we suggest, small clusters of items would need to be internally consistent, and direct representation of patterns of responses will be most useful to teachers to make instructional plans and decisions.

With a better understanding of the psychological constructs and their salience for activity settings, alternative "structures" or patterns of development may be identified for measurement, as is the goal with the cognitive structures perspective (Mislevy, 1989; Snow & Mandinach, 1991). Also, there will ultimately be an assessment framework that encourages teachers to view students' development in an integrated framework. This change in assessment orientation would support making decisions about instructional activities taking into account the full spectrum of cognitive and motivational structures in the development of learning.

Communication of Results

The implications for the communication of results are that a variety of formats for reporting assessment results needs to be available for teachers and students. The use of a framework such as the one here will result in extensive information, which teachers will want to access in different ways. Some teachers may want class-level summaries; others may want students clustered together on particular assessment items for instructional planning; others may want the responses of an individual to a set of items.[5] The need for flexibility and efficiency in access is critical for the use of more microlevel assessment information. Again, teacher collaborators will provide a needed perspective on the development of reporting systems, and a variety of formats for reporting assessment results needs to be available.

Another implication for the communication of classroom-level assessment results is the need to examine and justify levels of aggregation of results for individuals and classrooms. From one perspective, there is a justification for having results available only at the local classroom or student level. Because the assessment is focused here on mediating influences or processes, and not achievement outcomes per se, the information is needed only by teachers or learners, or others concerned directly with the instructional program. The broader framework for assessment requires smaller sets of information or responses from stu-

dents. Initially, they may be less consistent than we are accustomed to in the traditional reliability or error of measurement perspective. However, it can be expected that work will proceed to improve such indicators.

The processes or constructs described here are related to outcomes of interest for evaluation or accountability purposes at the school level. However, for teachers to be interested in such assessments, it is likely that there needs to be an agreement *not* to aggregate such information. Teachers are on solid ground with this point of view, for there are few descriptions in curricula guides on which to base instructional plans and activities, in contrast to the descriptions that exist for subject-matter topics.[6]

Integration of Assessment and Instruction

The implication for the integration of assessment and instruction is that assessment materials need to be accompanied by instructionally relevant materials. These materials can take a variety of forms: Materials could include suggestions of hypotheses or questions to be followed up to confirm or expand the assessment inferences, as is currently done with computer-based reports on intelligence testing; or materials could include instructional or intervention strategies for the classroom or clusters of students. This implication reinforces the need for the assessment development process to be collaborative. Only by working with teachers and others with extensive classroom experience can research and practice-based instructional suggestions be integrated with assessments in classrooms.

Summary

There have been major changes in the 25 years since the taxonomies provided a translation and adaptation of psychological theory into a structure for assessment theory and research for classrooms. These changes emphasize the need to understand thinking in the context of students' beliefs and self-directed cognitions. We have provided an organizing framework based on psychological constructs and classroom activity settings as a means to link assessment to classroom use by teachers of junior high school mathematics. We suggest that the psychological constructs that appear in active areas of subject-matter research are best assessed in the context of activity settings, in order to link them to classroom instructional planning.

The organization and framework for assessment we propose here is one of several that could be identified, building on existing theories. However, any framework for classroom assessment will need to build on a view of the student that places performance in the context of student cognition and conation—the thoughts, feelings, and beliefs about that performance in that subject matter. The development of such assessment procedures will need to be carried out in collaboration with teachers if the assessments are to have meaning and usefulness in classroom settings.

Notes

This article is a revised version of a paper presented at the NCME Annual Meeting in 1989. We wish to thank several anonymous reviews for helpful suggestions and to acknowledge the support of the Ford Foundation and The Aaron Diamond Foundation. New York city mathematics teachers and mathematics teacher educators, as well as Graduate School doctoral students Laura Alvarez, Amy Schmidt, and Dana Fusco made major contributions to the development of the project.

[1]The constructs for the proposed framework are in two particular areas: the student's thinking and beliefs related to self-direction, including metacognitive and self-regulatory skills; and the student's thinking and beliefs related to intentionality, including such constructs as motivation and attributions. By including constructs of self-direction, such as metacognition and self-regulation, the framework for assessment provides a bridge to the declarative knowledge and procedural skills (Glaser & Bassok, 1989) of the subject matter. By including constructs of intentionality, such as interests, values, motivations, and attributions, the framework provides for assessment of the structure of beliefs that underlies the initiation of the knowledge and procedural skill construction processes (e.g., see Snow, 1989).

[2]Data on pilot studies, reliability, and validity of the MAQ are reported in

Hecht and Tittle (1990). Briefly, large sample data were collected in the fall of 1988 in Grades 7–9 in urban schools, and data are reported for 1,737 students. Factor analysis data are reported for the self-regulatory statements of the MAQ; the factor analyses generally support the hypothesized structure of these statements. Although reliability data are reported (and are moderate, alphas averaging .4 to .7; alphas are higher for the factors), these MAQ statements are not scored and are used by examining individual statements. The reliability data for three-item clusters of the affective and motivational beliefs in each activity setting are moderate (about .5 to .6). Multidimensional scaling analyses of the affective and motivational beliefs across the three activity settings provide support for the classroom activity structure of the MAQ (Tittle, Weinberg, & Hecht, 1990).

[3]The MAQ was originally developed in paper-and-pencil format. It is available through ERIC (TM 015 633 or TM 015 811) and could be tallied by hand or by using a machine-scannable answer sheet. The student computer version and teacher-program disks are available for experimental use from the first author.

[4]All these different methods of accessing student information can be readily available with a computer. The teacher-program disk of the MAQ provides such access.

[5]A question could arise about legal issues. To the extent that an assessment tool such as the MAQ is obtained and used by individual classroom teachers for classroom instructional purposes, it is like other formal or informal assessments or curriculum materials that a teacher uses. To date, teachers and principals have used this assessment tool with no evident concern. This is largely due, we believe, to embedding of the constructs in the context of specific classroom activities in learning or doing a specific area of mathematics (mathematical word problems).

[6]The assessment perspective provided here can be viewed as complementary to measures of overall proficiency.

References

Artzt, A., & Armour-Thomas, E. (1992). Protocol analysis of group problem solving in mathematics: A cognitive-metacognitive framework for protocol analysis of group problem solving in mathematics. *Cognition and Instruction, 9*(2), 137–175.

Bandura, A. (1986). *Social foundations of thought and action.* Englewood Cliffs, NJ: Prentice-Hall.

Bloom, B. S. (Ed.). (1956). *Taxonomy of educational objectives I: Cognitive domain.* New York: Longman, Green.

Brophy, J., & Alleman, J. (1991). Activities as instructional tools: A framework for analysis and evaluation. *Educational Researcher, 20,* 9–23.

Brown, A. L. (1978). Knowing when, where, and how to remember: A problem of metacognition. In R. Glaser (Ed.), *Advances in instructional psychology* (Vol. 1, pp. 77–165). Hillsdale, NJ: Erlbaum.

Chi, M. T. H., Feltovich, P. J., & Glaser, R. (1981). Categorization and representation of physics problems by experts and novices. *Cognitive Science, 5,* 121–152.

Confrey, J. (1990). A review of the research on student conceptions in mathematics, science, and programming. In C. B. Cazden (Ed.), *Review of Research in Education: Vol. 16,* (pp. 3–56). Washington, DC: American Educational Research Association.

Connell, J. P. (1985). A new multidimensional measure of children's perception of control. *Child Development, 56,* 1018–1041.

Corno, L., & Mandinach, E. B. (1983). The role of cognitive engagement in classroom learning and motivation. *Educational Psychologist, 18,* 88–108.

Dweck, C. S. (1986). Motivational processes affecting learning. *American Psychologist, 41,* 1040–1048.

Eccles, J. S., Adler, T. F., Futterman, R., Goff, S. B., Kaczala, C. M., Meece, J. L., & Midgley, C. (1985). Self-perceptions, task perceptions, socializing influences, and the decision to enroll in mathematics. In S. F. Chipman, I. R. Brush, & D. M. Wilson (Eds.), *Women and mathematics* (pp. 95–121) Hillsdale, NJ: Erlbaum.

Ericsson, K. A., & Simon, H. A. (1984). *Protocol analysis.* Cambridge, MA: MIT Press.

Fennema, E., & Sherman, J. (1976). Fennema-Sherman Mathematics Attitude Scales. *JSAS Catalog of Selected Documents in Psychology, 6*(1), 31 (Ms. No. 1225).

Flavell, J. H. (1976). Metacognitive aspects of problem solving. In L. Resnick (Ed.), *The nature of intelligence* (pp. 231–236) Hillsdale, NJ: Erlbaum.

Ginsberg, H. (Ed.). (1983). *The development of mathematical thinking.* New York: Academic Press.

Glaser, R., & Bassok, M. (1989). Learning theory and the study of instruction. *Annual Review of Psychology, 40,* 631–666.

Hecht, D., & Tittle, C. K. (1990). *Mathematics Assessment Questionnaire: A survey of thoughts and feelings for students in grades 7–9.* (Tech. Rep. TM 015 811). New York: Graduate Center, City University of New York,

Center for Advanced Study in Education.

Krathwohl, D. R., Bloom, B. S., & Masia, B. B. (1964). *Taxonomy of educational objectives II: Affective domain.* New York: Longman.

Leinhardt, G., & Putnam, R. T. (1986, April). *The skill of learning from classroom lessons.* Paper presented at the Annual Meeting of the American Educational Research Association, San Francisco.

McLeod, D. B., & Adams, V. M. (Eds.). (1989). *Affect and mathematical problem solving: A new perspective.* New York: Springer-Verlag.

Meichenbaum, D. (1977). *Cognitive behavior modification: An integrative approach.* New York: Plenum Press.

Mislevy, R. J. (1989). *Foundations of a new test theory.* (Res. Rep. No. RR 89–52ONR). Princeton, NJ: Educational Testing Service.

National Council of Teachers of Mathematics (1989). *Curriculum and evaluation standards for school mathematics.* Reston, VA: Author.

Nickerson, R. S. (1989). New directions in educational assessment. *Educational Researcher, 18*(9), 3–7.

Schoenfeld, A. H. (1985). *Mathematical problem solving.* New York: Academic Press.

Schon, D. A. (1983). *The reflective practitioner.* New York: Basic Books.

Snow, R. E. (1989). Toward assessment of cognitive and conative structure in learning. *Educational Researcher, 18*(9), 8–14.

Snow, R. E., & Mandinach, E. G. (1991, February). *Integrating assessment and instruction: A research and development agenda.* (Research Report No. RR 91-8). Princeton, NJ: Educational Testing Service.

Steffe, L. P., & Cobb, P. (1988). *Construction of arithmetical meanings and strategies.* New York: Springer-Verlag.

Stodolsky, S. S. (1988). *The subject matters: Classroom activity in math and social studies.* Chicago, IL: University of Chicago.

Tittle, C. K. (1989). Validity: Whose construction is it in the teaching and learning context? *Educational Measurement: Issues and Practice, 8*(1), 5–13, 34.

Tittle, C. K., & Hecht, D. (1990). *Mathematics Assessment Questionnaire: A survey of thoughts and feelings for students in Grades 7–9: Manual for users.* (Tech. Rep. TM 015 633). New York: Graduate Center, City University of New York, Center for Advanced Study in Education.

Tittle, C. K., Weinberg, S., & Hecht, D. (1990, July). Dimensions of early adolescents' beliefs about learning mathematical word problems in school. Paper presented at the meeting of the International Association of Applied Psychology, Kyoto, Japan.

von Glaserfeld, E. (1987). Learning as a constructive activity. In C. Janvier (Ed.), *Problems of representation in the teaching and learning of mathematics* (pp. 3–17). Hillsdale, NJ: Erlbaum.

von Glaserfeld, E. (1989). Constructivism in education. In T. Husen & T. N. Postlewaite (Eds.), *International encyclopedia of education: Supplementary Vol. 1. Research and studies* (pp. 162–163). Oxford, England: Pergamon.

Weiner, B. (1986). *An attributional theory of motivation and emotion.* New York: Springer-Verlag.

Weinert, F. E. (1987). Introduction and overview: Metacognition and motivation as determinants of effective learning and understanding. In F. E. Weinert & R. H. Kluwe (Eds.), *Metacognition, motivation, and understanding.* Hillsdale, NJ: Erlbaum.

Weinert, F. E., & Kluwe, R. H. (Eds.). (1987). *Metacognition, motivation, and understanding.* Hillsdale, NJ: Erlbaum.

Wittrock, M. C. (1977). Learning as a generative process. In M. C. Wittrock (Ed.), *Learning and instruction* (pp. 621–631). Berkeley, CA: McCutchan.

Yen, W. M. (1987, June). *A Bayesian/IRT index of objective performance.* Paper presented at the Annual Meeting of the Psychometric Society, Montreal.

Zimmerman, B. J., & Schunk, D. H. (Eds.). (1989). *Self-regulated learning and academic achievement.* New York: Springer-Verlag.

An NCME Instructional Module on

Developing a Personal Grading Plan

David A. Frisbie and Kristie K. Waltman
University of Iowa

David A. Frisbie is a professor of measurement and statistics in the College of Education at the University of Iowa, 316 Lindquist Center, Iowa City, IA 52242.

Kristie K. Waltman is a doctoral student in the College of Education at the University of Iowa.

The purpose of this instructional module is to assist teachers in developing defensible grading practices that effectively and fairly communicate students' achievement status to their parents. In formulating such practices, it is essential that teachers first consider their personal grading philosophy and then create a compatible personal grading plan. The module delineates key philosophical issues that should be addressed and then outlines the procedural steps essential to establishing a grading plan. Finally, the features of several common methods of absolute and relative grading are compared.

This instructional module has been designed to help prospective and beginning teachers sort out the issues involved in formulating their grading procedures and to help experienced teachers reexamine the fairness and defensibility of their current grading practices. It can be applied at any grade level and in any subject matter area in which letter grades are assigned to students at the end of a reporting period. The content focus is limited to grading, so other modes of evaluating and reporting student progress are not addressed.

With regard to the purpose of grades, the position we will assume and defend is that grades are intended mainly to communicate the achievement status of students to their parents. The grade, then, symbolizes the extent to which a student has attained the important instructional goals of the reporting period for which the grade is assigned. Grades would not be needed if there were no need to communicate achievement to parents (or others outside the school setting). Grades are not essential to the instructional process: teachers can teach without them and students can and do learn without them.

Grades do serve several other important functions that are secondary to their school-to-home communication role, however. Grades provide incentives to learn for many students. Most students are motivated to attain the highest grades and to receive the recognition that often accompanies such grades, and they are motivated to avoid the lowest grades and the negative outcomes that sometimes are associated with those

grades. Grades also provide information to students for self-evaluation, for analysis of strengths and weaknesses, and for creating a general impression of academic promise, all of which may enter into educational and career planning. Finally, grades are used to communicate students' performance levels to others who want to know about past achievement or want to forecast future academic success. Prospective employers and teachers in subsequent classes use grades in these ways. So do those who are charged with deciding who qualifies for honor society, who is eligible for basketball, or who should be the class valedictorian.

This module is organized to demonstrate the process a teacher might follow in devising a grading plan. First, some of the philosophical issues inherent in the grading process are identified, and then steps to follow in creating a grading plan are outlined. Finally, some of the most common methods of assigning grades are analyzed. The primary objectives of this module are to enable the reader to (a) describe the main questions of value that need to be considered in formulating a personal grading philosophy; (b) explain how written district grading policies, district reporting forms, and building-level expectations can help or hinder the development of a personal grading philosophy; (c) identify the essential procedural questions that need to be resolved in developing a personal grading plan; (d) explain how the decisions about defining the grade symbols directly influence other subsequent decisions in creating a personal grading plan; and (e) analyze the strengths and weaknesses of each of several common methods of assigning grades.

Teachers who implement the recommendations of this module should end up with a defensible grading plan that is in harmony with their personal grading philosophy and the grading policy of the district in which the plan will be implemented.

Developing a Grading Philosophy

The process of grading requires teachers to make a number of

From *Educational Measurement: Issues and Practices,* Fall 1992, pp. 35-42. © 1992 by the National Council on Measurement in Education. Reprinted by permission of the publisher.

decisions that are grounded in their personal value system. What to do about grading or how to do it is often less a matter of correctness and more a matter of preference and perceived value or importance. In this section, we identify a number of "should" questions, questions about which reasonable people might disagree because of their personal beliefs, values, and experiences. "What should a B mean? Should any student be assigned an F grade? How many A grades should be assigned in a class?" These are questions for which research studies cannot provide answers, but they are the types of questions that must be answered by each teacher who issues grades.

1. What meaning should each grade symbol carry? A grade of C can tell how much Rudy knows, how he compares to his classmates, how hard he has tried, how much he has learned this quarter, or how well he has behaved this term. Since it cannot tell all of these things at once, what should it be limited to telling?

2. What should "failure" mean? There is undoubtedly more emotion associated with the F grade than any other, largely because of the negative consequences for many students who receive it. What does F mean? Should it mean the student knows nothing, knows the least within his class group, can do only the lowest level of work in the curriculum, hasn't tried to learn, or hasn't learned much in 9 weeks?

3. What elements of performance should be incorporated in a grade? Once a teacher has decided on the meaning the grade symbols should convey, much effort will be required to keep contaminating information out of the grade. Teachers are constantly making observations and judgments about a variety of characteristics of their students. Such information can be used to evaluate communication skills, interpersonal relations, attitude, and motivation, but not all information gathered need be funneled into the grading decisions. What should be included and what should be kept out?

4. How should the grades in a class be distributed? In some districts, written grading policies dictate the nature of grade distributions (e.g., the percentages of As, Bs, etc.); however, most districts seem not to have such policies. Thus, most teachers are probably faced with a decision about the percentage of A grades or C grades they should issue. Should the average grade be C? Is it okay if everyone gets an A? Should there be an equal number of B and D grades?

5. What should the components be like that go into a final grade? The separate scores or grades that are combined to form the final grade for a reporting period must, above all, convey the meaning the teacher previously decided upon for the grade symbols. Should rough drafts count? How about scores from a test that turned out to be too hard? What about practice trials for performance tests? How many components should there be as a minimum?

6. How should the components of the grade be combined? Suppose Mr. Voss uses three tests, a short paper, and an individual project for third quarter grading in his sixth-grade social studies class. Should each of the five components be worth 20% of the final grade or should some be more heavily weighted? What should he think about when making that decision?

7. What method should be used to assign grades? After component scores have been combined, a final grade needs to be assigned to each student. The method of assignment ought to be consistent with the decisions made earlier about the meaning each grade symbol should have. For example, it would be illogical to grade on the curve if grades are to be based on absolute standards of performance. Which of the several methods of absolute grading is best?

8. Should borderline cases be reviewed? If borderline cases are to be reexamined to decide on the appropriateness of the grades, here are some questions the teacher needs to address: How close to a cutoff point does a score need to be before it is considered borderline? Should only grades just below a cutoff be checked or should those just above be looked at also? What additional information should be examined to help make the borderline decisions? Should students be allowed to furnish extra credit work to raise a borderline grade?

9. What other factors can influence the philosophy of grading? A teacher's personal philosophy of grading also can be shaped by school district grading policies and building practices. For example, some district grade-report forms provide descriptive phrases to define each grade symbol. In such cases, written district policy is inherent in the reporting form even though grading procedures are not prescribed explicitly. In the absence of written policy, however, the most recent grades issued become the norm; practices that depart noticeably from the norm are likely to be squelched, regardless of the philosophy of the grader.

Establishing a Grading Plan

This section of the module details the sequential steps involved in applying a personal philosophy of grading to form a personal grading plan. It is a personal plan because it incorporates the personal values, beliefs, and attitudes of the particular teacher who will use it to assign grades. And though a philosophy of grading is the foundation for establishing a grading plan, the plan is also shaped and influenced by current research evidence, prevailing lore, reasoned judgment, and matters of practicality.

Step 1. Identify and implement written district policy. If there is written district policy on grading, teachers are obligated professionally (and probably legally) to follow it. The policy may be in the form of detailed rules or it may be a set of general statements from a school board resolution. It may simply be reflected in the reporting form sent to parents, in the statements of purpose on the report card, or in the explanations of the meanings of the grade symbols used.

What should you do if your philosophy and preferred grading procedures conflict with written policy? First, a discussion with your building administrator may be the most reasonable approach because the administrator is the first line of enforcement of district policy. If the results of such a meeting are not satisfactory, a next step would be to follow the existing policy while informally surveying your colleagues to see whether they would support a change. If so, efforts to alter the policy to fit the philosophies of the staff could be very productive.

Step 2. Decide what the meaning of each grade symbol will be. There are three facets to the meaning of a letter grade, and the teacher needs to make a decision about each facet for his or her plan. First, the grade compares performance either to a relative standard (norm-referenced) or to an absolute standard (criterion-referenced). For example, a relative comparison is being made if a C grade means "average performance compared to others in the class," but an absolute comparison is being made if it means "demonstrated attainment of the most important objectives." It is essential for the teacher who adopts a criterion-referenced meaning to develop a description of the student behavior that defines each grade symbol. Figure 1 illustrates the types of phrases that can be used to differentiate levels of performance on the absolute grading scale. These phrases are contrasted with descriptors of relative grades that depend entirely on average performance to obtain their meanings. Note that to describe a "B student" using absolute standards, no reference is made to the achievements of other students. Instead, the comparison is based on the knowledge and skills studied and the extent to which prerequisites for future learning have been attained. The selection of a relative or an absolute grading standard is very critical because, once

Grade	Absolute Scale, Criterion-referenced	Relative Scale, Norm-referenced
A	• Firm command of knowledge domain • High level of skill development • Exceptional preparation for later learning	Far above class average
B	• Command of knowledge beyond the minimum • Advanced development of most skills • Has prerequisites for later learning	Above class average
C	• Command of only the basic concepts of knowledge • Demonstrated ability to use basic skills • Lacks a few prerequisites for later learning	At the class average
D	• Lacks knowledge of some fundamental ideas • Some important skills not attained • Deficient in many of the prerequisites for later learning	Below class average
F	• Most of the basic concepts and principles not learned • Most essential skills cannot be demonstrated • Lacks most prerequisites needed for later learning	Far below class average

FIGURE 1. *Descriptors of grade-level performances using absolute or relative standards*

that selection is made, all of the tools of assessment that are used to obtain grading information should be designed in accord with that selection—either norm-referenced or criterion-referenced.

A second facet of the meaning of a grade indicates whether achievement or effort is being described. Obviously effort and achievement are not independent, but a single grade cannot describe both unambiguously. Ideally, separate grades or marks should be used for each trait so that the two can be described more purely at the same time. If only one grade can be issued, however, describing achievement rather than effort seems more beneficial.

The third facet is a time-related reference—growth vs. status. If a grade is to indicate the amount of growth from the beginning of the grading period until the end, the highest grades should be assigned to those who demonstrate the greatest gains. In many subject areas, those with high beginning achievement levels will likely be able to grow the least. In fact, in some units of instruction, the highest achieving student may grow very little, if at all. But, assigning a C or D grade to such a student seems counter to the general notion of what grades usually connote. In short, most parents, students, and teachers are interested in whether growth has occurred, as they should be. But more important to them is the level of achievement at a particular time and whether that level is sufficient for moving onto the next sequence of the instructional program.

Step 3. Check the grade meanings against your instructional approach for logical consistency. A teacher who uses an outcomes-based approach or a highly individualized approach to instruction would not logically choose to use grades that have a norm-referenced meaning. Another teacher who depends heavily on the principles of cooperative learning would not likely use norm-referenced grades because of the competition they breed. Teachers who are devoted to a specific instructional or teaching philosophy need to develop a grading plan that is compatible with their teaching philosophy.

Step 4. Identify evaluation variables, reporting variables, and grading variables separately. The interpretability of a course grade will be jeopardized if the grade is made to carry too many pieces of information. This is the main reason why effort should be separated from achievement and growth should be separated from status when establishing the meaning of each grade symbol. Failure to make these separations will introduce irrelevant noise; static in any communication leads to misunderstanding and subsequent inappropriate decisions and impressions. One way of guarding against the threats to clear communication involves planning for evaluation. That is, just as plans should be made about what to teach and how to teach, concurrent plans should be made about the type of evaluation information that should be gathered during instruction.

Teachers gather preinstructional information about students' entering behaviors, they gather additional information to monitor student and class progress, and they obtain further information to decide if students are ready to move on to a new instructional unit. Thus, the *evaluation variables* that teachers depend on include such learner characteristics as interests, preferences, academic ability, past achievements, attitudes, effort, conduct, study skills, interpersonal skills, and the like. There are too many such variables to enumerate, but teachers can identify many of them and make definite plans to gather information about them. But having gathered such a wealth of information, it is not their intention to report the outcomes or judgments about all of them to parents or students. Ordinarily they select a small subset of such variables, which can be called *reporting variables,* as required by the district reporting methods, and they will use symbols or narrative comments to pass on the selected information.

Finally, from the set of reporting variables described above, a teacher will select those that provide information that is consistent with the meaning of the grades the teacher plans to assign. This subset of reporting variables can be labeled *grading variables.* The teacher who is determined to use grades

Table 1

The Distribution of Instructional Objectives Within Grading Components for Three Units of Instruction

Grading Component	Unit 1		Unit 2		Unit 3	
	Objs. 1–12	(33%)	Objs. 13–24	(33%)	Objs. 25–36	(33%)
Tests	1–8	(22%)	13–20	(22%)	25–32	(22%)
Quizzes	3–5		13–15		25–27	
Lab reports	9–10	(5%)	22–24	(6%)	36	(3%)
Homework	8–9		23–24		35–36	(2%)
Lab practicals	11–12	(5%)	23	(3%)	34	(3%)
Performance tests	—		21	(3%)	33,36	(2%)

to describe achievement levels will temporarily set aside indicators of effort, demeanor, attitude, and congeniality in favor of performance assessments and scores on tests, papers, and projects. The latter reflect achievement more accurately.

Note that it is possible to distort the meaning and value of certain grading components that, on the surface, appear to be relevant grading variables. For example, if the social studies essay scores of some students are reduced because of deficiencies in writing mechanics, how well do those scores describe achievement in social studies? If the teacher assigns an A to a group project, what does that A mean for a member of the group who made little contribution to planning, conducting, or summarizing project activities? If the grade on a paper is dropped a full letter for each day it is late, what does the final grade on a late paper indicate about achievement in language arts? If a student has an unexcused absence on the day of a test, what does an F grade for that test contribute to a quarter grade that is supposed to describe achievement? This is not the place to argue the merits of such policies or to explore alternative actions, but it is germane to point out that "relevant" grading variables can be distorted. Tainted component scores cause tainted composites. Tainted composites lead to misinterpretation.

Step 5. Check to see what the grade distributions in your building have been like at your grade level in the subjects you teach. If no written district policy exists, the grades issued in the most recent years will be the norm against which the reasonableness of each teacher's grades will be judged. How would your principal (and other teachers) react if your outcomes-based approach resulted in A grades for all of your students? This hypothetical question can not be answered, but it points out that grading patterns that depart significantly from local history generally will be questioned.

Suppose you teach an honors class in algebra and also have a regular algebra class. Should the grade distributions be similar in the two classes? If the grades from the two classes were merged into a single distribution, should that large distribution have the same number of A grades as would be assigned in two regular classes (assuming no honors section)? If written policy does not speak to these issues, the grades from the past few years are probably the best indication of what the current outcomes should be like.

Step 6. Decide on the kinds and number of grading components needed. Is it reasonable to base a 9-week English grade only on the score from a single test? Most would say, "Definitely not." Would scores from only two tests be sufficient? "Better," most would probably say, "but far from ideal." Generally, the more *good* information available for assigning grades, the more likely those grades will represent actual achievement levels accurately. There is no minimum number

of tests or other grading components that should be used; the overriding concern is to assess attainment of as many of the instructional objectives as possible so that grades will represent accomplishments with respect to the entire domain. The types of grading components required should be determined by examining what the instructional objectives require.

At this stage, it is also important to rule out the use of certain achievement-oriented evaluation variables from the set of grading variables. All of the instructional activities and exercises that students complete for practice purposes should be regarded as evaluation variables that inform teachers about progress *during* learning, not status indicators at the *end* of a learning experience. Daily homework, periodic quizzes, and responses to oral questioning are examples of evaluation variables that generally should not be regarded as grading variables. As long as a grade is intended to describe achievement status at the end of an instructional segment, assessments designed mainly to monitor progress during instruction should be excluded.

Should the contribution of individual students to a group project be factored into the grading of the project or the quarter's work? Can individual contributions be teased out? Should all group members be assigned the same grade? Should teachers simply provide evaluative reactions to group work but not treat such results as grading variables? Surely a student's grade should not be embellished or tainted by the achievements of others. Again, tainted composites lead to misinterpretation.

Many assessment techniques require a particular communication skill—writing, reading, speaking, drawing—that may not be well developed in some students. For example, a preponderance of essay testing may favor good writers, or the use of only objective tests may disadvantage poor readers. Obviously, students with limited English proficiency will be at a disadvantage no matter which medium of communication is used. The components of a grade ought to be selected or developed so that achievement in the subject area of interest (e.g., social studies) will not be masked by the language skills required by the assessment method.

Step 7. Determine how much weight each grading component will have. The role of instructional objectives is central to the process of combining grading components, just as it is for deciding which components to use. The task of formulating weights involves deciding how important each component score or grade is in describing achievement at the end of a grading period. The information in Table 1 illustrates the process of determining weights.

Table 1 shows that three science units were completed during one quarter, each unit consisted of 12 objectives, and each unit was to have equal weight (about 33%) in the quarter grade. The objectives measured by each grading component are identified by their number. Here is the initial thinking for determining the weights for the components of Unit 1:

1. Since 8 of the 12 objectives were covered by the test, two-thirds ($8/12$) of the weight for Unit 1 (33%) should be designated for the tests (22%).
2. The objectives measured by the quizzes were also covered by the test. Since they were regarded as checks during the learning process, the quizzes should have zero weight.
3. The lab reports covered 2 of the 12 objectives (17%), and no other grading component measured those same objectives. Give 17% of the unit weight (33%) to lab reports (about 5%).
4. Homework, like quizzes, was considered practice and dealt with objectives measured by other components. The quality of homework could be influenced by the help of others or it might be copied. No weight should be given to homework in the final grade.
5. Lab practicals, like lab reports, covered two unique objectives. Therefore, the same rationale was used to allocate 5% weight to lab practicals.

What factors entered into the thinking about component weights in the scenario above? One factor was the importance of the component as indicated in part by the number of objectives it encompassed. Another factor was uniqueness. Two components that measured any objectives in common were given less weight individually than two components that measured an equal number of unique objectives. (Notice how Objective 36 in Table 1 was handled.) A third factor, not evident in the scenario or Table 1, is the accuracy of the scores obtained from a component. For measures of similar skills, the one that provides the most accurate scores ought to be given the most weight.

Step 8. Determine how components will be combined to create a composite score or final grade. Once component weights have been established, the teacher must decide how to combine components so that the desired weights and actual weights are the same. The considerations and procedures for proper weighting differ for the norm-referenced and criterion-referenced situations. The differences are detailed in another instructional module and will not be repeated here (Oosterhof, 1987). For norm-referenced purposes, the variability of the scores of each component influences the weight the component will have in the composite. For criterion-referenced purposes, it is the total points associated with each component that matters most.

Step 9. Choose a method for assigning grades. The relative merits of the various common methods of assigning grades to composite scores are reviewed below. At this stage of establishing a grading plan, it is important for the teacher to choose or adapt a method of grade assignment that is consistent with the meaning that the grade symbols are intended to carry. Unfortunately, some of the most common methods of assigning grades yield results that are neither norm-referenced nor criterion-referenced. Consequently, teachers need to look carefully at methods of grade assignment that seem worthy of adoption.

The final aspect of assigning grades is the matter of dealing with borderline grades. For some teachers, the question is not *how* to treat borderline cases; it's *whether* to do it at all. They regard their grading practices as rigid procedures that produce highly objective grade results. For them, a review of borderline cases could insert subjectivity into the process and lead to outcomes that they would feel uncomfortable defending. However, others are driven by the apparent subjectivity inherent in several aspects of the grading process and by the desire to be fair in grading. Their notion of fairness is to err in favor of the student (award the higher of two grades) if an error is going to

be made. The reconsideration of borderline cases, then, is one way to ensure that certain errors will not be too influential in determining a student's grade.

What basis should be used for deciding whether to raise a grade in a borderline situation? Nearly always, *achievement* information that was not used to assign the tentative final grade should be taken into consideration. This advice is consistent with the premise that a grade should describe achievement rather than effort or some other trait. Homework quality, quiz score average, quality of class participation, and contributions to cooperative learning experiences are all possible achievement-oriented evaluation variables that could be suitable for borderline reviews. Some teachers hold one high-quality piece of achievement data in reserve for just such purposes.

Some Relative Grading Methods

Grades derived from any of the relative grading methods will have certain shortcomings that are inherent in any grades intended to have a norm-referenced meaning. For example, unless the person interpreting the grade knows which reference group was used, the grade means very little. Was it the student's class, a combination of classes, or classes from the past two years? Further, by definition, a norm-referenced grade does not tell what a student can do; there is no content basis other than the name of the subject area associated with the grade.

Grading on the Curve

The curve referred to in the name of this method is the normal, bell-shaped curve that is often used to describe the achievements of individuals in a large heterogeneous group. The idea behind this method is that the grades in a class should follow a normal distribution, or one nearly like it. Under this assumption, the teacher determines the percentage of students who should be assigned each grade symbol so that the distribution is normal in appearance. For example, the teacher may decide that the percentages of A through F grades in the class should be 10%, 20%, 40%, 20%, and 10%, respectively.

Since some teachers who use the method rightly believe that classroom groups are too small for their achievement scores to resemble a normal curve, they choose percentages that, in their judgment, are more realistic. So they may decide on 20%, 35%, 30%, 10%, and 5%. The percentages are selected arbitrarily and are treated like grade quotas so that the top 20% of students in terms of their composite scores will earn an A, the next 35% would be assigned a B, and so on.

Grading on the curve is a simple method to use, but it has serious drawbacks. The fixed percentages are nearly always determined arbitrarily, and the percentages do not account for the possibility that some classes are superior and others are inferior relative to the phantom "typical" group the percentages are intended to represent. In addition, the use of the normal curve to model achievement in a single classroom is generally inappropriate, except in large required courses at the high school and college levels.

Distribution Gap Method

When the composite scores of a class are ranked from high to low, there will usually be several short intervals in the score range where no student actually scored. These are gaps. This method of grade assignment involves finding the gaps in the distribution and drawing grade cutoffs at those places. For example, if the highest composite scores in a class were 211, 209, 209, 205, 197, 196, . . ., then the teacher might use the gap between 205 and 197 to separate the A and B grades. The gap between 211 and 209 is too small and might produce too few A grades. The one between 209 and 205 might be large enough, but 205 seems more like 209 than 197.

In some score distributions there are many wide gaps; in others there are only a few narrow gaps. The sizes and locations of the gaps are determined by random errors of measurement as well as by actual differences among students in achievement. For example, Mike's 197 maybe would have been 203 (if there had been less error in his scores), and Theo's 205 maybe would have been 200. Under those circumstances, the A–B gap would be less obvious, and too many final grade decisions would have been made by reviewing borderline cases.

When gaps are wide enough, this method helps the teacher avoid disputes with students about near misses. But when the gaps are narrow, too much emphasis is placed on the borderline information, information that the teacher had decided was not relevant enough or accurate enough to be included among the set of grading components that formed the composite. Only occasionally will the gap distribution method yield results that are comparable to those obtained with more dependable and defensible methods.

Standard Deviation Method

This relative method is the most complicated computationally, but it also is the fairest in producing grades objectively. It uses the standard deviation, a statistic that tells the average number of points by which the scores of students differ from their class average. It is a number that describes the dispersion, variability, or spread of scores around the average score. In this method, the standard deviation is used like a ruler to identify grade cutoff points.

Suppose you have formed composite scores for your class of 25 students and that the average was 129 and the standard deviation was 10. (Consult an introductory measurement or statistics book to see how to compute these statistics simply.) Assuming C to be the average grade, we can find the cutoff between B and C by adding, for example, one-half of the standard deviation to the average $(129 + (0.5)(10) = 134)$. Then the A–B cutoff is found by adding 1.5 standard deviations (for example) to the average $(129 + (1.5)(10) = 144)$. By subtracting corresponding values from the average score, the C–D cutoff is found to be 124, and the D–F cutoff is 114. (Can you verify these values?) The ranges for each grade are the following: A = 145 and up, B = 135–144, C = 124–134, D = 123–114, and F = 113 and below. These ranges can be made smaller or larger for groups of higher or lower ability level by adjusting the number of standard deviations used to find the cutoffs. For a particularly able class, for example, the A–B cutoff might be only one standard deviation above the average and the B–C cutoff might be 0.3 above, rather than 0.5.

Unlike grading on the curve, this method requires no fixed percentages in advance, and unlike the distribution gap method, the cutoff points are not tied to random error. When the teacher has some notion of what the grade distribution should be like, some trial and error might be needed to decide how many standard deviations each grade cutoff should be from the composite average. When a relative grading method is desired, the standard deviation method is most attractive, despite its computational requirements.

Some Absolute Grading Methods

Absolute grading methods produce grades that share some general shortcomings, independent of the particular method that generated the grades. For example, unless they are accompanied by a description of the performance standards or the content domains that have been studied, the meaning of an absolute grade is obscure. Furthermore, no criterion-referenced grading method produces grades that are strictly absolute in meaning. Such grades are based on performance

standards that nearly always have a normative basis. A "B writer" in fourth grade should be able to use quotations in dialogues, the teacher may say, but if most fourth-grade students do not and cannot, the standard is likely to be lowered to reflect reality (the norm). Note that adjusting grades instead of modifying the standards would contribute to meaningless grades.

Fixed Percent Scale

This method uses fixed ranges of percent-correct scores as the basis for assigning grades to the components of a final grade. A popular grading scale is the following: 93–100 = A, 85–92 = B, 78–84 = C, etc. These ranges are fixed at the beginning of the reporting period and are applied to the scores from each grading component—written tests, demonstrations, papers, and performance assessments. Component grades are then weighted and averaged to get the final grade.

Unfortunately, a percent score will be meaningless unless the domain of tasks, behaviors, or knowledge upon which the assessment was based is defined explicitly. That is, a test score of 100% should mean that the student has complete or thorough attainment of the key elements of the area of knowledge that was sampled by the test. But if an assessment is developed in such a way that the underlying content domain is ill-defined or nebulous, the percent-correct scores from it will have no meaning beyond the specific tasks that comprise the assessment. Scores of 80% on a spelling test and 75% on a speech say little about performance unless we know the difficulty of the domain of spelling words and which important criteria were used to score the speech. In sum, percent scores cannot provide a reference to absolute performance standards unless the underlying knowledge domain is adequately described.

Another serious drawback of this grading method is the fact that the percent-score ranges for each grade symbol are fixed for all grading components. For example, the fact that 93% is needed for an A places severe and unnecessary restrictions on the teacher when he or she is developing each assessment tool. If the teacher believes there should be some A grades, a 20-point test must be easy enough so that some students will score 19 or higher; otherwise there will be no A grades. This circumstance creates two major problems for the teacher as assessment developer. First, it requires that assessment tasks be chosen more for their anticipated easiness than for their content representativeness. As a result, there may be an overrepresentation of easy concepts and ideas, an overemphasis on facts and knowledge, and an underrepresentation of tasks that require higher order thinking skills. The teacher may need to "fudge" on the domain definition to accommodate the fixed grading scale.

A further limitation of this method relates to the accuracy of the assessment information obtained. Since the grade cutoff scores usually are located between the 60% and 100% points on the percent scale, most of the scale points (0–60) are of no value in describing the different absolute levels of achievement. For example, if A and B performance must be in the range of 85–100%, the very best B achievement and the very worst B achievement are separated by only eight points (85–92), as are the very best and very worst A achievements (93–100). These are fairly narrow score ranges, especially considering the fact that a 100-point scale is available for use. Because these ranges are narrow *and* fixed, they will contribute to fairly inaccurate grades when the scores of any single grading component are not very dependable. If the grade ranges could be made larger when the scores of a certain component are fairly inaccurate, then more accurate grades would probably result.

The fixed percent scale method usually produces grades that have little meaning in terms of content standards, and it often yields grades that are of questionable accuracy. The percent cutoffs for each grade are arbitrary and, thus, not defensible. Why should the cutoff for an A be 93, 92, or 90? Further, why shouldn't the A cutoff be 88% for a certain test, 91% for another, and 83% for a certain simulation exercise? Is there any reason why the same numerical standards must be applied to every grading component when those standards are arbitrary and void of absolute meaning?

Total Point Method

Some teachers accumulate points earned by students throughout a reporting period and then assign grades to the point total at the end of the period. First the teacher decides which components will figure into the final grade and what the maximum point value of each component will be. (This is done before tests are developed and before the scoring criteria for projects are established.) For example, you may decide to use two tests (50 points each), two papers (40 points each), and a report (20 points) for a maximum of 200 points for the quarter. Then the grade cutoffs might be set as follows: 180–200 = A, 160–179 = B, 140–159 = C, 120–139 = D, and 0–119 = F. Implicit in this set of ranges is a percent scale with grade cutoffs of 90%, 80%, 70%, and 60%. All teachers who use this method do not necessarily adopt these same cutoffs, but it is easy to see that there is no rational way to set the cutoffs. They are as arbitrary, and nearly as meaningless, as those derived from the fixed percent scale method. Unlike the fixed percent scale method, however, grades are not assigned to components with the total point method. And unlike grading on the curve, the arbitrary cutoff points are established at the beginning of the reporting period, *before* assessment results are known.

One of the difficulties of using this method is that often a decision has to be made about the maximum score on a project or test before the teacher has had ample time to think about the key ingredients of the assessment. Here's how this circumstance can contribute to poor assessment development practices: Suppose I need a 50-point test to fit my grading scheme, but I find as I build the test that I need 32 multiple-choice items to sample the content domain thoroughly. I find this unsatisfactory (or inconvenient) because 32 does not divide into 50 very nicely (It's 1.56!). To make life simpler, I could drop 7 items and use a 25-item test with 2 points per item. If I did that, my point totals would be in fine shape, but my test would be an incomplete measure of the important unit objectives. The fact that I had to commit to 50 points prematurely dealt a serious blow to obtaining meaningful assessment results.

Another potential drawback to the total point method is the ease with which extra credit points can be incorporated to beef up low point totals. This practice can simultaneously distort the meaning of the content domain and final grade. When the extra tasks are challenging and relevant to current instruction, this seems like a reasonable way to individualize and motivate high achieving students. In such cases, the outcome is likely to make high point totals even higher. But extra credit that simply allows students to compensate for low test scores or inadequate papers is not reasonable, especially if the extra work does not help them overcome demonstrated deficiencies. The point here is that this method of grading makes it convenient for teachers to allow extra credit work of the latter form to compensate for low achievement. When that happens, the grades take on a new meaning because the relevant domain of knowledge and skills gets redefined by the nature of the extra credit tasks.

Content-Based Method

This method involves assigning a grade to each component of the final grade and then weighting the separate grades to obtain the final one. The teacher develops brief descriptions of the achievement levels (standards) associated with each grading symbol, somewhat like those shown in Figure 1. These standards for "A work" and "B work" and so on are then used to establish the grade cutoff scores for every component. Compared to the fixed percent scale method, which keeps cutoff scores constant for all components, this method keeps the performance standards for a grade constant but lets the cutoff scores change. Here is an example of how the method might be used:

Suppose you have prepared a 30-item test to measure the achievement of most of the objectives in a unit of instruction. Assuming that grades A through F will be assigned to test scores, you will need to develop a brief description of the performance levels you expect students to reach for each of the five possible grades. For example, you might describe C expectations as "knows basic concepts and can do the most important skills; lacks some prerequisites for later learning." Using descriptions like these, you can begin an item-by-item review of the test.

For question no. 1, ask whether a student with only minimum achievement (D) should be able to answer correctly. If so, record a D next to the item; if not, pose the same question for grade C achievement. This process continues until the first item has been classified. For items that the teacher believes most A students will not necessarily answer correctly, a symbol such as N can be used to indicate that no grade level applies. (For items worth more than a single point, you will need to decide the minimum number of points that students at each achievement level should be able to earn.)

After you have classified each item with a symbol, the D–F cutoff score is found by adding the number of D symbols. Then the C–D cutoff is obtained by adding the number of D and C symbols. The B–C cutoff is the sum of D, C, and B symbols, and the A cutoff is the sum of the D, C, B, and A symbols. To account for negative errors of measurement, you could lower each grade cutoff by one or two points. Such adjustments for error at this stage of grading would make it unnecessary to review borderline cases at a later time.

All grading methods involve subjectivity, and this one requires two main types of subjective decisions. The first type entails the development of explicit expectations for the achievers at each of the letter-grade levels. What is B achievement like and how is it different from C achievement? Good teachers might disagree with one another about how to define these performance standards. The other subjective decision making occurs when items are reviewed to determine the grade category to which each one belongs. Again, good teachers may disagree about whether a "B student" should be able to answer a particular item correctly. Notice that these two types of judgments do not require that subjective decisions be made about individual students. There is no need to decide, for example, whether Jana is a C student or whether Matt could answer a certain question correctly. The judgments required here are about standards and about the particular tasks that students at each level should be expected to do.

Personal Grading Practices Evolve

Since both philosophies and instructional approaches change as curriculum changes, teachers need to be prepared to adjust their grading plans accordingly. With experience in assigning grades, reporting to parents, and observing the impact of grading on learning, many teachers rethink their responses to the philosophical questions enumerated in the "Developing a Grading Philosophy" section. The meanings of the symbols, the characteristics to be judged, the components to include in a grade, and the method used for assigning grades are all issues of value that take on new importance or new meaning as teachers accumulate grading experience and observe the practices of colleagues.

6. ASSESSMENT

Grading practices also may change as a teacher's instructional approach changes. For example, a teacher who begins experimenting with cooperative learning strategies would start depending more on group projects and presentations for assessment information. The nature of the grading components being used may need to change, as would any grading practices that foster competition among learners.

In short, a teacher's grading practices are likely to evolve slowly over time as his or her grading philosophy changes, as experience in grading accumulates, and as a base of grading data from several classes becomes available. As the nature of the curriculum changes and teachers fine-tune or modify their instructional approaches, the procedures outlined here can be reviewed to adjust inconsistencies in philosophy and practice.

Reference

Oosterhof, A. C. (1987). Obtaining intended weights when combining students' scores. *Educational Measurement: Issues and Practice, 6*(4), 29–37.

Annotated References

The references in this section cover a broad range of topics on grading, as do several other excellent introductory measurement texts. We have chosen to highlight some of the unique or particularly strong parts of these references as an aid to those who seek additional reading.

Carey, L. M. (1988). *Measuring and evaluating school learning.* Newton, MA: Allyn and Bacon. Chapter 13.
   The section on designing a gradebook and managing daily records is unique. There also are ample illustrations of the selection and implementation of weights.

Ebel, R. L., & Frisbie, D. A. (1991). *Essentials of educational measurement* (5th edition). Englewood Cliffs, NJ: Prentice Hall. Chapter 15.
   Philosophical issues are discussed in depth and threats to the meaning of grades are considered. The standard deviation and content-based methods are illustrated.

Hills, J. R. (1981). *Measurement and evaluation in the classroom* (2nd edition). Columbus, OH: Bell & Howell. Chapters 14–19.
   The chapter on faulty grading practices provides good background for developing a grading philosophy and plan. Broad coverage is also given to reporting methods other than grading.

Oosterhof, A. C. (1990). *Classroom applications of educational measurement.* Columbus, OH: Merrill. Chapters 21–22.
   A helpful discussion of the sources of inconsistency in grades is given in one section and a chapter is devoted to weighting procedures for relative grading methods.

Self-Test

1. Which of these statements is most likely to be found in a school's grading policy handbook?
   A. "All teachers will assign grades by grading on the curve."
   B "Grades assigned by teachers are final and may not be appealed."
   C. "Quarter grades must be based on written test scores only."
   D. "The grade of C will be awarded to students whose performance is average compared with their classmates."

2. Which of the following statements indicates that Kathy's B represents her present achievement level compared to an absolute standard?
   A. Kathy is performing well above her peers.
   B. Kathy has shown considerable hard work and has adequate mastery of the primary objectives.
   C. Kathy is the most able student in the class and should have received an A.

   D. Kathy has mastered most of the material taught this grading period.

Use this situation to answer questions 3–5.
   Mr. Thompson is a fifth-grade teacher with a class of mixed ability. He has organized his social studies curriculum so that he covers four instructional units per quarter. The following is a list of evaluation data that he collects on each student during each of the four units.

   I. 5 homework assignment scores.
   II. 1 project
   III. 1 quiz (after the first week)
   IV. 1 unit test

   Mr. Thompson wants his quarter grades to reflect students' achievements at the end of the quarter compared with his absolute standards.

3. Given his grading plan, which information should he incorporate into the composite for the quarter?
   A. IV only
   B. II, III, and IV
   C. II and IV
   D. I, II, III, and IV

4. What additional information is needed to decide how to weight the projects in the final grade?

   A. The amount of time students spent in completing the projects
   B. The amount of variability of the scores within the class on each project
   C. The difficulty level of each project for the class as a whole
   D. The number of unique objectives each project measures compared to other components

5. Which is the best way for Mr. Thompson to grade the projects so that the meaning he wants in his social studies grades is obtained?
   A. Use scoring criteria that are based on content standards.
   B. Try to rank the projects in order from best to worst.
   C. Compare the quality of each student's four projects to look for improvement.
   D. Ask for amount of time spent and amount of help received from others to judge effort.

True–False

6. The objectivity of the standard deviation method for assigning grades makes it superior to the content-based method.

7. Grades that simultaneously incorporate effort, growth, achievement, organization, and ability are less useful than those that incorporate only achievement.

8. One of the advantages of the content-based method over the fixed-percent scale method is that it allows the performance standards for a grade to vary for each component.

9. Some evaluation variables are both reporting variables and grading variables.

10. Homework scores are better grading variables than evaluation variables.

11. If the achievement of a certain objective cannot be measured effectively by a written test, the objective should be excluded from the grading plan.

Answers to Self-Test

1. D. The first three choices are too restrictive or too detailed for most policies. (See Step 1.)
2. D. See Step 2.
3. C. The projects and tests provide information about

achievement status at the end of a unit. Homework assignments and quizzes relate to practice and monitoring progress. (See Steps 6–7.)

4. D. The number of objectives covered and the uniqueness of those objectives should be examined when determining component weights. (See Step 7.)

5. A. Components should be scored in a manner consistent with the meaning of the final grade. (See Step 2.)

6. False. The standard deviation method requires subjectivity also (e.g., which grade will be average, how many standard deviations to use to find a cutoff).

7. True. Incorporating more than achievement into a grade distorts the grade's meaning.

8. False. The content-based method allows the cutoff scores to change while keeping the standards constant. (See Content-based Method.)

9. True. Grading variables are a subset of reporting variables, which are in turn a subset of evaluation variables. (See Step 4.)

10. False. Homework is best used to monitor learning and provide practice throughout the instructional unit. (See Step 7.)

11. False. The achievement of such objectives could be assessed by other means—performance assessments, projects, or presentations.

Creating Tests Worth Taking

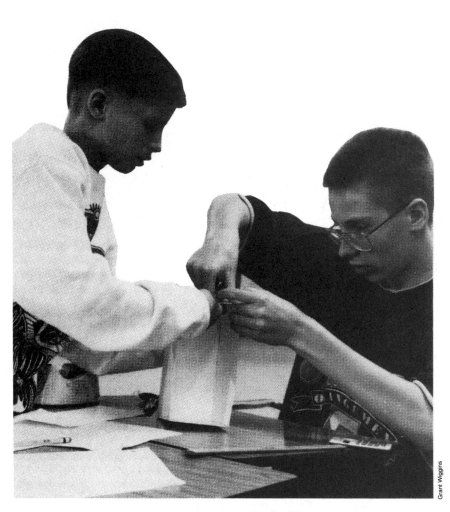

Grant Wiggins

The Director of Research at CLASS provides questions, criteria, and suggestions for test designers who want to engage students as well as evaluate their performance.

GRANT WIGGINS

Grant Wiggins is the Director of Research and Programs for the Center on Learning, Assessment, and School Structure (CLASS), 39 Main St., Geneseo, NY 14454. These design ideas derive from the work of CLASS in Frederick County, Md.; South Orange-Maplewood, N.J.; Urbandale, Iowa.; and with faculties in Monroe, Orange, Suffolk, Ulster, and Wayne counties, N.Y.

Should a test be enticing? I think so. And should tests more often be authentic simulations of how knowledge is tested in adult work and civic settings? Many of us believe so. "Performance assessment" calls upon test makers to be creative designers then, not just technicians.

In performance assessment the design issues resemble those facing the architect. There is ground to be covered (the syllabus), there are the logistics of making the design fit the site (making large-scale assessment work in the school), and there are building codes (psychometric norms) and town elders (school board members and district testing directors) to worry about. But designers have typically avoided another, more basic obligation: the need to serve the users — in this case, students and teachers. The clients must "own" the design; form must follow function. The more the tasks (like the house) fit seamlessly with both the environment and the client's aspirations, the better the design and the result.

In this article I offer some proven design tips, tools, and criteria for fashioning assessment tasks that are more enticing, feasible, and defensible — tests worth taking.

Questions and Criteria

Designers of performance assessments should use the following key questions as a tool to guide the design process:

- What kinds of essential tasks, achievements, habits of mind, or other valued "masteries" are falling through the cracks of conventional tests?
- What are the core performances, roles, or situations that all students should encounter and be expected to master?
- What are the most salient and insightful discriminators in judging actual performances?
- What does genuine mastery of each proposed assessment task look like? Do we have credible and appropriate exemplars to anchor our scoring system? Have we justified standards so they are more than local norms?
- Are the test's necessary constraints — imposed on help available from others, access to resources, time to revise, test secrecy, prior knowledge of standards — authentic?
- Do our assessment tasks have sufficient depth and breadth to allow valid generalizations about overall student competence?
- Have we ensured that the test will not be corrupted by well-intentioned judges of student work?
- Who are the audiences for assessment information, and how should assessment be designed, conducted, and reported to accommodate the needs of each audience? When are audit-tests appropriate and inappropriate?

These questions can be summarized and reframed to produce eight basic design criteria:

1. Assessment tasks should be, whenever possible, authentic and meaningful — worth mastering.
2. The set of tasks should be a valid sample from which apt generalizations about overall performance of complex capacities can be made.
3. The scoring criteria should be authentic, with points awarded or taken off for essential successes and errors, not for what is easy to count or observe.
4. The performance standards that anchor the scoring should be genuine

benchmarks, not arbitrary cut scores or provincial school norms.
5. The context of the problems should be rich, realistic, and enticing — with the inevitable constraints on access to time, resources, and advance knowledge of the tasks and standards appropriately minimized.
6. The tasks should be validated.
7. The scoring should be feasible and reliable.
8. Assessment results should be reported and used so that *all* customers for the data are satisfied.

The suggestions and observations that follow offer further assistance to would-be designers.

Choosing What to Test

Choose exit outcomes or areas of the curriculum that now tend to fall through the cracks of conventional testing. Typical tests, even demanding ones, tend to overassess student "knowledge" and underassess student "know-how with knowledge" — that is, intellectual performance. Auditing local tests with Bloom's taxonomy as criteria, for example, shows that synthesis is infrequently assessed at present, and is *inherently resistant* to assessment by multiple-choice tests because it requires "production of a unique communication" that bears the stamp of the student.[1]

Faculties should also consider their institutional "customers." What kinds of tasks must our *former* students master? Here, for example, is a question from a freshman final exam in European history at a prestigious college; it suggests how even our better students are often ill-prepared for real intellectual tasks:

> Imagine yourself Karl Marx, living half a century later. Write a brief evaluation of the programs of the Fabian socialists and the American reformers such as T. Roosevelt to present to the Socialist International.

Think of the knowledge to be tested as a tool for fashioning a performance or product. Successful task design requires making the essential material

of a course a *necessary means* to a successful performance *end*. Example: a 5th grade teacher assesses geography knowledge by having his students devise a complete itinerary, map, and travel packet for their favorite rock group's world tour, within certain budget, logistical, cultural, and demographic restrictions.

Another example: students are asked to design a museum exhibit around a theme studied in a history course, selecting from many real or facsimile artifacts; required to justify what is both included and excluded in the exhibit; and must seek funding from a "foundation" of teachers and peers for the exhibit.

We want to know: Can the student use knowledge and resources effectively, *to achieve a desired effect*? This is the question Bloom and his colleagues argued was at the heart of synthesis. These tasks should only be judged well done to the extent that the content is well used.

Designing the Tasks

Contextualize the task. The aim is to invent an authentic simulation, and like all simulations, case studies, or experiential exercises, the task must be rich in contextual detail. A context is rich if it supports multiple approaches, styles, and solutions and requires good judgments in achieving an effective result. One must please a real audience, make a design actually work, or achieve an aesthetic effect that causes pride or dismay in the result.

The test may be a contrivance, but it needn't *feel* like one.[2] Consider professional training and testing. Doctors and pilots in training confront situations that replicate the challenges to be later faced. Business and law students learn by the case method, fully immersed in the facts of real past cases. A context is realistic to the extent that we so accept the premises, constraints, and "feel" of the challenge that our desire to master it makes us lose sight of the extrinsic factors and motives at stake — namely that someone is evaluating us. In just this way, for example, putting out a school

6. ASSESSMENT

newspaper for a journalism course doesn't feel contrived.

Here's an example of how a teacher's attempt to design a performance task evolved as a concern for context was introduced. The original task, in a global studies course, required students to design a trip to China or Japan. But what kind of trip? For what customers? With what constraints of budget or time? The teacher then refined the task so that each student had a $10,000 budget for **designing a month-long, cultural-exchange trip for students their age. Still, the purpose is too abstract.** What must the tour designers accomplish? Are they trying to design a tour in the abstract or really attract tour-takers? The students were finally charged to be travel agents who develop an extensive brochure and research the cost and logistical information using a computer reservations system.

There is no such thing as performance-in-general. To understand what *kind* and *precision* of answer fits the problem at hand, the student needs contextual detail: it clarifies the desired result, hence the criteria and standards. Too many measurement tasks have an acceptable margin of error that is arbitrary. Are we measuring body temperature or roasts in the oven? It matters. The task's standard of performance (desired precision or quality of product) should be apparent. In fact, an important oversight by the global studies teacher was her failure to give the students model tour brochures.[3]

Aim to design "meaningful" tasks — not the same as "immediately relevant or practical" tasks. An assessment task will be meaningful to the extent that it provokes thought and thus engages the student's interest. But a task can be engaging without being of apparent, immediate usefulness. Whether it be mysteries, debates, mock trials, putting on plays — or, for that matter, Nintendo — students clearly respond to "irrelevant" but real challenges. What do such tasks have in common? Designers need to conduct better

empirical studies to discover the tasks that tap those twin intellectual needs: *our urge for efficacy and our need for meaningful connections.*

This caution about meaning vs. relevance is particularly warranted to avoid turning important theoretical problems into crude utilitarian ones. Many genuine problems do not have obvious practical value, but they nonetheless evoke interest and provide insight into student abilities. Consider two such problems, one in geometry and one in history/English:

> We all know the Pythagorean theorem: $A^2 + B^2 = C^2$; but does it have to be a square that we draw on each leg? Suppose we drew the same shape on each leg; would the areas on A and B add up to the area on C? Find other shapes that make the equation work, too, and try to derive a more general formula of the theorem.[4]

> You and your colleagues (groups of 3 or 4) have been asked to submit a proposal to write a U.S. history textbook for middle school students. The publishers demand two things: that the book hit the most important things, and that it be interesting to students. Because of your expertise in 18th-century American history, you will provide them a draft chapter on the 18th century, up to but not including the Revolution, and "field tested" on some middle school students. They also ask that you fill in an "importance" chart with your response to these questions: (1) Which event, person, or idea is most important in this time period, and why? (2) Which of three sources of history — ideas, people, events — is most important? You will be expected to justify your choices of "most important" and to demonstrate that the target population will likely be interested in your book.

Design performances, not drills. A test of many items (a drill) is not a test of knowledge in use. "Performance" is not just doing simplistic tasks that cue us for the desired bit of knowledge. It entails "putting it all together" with good judgment; good judgment cannot be tested through isolated, pat drills. As one teacher put it to me a few years ago: "The

trouble with kids today is that they don't know what to do when they don't know what to do." She is right — and a prime reason is that tests rarely put students in an authentic performance situation, where *thinking,* not just an obvious bit of knowledge, is required.

The designer's aim, then, is to avoid inventing a new round of (this time, hands-on) isolated items. Rather, we should consider the difference between drilled ability vs. performance ability and ask: *What is the equivalent of the game or recital in each subject matter?* What does the "doing" of mathematics, history, science, art, language use, and so forth, look and feel like in context? What are the projects and other kinds of synthesizing tasks performed all the time by professionals, consumers, or citizens that can be adapted to school use?

Such tasks are always "higher-order," and we would do well to use Lauren Resnick's criteria in our search for better-designed assessments. Higher-order thinking

• is *nonalgorithmic* — that is, the path of action is not fully specified in advance;

• is *complex*, with the total path not visible from any single vantage point;

• *often yields multiple solutions*, each with costs and benefits;

• involves *nuanced judgment* and interpretation;

• involves the *application of multiple criteria*, which sometimes conflict with one another;

• often involves *uncertainty*, because not everything that bears on the task is known;

• involves *self-regulation* of the thinking process, rather than coaching at each step;

• involves *imposing meaning*, finding structure in apparent disorder;

• is *effortful*, with considerable mental work involved.[5]

It may help to think of this problem as the search for larger, more interrelated but complex chunks of content to build tasks around. What, for example, might be 8 to 10 important performance tasks in a subject that

220

effectively and efficiently "map" the essential content? Vocational programs usually grapple well with this problem by casting the course objectives as a set of increasingly complex tasks to be mastered, in which the student in the last task(s) must literally put it all together, for example, build a house in carpentry.

Refine the tasks you design by building them backwards from the models and scoring criteria. A complex task is not a vague task, with the objective or specifications unknown. All real-world performers know the target and the standards, not just their task in advance; such knowledge guides their training and

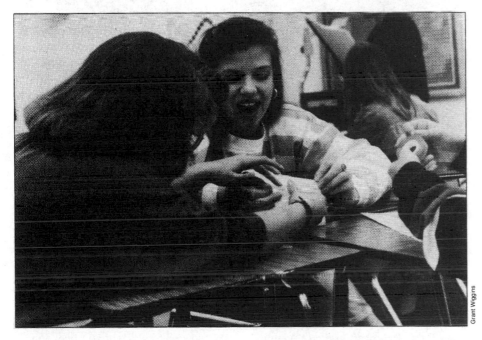

Grant Wiggins

rehearsals. Students should never have to wonder "Is this right?" "Am I finished?" "How am I doing?" "Is this what you want?" In a "real" problem the task is ill-structured but well-defined: the goal, specifications, or desired effect is known, but it is not obvious how to meet it. Knowing the *requirements of task mastery* — the "specs" — means the student must be habituated by testing to think of mastery as control over the *knowable* essentials, not as calculated cramming and good guesses. This requires providing the student with scoring criteria and models of excellent performance or production as part of instruction. (Think of diving and

debate.) Such practice is the norm throughout Carleton, Ontario, where students work from "exemplar booklets" to practice grading student work — in the same way now reserved for judges in our assessments.

"What does mastery at the task look like? What will we be able to properly infer from the collected student work?" These become the *key* questions to ask in the challenge of taking a basic idea and making a valid performance-assessment task out of it (as opposed to an instructional task). The questions properly focus on judging anticipated results and move away from design that produces merely pleasant or interesting work.

Scoring Considerations

Score what is most important for doing an effective job, not what is easiest to score. The scoring rubrics should represent generalizations about the traits found in an array of actual performances. But too often we resort to scoring what is easiest — or least controversial — to observe. A fine task can be rendered inauthentic by such bogus criteria.

Two key questions for setting up a scoring system therefore are: "What are the most salient characteristics of each level or quality of response?" and "What are the errors that are

most *justifiable* for use in lowering a score?" Obvious successes and errors (such as those that relate to spelling or computation) are not necessarily the most accurate indicators of mastery or its absence.[6] Too many essay scoring systems reward students for including merely *more* arguments or examples; quantity is not quality, and we teach a bad lesson by such scoring practices.

When possible, scoring criteria should rely on descriptive language, not evaluative and/or comparative language such as "excellent" or "fair." Judges should know specifically where in performance to look and what to look for. The ACTFL foreign language proficiency guidelines and the Victoria, Australia, "Literacy Profiles" are perhaps the best examples available of such empirically grounded criteria.[7] Teachers may also want to have students analyze a task and help devise the scoring system. This builds ownership of the evaluation, makes it clear that judgments need not be arbitrary, and makes it possible to hold students to higher standards because criteria are clear and reasonable.

"Benchmark" the standards for performance to ensure that your scoring standards are wisely chosen and suited to wider-world or next-level demands. Standard-setting for performance involves selecting exemplary samples of performance or production. The challenge is to avoid using local age-grade norms; the solution is to equate our exit-level standards at desirable colleges or professions. That advice, of course, begs a more fundamental question: Whose view of excellence should count? It is at least prudent to equate local standards of scoring to some credible wider-world or next-level standard—something routinely done in the performing arts, athletics, and vocational education.[8] *And, every so often, refer to next-level standards when scoring the work of younger students.* (I believe Illinois was the first state to assess both 6th and 8th grade writing samples against 8th grade exemplars, for instance.)

6. ASSESSMENT

Administering the Assessments

Since constraints always exist in testing, make them as authentic as possible. The question is not "Should there be constraints in testing?" but rather "When are constraints authentic, and when are they inauthentic?" It is often a matter of degree, but the principle needs to be maintained and defended.

Constraints facing the designer of authentic assessment tasks typically involve access or restrictions to the following resources: (1) time (including time to prepare, rethink, and revise), (2) reference material, (3) other people (including access to peers, experts, the test designer, and/or the judge), and (4) prior knowledge of the tasks and how they will be assessed (the issue of test security). The question then becomes: What are *appropriate* limits on the availability of these resources?

Traditional testing, because it involves indirect proxies for performance, requires numerous inauthentic constraints to preserve validity. The validity of most multiple-choice tests, for example, is compromised if questions are known in advance or if reference material can be consulted during the test. These habits of administration run deep; they seem obviously required. But what of the validity issues raised by denying students access to basic resources? Just what is being tested when the student cannot predict the historical periods or books that will be assessed, or cannot consult resources while writing?

We need not keep textbooks and other materials from students if the task is genuinely authentic. For example, in many of Connecticut's performance tasks in mathematics, the key formulas are given to the student as background to the problem. And why not allow the student to bring notes to the exam? A physics teacher I know allows students to bring an index card to the exam with anything on it; the card often reveals more about the student's knowledge than the exam answers!

Too little time for performing is not always the key issue either. Is the

Grant Wiggins

limiting of the test to *one sitting* authentic? If writing is indeed revision, for example, why not allow writing assessment to occur over three days, with each draft graded? Many districts now do so, including Jefferson County, Kentucky, and Cherry Creek, Colorado.[9]

I am not arguing that the student should have unlimited time and access in testing.[10] Let us ask: What kinds of constraints authentically simulate or replicate the constraints and opportunities facing the performer in context? What kinds of constraints tend to bring out the best in apprentice performers and producers?

Develop a written, thorough protocol that details how the task should be administered — especially so judges will know the proper limits of their interventions to student acts, comments, or questions. It is incred-

ibly easy to invalidate performance assessment by varying the instructions, the amount of assistance provided, and the depth of responses given to inevitable student questions. Determining beforehand what is acceptable response and intervention by adults is essential; test administrators must receive standard verbal responses for delicate situations, confusions, or problems that arise.

And don't forget that kids can do the darndest things with directions that aren't thought through. In a hands-on science experiment that asked whether "the sun" heated up different colored liquids at different rates, a student did not use the heat lamp provided, moved all his equipment to the window, saw it was a cloudy day, and wrote "no."

Make the tasks maximally self-sustaining and the record-keeping obligation mostly the student's. Many educators who have never seen large-scale performance assessment cannot fathom how all students can be efficiently and effectively assessed. But they assume that the teacher will have to guide activity every step of the way and record massive amounts of information simultaneously. Thoughtful preparation, designed to make the assessment self-running, frees the teacher to be a perceptive judge.

Creating a Tool Kit

Develop a districtwide "tool kit" of exemplary tasks, task templates, and design criteria for assessment tasks. Not all of us are good designers, but why should we have to be? Teachers can help their colleagues by providing a sampler of tasks and task templates. Kentucky has done this at the statewide level, providing dozens of tasks and task ideas to teachers as part of the new state performance-based assessment system. We should consider including not only current examples of model assessment tasks, but traditional performance-based challenges such as debates, treasure hunts, mysteries, design competitions, historical reenactments, science fairs, Odyssey of the Mind tasks, Scout Merit Badges, student-run banks and stores, and so forth.

The mathematics performance assessment team of the Connecticut Department of Education has identified the following types of problems as central to its work:

• Given data on graphs, write a story that represents the data or graph.

• Given headlines or claims with background data, explain whether or not the claims are reasonable.

• Given student work containing common errors, write a response to the student.

• Given equations or number facts, write a problem that the equations or facts could solve.

• Given trends or sample data, make and justify predictions.

• Given consumer- or job-related buying, selling, or measuring situations, solve a problem.

• Given multiple or competing interpretations of given data, justify each interpretation.

Job roles provide ample opportunities for task designers to create simulations. Here are some suggestions.

• Museum curator: design museum exhibits; compete for "grant" money.

• Engineer or surveyor: bid and meet specs for largest-volume oil container; build a working roller coaster; map or survey a region around school or in the building.

• Ad agency director: design advertising campaigns, book jackets, or blurbs for books read in class.

• Psychologist/sociologist: conduct surveys, perform statistical analyses, graph results, write newspaper articles on the meaning of results.

• Archaeologist: determine the culture or time frame of a mystery artifact or person.

• Newspaper editor and writer: write articles and editorials set in the studied historical time.

• Policy analyst: predict the future in a country being studied.

• Product designer: conduct research, design ad campaign, present proposal to panel.

• Job interviewee: present portfolio and try to get "hired" for a specific job related to skills of current course (interview conducted by other students or teacher).

• Expert witness to Congress: testify on behalf of or against advertising claims, regulation of children's TV, or current policy issue.

• Commercial designer: Propose artwork for public buildings.

Piloting and Reporting

Always pilot some or all of the test. Assessment design is like software design: one can *never* accurately and fully anticipate the naive user's response. A first design may not fit the purpose or maximally evoke the desired knowledge; a prompt might result in irrelevant responses that are nonetheless appropriate or reasonable to the student; the logistical constraints of a context can turn out to be more daunting than anticipated; the judges may be too self-interested in the results or insufficiently trained. A pilot is the only way to find out, even if it involves only a tiny sample of performers. And the de-bugging requires a *naive* "guinea pig" — a teacher from a different subject or a few students — if the hidden problems in the goal, directions, or procedures are to be found.

You are what you report: Make sure that your report cards, transcripts, and district accountability reports relate achievement and progress to essential performance tasks and exit-level standards. Few transcripts reflect achievement in reference to outcomes. They tend to certify that tests were passed on each isolated packet of content instead of documenting what the student can do and to what level of performance. Further, a one-shot test cannot validly assess many important capacities, as the phrases "habits of mind" or "consistency of performance" suggest. Grading and reporting thus need to move toward scoring that provides a "progress" measure — that is, work scored against exit-level performance standards. And no worthy performance is reducible to one aggregate score. Every student ought to have the equivalent of a baseball card — many different kinds of abilities measured and a brief narrative report — if we are seriously interested in accurately documenting and improving complex performance.

Assessment's Role in School Reform

An underlying premise of this kind of assessment reveals why I believe that assessment reform is the Trojan horse of real school reform. We badly need better definitions of mastery or *understanding* to guide assessment design, curriculum design, and teacher job descriptions and performance appraisal. Circling "correct" answers to problems only test makers care about is not "knowing," nor is it the aim of teaching. Authentic tests provide a stimulating challenge instead of an onerous obligation.

Perhaps more important for school restructuring is the need to build local

Horace's School: Redesigning the American High School

Theodore R. Sizer
Boston:
Houghton Mifflin Company, 1992

This book is a valuable tool for a school in the midst of a major assessment/restructuring process. Presented as an extended case study centering around the fictional teacher, Horace Smith, the book follows Horace through a series of restructuring committee meetings he is chairing at Franklin High School.

The meetings accurately capture the blend of tedium and excitement characteristic of the committee process. Flowing from the discussions of what it means to be well educated and how to best provide this education are several examples of "exhibitions." These are the means whereby students demonstrate their understanding of ideas and skills underlying the school's newly devised program. The exhibitions provide readers Sizer's best examples of performance assessments for high school students.

Interspersed with Sizer's commentary is his narrative. It is here I found him at his best. The chapter "Policy and Power" is as cogent and heartfelt a statement about reform as I have read.

The book draws from years of research and the author's work with the Coalition of Essential Schools. Sizer delineates the Coalition's "nine common principles," which recognize there is no one way for a good school to look or proceed. Likewise, there are no shortcuts in the restructuring process, especially as it seeks to challenge the underlying principles of our current schools. This book sheds light on the reform process and helps clarify the challenge. The rest is up to us.

Available from Houghton Mifflin Company, Two Park St., Boston, MA 02108, for $19.95 (paperback).

— Reviewed by Stephen Garger, University of Portland, Portland, Oregon.

---

educator capacity and interest in quality assessment.[11] Genuine faculty empowerment is impossible without deep ownership of local standards and measures. Farming all these problems out to distant "experts" is a grave mistake — one rarely made in any other country. Good teaching is inseparable from good assessing. It may well be that experts can design more rigorous tests, and that correlational/predictive validities exist in standardized tests. But schooling we can be proud of and held genuinely accountable for demands more locally useful, authentic, and enticing assessments.

---

[1]Bloom, (1954), pp. 163, 175. Serious would-be test designers would do well to reread the *text* of the taxonomy, not just the Appendix/list, as well as the follow-up handbook developed by Bloom, Madaus, and Hastings, (1981).

[2]"The student should [have] freedom from excessive tension . . . be made to feel that the product of his efforts need not conform to the views of the instructor . . . [and] have considerable freedom of activity . . . [including] freedom to determine the materials or other elements that go into the final product." In Bloom, (1954), p. 173.

[3]See Linn, Baker, and Dunbar, (1991), for further discussion of validity design issues.

[4]I have watched half a dozen classes immerse themselves in this problem and beg to continue when time ran out.

[5]From Resnick (1987).

[6]Describing key errors and using them in the rubric is a *very different* matter than building them into test answers as "distractors."

[7]A related issue that emerges in designing rubrics (and thus far unaddressed by measurement experts) is the difference between the degree of difficulty of the task and the desired quality of the performance — a distinction made in New York's music performance assessments.

[8]See Wiggins (1991).

[9]Yes, yes, I know the issue is *really* one of cheating. Let the teacher "sign off" on the papers, then, certify authorship, as they do in Australia and now in Vermont.

[10]Though many New York State tests do allow the student what amounts to unlimited time — all day — given the shortness of the test. And certifiably learning disabled students are allowed unlimited time on the SATs as well as many state achievement tests.

[11]See Stiggins (1991).

References and Readings

Bloom, B. S., ed. (1954). *Taxonomy of Educational Objectives: The Classification of Educational Goals; Handbook I: The Cognitive Domain.* New York: Longman Publishers.

Bloom, B. S., G. F. Madaus, and J. T. Hastings. (1981). *Evaluation to Improve Learning.* New York: McGraw-Hill. [A major revision of *Handbook on Formative and Summative Evaluation of Student Learning.* (1971). McGraw-Hill].

Linn, R. L., E. L. Baker, and S. B. Dunbar. (November 1991). "Complex, Performance-Based Assessment: Expectations and Validation Criteria." *Educational Researcher* 20, 8: 15-21.

Mitchell, R. (1992). *Testing for Learning: How New Approaches to Evaluation Can Improve American Schools.* New York: The Free Press.

National Council of Teachers of Mathematics. (Forthcoming). *Mathematics Assessment: Myths, Models, Good Questions, and Practical Suggestions.* Reston, Va.: NCTM.

Resnick, L. (1987). *Education and Learning to Think.* Washington, D.C.: National Academy Press.

Schwartz, J. L., and K. A. Viator, eds. (1990). "The Prices of Secrecy: The Social, Intellectual, and Psychological Costs of Testing in America." A Report to the Ford Foundation. Education Technology Center, Cambridge, Mass.: Harvard Graduate School of Education.

Stiggins, R. (March 1991). "Assessment Literacy." *Phi Delta Kappan* 72, 7: 534-539.

Victoria Ministry of Education. (1990). *Literacy Profiles: Handbook.* Victoria, Australia. [Distributed in the U. S. by TASA, Brewster, N.Y.]

Wiggins, G. (February 1991). "Standards, Not Standardization: Evoking Quality Student Work." *Educational Leadership* 48, 5:18-25.

Wiggins, G. (June 1990). "Finding Time." *Basic Education* 34, 10.

Wiggins, G. (May 1989). "A True Test: Toward More Authentic and Equitable Assessment." *Phi Delta Kappan* 70, 9: 703-713.

Wiggins, G. (April 1989). "Teaching to the (Authentic) Test." *Educational Leadership* 46, 7: 41-47.

Performance Assessment
The Realities That Will Influence the Rewards

**Carol Anne Pierson
and Shirley S. Beck**

Carol Anne Pierson is Associate Professor and Assistant Dean of Education, University of Central Arkansas, Conway. Shirley S. Beck is Assistant Professor, Department of Curriculum and Instruction, Southwest Texas State University, San Marcos.

As educators continually strive to improve evaluation methods, performance assessment has grown in popularity and use. Performance assessment is an authentic way to acquire accurate information about students' performance and comprehension (Perrone, 1991). Its appeal may be related to the growing need for local decision-making about student progress and instructional programs, as well to the interest in outcome-based education. Extensive debate about this type of assessment is carried on in education journals, professional meetings and education policy discussions. "Expert" perceptions of the "movement" range from skepticism to a belief that it is the solution to all of education's ills (Arter, 1991; Cizek, 1991).

At best, performance assessment could be the key to restructuring schools for higher standards and improved accountability. At the very least, it adds an expanded dimension to education assessment. At worst, performance assessment could become another promising idea tossed on the junk heap of discarded innovations if care is not taken to really understand its nature and limitations. As more schools move toward performance assessment for student evaluations, teachers and particularly administrators must become knowledgeable users.

Performance assessment is not a totally new idea. It is a common form of assessment in fields such as medicine and law. Industry uses performance assessment to make promotion decisions. Performance assessment was once the most common form of assessment in education, prior to the widespread use of standardized tests (Perrone, 1991). And it has been used regularly in such subjects as physical education, music and art.

> *At best, performance assessment could be the key to restructuring schools for higher standards and improved accountability.*

Language arts teachers, in particular, have embraced the concept of performance assessment, perhaps because they have been using performance testing to varying degrees for many years (i.e., to evaluate essays, speeches, book reports and various forms of oral reading). Their cry to legitimize teacher observations of students engaged in actual literacy tasks is being heard and supported by other teachers, administrators, governors and legislators. Performance assessment of reading and writing is becoming a reality in many classrooms across the United States.

As the "movement" generates increased enthusiasm and optimism, more and more administrators are seeking help to establish performance assessment procedures not only for reading and English programs, but also for other content areas, such as math and science. The authors, as assessment consultants, have discovered that enthusiasm for and acceptance of performance assessment often exceed knowledge about its nature and complexity. As they wrestle with the task of helping administrators develop environments and structures for moving toward performance assessment, the authors have identified three basic and critical questions that often go unanswered when schools rush to jump on the performance assessment bandwagon:

- What exactly is performance assessment?

From *Childhood Education*, Fall 1993, pp. 29-32. Reprinted by permission of the authors and the Association for Childhood Education International, 11501 Georgia Avenue, Suite 315, Wheaton, MD. © 1993 by the Association.

6. ASSESSMENT

- What advice is available from experts and the research?
- What issues and concerns must be addressed?

What Exactly Is Performance Assessment?

Few discussions of performance assessment clearly define the phrase. The authors found Berk's (1986) operational definition to be a fair and concise representation of current beliefs about performance assessment. He defines performance assessment as "the process of gathering data by systematic observation for making decisions about an individual" (p. ix). Stiggins and Bridgeford (1986) establish three criteria for a performance assessment. First, students must apply knowledge they have acquired. Second, students must complete a clearly specified task within the context of either a real or simulated exercise. Third, the task or completed product must be observed

Spontaneous assessment grows out of teachers' day-to-day intuitive observations and judgments . . .

and rated with respect to specified criteria in accordance with specified procedures, requiring students to actually demonstrate proficiency.

Stiggins and Bridgeford make a very important distinction between spontaneous and structured performance assessments. Spontaneous assessment grows out of teachers' day-to-day intuitive observations and judgments in the classroom. On the other hand, structured performance assessment must meet standards for reliability and validity and is systematically designed and planned for specific purposes. It uses clearly designed and specified scoring criteria and assesses very well-defined behaviors. Structured performance assessment is

the type most performance assessment experts want us to understand.

An example of the critical distinction between structured and unstructured assessments can be found in portfolio assessment. Many articles about portfolio assessment of writing, in particular, do not suggest rigorous criteria for the selection and analysis of portfolio entries. Gathering a collection of student products is certainly a legitimate task for a teacher or school. It must be understood, however, that an unstructured collection provides no data for analysis or comparison. If performance assessment is to become a viable alternative to conventional testing, it must be rigorous. Standards for selection and analysis must be a part of every performance assessment.

Cizek (1991) makes a distinction between indirect and direct measures of student assessment. He suggests that conventional paper-and-pencil tests are indirect measures of what students know about a topic, whereas performance tests are direct measures of students' ability to employ that knowledge during an actual task. Performance assessment goes beyond measuring what students *know* to measuring what students can *do* or *apply*.

What Advice Is Available from Experts and the Research?

Structured performance assessment has been used for decades in business, industry, fine arts and sports. The actual sales record, product, play and game are recognized as legitimate means of assessing knowledge and ability to perform. Managing, supervising, directing and coaching focus on end products or performances. Structured performance assessment is not new to academic subjects, but it has not always been considered as "legitimate" a form of assessment as so-called objective or norm-referenced tests. Performance assessment is more likely to develop into a long-lived innovation if we pay heed to the following five sug-

gestions offered by assessment experts and researchers.

- First, the use of performance assessment in other fields alerts us to the necessity of carefully and clearly describing and analyzing the tasks students will be expected to perform. Commenting on the business sector, Nathan and Cascio (1986) state, "A job analysis is necessary for showing the job-relatedness of all performance appraisal methods and is the basis for the performance standards fed back to employees" (p. 33). This same process must be applied to education. Analysis of the task that the student is to perform is a critical factor in making performance assessment a viable measurement. We cannot construct a list of criteria or a means of rating that criteria if we have not first determined what we expect students to produce.

- Second, all reliability, validity, administration and scoring standards relevant to conventional forms of assessment must also be applied to performance assessment (Brandt, 1992). Unless performance assessment is rigorous, its usefulness will be questioned. We must be wary of the misconception that any alternative assessment will automatically be a better assessment (Arter, 1991). Articles advocating portfolio assessment, for example,

Unless performance assessment is rigorous, its usefulness will be questioned.

often do not include detailed criteria for selecting and evaluating portfolio entries (Rief, 1990) and may lead practitioners to believe that evaluation can be accomplished simply by collecting and describing samples of student work.

■ Third, Grant Wiggins suggests that in order for structured performance assessment to be useful, models must be created and criteria and standards must be set (Brandt, 1992). Education does not have to invent this wheel. Established models in art, music, drama, speech and athletics may help educators develop new models appropriate for academic subjects. A significant step was taken in 1985 when a joint committee composed of representatives from American Educational Research Association, American Psychological Association and National Council on Measurement in Education established a set of standards for educational and psychological measurement that included performance assessment standards (AERA/APA/NCME Joint Committee, 1985). These standards are an excellent place for schools to begin their search for appropriate models. States such as Colorado have taken the lead in establishing

... evidence gathered from other professions ... indicates performance assessment is much more transferable to real world tasks.

models that can be tested and revised to meet local needs (Gilbert, 1990).

■ Fourth, education professionals need to recognize and respond to factors that may impede further development and use of performance assessment. Developing strategies and structures for dealing with these factors may be as important as developing the new assessment instruments themselves. Speed and low cost were two attractive features of conventional tests.

Performance tests, however, are much more time-consuming to construct and administer (Maeroff, 1991). Developing, administering and scoring performance assessments are labor-intensive tasks, and the teachers who develop these new instruments will require released time. The cost of performance assessments will necessarily be weighed against their usefulness. Widespread support, as well as funding, will be the essentials that keep performance assessment from being discarded as a nonviable innovation.

■ Finally, we must be aware that the performance assessment movement in education is really still in its infancy and the body of definitive research is very small. Nor do we have clear research evidence to determine if students who do poorly on conventional tests will do appreciably better on performance tests. Furthermore, there is insufficient research evidence to establish a clear link between re-

(John Ferraro/The Shore Line Times)

As a method for extending performance assessment, proper use of the computer in a learning situation provides another tool for tracking, in a very individualized way, the progress of a student.

sults of performance assessment and effective functioning in college or on the job. We can, however, use evidence gathered from other professions that indicates performance assessment is much more transferable to real world tasks. Educators must continue to share what they know about the state of performance assessment if this form of evaluation is to become increasingly useful.

What Issues and Concerns Must Be Addressed?

Issues and concerns specific to the unique applications of performance assessment in education must be addressed carefully and systematically. As more and more districts move toward performance assessment, more and more issues and concerns about the design and use of the new tests will be raised. The questions generated by the following issues do not yet have "right" answers, or even general agreement on possible answers. Performance assessment cannot move ahead, however, until education planners at least come up with answers that are appropriate to their local situations.

The authors have identified four major issues and related questions that are most frequently discussed in the literature and must be answered before performance assessment can be implemented.

Issue 1: Establishing Standards for Performance Testing

- Is the assigned task worthy of being assessed?
- Is the end product clearly defined through models of acceptable products?
- Are the criteria for administering and scoring the test precise and clear?
- Do the scoring rubrics, or guidelines and procedures, accurately represent the agreed-upon criteria?
- Who will decide on the criteria? Will parents and students be a part of these decisions?

- How will criteria and standards be conveyed to all stakeholders (teachers, administrators, students, parents, the political community, others)?

Issue 2: Assuring Precision of Performance Assessment Instruments

- Is a performance test the best way to assess the behavior under consideration?
- Are uniform operational definitions available for all terms used? For example, the term "composite portfolio" has several definitions in the literature and in practice. One definition must be agreed upon if this term is to be used in a local proposal.
- How carefully structured is the relationship between the performance assessment and other tests in use (predictive validity)? For example, if college admission is a concern for a school district, will its high school writing test predict success on SATs?
- How do the criteria to be judged match the rating items, the prompt and the end product (content validity for observable behavior, construct validity for abstract concepts)? For example, if the end product and the criteria of a speech test were focused on persuasive ability while the prompt required the student to give an informational speech, the content validity of the assessment would be questionable.
- Are the performance assessment tasks related to and transferable to real world tasks (ecological validity)? For example, reading assessment tasks that involve narrative text may not be related to technical types of reading demanded in the workplace (Quellmalz, 1986).
- Will all raters who administer the performance tests achieve a reasonable degree of concur-

rence or inter-rater reliability?
- Will multiple samples be assessed to achieve a more reliable view of performance?
- Will the performance instrument be systematically critiqued and revised as needed?

Issue 3: Using Performance Assessment Scores and Results

- How will performance assessment results be translated into grades for report cards, etc. (Jongsma, 1991)?
- How will performance assessment results be used to affect classroom decisions and instructional practices?
- Will performance assessment results be used to describe individual achievement, group performance or both?
- Will performance assessment results be used in concurrence with conventional test results?
- Will the performance assessment become the new high-stakes test?

Issue 4: Training Personnel To Use Performance Assessments

- Are personnel who will design, administer and interpret the performance instruments knowledgeable about assessment—are they assessment literate (Stiggins, 1991)?
- Who will train personnel to administer the assessments?
- How will quality training programs be guaranteed?
- Who will train students to interpret performance assessment feedback or participate in self-assessment?

Some Final Thoughts
As knowledge and understanding of learning continue to grow, the need for more flexible and diverse measurements will only increase. Performance assessment is a promising addition to the traditional tools. If this new tool is to fulfill its promise, performance assessment must be understood and used re-

sponsibly. Educators' professional judgments may finally achieve the legitimacy and worth they deserve, provided their assessment expertise grows as well. It is the authors' hope that educators will not leave the development of this new assessment tool solely to testing companies or so-called experts, but will strive to become experts themselves.

References

AERA/APA/NCME Joint Committee. (1985). *Standards for educational and psychological testing.* Washington, DC: American Psychological Association.

Arter, J. (1991). *Performance assessment: What's out there and how useful is it really?* Portland, OR: Northwest Regional Educational Lab. (ERIC Document Reproduction Service No. ED 333 051)

Berk, R. A. (Ed.). (1986). *Performance assessment.* Baltimore, MD: The Johns Hopkins University Press.

Brandt, R. (1992). On performance assessment: A conversation with Grant Wiggins. *Educational Leadership, 49,* 35-41.

Cizek, G. J. (1991). Innovation or enervation? Performance assessment in perspective. *Phi Delta Kappan, 72,* 695-699.

Gilbert, J. C. (1990). *Performance-based assessment resource guide.* Denver, CO: Colorado Department of Education. (ERIC Document Reproduction Service No. ED 327 304)

Jongsma, K. S. (1991). Rethinking grading practices. *The Reading Teacher, 45,* 318-320.

Maeroff, G. I. (1991). Assessing alternative assessment. *Phi Delta Kappan, 73,* 272-281.

Nathan, B. R., & Cascio, W. F. (1986). Technical and legal standards. In R. A. Berk (Ed.), *Performance assessment* (pp. 1-50). Baltimore, MD: The John Hopkins University Press.

Perrone, V. (Ed.). (1991). *Expanding student assessment.* Alexandria, VA: Association for Supervision and Curriculum Development.

Quellmalz, E. S. (1986). Writing skills assessment. In R. A. Berk (Ed.), *Performance assessment* (pp. 492-509). Baltimore, MD: The John Hopkins University Press.

Reif, L. (1990). Finding the value in evaluation: Self-assessment in a middle school classroom. *Educational Leadership, 47,* 24-29.

Stiggins, R. J. (1991). Assessment literacy. *Phi Delta Kappan, 72,* 534-539.

Stiggins, R. J., & Bridgeford, N. J. (1986). In R. A. Berk (Ed.), *Performance assessment* (pp. 469-492). Baltimore, MD: The Johns Hopkins University Press.

PLANNING FOR CLASSROOM
PORTFOLIO ASSESSMENT

Diana V. Lambdin
and Vicki L. Walker

Diana Lambdin teaches at Indiana University in Bloomington, IN 47405-1006. Her special interests include problem solving, curriculum development, assessment and evaluation, and writing to learn mathematics. Vicki Walker teaches middle school mathematics at Louisville Collegiate School, Louisville, KY 40207. She is interested in alternative methods of assessment, particularly portfolio assessment.

Three years ago, the mathematics teachers from grades 4–12 in our school met for two weeks during the summer for an in-service program related to assessment and decided to begin using portfolios with our students in the fall. I was enthusiastic, although I had no idea at that time how drastically my approach to assessment—and to teaching in general—would change as a result of the portfolio decision.

In the three years since that assessment meeting, I've struggled with learning how to use portfolios for classroom assessment and discovered many tips toward planning for their use. Among the most important things that I've learned are (*a*) the importance of having a clear

This article, although written in the first person singular, is actually a collaborative effort of the two authors, who shared equally in its conceptualization and writing. The authors became acquainted in 1990 when Louisville Collegiate School requested that mathematics educators at Indiana University give them some advice about bringing their mathematics teaching more in line with the NCTM's curriculum and evaluation standards. Frank Lester suggested the use of portfolio assessment as a catalyst for change. He and Diana Lambdin consulted with the Collegiate teachers for several years as they worked through the process of establishing the use of portfolio assessment in all their mathematics classes, grades 4–12. In 1992, the state of Kentucky began mandating the use of portfolios in mathematics assessment. For a related article see "Implementing the K–4 Mathematics Standards in Kentucky" in the November 1993 issue.

idea of the reason for assigning students to compile portfolios; (*b*) the importance of establishing workable routines for managing the production, organization, and storage of the portfolios; and (*c*) the importance of giving students clear guidance about expectations for their portfolios.

Portfolios are more than student folders.

Why Use Portfolios?

The mathematics teachers in my school established certain goals for our use of students' portfolios. First, we were looking for a better way to assess the whole

PLANNING FOR INSTRUCTION

child than just relying on test scores. Second, and perhaps most important, we wanted to help students develop better self-assessment skills and become less reliant on the grades we assign to their work. Third, we wanted to establish a better means of communication among students, parents, and teachers about the kinds of mathematical learning taking place in our classrooms.

These were lofty goals. Although it seemed that portfolios could help us attain them, early on it was not clear exactly how. In retrospect, I realize that I really had very little idea at first what good portfolios should look like, much less how I intended to manage or evaluate them. I discussed the portfolio project with my students during the first weeks of school and sent home a letter informing their parents, but for quite a while, I was actually just feeling my way along. As the year went on, the students and I all raised questions about portfolios, shared thoughts, and communicated about mathematics (and about what we thought demonstrated mathematical learning), and gradually a clearer picture developed. **Table 1,** taken from guidelines distributed in 1992 by the Kentucky Department of Education as part of an Educational Reform Act mandating the use of portfolios in mathematics assessment, furnishes an overview of the philosophy of portfolio assessment that I have gradually come to espouse. Although the process of searching for meaning has been important to my own growth as a professional, I might have been able to grow more quickly and efficiently had I realized certain things. In this article, I share some of the insights I've gained about portfolio assessment. (Resources I've found especially useful are listed in the **Bibliography.**)

From *Arithmetic Teacher*, February 1994, pp. 318-324. © 1994 by the National Council of Teachers of Mathematics. Reprinted by permission.

Portfolios Are Not the Same as Folders

In the beginning, I tended to equate portfolios with student folders in my mind. I'd often kept folders containing examples of students' work and conference comments, and I initially thought that was more or less what the portfolios would be like. I now realize that a very important element was missing in that conception of the portfolio process—the element of self-evaluation. In the portfolio process that has evolved in my classroom, students are much more in control when putting together their portfolios than they ever were with my old folders. Developing a portfolio involves reflection, writing, and self-critiquing in an effort to present a composite picture of oneself. This approach makes a portfolio much different from simply being a collection of sample pieces of a student's work.

Deciding what kind of envelopes or folders to use as portfolios and where to store them seemed at first to be relatively minor details, but I later realized that such routine decisions can have important implications. The department had decided that students would keep a *working portfolio* (a manila file folder) and a *permanent portfolio* (a dark blue, card-stock accordion-style folder). Throughout the grading period, students placed those papers they were considering as possible portfolio entries in their working portfolio, which served as a sort of holding tank for their selections. At the end of each grading period, students reevaluated their work and made the final selections to transfer to their permanent portfolio. During the first year, all the portfolios were kept in storage boxes that tended to float around my classroom, depending on where space was available at any given moment. When it came time for a class period devoted to working on portfolios, the storage boxes were pulled out usually from underneath a mass of papers, books, and dust.

> Portfolios can improve communication with students and parents.

Looking back, I can see that something was fundamentally wrong with my whole approach toward the management of the portfolios. The idea of having a working portfolio and a permanent portfolio was, and remains, an essential part of my portfolio procedures. Yet my early method of managing the working portfolios meant that portfolio selection was just one more thing to fit into all the many instructional activities I must orchestrate. In that first year, whenever the end of a grading period approached, I scrambled to squeeze in class time for portfolio work and processing. As the portfolios were dug out, I proclaimed to my classes that we all needed to value this process of compiling portfolios. Students were instructed to choose papers that would demonstrate their competencies and their insights. After the first grading period, when many portfolios appeared to be random selections of papers, I required students to attach a comment to each piece telling why they had chosen it for their portfolio. I pleaded that they reflect thoughtfully about their mathematical endeavors and hoped they would turn in masterpieces of mathematical revelation. Then I was extremely disappointed when many portfolios consisted primarily of computational work with comments such as "I chose this because it is neat" or "I chose this because I got all the right answers." Because I had talked about demonstrating good problem solving and displaying mathematical thinking and because I had set aside what I felt to be very valuable instructional time for students to select portfolio pieces and to write comments about them, I had naively assumed that my students would share my expectations about what constituted thoughtful reflection. That first year I sat at my desk facing a huge mound of blue folders, upset not only because most of my students' choices seemed to be off target and their reflections rather shallow but also because I had no earthly idea what I should do to evaluate the portfolios.

Tips for Getting Started with Portfolio Assessment

What seems obvious to me now is that by keeping portfolios in storage boxes and only pulling them out occasionally, I was inadvertently conveying a message to my students about the value of the portfolios that was quite contrary to my preachings. By stressing portfolio work only at the end of each grading period, I was defeating my own goal of having my students invest themselves in a process of self-reflection that would culminate in a product called a portfolio. I never imagined that I was instilling anything but positive ideas about maintaining portfolios in my students. Yet, little by little, I began to realize some important adjustments that needed to be made.

6. ASSESSMENT

Portfolios need to be accessible

First of all, I rearranged things in my room, purchased some inexpensive shelves, and made a permanent home for the portfolios. At present the shelves are located in the front of my room, the area is clearly labeled "Portfolios," and student samples and selection guidelines are posted on the wall directly above the shelves. Since the portfolios are visible and accessible every day, they are tended to more consistently. They are now an integral part of my classroom and of its activities.

Students need guidance in labeling and choosing

Getting my students to label their portfolio selections clearly is a challenge. I expect not just names and page numbers but also dates, assignment titles, and descriptions that clarify what the work is all about. I did not ask for this information initially, and consequently, I did not get it. As I began to give students more specific guidelines about how to label their entries, I began to see marked improvements in their portfolio work. Moreover, I believe my students began to be much more aware of the range of activities in which we were involved and the reasons we were doing these different types of work.

Initially I gave students key phrases for the types of items I expected to go into their portfolios: for example, *favorite piece, best effort, most improved, awesome problem-solving work.* I supplied self-stick notes on which they were to indicate the reasons for their selections; the notes were to be attached to the corresponding pieces. Some students spent considerable time thinking about which pieces of their work might qualify for inclusion in their portfolio and why. Most students, however, just raced through their notebooks and their working portfolios grabbing things they thought might fit the bill. Those who just wanted to get finished fast tended to focus primarily on superficial aspects like neatness and correctness and on computational tasks, rather than reflecting on the thinking they had done in solving nonroutine problems.

The many changes I have made in my guidelines for portfolio selections and portfolio writings have convinced me that I will probably continue to make adjustments with each passing year, but I can share some ideas about what I do currently. I give my students written guidelines about the different types of work to include in their portfolios (see **tables 2** and **3**). I also supply a handout of "thinking questions" for them to work through before preparing the written reflections that I now require to accompany each entry (see **table 4**). (These written reflections have replaced the self-stick notes, which I decided were too small and informal for my purposes.) In general, my goal is to guide students through a process of reflecting, and then writing, about why they've chosen specific pieces — in particular, what they've learned from the activities or work that they select and what kind of connections they can make between this work and other school topics or other aspects of

---

TABLE 2

Mathematics-portfolio entries

A complete portfolio will include—

- a completed table of contents;
- a letter to the reviewer written by the student that describes the portfolio;
- five best entries reflective of the topics studied and the activities completed in the course.

Each entry must include the original question, task, or problem posed; a title; the date; and the student's name. Entries must be in the same order as listed in the Table of Contents and must be numbered accordingly. If an entry is in the category of photographs, audiotapes, videotapes, or computer disks, then the entry must be accompanied by a brief paragraph describing the activity and its rationale.

(Adapted from Kentucky Department of Education [1992, 1–4])

TABLE 3

Mathematics-portfolio entry types

Writing
This type of entry includes journal entries, mathematics autobiographies, explanations, reflections, justifications, and so on.

Investigations or Discovery
This type of entry can be described as an exploration that leads to understanding of mathematical ideas or to the formulation of mathematical generalizations. Examples include gathering data, examining models, constructing arguments, and performing simulations.

Application
This type of entry is to include the selection and use of concepts, principles, and procedures to solve problems in a well-grounded, real-world context.

Interdisciplinary
This type of entry demonstrates the use of mathematics within other disciplines.

Nonroutine Problems
This type of entry includes problems for which the solution or strategies are not immediately evident. This category may include mathematical recreations such as puzzles and logic problems.

Projects
This type of entry includes activities that extend over a period of days and requires a formal presentation of the material learned. This category may include research projects, designs, constructions, and original computer programs.

Note: A portfolio entry may fall into more than one of the foregoing types.

(Adapted from Kentucky Department of Education [1992, 1–4])

TABLE 4

Portfolio "thinking questions"

Please think through these questions carefully as you begin finalizing your portfolio selections and preparing your written summaries.

- What activity or mathematical topic was involved?
- How did the activity help you learn something new?
- What did you learn from this experience?
- Can you describe any connections between the activity and other subject areas or real-life situations?
- Would you do anything differently if you had more time?
- What strategies did you use? (What did you *think* as you worked through the task?)
- What mathematical skills were used in your solution process?
- How would you rate your overall performance related to the activity?
- What are your areas of strength in mathematics?
- What goals have you set for yourself in mathematics?

their lives. (See **fig. 1** for an example of one student's work on an assignment involving estimation and her rationale for including that work in her portfolio.)

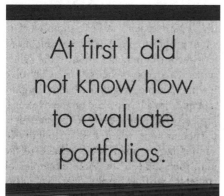

A table of contents is essential

I now require students to have a table of contents for their portfolios, and I have seen remarkable improvement in their portfolios since doing so. Offering students help in preparing a table of contents is fairly easy, yet extremely critical. I generally display a sample table of contents on the overhead projector (see **fig. 2**) so that students can take notes on the format. Since I've required a table of contents, I get far fewer portfolios that are just piles of papers with fragmented thoughts attached. Students seem to be more thorough regarding the layout of their work and the overall appearance of their portfolio, perhaps because they have more of a sense of a completed project. Each portfo-

lio now has a definite beginning and end and a clearer vision-at-a-glance of what it contains and what message it is meant to convey. Furthermore, the table of contents allows for easier perusal on my part and has saved me a great deal of time during my evaluation process.

Students Need Guidance in Being Reflective

I never realized before I began using portfolios the importance of giving students opportunities to categorize, edit, critique, and analyze their own work and the work of other students, so that they can develop an intuitive sense of what constitutes quality. Projecting transparencies of students' work for whole-class discussion about mathematical content and quality of work has now become a common instructional activity in my class. My students seem to benefit considerably from these whole-class discussions. Similarly, I have learned a lot about which areas of my instruction have made sense to them and on which topics they have remained confused. As we have begun to spend more time analyzing and processing material in class, my students and I have both become more engaged in reflecting on the value of various activities. Even though I had included problem-solving activities, writing tasks, group work, and special project work in

TABLE 5

Selected peer-evaluation portfolio reflections

Activity: Students engaged in partner conferences to discuss their portfolio selections, give advice to one another, and comment on stand-out selections

1. When I looked at the portfolio selections with Shawn, I noticed a lot of things I could have done better on. For instance, on my problem-solving section I did not do so good because it was the beginning of the year and I had not really gotten into school yet.

2. I worked with Jeff today. He helped me see many things about my papers but most of all he helped pick my best work. This is "How many books are in the library?" This work shows reasoning, estimation, observations, and many others things. This is why this work stands out so well. It shows what my work was. This was also challenging and exciting to me. Even though my estimation was 5600 and the actual was 19,000, I still think my reasoning and attitude towards this project was very good.

3. Today I worked with Andrew. He helped me see the things I was doing wrong. I had a codecracker which didn't show a lot but he helped me see how to make it work. He told me to add an explanation about it for it to fit. I think a standout piece is my million's project. It shows everything I need. It has the original problem plus it shows all my work. It has an explanation about the problem and what we did.

4. One piece of work I think I did super was the "Buckets of Trouble." Even though the explanation wasn't perfect, it showed what our group had done and had pictures to show strategies and the solution. This was a standout piece, and was a fun experiment too. Our group had to work with cups to visualize what we were doing and if it would work.

5. Today I conferenced with Jenny. She pointed out that some of my work needed explanation and helped me choose another piece of work that helps make my portfolio stand out. We chose the Library Book project. The piece was neat, colorful, and had a wonderful explanation!

FIGURE 1

Student work with portfolio reflection

Portfolio paragraph

Anne
5-25-93

I chose my "books in the library" project for an entry because it shows my work and has a clear explanation of the process I used. I enjoyed this project because we got to work our own way and find the answer alone. This project taught me to collect data, organize it, and to understand what I did enough to put it in words. Even though my answer wasn't very exact I feel that for the beginning of the year it is pretty good.

Anne
9/16/92

Books in the
Library

When I began the Library Books project I thought there might be 400 books. First of all I counted 3 shelves—1 full, 1 medium, and 1 with barely any. Next I averaged them. After that I counted the number of shelves upstairs and multiplied the average amount of books per shelf by the number of shelves. Then I went downstairs and counted the books on the spinners, counted the books in the Kiddie Library, and counted all the books on the downstairs shelves. The total amount of books in the library is ...

26,057

This is how I got my answer:

Upstairs: 51 per shelf
x 198 shelves
10,098 on the shelves
+ 97 countertop
10,195

Downstairs:
961 kiddie Room
14,770 all shelves
9 atlases
+ 122 spinners
15,862

Downstairs 10,195
+ 15,862
26,057 total

Upstairs

---

my classes for years, I was surprised to discover that many of my students had never thought about the distinctions among these types of learning activities. A case in point is one student who chose only computational selections for his portfolio and justified his selections with the statement that he had spent a lot of time working the "problems." Time spent was what made them problem *solving* for him.

Whole-class discussions prompt reflection.

In addition to having the whole class share and discuss examples presented on the overhead projector, I frequently engage students in peer-evaluation activities. I pair students or have them work in small groups to make portfolio selections and record comments about their selections. This type of activity may involve having students respond to some important questions I've placed on the overhead projector or may occur at the end of a particular unit when I ask students to summarize the main ideas related to the unit. (See **table 5** for some examples of students' writing from a peer-evaluation activity.)

I involve students in peer-evaluation activities a couple of times a month. During such activities, I am able to circulate around the room, take note of valuable comments I hear, make informal assessments of students, and exchange thoughts with small groups or individuals about the type or quality of work they've completed. In this manner, my instructional style and my assessment procedures have become more unified, and portfolio selection is no longer a one-day activity at the end of each marking period. The primary goal of my peer-evaluation activities is that the students spend time thinking about, and sharing their ideas related to, mathematics. The additional benefits of such activities are that students become more aware of what they have studied and what they have learned, I gain valuable insights

I place on reflection and on written expression.

Portfolios Facilitate Communication

Using portfolios has changed my communication with students and their parents in ways I had never considered before. For example, portfolios now serve as a powerful tool in parent-teacher or student-teacher conferences. As we examine together examples of such things as group work, problem solving, or written reflections, I can clarify my goals for such assignments, we can compare this type of work with more traditional textbook assignments, and students can ask questions or try to clarify thoughts that they might not have expressed well on paper. Valuable student-teacher communication also takes place through portfolio writings in which students are

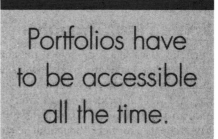

Portfolios have to be accessible all the time.

assigned to share their reactions to class activities or assignments and to reflect on their personal goals for mathematics learning. (**Fig. 3** presents an example of a student's reflection on his personal strengths and weaknesses in mathematics.)

Student-parent communication has also benefited from my use of portfolios, especially since I began requiring parental signatures on the portfolios and encouraging input from parents on students' selections. During my second year of using portfolios I began sending home a newsletter at the end of each grading period to summarize the major topics and ideas that had been covered in class. The newsletter not only has helped me review important ideas with my students as they prepare their portfolios but has facilitated student-parent communication about what has been stressed in class and why.

FIGURE 2

Sample portfolio table of contents

NAME_____
GRADE _____
DATE _____

TABLE OF CONTENTS

Title of Entry	Date Completed	Page
1. Will All Quadrilaterals Tessellate?	15 Nov. 1991	1
2. Buckets of Trouble	27 Oct. 1991	3
3. M&M Probability	16–18 Mar. 1992	5
4. Statistical Project on Immigration	2–12 Feb. 1992	8
5. My Sixth-Grade Mathematics Experience	19 Apr. 1992	10

---

about my instruction, and the entire portfolio-assessment process becomes an integral part of all that we do.

Portfolio Evaluation

Evaluating student portfolios is very time consuming. I have found it easier to handle if I evaluate one class of portfolios at a time rather than try to grade all classes at once. The letter grade that I assign to each portfolio is included as part of the overall grade for the marking period and is based on three things: the diversity of selections, written reflections about selections, and the organization of the portfolio. Note that I do not grade portfolios on the quality of the selections included (homework, group work, writing assignments, tests, etc.) because many of these have already been graded. Thus, it is possible for a student who gets below-average grades on the mathematics work to receive a better portfolio grade than a student with very high grades on her or his work if the former portfolio is more thoughtfully chosen and carefully documented than the latter.

I use a two-step procedure for portfolio assessment. First I read through all the portfolios and sort them into three piles: *excellent, satisfactory,* and *needs improvement.* Then I go back through each pile and assign a score to each portfolio by using a five-point scale (1–5) for each of my three categories (selection, reflection, and organization). Assigning these points is a difficult, fairly subjective, process. But I try to set general guidelines ahead of time.

When assigning points for the selection category, I consider the diversity of the entries, the time periods represented (work should be represented from throughout the school year thus far), and the overall appropriateness of the selections. Points assigned for reflection are based on the students' written reflections about their choices. I consider clarity of thought, analysis of the problem or the mathematical concepts being displayed, use of complete sentences, legibility, and overall quality of the reflections. The category for organization involves the more technical aspects of the portfolio, such as whether it contains a table of contents, has all its pieces correctly ordered and labeled, and includes the required parental signature. I generally assign five points per category for those portfolios that show excellent work, three points for those that are satisfactory, and one point for those needing improvement. (Four points and two points are assigned, as needed, for work that seems to fall in between.) For example, a student might receive four points for diversity of selection, three points for written reflections, and five points for organization, for a total of twelve points (of fifteen possible) for the portfolio.

The final step of the evaluation process involves writing personal comments to each student about the strengths and weaknesses of his or her portfolio. Although this writing takes a great deal of my time, it greatly enhances my communication with my students and reinforces the value

FIGURE 3

Student self-reflection

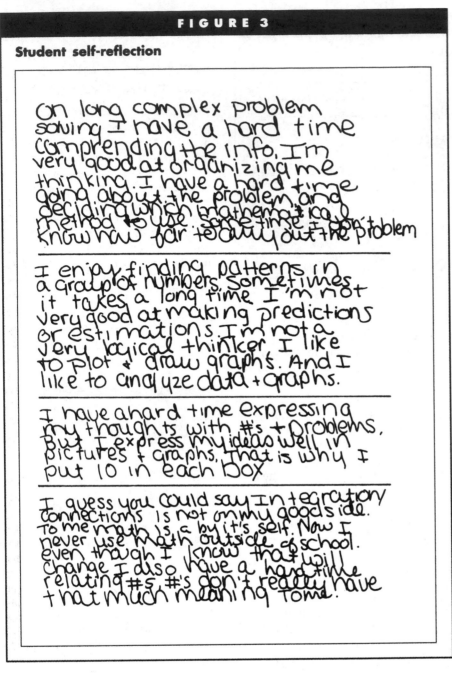

On long complex problem solving I have a hard time comprending the info. I'm very good at organizing me thinking. I have a hard time going about the problem and deciding which mathematical method to use. Sometimes I don't know how far to carry out the problem

I enjoy finding patterns in a group of numbers. Sometimes it takes a long time I'm not very good at making predictions or estimations I'm not a very logical thinker. I like to plot & draw graphs. And I like to analyze data + graphs.

I have a hard time expressing my thoughts with #'s + problems. But I express my ideas well in pictures + graphs. That is why I put 10 in each box

I guess you could say Integration connections is not on my good side. To me math is a by it's self. Now I never use math outside of school. even though I know that will change I also have a hard time relating #'s. #'s don't really have that much meaning to me.

Some Final Thoughts

Portfolio assessment has helped me and my students make progress toward a number of the goals recommended by the NCTM's *Curriculum and Evaluation Standards for School Mathematics* (1989). My students are more thoughtful about what mathematics they are studying and why. They seem to be developing a better understanding of what is meant by problem solving and mathematical reasoning, less often resorting to the blind application of computational algorithms when confronted with problems. In making portfolio selections, my students are learning to look for connections among mathematics topics (and between mathematics and other aspects of their lives), and they are learning to take personal responsibility for self-assessment. In writing their portfolio reflections, they are improving their abilities to communicate about mathematical ideas and about their own personal strengths and weaknesses.

I must admit, quite honestly, that portfolio assessment is time-consuming and labor-intensive for teachers, especially those who have many students. But careful planning and establishment of routines can eliminate much wasted effort and will make the job easier to do. I have found the results well worth it. Since using portfolios with my classes, I have no doubt that my students are learning more mathematics, and that has always been my ultimate goal.

Bibliography

Kentucky Department of Education. *Kentucky Mathematics Portfolio: Teacher's Guide.* Frankfort, Ky.: The Department, 1992.

Mumme, Judith. *Portfolio Assessment in Mathematics.* Santa Barbara, Calif.: University of California, 1990. (A publication from the California Mathematics Project.)

National Council of Teachers of Mathematics. *Curriculum and Evaluation Standards for School Mathematics.* Reston, Va.: The Council, 1989.

Petit, Marge. *Getting Started: Vermont Mathematics Portfolio—Learning How to Show Your Best!* Cabot, Vt.: Cabot School, 1992.

Stenmark, Jean Kerr, ed. *Assessment Alternatives in Mathematics: An Overview of Assessment Techniques That Promote Learning.* Berkeley: University of California, 1989.

———. *Mathematics Assessment: Myths, Models, Good Questions, and Practical Suggestions.* Reston Va.: National Council of Teachers of Mathematics, 1991.

Vermont Portfolio Committee. *The Vermont Mathematics Portfolio: What It Is, How To Use It.* Montpelier, Vt.: Vermont Department of Education, 1991.

Putting the Standardized Test Debate in Perspective

When used correctly, standardized tests do have value, but they provide only part of the picture and have limits—which we must understand and work to improve.

BLAINE R. WORTHEN AND VICKI SPANDEL

Blaine R. Worthen is Professor and Chair, Research and Evaluation Methodology Program, Utah State University, Psychology Department, Logan, UT 84322. **Vicki Spandel** is Senior Research Associate, Evaluation and Assessment Program, Northwest Regional Educational Laboratory, 101 S.W. Main St., Portland, OR 97204.

Are the criticisms of educational testing valid, or do most of the objections stem from the fact that such tests are often misused? By far the most common type of standardized test is the norm-referenced test—that in which a student's performance is systematically compared with the performance of other (presumably) similar students. Minimum competency and criterion-referenced tests—those that measure student performance against established criteria—can also be standardized. However, not coincidentally, most criticism has been leveled at standardized, norm-referenced tests.

Criticisms of Standardized Tests

Among the current criticisms, a few stand out as most pervasive and most bothersome to those who worry over whether to support or oppose standardized testing. In this article, we'll look at seven of the most common criticisms.

Criticism #1: Standardized achievement tests do not promote student learning. Critics charge that standardized achievement tests provide little direct support for the "real stuff" of education, namely, what goes on in the classroom. They do nothing, critics contend, to enhance the learning process, diagnose learning problems, or provide students rapid feedback.

True, standardized tests do paint student performance in broad brush strokes. They provide general performance information in content areas like math or reading—as the test developers have defined these areas. They do not, nor are they *meant* to, pick up the nuances of performance that characterize the full range of a student's skill, ability, and learning style. Of course, we hope that standardized test results are only a small portion of the assessment information a teacher relies on in making academic decisions about students or curriculum. Good classroom assessment begins with a teacher's own observations and measurement of what students are gaining from instruction every day. Standardized testing can never replace that teacher-centered assessment. But it *can* supplement it with additional information that may help clarify a larger picture of student performance.

Criticism #2: Standardized achievement and aptitude tests are poor predictors of individual students' performance. While some tests may accurately predict future performances of *groups*, critics of testing argue that they are often inaccurate predictors of *individual* performance. Remember Einstein flunked 6th grade math, the critics point out eagerly. Clearly, no test can tell everything. If standardized tests were thousands of items long and took days to administer, they'd probably be better predictors than they are now. But remember—there are predictions and predictions. When a person passes a driver's test, we can't say she'll never speed or run a red light. Similarly, when a child scores well on a standardized reading test, that doesn't mean we can kick back and say, "Well, he's a terrific reader, all right. That's how it will always be." Ridiculous. Maybe he felt extra confident. Maybe the test just happened to touch on those things he knew well. But if we look at *all* the students with high scores and *all* those with low scores, we can safely predict more reading difficulties among students with low scores.

What all this means is that in a standardized test we have the best of

237

one world—a measure that is relatively accurate, pretty good at what it does, but necessarily limited in scope.

Because there are so many drivers to be tested and only a finite amount of time, we cannot test each driver in every conceivable driving situation; and, similarly, we cannot measure all we might like to measure about a child's reading skills without creating a standardized test so cumbersome and complex no one would want to use it. The world of testing is, to a large extent, a world of compromise.

Criticism #3: The content of standardized achievement tests is often mismatched with the content emphasized in a school's curriculum and classrooms. Because standardized tests are intended for broad use, they make no pretense of fitting precisely and equally well the specific content being taught to 3rd graders in Salt Lake City's public schools and their counterparts at the Tickapoo School downstate. Instead, they attempt to sample what is typically taught to *most* 3rd graders in *most* school districts. The result is a test that reflects most curriculums a little, but reflects none precisely. For most users, there are big gaps—whole lessons and units and months of instruction skimmed over or left out altogether. Or the emphasis may seem wrong—too much attention to phonics, not enough on reading for meaning, perhaps. Again, the problem is the size of the test. We simply cannot cover in 10 or 20 test items the richness and diversity that characterize many current curriculums.

Criticism #4: Standardized tests dictate or restrict what is taught. Claims that standardized tests dominate school curriculums and result in "teaching to the test" are familiar and can be leveled at any type of standardized testing that has serious consequences for the schools in which it is used. On the surface it may seem inconsistent to claim that standardized tests are mismatched with what is taught in the schools and at the same time to complain that the tests "drive the curriculum." But those two allegations are not necessarily at odds. The first is grounded in a fear that in trying to represent everyone somewhat, standardized tests will wind up representing no one really well; the second arises from the consequent fear that everyone will try to emulate the ge-

neric curriculum suggested by the test content. This doesn't have to happen, of course.

Further, to the extent it does happen, it seems absurd to blame the test. The question we really need to be asking is "How are decisions about curriculum content being made?" There's often considerable fuzziness on that issue. Here's one sobering note:

Achievement test batteries are designed around what is thought to be the content of the school curriculum as determined by surveys of textbooks, teachers, and other tests. Textbooks and curriculums are designed, on the other hand, in part around the content of tests. One cannot discern which side leads and which follows; each side influences the other, yet nothing assures us that both are tied to an intelligent conceptualization of what an educated person ought to be.[1]

Criticism #5: Standardized achievement and aptitude tests categorize and label students in ways that cause damage to individuals. One of the most serious allegations against published tests is that their use harms students who are relentlessly trailed by low test scores. Call it categorizing, classifying, labeling (or mislabeling), or whatever, the result is the same, critics argue: individual children are subjected to demeaning and insulting placement into categories. The issue is really twofold: (1) tests are not infallible (students can and do change and can also be misclassified); and (2) even when tests *are* accurate, categorization of students into groups that carry a negative connotation may cause more harm than any gain that could possibly come from such classification.

Published tests, critics claim, have far too significant an effect on the life choices of young people. Some believe that achievement and intelligence tests are merely convenient and expedient means of classifying children and, in some cases, excluding them from regular education. But here again, it's important to raise the question of appropriate use. Even if we agree that it's okay to classify some children in some cases for some purposes, we must still ask whether standardized tests provide sufficient information to allow for intelligent decisions. We must also ask whether such tests provide any really useful information not already available from other sources.

Here's something to keep in mind, too. Some test results rank students along a percentile range. For instance, a student with a percentile ranking of 75 on a reading test may be said to have performed better than 75 percent of the other students who took the same test. But a difference in performance on even *one test item* could significantly raise or lower that percentile ranking. Knowing this, should we classify students on the basis of standardized tests? That probably depends on the consequences, on whether the information is appropriate and sufficient for the decision at hand, and on whether there is any corroborating evidence. Suppose we identify talented and gifted students on the basis of standardized math and reading tests. We ought, then, to at least be able to show that high performance on those tests is correlated directly with high probability of success in the talented and gifted program.

Criticism #6: Standardized achievement and aptitude measures are racially, culturally, and socially biased. Perhaps the most serious indictment aimed at both norm-referenced and minimum competency tests is that they are biased against ethnic and cultural minority children. Most published tests, critics claim, favor economically and socially advantaged children over their counterparts from lower socioeconomic families. Minority group members note that many tests have disproportionately negative impact on their chances for equal opportunities in education and employment. We must acknowledge that even well-intentioned uses of tests can disadvantage those unfamiliar with the concepts and language of the majority culture producing the tests. The predictable result is cultural and social bias—failure of the test to reflect or take into account the full range of the student's cultural and social background.

A conviction that testing is biased against minorities has led some critics to call for a moratorium on testing and has also prompted most of the legal challenges issued against minimum competency tests or the use of norm-referenced standardized tests to classify students. It is tempting, in the face of abuses, to outlaw testing. But simplistic solutions rarely work well. A more conservative, and far more challenging, solution is to improve our tests, to build in the sensitivity to cultural differences that would make them fair for all—and to interpret results with an honest awareness of any bias not yet weeded out.

Making such an effort is crucial, if one stops to consider one sobering thought. Assume for the moment that there *is* a bit of cultural bias in college entrance tests. Do away with them, right? Not unless you want to see college admission decisions revert to the still more biased "Good Old Boy" who-knows-whom type of system that excluded minorities effectively for decades before admissions tests, though admittedly imperfect, provided a less biased alternative.

Criticism #7: Standardized achievement and aptitude tests measure only limited and superficial student knowledge and behaviors. While test critics and supporters agree that tests only sample whatever is being tested, critics go on to argue that even what is measured may be trivial or irrelevant. No test items really ask "Who was buried in Grant's Tomb?" but some are nearly that bad.

They don't have to be. The notion that multiple choice tests can tap only recall is a myth. In fact, the best multiple choice items can—and do—measure students' ability to analyze, synthesize information, make comparisons, draw inferences, and evaluate ideas, products, or performances. In many cases, tests are improving, thanks in large part to critics who never give up.

Better Than the Alternatives

No test is perfect, and taken as a whole, educational and psychological measurement is still (and may always be) an imperfect science. Proponents of standardized tests may point to psychometric theory, statistical evidence, the merits of standardization, the predictive validity of many specific tests, and objective scoring procedures as arguments that tests are the most fair and bias-free of any procedures for assessing learning and other mental abilities. But no well-grounded psychometrician will claim that tests are flawless, only that they are enormously useful.

What do they offer us that we couldn't get without them? Comparability, for one thing. Comparability in the context of the "big picture," that is. It isn't very useful, usually, for one

teacher to compare his or her students' performance with that of the students one room down and then to make decisions about instruction based on that comparison. It's too limited. We have to back away to get perspective. This is what standardized test results enable us to do—to back off a bit and get the big, overall view on how we can answer global questions: In *general*, are 3rd graders learning basic math? Can 6th graders read at the predefined level of competency?

Thus, such tests will be useful to us if we use them as they were intended and do not ask them to do things they were never meant to do, such as giving us a microscopic view of an individual student's range of skills.

Appropriate Use Is the Key

On their own, tests are incapable of harming students. It is the way in which their results can be misused that is potentially harmful. Critics of testing often overlook this important distinction, preferring to target the instruments themselves, as if they were the real culprits. That is rather like blaming the hemlock for Socrates' fate. It is palpable nonsense to blame all testing problems on tests, no matter how poorly constructed, while absolving users of all responsibility—not that bad tests should be condoned, of course. But even the best tests can create problems if they're misused. Here are some important pitfalls to avoid.

1. *Using the wrong tests.* Schools often devise new goals and curriculum plans only to find their success being judged by tests that are not relevant to those goals or plans yet are imposed by those at higher administrative levels. Even if district or state level administrators, for example, have sound reasons for using such tests at *their* level, that does not excuse any school for allowing such tests to be the *only* measures of their programs. Teachers and local administrators should exert all the influence they can to see that any measures used are appropriate to the task at hand. They can either (1) persuade higher administrators to select new standardized achievement or minimum competency measures that better match the local curriculum or (2) supplement those tests with measures selected or constructed specifically to measure what the school is attempting to accomplish.

Subtle but absurd mismatches of purpose and test abound in education. Consider, for instance, use of state-wide minimum competency tests to make interschool comparisons, without regard for differences in student ability. Misuse of tests would be largely eliminated if every test were carefully linked with the decision at hand. And if no decision is in the offing, one should question why *any* testing is proposed.

2. *Assuming test scores are infallible.* Every test score contains possible error; a student's *observed* score is rarely identical to that student's *true* score (the score he or she would have obtained had there been no distractions during testing, no fatigue or illness, no "lucky guesses," and no other factors that either helped or hindered that score). Measurement experts can calculate the probability that an individual's *true* score will fall within a certain number of score points of the *obtained* score. Yet many educators ignore measurement error and use test scores as if they were highly precise measures.

3. *Using a single test score to make an important decision.* Given the possibility of error that exists for every test score, how wise is it to allow crucial decisions for individuals (or programs) to hinge on the single administration of a test? A single test score is too suspect—in the absence of supporting evidence of some type—to serve as the sole criterion for *any* crucial decision.

4. *Failing to supplement test scores with other information.* Doesn't the teacher's knowledge of the student's ability count for anything? It should. Though our individual perceptions as teachers and administrators may be subjective, they are not irrelevant. Private observations and practical awareness of students' abilities can and should supplement more objective test scores.

5. *Setting arbitrary minimums for performance on tests.* When minimum test scores are established as critical hurdles for selection and admissions, as dividing lines for placing students, or as the determining factor in awarding certificates, several issues become acute. Test validity, always important, becomes crucial; and the minimum standard itself must be carefully scrutinized. Is there any empirical evidence that the minimum standard is

set correctly, that those who score higher than the cutoff can be predicted to do better in subsequent academic or career pursuits? Or has the standard been set through some arbitrary or capricious process? Using arbitrary minimum scores to make critical decisions is potentially one of the most damaging misuses of educational tests.

6. *Assuming tests measure all the content, skills, or behaviors of interest.* Every test is limited in what it covers. Seldom is it feasible to test more than a sample of the relevant content, skills, or traits the test is designed to assess. Sometimes students do well on a test just because they happen to have read the *particular* chapters or studied the *particular* content sampled by that test. Given another test, with a different sampling of content from the same book, the students might fare less well.

7. *Accepting uncritically all claims made by test authors and publishers.* Most test authors or publishers are enthusiastic about their products, and excessive zeal can lead to risky and misleading promises. A so-called "creativity test" may really measure only verbal fluency. A math "achievement" test administered in English to a group of Inuit Eskimo children (for whom English is a second language) may test understanding of English much more than understanding of math.

8. *Interpreting test scores inappropriately.* The test score *per se* tells us nothing about *why* an individual obtained that score. We watched the SAT scores fall year after year, but there was nothing in the scores themselves to tell us *why* that trend was downward. There turned out, in fact, to be nearly as many interpretations of the trend as there were interpreters.

A student's test *score* is not a qualitative evaluation of performance, but rather, a mere numeric indicator that lacks meaning in the absence of some criteria defining what constitutes "good" or "bad" performance.

9. *Using test scores to draw inappropriate comparisons.* Unprofessional or careless comparisons of achievement test results can foster unhealthy competition among classmates, siblings, or even schools because of ready-made bases for comparisons, such as grade-level achievement. Such misuses of tests not only potentially harm both

the schools and the children involved, but also create an understandable backlash toward the tests, which should have been directed toward those who misused them in this way.

10. *Allowing tests to drive the curriculum.* Remember that *some* individual or group has selected those tests, for whatever reason. If a test unduly influences what goes on in a school's curriculum, then someone has allowed it to override priorities that educators, parents, and the school board have established.

11. *Using poor tests.* Why go to the effort of testing, then employ a poorly constructed or unreliable measure—especially if a better one is at hand? Tests can be flawed in a multitude of ways, from measuring the wrong content or skills (but doing it well) to measuring the correct content or skills (but doing it poorly). Every effort should be made to obtain or construct the best possible measures.

12. *Using tests unprofessionally.* When educational tests are used in misleading or harmful ways, inadequate training of educators is often at fault. When test scores are used to label children in harmful ways, the fault generally lies with those who affix the labels—not with the test. When scores are not kept confidential, that is the fault of the person who violated the confidence, not the test maker. In short, as educators, we have a serious ethical obligation to use tests *well*, if we use them at all.

In Search of a Balanced View

Not all criticisms of tests can be deflected by claiming that they merely reflect misuses of tests. There are also apparent weaknesses in many tests, partly because we have yet a good deal to learn about measurement. We know enough already, however, to state unequivocally that uncertainty and error will always be with us, and no test of learning or mental ability or other characteristics can ever be presumed absolutely precise in its measurements. The professional judgments of teachers and other educators will continue to be essential in sound educational decision making. But we also assert—as do test advocates—that tests are often a great deal better than the

alternatives. Thus, we find ourselves caught in the middle of the debate between testing critics and enthusiasts.

The stridency of that debate occasionally calls to mind the old rhyme, "When in danger or in doubt, run in circles, scream, and shout!" In more recent years, however, there has been some softening on both sides. Measurement experts spend less time defending tests and deriding their detractors and more time working to improve the science of measurement. At the same time, they have become more comfortable in acknowledging that test scores are approximations and less obsessed with claiming unflinching scientific support for every test they devise.

Meanwhile, critics seem less intent on diagnosing psychometric pimples as terminal acne. They seem more aware that many testing problems stem from misuse, and their calls for "testing reform" have quieted somewhat as they have recognized that even the best tests, if subjected to the same sorts of misuse, would prove no more helpful. Further, most critics are beginning to acknowledge that abolishing testing would leave us with many decisions still to make—and even less defensible bases on which to make them.

But even if there are no quick-fix answers to the testing dilemma, there are things we can do. We can: (1) scrupulously avoid any misuses of tests or test results; (2) educate ourselves and our colleagues about tests so that we understand their capabilities and limitations and do not ask them to tell us more than they can; (3) stretch to the limit our creative talents in test design, teaching ourselves to develop test items that not only resound with our own thoughtful understanding of critical content but that encourage students to think; and (4) recall, even when pressed for hasty or expedient decisions, that no matter how much any test may tell us, there is always so much more to be known.

[1]G. V. Glass, (1986), "Testing Old, Testing New: Schoolboy Psychology and the Allocation of Intellectual Resources," in *The Future of Testing*, Buros-Nebraska Symposium on Measurement and Testing, Vol. 2, p. 14, edited by B. S. Plake, J. C. Witt, and J. V. Mitchell, (Hillsdale, N.J.: Lawrence Erlbaum Associates).

Credits/ Acknowledgments

Cover design by Charles Vitelli

1. Perspectives on Teaching

Facing overview—© A. Reininger/Woodfin Camp.

2. Development

Facing overview—Courtesy of Leslie Holmes Lawlor.

3. Exceptional and Culturally Diverse Students

Facing overview—United Nations by Marta Pinter.

4. Learning and Instruction

Facing overview—Sara Krulwich/The New York Times.

5. Motivation and Classroom Management

Facing overview—Louie Psihoyos/Woodfin Camp.

6. Assessment

Facing overview—Dushkin Publishing Group.

ANNUAL EDITIONS ARTICLE REVIEW FORM

■ NAME: _____ DATE: _____

■ TITLE AND NUMBER OF ARTICLE: _____

■ BRIEFLY STATE THE MAIN IDEA OF THIS ARTICLE: _____

_____

_____

_____

_____

■ LIST THREE IMPORTANT FACTS THAT THE AUTHOR USES TO SUPPORT THE MAIN IDEA:

_____

_____

_____

_____

_____

_____

■ WHAT INFORMATION OR IDEAS DISCUSSED IN THIS ARTICLE ARE ALSO DISCUSSED IN YOUR
TEXTBOOK OR OTHER READING YOU HAVE DONE? LIST THE TEXTBOOK CHAPTERS AND PAGE
NUMBERS:

_____

_____

_____

_____

_____

_____

_____

■ LIST ANY EXAMPLES OF BIAS OR FAULTY REASONING THAT YOU FOUND IN THE ARTICLE:

_____

_____

_____

_____

_____

■ LIST ANY NEW TERMS/CONCEPTS THAT WERE DISCUSSED IN THE ARTICLE AND WRITE A
SHORT DEFINITION:

_____

_____

_____

_____

_____

ANNUAL EDITIONS:
EDUCATIONAL PSYCHOLOGY 95/96
Article Rating Form

Here is an opportunity for you to have direct input into the next revision of this volume. We would like you to rate each of the 41 articles listed below, using the following scale:

1. **Excellent: should definitely be retained**
2. **Above average: should probably be retained**
3. **Below average: should probably be deleted**
4. **Poor: should definitely be deleted**

Your ratings will play a vital part in the next revision. So please mail this prepaid form to us just as soon as you complete it.
Thanks for your help!

Annual Editions revisions depend on two major opinion sources: one is our Advisory Board, listed in the front of this volume, which works with us in scanning the thousands of articles published in the public press each year; the other is you—the person actually using the book. Please help us and the users of the next edition by completing the prepaid article rating form on this page and returning it to us. Thank you.

Rating	Article	Rating	Article
	1. We Need a Third Wave of Education Reform		24. Five Standards of Authentic Instruction
	2. The Six National Goals: A Road to Disappointment		25. Optimizing the Instructional Moment: A Guide to Using Socratic, Didactic, Inquiry, and Discovery Methods
	3. Where Can Teacher Research Lead? One Teacher's Daydream		26. The Culture/Learning Style Connection
	4. Myths Associated with Developmentally Appropriate Programs		27. Paradigm Shifts in Designed Instruction: From Behaviorism to Cognitivism to Constructivism
	5. Helping Children Develop Self-Control		28. The Link between Technology and Authentic Learning
	6. Young Children's Understanding of Everyday Emotions		29. Choices for Children: Why and How to Let Students Decide
	7. Encouraging Positive Social Development in Young Children		30. Motivating Underachievers: Make Them *Want* to Try
	8. Developmentally Appropriate Middle Level Schools		31. Educating and Motivating African American Males to Succeed
	9. At-Risk Students and Resiliency: Factors Contributing to Academic Success		32. Beginning Teachers and Classroom Management: Questions from Practice, Answers from Research
	10. Young Children with Attention Deficits		33. Rule-Creating in a Constructivist Classroom Community
	11. Enabling the Learning Disabled		34. Helping Students Develop Self-Discipline
	12. Ability Grouping: Geared for the Gifted		35. Effective Classroom Discipline: Advice for Educators
	13. Meeting the Needs of Your High-Ability Students		36. Assessment Theory and Research for Classrooms: From *Taxonomies* to Constructing Meaning in Context
	14. What We Can Learn from Multicultural Education Research		37. Developing a Personal Grading Plan
	15. Authentic Multicultural Activities		38. Creating Tests Worth Taking
	16. Student Diversity: Implications for Classroom Teachers		39. Performance Assessment: The Realities That Will Influence the Rewards
	17. Remembering the Forgotten Art of Memory		40. Planning for Classroom Portfolio Assessment
	18. The Mind's Journey from Novice to Expert		41. Putting the Standardized Test Debate in Perspective
	19. The Rewards of Learning		
	20. Rewards versus Learning: A Response to Paul Chance		
	21. Sticking Up for Rewards		
	22. The Return of Character Education		
	23. Synthesis of Research on Cooperative Learning		

(Continued on next page)

ABOUT YOU

Name_____ Date_____

Are you a teacher? ☐   Or student? ☐

Your School Name _____

Department _____

Address _____

City_____ State _____ Zip _____

School Telephone # _____

YOUR COMMENTS ARE IMPORTANT TO US!

Please fill in the following information:

For which course did you use this book? _____

Did you use a text with this Annual Edition?   ☐ yes   ☐ no

The title of the text? _____

What are your general reactions to the Annual Editions concept?

Have you read any particular articles recently that you think should be included in the next edition?

Are there any articles you feel should be replaced in the next edition? Why?

Are there other areas that you feel would utilize an Annual Edition?

May we contact you for editorial input?

May we quote you from above?

ANNUAL EDITIONS: EDUCATIONAL PSYCHOLOGY 95/96

BUSINESS REPLY MAIL

First Class   Permit No. 84   Guilford, CT

Postage will be paid by addressee

**The Dushkin Publishing Group/
Brown & Benchmark Publishers**
DPG   **Sluice Dock
Guilford, Connecticut 06437**